Study Guide

to accompany

The Economy Today

Study Guide

to accompany

The Economy Today

Eighth Edition

Bradley R. Schiller
The American University

Prepared by
Linda Wilson
University of Texas-Arlington

Tom Anderson
Montgomery College

Mc Graw Hill **Irwin McGraw-Hill**

Boston   Burr Ridge, IL   Dubuque, IA   Madison, WI   New York   San Francisco   St. Louis
Bangkok   Bogotá   Caracas   Lisbon   London   Madrid
Mexico City   Milan   New Delhi   Seoul   Singapore   Sydney   Taipei   Toronto

McGraw-Hill Higher Education

A Division of The *McGraw-Hill* Companies

Study Guide to accompany
THE ECONOMY TODAY

Copyright © 2000, 1997 by The McGraw-Hill Companies, Inc. All rights reserved.
Printed in the United States of America.
The contents of, or parts thereof, may be reproduced for use with
THE ECONOMY TODAY
Bradley R. Schiller
provided such reproductions bear copyright notice and may be reproduced in
any form for any other purpose without permission of the publisher.

1 2 3 4 5 6 7 8 9 0 QPD/QPD 9 0 9 8 7 6 5 4 3 2 1 0

ISBN 0-07-242955-0

http://www.mhhe.com

STUDY GUIDE

Table of Contents

Preface

This study guide is written to accompany *The Economy Today*, 8th edition, by Bradley R. Schiller. The overall focus of the Study Guide is to reinforce the economic principles and concepts presented in the textbook. Each section of each chapter has a particular objective.

The *Quick Review* and *Learning Objectives* sections provide brief summaries of the basic contents of the corresponding text chapters.

The *Using Key Terms* section allows students to practice using the words defined in each chapter in a crossword puzzle format.

The *True or False* and *Multiple Choice* sections help students apply economic principles in a familiar problem-solving setting. This will help greatly in the preparation for exams.

The *Problems and Applications* section lets students discover economic principles for themselves. Students not only learn the techniques that economists use, but they also discover the basis for the economic concepts they have learned.

Semester after semester, students have difficulty with the same concepts and make the same mistakes. The section called *Common Errors* addresses some of these problems, and provides an explanation using appropriate economic principles.

STUDY GUIDE
Acknowledgments

We thank the McGraw-Hill staff for their support, especially Paul Shensa and Miller Murray. We also thank Thomas Jarrett for providing graphic design, layout modifications, and technical support for this edition.

Linda L. Wilson
The University of Texas at Arlington

Thomas Anderson
Montgomery College, Maryland

CHAPTER 1

Economics: The Core Issues

Quick Review

Throughout history, people have strived to increase the level of output given the available resources and technology. As we move into the 21st century, the quest for more output continues. But what approach should be used to manage society's scarce resources? This question has generated much debate. Adam Smith believed we should allow the market mechanism to allocate resources and rely on a minimum of government intervention. Karl Marx said the government should decide the allocation of all resources and should even own the resources or factors of production. John Maynard Keynes called on government to play an active role in maintaining balance in the economy to prevent the excesses which result from a "hands off" approach.

The debate over how resources should be allocated is not unique to the United States, and is heard increasingly in other parts of the world as countries try to adjust to the collapse of the communist systems in Eastern Europe and elsewhere. The emerging consensus indicates that the market mechanism relied on in the United States (and elsewhere) is vastly superior to the central-planning mechanism which characterized the communist world. This result leads us to focus on two central questions:

- What forces determine economic outcomes?
- What can we do to improve economic outcomes?

To begin the study of economics, we note that the U.S. economy produces an output of over $7 trillion per year. In the process it must allocate its land, labor, capital, and entrepreneurship to competing uses. Resources are considered scarce, even when they seem abundant, because there are not enough of them to satisfy all of society's wants. Thus, every society confronts the problem of scarcity and must somehow answer these basic questions:

- WHAT is to be produced?
- HOW should it be produced?
- FOR WHOM should the output be produced?

Because of the imbalance between society's wants and resources, choosing to produce one thing means choosing not to produce something else. Economists illustrate these choices by drawing a production-possibilities curve. This curve shows the combinations of goods and services a society could produce if it were operating efficiently and all of its resources were fully employed. The production-possibilities curve appears bowed out from the origin because of the law of increasing opportunity costs. To an economist, cost is measured by the best alternative opportunity forgone when choosing a course of action.

In the United States, our choices are largely accomplished through the market mechanism. The "invisible hand" of the market mechanism coordinates the production and consumption decisions of millions of individuals and directly affects the allocation of the economy's resources. Changes in relative prices (called price signals) are what make the system go.

The individual decisions of households and firms are supplemented with generous doses of public-sector activity. When the market mechanism fails to provide goods and services efficiently and equitably – a situation called "market failure" – the public sector must provide assistance. For example, market systems do not automatically generate pollution-control mechanisms which assure us of clean air and water. Such market imperfections must be overcome by government activity. In some economies the market mechanism has not been allowed to work. Planned (or command) economies, like that of the old Soviet Union, are good examples of this. But even in mixed economies "government failure" can make things worse.

In the study of the economy, it is useful to break economics into two categories: microeconomics and macroeconomics. Microeconomics focuses on a specific individual, firm, industry, or government agency; macroeconomics focuses on the entire economy. It should be noted that economics is not a settled body of doctrine. There is much controversy over how the economy works. That is what makes it so interesting.

Learning Objectives

After reading Chapter 1 and doing the following exercises, you should:

1. Understand the debate concerning market allocation vs. government allocation of resources.
2. Understand that economics is the study of how to allocate society's scarce resources – land, labor, capital, and entrepreneurship.
3. Know that scarcity results because resources are not sufficient to satisfy all of society's wants.
4. Be able to define and illustrate opportunity costs using a production-possibilities curve.
5. Understand the law of increasing opportunity costs.
6. Be able to demonstrate efficiency, growth, unemployment, and underemployment using a production-possibilities curve.
7. Know why every economy must answer the same basic questions – WHAT, HOW, FOR WHOM.
8. Be able to distinguish macroeconomic issues from microeconomic issues.
9. Be able to describe how the market mechanism seeks to allocate society's resources to their most valued use.
10. Be aware that there is serious debate and controversy over how the economy works.
11. Be able to discuss the tradeoffs inherent in the "peace dividend."
12. Be able to describe the mixed economy and distinguish market failure from government failure.

Using Key Terms

Fill in the puzzle on the opposite page with the appropriate term from the list of Key Terms at the end of the chapter in the text.

Across

1. The reason there is no such thing as a "free lunch".
3. Occurs when government intervention fails to improve economic outcomes.
6. Represented by land, labor, capital, and entrepreneurship.
7. Economic study concerned with the behavior of individuals, firms, and government agencies.
11. The study of how best to allocate society's scarce resources.
14. Referred to as the "invisible hand" by Adam Smith.
16. Latin term meaning "other things remaining equal."
17. Economic policy supported by Adam Smith.

Down

2. The curve represented in Figure 1.1 in the text.
4. The assembling of resources to produce new or better products.

5. The study of the economy as a whole.
8. The use of both market signals and government directives to select the mix of output.
9. Illustrated in Figure 1.4 in the text by the outward shift of the production-possibilities curve.
10. Occurs when the market mechanism results in the wrong mix of output.
12. Final goods used to produce other goods.
13. The idea that there are not enough resources available to satisfy all desires.
15. According to the *World View* article on page 5 in the text, the Chinese government has been experimenting with a market-driven economy to increase output and _____.

Puzzle 1.1

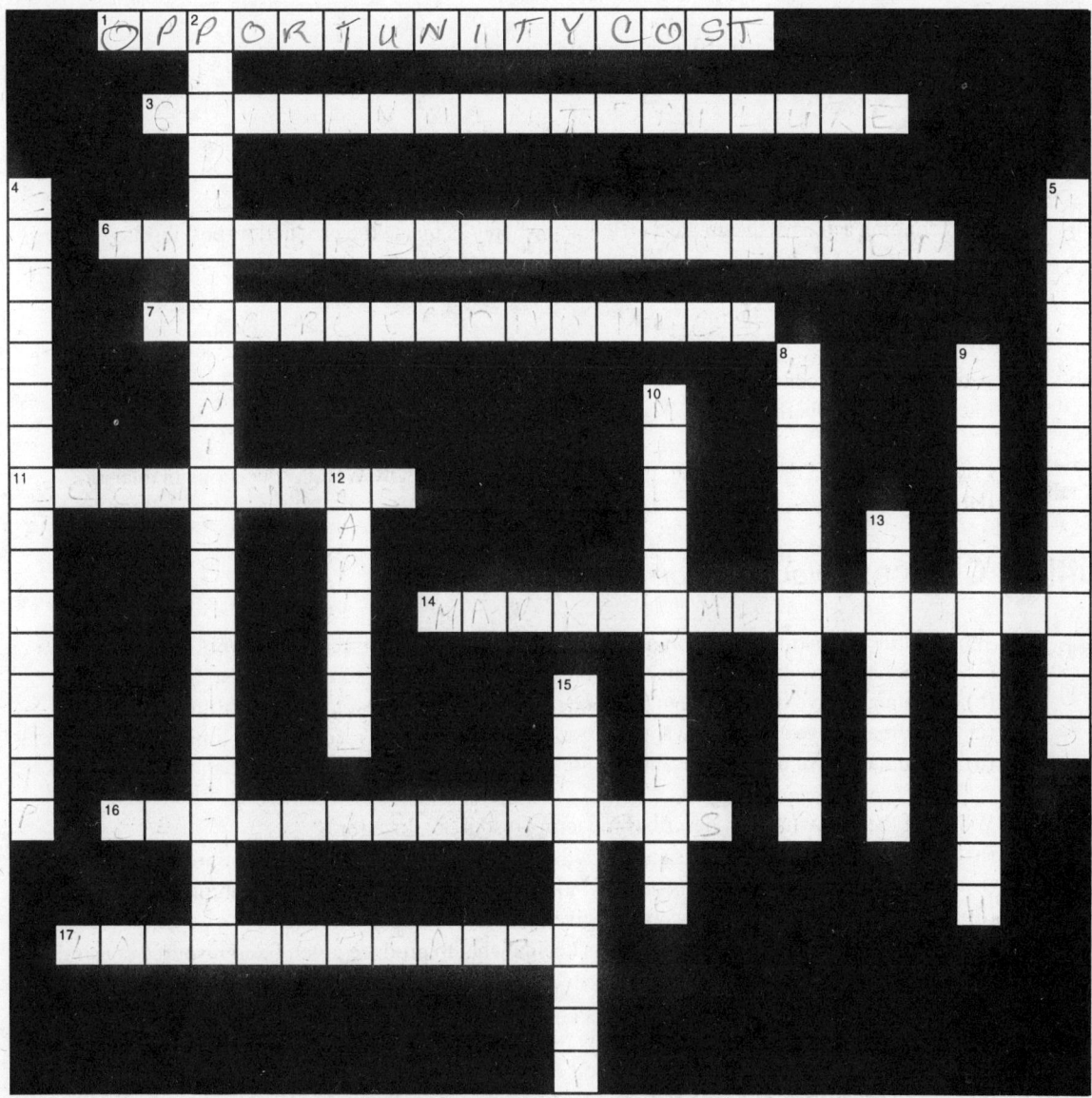

True or False: *Circle your choice and explain why any false statements are incorrect.*

T **F** 1. Scarcity is only a problem in the very poor countries of the world.

T **F** 2. Students do not pay tuition in elementary school, so from society's point of view, there is no opportunity cost involved in their education.

T F 3. A production-possibilities curve can be drawn only if a scarce resource prevents unlimited production of a product.

T **F** 4. One reason that the production-possibilities curve is bowed outward is that more production means the economy is less efficient in producing output.

T F 5. If the economy is fully and efficiently employing its resources, then the only way to acquire more of one good, *ceteris paribus*, is to accept less of something else.

T F 6. The opportunity cost of a good increases as more of the good is produced because resources are not equally well suited to the production of all goods.

T **F** 7. The economy achieves the greatest efficiency when it is inside the production-possibilities curve.

T **F** 8. An economy will never be able to produce a combination of goods and services outside of its existing production-possibilities curve.

T F 9. A market driven economy is not capable of solving the problems created by pollution without intervention by government.

T F 10. Price signals direct the answers to the WHAT, HOW, and FOR WHOM decisions in a laissez-faire economy.

Multiple Choice: *Select the correct answer.*

C 1. Which of the following is the best description of the origin of the economic problem of scarcity?
    (a) Humans have limited wants for goods and services and resources are also limited.
    (b) Humans have limited wants for goods and services and resources are unlimited.
    (c) Humans have unlimited wants for goods and services but resources are limited.
    (d) Humans have unlimited wants for goods and services and resources are also unlimited.

A 2. Which of the following best describes the term "resource allocation"?
    (a) Which goods and services society will produce with available factors of production.
    (b) How society spends the income of individuals based on resource availability.
    (c) How society purchases resources, given its macroeconomic goals.
    (d) How individual market participants decide what to produce given fixed resource constraints.

A 3. A consequence of the economic problem of scarcity is that:
    (a) Choices have to be made about how resources are used.
    (b) There is never too much of any good or service produced.
    (c) The production of goods and services has to be controlled by the government.
    (d) The production possibilities curve is bowed outward.

C 4. Which of the following is *not* a factor of production?
   (a) A teacher.
   (b) A ball-point pen.
   (c) The $100,000 used to start a new business.
   (d) Ten acres of forest.

D 5. Centrally planned economies are most likely to underestimate the value of:
   (a) Land.
   (b) Labor.
   (c) Capital.
   (d) Entrepreneurship.

C 6. Which of the following describes how resources are typically allocated in the U.S. economy?
   (a) By tradition.
   (b) By democratic vote.
   (c) By markets.
   (d) By government.

C 7. I plan on going to a $5 movie this evening instead of studying for an exam. The total opportunity cost of the movie:
   (a) Depends on how I score on the exam.
   (b) Is $5.
   (c) Is what I could have purchased with the $5 plus the study time I forgo.
   (d) Is the forgone studying I could have done in the same time.

B 8. The opportunity cost of installing a traffic light at a dangerous intersection is:
   (a) Negative, since it will reduce accidents.
   (b) The best possible alternative bundle of other goods or services that must be forgone in order to build and install the traffic light.
   (c) The time lost by drivers who approach the intersection when the light is red.
   (d) The cost of the stoplight plus the cost savings from a reduction in the number of accidents.

B 9. Which of the following events would cause the production-possibilities curve to shift inward?
   (a) The labor supply grows.
   (b) An unexpected freeze destroys many U.S. crops.
   (c) A technological breakthrough occurs.
   (d) New factories are built.

D 10. Which of the following events would cause the production-possibilities curve to shift outward?
   (a) The economy's capital stock increases.
   (b) A new, strong plastic is developed for use in building houses.
   (c) More women enter the labor force.
   (d) All of the above.

C 11. The slope of the production-possibilities curve provides information about:
   (a) The growth of the economy.
   (b) Technological change in the economy.
   (c) Opportunity costs in the economy.
   (d) All of the above.

B 12. The law of increasing opportunity cost explains:
   (a) How everything becomes more expensive as the economy grows.
   (b) The shape of the production-possibilities curve.
   (c) Inflation.
   (d) All of the above.

_B_ 13. When an economy is producing efficiently it is:
  (a) Producing a combination of goods and services outside the production-possiblities curve.
  (b) Getting the most goods and services from the available resources.
  (c) Experiencing decreasing opportunity costs.
  (d) All of the above are correct.

_B_ 14. In a market economy, the answer to the WHAT to produce question is determined by:
  (a) Direct negotiations between consumers and producers.
  (b) Producer profits and sales.
  (c) Government directives.
  (d) A democratic vote of all producers.

_C_ 15. In a market economy, the answer to the HOW to produce question is determined by:
  (a) Government planners.
  (b) The production possibilities curve.
  (c) The least-cost method of production.
  (d) The method of production which uses the least amount of labor.

_A_ 16. The trend toward greater reliance on the market mechanism by former communist societies is evidence of:
  (a) Government failure.
  (b) Market failure.
  (c) The failure of a mixed economy.
  (d) *Ceteris paribus*.

_D_ 17. Which of the following are major macroeconomic goals of the economy?
  (a) Full employment.
  (b) Control of inflation.
  (c) Economic growth.
  (d) All of the above.

_A_ 18. Microeconomics focuses on the performance of:
  (a) Individual consumers, firms and government agencies.
  (b) Firms only.
  (c) Government agencies only.
  (d) The economy as a whole.

_____ 19. Reread the *World View* article "Free Enterprise Blooms in Wenzhou, China, Out of the Party's Sight." The article best illustrates:
  (a) The success of Karl Marx's view of market-based economies.
  (b) Market failure.
  (c) The concepts described in *The Wealth of Nations*.
  (d) The scarcity of resources.

_____ 20. Reread the *World View* article "North Korea Says It Is Running out of Food." Implicitly, the article is suggesting that the maintenance of an army results in:
  (a) An opportunity cost in terms of consumer goods.
  (b) An opportunity cost in terms of investment goods only.
  (c) No opportunity cost because the army keeps the country safe.
  (d) No opportunity cost because the soldiers are being paid.

_A_ 21. The slope of a curve at any point is given by the formula:
  (a) The change in y coordinates between two points divided by the change in their x coordinates.
  (b) The change in x coordinates between two points divided by the change in their y coordinates.
  (c) The percentage change in y coordinates between two points divided by the percentage change in their x coordinates.
  (d) The percentage change in x coordinates between two points divided by the percentage change in their y coordinates.

_B_ 22. When the relationship between two variables changes:
  (a) There is movement from one point on a linear curve to another point on the same curve.
  (b) The entire curve shifts.
  (c) The labels on the axes must be changed.
  (d) The curve becomes linear.

_B_ 23. A linear curve can be distinguished by:
  (a) The continuous change in its slope.
  (b) The same slope throughout the curve.
  (c) The changing relationship between the two variables.
  (d) A shift in the curve.

Problems and Applications

Exercise 1

Suppose you have only 20 hours per week to allocate to study or leisure. The following table indicates the tradeoff between leisure time (not studying) and the grade-point average achieved as a result of studying.

Table 1.1

	(a)	(b)	(c)	(d)	(e)
Leisure time (hours / week)	20	18	14.5	10	0
Grade-point average	0	1.0	2.0	3.0	4.0

1. In Figure 1.1, draw the production-possibilities curve that represents the possible combinations from Table 1.1.

Figure 1.1

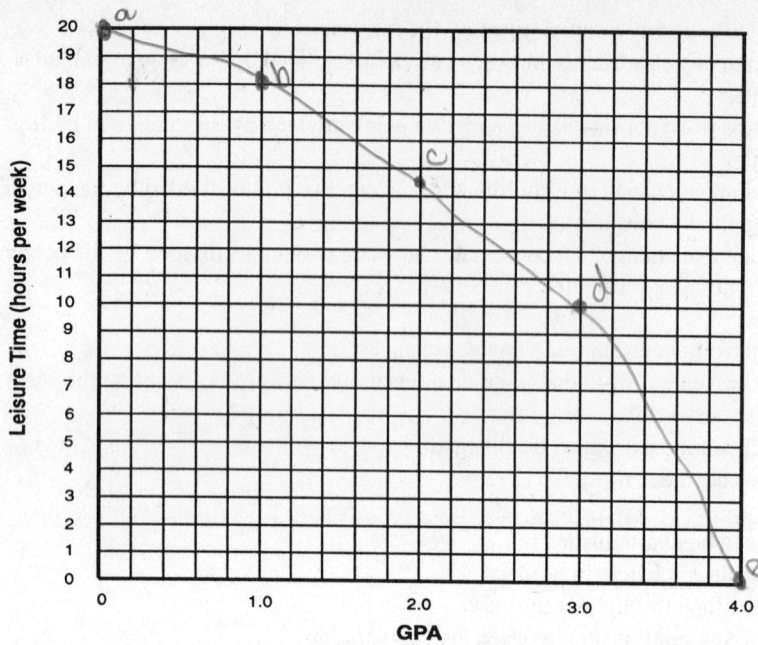

2. Using the information above, what is the opportunity cost of raising your grade-point average from 2.0 to 3.0? _Decrease in leisure time by 4.5 hours_

3. What is the opportunity cost of raising your grade-point average from 3.0 to 4.0?
   Decrease in leisure time by 10 hours.

4. Why does the opportunity cost of improving your grade-point average increase?
   Because leisure time is decreasing, which leaves more room for study time.

Exercise 2

This exercise is similar to the problem at the end of Chapter 1 in the text. It provides practice in drawing and interpreting a production-possibilities curve and demonstrating shifts of such a curve.

1. A production-possibilities schedule showing the production alternatives between corn and lumber is presented in Table 1.2. Plot combination *A* in Figure 1.2 and label it. Do the same for combination *B*. In going from combination *A* to combination *B*, the economy has sacrificed __2__ billion board feet of lumber production per year and has transferred the land to production of __1__ billion bushels of corn per year. The opportunity cost of corn in terms of lumber is __2__ board feet per bushel.

Table 1.2

Combination	Quantity of corn (billions of bushels per year)	Quantity of lumber (billions of board feet per year)
A	0	50
B	1	48
C	2	44
D	3	38
E	4	30
F	5	20
G	6	0

2. In answering Question 1 you determined the opportunity cost of corn when the economy is initially producing only lumber (combination *A*). Using the information in Table 1.2, plot the rest of the production-possibilities combinations in Figure 1.2 and label each of the points with the appropriate letter.

Figure 1.2

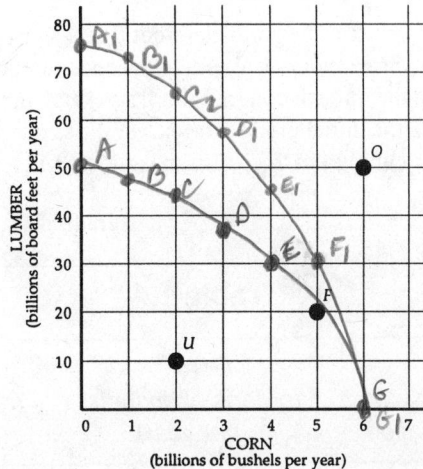

3. When Table 1.3 is completed, it should show the opportunity cost of corn at each possible combination of lumber and corn production in the economy. Opposite "1st billion bushels" insert the number of board feet per year of lumber sacrificed when the economy shifts from combination *A* to combination *B*. Complete the table for each of the remaining combinations.

Table 1.3

Corn production (billions of bushels per year)	Opportunity cost of corn in terms of lumber (billions of board feet per year)
1st billion bushels	2
2nd billion bushels	4
3rd billion bushels	6
4th billion bushels	8
5th billion bushels	10
6th billion bushels	20

4. In Table 1.3, as more corn is produced (as the economy moves from combination *A* toward combination *G*), the opportunity cost of corn (falls, *rises*, remains the same), which illustrates the law of _____ increasing opportunity cost.

5. Suppose that lumber companies begin to clear-cut forest areas instead of cutting them selectively. Clear-cutting improves the economy's ability to produce lumber but not corn. Table 1.4 describes such a situation. Using the information in Table 1.4, sketch the new production-possibilities curve in Figure 1.2 as you did the initial production-possibilities curve based on Table 1.3. For which combination does clear-cutting fail to change the amount of corn and lumber produced? _____ G

Table 1.4

Combination	Corn (billions of bushels per year)	Lumber (billions of board feet per year)
A'	0	75
B'	1	72
C'	2	66
D'	3	57
E'	4	45
F'	5	30
G'	6	0

6. After the introduction of clear-cutting most of the new production-possibilities curve is (*outside*, inside, the same as) the earlier curve. The opportunity cost of corn has (*increased*, decreased) as a result of clear-cutting.

7. Study your original production-possibilities curve in Figure 1.2 and decide which of the combinations shown (*U, F, O*) demonstrates each of the following. (*Hint:* Check the answers at the end of the chapter to make sure you have diagrammed the production-possibilities curve in Figure 1.2 correctly.)
   (a) Society is producing at its maximum potential. Combination _F_.
   (b) Society has some unemployed or underemployed resources. Combination _U_.
   (c) Society cannot produce this combination. Combination _O_.
   (d) Society might be able to produce this combination if technology improved but cannot produce it with current technology. Combination _O_.
   (e) If society produces this combination, some of society's wants will go unsatisfied unnecessarily. Combination _U_.

Exercise 3

This exercise requires the understanding of scarcity, opportunity cost and production possibilities. Answer the following questions based on the information on pages 4 through 9 in the text.

_B_   1. The term "peace dividend," refers to the:
   (a) Difference between a market economy and a mixed economy.
   (b) Availability of scare resources for the production of civilian goods.
   (c) Tradeoff between consumption and investment.
   (d) Tradeoff between food and civilian goods.

_C_   2. For the U.S., the share of total output devoted to military goods:
   (a) Has remained fairly constant since 1940.
   (b) Is currently about 25 percent.
   (c) Has decreased since the end of the Cold War.
   (d) Is fairly low and results in no opportunity cost.

_A_   3. According to Figure 1.1 in the text, as the mix of output moves from point *B* to point *C*:
   (a) There is an increase in the production of televisions.
   (b) There is no opportunity cost because point *C* represents the optimal mix of output.
   (c) More factors of production are available for both shoes and televisions.
   (d) All of the above are true.

_B_   4. According to the text, the North Korean army:
   (a) Is the largest in the world in terms of number of personnel.
   (b) Absorbs approximately 25 percent of the country's resources.
   (c) Absorbs a large share of output because North Korea is such a large country.
   (d) All of the above are true.

_D_   5. Which of the following is the opportunity cost of maintaining an army in North Korea?
   (a) There is no opportunity cost because North Korea needs a large army to protect its citizens.
   (b) There is no opportunity cost because North Korea is producing the optimal mix of output.
   (c) Only the money spent on military equipment and salaries.
   (d) The food and other consumer goods that must be given up.

Exercise 4

This exercise provides practice in the use of graphs.

Use Figure 1.3 below to answer the following questions.

Figure 1.3

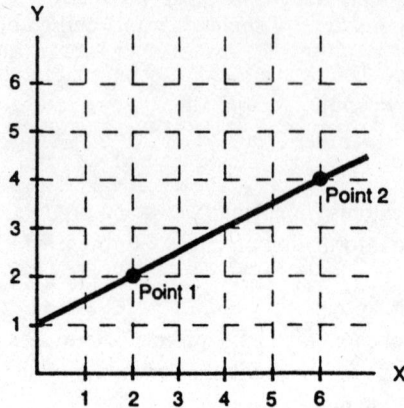

The slope of a line is the rate of change between two points or the vertical change divided by the horizontal change.

1.   The vertical distance between the two points equals ___2___ .

2.   The horizontal distance between the two points equals ___4___ .

3.   The slope of the line equals ___½___ .

4.   The slope of the line is (positive, negative) because as one variable increases the other variable (increases, decreases).

5.   The line has the same slope at every point implying a (constant, changing) relationship between the two variables.

6.   When the slope of a line is the same at every point, the curve is (linear, nonlinear).

Common Errors

The first statement in each "common error" below is incorrect. Each incorrect statement is followed by a corrected version and an explanation.

1. Words mean the same thing in economics that they do in our everyday conversation. WRONG!

    Words used in everyday conversation *very often* have different meanings when they are used in economics. RIGHT!

    You'll have to be very careful here. Words are used with precision in economics. You'll have difficulty if you confuse their everyday meanings with their economic meanings. For example, the term "capital" in economics means simply "man-made instruments of production." In everyday usage it may mean money, machines, a loan, or even the British response to the question "How are you feeling?"

2. Economic models are abstractions from the real world and are therefore useless in predicting and explaining economic behavior. WRONG!

    Economic models are abstractions from the real world and *as a result* are useful in predicting and explaining economic behavior. RIGHT!

    You have to be willing to deal with abstractions if you want to get anything accomplished in economics. By using economic models based on specific assumptions, we can make reasonable judgments about what's going on around us. We try not to disregard any useful information. However, to try to include everything (such as what cereal we like for breakfast) would be fruitless. For example, the production-possibilities frontier is an abstraction. No economist would argue that it is an economy! But it certainly is useful in focusing on public-policy choices, such as the choice between guns and butter.

3. Because economics is a "science," all economists should come up with the same answer to any given question. WRONG!

    Economics is a science, but there is often room for disagreement in trying to answer a given question. RIGHT!

    Economics is a social science, and the entire society and economy represent the economist's laboratory. Economists cannot run the kind of experiments that are done by physical scientists. As a result, two economists may attack a given problem or question in different ways using different models. They may come up with different answers, but since there is no answer book, you cannot say which is right. The solution is, then, to do more testing, refine our models, compare results, and so on. By the way, the recent space probes have given physicists cause to reevaluate much of their theory concerning the solar system, and there is much controversy concerning what the new evidence means. But physics is still a science, as is economics!

4. Increasing opportunity cost results from increasing inefficiency. WRONG!

    Increasing opportunity cost occurs even when resources are being used at their peak efficiency. RIGHT!

    Increasing opportunity cost and inefficiency are confused because both result in a lower amount of output per unit of input. However, inefficiency results from poor utilization or underemployment of resources, while increasing opportunity results from the increasing difficulty of adapting resources to production as more of a good is produced. Inefficiency can be represented as a movement inward from the production-possibilities curve, while increasing opportunity cost can be measured in movements along the production-possibilities curve. As the slope becomes steeper because of a movement down the production-possibilities curve, the good on the *x*-axis experiences increasing opportunity cost (a steeper slope). Similarly, a movement up along the production-possibilities curve represents a higher opportunity cost for the good on the *y*-axis – this time in the form of a flatter slope as more of the good on the *y*-axis is produced.

•ANSWERS•

Using Key Terms

Across

1. opportunity cost
3. government failure
6. factors of production
7. microeconomics
11. economics
14. market mechanism
16. ceteris paribus
17. laissez faire

Down

2. production possibilities
4. entrepreneurship
5. macroeconomics
8. mixed economy
9. economic growth
10. market failure
12. capital
13. scarcity
15. efficiency

True or False

1. F   All societies experience the problem of scarcity because human wants for goods and services will always exceed society's ability to produce goods and services.
2. F   Factors of production are required to produce education. These factors could have been used to produce other goods and services. The opportunity cost of education is the value of the best goods and services given up to get education.
3. T
4. F   Efficiency is maximized along a given production-possibilities curve. The production-possibilities curve bows outward because of the law of increasing opportunity costs, i.e. resources are not perfectly transferable from the production of one good to the production of another. Efficiency means "getting the most from what you have."
5. T
6. T
7. F   The economy achieves the greatest efficiency when it is on the curve.
8. F   An economy could produce a combination of goods and services outside its existing curve in the future if technology improves and/or the quantity of resources increase sufficiently.
9. T
10. T

Multiple Choice

1.	c	5.	d	9.	b	13.	b	17.	d	21.	a
2.	a	6.	c	10.	d	14.	b	18.	a	22.	b
3.	a	7.	c	11.	c	15.	c	19.	c	23.	b
4.	c	8.	b	12.	b	16.	a	20.	a		

Problems and Applications

Exercise 1

1. **Figure 1.1 Answer**

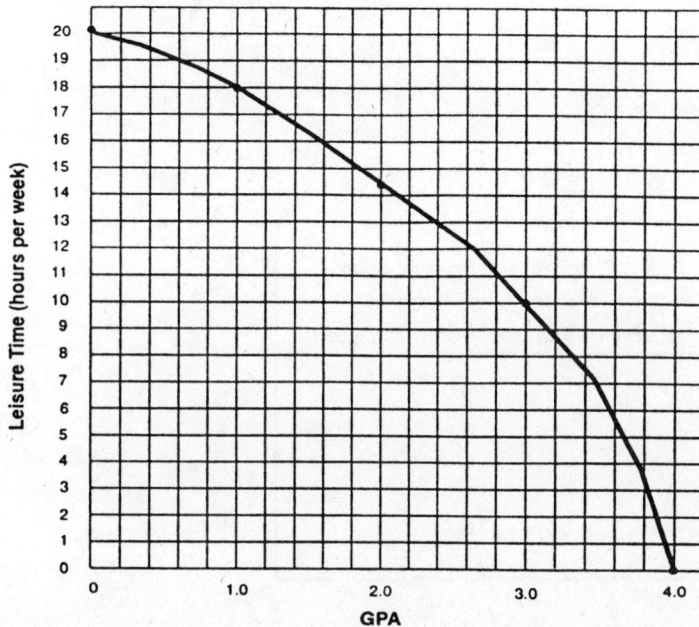

2. 4.5 hours of leisure time.

3. 10 hours of leisure time.

4. Higher grades are harder to get, particularly if the class is graded on a curve, with higher grades being received by a decreasing number of students. The "law" of increasing opportunity cost is evident in the economy and in the classroom.

Exercise 2

1. 2, 1, 2

2. **Figure 1.2 Answer**

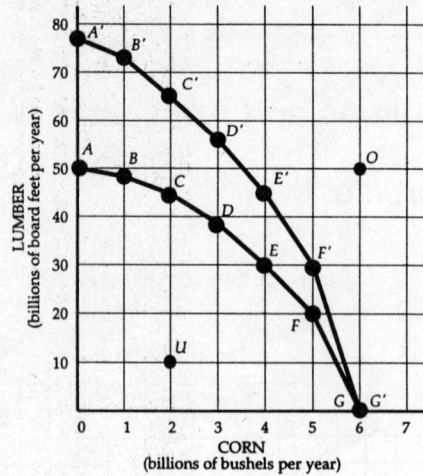

3. **Table 1.3 Answer**

Corn production (billions of bushels per year)	Opportunity cost of corn in terms of lumber (billions of board feet per year)
1st billion bushels	2
2nd billion bushels	4
3rd billion bushels	6
4th billion bushels	8
5th billion bushels	10
6th billion bushels	20

4. Rises, increasing opportunity costs
5. See Figure 1.2 answer; combination *G*.
6. Outside, increased
7. a. *F*; b. *U*; c. *O*; d. *O*; e. *U*

Exercise 3

1. b
2. c
3. a
4. b
5. d

16

Exercise 4

1. 2
2. 4
3. Slope = vertical change/horizontal change = 2/4 = 1/2 or 0.5
4. Positive, increases
5. Constant
6. Linear

CHAPTER 2

The U.S. Economy: A Global View

Quick Review

To understand the American economy, we must look to the answers it generates to the following questions:

- WHAT goods and services does the United States produce?
- HOW is that output distributed?
- FOR WHOM is the output produced?

The WHAT question is answered by a summary measure called gross domestic product (GDP). GDP is the total dollar value of all final goods and services produced *in a country* during a given time period. Although there are several ways to break up the GDP, a frequently used technique is to classify the *output which is produced* by the groups which purchase it: consumer goods by households, investment goods by business, and output taken by government at the federal, state, and local levels. In addition we must account for goods and services produced here and sold abroad (exports) and those which are produced abroad and sold here (imports).

The HOW question is answered by entrepreneurs who make decisions about how the nation's factors of production (which vary in quantity, quality and mobility) will be allocated within the framework provided by government. Government provides the legal rules of the game under which economic activity takes place. Government also intervenes to protect the environment from the negative third-party effects which accompany the pursuit of profits within the market mechanism. Government provides protection to consumers, labor and the environment through laws and regulations.

The economy never stands still, and we have observed in this century both the decline of agriculture and manufacturing and the rise of the service sector in the U.S. economy. The relative importance (both in size and numbers) of various forms of business organization – proprietorships, partnerships and corporations – has undergone substantial revision as well.

The FOR WHOM question is answered by the nation's income distribution, where those at the upper end of the distribution receive incomes which are disproportionate to their numbers.

In the future society will demand different answers to the WHAT, HOW, and FOR WHOM questions as new concerns cause us to revise our priorities. Both market signals and government directives will be assigned significant roles as questions concerning possible income stagnation, environmental destruction, and widening inequality and others are debated.

Learning Objectives

After reading Chapter 2 and doing the following exercises, you should:

1. Be able explain why GDP and its components are an answer to the WHAT question.
2. Understand that factors of production differ in quantity, quality, and mobility in the United States and elsewhere.
3. Be able to trace the broad changes in industry structure in the United States from 1900 to the present.
4. Understand the role of government intervention as the economy answers the HOW question.
5. Know the basic types and relative importance of business organizations in the United States.
6. Understand that the economy's answer to the FOR WHOM question lies in the income distribution.
7. Expect that new market signals and government directives will change the answers to the WHAT, HOW, and FOR WHOM questions.

Using Key Terms

Fill in the puzzle on the opposite page with the appropriate term from the of Key Terms at the end of the chapter in the text.

Across

1. Account for nearly half of all federal government spending but are not part of GDP.
6. Used in Table 2.2 in the text to divide the population and then rank by income level.
9. The ability of a country to produce a good at a lower opportunity cost than another country.
10. The high level of _____ in the U.S. is explained to some extent by the level of education according to the article on page 34 in the text.
12. Goods and services bought from other countries.
13. A market situation in which the government intervenes to protect consumers from exploitation.
14. The costs or benefits of a market activity that affect a third party.
15. The resources used to produce goods and services.
16. A high ratio of capital to labor in the production process.

Down

2. Goods and services sold to other countries.
3. The sum of consumption, investment, government expenditure, and net exports.
4. The knowledge and skills possessed by the labor force.
5. An expansion of production possibilities.
7. Used to compare the average living standards in the article on page 28 in the text.
8. The value of exports minus imports.
11. Equals 15 percent of GDP in Figure 2.3 in the text.

Puzzle 2.1

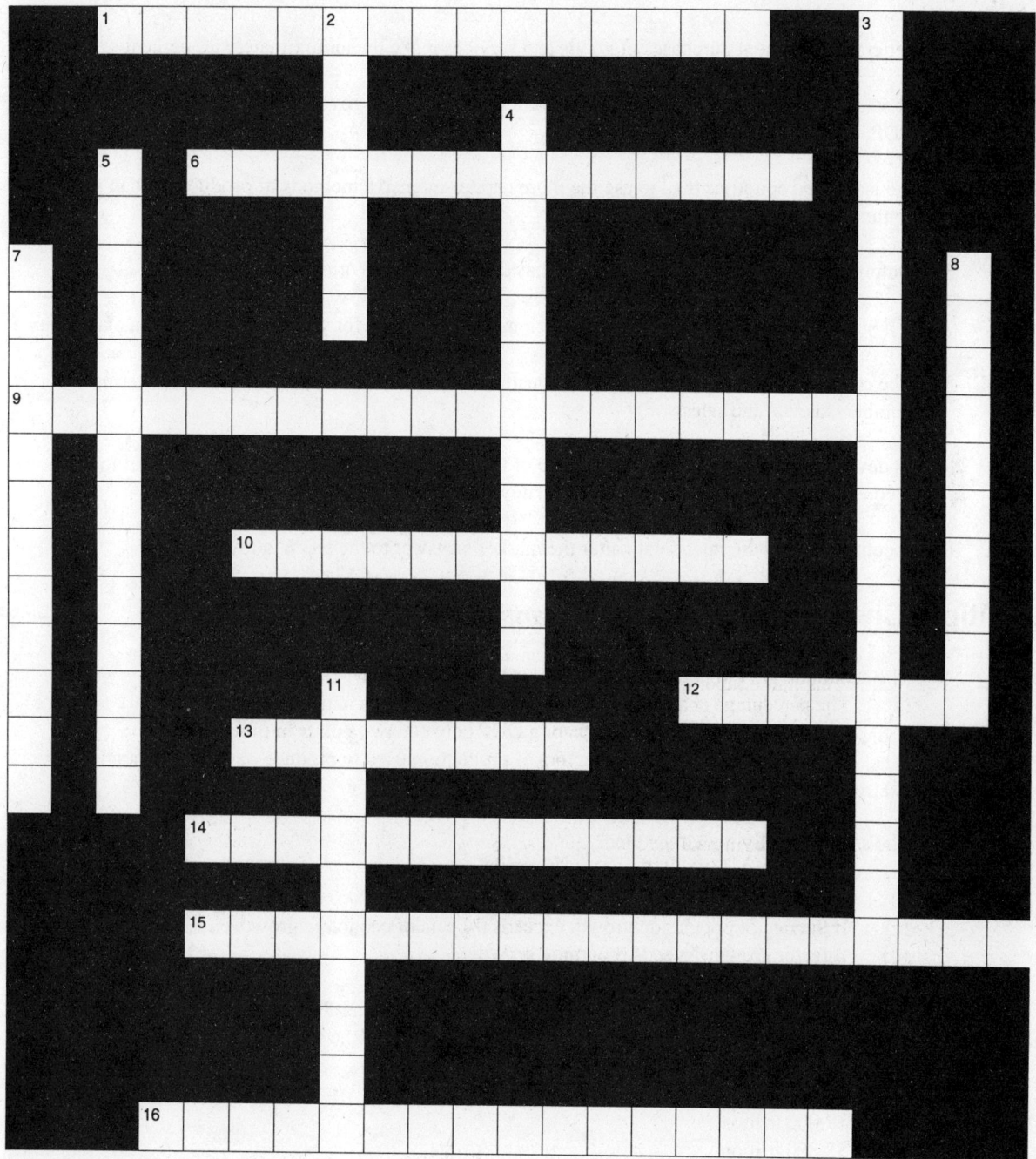

True or False: *Circle your choice and explain why any false statements are incorrect.*

T F 1. The United States produces about 25 percent of the world's output.

T F 2. If the economic growth rate exceeds the population growth rate, per capita GDP will increase.

T F 3. Federal government purchases of goods and services make up approximately 20 percent of GDP.

T F 4. Food stamps, medicare, and veterans' benefits are counted as government expenditures in the GDP.

T F 5. Industrialized countries tend to use the more capital-intensive methods of production than poor countries.

T F 6. Output by the U.S. manufacturing sector has declined since World War II.

T F 7. If a business installs outdoor lighting which makes it difficult for you to sleep, this is an externality.

T F 8. The corporation is the dominant form of business organization in the United States in terms of numbers, assets, and sales.

T F 9. In developed countries the richest quintile of the population gets a smaller proportion of total income than that quintile receives in poor, developing nations.

T F 10. Income transfers are intended to alter the market's answer to the HOW question.

Multiple Choice: *Select the correct answer.*

_____ 1. The economic growth rate of the economy is best measured by:
  (a) The percentage change in the GDP between two points in time.
  (b) The percentage change in per capita GDP between two points in time.
  (c) The sum of the value of the factors of production used to produce output in a country.
  (d) A measure of output divided by a measure of population.

_____ 2. The standard of living will decline:
  (a) Whenever the GDP falls.
  (b) If the percentage change in per capita GDP rises.
  (c) If the rate of population growth exceeds the rate of economic growth.
  (d) If factor growth exceeds economic growth.

_____ 3. Suppose that during the course of a year, an economy produces $4.8 trillion consumer goods, $1.2 trillion investment goods, $1.4 trillion government services, $0.6 trillion exports, and $0.8 trillion imports. For that economy, GDP would be:
  (a) $8,000 trillion.
  (b) $7,000 trillion.
  (c) $8,800 trillion.
  (d) $7,200 trillion.

_____ 4. Which of the following countries (or regions) annually produces the most output?
  (a) Japan.
  (b) United States.
  (c) China.
  (d) The combined European Union.

_____ 5. Since 1900 the change in the relative importance of different sectors in the U.S. economy is best characterized as:
   (a) Relative growth in farm output share.
   (b) Relative growth in manufacturing output share.
   (c) Relative growth in service output share.
   (d) Relative decrease in service output share.

_____ 6. As the United States economy relies more and more heavily on the production of services rather than goods:
   (a) GDP will decrease since there will be less "real" production.
   (b) International trade will become more difficult.
   (c) Mass unemployment will result.
   (d) None of the above are likely to occur.

_____ 7. Which of the following has contributed to the increase in international trade in the United States since the 1920s?
   (a) Reduced trade barriers.
   (b) Improved communication systems.
   (c) The growing share of services in U.S. production.
   (d) All of the above.

_____ 8. Most of the United States GDP is used by:
   (a) Consumers.
   (b) Federal, state and local governments.
   (c) Businesses.
   (d) Foreign individuals and businesses.

_____ 9. Investment goods:
   (a) Both maintain and expand production possibilities.
   (b) Maintain production possibilities but do not expand them.
   (c) Expand production possibilities but do not maintain them.
   (d) Include consumption goods.

_____ 10. Which of the following are included in the GDP?
   (a) Social security benefits.
   (b) Net exports.
   (c) Imports.
   (d) Welfare checks.

_____ 11. Which of the following explains the low productivity of workers in poor, developing countries?
   (a) Labor intensity of their production processes.
   (b) The low factor mobility.
   (c) The low quality of labor as a result of poor education.
   (d) All of the above.

_____ 12. An increase in the level of human capital in an economy, *ceteris paribus*, will have the following effect on the economy's production possibilities curve.
   (a) Shift the curve inward.
   (b) Result in a movement from inside the curve to a point on the curve.
   (c) Shift the curve outward.
   (d) Result in a movement along the curve.

_____ 13. The primary way to distinguish among corporations, partnerships, and proprietorships is through:
   (a) Their ownership characteristics.
   (b) The size of firms.
   (c) The market share of leading firms.
   (d) The number of firms in each classification.

_____ 14. Which of the following would *not* be a common government activity in the U.S. economy?
   (a) The distribution of goods and services.
   (b) The regulation of water pollution.
   (c) Enforcing child labor laws.
   (d) Requiring producers to label the contents of baby food.

_____ 15. When the production of a good creates external costs:
   (a) Profits for the producer of the good will be lower.
   (b) Production of the good will be lower.
   (c) Society's collective well being will be lower.
   (d) The level of environment pollution will be lower.

_____ 16. When monopolies exist:
   (a) Prices tend to be higher.
   (b) Production tends to be lower.
   (c) Quality tends to be lower.
   (d) All of the above can occur.

_____ 17. The result of government intervention in the market in the case of market failure is that:
   (a) Society is always better off.
   (b) The production possibilities curve will always shift outward.
   (c) Society may be worse off.
   (d) Society will always be worse off.

_____ 18. Which of the following statements about the way markets allocate resources is most accurate from society's perspective?
   (a) The market always allocates resources in the best way.
   (b) The market may allocate resources in a way that is not in society's best interest.
   (c) Resource allocation by markets may not be perfect but it is always better than when the government allocates resources.
   (d) Markets often fail to allocate resources properly so we must rely on governments to determine the proper use of our resources.

_____ 19. Inequalities in income caused by market forces:
   (a) Are always undesirable.
   (b) Can provide incentives and rewards for achievements.
   (c) Cannot be addressed by government action.
   (d) Inequalities in income caused by market forces do not exist.

_____ 20. Market signals:
   (a) Are sent by consumer purchases.
   (b) Provide incentives for improving efficiency.
   (c) Are answered by resource reallocations.
   (d) All of the above.

Problems and Applications

Exercise 1

Each January the president has the Council of Economic Advisers prepare an economic report on the state of the U.S. economy called *The Economic Report of the President.* It summarizes the essential features of the economy's performance and describes the policy initiatives that are likely to be undertaken. This exercise uses the kind of information that is developed in this publication.

1. Table 2.1 shows the real GDP and the nominal GDP for the years 1990-97.

Table 2.1
Real GDP and nominal GDP, 1990-97

Year	Real GDP (in billions of dollars per year)	Nominal GDP (in billions of dollars per year)	Percentage growth in real GDP	Percentage growth in nominal GDP	U.S. population (in millions)	Real GDP per capita
1990	6,136.3	5,743.8	------------	-----------	249.9	_____
1991	6,079.4	5,916.7	_____	_____	252.6	_____
1992	6,244.4	6,244.4	_____	_____	255.4	_____
1993	6,389.6	6,558.1	_____	_____	258.1	_____
1994	6,610.7	6,947.0	_____	_____	260.6	_____
1995	6,742.1	7,265.4	_____	_____	263.0	_____
1996	6,928.4	7,636.0	_____	_____	265.5	_____
1997	7,191.4	8,083.4	_____	_____	267.9	_____

2. From the information in Table 2.1, calculate the percentage growth in nominal and real GDP for each of the years 1991-97 and insert your answers in the appropriate columns. Use the following formula:

$$\text{Percentage growth in real GDP} = \frac{\text{real GDP}_t - \text{real GDP}_{t-1}}{\text{real GDP}_{t-1}} \times 100\%$$

where t = current year

   $t - 1$ = previous year

For example, for 1991 real GDP grew by the following percentage:

$$\frac{\text{real GDP}_t - \text{real GDP}_{t-1}}{\text{real GDP}_{t-1}} = \frac{\$6{,}079.4 - \$6{,}136.3}{\$6{,}136.3} \times 100\% = -0.9\%$$

3. T   F   When nominal GDP grows, real GDP must grow.
4. By what nominal-dollar amount did nominal GDP grow from 1990 to 1997? \$_____
5. By what constant-dollar amount did real GDP grow from 1990 to 1997? \$_____
6. The U.S. population for the years 1990–97 is presented in column 6 of Table 2.1. Calculate the real GDP per capita in column 7.
7. T   F   When real GDP rises, real GDP per capita must also rise.

25

Exercise 2

This problem is designed to help you understand the mix of output in the United States.

1. Calculate the percentage of total output accounted for by each of the expenditure categories in Table 2.2. Then compare your answers to Figure 2.3 in the text. Figures will not be exact due to rounding.

Table 2.2. U.S. national-income aggregates, 1997 (billions of dollars per year)

Expenditure categories		Percentage of total output
Consumption goods and services	$5,489	_____
Investment goods	1,238	_____
Exports	959	_____
Imports	1,056	_____
Federal government purchases	525	_____
State and local government purchases	929	_____

2. Are net exports positive or negative in Table 2.2? _____

3. T   F   When net exports are negative, an economy uses more goods and services than it produces.

Exercise 3

This exercise focuses on the growth rates for GDP, population, and per capita GDP.

Refer to Table 2.1 in the text to answer questions 1-5.

1. Which country had the lowest growth rate of per capita GDP during this time period? _____

2. Which country had the highest growth rate of per capita GDP during this time period? _____

3. In Kenya, the growth rate of GDP during this time period was ____ percent and the growth rate of population was _____ percent. When the population growth rate is greater than the GDP growth rate, then per capita GDP must (increase, decrease).

4. In general, the population of high-income countries grew more (rapidly, slowly) which made it easier to raise living standards.

5. T   F   Since the GDP growth rate for Nigeria was greater than the GDP growth rate for Zimbabwe, during this time period, then Nigeria experienced a greater increase in per capita GDP than did Zimbabwe.

Common Errors

The first statement in each "common error" below is incorrect. Each incorrect statement is followed by a corrected version and an explanation.

1. A higher GDP means an increase in the standard of living. WRONG!

   A high per capita GDP is an imperfect measure of the standard of living. RIGHT!

   Many developing countries experience a rise in GDP, but their population grows faster. This means that there is actually less income per person and the standard of living falls! The growth in population must be taken into account in measuring the standard of living, which is the reason that the per capita GDP, not just the GDP, is used. However, even the per capita GDP measure fails to take into account the distribution of income.

2. Investors make an economic investment when they invest in the stock market. WRONG!

   Economic investment occurs only with the *tangible* creation or maintenance of capital goods. RIGHT!

   A distinction must be made between financial investment and economic investment. Common usage usually refers to financial investment in which individuals purchase a financial security backed by a financial institution. Such an activity is called saving, which is the alternative to immediate consumption. Such saving may eventually be used by financial corporations to make loans that will eventually lead to economic investment. But economists have found that there are a lot of things that can happen to saving before it turns into tangible production of capital goods. Therefore economists analyze saving and investment separately.

3. As the United States imports more, consumption rises and therefore so does the GDP. WRONG!

   Imports replace consumption of goods produced in the United States and lower the GDP. RIGHT!

   The GDP is the sum of consumption, investment, government purchases and *net exports*. Net exports are computed by *subtracting* imports from exports. So, let's look at the GDP as an equation:
   GDP = consumption + investment + government purchases + exports - imports

   Greater imports mean a lower GDP, *ceteris paribus*! Consumption of foreign goods is not the concept of U.S. consumption used by economists. Economists focus on the output that is actually produced *in the United States* to satisfy U.S. consumers, not all of the expenditures that consumers make.

4. Export goods are not included in the GDP because they are not consumed by Americans. WRONG!

   Export goods are produced in the United States and therefore are included in the GDP. RIGHT!

   The GDP is the sum of consumption, investment, government purchases and *net exports*. Once again the equation appears as follows:
   GDP = consumption + investment + government purchases + exports - imports

   Larger exports mean a higher GDP! The GDP focuses on the output of the economy and our use of resources to produce that output, regardless of who consumes it.

•ANSWERS•

Using Key Terms

Across

1. income transfers
6. income quintile
9. comparative advantage
10. productivity
12. imports
13. monopoly
14. externalities
15. factors of production
16. capital intensive

Down

2. exports
3. gross domestic product
4. human capital
5. economic growth
7. per capita GDP
8. net exports
11. investment

True or False

1. T
2. T
3. F   Federal government purchases of goods and services only make up approximately 8 percent of GDP.
4. F   These are income transfers and are not included in GDP. No good or service is directly provided in exchange for these payments.
5. T
6. F   Manufacturing output has increased by approximately 4 times since just 1950. However, since GDP has increased by more than 4 times since 1950, manufacturing's share of total GDP has decreased.
7. T
8. F   The corporation is dominant in sales and assets, but the single proprietorship is the most common form of business structure in the U.S.
9. T
10. F   Income transfers alter the market's answer to the FOR WHOM question.

Multiple Choice

1.	a	5.	c	9.	a	13.	a	17.	c
2.	c	6.	d	10.	b	14.	a	18.	b
3.	d	7.	d	11.	d	15.	c	19.	b
4.	b	8.	a	12.	c	16.	d	20.	d

Problems and Applications

Exercise 1

1. **Table 2.1 Answer**

Year	Real GDP (in billions of dollars per year)	Nominal GDP (in billions of dollars per year)	Percentage growth in real GDP	Percentage growth in nominal GDP	U.S. population (in millions)	Real GDP per capita
1990	6,136.3	5,743.8	----	----	249.9	24,555
1991	6,079.4	5,916.7	-0.9	3.0	252.6	24,067
1992	6,244.4	6,244.4	2.7	5.5	255.4	24,449
1993	6,389.6	6,558.1	2.3	5.0	258.1	24,756
1994	6,610.7	6,947.0	3.5	5.9	260.6	25,367
1995	6,742.1	7,265.4	2.0	4.6	263.0	25,635
1996	6,928.4	7,636.0	2.8	5.1	265.5	26,096
1997	7,191.4	8,083.4	3.8	5.9	267.9	26,844

2. See Table 2.1 answer, columns 4, 5
3. F
4. $2,339.6 billion

5. $1,055.1 billion
6. See Table 2.1 answer, column 7
7. F

Exercise 2

1. **Table 2.2 Answer**

Expenditure categories		Percentage of total output
Consumption goods and services	$5,489	67.9
Investment goods	1,238	15.3
Exports	959	11.9
Imports	1,056	13.1
Federal government purchases	525	6.5
State and local government purchases	929	11.5

2. Negative
3. T

Exercise 3

1. Haiti
2. China
3. 2.0, 2.6, decrease
4. slowly
5. F

CHAPTER 3
Supply and Demand

Quick Review

Nations around the world have abandoned central planning as a means of answering the WHAT, HOW, and FOR WHOM questions and are hastily turning to free markets for solutions instead. To understand how a market economy solves these same questions requires an understanding of the essential features of market-directed activity—demand and supply. To focus our discussion, we examine the following questions:

- What determines the price of a good or service?
- How does the price of a product affect its production or consumption?
- Why do prices and production levels often change?

All market participants have a common characteristic. They try to maximize some goal subject to one or more constraints. They do so by participating in markets.

Let's look at some market participants and see how they interact. Households and firms exchange factors of production in factor markets and goods and services in product markets. The quantity supplied of factors or products in a market is the quantity that sellers are willing and able to sell at a particular price. Market prices are likely to affect the quantity supplied. Economists represent the relationship between price and the quantity supplied in a supply schedule or supply curve. Supply represents the ability and willingness to sell specific quantities of a good at alternative prices in a given time period, *ceteris paribus*.

The quantity demanded of factors or products in a market is the quantity that buyers are willing and able to buy at a particular price. When prices fall, people tend to buy more. Economists represent the relationship between price and the quantity purchased in the form of a demand schedule or demand curve. Demand is the ability and willingness to buy specific quantities of a good at alternative prices in a given time period, *ceteris paribus*. Demand and supply do not determine what is actually exchanged, nor do they tell why an exchange occurs.

Market supply and market demand curves can be used to find the equilibrium price and rate of production in a market. A market supply curve is the sum of the supply curves of the sellers in the market. Similarly, a market demand curve is the sum of the individual demand curves of buyers in the market. When the market demand curve intersects the market supply curve, the market is in equilibrium. The market mechanism moves price toward the equilibrium price level as follows:

1. If the market price is above the equilibrium price, surpluses appear. To get rid of the surplus, sellers lower prices and production rates. Buyers purchase more at lower prices.
2. If the market price is below equilibrium price, shortages occur. Buyers bid up the price of the commodity and sellers raise production rates in response to the increased price.

In both cases, price and production rates change until the market reaches the equilibrium price and equilibrium

31

quantity production rate - the price and quantity that clears the market. The market mechanism is not perfect and may fail if there are externalities. It may not allocate income in a desirable way, but it does answer the questions WHAT to produce, HOW to produce, and FOR WHOM to produce.

Market demand and market supply curves shift for a variety of reasons. Changes in the price or availability of other goods, tastes, income, expectations, and the number of buyers can alter market demand. Changes in resource prices, in technology, in expectations, in taxes, and in the number of sellers can alter market supply. With each shift the market finds its way, through trial and error, back to equilibrium. Governments sometimes feel compelled to interfere with the market mechanism by establishing maximum prices (price ceilings) for certain things. No matter how laudable the goals of the program for which they are instituted, price ceilings result in shortages. In some cases the results have been so perverse that public-sector intervention moves society away from, rather than toward, preferred economic outcomes. Participants in the market for rent-controlled apartments in New York and Moscow can attest to this.

Learning Objectives

After reading Chapter 3 and doing the following exercises, you should:

1. Know the basic questions in economics and how the U.S. economy answers the questions.
2. Be able to describe the different types of markets and the motivations of participants in those markets.
3. Understand how a demand schedule represents demand and how a supply schedule represents supply.
4. Be able to define and graph supply and demand curves.
5. Know why supply and demand curves shift.
6. Know what causes movements along demand and supply curves.
7. Know the difference between individual demand and supply vs. market demand and market supply.
8. Be able to explain shortages and surpluses and the effects of price ceilings and price floors.
9. Be able to describe how and why markets move toward equilibrium.

Using Key Terms

Fill in the puzzle on the opposite page with the appropriate term from the list of Key Terms at the end of the chapter in the text.

Across

3.	The result of rent controls discussed on page 62-63 in the text.
6.	Changes from $2.00 to $3.00 in Figure 3.7 in the text.
7.	The willingness and ability to sell various quantities of a good at alternative prices.
10.	The willingness and ability to buy a particular good at some price.
12.	The assumption by economists that nothing else changes.
15.	Where businesses purchase the factors of production.
16.	The use of market price and sales to signal desired output.
17.	Refers to the inverse relationship between price and quantity.

Down

1.	The result of an income change in Figure 3.3 in the text.
2.	According to the cyber note on page 50 in the text, consumers reveal their _____ to Priceline.
3.	The sum of all producers' sales intentions.
4.	The name of the table from which Figure 3.2 in the text is drawn.
5.	Where goods and services are exchanged.
8.	According to Figure 3.6 in the text, at a price of $2.50 per page, a _____ of 32 pages per semester exists.
9.	The response of some local governments, including New York City, to high rent prices according to the text.
11.	Explains why the curve in Figure 3.5 in the text is upward sloping.

13. The value of the most desirable forgone alternative.
14. The name for the final curve on the right in Figure 3.4 in the text.

Puzzle 3.1

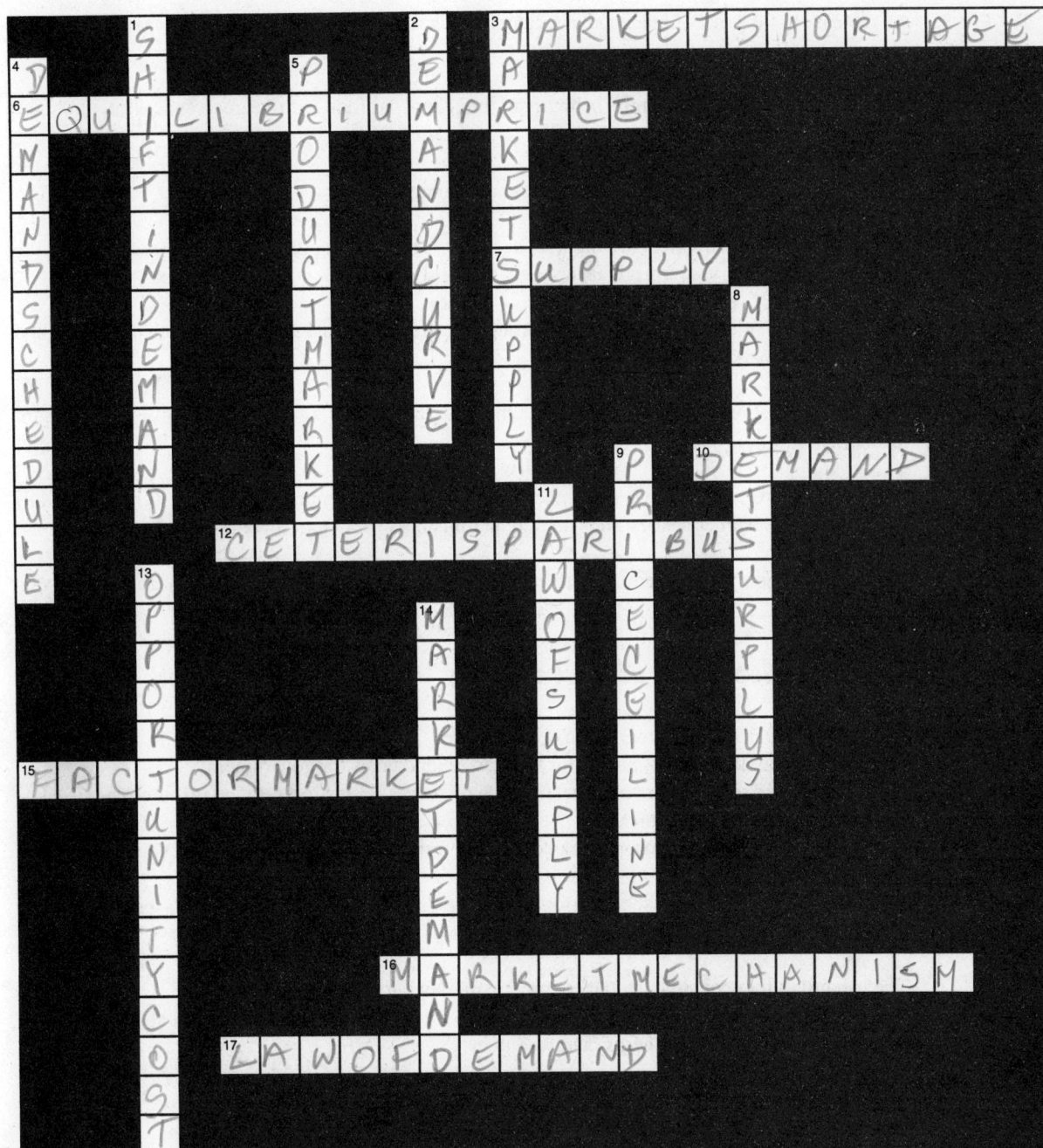

True or False: *Circle your choice and explain why any false statements are incorrect.*

T (F) 1. The demand curve shows how much of a good a buyer will actually buy at a given price.

T (F) 2. A change in one of the determinants of demand causes a movement along the demand curve for the good.

(T) F 3. An increase in the price of one good can cause the demand for another good to increase if the goods are substitutes.

(T) F 4. Supply curves reflect the potential behavior of the sellers or producers of a good or service, not of the buyers.

T (F) 5. The "law of supply" has nothing to do with opportunity costs.

(T) F 6. When the number of suppliers in a market changes, the market supply curve also changes, even if the individual supply curves of original suppliers do not shift.

(T) F 7. The equilibrium price can be determined through the process of trial and error by both the buyers and the sellers in a market.

(T) F 8. There are never shortages or surpluses when the price in a market is equal to the equilibrium price for the market.

T (F) 9. When economists say that the market mechanism provides an "optimal" allocation of resources they mean that all consumer desires are satisfied and business profits are maximized.

T (F) 10. In a market economy, producers earn profits by producing the goods and services that consumers want the most.

Multiple Choice: *Select the correct answer.*

___C___ 1. The goals of the principal actors in the economy are:
   (a) Income for consumers, profits for businesses, and taxes for government.
   (b) Goods and services for consumers, scarce resources for businesses, and resources not used by businesses for government.
   (c) Satisfaction from purchases for consumers, profits for businesses, and general welfare for government.
   (d) Available goods and services for consumers, scarce resources for businesses, and general welfare for government.

___D___ 2. The incentives for economic interaction among market participants include:
   (a) Limited ability to produce what we need.
   (b) Constraints on time, energy, and resources.
   (c) The gains possible from specialization.
   (d) All of the above.

___A___ 3. Consumers:
   (a) Provide dollars to the product market.
   (b) Receive dollars from the product market.
   (c) Provide dollars to the factor market.
   (d) Receive goods and services from the factor market.

✗ *B* 4. The law of demand states that:
   (a) As price falls, quantity demanded falls, *ceteris paribus*.
   (b) As price falls, quantity demanded increases, *ceteris paribus*.
   (c) As price falls, demand falls, *ceteris paribus*.
   (d) As price falls, demand increases, *ceteris paribus*.

C 5. Which of the following must be held constant according to the *ceteris paribus* assumption in defining a demand schedule?
   (a) The price of the good itself.
   (b) Expectations of sellers.
   (c) Income.
   (d) Technology.

D 6. The quantity of a good that a consumer is willing to buy depends on:
   (a) The price of the good.
   (b) The consumer's income.
   (c) The opportunity cost of purchasing that good.
   d) All of the above.

B 7. Jon's demand schedule for donuts indicates:
   (a) How much he likes donuts.
   (b) His opportunity cost of buying donuts.
   (c) Why he likes donuts.
   (d) How many donuts he will actually buy.

B 8. According to the law of supply, a supply curve:
   (a) Has a negative slope.
   (b) Has a positive slope.
   (c) Is a horizontal, or flat, line.
   (d) Will always be less than the demand curve.

A 9. When a seller sells a good, *ceteris paribus*:
   (a) There is no change in supply or the quantity supplied.
   (b) The supply curve shifts to the left, but quantity supplied remains the same.
   (c) The quantity supplied of the good falls, but supply remains unchanged.
   (d) The supply curve shifts to the left, and the quantity supplied falls.

B 10. If corn and wheat are alternative pursuits for a farmer, a change in the supply of corn will take place:
   (a) When the price of corn changes.
   (b) When the price of wheat changes.
   (c) When the demand for corn changes.
   (d) When consumers want to buy more corn at the same price.

C 11. Suppose that this spring the MC birdhouse Co. announced that they need higher prices than last year to sell the same quantity of birdhouses. We can conclude that:
   (a) There has been an increase in demand.
   (b) There has been a decrease in demand.
   (c) There has been a decrease in the company's supply.
   (d) There has been an increase in the company's supply.

✗ *A* 12. To calculate market supply we:
   (a) Add the quantities supplied for each individual supply schedule horizontally.
   (b) Add the quantities supplied for each individual supply schedule vertically.
   (c) Find the average quantity supplied at each price.
   (d) Find the difference between the quantity supplied and the quantity demanded at each price.

B 13. Market supply and market demand are similar in that both:
   (a) Involve the willingness and ability of a supplier to sell a product or service.
   (b) Can be derived by adding horizontally all the respective supply and demand curves of the individuals in the market.
   (c) Are affected by income.
   (d) Have price on the x-axis and production rate(quantity) on the y-axis.

C 14. In a market, the equilibrium price is determined by:
   (a) What buyers are willing and able to purchase.
   (b) What sellers are willing and able to offer for sale.
   (c) Both demand and supply.
   (d) The government.

A 15. A leftward shift in a demand curve and a leftward shift in a supply curve both result in a:
   (a) Lower equilibrium quantity.
   (b) Higher equilibrium quantity.
   (c) Lower equilibrium price.
   (d) Higher equilibrium price.

D 16. Supply and demand do not necessarily tell us:
   (a) The actual quantities produced and bought in a market.
   (b) The reasons that a particular quantity is demanded or supplied.
   (c) Who actually produces or receives the quantity supplied or demand.
   (d) All of the above.

D 17. In a market economy, the people who receive the goods and services produced are the people who:
   (a) Need the goods and services.
   (b) Want the goods and services the most.
   (c) Have the most political power.
   (d) Are willing and able to pay the market price.

C 18. When economists talk about "optimal outcomes" in the marketplace, they mean that:
   (a) The allocation of resources by the market is perfect.
   (b) All consumer desires are satisfied and business profits are maximized.
   (c) The allocation of resources by the market is likely to be the best possible given scare resources and income constraints.
   (d) Everyone that wants a good or service can get it.

___ 19. When effective price ceilings are set for a market:
   (a) Quantity supplied will be less than the equilibrium quantity, and price will be less than the equilibrium price.
   (b) Quantity supplied will be less than the equilibrium quantity, and price will be greater than the equilibrium price.
   (c) Quantity supplied will be greater than the equilibrium quantity, and price will be less than the equilibrium price.
   (d) Quantity supplied will be greater than the equilibrium quantity, and price will be greater than the equilibrium price.

_B_ 20. One *World View* article described the difficulty faced by consumers of electricity who were already "severely pinched by . . . the new, real-world prices for food, rents, and other services." The determinant that is shifting the market demand for electricity on the basis of this quotation is:

 (a) The price of electricity.
 (b) The price of other goods.
 (c) Seller expectations.
 (d) Income.

Problems and Applications

Exercise 1

This exercise provides practice in graphing demand and supply curves for individual buyers and sellers as well as graphing market demand and market supply curves.

1. Suppose you are willing and able to buy 20 gallons of gasoline per week if the price is $1 per gallon, but if the price is $3 per gallon you are willing and able to buy only the bare minimum of 10 gallons. Complete the demand schedule in Table 3.1.

Table 3.1
Your demand schedule for gasoline

Price (dollars per gallon)	Quantity (gallons per week)
$1	20
3	10

2. Use the demand schedule in Table 3.1 to draw the demand curve in Figure 3.1. Assume the demand curve is a straight line.

Figure 3.1
Your demand curve for gasoline.

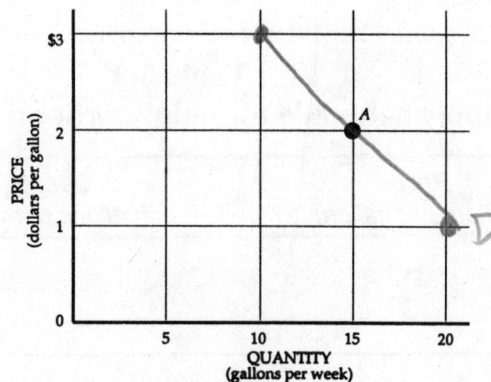

If you have drawn your demand curve correctly, it should go through point *A*.

3. Suppose that 999 other people in your town have demand curves for gasoline that are just like yours in Figure 3.1. Fill out the town's market-demand schedule in Table 3.2 at each price. (Remember to include your own quantity demanded along with everyone else's at each price.)

Table 3.2
Market-demand schedule for gasoline in your town

Price (dollars per gallon)	Quantity (gallons per week)
$1	20,000
3	10,000

4. Using the market-demand schedule in Table 3.2, draw the market-demand curve for gasoline for your town in Figure 3.2. Assume that the curve is a straight line, and label it D.

Figure 3.2
Market supply and demand curves for gasoline in your town

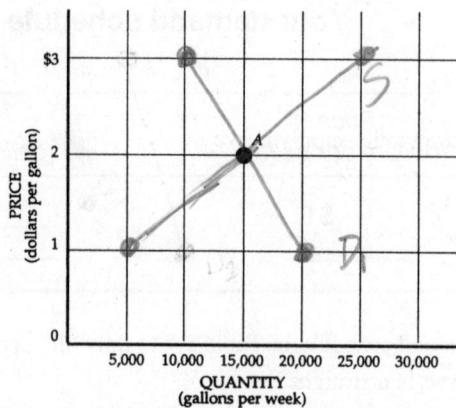

If you have drawn the demand curve correctly, it should pass through point A.

5. Suppose the friendly neighborhood gas station is willing to sell 250 gallons of gasoline per week at $1 per gallon and 1,250 gallons per week at $3 per gallon. Fill in the supply schedule for this gas station in Table 3.3.

Table 3.3
Supply schedule for neighborhood gas station

Price (dollars per gallon)	Quantity (gallons per week)
$1	250
3	1250

6. Graph the supply curve for the gas station in Figure 3.3 using the information in Table 3.3. Assume that the supply curve is a straight line.

Figure 3.3
Supply curve for neighborhood gas station

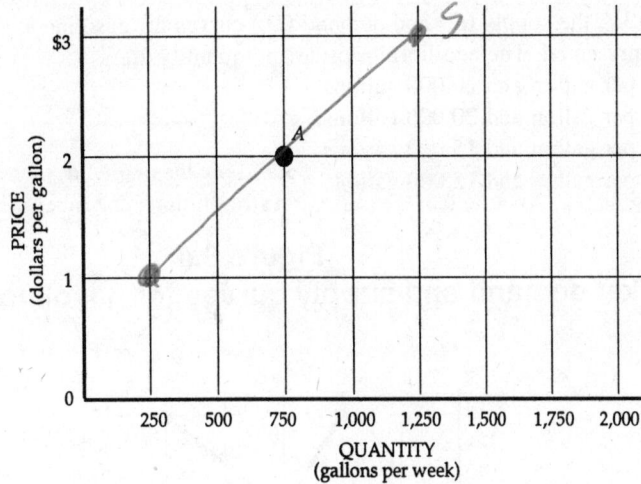

If you have drawn the supply curve correctly, it should pass through point A.

7. Suppose that nineteen other gas stations in your town have the same supply schedule as your neighborhood gas station (Table 3.3). Fill out the market-supply schedule for gasoline of the 20 gas stations in your town in Table 3.4.

Table 3.4
Market supply schedule for gasoline in your town

Price (dollars per gallon)	Quantity (gallons per week)
$1	5000
3	25000

why?
$20 \times 250 = \$5000$
$20 \times 1250 = 25000$

8. Using the market supply schedule in Table 3.4, draw the market supply curve for gasoline for your town in Figure 3.2. Assume that the market supply curve is a straight line. If you have drawn the curve correctly, it should pass through point A. Label the supply curve S.

9. The equilibrium price for gasoline for your town's 20 gas stations and 1,000 buyers of gasoline (see Figure 3.2) is:
   (a) Above $2.
   (b) Exactly $2.
   (c) Below $2.

10. At the equilibrium price:
   (a) There is a shortage.
   (b) There is a surplus.
   (c) There is an excess of inventory.
   (d) The quantity demanded equals the quantity supplied.

Exercise 2

This exercise shows the market mechanics at work in shifting market-demand curves.

1. In Figure 3.4, the supply (S_1) and demand (D_1) curves for gasoline as they might appear in your town are presented. The equilibrium price and quantity are:
   (a) $3 per gallon and 20,000 gallons.
   (b) $2 per gallon and 20,000 gallons.
   (c) $2 per gallon and 15,000 gallons.
   (d) $1 per gallon and 15,000 gallons.

Figure 3.4
Market demand and supply curves for gasoline in your town

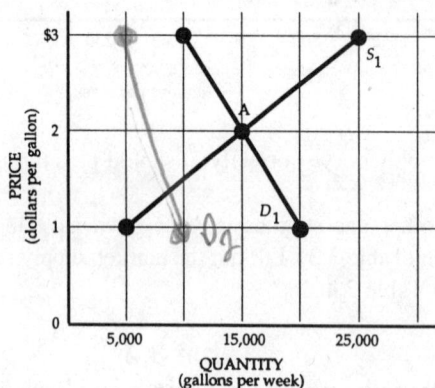

2. Assume that one-half of the people in your town move away. Because of this, suppose that the remaining buyers are willing and able to buy only half as much gasoline at each price as was bought before. Draw the new demand curve in Figure 3.4 and label it D_2.

3. When the number of buyers in a market changes, the market demand curve for goods and services shifts and there is a change in (demand, quantity demanded).

4. When half of the buyers move from your town and the demand curve shifts, the new equilibrium price:
   (a) Is above the old equilibrium price.
   (b) Remains the same as the old equilibrium price.
   (c) Is below the old equilibrium price.
   (*Hint:* See the second demand curve, D_2, in Figure 3.4.)

40

5. Given the new demand curve, if the market price remains at the old equilibrium price of $2 then:
   - (a) A surplus of gasoline will occur.
   - (b) A shortage of gasoline will occur.
   - (c) The quantity demanded will equal the quantity supplied.

6. When there is a surplus in a market:
   - (a) Buyers do not wish to buy as much as sellers want to sell.
   - (b) Sellers are likely to offer discounts to eliminate expensive excess inventories.
   - (c) Buyers who cannot buy commodities at the current market price are likely to make offers to buy at lower prices that sellers will now accept.
   - (d) All the above.

7. When there is a leftward shift of the market-demand curve, market forces should push:
   - (a) Market prices upward and market quantity downward.
   - (b) Market prices upward and market quantity upward.
   - (c) Market prices downward and market quantity upward.
   - (d) Market prices downward and market quantity downward.

8. Whenever there is a rightward shift of the market demand curve, market forces should push:
   - (a) Market prices upward and market quantity downward.
   - (b) Market prices upward and market quantity upward.
   - (c) Market prices downward and market quantity upward.
   - (d) Market prices downward and market quantity downward.

Exercise 3

This exercise gives practice in computing market demand and market supply curves using the demand and supply curves of individuals in a market. It is similar to a problem for chapter 3 in the text.

1. Table 3.5 shows the weekly demand and supply schedules for various individuals. Fill in the total market quantity that these individuals demand and supply.

Table 3.5
Individual demand and supply schedules

Price	$4	$3	$2	$1
Buyers				
Al's quantity demanded	2	3	5	6
Betsy's quantity demanded	2	2	2	3
Casey's quantity demanded	1	2.5	3	3.5
Total market quantity demanded	5	7.5	10	12.5
Sellers				
Alice's quantity supplied	4	3	2	1
Butch's quantity supplied	6	5	4	2
Connie's quantity supplied	5	4	3	2
Ellen's quantity supplied	5	3	1	0
Total market quantity supplied	20	15	10	5

Use the data in Table 3.5 to answer questions 2-4.

2. Construct and label market-supply and market-demand curves in Figure 3.5.

3. Identify the equilibrium point and label it *EQ* in Figure 3.5.

4. What is the situation in terms of quantity demanded versus quantity supplied at a price of $1 in Figure 3.5?

Figure 3.5
Market-supply and market-demand curves for buyers and sellers

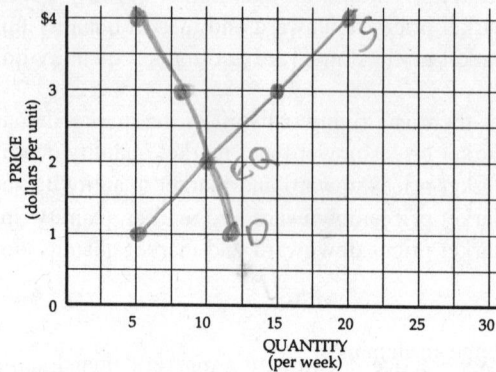

Exercise 4

This exercise provides examples of events that would shift demand or supply curves. It is similar to a problem at the end of the chapter in the text.

Figure 3.6
Shifts of curves

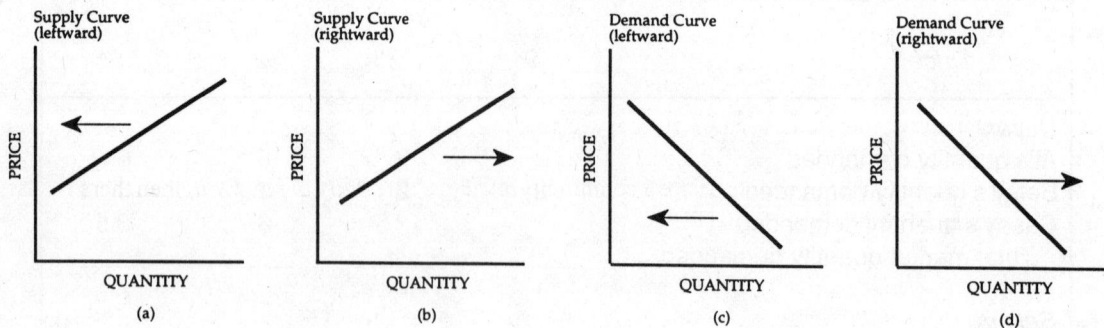

Choose the letter of the appropriate diagram in Figure 3.6 that best describes the shift that would occur in each of the following situations. The shifts are occurring in the market for U.S. defense goods. (*Hint:* Ask yourself if the change first affects buyers or the sellers. Refer to the nonprice determinants for demand and supply listed in the text if necessary).

42

_A_ 1. Because of increased protectionism for steel, steel producers are able to raise the price of specialty steel, which is a key resource in the production of defense goods.

_B_ 2. A new superior engineering design is developed that reduces the amount of materials needed to produce nuclear submarines.

_D_ 3. New buyers enter the market to purchase defense goods.

_A_ 4. A large firm in the defense industry closes down when it loses a defense contract.

_C_ 5. A country that previously bought U.S. defense goods enters into a peace agreement.

Exercise 5

The media often provide information about supply and demand shifts. This exercise uses one of the articles in the text to show the kind of information to look for.

Reread the *In the News* article entitled "Orange Prices Start to Rise After California Freeze." Then answer the following questions:

1. Which of the four diagrams in Figure 3.6 in the previous exercise best represents the shift in the orange market caused by the freeze? a b c d   (circle one)

2. The change in the orange market is referred to as a:
    (a) Change in demand.
    (b) Change in quantity demanded.
    (c) Change in supply.
    (d) Change in quantity supplied.

3. What is the expected change in price and quantity in the orange market?
    _____

Common Errors

The first statement in each "common error" below is incorrect. Each incorrect statement is followed by a corrected version and an explanation.

1. If a large number of people petition the government in order to get something, then there is a large demand for that item. WRONG!

    If a large number of people desire a commodity *and have the ability to pay for it,* then there is a large demand for that item. RIGHT!

    People want something, but there is no "demand" for it unless they are able to pay for it. Economists use the word "demand" in a way that is quite different from normal usage. People who want (desire; have preferences, a taste, or liking for) a commodity are seen as going to a market to purchase the commodity with money. "Demand" does not mean claiming the right to something when a person hasn't the ability to buy it.

2. Market price is the same thing as equilibrium price. WRONG!

    The market price moves by trial and error (via the market mechanism) toward the equilibrium price. RIGHT!

    When demand and supply curves shift, the market is temporarily out of equilibrium. The price may move along a demand or supply curve toward the new equilibrium.

3. Since the quantity bought must equal the quantity sold, every market is always in equilibrium by definition. WRONG!

    Although quantity bought equals quantity sold, there may be shortages or surpluses. RIGHT!

    Although the quantity actually bought does equal the quantity actually sold, there may still be buyers who are willing and able to buy more of the good at the market price (market shortages exist) or sellers who are willing and able to sell more of the good at the market price (market surpluses exist). If the market price is above the equilibrium price, there will be queues of goods (inventories). Prices will be lowered by sellers toward the equilibrium price. If the market price is below the equilibrium price, there will be queues of buyers (shortages). Prices will be bid up by buyers toward the equilibrium price.

4. The intersection of supply and demand curves determines how much of a good or service will actually be exchanged and the actual price of the exchange. WRONG!

    The intersection of supply and demand curves shows only where buyers and sellers intend and have the ability to exchange the same amount of a commodity. RIGHT!

    Many institutional interferences may prevent the market from ever reaching the equilibrium point, where supply and demand curves intersect. All that can be said is that, given a free market, prices and production will tend to move toward equilibrium levels.

5. A change in price changes the demand for goods by consumers. WRONG!

    A change in price changes the quantity demanded by consumers in a given time period. RIGHT!

    Economists differentiate the terms "quantity demanded" and "demand." A change in the quantity demanded usually refers to a movement along the demand curve as a result of a change in price. A change in demand refers to a shift of the demand curve as a result of a change in incomes, tastes, prices or availability of other goods, or expectations.

6. A change in price changes the supply of goods produced by a firm. WRONG!

    A change in price changes the quantity supplied of a good by a firm in a given time period. RIGHT!

    Economists differentiate the terms "quantity supplied" and "supply." A change in the quantity supplied usually refers to a movement along a supply curve as a result of a change in price or production rate. A change in supply refers to a shift of the supply curve as a result of a change in technology, prices of resources, number of sellers, other goods, expectations, or taxes.

•ANSWERS•

Using Key Terms

Across

3. market shortage
6. equilibrium price
7. supply
10. demand
12. ceteris paribus
15. factor market
16. market mechanism
17. law of demand

Down

1. shift in demand
2. demand curve
3. market supply
4. demand schedule
5. product market
8. market surplus
9. price ceiling
11. law of supply
13. opportunity cost
14. market demand

True or False

1. F   The demand curve indicates how much a buyer would like to buy and is able to pay for. How much is actually bought also depends on supply.
2. F   A change in one of the determinants of demand results in a shift in the demand curve.
3. T
4. T
5. F   The quantity of a good that a producer is willing and able to produce and offer for sale at any price depends on the value of the alternative goods that could have been produced with those same resources, i.e. the opportunity costs.
6. T
7. T
8. T
9. F   An optimal outcome does not mean that all consumer desires are satisfied and business profits are maximized. It simply means that the market outcome is likely to be the best possible given scarce resources and income constraints.
10. F   In a market economy, producers earn profits by producing the goods and services that consumers demand, i.e. are willing and able to pay for.

Multiple Choice

Problems and Applications

Exercise 1

1. **Table 3.1 Answer**

p	q
$1	20
3	10

2. **Figure 3.1 Answer**

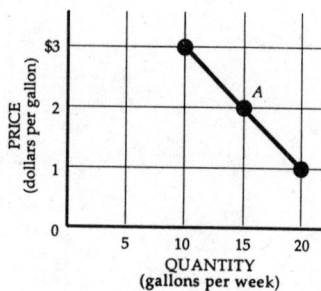

3. **Table 3.2 Answer**

p	q
$1	20,000
3	10,000

4. See Figure 3.2 Answer, curve D.

Figure 3.2 Answer

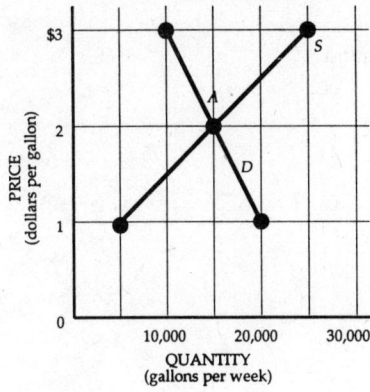

5. ## Table 3.3 Answer

p	q
$1	250
3	1,250

6. ## Figure 3.3 Answer

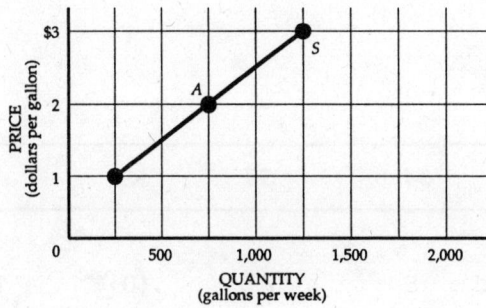

7. ## Table 3.4 Answer

p	q
$1	5,000
3	25,000

8. See Figure 3.2 Answer, curve S.

9. b
10. d

Exercise 2

1. c

2. Figure 3.4 Answer

3. demand
4. c
5. a
6. d
7. d
8. b

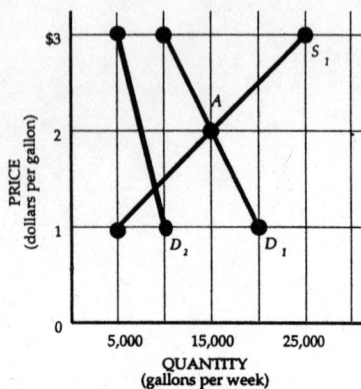

Exercise 3

1. **Table 3.5 Answer**

Price	$4	$3	$2	$1
Buyers Total market quantity demanded	5	7.5	10	12.5
Sellers Total market quantity supplied	20	15	10	5

2.   **Figure 3.5 Answer.**

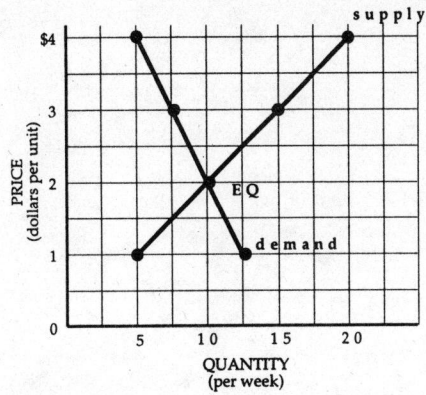

3.   See point *EQ* in Figure 3.5.
4.   The quantity demanded is greater than the quantity supplied or there is a shortage of 7.5 units (12.5 minus 5).

Exercise 4

1. a
2. b
3. d
4. a
5. c

Exercise 5

1. a
2. c
3. an increase in price and a decrease in quantity

CHAPTER 4

The Public Sector

Quick Review

The combined levels of government—federal, state, and local—have a tremendous impact on the answers to the questions WHAT, HOW, and FOR WHOM in the U.S. economy. In this chapter we focus initially on the following questions:

- Do we need a public sector?
- What goods and services are best produced by the government?
- How large a public sector is desirable?

There are several ways to justify the existence of the public sector. One justification is market failure, the failure of the market mechanism when left on its own to produce an "optimal mix" of output. This first justification for government intervention resides in the concept of "public goods." These goods and services are consumed jointly, both by those who pay and by those who don't. Those who don't pay are termed "free riders." National defense is a good example, because the consumption of national defense is communal. Consumption by one person does not preclude consumption by another. Public goods are different from private goods, because consumption of a private good by one person generally does preclude consumption by another.

The existence of externalities—costs or benefits of a market activity that are borne by a third party—is often cited as justification of public-sector activity, too. Externalities can be negative (such as the pollution from a steel mill) or positive (such as the enrichment of the surrounding community when education is produced and consumed). Because the market has no way of accounting for all the costs and benefits of some forms of economic activity, it tends to underproduce those that generate external benefits and overproduce those that generate external costs.

The existence of market power—the ability of a single firm to alter the market price of a specific product—also justifies public-sector intervention. Market power—whether bestowed by a legal sanction (copyrights, patents, and the like), efficiencies of large-scale production, or some other factor—can be used to restrict output and raise prices. The public sector counters market power by antitrust activity and/or regulation (as with cable TV).

Finally, lack of equity in the answer to the FOR WHOM question is the basis for a large measure of public-sector activity. The market mechanism, left on its own, would provide too little for some (the aged, the infirm, some of the very young) than is thought fair. Since the public at large is thought to benefit from expenditures made to address this problem, income redistribution—for example, through transfer payments—is considered a public good.

The examples above focus on micro failures (i.e., where *we are on* the production-possibilities curve). Macro failures can also occur, such as when *we fail to reach* our production-possibilities curve or experience inflation. Thus, government is expected to intervene at the macro level to alleviate the problem of unemployment and stabilize the price level.

The role of government has grown dramatically in recent decades. The budget of the federal government is $1.8 trillion per year, but it still takes a slightly smaller share (of the now much larger economy) than it did in 1950. State and local government activity exceeds that of the federal government and has grown much more rapidly in recent decades. Transfer payments have increased much faster than purchases of goods and services, and they account for the largest part of the observed increase in the size of the entire public sector.

Federal expenditures on goods and services, transfer payments, interest on the public debt, and general aid to state and local governments are supported by the federal personal income tax, social security taxes, corporate income taxes, excise taxes, and other taxes. State and local governments rely most heavily on sales taxes and on property taxes, respectively. Their expenditures go primarily to education, streets and highways, and other services we find close to home.

Whether government is "too big" depends on one's perception of the private-sector activity forgone when government absorbs resources and changes the mix of the economy's output. Cost-benefit analysis and mechanisms that allow taxpayers to vote on projects are ways of trying to ensure that we get the amount and kind of government we want.

Critics of public-sector activity emphasize the role of public officials' self-interest in the decision-making process. In fact, public-choice theory essentially extends the analysis of market behavior to political behavior. Public officials are viewed as utility maximizers pursuing their own individual goals rather than public goals.

Learning Objectives

After reading Chapter 4 and doing the following exercises, you should:

1. Be able to explain the different types of micro failure that justify public-sector intervention.
2. Understand how macro failure justifies public-sector activity.
3. Recognize the opportunity costs of public-sector activity.
4. Know how the mechanism of public decision making differs from the market mechanism.
5. Be able to compute and use cost-benefit ratios.
6. Know the effects of externalities and how they should be handled in the economy.
7. Know the different tax structures and the level of government for which they are particularly important.
8. Be able to determine whether a given tax is progressive or regressive.
9. Know some of the important policy issues connected with taxation, expenditure and borrowing.
10. Understand the essentials of public choice.

Using Key Terms

Fill in the puzzle on the opposite page with the appropriate term from the list of Key Terms at the end of the chapter in the text.

Across

1. The most desired goods and services that are given up in order to obtain something else.
5. An increase in the average level of prices.
8. Referred to as the "invisible hand."
10. The likely outcome of government intervention according to the survey titled "Rising Doubts about Government Waste" in the text.
14. An industry in which a single firm achieves economies of scale over the entire range of output.
16. State lotteries are categorized in this way according to the article titled "Some Taxing Facts about Lotteries" in the text.
18. A form of government intervention to address the FOR WHOM question.
19. Theory which emphasizes the role of self-interest in public decision making.
20. The ability to alter the market price of a good or service.
21. The fee paid for the use of a public-sector good or service.

Down

2. Labeled as point X in Figure 4.1 in the text.
3. Occurs when people are willing to work but are unable to find jobs.

4. The market failure discussed in the article "The Human Cost of Secondhand Smoke" in the text.
6. A tax system in which tax rates rise as incomes rise.
7. For a _____, consumption by one person excludes consumption by others.
9. Federal grants to state and local governments for specific purposes.
11. Represented by point M in Figure 4.1 in the text.
12. Can be consumed jointly.
13. Only one producer in an industry.
15. One who does not pay but still enjoys the benefits.
17. The legislation used to prevent or break up concentrations of market power such as Microsoft.

Puzzle 4.1

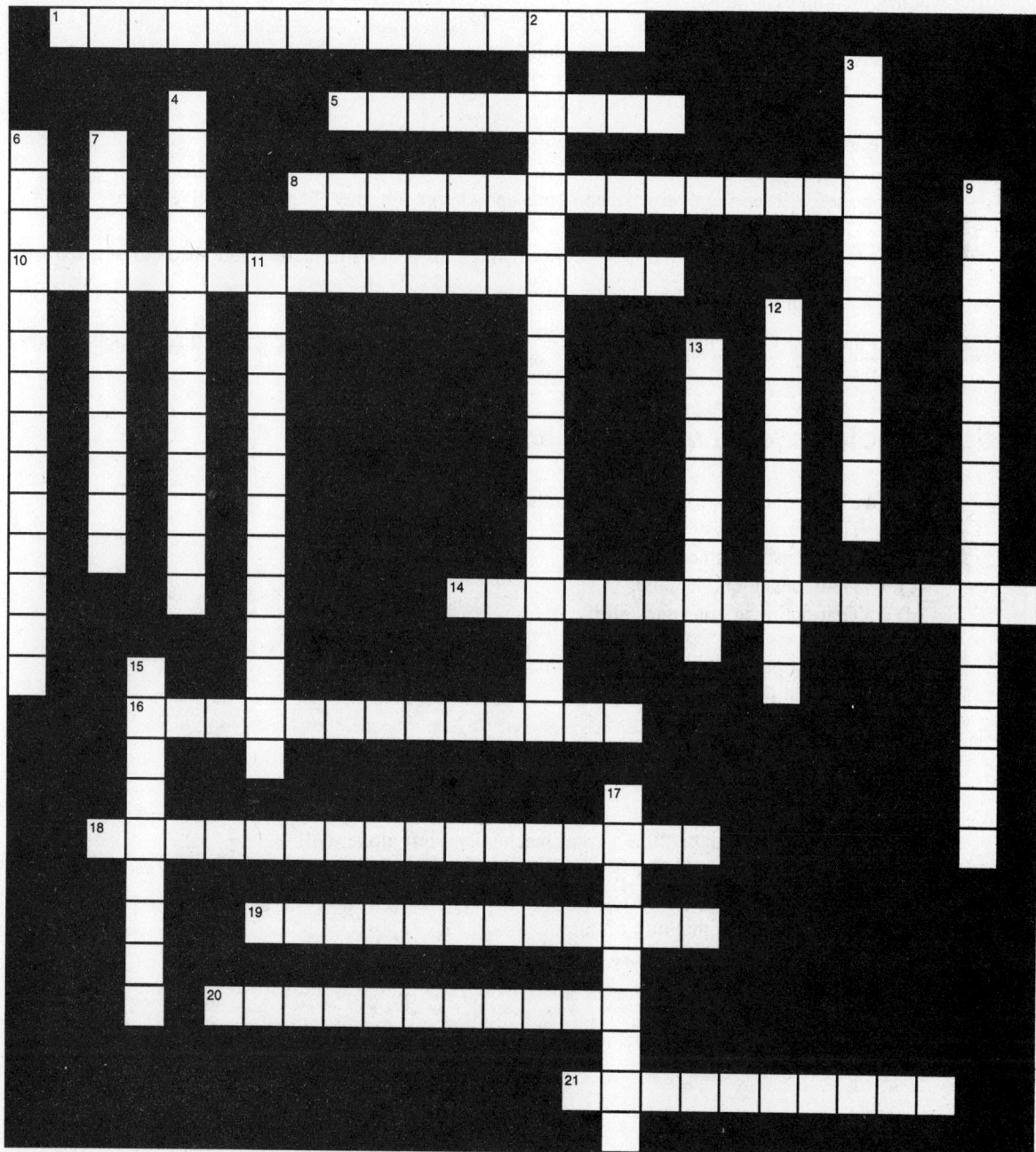

True or False: *Circle your choice and explain why any false statements are incorrect.*

T F 1. Market failure implies that the forces of supply and demand have not led to the best point on the production-possibilities curve.

T F 2. Government intervention is not necessary even when the market mix of output equals the optimal mix of output.

T F 3. The existence of public goods and externalities causes resource misallocations.

T F 4. Police protection is an example of a service that involves the free-rider problem.

T F 5. If you burn garbage in your backyard and the smoke damages a neighbor's house, the damage is considered an externality.

T F 6. Markets will overproduce goods that yield external benefits and underproduce goods that yield external costs.

T F 7. Market power creates a flawed response to an accurate price signal.

T F 8. Monopolies will tend to overproduce goods and charge a higher than competitive price.

T F 9. The federal government in the U.S. economy has grown in both relative and absolute terms since the 1950s.

T F 10. When the government intervenes in the economy, the market mix of goods and services is always improved.

Multiple Choice: *Select the correct answer.*

_____ 1. In a market economy, producers will produce the goods and services:
  (a) That consumers desire the most.
  (b) That consumers need the most.
  (c) That consumers demand.
  (d) That optimize consumer utility.

_____ 2. Market failure includes:
  (a) Externalities.
  (b) Market power.
  (c) Inequity in the distribution of goods and services.
  (d) All of the above.

_____ 3. Market failure suggests that the market mechanism, left alone, will:
  (a) Produce too many public goods and too few private goods.
  (b) Produce too many private goods and too few public goods.
  (c) Produce the optimal mix of output.
  (d) Result in too few resources being allocated to private goods.

4. The market will sometimes fail to produce society's optimum output because:
   (a) Producers do not always measure the same benefits and costs as society.
   (b) Producers will not produce certain types of important goods and services that cannot be kept from consumers who do not pay.
   (c) When producers have market power, they will tend to underproduce goods and services.
   (d) All of the above are correct.

5. When the market fails, which of the following is true?
   (a) The mix of goods and services is inside the production-possibilities curve.
   (b) Government intervention will improve the mix of goods and services.
   (c) The mix of goods and services is at the wrong point on the production-possibilities curve.
   (d) All of the above could be true.

6. Which of the following is most likely a private good?
   (a) Computers.
   (b) National defense.
   (c) Roads.
   (d) Flood control dams.

7. When public goods are marketed like private goods:
   (a) Public goods are underproduced.
   (b) Many consumers want to buy the goods.
   (c) Public goods are overproduced.
   (d) Government failure results.

8. For which of the following goods and services is the government likely to encourage production because of the existence of external benefits?
   (a) Education.
   (b) Health services for the poor.
   (c) A neighborhood renovation project.
   (d) All of the above.

9. The federal government's role in antitrust enforcement is justified by considerations of:
   (a) Equity in the distribution of goods and services.
   (b) Public goods and externalities.
   (c) Underproduction by firms with market power.
   (d) Macro failure.

10. The development of market power by a firm is considered to be a market failure because firms with market power:
    (a) Produce more and charge a lower price than what is socially optimal.
    (b) Tend to ignore external costs.
    (c) Produce less and charge a higher price than what is socially optimal.
    (d) Do not respond to consumer demand.

11. Transfer payments are an appropriate mechanism for correcting:
    (a) Market power.
    (b) Government failure.
    (c) Inflation.
    (d) Inequity in the distribution of goods and services.

_____ 12. Which of the following are both examples of macro failure?
    (a)   Externalities and market power.
    (b)   Inflation and unemployment.
    (c)   Inflation and regulation.
    (d)   Regulation and antitrust.

_____ 13. The primary function of taxes is to:
    (a)   Transfer command over resources from the private sector to the public sector.
    (b)   Increase the purchasing power of the private sector.
    (c)   Increase private saving.
    (d)   Make it possible to sell bonds to finance the U.S. budget deficit.

_____ 14. Government intervention in the market:
    (a)   Involves an opportunity cost.
    (b)   Never involves an opportunity cost because only market activities result in other goods and services being given up.
    (c)   Does not involve an opportunity cost if market outcomes are improved.
    (d)   Results in the "free-rider dilemma."

_____ 15. The largest single source of revenue for the federal government is:
    (a)   Borrowing (selling government bonds).
    (b)   Social security taxes.
    (c)   The corporate profits tax.
    (d)   The personal income tax.

_____ 16. Which of the following can be classified as a regressive tax?
    (a)   The federal corporate income tax.
    (b)   The federal personal income tax.
    (c)   The state sales tax.
    (d)   All of the above.

_____ 17. Which of the following is an example of a progressive tax?
    (a)   The excise tax on distilled spirits.
    (b)   The federal tax on gasoline.
    (c)   The federal personal income tax.
    (d)   All of the above.

_____ 18. States receive most of their tax revenues from :
    (a)   Sales taxes.
    (b)   State income taxes.
    (c)   Property taxes.
    (d)   User charges.

_____ 19. If government production forces the economy inside the production-possibilities curve, the following will occur:
    (a)   Government failure.
    (b)   Waste.
    (c)   Inefficiency.
    (d)   All of the above.

_____ 20. Which of the following would *not* support the theory of public choice?
- (a) The governor of the state vetoes a highway bill even though the highway would enhance the value of property he owns.
- (b) The local mayor campaigns in favor of a bond issue for the construction of sewer lines that will raise the value of his property.
- (c) The local police chief fails to give the mayor a speeding ticket because the mayor might fire him.
- (d) A college president asks the board of regents to allow her to remain in office so she can bolster her retirement income, even though she has reached the mandatory retirement age.

Problems and Applications

Exercise 1

Assume point *A* represents the optimal mix of output in Figure 4.1. Determine which letter best represents the following situations. Then answer questions 4-7.

Figure 4.1

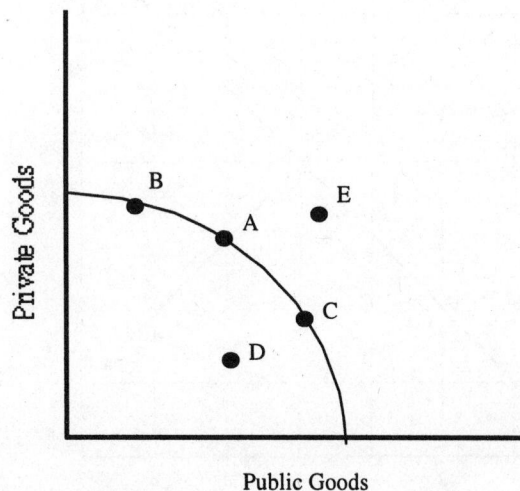

Public Goods

_____ 1. Government failure at the micro level that results in an overproduction of public goods.

_____ 2. The free-rider dilemma.

_____ 3. Macro failure in the marketplace.

4. The market mechanism tends to _____ private goods and _____ public goods.

5. In terms of the production-possibilities curve, _____ failures imply that society is at the wrong point on the curve and _____ failures imply that society is inside the curve.

6. Market failures justify government _____.

7. If government involvement fails to improve market outcomes then there is _____
_____.

Exercise 2

This exercise examines the difference between internal and external costs and the impact on the demand curve.

Assume that the consumption of the good represented in Figure 4.2 generates external costs of $2 per unit.

1. Draw the social demand curve in Figure 4.2 and label it.

Figure 4.2

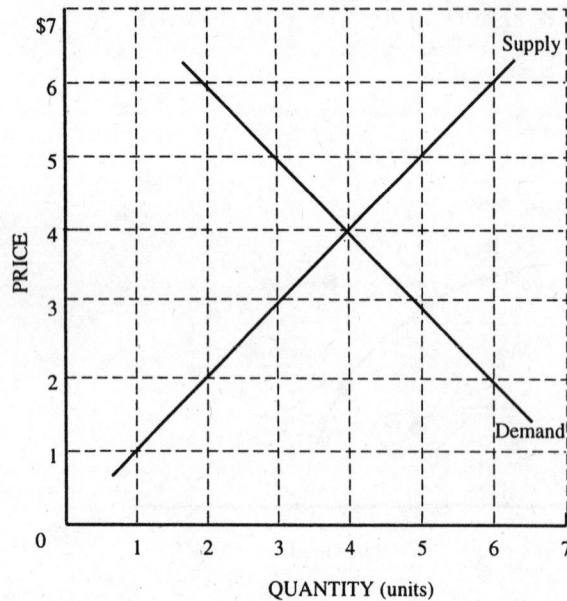

2. Market equilibrium occurs at a price of _____ and a quantity of _____ in Figure 4.3.

3. The socially optimal level of production occurs at a price of _____ and a quantity of _____.

4. External costs cause the market to produce (more, less) of a good than is optimal.

5. T   F   The market price of $4.00 does not reflect the external costs.

58

Exercise 3

This exercise focuses on the changes in public-sector spending in the U.S.

Refer to figure 4.4 in the text titled "Government Growth" to answer questions 1-4.

1. The large increase in total government purchases between 1940 and 1945 was the result of an increase in (only federal, both state and local and federal) government spending.

2. Compared to the level of federal spending in 1960, the projected level of federal spending for 2000 is (greater, less, the same).

3. State and local government spending increased from approximately 6 percent of national output in 1950 to approximately _____ percent in 1990.

4. The decrease in total government purchases during the 1990s was primarily due to the decrease in (federal, state and local) purchases.

Exercise 4

This exercise examines progressive and regressive tax structures.

Table 4.1.

	Income	Tax paid	Percentage of income paid in taxes
Country A	$30,000	$3,000	_____
	$60,000	$7,200	_____
Country B	$30,000	$4,500	_____
	$60,000	$7,800	_____

1. Calculate the percentage of income paid in taxes in Table 4.1.

2. According to Table 4.1, the tax structure in Country A is _____ because the tax rate _____ as income rises.

3. According to Table 4.1, the tax structure in Country B is _____ because the tax rate _____ as income rises.

Common Errors

The first statement in the "common error" below is incorrect. The incorrect statement is followed by a corrected version and an explanation.

1. Fire protection, police protection, education, and other services can be produced more efficiently by the private sector than by the public sector. WRONG!

    The public sector can produce many services more efficiently than the private sector. RIGHT!

    You should recognize now that the existence of externalities and the free-rider problem force society to produce some goods and services through public-sector expenditures. Many of the goods and services we take for granted (such as education) would not be produced in sufficient quantities if left to the private sector. And can you imagine trying to provide for your own defense against foreign countries?

•ANSWERS•

Using Key Terms
Across
1.   opportunity cost
5.   inflation
8.   market mechanism
10. government failure
14. natural monopoly
16. regressive tax
18. transfer payments
19. public choice
20. market power
21. user charge

Down
2.   optimal mix of output
3.   unemployment
4.   externalities
6.   progressive tax
7.   private good
9.   categorical grants
11. market failure
12. public good
13. monopoly
15. free rider
17. antitrust

True or False

1. T
2. F Equity considerations may necessitate government intervention.
3. T
4. T
5. T
6. F Markets will underproduce goods that yield external benefits and overproduce goods that yield external costs.

7. T
8. F Monopolies will tend to underproduce goods and are therefore able to charge a higher price.
9. F The federal government has grown in absolute terms since the 1950s but its relative share of production has declined, i.e. it has grown more slowly than the private sector.
10. F Sometimes government intervention worsens the market mix of goods and services. This is an example of "government failure."

Multiple Choice

1. c	5. d	9. c	13. a	17. c
2. d	6. a	10. c	14. a	18. a
3. b	7. a	11. d	15. d	19. d
4. d	8. d	12. b	16. c	20. a

Problems and Applications

Exercise 1

1. c
2. b
3. d
4. overproduce, underproduce

5. micro, macro
6. intervention
7. government failure

Exercise 2

1. See Figure 4.2 answer

Figure 4.2 Answer

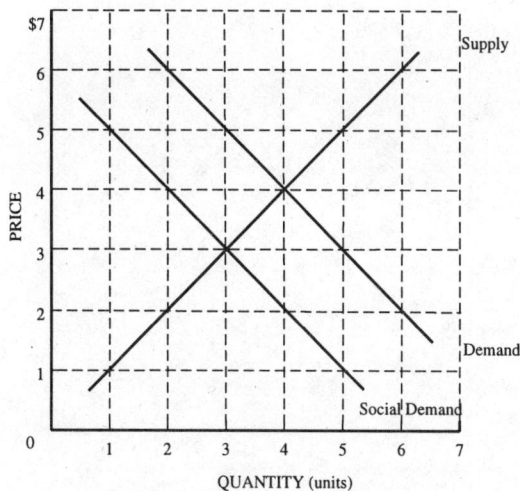

2. $4.00, 4 units
3. $3.00, 3 units
4. more
5. T

Exercise 3

1. only federal
2. less
3. 12 percent
4. federal

Exercise 4

1. See Table 4.1 Answer

Table 4.1 Answer

	Income	Tax Paid	Percentage of income paid in taxes
Country A	$30,000	$3,000	10%
	$60,000	$7,200	12%
Country B	$30,000	$4,500	15%
	$60,000	$7,800	13%

2. progressive, rises
3. regressive, falls

CHAPTER 5
National-Income Accounting

Quick Review

In this chapter we begin the task of measuring the economy's performance. The need for performance measures became obvious during the Great Depression of the 1930's when everyone knew the economy was in trouble but there was no way to find out just how bad things were. National-income accounting addresses this problem, and helps us answer such questions as:

- How much output is being produced? What's it being used for?
- How much income is being generated in the marketplace?
- What's happening to prices and wages?

National-income accounting is a process by which we measure the nation's economic activity. Several national-income aggregates allow the national-income accountant to add together the production of goods and services using dollar value as a single common denominator.

The most often used economic aggregate is gross domestic product (GDP)—the total market value of all final goods and services produced within a nation's borders over a year. When our total output is calculated in dollar terms and compared with *what could have been* produced by the economy over the same period, appropriate economic policies can be developed.

The GDP does not include all types of transactions. It includes only those involving production of new products and services; for example, sales of new cars are included, but sales of used cars are not. Some transactions are not included in the GDP, such as paying Junior for mowing the lawn. The services of homemakers and bartering are not included in the GDP. There is also a large underground economy that the GDP never captures. Finally, only transactions involving goods and services that are sold for final consumption are included—whether they are purchased by households, business, government, or foreign buyers. Intermediate goods are not included in the GDP in order to avoid distortions resulting from double counting.

The GDP serves as an excellent standard for comparing different economies and the changes in the output of a single economy over time. There are, however, several alternative measures of output, each calculated with a different purpose in mind. The net domestic product (NDP) corrects for the consumption of capital and therefore serves as a better measure of the changes in the production possibilities of the economy. When indirect business taxes are subtracted from net domestic product, we get national income, which shows what the factors of production earned in the process of producing the nation's output. Finally, to find out how much of the income earned is actually received, we calculate personal income and disposable income, the latter being how much is available to spend after personal taxes are taken out.

GDP is a price-times-quantity measure. It can increase because prices go up, because quantities go up, or both. Because our standard of living is based on real goods and services, we distinguish between real GDP and nominal GDP. When prices are rising, we deflate the GDP by dividing by an appropriate index. When prices fall, we inflate it. When comparing the output of different countries, it is good practice to divide GDP by population to find the income per capita.

The national-income accounts tell us a lot about how the economy is doing and, thus, how our society is doing. But there's much more to the nation's well-being than the monetary measures might imply. Some of the things we produce (automobiles, for example) add to our well-being by providing transportation, and subtract from it at the same by raising the level of pollution when they are driven. Similarly, we value leisure time, peace and security, and other non-material things. How should these be counted? Researchers who wrestle with these problems have developed indices which rely on non-monetary measures to determine how well society is doing. Two Fordham University professors claim their index shows that social well-being in the United States has declined for two decades even though the GDP has risen!

Learning Objectives

After reading Chapter 5 and doing the following exercises, you should:

1. Know the purposes of national-income accounting.
2. Be able to describe the different measures of output and income.
3. Know why the GDP per capita is computed.
4. Be able to explain the conceptual problems encountered in estimating GDP, including the underground economy
5. Understand the difference between GDP and GNP.
6. Know the difference between real GDP and nominal GDP and be able to calculate each.
7. Know the definitions and uses of the important national-income aggregates.
8. Be able to calculate GDP and other aggregates from a given set of data on the national accounts.
9. Be able to distinguish GDP from NDP.

Using Key Terms

Fill in the puzzle on the opposite page with the appropriate term from the list of Key Terms at the end of the chapter in the text.

Across

1. Calculated as nominal GDP divided by the price index.
3. Equal to GDP minus depreciation and indirect business taxes.
4. Total investment expenditure in a given time period.
9. Alternative combinations of goods and services that can be produced with the available resources and technology.
10. Equal to $0.12 in the first stage of production according to Table 5.2 in the text.
11. Equal to disposable income minus consumption.
13. The wearing out of plant and equipment.
16. The amount of output that can be consumed without reducing a country's capital stock.
18. The income received by households before the payment of taxes.
19. Equal to $6,028 billion in Table 5.6 in the text.
20. Used as a measure of the relative standard of living.

Down

2. Equal to $8,511 billion according to Table 5.6 in the text.
3. The measurement of aggregate economic activity.
5. Persistent increases in the price level.
6. Goods purchased for use as input in further stages of production.
7. Equal to real GDP in 1992 according to Figure 5.1 in the text.

8. Expenditures on new plant, equipment and structures plus changes in inventories.
12. Gross investment minus depreciation.
14. Goods and services purchased from other countries.
15. The basis for indexing price changes.
16. Equal to exports minus imports.
17. Goods and services sold to other countries.

Puzzle 5.1

True or False: *Circle your choice and explain why any false statements are incorrect.*

T F 1. Without prices, it would be impossible to add up the outputs produced in different sectors of the economy in a meaningful way.

✗ (T) F 2. Intermediate goods are not counted in GDP because their value is included in the value of the final product. *P. 87*

✗ (T) F 3. If drugs that are now illegal in the U.S. were legalized (e.g. marijuana), U.S. GDP would increase, *ceteris paribus.*

✗ T (F) 4. Per capita GDP provides information about the distribution of GDP within a country.

✗ (T) F 5. Real GDP and nominal GDP are equal during the base year for which an index is constructed.

✗ T (F) 6. In a period of rising prices, real GDP will rise more rapidly than nominal GDP.

T F 7. NDP provides information about future production possibilities because it measures gross investment.

✗ (T) F 8. According to the expenditures approach to calculating GDP, GDP equals Consumption + Gross Investment + Government Expenditures + (Exports - Imports).

T F 9. State and local government expenditures on goods and services are *not* included in GDP because to do so would result in double counting.

✗ (T) F 10. The total value of market incomes must equal the total value of final output, or GDP.

Multiple Choice: *Select the correct answer.*

✗ *d* 1. A basic function of the national-income accounting system is to:
  (a)   Identify economic problems.
  (b)   Evaluate economic policy.
  (c)   Provide a framework for policy.
  (d)   All of the above.

✗ *d* 2. GDP can be found by:
  (a)   Adding up the spending by business, government, households, and foreigners, and subtracting imports.
  (b)   Adding up the value added at every stage of production in the economy.
  (c)   Adding up all the receipts of households, government, and business.
  (d)   All of the above.

✗ *b* 3. Suppose that a friend of yours claims that he is helping the economy by throwing trash on the street rather than in trash cans because the extra expenditures necessary to clean up the streets will increase GDP. Your friend is:
  (a)   Wrong. GDP will not be affected because nothing new is being produced.
  (b)   Right. GDP will increase because the dollars spent money to clean up the trash will increase government spending, *ceteris paribus.*
  (c)   Wrong. GDP will not be affected because this is not a socially desirable use of resources and will therefore not be included in GDP.
  (d)   Wrong. GDP will decline because cleaning the streets will take resources away from more productive work.

4. If the real U.S. GDP was $6,928.8 billion in 1996 and the U.S. population was 266 million, the per capita real GDP would have been closest to:
   - (a) $462,700 per person.
   - (b) $12,194 per person.
   - (c) $26,048 per person.
   - (d) $38,390 per person.

5. A housewife takes over the job of a deceased family member in running the family business and hires help to clean house and babysit. As a result, the GDP of the economy, *ceteris paribus:*
   - (a) Remains unchanged, since the amount of productive activity remains unchanged.
   - (b) Rises by the amount paid to house cleaners and babysitters.
   - (c) Falls by the amount of household work left undone by the house cleaners and babysitters.
   - (d) Falls by the amount of income generated previously by the deceased family member.

6. The underground economy exists because.
   - (a) People wish to avoid taxes.
   - (b) Illegal activities are often highly profitable.
   - (c) It is difficult to trace transactions in the underground economy.
   - (d) All of the above are reasons.

7. An electronic calculator manufacturer sells assembled calculators for $25 each. If the manufacturer pays $10 for components in each calculator, the value added to each calculator by manufacturing is:
   - (a) $25.
   - (b) $10.
   - (c) $35.
   - (d) $15.

8. Which of the following is *not* a final good or service?
   - (a) A printing press purchased by a publishing company.
   - (b) Automobile tires purchased by an auto manufacturing company.
   - (c) Gasoline purchased for personal use by a car owner.
   - (d) The preparation of your tax return by a CPA.

9. The difference between real GDP and nominal GDP is that:
   - (a) Nominal GDP is the value of output measured in constant prices.
   - (b) Real GDP is the value of output measured in constant prices.
   - (c) Real GDP is the value of output measured in current prices.
   - (d) Real GDP can give a distorted view of economic activity because of price level changes.

10. Real GDP measures changes in:
    - (a) Prices.
    - (b) Production.
    - (c) Prices and production.
    - (d) Wages.

11. Suppose that the total market value of all the final goods and services produced in the country of GDPLAND was $10 billion in 1999 (measured in 1999 prices) and $12 billion in the year 2000 (measured in 2000 prices). Which of the following statements is definitely correct?
    - (a) Production increased in GDPLAND between 1999 and 2000.
    - (b) Average price levels increased in GDPLAND between 1999 and 2000.
    - (c) Nominal GDP increased in GDPLAND between 1999 and 2000.
    - (d) All of these statements are definitely correct.

_____ 12. If depreciation exceeds gross investment, then:
    (a)   Net investment exceeds depreciation.
    (b)   Gross investment is negative.
    (c)   The difference between GDP and NDP is smaller than gross investment.
    (d)   The nation's capital stock is being depleted.

_____ 13. The stock of capital in the United States can grow only if:
    (a)   Depreciation is positive.
    (b)   Gross investment minus depreciation is positive.
    (c)   GDP minus NDP is positive.
    (d)   All of the above.

_____ 14. An increase in business inventories during some time period, _ceteris paribus_, will:
    (a)   Decrease GDP during that period.
    (b)   Increase GDP during that period.
    (c)   Not affect GDP during that period but will increase GDP in later periods when the inventory is sold.
    (d)   Never affect GDP because changes in inventories are not included in the calculation of GDP.

_____ 15. Which of the following types of government spending is included in the calculation of GDP?
    (a)   Federal government spending only.
    (b)   Federal, state and local government spending for any purpose.
    (c)   Federal, state and local government spending on goods and services only.
    (d)   Federal, state and local spending on transfer payments only.

_____ 16. In calculating GDP:
    (a)   Imports are subtracted from exports because they represent the value of production and resources absorbed in foreign economies.
    (b)   Imports are added to exports because both represent purchases of final goods.
    (c)   Imports are subtracted from exports to obtain gross exports.
    (d)   Imports are subtracted from exports and included in gross investment.

_____ 17. _DI_ is the most practical way to:
    (a)   Measure how much income households can spend and save.
    (b)   Measure how much output can be consumed on a sustainable basis.
    (c)   Make international comparisons of the standard of living.
    (d)   Analyze the growth rate of the economy over time.

_____ 18. Businesses return purchasing power to the circular flow in the form of:
    (a)   Retained earnings.
    (b)   Depreciation charges.
    (c)   Business investment.
    (d)   Profit.

_____ 19. The value of total output must equal the value of total income in an economy because:
    (a)   One person's expenditures on goods and services is another person's income.
    (b)   Income earned is spent on goods and services which creates additional production.
    (c)   Of the circular nature of the economy.
    (d)   All of the above are reasons.

_____ 20. The social well-being of a country:
    (a)   Is best measured by per capita GDP.
    (b)   Always increases when real GDP increases.
    (c)   Decreases when real GDP decreases.
    (d)   Is measured by more than changes in real GDP.

Problems and Applications

Exercise 1

This exercise demonstrates the concept of value added. It is similar to Problem 1 in the text.

Assume that orange juice production involves the following steps.

Step 1: A juice company grows its own oranges to reduce costs.
Step 2: The juice company sells a jug of orange juice to the grocery store for $1.85.
Step 3: The grocery store sells the jug of juice to the consumer for $3.25.

1. The value added from step 1 to step 2 is equal to _____.

2. The value added from step 2 to step 3 is equal to _____.

3. If the juice company bought the oranges from a farmer, the oranges would be considered a(an) (intermediate, final) good.

4. What is the total contribution made to GDP by one jug of orange juice? _____

Exercise 2

This exercise demonstrates how to calculate real GDP and emphasizes the difference between nominal and real GDP.

Table 5.1 GDP Data

	Nominal GDP (billions of dollars per year)	Price index	Real GDP (billions of dollars per year)
Year 1	$3,300	100	_____
Year 2	$3,500	103	_____
Year 3	$3,800	111	_____
Year 4	$4,050	120	_____

1. Calculate real GDP in Table 5.1. Use the formula:

$$\text{Real GDP} = \frac{\text{Nominal GDP}}{\text{Price index}} \times 100$$

2. According to Table 5.1, in which year is the real level of output greatest? _____

3. The measurement of goods and services produced without the impact of price level changes is referred to as _____.

4. In Figure 5.1 in the text, nominal GDP rises more rapidly than real GDP because nominal GDP includes _____.

5. The best measure of physical changes in output in Figure 5.1 is _____.

Exercise 3

This exercise provides practice in calculating GDP and other national income accounts. (The chart below can be referred to as you work this exercise.)

Flow chart 5.1

Add items in this column to get the next account	National income account	Subtract items in this column to get the next account
	GDP	
		Depreciation
	NDP	
		Indirect business taxes
	NI	
Transfer payments Net interest		Corporate taxes Retained earnings Social Security taxes
	PI	
		Personal income taxes
	DI	
		Consumption
	Saving	

Table 5.2 National Income Data

Consumption	$300 billion
Depreciation	10 billion
Exports	30 billion
Corporate Taxes	15 billion
Personal Income Taxes	60 billion
Gross Investment	30 billion
Indirect business taxes	5 billion
Retained earnings	10 billion
Imports	35 billion
Government Purchases	80 billion
Social Security Taxes	15 billion
Transfer Payments	30 billion
Net Interest	5 billion

Use the information in Table 5.2 to make the following calculations.

1. GDP   _____

2. NDP   _____

3. NI   _____

4. PI   _____

5. DI   _____

6. Savings   _____

7. Net investment _____

8. Which of the accounts above is the best indicator of future production possibilities? _____

9. Which of the accounts above is equal to the total income earned by the factors of production? _____.

Common Errors

The first statement in each "common error" below is incorrect. Each incorrect statement is followed by a corrected version and an explanation.

1. Income and output are two entirely different things. WRONG!

   Income and output are two sides of the same coin. RIGHT!

   This is fundamental. Every time a dollar's worth of final spending takes place, the seller must receive a dollar's worth of income. It could not be otherwise. Remember, profits are used as a balancing item. Don't confuse the term "income" with the term "profit." Profits can be negative, whereas output for the economy cannot.

2. Comparisons of per capita GDP between countries tell you which population is better off. WRONG!

   Comparisons of per capita GDP between countries are only indicators of which population is better off. RIGHT!

   Simple comparisons of per capita GDP ignore how the GDP is distributed. A country with a very high per capita GDP that is unequally distributed may well provide a standard of living that is below that of another country with a lower per capita GDP which is more equally distributed. There are other problems with comparisons of per capita GDP between countries because of exchange-rate distortions, differences in mix of output in two countries, and how the economy is organized. GDP per capita is an indicator only of the amount of goods and services each person could have, not what each person does have.

3. Value added is a measure of a firm's profit. WRONG!

   Value added includes all factor payments to land, labor, and capital in addition to the residual (profit) that goes to the entrepreneur for taking risks. RIGHT!

   In computing value added, a firm subtracts *from* total revenue the cost of items sold to the firm. There are additional cost items that normally would be subtracted to calculate "profit" which are not subtracted in the computation of value added. Those items include the cost of capital, land, and labor. When value added for all economic units is combined, the total of payments to capital (interest), land (rent), labor (wages), and risk taking (profits) will equal the total gross national product.

71

•ANSWERS•

Using Key Terms

Across

1. real GDP
3. national income
4. gross investment
9. production possibilities
10. value added
11. saving
13. depreciation
16. net domestic product
18. personal income
19. disposable income
20. GDP per capita

Down

2. gross domestic product
3. national income accounting
5. inflation
6. intermediate goods
7. nominal GDP
8. investment
12. net investment
14. imports
15. base period
16. net exports
17. exports

True or False

1. T
2. T
3. T
4. F   GDP per capita is simply a statistical average and tells us nothing about the way GDP is distributed.
5. T
6. F   Nominal GDP is affected by inflation and will increase faster than real GDP. Real GDP is not affected by changing price levels.
7. F   NDP provides information about future growth potential because it measures net investment.
8. T
9. F   State and local government expenditures on goods and services are included in GDP. These expenditures measure additional production beyond the goods and services the federal government consumes so there is no double counting.
10. T

Multiple Choice

1.	d	5.	b	9.	b	13.	b	17.	a
2.	d	6.	d	10.	b	14.	b	18.	c
3.	b	7.	d	11.	c	15.	c	19.	d
4.	c	8.	b	12.	d	16.	a	20.	d

Problems and Applications

Exercise 1

1. $1.85

2. $1.40

3. Intermediate

4. $3.25

Exercise 2

1.

Table 5.1 answer.

	Nominal GDP (billions of dollars per year)	Price index	Real GDP (billions of dollars per year)
Year 1	$3,300	100	**$3,300**
Year 2	$3,500	103	**$3,398**
Year 3	$3,800	111	**$3,423**
Year 4	$4,050	120	**$3,375**

2. Year 3
3. Real GDP
4. An increase in the price level or inflation.
5. Real GDP

Exercise 3

1. $405 billion
2. $395 billion
3. $390 billion
4. $385 billion
5. $325 billion
6. $25 billion
7. $20 billion
8. NDP
9. NI

73

CHAPTER 6
Unemployment

Quick Review

Unemployment concerns policymakers because it causes people to lose their income and creates social unrest. Society also loses its potential output. In the Employment Act of 1946 a low unemployment rate became one of the country's important national goals. But unemployment is difficult to measure, its causes are numerous, and its impact is hard to gauge. Thus we need to answer several questions:

- When is a person "unemployed"?
- What are the costs of unemployment?
- What is an appropriate goal for "full employment"?

Unemployment is measured in terms of only those people in the labor force who have no job but are actively seeking employment. If you're a civilian under 16 or you're not looking for work, then you're not in the labor force and you are not considered unemployed. This criterion eliminates children, parents at home, and people in the armed forces. The number of unemployed is determined through surveys of households across the country. To find the unemployment rate, divide the number of unemployed by the number in the labor force.

Making the distinction between the labor force and the total population allows us to distinguish also between physical production possibilities, the maximum amount that could be produced with all resources and technology, and institutional production possibilities, which defines the annual output we could produce if we efficiently employed our resources within the limits imposed by available resources, technology, and social constraints on their use. The labor force is smaller than the entire population because of institutional constraints such as compulsory education or child labor laws. The resulting institutional production-possibilities curve lies inside the physical production-possibilities curve.

Thus the country's labor-force participation rate is calculated by dividing the number of people working (or seeking work) by the population. Those who are unemployed do not stay unemployed, however, and how long it takes to get a new job (the duration of unemployment) is important. The duration grows longer in recessions and can be very short when the economy approaches capacity. Finally, the unemployment rate varies by a number of socioeconomic variables—race, age, sex, education, and so on. Besides causing a loss of output, unemployment imposes other costs on society as well—alcoholism, suicide, divorce, crime, and the like, are all positively related to the unemployment rate, i.e., when unemployment goes up, the other problems increase. The underemployed and discouraged workers are not part of the unemployment rate, but they do have an impact on society. As unemployment goes up, GDP goes down. According to Okun's Law the relationship is systematic – each one percentage point increase in the unemployment rate leads to a two percentage point reduction in GDP.

Economists typically distinguish four kinds of unemployment: frictional (short-term unemployment between jobs), seasonal (unemployment that varies with the seasons), structural (caused by a mismatch of available labor with skill requirements or job locations), and cyclical (caused by deficient aggregate demand).

For these reasons, several million people are unemployed in the United States during any period of time.

During the 1960s the Council of Economic Advisers thought that an unemployment rate of 4 percent provided the optimal balance between employment and price-level goals. In the 1970s and 1980s this figure was revised upward to 6 to 7 percent to reflect the increased importance of structural unemployment. Changes in the age-sex composition of the labor force, and more liberal transfer payments, were among the reasons for this upward revision. As structural barriers declined in the 1990s, the nation's unemployment goal was changed to 5.3 percent.

The U.S. labor force has doubled in size since 1950 because of increases in the population size and because of a higher labor force participation rate, especially among women. During this time, the kind of labor needed has also changed. Technological advances, declining industries, and corporate downsizing are all conspiring to require a more educated labor force with increased emphasis on skills. If the United States does not address the potential skills gap, structural unemployment will increase.

Learning Objectives

After reading Chapter 6 and doing the following exercises, you should:

1. Know who is included in the labor force.
2. Know why the physical production possibilities and institutional production possibilities differ.
3. Understand why unemployment is a major social concern.
4. Be able to calculate the unemployment rate.
5. Be able to explain why and how the unemployment rate varies with age, sex, education, and race.
6. Be able to distinguish between unemployment and underemployment.
7. Be aware of programs designed to alleviate unemployment.
8. Be aware of the ways in which the unemployment rate may understate or overstate the true dimensions of the unemployment problem.
9. Know the meaning of "full employment."
10. Be able to distinguish the nature and causes of cyclical, frictional, structural, and seasonal unemployment.
11. Be able to calculate the nation's loss of output owing to rising unemployment using Okun's Law.
12. Know the dimensions, causes and cures of the emerging "skills gap."

Using Key Terms

Fill in the puzzle on the opposite page with the appropriate term from the list of Key Terms at the end of the chapter in the text.

Across

1. The number of unemployed people divided by the size of the labor force.
6. Unemployment experienced by people moving between jobs.
7. The percentage of the population working or seeking work.
11. Education and training can be used to narrow the _____ which reduces structural unemployment.
12. Unemployment due to seasonal changes.
13. Individuals who are not looking for a job but would accept a job if one were available.
14. Situation in which people work at jobs below their capacity.
15. The inability of labor-force participants to find jobs.

Down

2. The rate of unemployment that prevails in the long run.
3. Alternative combinations of goods and services that can be produced with available resources and technology.

4. The type of unemployment most often experienced by teenagers with few jobs skills and an inadequate education.
5. Unemployment that occurs when there are not enough jobs.
8. Quantifies the relationship between the shortfall in output and unemployment.
9. The lowest rate of unemployment compatible with price stability.
10. Everyone sixteen and older who is working for pay or looking for a job.

Puzzle 6.1

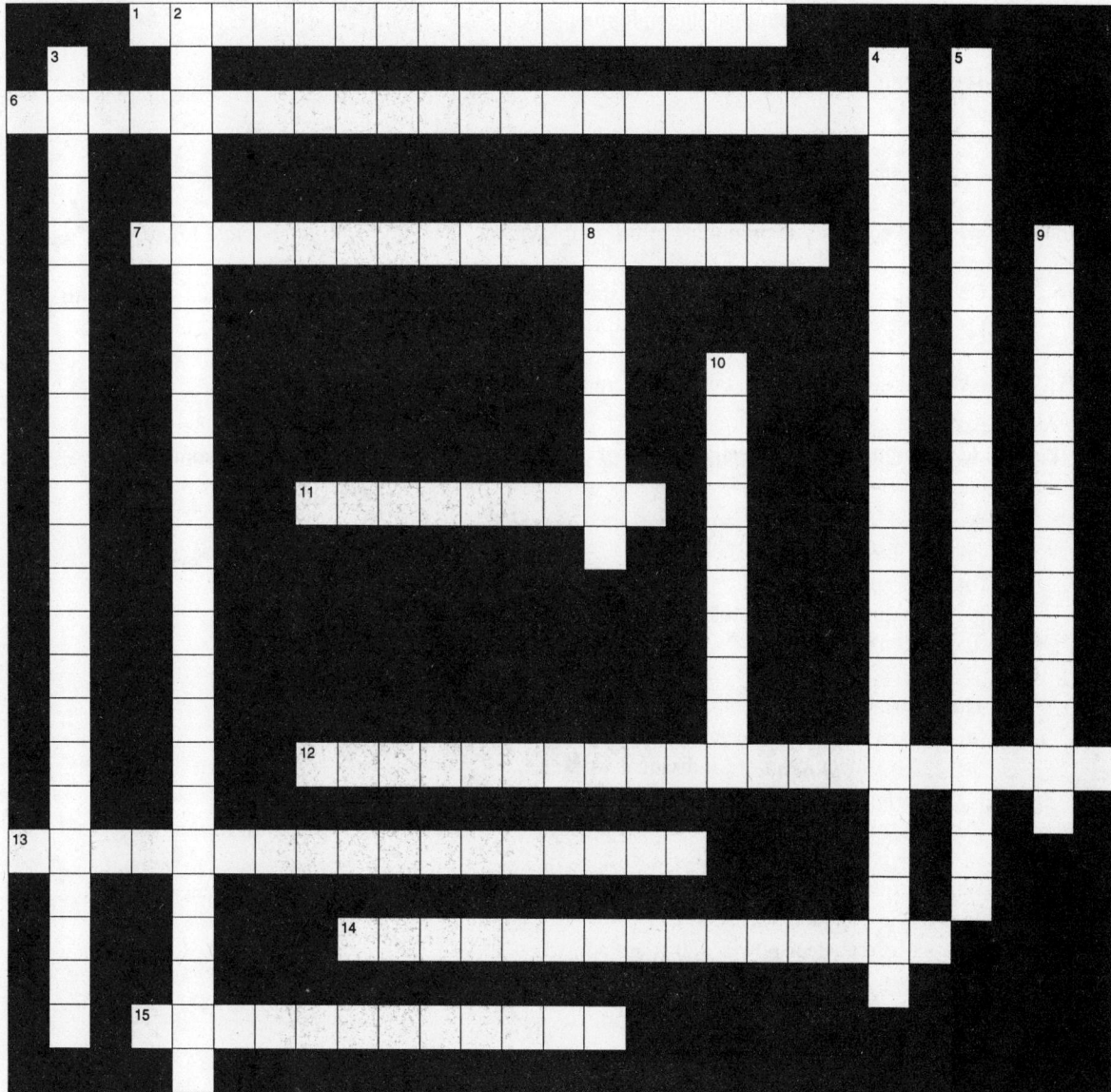

True or False: *Circle your choice and explain why any false statements are incorrect.*

T (F) 1. Ed says he would like to have a job but hasn't applied for a job in 6 months. Ed is counted as being unemployed in the calculation of the unemployment rate.

T F 2. When the number of unemployed workers increases, the unemployment rate will always rise.

T F 3. When the economy is growing, the average duration of unemployment declines.

T (F) 4. Those who get discouraged and no longer seek work are counted as unemployed.

T F 5. The transition from manufacturing to service industries has accompanied GDP growth, but it has also led to greater frictional unemployment.

(T) F 6. Teenage unemployment is high because of teenagers' lack of job experience and marketable skills.

T F 7. Cyclical unemployment stems from insufficient aggregate demand.

T (F) 8. When an economy is producing at full employment, everyone willing and able to work has a job.

T F 9. One of the main reasons for revising the full-employment goal during the 1980s was a change in the age-sex composition of the labor force.

T F 10. As the skills gap widens, cyclical unemployment increases, *ceteris paribus*.

Multiple Choice: *Select the correct answer.*

_____ 1. People become labor force participants when they:
(a) Take a full-time job.
(b) Go back to school.
(c) Return solely to household activities.
(d) Retire.

A 2. The macro consequence of unemployment is:
(a) Lost output for the economy.
(b) Lost income for the individual worker.
(c) A leftward shift in the institutional production-possibilities curve.
(d) A 4 percent decrease in GDP for every 1 percent increase in unemployment.

_____ 3. Which of the following would cause the institutional production-possibilities curve to shift outward in the short run?
(a) More nuclear power plants are constructed.
(b) The federal government eliminates its student loan program.
(c) The child labor laws are relaxed.
(d) All of the above.

_____ 4. As economic output increases and an economy moves toward full employment:
(a) Production moves closer to the institutional production-possibilities curve, but not beyond it.
(b) Production moves beyond the physical production-possibilities curve.
(c) The institutional production-possibilities curve shifts outward but not the physical production-possibilities curve.
(d) The physical production-possibilities curve shifts outward but not the institutional production-possibilities curve.

78

_____ 5. When the labor force participation rate increases in an economy, *ceteris paribus*:
   (a) Production moves closer to the institutional production-possibilities curve, but not beyond it.
   (b) Production moves beyond the physical production-possibilities curve.
   (c) The institutional production possibilities curve shifts outward.
   (d) The physical production-possibilities curve shifts outward but not the institutional production-possibilities curve.

※ _C_ 6. When the growth rate of the labor force is more rapid than the growth rate of the unemployed, then it is certain that:
   (a) The unemployment rate is rising.
   (b) The labor-force participation rate is rising.
   (c) The percentage of the labor force that is employed is rising.
   (d) The labor-force participation rate is falling.

※ _d_ 7. When an economy enters a recession, then:
   (a) The duration of unemployment rises.
   (b) The number of discouraged workers rises.
   (c) The unemployment rate rises.
   (d) All of the above.

_____ 8. Which of the following statements is most accurate?
   (a) Most unemployed workers take a significant length of time (i.e. more than six months) to find another job.
   (b) Most unemployed workers never find another job.
   (c) Most unemployed workers do not find another job without retraining and/or relocation.
   (d) Most people who become unemployed find jobs in a relatively short period of time (i.e. 2 to 3 months).

※ _b_ 9. Individuals who are working part-time while seeking full-time employment are classified as:
   (a) Unemployed.
   (b) Underemployed.
   (c) Discouraged workers.
   (d) Phantom unemployed.

_____ 10. The official unemployment statistics may exaggerate the significance of unemployment by including the:
   (a) Underemployed.
   (b) Phantom unemployed.
   (c) Discouraged workers.
   (d) High school dropouts.

※ _d_ 11. Which of the following are considered possible side effects of increased unemployment?
   (a) Suicides, homicides, and other crimes.
   (b) Heart attacks and strokes.
   (c) Admissions to mental hospitals.
   (d) All of the above.

※ _b_ 12. When migrant workers seek employment after the crops have been picked, the unemployment rate goes up. This situation is an example of:
   (a) Frictional unemployment.
   (b) Seasonal unemployment.
   (c) Structural unemployment.
   (d) Cyclical unemployment.

_____ 13. Frictional unemployment goes up when:
- (a) A student quits work to return to school at the end of the summer.
- (b) A corporation transfers a worker to another city.
- (c) A worker quits one job in order to search for another.
- (d) There is inadequate demand for labor.

_____ 14. Which of the following is believed to have contributed to an increase in the level of structural unemployment during the 1970s and 1980s?
- (a) More youth and women in the labor force.
- (b) Increased transfer payments.
- (c) Structural changes in demand.
- (d) All of the above.

_____ 15. In terms of the musical chairs analogy in the text, which of the following is a description of cyclical unemployment?
- (a) There are too few chairs.
- (b) There are too many chairs.
- (c) There are enough chairs, but some are not the right size.
- (d) There are enough chairs, but it takes time to find one.

_____ 16. Which of the following government programs would be most appropriate to counteract cyclical unemployment?
- (a) Those which stimulate economic growth.
- (b) Those that provide additional health services.
- (c) Those that provide job placement services.
- (d) Those that provide job training.

_____ 17. Inflation is most likely to be a problem in an economy that:
- (a) Is producing inside the institutional production-possibilities curve.
- (b) Is producing on the institutional production-possibilities curve.
- (c) Has large quantities of unemployed resources.
- (d) Is producing between the institutional production-possibilities curve and the physical production-possibilities curve.

_____ 18. Which of the following groups would be the most likely to qualify for unemployment benefits?
- (a) People who quit their last jobs.
- (b) People who lose their jobs due to increased foreign competition and are looking for work.
- (c) Mothers who have not worked recently.
- (d) People who are fired from one of the three part-time jobs that they have been working.

_____ 19. During which one of the following decades did unemployment levels first rise significantly above the 4 percent level as the result of increasing proportions of both teenagers and women entering the labor force?
- (a) 1960s.
- (b) 1970s.
- (c) 1980s.
- (d) 1990s.

_____ 20. As the gap between the skills required for emerging jobs and the skills of workers widens:
- (a) Only those workers entering the job market are affected.
- (b) Structural unemployment decreases.
- (c) Structural unemployment increases.
- (d) Cyclical unemployment increases.

Problems and Applications

Exercise 1

The following exercise provides practice in categorizing the population according to labor force participation, employment, and unemployment.

Suppose the population of a country is 1.4 million and the labor force is 1 million, of whom 900,000 are employed. Assume that the full-employment level occurs at a 5 percent unemployment rate and at a real GDP of $100 billion. Answer the indicated questions on the basis of this information:

1. What is the unemployment rate? _____

2. Assume "full employment" is equal to 5 percent unemployment. How many more members of the labor force must find jobs for the economy to achieve full employment? _____

3. On the basis of the information above and the revised version of Okun's Law stated in the text, how much potential GDP has been lost because the economy is not at full employment? _____

4. On the basis of the information above and the revised version of Okun's Law, what is the GDP of the economy? _____

Exercise 2

This exercise shows how to calculate the unemployment rate and indicates the relationship between the unemployment rate and GDP.

1. Compute the unemployment rate based on the information in Table 6.1, and insert it in column 4.

Table 6.1
Unemployment and real GDP, 1981-95

Year	(1) Noninstitutional population	(2) Civilian labor force (thousands of persons 16 and over)	(3) Unemployment (thousands of persons 16 and over)	(4) Unemployment rate (percent)	(5) Percentage change in real GDP
1981	170,130	108,670	8,273	_____	2.5
1982	172,271	110,204	10,678	_____	−2.1
1983	174,215	111,550	10,717	_____	4.0
1984	176,383	113,544	8,539	_____	6.8
1985	178,206	115,461	8,312	_____	3.7
1986	180,587	117,834	8,237	_____	3.0
1987	182,753	119,865	7,425	_____	2.9
1988	184,613	121,669	6,701	_____	3.8
1989	186,393	123,869	6,528	_____	3.4
1990	188,049	124,787	6,874	_____	1.3
1991	189,765	125,303	8,426	_____	−1.0
1992	191,576	126,982	9,384	_____	2.7
1993	193,550	128,040	8,734	_____	2.2
1994	196,814	131,056	7,996	_____	3.5
1995	198,584	132,304	7,404	_____	2.0

2. In Figure 6.1 graph both the unemployment rate (column 4 of Table 6.1) and the percentage change in real GDP (column 5).

Figure 6.1

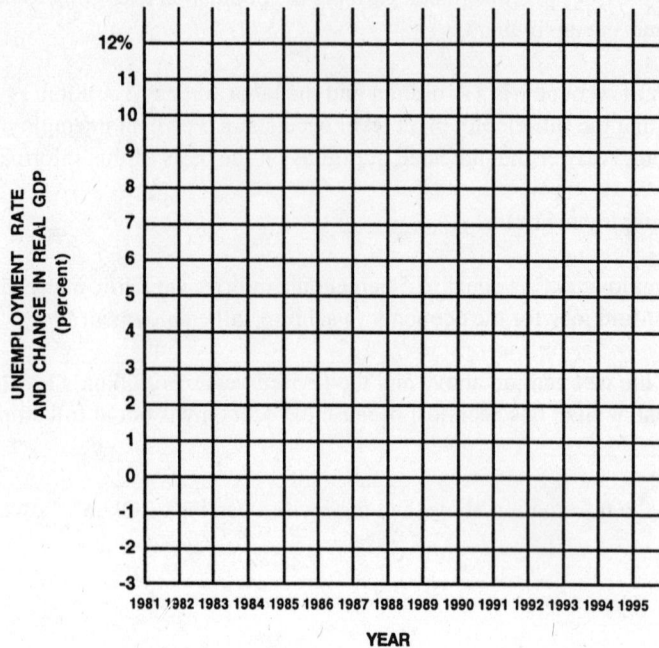

3. The relationship between the unemployment rate and the percentage change in the real GDP is best characterized as:
   (a) A direct relationship (the two indicators go up and down together).
   (b) An inverse relationship (the two indicators move in opposite directions).

4. Which indicator seems to change direction first as time passes?
   (a) Percentage change in real GDP.
   (b) The unemployment rate.

5. Which of the following types of unemployment had the largest impact on the unemployment rate from 1981 to 1982 in Figure 6.1?
   (a) Structural unemployment.
   (b) Seasonal unemployment.
   (c) Cyclical unemployment.
   (d) Frictional unemployment.

6. If "full employment" is defined as an unemployment rate of 5.5 percent, in what years was full employment achieved between 1981 and 1995? _____

Exercise 3

This exercise shows the relationship between unemployment and population. It is similar to the problem at the end of the chapter.

Suppose the data in Table 6.2 describe a nation's population.

Table 6.2
Employment and unemployment

	Year 1	Year 2
Population	400 million	460 million
Labor force	250 million	250 million
Unemployment rate	8 percent	8 percent
Number of unemployed	_____	_____
Number of employed	_____	_____

1. Fill in the blanks in Table 6.2 to show the number of unemployed and the number of employed.

2. When the population grows but the labor force and the unemployment rate remain constant, the number employed (rises, remains the same, falls).

3. If both the population and the number employed remain constant, but a larger percentage of the population passes through to retirement, the unemployment rate should (rise, remain the same, fall), *ceteris paribus*.

4. The people who immigrate to the United States are generally young and of working age compared to the existing population of the United States. As greater immigration rates are permitted and if the unemployment rate stays constant, the number employed would (rise, remain the same, fall), *ceteris paribus*.

Exercise 4

The following exercise provides practice in categorizing the various types of unemployment. Identify each of the following cases as an example of seasonal unemployment, frictional unemployment, structural unemployment, or cyclical unemployment.

1. During the summer illegal immigrants cross the border to pick crops but some cannot find jobs.
   _____

2. People who are fired from jobs with high salaries take longer to find new jobs than those with low salaries. _____

3. At the worst point of the Great Depression nearly one-fourth of the labor force in the United States was unemployed. _____

4. A city experiences an extreme shortage of labor and, at the same time, a substantial level of unemployment. The problem is that the shortage occurs in high-tech industries while the unemployment occurs for unskilled workers. _____

Common Errors

The first statement in each "common error" below is incorrect. Each incorrect statement is followed by a corrected version and an explanation.

1. The government should eliminate unemployment. WRONG!

   The government must reduce unemployment at the same time that it accomplishes other goals. RIGHT!

   Under the Full Employment and Balanced Growth Act of 1978, the government sets an unemployment goal for itself, but this goal is well short of a zero unemployment rate. As we shall see in subsequent chapters, the government may have to sacrifice such goals as price stability if it lowers unemployment too much. In this chapter we have seen that it would be very difficult and even undesirable to eliminate frictional or seasonal unemployment.

2. A rise in the unemployment rate of 0.1 or 0.2 percent for a month is bad. WRONG!

   Monthly changes in the unemployment rate may not have any significant economic implications. RIGHT!

   Small changes in the unemployment rate tell us nothing about what is happening in the labor force; large changes in seasonal or frictional unemployment are not necessarily bad and could not be easily remedied even if they were. Be careful in interpreting short-run changes in the unemployment rate.

3. Everyone who is counted as unemployed qualifies for unemployment benefits. WRONG!

   To qualify for unemployment benefits, certain conditions must be met. RIGHT!

   Many of those who are counted as unemployed do not qualify for unemployment benefits. Those who are new entrants to the labor force, those who have not worked at their last job for an extended period, and those who quit their last job are ineligible in many states. In addition some who are among the "seasonally unemployed" may not qualify for benefits.

•ANSWERS•

Using Key Terms

Across
1. unemployment rate
6. frictional unemployment
7. participation rate
11. skills gap
12. seasonal unemployment
13. discouraged worker
14. underemployment
15. unemployment

Down

2. natural rate of unemployment
3. production possibilities
4. structural unemployment
5. cyclical unemployment
8. Okun's Law
9. full employment
10. labor force

True or False

1. F Ed is counted as being out of the labor force because he is not actively looking for a job.
2. F When the number of unemployed workers increases, the unemployment rate will rise only if the labor force increases at a slower rate (or decreases).
3. T
4. F Discouraged workers are counted as not being in the labor force because they are not actively looking for a job.
5. F This transition has led to greater structural unemployment.
6 T
7. T
8. F Full employment does not imply a zero unemployment rate. It is usually defined as between 4 and 6 percent unemployment.
9. T
10. F As the skills gap widens, structural unemployment increases.

Multiple Choice

1. a	5. c	9. b	13. c	17. d
2. a	6. c	10. b	14. d	18. b
3. d	7. d	11. d	15. a	19. b
4. a	8. d	12. b	16. a	20. c

Problems and Applications

Exercise 1

1. The unemployment rate is found as follows:

$$\text{Unemployment rate} = \frac{\text{Unemployed}}{\text{Labor force}} = \frac{(\text{Labor force minus employed})}{\text{Labor force}}$$

$$= \frac{(1,000,000 - 900,000)}{1,000,000} = 10\%$$

2. 50,000. The unemployment rate is 10 percent which is 5 percent above full employment. Multiplying 5 percent by the labor force of 1 million gives 50,000.

3. Unemployment is 5 percentage points above the full employment level. Okun's Law suggests that each percentage point costs the economy 2 percent of full employment GDP. Multiplying 5 percent unemployment times 2 equals 10 percent. Then multiplying 10 percent times $100 billion equals $10 billion.

4. Full employment GDP = $100 billion. Lost output = $10 billion. Thus, GDP = $90 billion.

Exercise 2

1. **Table 6.1 Answer**

Year	(4) Unemployment rate (percent)
1981	7.6
1982	9.7
1983	9.6
1984	7.5
1985	7.2
1986	7.0
1987	6.2
1988	5.5
1989	5.3
1990	5.5
1991	6.7
1992	7.4
1993	6.8
1994	6.1
1995	5.6

2. **Figure 6.1 Answer**

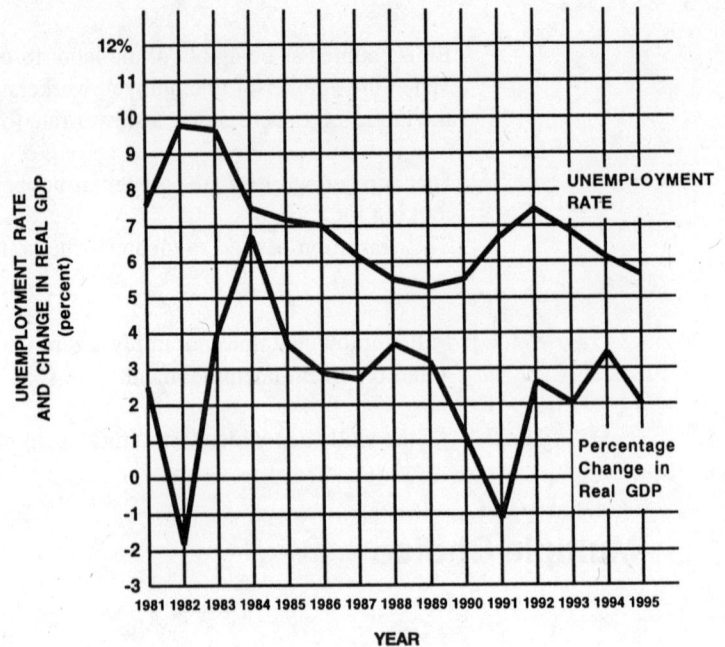

3. b
4. a   After a dramatic rise in real GDP, it takes several years for the unemployment rate to reach the lowest level.
5. c
6. 1988, 1989, 1990

Exercise 3

1. **Table 6.2 Answer**

	Year 1	Year 2
Population	400 million	460 million
Labor force	250 million	250 million
Unemployment rate	8 percent	8 percent
Number of unemployed	20 million (= 250 x 0.08)	20 million
Number of employed	230 million (= 250 – 20)	230 million

2. Remains the same
3. Fall
4. Rise

Exercise 4

1. seasonal
2. frictional
3. cyclical
4. structural

CHAPTER 7

Inflation

Quick Review

It is generally agreed that inflation was the nation's number one problem in the 1980s. Fear of its ravaging effects led to dramatic and desperate steps to tame the process. And, while inflation has retreated it is still a matter of great concern according to public opinion polls. To understand inflation we pose the following questions:

- What kind of price increases are referred to as "inflation"?
- Who is hurt (or helped) by inflation?
- What is an appropriate goal for "price stability"?

Inflation is defined as an increase in the average level of prices, and deflation is a decrease in the same measure. The average is a weighted one, so some prices may be falling while the *average* increases.

Inflation is not an equal opportunity phenomenon. It makes some worse off, while at the same time, others benefit from inflation. The price, income, and wealth effects spawned by the increase in average prices cause a redistribution of income and wealth. During an inflationary period, the prices of some goods rise faster than the average. Incomes may not rise as fast as the rate of inflation, and some forms of wealth may lose value. Of course, if the opposite occurs, there are benefits from the inflationary process.

On a macro (economy wide) level, inflation's effects are damaging too, as it is hard to make business and household decisions when you haven't a good idea of what the price level will be in the future. This leads decision makers to shorten their time horizons, diverts resources to speculative activities, and wreaks havoc on taxpayers whose tax bill is calculated in nominal terms, while their well-being is measured in real terms.

The rate of inflation is measured most frequently by using the Consumer Price Index (CPI), a weighted average of the price of a given basket of goods. Increases in the average price of the basket represent the inflationary process. Other indexes—the Producer Price Index (PPI) and the GDP deflator—can be used to answer questions about inflation too.

The goal of stable prices does not necessarily mean we wish to have a zero rate of change in the price level. Other macro goals, such as full employment and economic growth, must be considered too, and tradeoffs seem inevitable. Moreover, the CPI itself has some flaws which make zero inflation less desirable.

Inflationary problems experienced in the 1980s led to the development of some practical protective measures such as cost-of-living-adjustment (COLA) clauses in various contractual arrangements and adjustable-rate mortgages (ARMs) for lenders, both of which are tied to the CPI.

Still some feel that given the negative impact of the inflationary process, the best policy is to aim for zero inflation. Data indicate that countries with the lowest rates of inflation are also the ones with the lowest rates of unemployment. This makes sense if we consider that inflation interferes with the ability of prices to provide information about relative scarcity in the market.

Learning Objectives

After reading Chapter 7 and doing the following exercises, you should:

1. Understand that inflation is measured as an increase in the *average* level of prices.
2. Understand the difference between average prices and relative prices.
3. Be able to describe how price, income, and wealth effects accomplish redistributions in the economy.
4. Understand that some members of society are subject to money illusion.
5. Be able to explain why the inflationary process causes uncertainty and shortened time horizons, and diverts resources to speculative activity.
6. Be able to calculate and interpret a price index like the Consumer Price Index (CPI), and understand why other measures are also useful.
7. Understand why price stability does not necessarily mean a zero rate of increase in the price level.
8. Know that when quality improvements occur, the CPI will overstate the rate of inflation.
9. Be able to discuss mechanisms developed to protect various groups from the redistributive effects of inflation.
10. Understand why many knowledgeable people advocate policies designed to yield zero inflation worldwide.

Using Key Terms

Fill in the puzzle on the opposite page with the appropriate term from the list of Key Terms at the end of the chapter in the text.

Across

1. The price of apples compared to the price of other fruit.
5. Computed by the Bureau of Labor Statistics as the average price of consumer goods.
7. The nominal interest rate minus the anticipated rate of inflation.
8. The inflation adjusted value of output.
11. The increase in the average price level over a particular time period.
12. Used to express the purchasing power of income.
13. A decrease in average prices.
14. The price index that refers to all final goods and services.
15. Used in lease and wage agreements to protect real income from inflation.
16. Established at a rate of less than 3 percent inflation in the Full Employment and Balanced Growth Act of 1978.
17. The current dollar value of output.
18. The process in which inflation pushes people into higher tax brackets.
19. The use of nominal dollars, instead of real dollars, to guage changes in income or wealth.

Down

2. A home loan used to protect the lender during inflationary periods.
3. The time period used for comparative analysis.
4. The situation discussed in the article in this chapter of the text about the Weimar Republic.
6. The percentage of a typical consumer budget spent on a good; used to compute inflation indexes.
9. Results in a redistribution of income and wealth.
10. Income received in a given time period measured in current dollars.

Puzzle 7.1

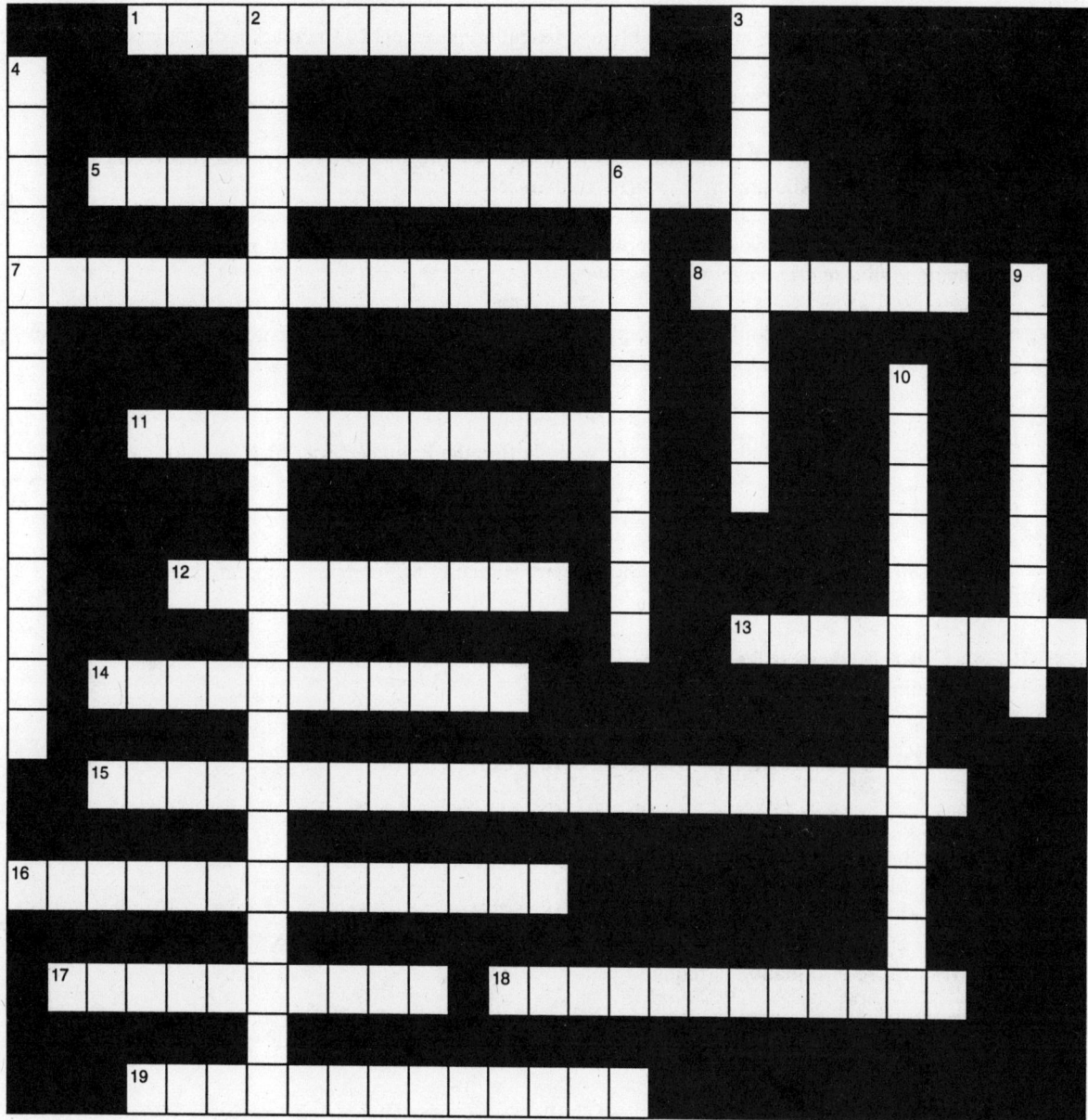

True or False: *Circle your choice and explain why any false statements are incorrect.*

T F 1. It is possible for individual prices to rise or fall during periods of inflation.

T F 2. Relative price changes are a desirable and essential ingredient of the market mechanism.

T F 3. Everyone is made worse off by inflation.

T F 4. When doctors' fees rise faster than aspirin prices, real income falls for people who visit a doctor relative to those who prescribe aspirin for themselves.

T F 5. If the prices of things you buy do not increase, but the inflation rate is 10 percent, then your real income falls, *ceteris paribus*.

T F 6. If all individuals were able to anticipate inflation correctly and make appropriate adjustments in their market behavior, there would be no redistribution of real income or real wealth as a result of inflation.

T F 7. The Consumer Price Index usually increases before the Producer Price Index.

T F 8. The official goal set by congress for inflation in the U.S. is zero percent.

T F 9. The CPI overstates the rate of inflation when the quality of the items in the market basket improves.

T F 10. A COLA counteracts the redistributive effects of inflation by adjusting nominal income according to the rate of inflation.

Multiple Choice: *Select the correct answer.*

_____ 1. If the price of computers falls 5 percent during a period when the level of average prices falls 10 percent, the relative price of computers compared with other goods:
(a) Stays the same.
(b) Increases.
(c) Decreases.
(d) More information is required.

_____ 2. When an economy experiences a zero rate of inflation, which of the following statements is definitely true?
(a) Real incomes do not change.
(b) Relative prices do not change.
(c) There is no redistribution of income and wealth because of inflation.
(d) All of the above.

_____ 3. Income redistribution occurs during inflation because:
(a) Not all prices rise by the same amount as average prices.
(b) Some taxes cause inflation to hit certain income groups harder than others.
(c) Not all groups can protect their incomes against inflation.
(d) All of the above.

_____ 4. Which of the following is a micro consequence of inflation that causes redistribution of income?
   (a)   A price effect.
   (b)   An income effect.
   (c)   A wealth effect.
   (d)   All of the above.

_____ 5. If actual inflation is greater than anticipated inflation in an economy:
   (a)   Borrowers would experience an increase in real income.
   (b)   Lenders would experience an increase in real income.
   (c)   All workers would experience a decrease in real income.
   (d)   The wealth effect would redistribute purchasing power to people on fixed incomes.

_____ 6. Which of the following groups is likely to lose as a result of unanticipated deflation?
   (a)   Borrowers who have loans at fixed interest rates.
   (b)   Fixed-income groups.
   (c)   Workers who receive fixed wages under multi-year contracts.
   (d)   Mortgage lenders who make adjustable-rate mortgages.

_____ 7. Suppose you get a 10 percent raise during a year in which the price level rises by 10 percent. Then over the year:
   (a)   Your real income falls, but your nominal income remains unchanged.
   (b)   Your real and nominal income both fall.
   (c)   Your real income remains unchanged, but your nominal income rises.
   (d)   Your real income remains unchanged, but your nominal income falls.

_____ 8. Because some people's incomes rise faster than inflation, while others rise more slowly:
   (a)   There are no adverse effects from inflation.
   (b)   There are redistribution effects from inflation.
   (c)   ARMs were created.
   (d)   People shorten their time horizons.

_____ 9. Which of the following characterizes consumers' or businesses' reactions to the uncertainties caused by inflation?
   (a)   Consumers cut back on consumption because they fear that future cost increases will make it difficult to make payments on what they consume.
   (b)   Consumption increases as consumers try to buy products before their prices rise.
   (c)   Businesses decrease investment spending in an attempt to avoid being caught with unprofitable plant and equipment.
   (d)   All of the above.

_____ 10. Which of the following is a macro consequence of inflation?
   (a)   Increased uncertainty.
   (b)   Lengthened time horizons.
   (c)   The wealth effect.
   (d)   The price effect.

_____ 11. Speculation during periods of inflation can result in:
   (a)   People buying resources for resale later rather than using the resources for current production.
   (b)   A movement inside the institutional production-possibilities curve.
   (c)   People buying gold, silver, jewelry, etc. instead of capital for production.
   (d)   All of the above.

_____ 12. At the beginning of 1960 the CPI was 29.6. At the end of 2000 it was approximately 170.8. Which of the following most closely approximates the forty-year rate of inflation?
- (a) 141 percent
- (b) 477 percent
- (c) 350 percent
- (d) 550 percent

_____ 13. If you were interested in charting prices charged by producers of energy, which of the following would be the most appropriate?
- (a) The CPI.
- (b) The PPI.
- (c) The GDP deflator.
- (d) The COLA.

_____ 14. The reason that policy makers are reluctant to force the economy to a zero percent inflation rate is that:
- (a) Unacceptable levels of unemployment might result.
- (b) Businesses would not be able to raise prices.
- (c) Real incomes would fall.
- (d) Businesses would postpone production decisions.

_____ 15. If the CPI doesn't adjust for product quality improvements, then the CPI tends to:
- (a) Understate the inflation rate.
- (b) Overstate the inflation rate.
- (c) Understate economic growth.
- (d) Be artificially low.

_____ 16. Which one of the following statements about inflation in the U.S. is correct?
- (a) Prior to World War II, the U.S. experienced periods of both deflation and inflation.
- (b) The U.S. experienced inflation virtually every year since 1800.
- (c) Since World War II, the U.S. has consistently met its inflation goal of 3 percent or lower.
- (d) Prior to World War II, the U.S. experienced deflation virtually every year; since World War II, the U.S. has consistently experienced inflation.

_____ 17. COLAs are desired because:
- (a) The real value of wages can be maintained, since COLAs correct for the effects of inflation.
- (b) COLAs help reduce the rate of inflation.
- (c) COLAs help stimulate employment.
- (d) All of the above.

_____ 18. For an economy in which nominal interest rates are higher than real interest rates, which of the following statements is definitely true?
- (a) Anticipated inflation was greater than actual inflation.
- (b) Actual inflation was greater than anticipated inflation.
- (c) Inflation was anticipated.
- (d) No inflation occurred.

_____ 19. The most fundamental function of prices in a market economy is to provide:
- (a) The data necessary to calculate rates of inflation.
- (b) The basis for the calculation of sales tax.
- (c) Information about the relative scarcities of resources and goods and services.
- (d) Maximum profits to producers.

_____ 20. The most desirable inflation rate is the rate that:
   (a)   Equals the official goal of 3 percent.
   (b)   Least affects the behavior of companies, investors, consumers and workers.
   (c)   Maximizes the "wealth effect" of inflation.
   (d)   Coincides with an unemployment rate of zero percent.

Problems and Applications

Exercise 1

This exercise emphasizes the redistribution of inflation and deflation.

1. During a period of inflation a person who owns no assets and has no COLA is likely to experience a (negative, positive) (wealth, income) effect.

2. During a period of inflation a family has a COLA that protects their income, but their rent payment rises more rapidly than the rate of inflation. This family experiences a (negative, positive) (price, wealth) effect.

3. During a period of inflation a person owns stock which increases in value at a rate greater than the rate of inflation. This person experiences a (negative, positive) (wealth, price) effect.

4. During a period of deflation a person's income remains constant. This results in a (positive, negative) (price, income) effect.

5. During a period of deflation a person owns a home that decreases in value at a rate greater than the rate of deflation. The result of this situation is a (positive, negative) (wealth, income) effect.

Exercise 2

This exercise refers to an article in the text titled "Inflation and the Weimar Republic." Read the article and then answer questions 1-5.

1. What country does the article refer to concerning hyperinflation and what is the time period?
   _____

2. What is the historical event that the article links to inflation? _____

3. What are some of the more obvious consequences of hyperinflation? _____
   _____

4. Because of the above consequences unemployment (fell, rose) significantly.

5. Who benefited during this period of hyperinflation? _____

Exercise 3

This exercise emphasizes the calculation of real GDP, real income, and the real interest rate.

Use the information in Table 7.1 to answer questions 1-6. Assume 1996 is the base period.

Table 7.1

	Nominal GDP (billions of dollars)	Jarrett's nominal income	GDP deflator	CPI	Nominal interest rate
1996	$3,200	$28,000	100	100	7%
1997	3,500	31,000	105	108	10%
1998	3,700	35,000	112	114	12%

1. Calculate real GDP for 1997. Use the formula:

$$\text{Real GDP1997} = \frac{\text{Nominal GDP}_{1997}}{\text{GDP deflator}_{1997}} \times 100$$

_____

2. Calculate real GDP for 1998. _____

3. Calculate Jarrett's real income for 1998. Use the formula:

$$\text{Real income1998} = \frac{\text{Nominal income}_{1998}}{\text{CPI}_{1998}} \times 100$$

_____

4. By what percentage did consumer prices rise from 1996 to 1997? _____

5. By what percentage did consumer prices rise from 1996 to 1998? _____

6. Use the Consumer Price Index as a measure of the anticipated rate of inflation. Calculate the real interest rate for 1997. (The formula is on page 139 in the text.) _____

Exercise 4

This exercise focuses on the causes of inflation and the different impacts on the economy.

1. When consumers seek to buy more goods than the economy can produce, the result is _____ inflation.

2. When production costs rise for numerous industries, the result is _____ inflation.

Figure 7.1

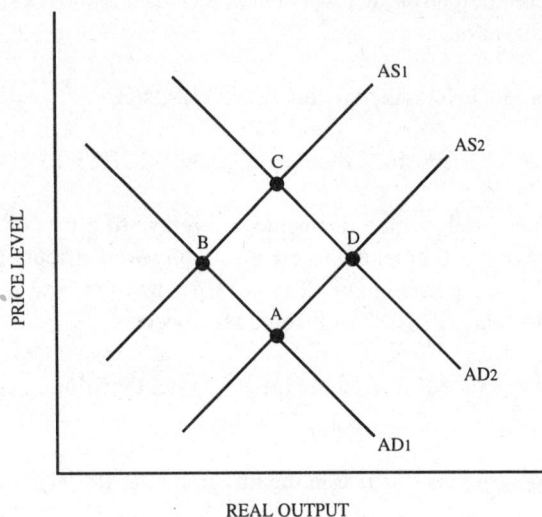

3. Assume the economy is in equilibrium at point A in Figure 7.1. As a result of cost-push inflation, the economy would move to point _____. The price level would _____ and the level of output would _____.

4. Assume the economy is in equilibrium at point B in Figure 7.1. As a result of demand-pull inflation, the economy would move to point _____. The price level would _____ and the level of output would _____.

Exercise 5

This exercise will help you see the impact of different inflation rates on the value of money held for different periods of time.

1. Use Table 7.6 in the text to find the value of $1000 for the given inflation rate and period of time.
   a. Four years at 8% inflation: _____
   b. Five years at 4% inflation: _____
   c. Eight years at 4% inflation: _____
   d. Ten years at 2% inflation: _____
   e. Seven years at 10% inflation: _____

2. In which of the two cases above does the $1000 come closest to being worth the same amount? _____

3. In which case above is the $1000 worth the least amount?_____

4. Would you lose more money if you placed $1000 under your mattress for ten years at 2% inflation or if you placed $1000 in a cookie jar for four years at 8% inflation?_____ _____

Common Errors

The first statement in each "common error" below is incorrect. Each incorrect statement is followed by a corrected version and an explanation.

1. When the price of a product rises, there is inflation. WRONG!

    When the average level of prices rises, there is inflation. RIGHT!

    The price of a single product may rise while an average of prices of all products falls. Such adjustments in relative prices is essential to the most *efficient* distribution of goods and services through the market. When the average of all prices is rising, however, distribution may not be efficient and capricious redistributions of income may occur.

2. As long as price increases do not exceed the inflation rate, they do not contribute to inflation. WRONG!

    Every price increase contributes to a rise in the inflation rate. RIGHT!

    Since the inflation rate is an average of all price increases, the increase in any price by any amount raises the average. Firms that buy commodities from other firms that raise prices will, in turn, attempt to pass the increase on to their own customers; an increased price may have indirect effects in raising the inflation rate.

3. Indexation, such as a COLA clause in a contract, protects the *economy* against the effects of inflation. WRONG!

    A COLA clause protects an individual against the effects of inflation. RIGHT!

    Indexation can protect the real incomes of specific groups for which indexation is applied. In other words, it can address some of the micro consequences of inflation. However, if everyone's income is not indexed, then even the micro consequences may not be adequately addressed. In fact, indexation can lead to dramatic changes in relative prices. Furthermore, indexation may lead to anticipation of higher rates of inflation; high current inflation rates may guarantee higher future rates as a result of indexation.

•ANSWERS•

Using Key Terms

Across

1. relative price
5. consumer price index
7. real interest rate
8. real GDP
11. inflation rate
12. real income
13. deflation
14. GDP deflator
15. cost-of-living adjustment (COLA)
16. price stability
17. nominal GDP

18. bracket creep
19. money illusion

Down

2. adjustable rate mortgage
3. base period
4. hyperinflation
6. item weight
9. inflation
10. nominal income

True or False

1. T
2. T
3. F   There are winners and losers during periods of inflation because of the price, wealth and income effects.
4. T
5. F   If your purchasing power does not change, then your real income hasn't changed.
6. T
7. F   The PPI measures changes in average prices at the producer level, which typically occurs before changes in the CPI.
8. F   The official goal set by the Full Employment and Balanced Growth Act of 1978 was 3 percent inflation.
9. T
10. T

Multiple Choice

1. b	5. a	9. d	13. b	17. a
2. c	6. a	10. a	14. a	18. d
3. d	7 c	11. d	15. b	19. c
4. d	8. b	12. b	16. a	20. b

Problems and Applications

Exercise 1

1. negative, income
2. negative, price
3. positive, wealth
4. positive, income
5. negative, wealth

Exercise 2

1. Germany; after World War I, specifically from 1921-1923
2. War
3. Decrease in profits, increase in speculation, shortened time horizons.
4. rose
5. debtors, such as farmers

Exercise 3

1. $3,333.33 billion
2. $3,303.57 billion
3. $30,701.75 billion
4. 8 percent
5. 14 percent
6. 2 percent

Exercise 4

1. demand-pull
2. cost-push
3. B, increase, decrease
4. C, increase, increase

Exercise 5

1. a. $735
   b. $822
   c. $731
   d. $820
   e. $513
2. b and d
3. e
4. $1000 in a cookie jar for four years at 8% inflation

C H A P T E R 8
The Business Cycle

Quick Review

The Great Depression of the 1930s was a worldwide phenomenon. No market economy seemed to avoid it. High unemployment and low production for a decade led to despair nearly everywhere. They also caused a major rethinking of our views on the U.S. economy. Serious questions were raised, including:

- How stable is a market-driven economy?
- What forces cause instability?
- What, if anything, can the government do to promote steady economic growth?

The basic purpose of macroeconomics is to answer these questions—that is, to explain the alternating periods of expansion and contraction in gross domestic product (GDP) known as the business cycle. If we can develop a macro theory to explain such changes, perhaps we can develop macro policies to control them.

The Classical school of thought, which was largely in vogue prior to the 1930s, stressed the self-adjusting nature of the economy. Automatic adjustment mechanisms—such as flexible wages and prices, falling interest rates, and the like—were thought to ensure that any downswing would be short if the economy was left alone, that is, if a laissez faire attitude prevailed. This optimistic view was summarized in Say's Law—"supply creates its own demand."

The Great Depression lasted a long time, and economists and politicians everywhere began to question Classical theory. The great British economist John Maynard Keynes developed an alternative theory that took issue with the self-adjusting view of Classical economics. Keynes asserted that the economy was, in fact, inherently *unstable*. To leave the economy alone was poor policy. Instead, he prescribed increased government spending, income transfers, and lower interest rates to get the economy moving again.

The arguments about business cycles are still not settled, but we have learned a great deal and agree to measure the cycle from peak to trough by watching the fluctuation in real GDP. Two consecutive quarters of decline in real GDP is considered a recession. Growth for a period below the 3 percent long-run historical trend of the economy is called a "growth recession." The statistics presented in this chapter make it clear that business cycles vary greatly in length, frequency, and intensity.

It is sometimes useful to visualize the macro economy as a set of outcomes—output, jobs, prices, growth and international balances—which depend on a finite set of determinants—internal market forces, external shocks, and policy levers. Modern economists combine these insights with aggregate demand and aggregate supply curves to see how the economy works. The aggregate demand curve slopes downward and to the right when plotted against the price level because of the real-balances effect, the foreign trade effect and the interest rate effect. The aggregate supply curve slopes upward and to the right when plotted on the same grid because of the profit effect and the cost effect (though in the long run it may be vertical!). The intersection of the aggregate demand and supply curves defines the macro equilibrium. The equilibrium may be undesirable because it may not provide the level of employment and output we desire. Even if it does, it may be unstable and not last for long because the forces behind the equilibrium can change. Shifts in aggregate demand and/or aggregate supply can lead to unemployment, inflation, or, worse yet, stagflation—a combination of the two.

The aggregate-demand and aggregate-supply framework provides a convenient way to compare various theories about how the economy works. The theories can be classified as demand-side, supply-side, or eclectic. The three policy levers used to discuss and demonstrate the several theories are:

1. Fiscal policy—changes in taxes and government spending to alter economic outcomes.
2. Monetary policy—the use of money and credit to control economic outcomes.
3. Supply-side policy—favors tax cuts and other policies to increase incentives for producers.

The next several chapters are devoted to explaining the policies above and the impact they can have on the macroeconomy.

Learning Objectives

After reading Chapter 8 and doing the following exercises, you should:

1. Understand the dimensions of the business cycle.
2. Have in mind a historical perspective on the business cycle from the Great Depression to the present.
3. Be able to distinguish the Keynesian and Classical positions on how the macro economy works.
4. Understand why the aggregate supply curve slopes upward to the right, and why the aggregate demand curve slopes downward to the right.
5. Recognize that a given macro equilibrium may not be desirable, and that it may also be unstable.
6. Understand the different explanations of the business cycle—demand-side, supply-side, and eclectic.

Using Key Terms

Fill in the puzzle on the opposite page with the appropriate term from the list of Key Terms at the end of the chapter in the text.

Across

2. The value of final output produced in a given period, adjusted for changing prices.
3. The idea that whatever is produced by suppliers will always be sold.
9. The output level represented by point Q_F in Figure 8.8 in the text.
12. The use of tax cuts and government deregulation to shift the aggregate supply curve.
13. The portion of the business cycle when total output decreases.
14. The macro failure in Figure 8.8 in the text because the equilibrium price level exceeds the desired price level.
15. The concept of nonintervention by government in the market mechanism.

Down

1. A situation in which the economy grows but at a very slow rate.
4. States that an increase in price causes a decrease in quantity demanded of a good.
5. The upward sloping curve in Figure 8.7 in the text.
6. Represented by point E in Figure 8.7 in the text.
7. The area of study that focuses on output, jobs, prices, and growth for the entire economy.
8. The use of money and credit controls to shift the aggregate demand curve.
9. The use of government spending and taxes to shift the aggregate demand curve.
10. Occurs as a result of shifts in aggregate demand and aggregate supply.
11. The curve drawn in Figure 8.5 in the text.

Puzzle 8.1

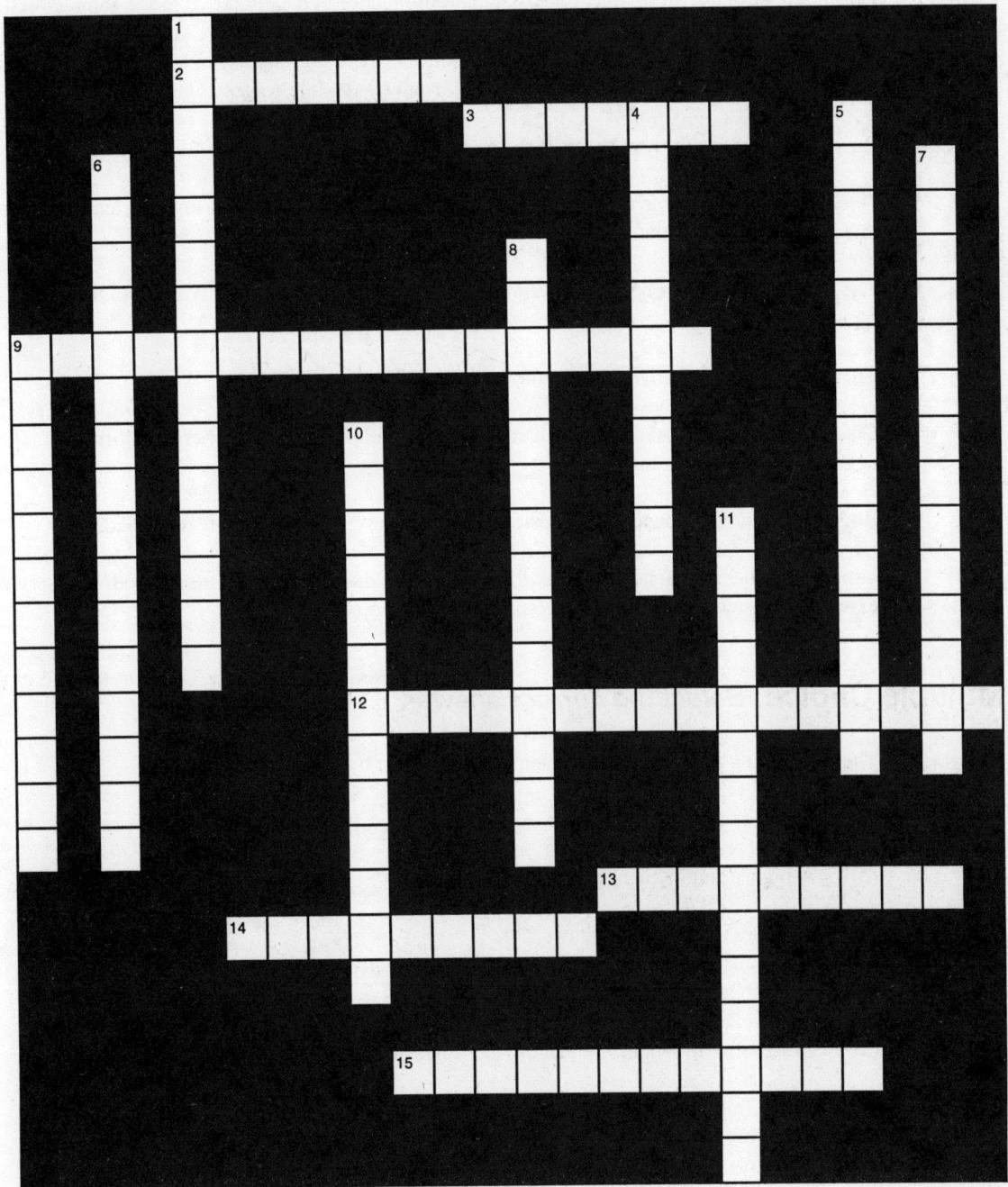

True or False: *Circle your choice and explain why any false statements are incorrect.*

T **F** 1. Business cycles are measured by changes in nominal GDP.

T **F** 2. During the business cycle, unemployment and production typically move in the same direction.

T F 3. In the Classical view of the economy, the product market is brought into equilibrium by flexible prices, the labor market is brought into equilibrium by flexible wages.

T F 4. Business cycles result from shifts of the aggregate supply and aggregate demand curves.

T F 5. One reason the aggregate demand curve is downward sloping is that at lower price levels interest rates tend to be lower thus stimulating more borrowing and spending.

T F 6. The profit effect occurs because, in the short run, resource costs typically do not increase as rapidly as the prices of goods and services.

T **F** 7. The full-employment GDP is the same as the equilibrium GDP.

T **F** 8. Classical economists believed that unemployment could exist for long periods of time if aggregate demand was inadequate.

T F 9. Both Keynesian and monetarist theories of the business cycle are supply-side theories.

T F 10. Supply-side theorists believe the unwillingness of producers to supply more goods and services at existing prices can prolong an economic downturn.

Multiple Choice: *Select the correct answer.*

_____ 1. The downswing in the business cycle is characterized by:
   (a) Higher real output.
   (b) A higher unemployment rate.
   (c) Higher prices.
   (d) A higher employment rate.

_____ 2. Business cycles in the United States:
   (a) Are remarkably similar in length but vary greatly in intensity.
   (b) Vary greatly in length, frequency, and intensity.
   (c) Are similar in frequency and intensity.
   (d) Are similar in length, frequency, and intensity.

_____ 3. Which of the following is inherent in the Classical view of a self-adjusting economy?
   (a) Inflexible wages.
   (b) Inflexible prices.
   (c) Say's Law.
   (d) Instability.

_____ 4. Keynesian theory became important when Classical economic theory did not adequately explain:
   (a) A prolonged period of both inflation and unemployment.
   (b) A prolonged growth recession.
   (c) A depression.
   (d) A prolonged period of inflation.

_____ 5. In the aggregate demand-aggregate supply diagram:
  (a) More than one equilibrium can occur.
  (b) The horizontal axis measures the average price level.
  (c) The intersection of the two curves marks the macro equilibrium.
  (d) The equilibrium level of output is always at the full employment level.

_____ 6. A decrease in business inventories, *ceteris paribus*, is best represented by:
  (a) An increase in AD.
  (b) A decrease in AD.
  (c) An increase in AS.
  (d) A decrease in AS.

_____ 7. The difference between market demand and aggregate demand is:
  (a) Market demand applies to all individuals, and aggregate demand does not.
  (b) Aggregate demand applies to a specific good, and market demand does not.
  (c) Policy levers work only through market demand.
  (d) Market demand applies to a given market while aggregate demand applies to the entire economy.

_____ 8. The real-balances effect relies on the idea that as the price level falls:
  (a) Each dollar you own will purchase more goods and services.
  (b) Each bond you own will increase in value, thus increasing your wealth.
  (c) You will begin to save less because your wealth has increased.
  (d) All of the above.

_____ 9. When the average price level falls in our economy, consumers tend to:
  (a) Buy more imported goods and fewer domestic goods, *ceteris paribus*.
  (b) Buy more imported goods and more domestic goods, *ceteris paribus*.
  (c) Buy fewer imported goods and more domestic goods, *ceteris paribus*.
  (d) Buy fewer imported goods and fewer domestic goods, *ceteris paribus*.

_____ 10. Which of the following is a reason why the aggregate supply curve is upward sloping?
  (a) Profit effect.
  (b) Interest rate effect.
  (c) Real-balances effect.
  (d) Foreign trade effect.

_____ 11. The cost effect implies:
  (a) That greater output results in increasingly higher costs.
  (b) A curved, upward-sloping aggregate supply curve.
  (c) That higher costs are reflected in higher average prices.
  (d) All of the above.

_____ 12. In macro equilibrium:
  (a) Aggregate quantity demanded equals aggregate quantity supplied.
  (b) The equilibrium price level and rate of output are both stable.
  (c) Both buyers' and sellers' intentions are satisfied.
  (d) All of the above.

_____ 13. When aggregate supply exceeds aggregate demand, what will happen to the price level?
  (a) Prices will rise.
  (b) Prices will remain the same.
  (c) Prices will fall.
  (d) Prices may either rise or fall depending on the business cycle.

_____ 14. Which of the following combination of shifts of aggregate demand and supply curves would definitely result in higher unemployment?
    (a)   Demand shifts to the left and supply shifts to the right.
    (b)   Demand shifts to the left and supply shifts to the left.
    (c)   Demand shifts to the right and supply shifts to the right.
    (d)   Demand shifts to the right and supply shifts to the left.

_____ 15. Controversies between Keynesian, monetarist, supply-side, and eclectic theories focus on:
    (a)   The shape and sensitivity of aggregate demand and aggregate supply curves.
    (b)   The existence or nonexistence of the aggregate supply curve.
    (c)   The importance of international balances to the economy.
    (d)   All of the above.

_____ 16. According to Keynes, policy makers should respond to a downturn in the business cycle by:
    (a)   Cutting taxes and increasing government spending.
    (b)   Cutting taxes and reducing government spending.
    (c)   Raising taxes and increasing government spending.
    (d)   Raising taxes and reducing government spending.

_____ 17. The eclectic approach to macroeconomic policy relies on:
    (a)   Demand-side policy.
    (b)   A laissez faire approach.
    (c)   Supply-side policy.
    (d)   Any or all of the above approaches.

_____ 18. A vertical supply curve:
    (a)   Implies that supply side policies will have no effect on the macro equilibrium.
    (b)   Means aggregate demand shifts have no impact on output.
    (c)   Is likely in the short run.
    (d)   Reflects the inflexibility of prices and wages.

_____ 19. If equilibrium GDP is less than full employment GDP, an appropriate fiscal policy lever would be to:
    (a)   Increase AD by increasing income taxes.
    (b)   Increase AD by increasing government spending.
    (c)   Increase AS by reducing government regulations.
    (d)   Reduce AS by tightening air pollution standards in order to improve air quality.

_____ 20. If an economy is suffering from excessively high rates of inflation, an appropriate monetary policy lever would be to:
    (a)   Decrease AS by decreasing the money supply.
    (b)   Decrease AD by increasing interest rates.
    (c)   Decrease AD by increasing income taxes.
    (d)   Increase AS by increasing the money supply.

Problems and Applications

Exercise 1

This exercise examines the effects of fiscal policy using aggregate supply and demand curves.

Assume the aggregate demand and supply curves are those shown in Figure 8.1. Then suppose the government increases spending, which causes the quantity of output demanded in the economy to rise by $1 trillion per year at every price level. Decide whether the change shifts aggregate demand or aggregate supply from its initial position.

Figure 8.1

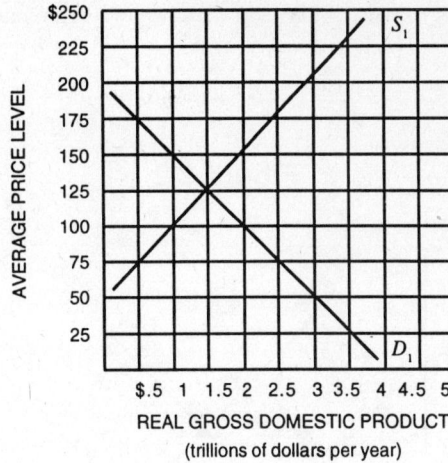

AVERAGE PRICE LEVEL

REAL GROSS DOMESTIC PRODUCT
(trillions of dollars per year)

1. Draw the new aggregate demand curve (label it D_2) or aggregate supply curve (label it S_2) in Figure 8.1.

2. What is the new equilibrium average price?_____

3. What is the new equilibrium output level?_____

4. Which school of thought would be most likely to prescribe the use of fiscal policy in this way?
_____

5. The shift that occurred in question 1 (above) is consistent with:
   (a) Inflation and a higher unemployment rate.
   (b) Inflation and a lower unemployment rate.
   (c) Deflation and a higher unemployment rate.
   (d) Lower inflation and a lower unemployment rate.

Exercise 2

This exercise will demonstrate the impact of inflation on savings.

1. Suppose you have $300 in savings at the beginning of the year and the price level is 100. If inflation pushes the price level up by 10 percent during the year, what will be the real value of your savings at year-end? (*Hint:* Refer to the formula on page 154 in the text.)
_____

2. The change in purchasing power in question 1 above, because of a change in the price level, is one explanation for the downward slope of the aggregate demand curve. This explanation is referred to as the _____.

3. The impact of the change in purchasing power in question 1 above would cause a (movement up, leftward shift in) the aggregate demand curve.

Exercise 3

This exercise will demonstrate the impact of shifts in demand and aggregate supply. Answer choices are AD, AS, or both AD and AS.

Use Figure 8.2 to answer questions 1-4.

Figure 8.2

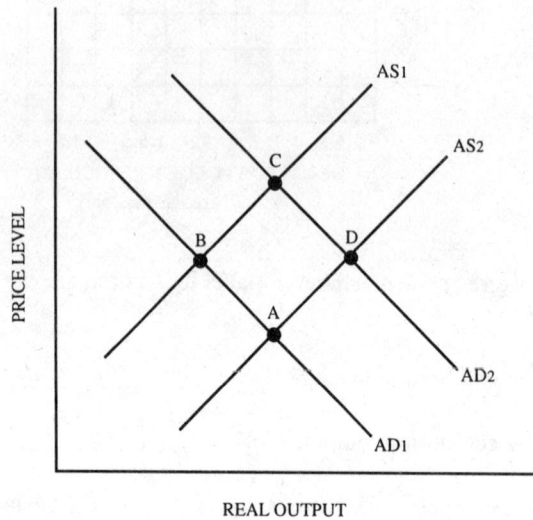

1. Assume the economy is initially in equilibrium at point B in Figure 8.2. Which curve would have shifted if a new equilibrium were to occur at point C? _____

2. Assume the economy is initially in equilibrium at point D in Figure 8.2. Which curve would have shifted if a new equilibrium were to occur at point C? _____

3. Assume the economy is initially in equilibrium at point B in Figure 8.2. Which curve would have shifted if a new equilibrium were to occur at point A? _____

4. Assume the economy is initially in equilibrium at point A in Figure 8.2. Which curve would have shifted if a new equilibrium were to occur at point C? _____

Exercise 4

This exercise focuses on the long-run aggregate supply curve and the impact of fiscal policy.

Use Figure 8.3 to answer questions 1-7.

Figure 8.3

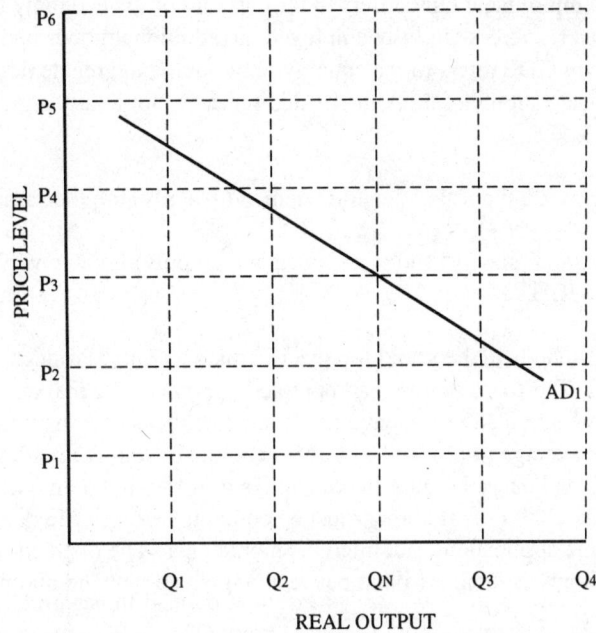

1. In Figure 8.3, aggregate demand is given as AD_1. Draw the long-run aggregate supply curve according to the classical/monetarist view of long-run stability. The equilibrium level of output should occur at Q_N. Label the curve AS. Label the equilibrium point E_1.

2. T   F Q_N represents the long-run equilibrium output level.

3. What is the equilibrium price level in Figure 8.3, given the long-run aggregate supply curve and AD_1? _____

4. Suppose the government uses fiscal policy to shift the aggregate demand curve in Figure 8.3 to the right. Draw the new aggregate demand curve and label it AD_2. Label the new equilibrium point E_2.

5. The fiscal policy action in question 4 above caused the price level to (rise, fall, stay the same).

6. The fiscal policy action in question 4 above caused the level of real output to (rise, fall, stay the same).

7. T   F   With a vertical long-run aggregate supply curve, fiscal policy is effective in changing the level of real output.

Common Errors

The first statement in each "common error" below is incorrect. Each incorrect statement is followed by a corrected version and an explanation.

1. The full-employment GDP is the same as the equilibrium GDP. WRONG!

    The full-employment GDP is not necessarily the same as the equilibrium GDP. RIGHT!

    The full-employment GDP refers to the capacity of the economy to produce goods and services. When resources are fully employed, no additional goods and services can be produced. The equilibrium GDP refers to the equality between the aggregate demand for goods and services and the aggregate supply of those goods and services, not to any particular level of resource employment.

2. Aggregate demand (supply) and market demand (supply) are the same. WRONG!

    Aggregate demand (supply) and market demand (supply) involve very different levels of aggregation. RIGHT!

    Market demand can be found for specific markets only. Products in that market must be homogeneous. The firms in that market are competitors. The market demand is used for microeconomic applications. Aggregate demand applies to all markets within the economy and involves their average prices. It is not even possible to sum the market demand curves to find the aggregate demand curve because the quantities of different commodities cannot be measured in the same units; GDP or real output must be computed. Aggregate demand is used for macroeconomic applications, not microeconomic ones. The distinction between aggregate supply and market supply is similar to that between aggregate demand and market demand.

3. A downward-sloping trend of the economic growth rate indicates a recession. WRONG!

    A downward-sloping trend of the real GDP indicates a recession. RIGHT!

    The economic growth rate is measured by the *percentage change* in the real GDP. A recession occurs whenever that percentage change is negative for two quarters. By contrast, in a graph of the real GDP, without any computation of year-to-year changes, it is necessary to look for a downward dip in the real GDP to spot a recession. Three rules for the relationship between the levels and percentage changes of the real GDP should always be remembered when either graph is being examined:
    1. Whenever there is a downward slope to a graph of the real GDP, there will be a negative percentage change in real GDP.
    2. Whenever the graph of the real GDP flattens, the percentage change in the real GDP will approach zero.
    3. Whenever there is an upward slope to a graph of the real GDP, there will be a positive percentage change in real GDP.

Using Key Terms

Across
2. real GDP
3. Say's Law
9. full employment GDP
12. supply-side policy
13. recession
14. inflation
15. laissez-faire

Down
1. growth recession
4. law of demand
5. aggregate supply
6. equilibrium macro
7. macroeconomics
8. monetary policy
9. fiscal policy
10. business cycle
11. aggregate demand

True or False

1. F   Business cycles are measured by changes in real GDP.
2. F   Unemployment and production typically move in opposite directions.
3. T
4. T
5. T
6. T
7. F   Equilibrium GDP does not guarantee full employment. Equilibrium GDP can be greater than, less than, or equal to full employment GDP.
8. F   Classical economists believed that the economy would adjust on its own to full employment. Keynes believed that unemployment could exist for long periods of time if aggregate demand was inadequate.
9. F   These are demand-side theories.
10. T

Multiple Choice

1. b	5. c	9. c	13. c	17. d
2. b	6. b	10. a	14. b	18. b
3. c	7. d	11. d	15. a	19. b
4. c	8. d	12. d	16. a	20. b

Problems and Applications

Exercise 1

1. See Figure 8.1 Answer, D_2

Figure 8.1 Answer

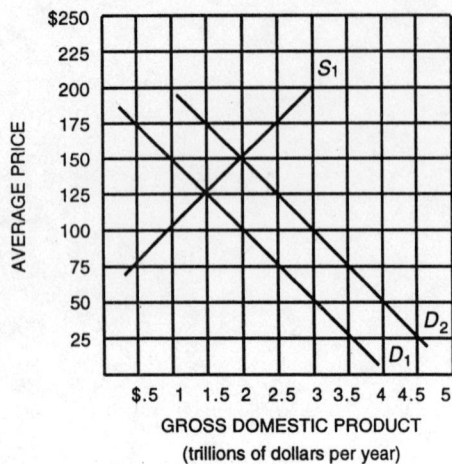

2. $150
3. $2 trillion
4. Keynesian
5. b

Exercise 2

1. $300/(110/100) = $300/(1.1) = $272.73
2. real-balances effect
3. movement up

Exercise 3

1. AD
2. AS
3. AS
4. both AD and AS

Exercise 4

Figure 8.3 answer

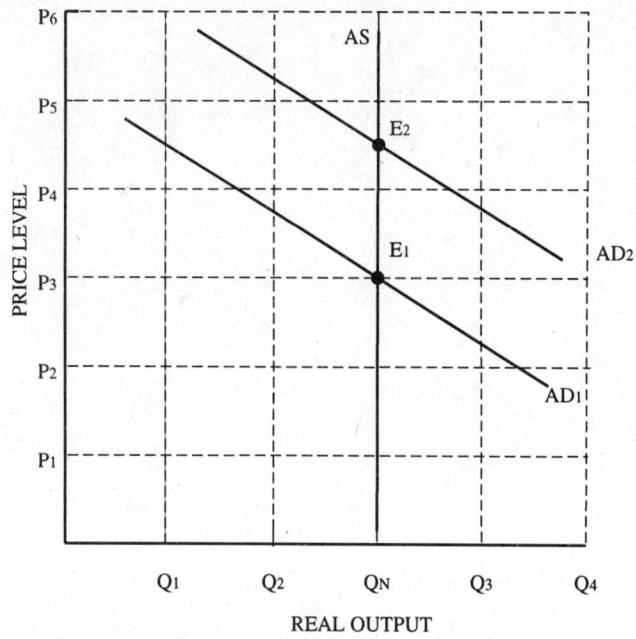

1. See AS and E_1 in Figure 8.3 Answer
2. T
3. P_3
4. See AD_2 and E_2 in Figure 8.3 Answer
5. Rise
6. Stay the same
7. F

CHAPTER 9

Aggregate Spending

Quick Review

The Great Depression caused economists to change the way they thought about the macroeconomy. John Maynard Keynes concluded that a *market-driven economy* could fall into a recessionary trap *and* that the problem was on the demand side of the economy. He posed the following questions:

- What are the components of aggregate demand?
- What determines the level of spending for each component?
- Will there ever be enough demand to maintain full employment?

Macroequilibrium only requires that aggregate supply equal aggregate demand, but the goal of full employment requires that the equilibrium occur at a unique level of output and price level. Keynes was concerned about the four components of aggregate demand:

- Consumption (C).
- Investment (I).
- Government spending (G).
- Net exports ($X - IM$).

He questioned whether aggregate demand would be sufficient to generate full employment and, if not, he wondered if it would shift on its own to solve the problem. He focused first on consumption and concluded that it is determined mostly by disposable income.

Disposable income must be divided into two parts—that which is spent and that which is saved. The amount spent out of any level of disposable income can be anticipated using the consumption function (a Keynesian invention) of the form $C = a + bY_D$, where the coefficients a and b describe consumer behavior. Here a depends on wealth, credit, age, and the like, and is referred to as "autonomous spending"; b is the percentage of current disposable income which is spent.

Income which is not spent is, by definition, saved. Household saving is a leakage from the circular flow of income as are business saving, imports, and taxes. If the economy is to prosper, some way must be found to inject the income which "leaks out" back into the income stream. There are several injections. Investment spending is done by firms as they purchase final output, and this category depends on interest rates, expectations, the development of new technologies, and innovation *but not* on current income. Government purchases (federal, state, and local) are a significant force in the economy, and decisions on how much to spend are independent of the level of real income. Foreign buyers purchase exports from the U.S. economy; Americans gladly purchase imports from foreign countries. The difference is called net exports. We can summarize as follows:

$$\text{Aggregate expenditures} = C + I + G + (X - IM)$$

Using spending categories, we can predict how much spending will take place at any level of income, and whether it will be sufficient to create full employment. Obviously, twin problems loom—aggregate spending may be too little and a recessionary gap may develop, or it may be too much and an inflationary gap may occur. The former causes cyclical unemployment; the latter, inflation arising from too much aggregate demand.

Learning Objectives

After reading Chapter 9 and doing the following exercises, you should:

1. Know the Keynesian theory of aggregate demand.
2. Understand the difference between aggregate demand and aggregate expenditure.
3. Know the four components of aggregate demand.
4. Be able to interpret the consumption function.
5. Know how to find the average and marginal propensities to consume.
6. Know how to use the aggregate spending function and the 45-degree line to calculate saving or dissaving.
7. Understand how a shift in the consumption function leads to a shift in aggregate demand.
8. Understand the nature and role of both leakages and injections.
9. Be able to describe the determinants of C, I, G, and $(X - IM)$.
10. Understand the role of saving, its relationship to investment, and the effect it has on equilibrium income.
11. Be able to graph the aggregate expenditure function and determine the resulting level of income.
12. Be able to graph a recessionary or an inflationary gap, explain what occurs, and describe appropriate government intervention.

Using Key Terms

Across

3. The distance from point h to point f in Figure 9.13 in the text.
5. Determined by expectations, interest rates, and technology.
8. Equal to 0.75 in Figure 9.4 in the text.
10. After tax income of consumers.
11. The downward-sloping curve in Figure 9:1 in the text.
17. The largest component of aggregate demand.
18. Savings, imports, and taxes represent a _____ from the circular flow.
19. Potential GDP.
20. The upward-sloping line in Figure 9.11 in the text.
21. The proportion of total disposable income spent on consumption.
22. Depreciation allowances plus retained earnings.

Down

1. The rate of output where desired expenditure equals the value of output.
2. Demonstrated on the right-hand side of Figure 9.14 in the text.
4. The upward-sloping curve in Figure 9.1 in the text.
6. Equal to 1 - MPC.
7. Provides a basis for predicting how changes in income will affect consumer spending.
9. Unemployment because of an inadequate level of aggregate demand.
12. The negative saving discussed in the article titled "Savings Rate Hits Negative Territory" in the text.
13. Exports, government spending, and investment in Figure 9.9 in the text.
14. The difference between point g and point f in Figure 9.12 in the text.
15. The difference between the consumption function and the 45 degree line at a disposable income of $300 in Figure 9.4 in the text.
16. The combination of price level and real output that is compatible with both aggregate demand and aggregate supply.

True or False: *Circle your choice and explain why any false statements are incorrect.*

T F 1. Keynes believed that if market participants were unwilling to buy all of the output produced, the government would have to intervene if the economy were to pull itself out of a recessionary gap.

T F 2. The four components of aggregate demand are consumption, investment, government spending, and net exports.

T F 3. The largest component of aggregate demand is government spending.

T F 4. The question "What fraction of total disposable income is spent on consumption?" can be answered by calculating the marginal propensity to consume.

T F 5. The slope of the consumption function equals the marginal propensity to consume.

T F 6. The consumption function will shift because of a change in current disposable income.

T F 7. Because saving is a leakage, a sudden increase in saving results in lower equilibrium income for society, *ceteris paribus*.

T F 8. Investment, government expenditures and exports are all injections into the circular flow.

T F 9. Investment depends primarily upon the current level of income.

T F 10. If desired spending at full-employment output is greater than full-employment output, there is an inflationary gap.

Multiple Choice: *Select the correct answer.*

_____ 1. Keynes argued that the level of economic activity is predominantly determined by the level of:
   (a) Aggregate supply.
   (b) Aggregate demand.
   (c) Unemployment.
   (d) Interest rates.

_____ 2. If, in the aggregate, consumers spend 90 cents out of every extra dollar received:
   (a) The *APC* is 1.11.
   (b) The *APC* is 0.90.
   (c) The *MPS* is 0.10.
   (d) The *MPC* is 0.10.

_____ 3. Suppose the MPC in an economy is 0.8 and the level of consumption spending independent of current disposable income is $1 billion. If disposable income is $14 billion, what is the level of consumption?
   (a) $11.2 billion.
   (b) $12.2 billion.
   (c) $8.0 billion.
   (d) $12.0 billion.

_____ 4. Autonomous consumption is found where the consumption function intersects the:
   (a) Vertical axis.
   (b) Horizontal axis.
   (c) 45-degree line.
   (d) Aggregate spending curve.

5. A change in autonomous consumption would correspond to:
   (a) A shift of both the consumption function and the aggregate demand curve.
   (b) A shift of the consumption function and a movement along the aggregate demand curve.
   (c) A movement along the consumption function and a shift of the aggregate demand curve.
   (d) A movement along both the consumption function and the aggregate demand curve.

6. In the consumption function $C = a + bY_D$, the value of a is determined in part by:
   (a) Disposable income.
   (b) The level of imports.
   (c) Consumer confidence.
   (d) All of the above.

7. The line described by the consumption function $C = a + bY_D$ will change its slope when:
   (a) The MPC changes.
   (b) Consumer confidence changes.
   (c) Disposable income changes.
   (d) The MPS is greater than 1.0.

8. Which of the following would shift the consumption function?
   (a) A change in the level of interest rates.
   (b) A change in disposable income.
   (c) A change in technology.
   (d) All of the above.

9. An increase in interest rates would result in:
   (a) A decrease in both aggregate demand and the aggregate expenditure line.
   (b) A decrease in aggregate demand and an increase in aggregate supply.
   (c) An increase in both aggregate demand and the aggregate expenditure line.
   (d) An increase in both aggregate demand and aggregate supply.

10. With respect to the aggregate demand curve, improved consumer confidence would:
    (a) Shift the curve rightward.
    (b) Shift the curve leftward.
    (c) Move the economy down along the curve.
    (d) Move the economy up along the curve.

11. Which of the following is a leakage?
    (a) Savings.
    (b) Imports.
    (c) Taxes.
    (d) All of the above.

12. In graphs with output on the horizontal axis and aggregate expenditures on the vertical axis, a 45-degree line represents:
    (a) The potential growth path for consumption.
    (b) A line marking where aggregate demand and supply intersect for equilibrium (macro).
    (c) The points on which aggregate expenditure equals output.
    (d) Points where consumption equals saving.

13. Which of the following would be included in investment spending?
    (a) The purchase of a new share of stock issued by IBM.
    (b) The purchase of a previously owned home.
    (c) The purchase of a used Sears delivery van by a small business.
    (d) The purchase of a new computer by a local merchant.

14. Which of the following causes a movement along the investment demand curve?
    (a) A change in expenditures.
    (b) A change in technology.
    (c) A change in the rate of interest.
    (d) The current level of income.

15. Assuming investment, government expenditures and net exports are all autonomous, the slope of the aggregate expenditure line is equal to:
    (a) 1.0.
    (b) The MPC.
    (c) The MPS.
    (d) Zero.

16. Equilibrium (macro) occurs at the output at which:
    (a) The aggregate expenditure curve intersects the 45-degree line.
    (b) The aggregate demand curve intersects the aggregate supply curve.
    (c) Desired expenditure equals the value of output.
    (d) All of the above.

17. If at full employment output, desired leakages exceed desired injections, then:
    (a) Keynesians believe government has a responsibility to increase injections by spending more.
    (b) Classical economists believe the economy will self-adjust.
    (c) The economy cannot sustain itself at full employment.
    (d) All of the above.

18. The amount by which the desired rate of total expenditure at full employment is less than full-employment output is the:
    (a) GDP gap.
    (b) Recessionary gap.
    (c) Inflationary gap.
    (d) Budget deficit.

19. When consumers, government, businesses, and the foreign sector do not buy all of the output that is produced, then:
    (a) Inventories accumulate.
    (b) There is an inflationary gap.
    (c) The economy will sustain itself at its potential GDP.
    (d) The aggregate expenditure line should decrease.

20. When aggregate expenditures fall below the full-employment level of output, which of the following types of unemployment is most likely to increase?
    (a) Cyclical.
    (b) Seasonal.
    (c) Frictional.
    (d) Structural.

Problems and Applications

Exercise 1

This exercise emphasizes the relationship between consumption and disposable income.

1. Complete columns 4, 5, and 7 in Table 9.1, and then compute the average propensity to consume and the marginal propensity to consume in columns 3 and 6.

Table 9.1
Marginal and average propensity to consume
(billions of dollars per year)

(1) Disposable income	(2) Total consumption	(3) Average propensity to consume	(4) Change in consumption	(5) Change in income	(6) Marginal propensity to consume	(7) Saving
$ 0	$100	----	----	----	----	$____
500	500	____	$400	$500	____	____
1,000	900	____	____	____	____	____

2. What is the level of consumption if disposable income increases to $1,200?_____

3. Write the consumption function based on the information in Table 9.1. _____

Exercise 2

This exercise provides practice in using the consumption function and in distinguishing shifts of the consumption function from movements along it.

1. Assume the following consumption function:

$$C = \$200 \text{ billion} + 0.75Y_D$$

In Table 9.2, compute a consumption schedule from the formula.

Table 9.2
Computation of a consumption schedule
(billions of dollars per year)

Disposable income (Y_D)	Autonomous consumption (a)	+	Income-dependent consumption (bY_D)	=	Total consumption (C)
$ 0	____		____		$____
400	____		____		____
1,200	200		0.75 x 1,200		1,100

2. Using the consumption schedule in Table 9.2, draw the consumption function in Figure 9.1 and label it 1. The curve should pass through point B if it is correctly drawn.

3. In Table 9.3, fill in the schedule for the consumption function $C = \$300 \text{ billion} + 0.75Y_D$.

4. What is the marginal propensity to consume in Table 9.3? _____

Table 9.3
Consumption function shift
(billions of dollars per year)

Disposable income (Y_D)	Autonomous consumption (a)	+	Income-dependent consumption $(0.75 \times Y_D)$	=	Total consumption (C)
$ 0	$300		_____		$_____
400	300		_____		_____
800	300		_____		_____
1,200	300		_____		_____

5. Using the schedule in Table 9.3, graph the consumption function in Figure 9.1 (label it 2) and draw a 45-degree line from the origin.

6. T   F   In Figure 9.1, the shift in the consumption function from curve 1 to curve 2 shows that at any given level of disposable income, consumption will be greater and savings will be less.

Figure 9.1
Consumption functions

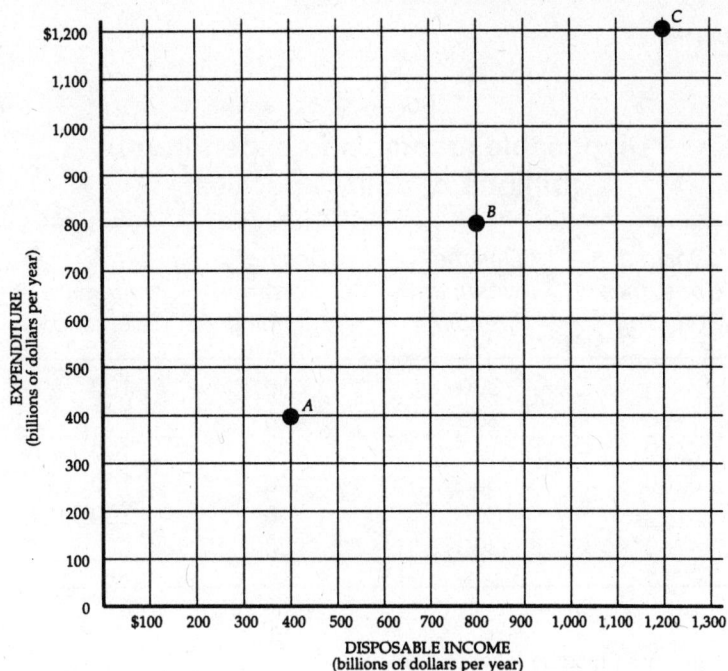

Exercise 3

Choose the diagram (a or b) in Figure 9.2 that best represents the shift in the consumption function that accompanies each of the events described in questions 1-4. Then, try to decide what impact each shift in the consumption function would have on the aggregate demand curve (c or d) for the economy. Place your answers in the blanks provided.

Figure 9.2

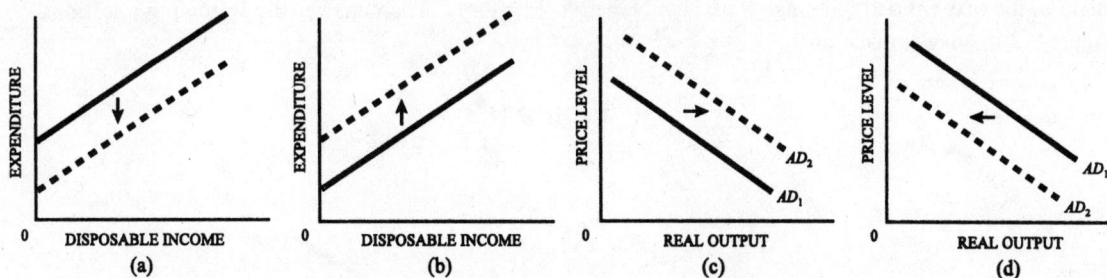

1. Consumer confidence falters as a recession becomes more likely. ____ ____

2. U.S. households experience a significant increase in their personal wealth. ____ ____

3. Congress passes new, strict regulations on the distribution and use of credit cards. ____ ____

4. Consumer interest rates are reduced to stimulate the economy. ____ ____

Exercise 4

This examines the relationship between the components of aggregate expenditure (consumption, investment, government spending, and net exports) and the level of income.

1. Complete Table 9.4.

Table 9.4
Disposable income and expenditures
(billions of dollars per year)

At Income (output) of	Desired Consumer Spending	Desired Investment Spending	Desired Government Spending	Net export Spending	Aggregate Expenditure
1000	_____	300	400	100	1750
2000	1700	300	400	100	_____
3000	2450	_____	400	100	3250
4000	3200	300	400	100	_____
5000	_____	300	400	100	4750
6000	4700	300	400	_____	5500

2. What is the equilibrium income level in Table 9.4?_____

3. What is the MPC from Table 9.4?_____

4. If full-employment output occurs at $6000 billion, there is a _____ gap and aggregate expenditure is (less than, greater than) the full employment level of output.

5. If full-employment output occurs at $2000 billion, there is a _____ gap and aggregate expenditure is (less than, greater than) the full employment level of output.

Exercise 5

The media continually present information about events that shift aggregate expenditure for the U.S. economy. This exercise uses one of the articles in the text to show the kind of information to look for. Reread the article in the text entitled "Savings Rate Hits Negative Territory." Then answer the following questions. Use Figure 9.3 to answer question 1.

Figure 9.3

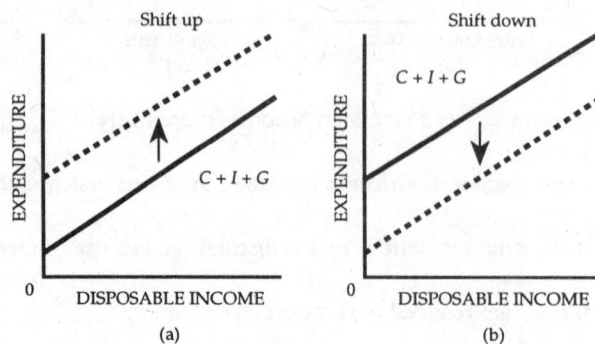

(a)

(b)

1. Which diagram in Figure 9.3 best represents the shift in aggregate expenditure that the article is describing?

2. Which of the following changes best represents the change to the circular flow?
   (a) More of a leakage.
   (b) Less of a leakage.
   (c) More of an injection.
   (d) Less consumption.

3. What should happen to the aggregate demand curve as a result of the change described in the article? _____

4. What phrase or sentence in the article describes the relationship between consumption and disposable income? _____
   _____

5. What passage indicates the reason for the consumption shift? _____
   _____

Common Errors

The first statement in each "common error" below is incorrect. Each incorrect statement is followed by a corrected version and an explanation.

1. The economy can spend no more than its income. WRONG!

   The economy *can* spend more than its income. RIGHT!

   The economy can spend more than its income by drawing down inventories of both public and private goods or by consuming capital (allowing it to depreciate) without replacing it. If the economy consumes more than its income, it will actually dissave and experience negative investment.

2. When a person invests in stocks, investment expenditure is increased. WRONG!

   The purchase of stocks has only an indirect relationship to investment expenditure in the economy. RIGHT!

   Investment expenditure refers to purchases of new capital goods (plant, machinery, and the like), inventories, or residential structures. A purchase of stock represents a transfer of ownership from one person to another. Sometimes such purchases are called "financial investments," but they do not represent economic investment.

3. The aggregate expenditure curve is the same as the aggregate demand curve. WRONG!

   The aggregate expenditure curve and aggregate demand curve are related to each other only indirectly. RIGHT!

   The aggregate expenditure curve and aggregate demand curve are two quite different concepts. They have different units on the axes; aggregate expenditure represents the intended expenditures at each *income* level; aggregate demand represents quantity demanded at each average price level for all goods and services.

4. The marginal propensity to consume is consumption divided by income. WRONG!

The average propensity to consume is consumption divided by income. RIGHT!

There is a big difference between total consumption and a change in consumption. While the average propensity to consume involves total consumption and total income, the marginal propensity to consume involves changes in consumption and changes in income.

5. Dissaving is the difference between the 45-degree line and aggregate expenditure curve. WRONG!

Dissaving is the difference between a curve representing the consumption function and the 45-degree line. RIGHT!

Both saving and dissaving are defined as the difference between disposable income and consumption. The 45-degree line shows the points at which expenditure equals income. So, when consumption expenditure equals income (the consumption function intersects the 45-degree line), there is zero saving. When the consumption expenditure exceeds income (the consumption function is above the 45-degree line), there will be dissaving.

6. Aggregate expenditure rises when people buy more imports. WRONG!

Aggregate expenditure falls when people buy more imports, *ceteris paribus*. RIGHT!

Students often think of imports as expenditures and therefore believe that increased spending on imports will have the same effect on the economy as an increase in consumption. Expenditures on imports, however, do not generate domestic income. If imports increase, they do so at the expense of purchases of U.S. goods, meaning fewer jobs in the United States. Because employment declines, there is less income with which to purchase goods; consumption falls and so does aggregate spending.

•ANSWERS•

Using Key Terms

Across

3. inflationary gap
5. investment
8. marginal propensity to consume
10. disposable income
11. aggregate demand
17. consumption
18. leakage
19. full employment GDP
20. aggregate expenditure
21. average propensity to consume
22. gross business saving

Down

1. expenditure equilibrium
2. demand-pull inflation
4. aggregate supply
6. marginal propensity to save
7. consumption function
9. cyclical unemployment
12. dissaving
13. injection
14. recessionary gap
15. saving
16. equilibrium macro

True or False

1. T
2. T
3. F Consumption is the largest component of aggregate spending.
4. F The marginal propensity to consume measures the fraction of additional disposable income that is spent on consumption.
5. T
6. F There is a movement along a given consumption function when disposable income changes.
7. T
8. T
9. F Investment changes a business's future capacity to produce, so expectations of future sales (i.e. income) are more relevant than current income.
10. T

Multiple Choice

1. b	5. a	9. a	13. d	17. d
2. c	6. c	10. a	14. c	18. b
3. b	7. a	11. d	15. b	19. a
4. a	8. a	12. c	16. d	20. a

Problems and Applications

Exercise 1

1. **Table 9.1 Answer**

(1) Disposable income	(2) Total consumption	(3) Average propensity to consume	(4) Change in consumption	(5) Change in income	(6) Marginal propensity to consume	(7) Saving
$ 0	$100	----	----	----	----	$ -100
500	500	1.0	$400	$500	0.8	0
1,000	900	0.9	400	500	0.8	100

127

2. $1060

3. $C = 100 + .8Y_D$

Exercise 2

1. **Table 9.2 Answer**

Disposable income (Y_D)	Autonomous consumption (a)	+	Income-dependent consumption (bY_D)	=	Total consumption (C)
$ 0	200		0		$ 200
400	200		0.75 x 400		500
1,200	200		0.75 x 1,200		1,100

2. **Figure 9.1 Answer**

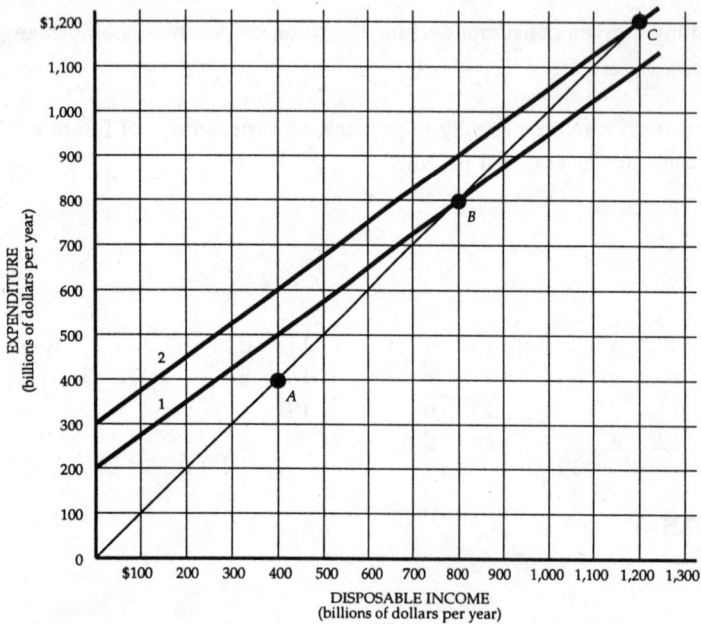

3. **Table 9.3 Answer**

Disposable income (Y_D)	Autonomous consumption (a)	+	Income-dependent consumption $(0.75 \times Y_D)$	=	Total consumption (C)
$ 0	$300		0		$ 300
400	300		0.75 x 400		600
800	300		0.75 x 800		900
1,200	300		0.75 x 1200		1200

4. 0.75. The marginal propensity to consume is the change in consumption (e.g., $600 - $300 billion per year) divided by the corresponding change in income ($400 - $0 billion per year).
5. See Figure 9.1 Answer, line 2
6. T

Exercise 3

1. a,d
2. b,c
3. a,d
4. b,c

Exercise 4

1. **Table 9.4 Answer**

At Income (output) of	Desired Consumer Spending	Desired Investment Spending	Desired Government Spending	Net export Spending	Aggregate Expenditure
1000	950	300	400	100	1750
2000	1700	300	400	100	2500
3000	2450	300	400	100	3250
4000	3200	300	400	100	4000
5000	3950	300	400	100	4750
6000	4700	300	400	100	5500

2. $4,000 billion
3. MPC = 0.75
4. recessionary, less than
5. inflationary, greater than

Exercise 5

1. a
2. b
3. Aggregate demand should shift to the right.
4. "Americans spent more money buying goods and services than they received in after-tax income . . ."
5. " . . . Consumers have been encouraged to spend so much by the soaring value of U.S. stocks - the so-called wealth effect . . ."

CHAPTER 10

Self-Adjustment or Instability?

Quick Review

In the Keynesian view of a market-driven economy, macro failure is both likely to occur and persist. This runs counter to the Classical view that, if left alone, it would quickly self-adjust to a full employment level of output. In this chapter we focus on the adjustment process and take an in-depth look at the following questions:

- What forces might derail the economy from its full-employment track?
- How will consumers and investors respond to a sudden imbalance between spending and output?
- What macro outcomes will these responses create?

Imbalances between saving (a leakage) and investment (an injection) are likely sources of aggregate expenditure imbalance. A two-sector model (households and business) is the easiest way to examine the imbalance. Actual investment consists of two components:

$$Actual\ investment = desired\ investment + undesired\ investment$$

If desired saving exceeds desired investment at full employment GDP, the economy experiences a recessionary gap. This "excess saving" causes inventory accumulation for business, which is *undesired investment.* As inventories pile up, prices fall, more workers are let go, wages fall, capacity is allowed to deteriorate, and interest rates fall.

The recessionary gap is measured at full employment. It is equal to the amount by which desired saving exceeds desired investment or the amount by which full-employment output exceeds desired spending. Any recessionary gap is compounded by the multiplier effect into a much larger cutback in production and employment. The multiplier in this two sector model is calculated as 1/(1-MPC). The multiplier process takes into account the circular flow of economic activity by recognizing that:

- Producers cut output and employment when output exceeds desired spending.
- The resulting loss of income causes a decline in consumer spending.
- Declines in consumer spending lead to further production cutbacks, more lost income, and still less consumption.

The real GDP gap is the amount by which equilibrium GDP falls short of the full-employment GDP. The dilemma is that there is no automatic adjustment back to full employment.

The inflationary gap is also measured at full employment as the amount by which desired spending exceeds full-employment output or the amount by which desired investment exceeds desired saving. In this case inventories are drawn down, prices rise, more people are hired, wages rise, there is an attempt to expand capacity, and interest rates rise. The problem here also is the accompanying multiplier effect. Keynes felt that a market-driven economy would fail to achieve equilibrium at full employment when there was a recessionary or an inflationary gap.

A weakness of the Keynesian model is that it does not separate out real output effects from price effects. To do this, we need to use the aggregate-demand—aggregate-supply framework introduced in Chapter 8. That model allows us to observe changes in both the GDP gap (measured horizontally) and the price level (measured vertically). The multiplier determines how far the aggregate demand curve shifts, while the slope of the aggregate supply curve determines how much of the shift is dissipated into price changes. This emphasizes the inherent inflation-unemployment tradeoff. It is clear that consumer confidence plays a critical role in achieving and maintaining macro stability.

Learning Objectives

After reading Chapter 10 and doing the following exercises you should:

1. Be able to distinguish between the Keynesian and Classical views of the adjustment process in a market-driven economy.
2. Be able to define and calculate both a recessionary gap and an inflationary gap.
3. Understand the critical distinction between desired investment and actual investment.
4. Be able to describe how the economy responds to a recessionary gap.
5. Be able to describe the multiplier process and calculate the multiplier.
6. Understand the possible divergence between equilibrium GDP and full-employment GDP.
7. Be able to describe and demonstrate price and output effects and the inflation-unemployment tradeoff in an AS-AD framework.
8. Understand the dual role of saving, that is, as a leakage in the short run and as a source of resources for net investment and growth in the long run.

Using Key Terms

Fill in the puzzle on the opposite page with the appropriate term from the list of Key Terms at the end of the chapter in the text.

Across

2. The downward-sloping curve in Figure 10.1 in the text.
5. Drawn as upward-sloping in the short run as illustrated in Figure 10.8 in the text.
8. Unemployment because of a recessionary gap.
9. Equal to 4 in Table 10.1 in the text.

Down

1. The fraction of additional income spent by consumers.
3. The rate of real output at which aggregate demand equals aggregate supply.
4. The situation that results in Figure 10.9 in the text because of excessive aggregate demand.
6. The difference between Q_F and Q_E in Figure 10.7 in the text.
7. The lowest rate of unemployment compatible with price stability.

Puzzle 10.1

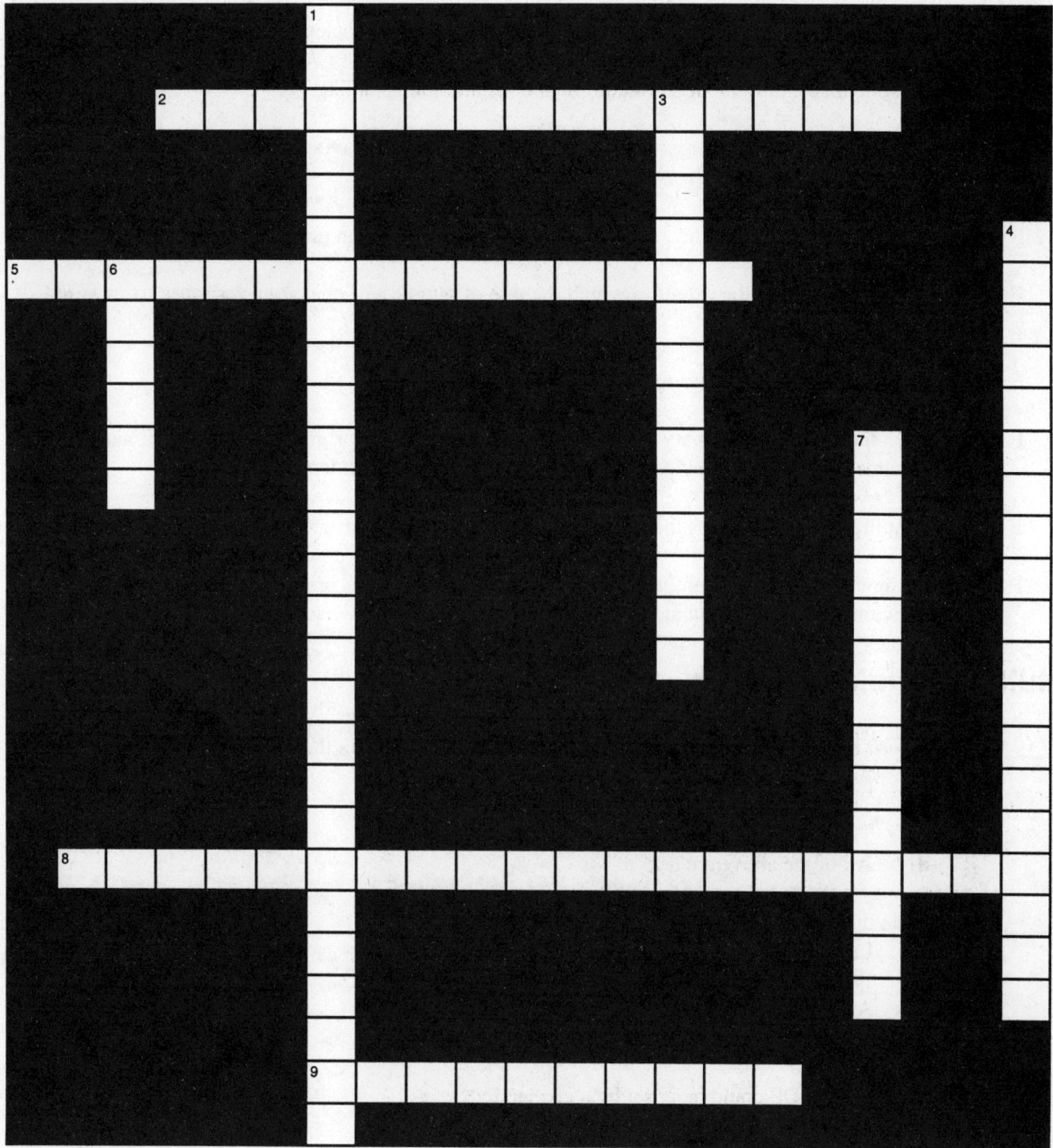

True or False: *Circle your choice and tell why any false statements are incorrect.*

T F 1. The larger the MPC, the smaller will be the multiplier.

T F 2. Reductions in saving result in lower equilibrium income for society, *ceteris paribus*.

T F 3. Investment spending is more volatile than consumption spending.

T F 4. In a purely private economy, the difference between desired saving and desired investment measures the undesired change in inventory.

T F 5. In a closed private economy, desired investment is greater than desired saving at equilibrium.

T F 6. The multiplier tells the extent to which the rate of output will change in response to an initial change in spending.

T F 7. Equilibrium GDP is always the most desired level of GDP for an economy.

T F 8. When there is an inflationary spiral, there is excess demand for goods and services, and consumers bid up prices by competing for those goods and services.

T F 9. If equilibrium GDP is less than full-employment GDP, then structural unemployment results.

T F 10. The aggregate supply-aggregate demand model can be used to predict how changes in spending behavior will affect output and prices.

Multiple Choice: *Select the correct answer.*

_____ 1. According to the Keynesian view of the macro economy, when the economy is at equilibrium:
  (a) Aggregate supply equals aggregate demand.
  (b) The economy is at full employment.
  (c) The price level is stable.
  (d) All of the above are true.

_____ 2. When the economy is at equilibrium:
  (a) Leakages equal injections.
  (b) Inventories are at desired levels.
  (c) Aggregate supply equals aggregate demand.
  (d) All of the above are true.

_____ 3. Equilibrium GDP could be upset by a change in:
  (a) Investment only.
  (b) Injections only.
  (c) Leakages only.
  (d) Any leakage or injection.

_____ 4. When investment spending decreases, all other levels of spending remaining constant:
  (a) Aggregate demand decreases.
  (b) Aggregate demand increases.
  (c) Aggregate supply decreases.
  (d) Aggregate supply increases.

5. When an economy is at full employment and consumption spending decreases, all other levels of spending remaining constant:
   (a) Increased unemployment results.
   (b) Any GDP gap disappears.
   (c) Inventory levels are less than desired until a new equilibrium is reached.
   (d) Changes in consumption spending have no impact on GDP.

6. The multiplier effect exists because:
   (a) Of the circular nature of the economy.
   (b) One person's expenditures become another person's income.
   (c) A change in autonomous spending results in changes to household income.
   (d) All of the above are reasons.

7. If actual investment exceeds desired investment then:
   (a) Inventories are increasing.
   (b) Output will increase as a result.
   (c) Demand-pull inflation exists.
   (d) Inventories are being depleted.

8. Keynes emphasized that because there is no automatic adjustment back to full employment:
   (a) Equilibrium GDP might be less than full-employment GDP.
   (b) A long-term recessionary gap could occur.
   (c) Cyclical unemployment could persist.
   (d) All of the above.

9. Suppose that as a result of higher interest rates, desired investment and aggregate demand decrease. Additional decreases in aggregate demand will be the result of:
   (a) Decreases in consumption.
   (b) Decreases in induced expenditures.
   (c) The multiplier effect.
   (d) All of the above.

10. Assuming an upward-sloping aggregate supply curve, when aggregate demand increases:
    (a) Unemployment decreases and the price level decreases.
    (b) Unemployment decreases and the price level increases.
    (c) Unemployment increases and the price level decreases.
    (d) Unemployment increases and the price level increases.

11. Suppose that an economy has an upward-sloping aggregate supply curve and a GDP gap equal to $45 billion. If aggregate demand increases by a total of $45 billion:
    (a) The GDP gap will be eliminated.
    (b) The resulting equilibrium GDP will be lower than full employment GDP because some of the additional spending will drive up prices instead of increasing output.
    (c) The resulting equilibrium GDP will be greater than full employment GDP because of demand-pull inflation.
    (d) Any of the above could occur depending on the size of the multiplier.

_____ 12. Using a consumption function of the form $C = a + bY_D$, which of the following would best measure the total impact on output of a change in autonomous spending?

(a) $\dfrac{1}{MPS}$

(b) $\dfrac{1}{1-b}$

(c) $\dfrac{1}{1-MPC}$

(d) All of the above.

_____ 13. When output exceeds desired spending, which of the following is included in the Keynesian adjustment process?
(a) Producers cut output and employment.
(b) Lost income causes a decline in consumer spending.
(c) Lower consumer spending results in additional loss of income.
(d) All of the above.

_____ 14. Because the aggregate supply curve rises more steeply as the economy approaches full employment:
(a) Inflation tends to accelerate.
(b) The GDP gap becomes larger.
(c) Aggregate demand shifts to the left.
(d) The multiplier effect becomes greater.

_____ 15. In which of the following cases would cyclical unemployment tend to increase, _ceteris paribus_?
(a) Undesired inventory depletion.
(b) Total value of goods supplied exceeds the total value of goods demanded.
(c) A period of significant inflation.
(d) Desired investment exceeds desired saving.

_____ 16. In the short run, one reason we do not define full employment as zero percent unemployment is because:
(a) Of the direct relationship between unemployment and inflation.
(b) The closer the economy gets to full capacity, the greater the risk of inflation.
(c) Of the vertical aggregate supply curve.
(d) All of the above.

_____ 17. An inflationary gap indicates that, there are not enough:
(a) Goods available and consumers bid up prices.
(b) Resources available and businesses bid up wages.
(c) Savings available and investors bid up interest rates.
(d) All of the above.

_____ 18. A rightward shift in the aggregate demand curve will cause:
(a) Both higher prices and higher output if the aggregate supply curve is upward-sloping.
(b) Higher prices and lower output if the aggregate supply curve is upward-sloping.
(c) No change in prices, but higher output, if the aggregate supply curve is upward-sloping.
(d) Lower prices and higher output if the aggregate supply curve is upward-sloping.

_____ 19. With an MPC of 0.50, an increase of $2 billion in autonomous consumption would cause:
(a) An initial increase of $1 billion in income.
(b) $500 million in multiplier effects.
(c) Income to change by a total of $4 billion.
(d) Income to change by a total of $2 billion.

_____ 20. A basic conclusion of Keynesian analysis is that:
  (a) Small macro disturbances can lead to much larger macro problems.
  (b) The economy does not self adjust to reach full employment or stable price levels.
  (c) Equilibrium GDP may not be consistent with full employment or price stability.
  (d) All of the above are conclusions.

Problems and Applications

Exercise 1

This exercise focuses on a recessionary gap caused by a change in investment spending.

Assume the economy is initially in equilibrium on AD_3 in Figure 10.1 and full-employment GDP occurs at Q_3. Use Figure 10.1 to answer questions 1-7.

Figure 10.1

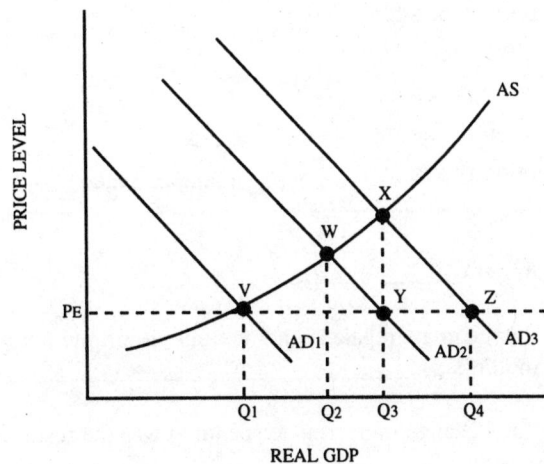

1. Suppose the rate of investment decreases and aggregate demand shifts initially to AD_2. The new equilibrium real GDP occurs at _____.

2. The decline in investment spending causes a (decrease, increase) in household income and consumption. Aggregate demand shifts to the (right, left) to (AD_1, AD_3). The final equilibrium is at a real GDP level of _____.

3. T F The real GDP gap is equal to the distance $Q_3 - Q_1$.

4. When equilibrium output is less than full-employment, there is a (recessionary, inflationary) gap.

5. When equilibrium output is less than full-employment output, at the full-employment level actual investment is (less than, greater than, equal to) desired investment because undesired inventories are (less than, greater than, equal to) zero.

6. When aggregate expenditure is (less than, greater than, equal to) the full-employment level of output, a recessionary gap exists.

7. A recessionary gap causes (seasonal, structural, cyclical, frictional) unemployment.

Exercise 2

The following exercise shows how the multiplier works and how to calculate it.

1. Suppose the economy were at full employment but suddenly experienced a $200 billion drop in business expenditures due to an abrupt cancellation of investment plans. Follow the impact of this sudden change through the economy by completing Table 10.1. (Refer to Table 10.1 in the text.) Assume the marginal propensity to consume is 0.90. (Hint: Consumption will drop by the "amount of the change in spending in the previous cycle" times the MPC.) Then use Table 10.1 to answer questions 2-7.

Table 10.1

Spending cycles	Drop in investment expenditure	Change in spending (billions of dollars per year)	Cumulative decrease in aggregate spending (billions of dollars per year)
First cycle:	GDP gap emerges	$200	$200
Second cycle:	consumption drops by	_____	_____
Third cycle:	consumption drops by	_____	_____
Fourth cycle:	consumption drops by	_____	_____
Fifth cycle:	consumption drops by	_____	_____
Sixth cycle:	consumption drops by	_____	_____
Seventh cycle:	consumption drops by	_____	_____

2. Compute the multiplier. _____

3. What is the total change in aggregate spending after an infinite number of cycles? (Multiply $200 billion times the multiplier.) _____

4. How much of the total change in aggregate spending was the result of a change in investment? _____

5. How much of the total change in aggregate spending was the result of a change in consumption? _____

6. T   F   A large portion of the change in aggregate spending in question 3 was due to the multiplier effect.

Exercise 3

This exercise emphasizes the short-run trade-off between unemployment and inflation.

Assume the economy is initially on AD_1. The full-employment level of output is Q_1 and the desired price level is P_2. Use Figure 10.2 to answer questions 1-3.

Figure 10.2

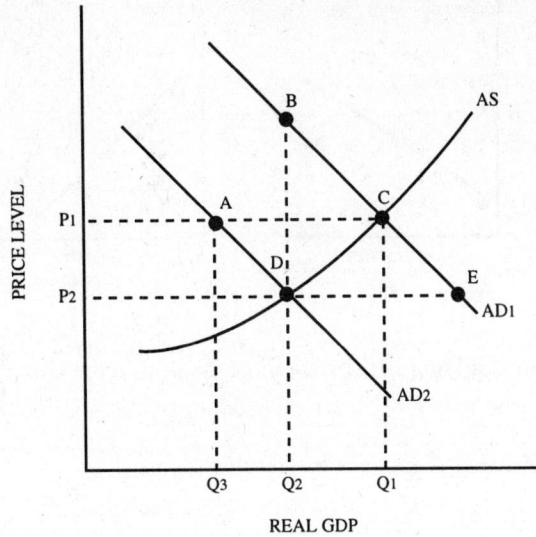

1. Assume price level P_1 is considered inflationary. If the AD curve is shifted to AD_2 to reduce the price level, the result is a _____ in the level of output and an _____ in the level of unemployment.

2. If AD is shifted back to the right to AD_1, output returns to the full-employment level, but the price level _____.

3. Because the AS curve is _____ sloping, any shift in AD will cause a trade-off between _____.

Exercise 4

This exercise focuses on an inflationary gap situation.

1. Figure 10.9 in the text illustrates an inflationary gap situation. An increase in investment caused AD to shift to _____ and the resulting multiplier effects caused AD to shift again to _____.

2. When AD shifts to the right, the price level _____.

3. In the situation in question 2, actual investment is (less than, greater than, equal to) desired investment and _____ are being depleted.

4. Producers will respond to the increased demand by (increasing, decreasing) production.

5. The resulting economic situation is referred to as _____ inflation.

Exercise 5

Reread the article in the text titled "U.S. Manufacturers Continue to Suffer From Impact of Asian Economic Crisis." Then answer questions 1-4.

Figure 10.3

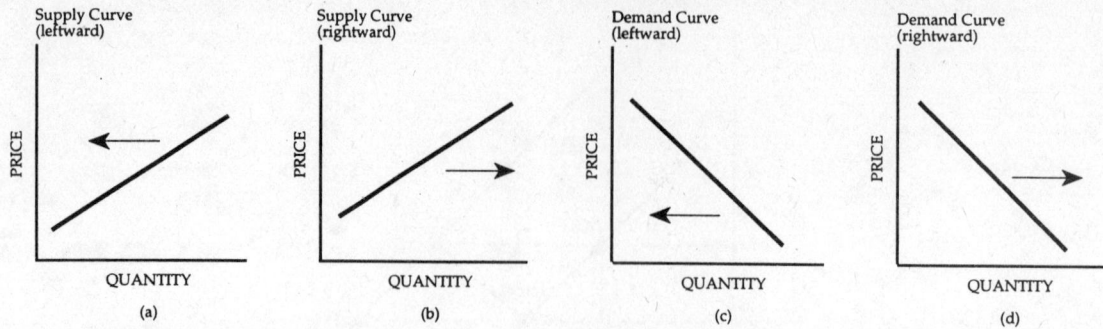

1. Which of the diagrams in Figure 10.3 represents the shift in the U.S. economy because of the Asian crisis?

2. The downturn in the Asian economies has resulted in a _____ in demand for U.S. exports.

3. Which areas of manufacturing have been most affected by the downturn?_____
    _____

4. How have U.S. manufacturers responded to the downturn? _____
    _____

Common Errors

The first statement in each "common error" below is incorrect. Each incorrect statement is followed by a corrected version and an explanation.

1. Since saving and investment must be the same by definition, a closed economy must be at expenditure equilibrium because investment equals saving. WRONG!

    Intended investment equals intended saving at expenditure equilibrium in a closed economy. RIGHT!

    If there are excess inventories or if people are forced to save because they cannot spend on desired goods and services, then the income level may be different from equilibrium income. Do not confuse actual investment and actual saving with intended investment and intended saving.

2. If consumers save more, interest rates will fall and investment will rise. WRONG!

    When consumption falls as a result of increased saving, investment may be discouraged. RIGHT!

    Interest rates *may* fall because of increased saving. However, Keynes showed that businesses may invest less when they expect to sell less. The lower consumption which results from increased saving may actually cause businesses to reduce investment.

3. Expenditure equilibrium and full-employment GDP are always the same. WRONG!

    Expenditure equilibrium and full-employment GDP are determined in different ways. RIGHT!
    Expenditure equilibrium occurs where the aggregate expenditure curve and the 45-degree line intersect. The full-employment GDP occurs at the GDP level where the market supply and

market demand curves for labor are in equilibrium. For most purposes, we can consider the two levels to be independent of each other.

Be careful! While it is possible to determine the expenditure equilibrium or income level by glancing at the aggregate spending curve and the 45-degree line, it is not possible to determine full-employment GDP this way. Full-employment GDP is shown simply as a vertical line.

•ANSWERS•

Using Key Terms

Across
2. aggregate demand
5. aggregate supply
8. cyclical unemployment
9. multiplier

Down
1. marginal propensity to consume
3. equilibrium GDP
4. demand-pull inflation
6. GDP gap
7. full employment

True or False
1. F   The larger the MPC, the larger the multiplier because there is less leakage (i.e. saving) each spending cycle.
2. F   Reductions in saving result in increase in consumption which increase equilibrium income.
3. T
4. T
5. F   At equilibrium, leakages must equal injections. In a closed private economy, the only leakages and injections are saving and investment.
6. F   The multiplier tells how much total spending will change in response to an initial change in spending.   Whenever the AS curve is upward sloping, the total change in output will be less than the total change in spending.
7. F   Equilibrium GDP does not necessarily mean that the economy is experiencing full employment or stable price levels.
8. T
9. F   Cyclical unemployment results.
10. T

Multiple Choice

1. a	5. a	9. d	13. d	17. d
2. d	6. d	10. b	14. a	18. a
3. d	7. a	11. b	15. b	19. c
4. a	8. d	12. d	16. b	20. d

Problems and Applications

Exercise 1

1. Q_2
2. decrease, left, AD_1, Q_1
3. T
4. recessionary
5. greater than, greater than
6. less than
7. cyclical

Exercise 2

1. **Table 10.1 Answer**

Spending cycles	Amount	Cumulative decrease in aggregate spending
First cycle:	$200.0	$200.0
Second cycle:	180.0	380.0
Third cycle:	162.0	542.0
Fourth cycle:	145.8	687.8
Fifth cycle:	131.2	819.0
Sixth cycle:	118.1	937.1
Seventh cycle:	106.3	1043.4

2. Multiplier = 1/(1-MPC) = 1/(1-0.9) = 10
3. $2 trillion
4. $200 billion
5. $1.8 trillion
6. T

Exercise 3

1. decrease, increase
2. increases
3. upward sloping, inflation, and unemployment

Exercise 4

1. AD_5, AD_6
2. increases
3. less than, inventories
4. increasing
5. demand-pull

Exercise 5

1. c
2. decrease
3. steel and farm equipment production
4. controlled costs, announced lay-offs, decreased production

CHAPTER 11

Fiscal Policy

Quick Review

Keynes concluded that unregulated economies would frequently suffer from either too little aggregate demand with accompanying unemployment, or too much aggregate demand leading to inflation. The solution to both problems, as he saw it, was government intervention to shift the economy's aggregate demand in the appropriate direction. Successful intervention, however, requires the careful assessment of policy alternatives. We consider this topic by raising the following questions:

- Can government spending and tax policies help ensure full employment?
- What policy actions will help fight inflation?
- What are the risks of government intervention?

The primary tools of government intervention through fiscal policy are changes in taxes, in government spending and in income transfers. Federal tax revenues have grown from $650 *million* at the beginning of the 1900s to over $1.8 *trillion* today. Remarkably, government spending has grown even faster. Income transfers have grown dramatically as well and are the subject of much current debate.

This chapter focuses on the aggregate demand side of the AD-AS framework introduced in the preceding chapter. The goal of fiscal policy is to enable the economy to achieve full-employment output with a stable price level. We begin our study by asking two additional questions:

- How can we induce a shift in AD?
- By how much do we want to shift the AD curve?

The primary tools of fiscal policy are government spending on goods and services, income transfers, and taxes. We look first at policies required to cure a recession. If the AS curve slopes upward, part of any increase in AD is siphoned off as price increases. Under these conditions, we must distinguish between:

- The GDP gap, the difference between equilibrium GDP and the GDP required for full employment, and
- The aggregate-demand shortfall—the amount of additional AD needed to achieve full employment after allowing for price level changes.

Fiscal expansion can be accomplished with an increase in government spending. The required increase in AD does not come completely from government purchases. Successive rounds of spending, kicked off by the initial government purchases, ripple through the economy through the multiplier process. The value of the multiplier is calculated as:

The multiplier can be used to estimate the fiscal stimulus required to get the economy to full employment by the following:

$$\text{Desired fiscal stimulus} = (AD \text{ desired increase/the multiplier})$$

The same thing could be accomplished with a tax cut which can again be estimated in two steps. First determine the desired fiscal stimulus and then determine the desired tax cut with:

$$\text{Desired tax cut} = (\text{desired fiscal stimulus}/MPC)$$

A tax cut of a given size will be less expansionary than a spending increase of the same size because part of the tax cut leaks into saving before the first private-sector spending takes place.

If aggregate demand is excessive and the economy suffers from inflation, the process must be reversed. Fiscal restraint can be accomplished with cuts in government spending, increased taxes, or reduced income transfers. The desired fiscal restraint is the same as the fiscal stimulus except it causes a decrease in AD.

Just getting to full employment GDP is important, but we should also be concerned about the mix of output when we get there. Greater borrowing by government might crowd out an equal amount of private spending. More G (defense goods or highways), and less I (fewer factories) as an example. Tax cuts can go to businesses or households and favor investors or consumers. Either way, the mix of output is affected. Changes in transfers lead to a different mix of output also.

Learning Objectives

After reading Chapter 11 and doing the following exercises, you should:

1. Know the major sources of federal government revenue.
2. Know the history of federal government expenditures.
3. Be able to distinguish the effects of government purchases from those of government transfers.
4. Understand how the components of fiscal policy can be used to stabilize the economy.
5. Be able to describe the AD shortfall.
6. Be able to calculate the AD shortfall, the multiplier, and the desired fiscal stimulus.
7. Be able to explain why tax cuts are less expansionary than increases in government purchases of an equal size.
8. Understand that fiscal restraint of a predictable size is required when aggregate demand is excessive.
9. Be able to explain why changes in transfer payments are seldom used to provide fiscal stimulus (or restraint).
10. Be able to explain how fiscal stimulus can be offset by the "crowding out" of private expenditure.
11. Be able to discuss the concern for the content of GDP at full employment.

Using Key Terms

Fill in the puzzle on the opposite page with the appropriate term from the list of Key Terms at the end of the chapter in the text.

Across

3. The use of fiscal policy to reduce aggregate demand.
5. The use of the federal government budget to change macroeconomic outcomes.
9. Personal income minus personal taxes.
10. The downward-sloping curve in Figure 11.1 in the text.
11. Government spending in the form of Social Security, welfare, and unemployment benefits.
12. The upward-sloping curve in Figure 11.1 in the text.
13. The difference between full-employment GDP and equilibrium GDP.

Down

1. Occurs at an output level of $5.6 trillion in Figure 11.2 in the text.
2. The change in consumption divided by the change in disposable income.
3. Tax cuts or spending increases intended to shift aggregate demand to the right.
4. A decrease in private-sector borrowing caused by increased government borrowing.
6. The amount aggregate demand must increase to achieve full-employment, after allowing for price-level changes.
7. Equal to 1/(1-MPC).
8. Equal to $400 billion in Figure 11.6 in the text.

Puzzle 11.1

True or False: *Circle your choice and indicate why any false statements are incorrect.*

T F 1. Fiscal policy works principally through shifts of the aggregate supply curve.

T F 2. From a Keynesian perspective, the way out of a recession includes an increase in government spending, a tax cut, or an increase in transfer payments.

T F 3. If the AS curve is horizontal (i.e. flat), the GDP gap is equal to the desired fiscal stimulus (or restraint).

T F 4. Increasing government expenditures by the amount of the AD shortfall will achieve full employment.

T F 5. The cumulative AD stimulus of increased transfer payments is given by:
Total AD stimulus = *MPC* × increase in transfer payments

T F 6. When there is excess aggregate demand, desired fiscal restraint equals the desired AD reduction divided by the multiplier.

T F 7. A tax cut contains less stimulus to the economy than an increase in government spending of the same size because some of the tax cut is saved.

T F 8. Both government purchases of goods and services and government transfer payments are part of AD.

T F 9. Every dollar of new government spending has a multiplied impact on aggregate demand.

T F 10. Crowding out is the idea that an increase in government spending may cause a reduction in private-sector spending.

Multiple Choice: *Select the correct answer.*

_____ 1. Fiscal policy works principally through shifts of:
(a) The aggregate supply curve.
(b) The aggregate demand curve.
(c) The full-employment output line.
(d) The 45-degree line.

_____ 2. Which of the following is a tool of fiscal policy?
(a) Increasing government purchases of goods and services.
(b) Increasing taxes.
(c) Increasing income transfers.
(d) All of the above.

_____ 3. In a diagram of aggregate demand and aggregate supply curves, the GDP gap is measured:
(a) As the vertical distance between the equilibrium price and the price at which the aggregate demand would intersect aggregate supply at full employment.
(b) As the horizontal distance between the equilibrium output and the full employment output.
(c) As the horizontal distance between the aggregate demand and the aggregate supply curves at the equilibrium price.
(d) As the amount of the AD shortfall or excess.

146

_____ 4. The "naïve" Keynesian model is unrealistic because it:
- (a) Does not take into account probable changes in the price level as the economy approaches full employment.
- (b) Assumes that the price level decreases as AD increases.
- (c) Assumes that AS is upward sloping when it is more probably horizontal.
- (d) Does not account for changes in output due to the multiplier.

_____ 5. The GDP gap will differ from the AD shortfall when:
- (a) The aggregate supply curve slopes upward.
- (b) The multiplier effect raises spending.
- (c) The budget us balanced.
- (d) All of the above.

_____ 6. To eliminate the AD shortfall of $100 billion when the economy has an *MPC* of 0.80, the government should increase its purchases by:
- (a) $20 billion.
- (b) $100 billion.
- (c) $500 billion.
- (d) $800 billion.

_____ 7. Assuming an *MPC* of 0.90, the change in total spending for the economy as a result of a $100 billion new government spending injection would be:
- (a) $10 billion.
- (b) $100 billion.
- (c) $90 billion.
- (d) $1 trillion.

_____ 8. $1 \div (1 - MPC)$ multiplied by a new spending injection gives the:
- (a) *MPC*.
- (b) Multiplier.
- (c) Total change in income generated from the new spending.
- (d) First-round income that is gained from the new spending.

_____ 9. An *MPS* of 0.25 means a $100 tax increase ultimately causes:
- (a) Spending to fall by $25.
- (b) Spending to fall by $300.
- (c) Spending to rise by $75.
- (d) Spending to rise by $400.

_____ 10. Suppose the consumption function is $C=100+.5Y$. If the government stimulates the economy with $100 billion in increased income transfers, aggregate expenditure would rise ultimately by:
- (a) $50 billion.
- (b) $80 billion.
- (c) $200 billion.
- (d) $400 billion.

_____ 11. When the government tries to correct for an aggregate demand shortfall in the economy, it must take into account that:
- (a) The total change in spending equals the government's spending and the multiplier effects of that spending.
- (b) The desired stimulus should be set at the AD shortfall divided by the multiplier.
- (c) Prices will rise unless the AS curve is horizontal.
- (d) All of the above.

_____ 12. The desired fiscal stimulus that will eliminate an AD shortfall should equal the:
  (a) Desired AD increase ÷ the multiplier.
  (b) Desired tax cut × *MPC*.
  (c) Desired income transfer × *MPC*.
  (d) All of the above.

_____ 13. The desired tax cut necessary to close an AD shortfall is given by:
  (a) Desired fiscal stimulus ÷ multiplier.
  (b) Desired fiscal stimulus ÷ *MPC*.
  (c) (Desired fiscal stimulus ÷ multiplier) ÷ *MPC*.
  (d) Desired fiscal stimulus times MPC.

_____ 14. For the balanced-budget multiplier to equal 1:
  (a) The budget need not be balanced, but the changes in taxes and spending must be equal.
  (b) The budget must be balanced before the changes in taxes and spending take place.
  (c) The budget must be balanced and the change in spending must equal the change in taxes.
  (d) The budget must be balanced, but the changes in taxes and spending may be unequal amounts.

_____ 15. Which of the following is most powerful in shifting the aggregate demand curve?
  (a) A $1 increase in government purchases.
  (b) A $1 reduction in taxes.
  (c) A $1 increase in transfer payments.
  (d) All are equally powerful.

_____ 16. The AD excess divided by the multiplier is equal to the:
  (a) *MPC*.
  (b) Desired fiscal restraint.
  (c) Total gain in income generated from lower spending.
  (d) First-round consumption that is lost from higher taxes.

_____ 17. If the desired fiscal restraint is $10 billion and the desired AD decrease is $100 billion, we can conclude that the desired:
  (a) Tax increase is $11.11 billion.
  (b) Tax increase is $10 billion.
  (c) Tax cut is $11.11 billion.
  (d) Tax cut is $10 billion.

_____ 18. Crowding out occurs when the government:
  (a) Increases taxes, thus causing a decrease in consumption.
  (b) Issues debt, thus making it more difficult for the private sector to issue debt.
  (c) Prints money, which displaces currency.
  (d) Does all of the above.

_____ 19. Which of the following are factors which may limit the effectiveness of fiscal policy in the real world?
  (a) The crowding out effect.
  (b) Time lags between the recognition of a macro problem and the implementation of corrective measures.
  (c) Political considerations which could alter the content and timing of fiscal policy.
  (d) All of the above are factors.

_____ 20. The "second crisis of economic theory" refers to:
   (a)   The typical fiscal policy tradeoff between
         unemployment and inflation.
   (b)   The dominance of Keynesian views in fiscal policy to the exclusion of newer, more
         enlightened viewpoints.
   (c)   The sometimes exclusive emphasis in fiscal policy on the level of output to the neglect of
         the content of output.
   (d)   Our inability to maintain full employment output over any significant period of time.

Problems and Applications

Exercise 1

This exercise shows how to use the aggregate demand and supply curves to analyze macro equilibrium, the AD shortfall, excess AD, and the GDP gap.

Table 11.1
Aggregate demand and supply*

Price Index (1)	Aggregate Supply (Qs) (2)	Aggregate Demand (Qd) Full Employment (3)	Aggregate Demand (Qd) AD1 (4)	Aggregate Demand (Qd) AD2 (5)
2.6	24	-	-	-
2.2	23	0	-	14
1.8	22	6	0	22
1.0	18	18	8	-
0.8	16	21	10	-
0.6	12	·24	12	-
0.4	4	27	14	-

* Quantity is measured in billions of units in columns 2 through 5.

1. Use the first two columns in Table 11.1 to draw the aggregate supply curve for an economy in Figure 11.1. Then use columns 1 and 3 to draw the aggregate demand curve at full employment. Label the aggregate supply curve AS and the aggregate demand curve at full employment AD_F.

Figure 11.1
Aggregate demand and supply

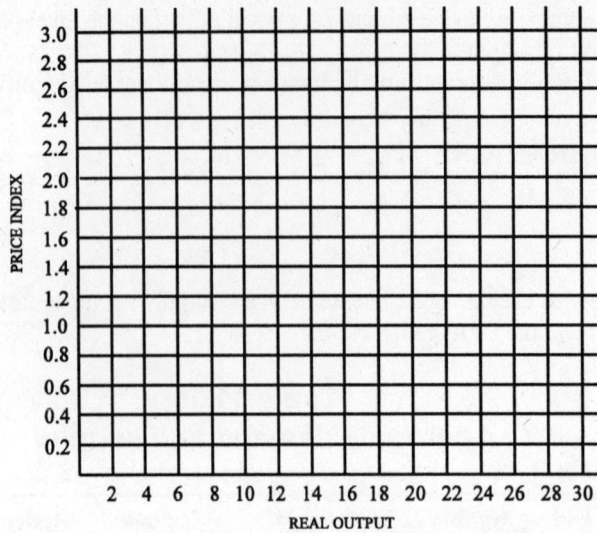

2. When macro equilibrium is achieved at full employment, the full-employment real output is
   _____. The corresponding full-employment price index is _____.

3. Now draw the aggregate demand curve corresponding to columns 1 and 4 labeling it AD_1 . For
   this aggregate demand curve, the equilibrium real output is _____. The corresponding
   equilibrium price index is _____.

4. Assume the economy is on AD_1. In Figure 11.1 indicate the GDP gap, which is _____
   billion units of output, and the AD (excess, shortfall), which is _____ billion units of
   output.

5. Which of the following government policies could be used to shift AD to full employment?
   (a) The government increases taxes.
   (b) The government provides tax incentives to encourage more saving.
   (c) The government eliminates investment tax credits, which results effectively in higher
       taxes on investment goods.
   (d) A trade agreement is approved, which suddenly results in U.S. exports rising faster than
       imports.
   (e) Foreign governments place limits on imports from the U.S.
   (f) Government cuts back on its expenditures.

6. Now draw the aggregate demand curve corresponding to columns 1 and 5 labeling it AD_2 . For
   this aggregate demand curve, the equilibrium real output is _____. The corresponding
   equilibrium average price index is _____.

7. Assume the economy is on AD_2. In Figure 11.1 indicate the GDP gap, which is _____ units
   of output, and the AD (excess, shortfall), which is _____ units of output.

8. Which of the following government policies could be used to shift AD to full employment?
   (a) The government lowers interest rates.
   (b) The government cuts taxes.
   (c) The government cuts its expenditures.
   (d) The government raises tariffs, which increases the cost of imports.
   (e) The government subsidizes exports to help domestic firms sell abroad.
   (f) The government eliminates IRAs and other instruments that encourage saving which results in greater autonomous consumption.

Exercise 2

This exercise emphasizes the impact of various fiscal policies on total spending.

Assume the economy can be described by the consumption function: $C = \$300$ billion $+ 0.9Y$.

1. Calculate the cumulative change in total spending if the government increases purchases of goods and services by $100 million. _____

2. Calculate the cumulative change in total spending if the government reduces taxes by $100 million. _____

3. Calculate the cumulative change in total spending if the government increases transfer payments by $100 million. _____

4. The $100 million increase in government spending on goods and services had a (smaller, larger) impact on total spending than the $100 million increase in transfer payments because there is a savings (leakage, injection) out of transfer payments.

5. Calculate the cumulative change in total spending if the government increases purchases of goods and services by $100 million and at the same time increases taxes by $100 million.

   _____

6. The situation described in question 5 represents a _____ _____ expenditure.

Exercise 3

The media often provide information on multiplier effects in the economy. This exercise will use one of the articles in the text to show the kind of information to look for.

Reread the article "Economy Is Already Feeling the Impact of Federal Government's Spending Cuts" in the text. Then answer the following questions:

1. Which passages indicate the cause of the change in the economy? _____
   _____

2. The change in the economy is (more, less) of the (injection, leakage).

3. What statement indicates the estimated impact of the "belt tightening" on GDP? _____
   _____

4. What evidence of secondary changes in income are reported? _____
   _____

151

Exercise 4

This exercise shows how the multiplier works to eliminate a GDP gap.

Refer to Figure 11.2 to answer questions 1-4. Assume the MPC equals 0.80 and the current level of aggregate demand is equal to AD_1.

Figure 11.2

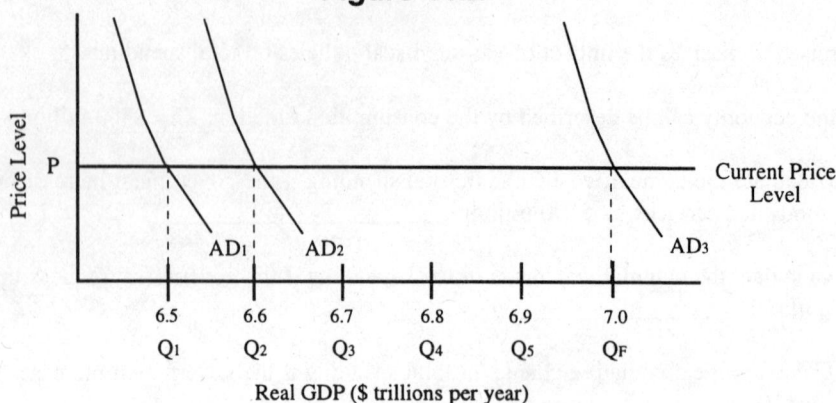

Real GDP ($ trillions per year)

1. What is the size of the GDP gap? _____

2. What is the value of the multiplier? _____

3. An increase in government spending of $100 billion would cause consumption to increase by $ _____ billion in the second spending cycle.

4. An increase in government spending of $100 billion would cause a cumulative increase in aggregate demand equal to $ _____ billion and would result in an equilibrium real GDP equal to $ _____ trillion.

Common Errors

The first statement in each "common error" below is incorrect. Each incorrect statement is followed by a corrected version and an explanation.

1. Government deficits always lead to inflation. WRONG!

    Government deficits may result from government spending to reach full employment with price stability. RIGHT!

    You should focus on what is happening to aggregate supply and demand, not just deficits, when looking for the sources of inflation. By looking at the deficit, you cannot tell if there is adequate aggregate demand in the economy. If there is a shortfall in aggregate demand, government spending and resulting deficits may restore full employment with price stability! If there is an excess aggregate demand, demand-pull inflation can result from increased consumption, investment, or export expenditures, just as much as from increased government spending. It is all too easy to point the finger at the government and forget the contribution to inflation of all the other sectors of the economy.

2. If the government increases spending and taxes by the same amount, there will be no effect on income. WRONG!

Income increases by the amount of government spending, even if taxes are increased by the same amount. RIGHT!

The full impact of the increased government spending turns into income for the people who provide goods and services to the government. Part of the increased taxes, however, comes from people's savings, which had been leakages from the economy. So consumption decreases by less than the loss of taxes. This in turn means that income generated by consumption spending is not cut back by the amount of taxes. Therefore, the economy experiences a smaller cutback in incomes as a result of increased taxes than from stimulus from increased government spending.

•ANSWERS•

Using Key Terms
Across
3. fiscal restraint
5. fiscal policy
9. disposable income
10. aggregate demand
11. income transfer
12. aggregate supply
13. real GDP gap

Down

1. macro equilibrium
2. marginal propensity to consume
3. fiscal stimulus
4. crowding out
6. AD shortfall
7. multiplier
8. AD excess

True or False
1. F   Fiscal policy works through shifts in the AD curve.
2. T
3. F   If the AS curve is horizontal (i.e. flat), the GDP gap is equal to the AD shortfall (or excess).
4. F   The effect of the multiplier must be taken into account even when AS is flat. In this case, government expenditures should be increased by an amount equal to the AD shortfall divided by the multiplier.
5. F   The total increase in AD is equal to MPC times the increase in transfer payments times the multiplier.
6. T
7. T
8. F   Only government purchases of goods and services are part of AD. Government transfer payments are not part of AD because they do not represent a direct purchase of goods and services.
9. T
10. T

Multiple Choice

1.	b	5.	a	9.	b	13.	c	17.	a
2.	d	6.	a	10.	c	14.	a	18.	b
3.	b	7.	d	11.	d	15.	a	19.	d
4.	a	8.	c	12.	d	16.	b	20.	c

Problems and Applications

Exercise 1

1. See Figure 11.1 Answer, AS and AD_F.

Figure 11.1 Answer

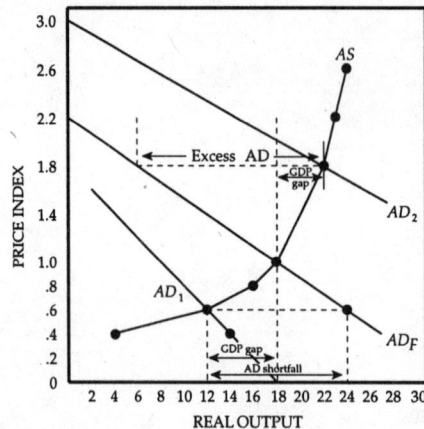

2. At full employment, the price index is 1.0 at an output of 18 units.
3. See Figure 11.1 Answer, AD_1. At AD_1, the price index is 0.6 at an output of 12 units.
4. See Figure 11.1 Answer. GDP gap = 6.0 units; AD shortfall = 12 units.
5. d We are looking for more of an injection or less of a leakage, and we find higher United States exports, which is more of an injection.
6. See Figure 11.1 Answer, AD_2. At AD_2, the price index is 1.8 at an output of 22 units.
7. See Figure 11.1 Answer. GDP gap = -4.0 units; excess AD = 16 units.
8. c We are looking for more of a leakage or less of an injection, and we find lower government expenditures, which is less of an injection.

Exercise 2

1. $1 billion increase
2. $900 million increase
3. $900 million increase
4. larger, leakage
5. $100 million increase
6. balanced budget

154

Exercise 3

1. "Skeptical about the federal government's pledge to tighten its belt?" and "Federal purchases of goods and services dropped 3.3% in 1992 . . . " tell us that *G* has been reduced.
2. An injection
3. Less of an injection
4. ". . . cuts in purchases by the federal government knocked as much as 0.5 percentage point off the gross domestic product last year . . . "
5. 400,000 jobs were lost in 1992 and the same was expected for the next year

Exercise 4

1. $7 trillion - $6.5 trillion = $500 billion
2. multiplier = $1/(1-MPC) = 1/(1-0.8) = 5$
3. $80 billion
4. 5 x $100 billion = $500 billion, $7.0 trillion

CHAPTER 12

Deficits, Surpluses, and Debts

Quick Review

This chapter concerns federal budget deficits and the national debt. The focus is on the following questions:

- How do deficits and surpluses arise?
- What harm (good) do deficits (surpluses) cause?
- Who will pay off the accumulated national debt?

When the federal government's revenues fall short of its expenditures in any fiscal year, the U.S. Treasury issues IOUs (e.g., Treasury bonds) and sells them to cover the difference. The difference is called the "deficit." It is a flow concept because it has a time dimension. If you add up all of the Treasury's IOUs that are outstanding, the sum is the national debt. It is a stock concept, because it can be measured at a point in time.

Budget deficits are closely related to fiscal policy even though almost 80 percent of the budget is uncontrollable, i.e., spending programs that are locked in from previous legislative commitments. For example, "automatic stabilizers" such as unemployment compensation *increase* as the economy weakens and decrease when the economy improves. Only twenty percent of the budget is "controllable." This is why economists and policy makers distinguish between "cyclical deficits" which are related to economic conditions, and the "structural deficit," which is the deficit which would result if the economy were at full employment. The cyclical deficit widens automatically when unemployment increases or inflation subsides, and thus shrinks when unemployment decreases or inflation accelerates. The structural deficit measures the thrust of fiscal policy. Discretionary fiscal policy is stimulative if the structural deficit is increasing (or the surplus shrinking), and restrictive if the structural deficit is shrinking (or the surplus is growing).

The national debt is a liability of the government (and its citizen-taxpayers), but it represents an asset to those who own it. Most of the debt is owned "internally" by banks and other financial institutions, the Federal Reserve, and individuals. The interest earned from holding government debt is an important source of income for the private sector.

Most of the debt that accrued in the first 200 years of our history was incurred to fight wars and recessions and seems modest by today's standards. Since 1980, the debt has jumped by roughly an additional $2 trillion fueled by recessions in (1980-82 and 1990-92) and the massive tax cuts passed in the first Reagan administration. The trend continued in the 90s, and the deficits incurred from 1993-1996 pushed the total over $5 trillion.

About 22 percent of the debt is owned by foreigners. Payment on foreign holdings of U.S. debt means that dollars must flow out of the country, which in turn has an impact on exchange rates. Debt that is purchased and held by foreigners allows us to avoid opportunity costs by providing the wherewithal to import goods and services. But, if foreigners in the future turn in their bonds for dollars and use them to increase their imports from us, future generations will have less output to consume. This situation *would* be a real burden.

The national debt may never be paid off; when some of it comes due, the Treasury just issues more IOUs to obtain funds. This "refinancing" is done routinely. The debt also has to be "serviced"—interest must be paid to those who own it. The interest payments restrict the government's ability to spend and redistribute income from taxpayers to bondholders without imposing opportunity costs.

Only when the debt takes resources that would be employed other places *or* causes resources to be misallocated does society incur an opportunity cost. When government purchases goods and services, the resources used to produce them are denied to the rest of society. The mix of output is definitely changed. This is referred to as "crowding out." Rates of investment and economic growth may both be reduced when government borrowing pushes interest rates up. Because of crowding out, future generations will have less capital to work with and thus less productive capacity. Of course, some of the things that government purchases benefit future generations too.

For the first time in a generation, the federal government budget was balanced in 1998. The attempt to gain control of the budget and the debt had been going on for some time. The Gramm-Rudman-Hollings Act (1985), the Budget Enforcement Act of 1990, and the Republican party's Contract With America were all efforts to stop the continuation of budget deficits and the resulting debt.

Learning Objectives

After reading Chapter 12 and doing the following exercises, you should:

1. Understand the cause of budget deficits and the relationship between deficits and the national debt.
2. Be able to discuss the recent history of the national debt.
3. Be able to distinguish between discretionary spending and uncontrollables.
4. Be able to describe the operation and importance of automatic stabilizers.
5. Be able to distinguish cyclical deficits from structural deficits.
6. Understand the economic effects of deficits and be able to explain "crowding out."
7. Understand the history of the national debt and how it reached its present size.
8. Know who owns the debt, and understand the implications of internal and external ownership.
9. Understand the real burden of the debt.
10. Understand that the only way to stop the debt from growing is to eliminate budget deficits.
11. Be aware of attempts to address the deficit problem.

Using Key Terms

Fill in the puzzle on the opposite page with the appropriate term from the list of Key Terms at the end of the chapter in the text.

Across

1. Represented by the movement from point a to point b in Figure 12.2 in the text.
6. Tax increases or spending cuts designed to reduce aggregate demand.
10. A spending or revenue item that responds automatically and countercyclically to national income.
12. The twelve-month accounting period used by the federal government.
13. When the government borrows funds to pay for spending that exceeds tax revenues.
14. Promissory notes issued by the U.S. Treasury.
15. The amount by which government spending exceeds revenues.
17. The idea that in order to get more public-sector goods some private-sector goods must be given up.
18. Equal to the total stock of all outstanding treasury bonds.
20. Tax cuts or spending increases designed to shift aggregate demand to the right.
21. Equal to $70 billion for 1998 according to Table 12.1 in the text.
22. Equal to 17 percent of the national debt according to Figure 12.4 in the text.
23. The issuance of new bonds to replace the bonds that mature.
24. An explicit limit on the size of the annual budget deficit.
25. An explicit limit on the size of the national debt.

Down

2. Spending decisions not determined by past legislative commitments.
3. The most desirable combination of output given the available resources and technology.
4. U.S. treasury bonds are an _____ for the people who own them.
5. Payments to individuals for which no current goods or services are exchanged.
7. The U.S. treasury bonds are a _____ for the federal government.
8. The portion of the budget deficit that widens when unemployment or inflation increases.
9. Use of the government budget to stabilize the economy.
11. The portion of the budget deficit that reflects fiscal-policy decisions.
16. The U.S. government debt owned by U.S. households, institutions, and government agencies.
19. The interest required to be paid each year on outstanding debt.

Puzzle 12.1

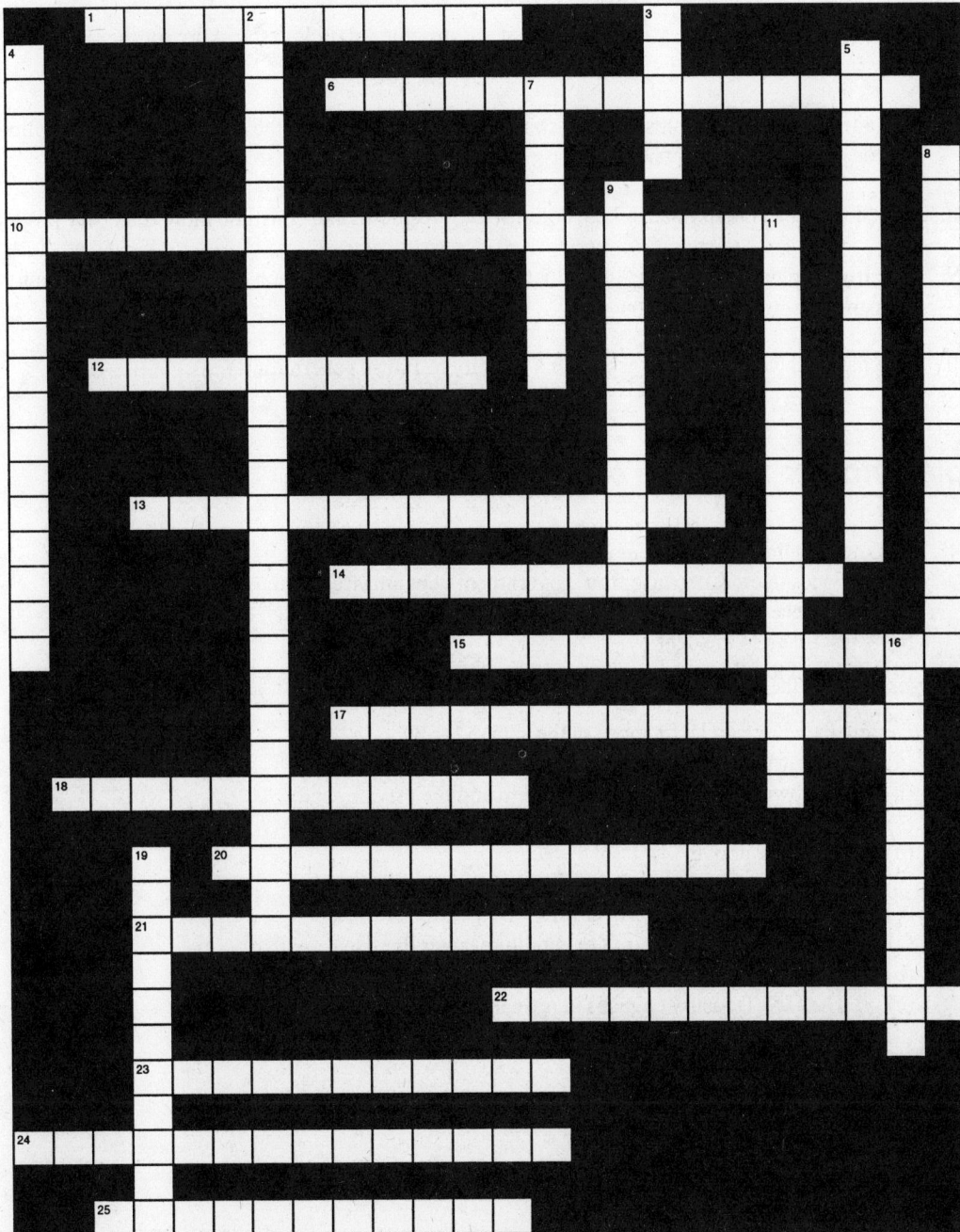

True or False: *Circle your choice and explain why any false statements are incorrect.*

T F 1. According to Keynes, a balanced budget would be appropriate only if all other injections and leakages were in balance and the economy was in full employment.

T F 2. Automatic stabilizers reduce government expenditures and decrease budget deficits when the economy is in a recession.

T F 3. Approximately 20 percent of the expenditures in the federal budget are "uncontrollable."

T F 4. The cyclical deficit narrows when unemployment or inflation increase.

T F 5. Part of the deficit arises from cyclical changes in the economy; the rest is the result of discretionary fiscal policy.

T F 6. Discretionary fiscal policy is stimulative if the structural deficit is shrinking (or the surplus is growing).

T F 7. In general, a budget surplus tends to change the mix of output in the direction of more public-sector goods and fewer private-sector goods.

T F 8. When foreigners help finance U.S. deficits, U.S. residents can consume more than they produce.

T F 9. The true burden of the debt is the reduction in national wealth when the federal government borrows money by selling bonds.

T F 10. The national debt is both an asset and a liability to future generations.

Multiple Choice: *Select the correct answer.*

_____ 1. Deficit spending results whenever the government:
  (a) Faces interest expense from government debt amassed from previous deficits.
  (b) Finances expenditures that exceed tax revenues.
  (c) Refinances the debt.
  (d) All of the above.

_____ 2. Deficit spending can be financed in the same year by:
  (a) Borrowing from foreign sources.
  (b) Borrowing from the banking system and the private sector.
  (c) U.S. treasury bonds.
  (d) All of the above.

_____ 3. A budget deficit is incurred whenever:
  (a) Tax revenues fall short of expenditures over the fiscal year.
  (b) Discretionary fiscal spending is used to achieve macro equilibrium.
  (c) The U.S. Treasury engages in refinancing activities.
  (d) The government uses fiscal policy.

_____ 4. Between the years 1969 and 1998, the federal budget:
(a) Experienced deficits in every year.
(b) Experienced surpluses in every year.
(c) Allocated funds to reduce the national debt.
(d) Experienced both deficits and surpluses.

_____ 5. Examples of discretionary fiscal spending include:
(a) Income taxes.
(b) Unemployment benefits.
(c) Social security payments.
(d) Expenditures for highways.

_____ 6. Uncontrollables:
(a) Include the major automatic stabilizers.
(b) Limit the use of discretionary fiscal policy.
(c) Make it difficult to achieve short-run stimulus or restraint.
(d) All of the above.

_____ 7. Automatic stabilizers tend to stabilize the level of economic activity because:
(a) They are changed quickly by Congress.
(b) They increase the size of the multiplier.
(c) They increase spending during recessions and decrease spending during inflationary periods.
(d) They control the rate of change in prices.

_____ 8. The major reason budget deficits were reduced during the 1990s and that 1998 experienced a surplus was:
(a) President Clinton's deficit reduction policies.
(b) The significant reductions in federal spending implemented by Congress.
(c) Structural surpluses during the period.
(d) The growing U.S. economy.

_____ 9. In contrast to the structural deficit, the cyclical deficit reflects:
(a) Fluctuations in economic activity.
(b) Fiscal-policy decisions.
(c) Changes in discretionary fiscal policy.
(d) Changes in the "full-employment" deficit.

_____ 10. The structural deficit represents:
(a) Federal revenues minus federal expenditures at full employment under current fiscal policy.
(b) Federal revenues minus expenditures under current fiscal policy at current output.
(c) A measure of the size of recessionary or inflationary gaps.
(d) The difference between expenditures at full employment and expenditures at cyclical unemployment.

_____ 11. The magnitude of a fiscal stimulus is measured by the:
(a) Decrease in the structural deficit (or increase in the structural surplus).
(b) Increase in the structural deficit (or decrease in the structural surplus).
(c) Increase in the total budget deficit.
(d) Increase in the cyclical deficit (or decrease in the cyclical surplus).

_____ 12. Crowding out occurs when the government:
(a) Increases taxes, causing a decrease in consumption.
(b) Prints money, which displaces currency.
(c) Borrows, making it more difficult for the private sector to borrow.
(d) Expenditures displace saving.

_____ 13. When the federal government runs a budget surplus, it is:
  (a) Providing a fiscal stimulus to the economy.
  (b) Adding a leakage to the circular flow.
  (c) Adding an injection to the circular flow.
  (d) Reducing leakages to the circular flow.

_____ 14. Which of the following uses of a budget surplus has the potential of increasing the private sector's proportion of output?
  (a) Cutting taxes.
  (b) Paying off a portion of the national debt.
  (c) Increasing transfer payments.
  (d) All of the above have the potential.

_____ 15. When the U.S. Treasury issues new bonds to replace bonds that have matured, it is engaging in:
  (a) Debt refinancing.
  (b) Debt servicing.
  (c) Income transfers.
  (d) Discretionary fiscal spending.

_____ 16. If all of the national debt were owned internally, then:
  (a) We would not have to worry about raising taxes to pay the interest on the debt.
  (b) We would still have to worry about the effect of interest payments on the distribution of income.
  (c) The federal government would have to stop refinancing the debt.
  (d) The Federal Reserve System would have no use for government debt.

_____ 17. Externally held U.S. debt results in:
  (a) A burden to the United States when newly issued bonds are sold to foreigners.
  (b) A burden to the United States when foreign-owned bonds are cashed in and proceeds are used to buy goods and services produced in the United States.
  (c) A burden incurred by foreigners when bonds are sold in the United States.
  (d) No burden to the United States.

_____ 18. A deficit ceiling limits:
  (a) The amount by which government spending can exceed government revenue.
  (b) The amount of the national debt.
  (c) The trade deficit.
  (d) Inflation.

_____ 19. Which of the following statements about the U.S. national debt is not correct?
  (a) The primary economic costs of the debt are being passed on to future generations.
  (b) The primary burden of the debt is incurred when the deficit-financed activity takes place.
  (c) The national debt represents both a liability and asset to future generations.
  (d) Future generations will bear some of the debt burden when crowding out occurs.

_____ 20. To pay off the debt would require that:
  (a) Current government expenditures be less than current government receipts.
  (b) The federal government run a budget surplus.
  (c) There be a transfer of revenue from taxpayers to bondholders.
  (d) All of the above.

Problems and Applications

Exercise 1

After doing this exercise you should understand the relationships among deficits, bonds, debt, and interest payments. You should see how continual deficits lead to larger and larger interest payments and larger and larger debt. Keep in mind that it is difficult to eliminate deficits when interest payments are an important factor contributing to the deficits.

1. Suppose the federal government expenditures in the year 2000 are $1 trillion and taxes are $800 billion. Compute the deficit and place the answer in column 1 of Table 12.1 for the year 2000.

Table 12.1
Deficits, bonds, debts, and interest payments
(billions of dollars per year)

Year	(1) Deficit	(2) Newly issued bonds	(3) Total debt	(4) Interest payment
1999	$0	$0	$0	$0
2000	_____	_____	_____	_____
2001	_____	_____	_____	_____
2002	_____	_____	_____	_____
2003	_____	_____	_____	_____
2004	_____	_____	_____	_____
2005	_____	_____	_____	_____
2006	_____	_____	_____	_____
2007	_____	_____	_____	_____

2. To finance the deficit, the government must sell bonds of an equivalent amount to cover the revenue shortfall. What is the dollar amount necessary to finance the debt? Place the answer in column 2 of Table 12.1 for the year 2000.

3. Assume that up to 1999 the government had zero debt (as shown in the 1999 row of Table 12.1). What is the total debt after the government has borrowed to cover the deficit in the year 2000? Place the answer in column 3 of Table 12.1 for the year 2000.

4. What will be the interest payment on the total debt in the year 2000 if the interest rate is 10 percent per year? Place the answer in column 4 of Table 12.1 for the year 2000. Assume all bonds are sold January 1 with interest due December 31.

5. For the years 2001 through 2007, the government spends $1 trillion each year plus any interest payment on the previous years' debt and receives tax revenues of only $800 billion each year. The interest rate is still 10 percent per year. Fill in the rest of Table 12.1.

6. Graph and label the deficit (column 1 of Table 12.1) and interest payment (column 4) in Figure 12.1.

Figure 12.1

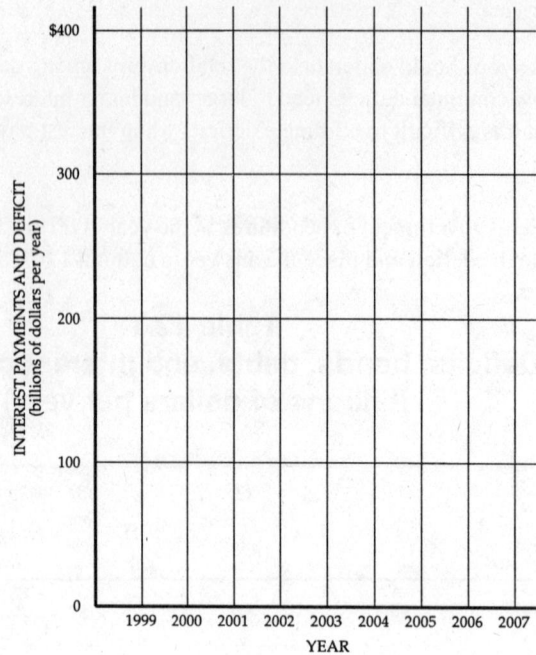

INTEREST PAYMENTS AND DEFICIT (billions of dollars per year) vs YEAR (1999–2007)

7. T   F   With continual deficits, interest payments on past deficits will become a bigger part of current deficits, *ceteris paribus*.

8. T   F   In this example, if both taxes and government expenditures increased at 5 percent per year as a result of bigger government, both the deficit and the debt would become smaller.

Exercise 2

This exercise focuses on the ratio of the national debt to GDP, which is an important measure of the burden of the debt.

Table 12.2 National debt and GDP
(billions of dollars per year)

Year	Country A			Country B		
	Debt	GDP	Debt/GDP	Debt	GDP	Debt/GDP
1999	$200	$1000	_____	$200	$1000	_____
2000	250	1250	_____	250	1150	_____
2001	280	1400	_____	280	1000	_____
2002	320	1600	_____	320	1000	_____
2003	400	2000	_____	400	1200	_____

1. Calculate the debt/GDP ratio for Country A and Country B in Table 12.2.

2. During the period from 1999 to 2003 both countries in Table 12.2 are experiencing (budget deficits, budget surpluses, a balanced budget) each year.

3. Even though the size of the debt is the same for the two countries in Table 12.2 for each year, the debt is likely to be a greater burden for Country _____ because the debt/GDP ratio is _____.

4. Given the information in Table 12.2, what is the most likely cause for the increase in the debt/GDP ratio from 2000 to 2001 for Country B? _____

5. The actual amount of debt increases each year for Country A in Table 12.2. The size of the debt/GDP ratio (increases, decreases, stays the same) because GDP (increases, decreases, stays the same) each year.

Exercise 3

This exercise explores the impact of government spending on private-sector spending.

Use Figure 12.2 to answer questions 1-6.

Figure 12.2

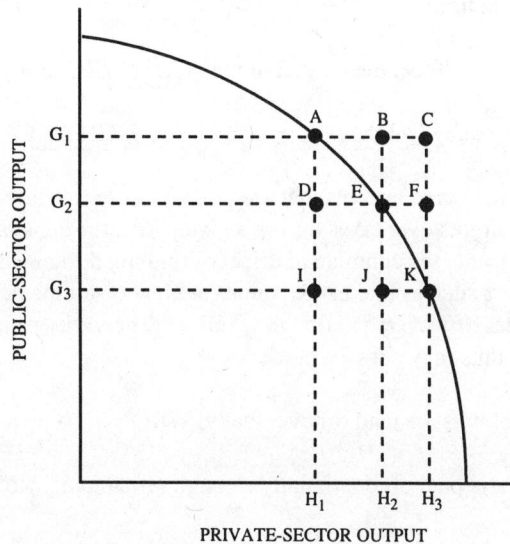

PRIVATE-SECTOR OUTPUT

1. If all debt is held internally and the government finances additional spending by borrowing, then an increase in government purchases would move the economy from point E to point ___.

2. If the economy moves from point K to point A because of increased government spending, the amount of private sector spending crowded out is equal to the distance _____.

3. Assume the government has a budget surplus and uses it to reduce the accumulated debt. As a result interest rates (rise, fall) and the economy moves from point E to point ____.

4. The situation described in questions 3 is referred to in the text as the _____ effect.

5. External financing of the debt allows the economy to move from point E to point _____.

6. In question 5, external financing allows public-sector goods to (increase, decrease, stay the same) while private-sector goods (increase, decrease, stay the same).

Exercise 4

Reports on fiscal policy typically involve changes in the deficit and the debt.

Reread the article titled "Fiscal Policy in the Great Depression" in the text.

1. President Hoover believed that the federal budget should always be (balanced, in deficit, in surplus).

2. What did President Hoover propose to resolve the problem with the federal budget?
   _____

3. From 1931 to 1933 the structural deficit _____. This fiscal restraint caused the _____ curve to shift to the (left, right).

4. What finally occurred that caused a huge increase in government spending which ended the Great Depression? _____

Common Errors

The first statement in each "common error" below is incorrect. Each incorrect statement is followed by a corrected version and an explanation.

1. Our grandchildren will feel the burden of the deficit. WRONG!

   Our grandchildren may feel the burden of the debt. RIGHT!

   Deficit and debt are concepts that are often confused. While deficits occur because of the excess of expenditures over taxes during a given year, the debt can be calculated at any given point in time and represents the cumulative effect of running deficits over our entire history. It is the debt on which transfers such as interest payments are made, not the deficit. Such transfers may result in opportunity costs. However, a deficit may reflect expenditures on capital which will benefit future generations and thus may not be a burden.

2. The national debt must be paid off eventually. WRONG!

   The national debt is paid off continually through refinancing. RIGHT!

   No Treasury bond has a maturity date more than thirty years in the future. Some bonds have maturity dates that come much sooner—in ten or twenty years. Treasury bills are sold at auction and have maturity dates of 360 days or less with 30-day intervals (i.e., 30, 60, 90, and so on). Suppose the federal government has balanced budgets for the next thirty years. The entire debt will have come due at some point. What will happen? It would be refinanced as it comes due and replaced with new debt.

3. There is nothing "behind" the national debt. WRONG!

   The federal government owns many physical assets and has the ability to tax. RIGHT!

   The proceeds of bond sales by the federal government are used to do many things, including the purchase of assets. Every item owned by the federal government—from the White House to

Old Faithful—is an asset that could be sold to help pay off the national debt. Stealth bombers, office buildings, computers, and the like, are all assets that were needed over the years and are as much an asset as the debt is a liability. By raising taxes, the government can at least theoretically run a surplus and pay off the debt.

•ANSWERS•

Using Key Terms

Across

1. crowding out
6. fiscal restraint
10. automatic stabilizers
12. fiscal year
13. deficit spending
14. treasury bonds
15. budget deficit
17. opportunity costs
18. national debt
20. fiscal stimulus
21. budget surplus
22. external debt
23. refinancing
24. deficit ceiling
25. debt ceiling

Down

2. discretionary fiscal spending
3. asset
4. optimal mix of output
5. income transfers
7. liability
8. cyclical deficit
9. fiscal policy
11. structural deficit
16. internal debt
19. debt service

True or False

1. T
2. F As an economy falls into a recession, automatic stabilizers tend to increase government spending (and reduce tax receipts) thus making budget deficits larger.
3. F Approximately 80 percent of the expenditures in the federal budget are uncontrollable.
4. F The cyclical deficit widens when unemployment or inflation increases.
5. T
6. F Such policies are restrictive.
7. F Unless the government spends the surplus, the proportion of private goods and services produced will tend to increase.
8. T
9. F The true burden of the national debt is the private goods and services that are foregone (i.e. crowded out) as a result of government borrowing.
10. T

Multiple Choice

1.	b	5.	d	9.	a	13.	b	17.	b
2.	d	6.	d	10.	a	14.	d	18.	a
3.	a	7.	c	11.	b	15.	a	19.	a
4.	a	8.	d	12.	c	16.	b	20.	d

Problems and Applications

Exercise 1

1-5.   **Table 12.1 Answer**

Year	(1) Deficit	(2) Newly issued bonds	(3) Total debt	(4) Interest payment
2000	$200	$200	$ 200	$ 20 = (0.10 x 200)
2001	220	220	420 = (200 + 220)	42 = (0.10 x 420)
2002	242	242	662 = (420 + 242)	66 = (0.10 x 662)
2003	266	266	928 = (662 + 266)	93 = (0.10 x 928)
2004	293	293	1,221 = (928 + 293)	122 = (0.10 x 1,221)
2005	322	322	1,543 = (1,221 + 322)	154 = (0.10 x 1,543)
2006	354	354	1,897 = (1,543 + 354)	190 = (0.10 x 1,897)
2007	390	390	2,287 = (1,897 + 390)	229 = (0.10 x 2,287)

6.   **Figure 12.1 Answer**

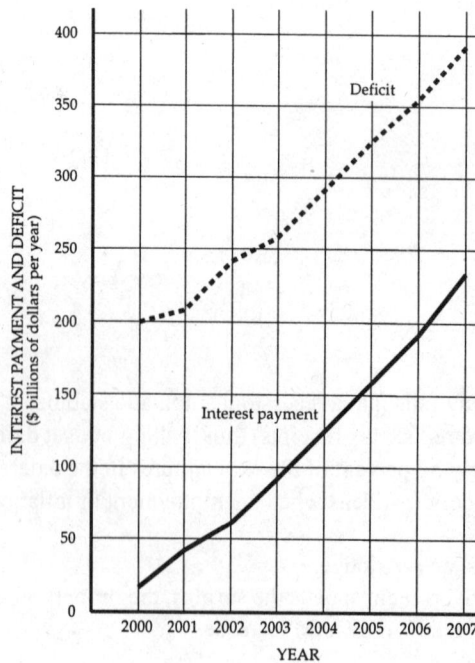

7. T   Compare relative sizes of columns 1 and 4 in Table 12.1 Answer.
8. F

Exercise 2

1. **Table 12.2 Answer**

Year	Country A				Country B		
	Debt	GDP	Debt/GDP		Debt	GDP	Debt/GDP
1999	$200	$1000	0.20		$200	$1000	0.20
2000	250	1250	0.20		250	1150	0.22
2001	280	1400	0.20		280	1000	0.28
2002	320	1600	0.20		320	1000	0.32
2003	400	2000	0.20		400	1200	0.33

2. budget deficits
3. B, greater
4. recession
5. stays the same, increases.

Exercise 3

1. A
2. H_3-H_1
3. fall, K
4. crowding-in
5. B
6. increase, stay the same

Exercise 4

1. balanced
2. a decrease in government spending and an increase in taxes
3. decreased, AD, left
4. World War II

CHAPTER 13
Money and Banks

Quick Review

Money is clearly very important to the operation of the U.S. economy. The study of money begins with some very basic questions:

- What is money?
- How is money created?
- What role do banks play in the circular flow of income and spending?

Let's begin by examining what money does for us. Money has three functions; it serves as a

- Medium of exchange: is accepted as payment for goods and services (and debts).
- Store of value: can be held for future purchases.
- Standard of value: serves as yardstick for measuring the prices of goods and services.

Money consists of all of those things that are generally acceptable as a medium of exchange. The narrowest definition of the "money supply" is $M1$, the sum of currency held by the public and balances held in transactions accounts and traveler's checks. The most watched monetary aggregate is $M2$. It includes $M1$ as well as savings accounts, certain time deposits and money-market mutual funds. Most of the basic money supply, $M1$, is in the form of transactions-account balances, commonly referred to as checking accounts. Most of the checking accounts come into existence when banks perform their lending function. When you borrow from a bank, you receive an increase in your checking account. You have more money, and no other member of the public has less. Thus the money supply expands.

Our banking system is based on the fractional-reserve principle. The Federal Reserve System (the Fed) requires banks to maintain reserves equal to some fraction of their transactions-account balances. As a result of this reserve requirement, and the fact that banks may lose reserves to other banks via the check-clearing process, a single bank can only make new loans if it has excess reserves. The banking system, however, can make loans equal to a multiple (1 ÷ reserve requirement) of any existing reserves. Banks and other depository institutions control the money supply by making loans and creating transactions-account balances. Banks also hold savings accounts and thus assist in the transfer of purchasing power from savers (those who choose not to spend all of their incomes) to borrowers (those who wish to spend more than their incomes). In addition to the reserve requirement, deposit creation is limited by the willingness of consumers and businesses to hold deposits and borrow money.

The Monetary Control Act of 1980 ended a set of regulations that discriminated among financial institutions. The changes set in motion by the act (which continue today) have blurred the distinction between commercial banks and other depository institutions. There have been significant and well-publicized problems in the financial sector in recent years. Fraud, inflation, high interest rates, increased competition from money market mutual funds, and falling oil prices all conspired to wreak havoc among the S&Ls and banks. While some of the losses suffered by depositors were covered by deposit insurance, others were not. So many S&Ls failed that Congress had to appropriate ever larger sums for the "bailout." The Resolution Trust Corporation (RTC) was created to manage the loans of failed financial institutions.

Learning Objectives

After reading Chapter 13 and doing the following exercises, you should:

1. Know the basic characteristics, history, and functions of money.
2. Know some of the differences between various accounts permitting transfer by check.
3. Understand how the Monetary Control Act of 1980 caused changes in the way financial institutions conduct business.
4. Be familiar with the composition and various definitions of the money supply ($M1$, $M2$, etc.).
5. Be able to summarize the important differences between banks and other financial institutions.
6. Know how banks create money with new loans.
7. Know the purpose of the reserve requirement.
8. Know the difference between required and excess reserves.
9. Be able to work through the steps of deposit creation using balance sheets (T-accounts).
10. Be able to calculate and explain the money multiplier.
11. Know the banking system's role in financing the circular flow of economic activity.
12. Know the history of the recent financial crises.

Using Key Terms

Fill in the puzzle on the opposite page with the appropriate term from the list of Key Terms at the end of the chapter in the text.

Across

1. Assets held by a bank to fulfill its deposit obligations.
5. Total reserves minus required reserves.
7. An account that allows direct payment to a third party.
9. Represent a leakage from the flow of money because they cannot be used to make loans.
10. The reciprocal of the required reserve ratio.

Down

2. Tends to increase with an increase in the money supply because new loans are used to purchase additional goods and services.
3. The process by which bank lending causes the money supply to increase.
4. The system of exchange in Russia described in the article in the text titled "The Cashless Society."
6. Equal to $1,087 billion according to Figure 13.1 in the text.
8. Equal to 0.20 in Figure 13.4 in the text.
10. Throughout history gold coins, tobacco, and bullets have functioned in this role.

Puzzle 13.1

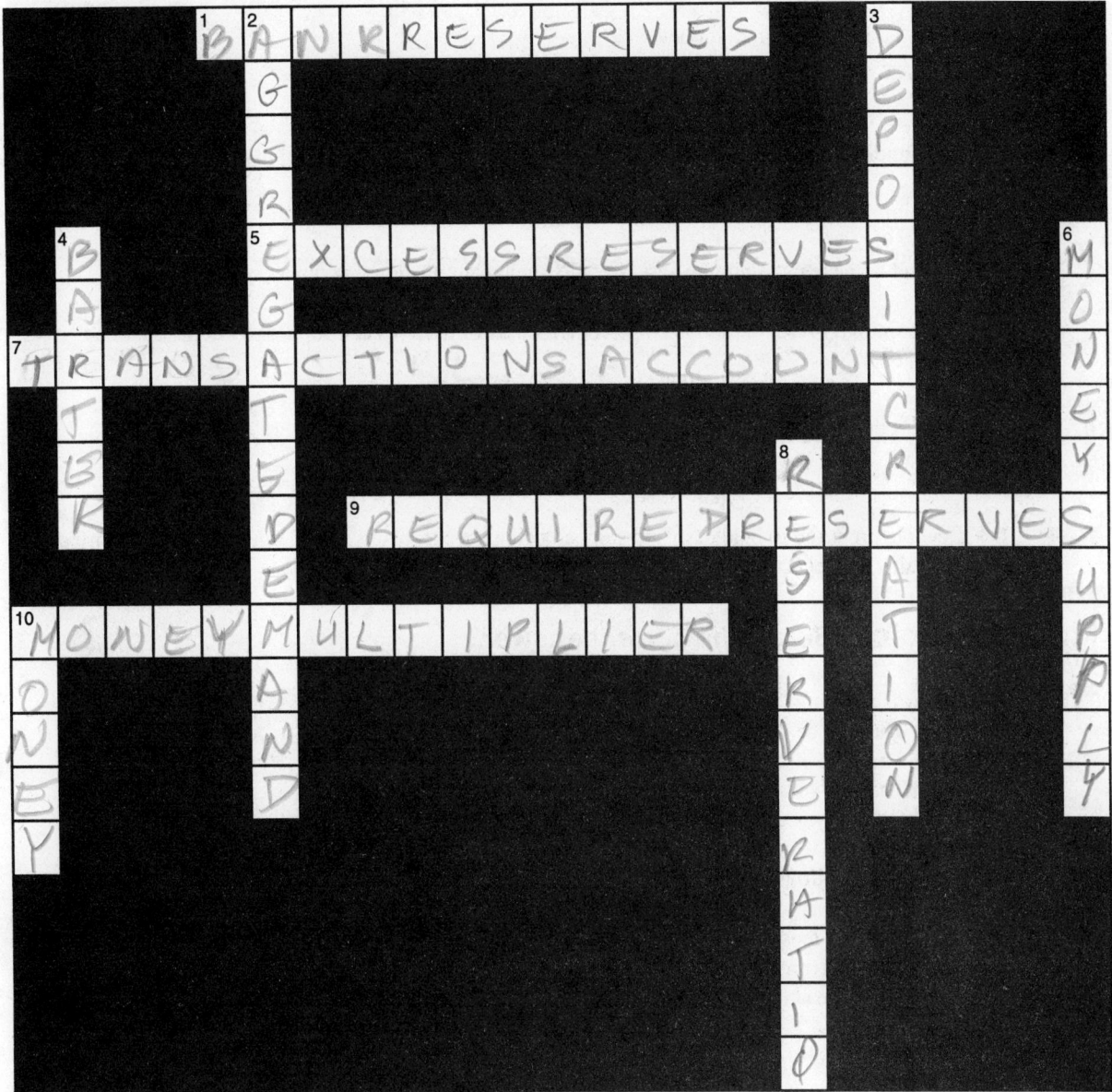

True or False: *Circle your choice and explain why any false statements are incorrect.*

T (F) 1. The terms "transactions-account balances" and "checking accounts" mean the same thing. F

T (F) 2. Credit cards are a form of money. F

(T) F 3. When you get a loan at a bank, the bank creates money. T

T (F) 4. The withdrawal of money from a checking account causes the money supply to get smaller. F

(T) F 5. The minimum-reserve ratio is established by the Federal Reserve System. T

T (F) 6. The higher the legal minimum-reserve ratio, the greater the lending power of the banks. F

(T) F 7. If the minimum-reserve ratio is 20 percent, then $1 of reserves can support $5 in transactions-account balances. T

T (F) 8. The amount any one bank can lend is equal to its total reserves. F

(T) F 9. Banks transfer money from savers to spenders by lending funds held on deposit. T

(T) F 10. If people preferred to hold cash and stopped using checks, banks would not be able to acquire or maintain reserves and would be forced to halt lending. T

Multiple Choice: *Select the correct answer.*

_d_ 1. Money is anything:
   (a) That can be used to barter.
   (b) That a government declares to have value.
   (c) That has value.
   (d) Generally accepted as a medium of exchange. ✓

_a_ 2. Which of the following is a necessary characteristic of money?
   (a) It serves as a medium of exchange. ✓
   (b) Its value must be supported by government reserves of gold and silver.
   (c) The government declares it to have value.
   (d) All of the above are necessary characteristics.

_c_ 3. Barter:
   (a) Facilitates specialization in production.
   (b) Is most efficient for an economy.
   (c) Is the direct exchange of one good or service for another. ✓
   (d) All of the above are correct.

_a_ 4. The different components of the money supply reflect:
   (a) Variations in liquidity and accessibility of assets. ✓
   (b) Whether deposits are domestic or international.
   (c) How often depositors use their accounts.
   (d) All of the above.

d 5. *M*1 refers to:
   (a) One component of the money supply.
   (b) Currency held by the public plus transactions-account balances.
   (c) The smallest of the money-supply aggregates watched by the Fed.
   (d) All of the above. ✓

c 6. Which of the following appears in *M*2 but not in *M*1?
   (a) Credit-union share drafts.
   (b) Treasury bills.
   (c) Saving account balances. ✓
   (d) U.S. savings bonds.

c 7. Money creation occurs when:
   (a) A person puts cash in a bank.
   (b) A person deposits a payroll check in their checking account.
   (c) Banks make loans to borrowers. ✓
   (d) The Federal Reserve increases the reserve requirement.

c 8. Suppose the total amount of transactions accounts on the books of all of the banks in the system is $1 million and the minimum-reserve ratio is 0.10. The amount of required reserves for the banking system is, then:
   (a) $10,000,000.
   (b) $1,000,000.
   (c) $100,000.
   (d) $900,000.

d 9. When the reserve requirement changes, which of the following will change for an individual bank?
   (a) Transactions-account balances, lending capacity.
   (b) Transactions-account balances, total reserves, excess reserves.
   (c) Total reserves, required reserves, excess reserves.
   (d) Required reserves, excess reserves, lending capacity.

d 10. Banks are required to keep a minimum amount of funds in reserve because:
   (a) Depositors may decide to withdraw funds.
   (b) It provides a constraint on the bank's ability to create money.
   (c) It provides a constraint on the bank's ability to affect aggregate demand.
   (d) All of the above are correct.

d 11. Suppose a bank has $2 million in deposits, a required reserve ratio of 20 percent, and reserves of $500,000. Then it has excess reserves of:
   (a) $200,000.
   (b) $300,000.
   (c) $400,000.
   (d) $100,000.

a 12. Suppose a bank has $100,000 in deposits, a required reserve ratio of 5 percent, and bank reserves of $45,000. Then it can make new loans in the amount of:
   (a) $40,000.
   (b) $5,000.
   (c) $2,500.
   (d) $45,000.

_a_ 13. A higher reserve requirement:
   (a)   Further limits deposit creation.
   (b)   Increases the ability of banks to make loans.
   (c)   Lowers the interest rate.
   (d)   Increases the borrowing capability of borrowers.

_d_ 14. If people never withdrew cash from banks and there was no reserve requirement, how much money could the banking system potentially create for a given amount of new deposits?
   (a)   Zero.
   (b)   The same amount as the new deposits.
   (c)   The amount of new deposits multiplied by the reserve ratio.
   (d)   An infinite amount of money.

_b_ 15. If the minimum-reserve ratio is 20 percent, the money multiplier is:
   (a)   25.
   (b)   5.
   (c)   4.
   (d)   0.25.

_____ 16. Suppose a banking system has $100,000 in deposits, a required reserve ratio of 10 percent, and total bank reserves for the whole system of $25,000. Then the whole system can potentially make new loans in the amount of:
   (a) $10,000.
   (b) $15,000.
   (c) $150,000.
   (d) $250,000.

_a_ 17. The main goal of banks is to:
   (a)   Earn a profit.
   (b)   Create money.
   (c)   Lend all of its deposits.
   (d)   Minimize its reserve ratio.

_d_ 18. Which of the following are constraints on the deposit-creation process of the banking system?
   (a)   The willingness of consumers and businesses to continue using and accepting checks rather than cash.
   (b)   The willingness of consumers, businesses, and government to borrow money.
   (c)   The reserve requirement.
   (d)   All of the above.

_b_ 19. Deposit insurance:
   (a)   Lowers the bankruptcy rate for banks.
   (b)   Lowers the number and magnitude of bank runs.
   (c)   Must be subsidized and run by the government in order to have credibility.
   (d)   All of the above.

_a_ 20. The primary purpose of both the FDIC and the Savings Association Insurance Fund (SAIF) is to:
   (a)   Increase depositor confidence in the banking system.
   (b)   Control the nation's money supply.
   (c)   Set reserve requirements for the banking system.
   (d)   Provide funds for home mortgages.

176

Problems and Applications

Exercise 1

Use the information from the Balance Sheet in Table 13.1 to answer Questions 1–5.

Table 13.1. Bank of Arlington

Assets		Liabilities	
Required reserves	$250,000	Transaction accounts	$1,000,000
Other assets	750,000		
Total	$1,000,000	Total	$1,000,000

1. Suppose that the Bank of Arlington is just meeting its reserve requirement. The reserve ratio must be ___.25___, and the money multiplier must be ___4___.

2. To be in a position to make loans, the Bank of Arlington must acquire some _____ (required reserves, *excess reserves*).

3. If we assume that the reserve ratio is changed to 15 percent, the Bank of Arlington would have required reserves of _150,500_ and excess reserves of _100,000_.

4. With a 15 percent reserve ratio the Bank of Arlington is in a position to make new loans totaling _100,000_.

5. With a 15 percent reserve ratio, the entire banking system can increase the volume of loans by _____.

Exercise 2

This exercise shows how the multiplier process works.

Assume that all banks in the system lend all of their excess reserves, that the reserve ratio for all banks is 0.20, and that all loans are returned to the banking system in the form of transactions deposits. Use the information from the Balance Sheets in Table 13.2, Table 13.3, Table 13.4, and Table 13.5 to answer Questions 1–6.

Table 13.2 Bank A - Initial Balance Sheet

Assets		Liabilities	
Required reserves	$20,000	Transaction accounts	$100,000
Excess reserves	0		
Other assets	80,000		
Total	$100,000	Total	$100,000

1. Bill takes $10,000 out of his cookie jar and deposits it in a transactions account in Bank A. Fill in the blanks in Bank A's balance sheet in Table 13.3 after the deposit. (Remember that some of the deposit will show up in required reserves and the remainder will become part of excess reserves.)

Table 13.3. Bank A - Balance Sheet After Bill's Deposit

Assets		Liabilities	
Required reserves	$_____	Transaction accounts	$_____
Excess reserves	_8,000_		
Other assets	80,000		
Total	$_____	Total	$_____

Now assume that Bank A lends all of its excess reserves to Pat, who spends the money on a car. The car dealership deposits the money in its transactions account in Bank B. Bank B's initial balance sheet is the same as Bank A's initial balance sheet.

2. Fill in the blanks in Bank B's balance sheet after the car dealership makes its deposit.

Table 13.4. Bank B - Balance Sheet After Car Dealership's Deposit

Assets		Liabilities	
Required reserves	$_____	Transaction accounts	$_____
Excess reserves	_____		
Other assets	80,000		
Total	$_____	Total	$_____

Now assume Bank B lends all of its excess reserves to Mary, who spends the money on college tuition. The university deposits the money in Bank C. Bank C's initial balance sheet is the same as Bank A's initial balance sheet.

3. Fill in the blanks in Bank C's balance sheet after the university makes its deposit.

Table 13.5. Bank C - Balance Sheet After University's Deposit

Assets		Liabilities	
Required reserves	$_____	Transaction accounts	$_____
Excess reserves	_____		
Other assets	80,000		
Total	$_____	Total	$_____

4. Add together the loans made by each bank because of the initial $10,000 deposit made by Bill.

Bank A lent $_____
Bank B lent $_____
Bank C lent $_____

Total loans made so far $_____

5. The money multiplier for this exercise equals _____.

6. The potential deposit creation for the banking system in this exercise is _____.

Exercise 3

Reread the article "The Cashless Society" and the article "Furniture Chain Won't Take Cash" in the text. Use these two articles to answer the following questions.

1. Which form of money ($M1$, $M2$,... etc.) is most affected in both articles? _____

2. According to the article about the furniture store, currency no longer performs which of the functions of money? _____

3. Which passage indicates the impact the no-cash policy will have on the furniture store?
   _____

4. Because the ruble has lost its value, people are using _____ to acquire goods and services.

5. Which passage indicates the impact on the Russian economy as a result of barter? _____
   _____

Exercise 4

This exercise focuses on the reserve requirement and its impact on the money supply.

1. Given the following reserve ratios, calculate the money multiplier for each.

   a. Reserve ratio = 10 percent   Money multiplier = _____
   b. Reserve ratio = 20 percent   Money multiplier = _____
   c. Reserve ratio = 30 percent   Money multiplier = _____

2. As the reserve ratio increases, the money multiplier (increases, decreases).

3. As the money multiplier decreases, potential deposit creation (increases, decreases).

4. T   F   An increase in the reserve ratio functions as a constraint on the deposit creation of the banking system.

Common Errors

The first statement in each "common error" below is incorrect. Each incorrect statement is followed by a corrected version and an explanation.

1. Banks can't create money. WRONG!

   Banks can and do create money. RIGHT!

It should be obvious by now that banks and other depository institutions are very important participants in the money-supply process. They create money by granting loans to borrowers and accomplish their role by adding to their customers' transactions accounts. The accounts are money just as much as the coins and currency in your wallet are money. The banks create (supply) money, but only in response to borrowers' demands for it. Without customers demanding loans, banks wouldn't be able to create money at all.

2. Banks hold your deposits in their vaults. WRONG!

Banks don't hold your deposits in their vaults. (And neither do other depository institutions.) RIGHT!

You can look at this two ways. First, when you deposit your paycheck, there's nothing for the bank to "hold" in its vault, except the check, and that is returned to the person who wrote it. Second, if you deposited coin or cash, it's all put together and you can't distinguish any one person's deposit from any other person's deposit. Even then, when "cash in vault" becomes too large, much of it is shipped away by armored truck to the Federal Reserve Bank. (This is described in Chapter 14.) Thus, banks don't hold your deposits in their vaults.

3. Gold and silver are intrinsically valuable and are necessary to secure the value of a currency. WRONG!

Money can serve as a store of value, a standard of value, and a medium of exchange without being backed by gold and silver. RIGHT!

While precious metals such as gold and silver have frequently been used to back currencies, they do not back the dollar today. Like other commodities, their value in terms of dollars continually fluctuates in response to supply and demand conditions. International monetary authorities have attempted to "demonetize" the precious metals and have been successful in holding the price of these metals down in terms of the major currencies. Nevertheless, during periods of calamity and fear, these precious metals are hoarded because people believe these items have intrinsic value; they then do take the role of a store of value.

4. Banks are irresponsible if they fail to store all of the money that is deposited with them so that it is available on demand. WRONG!

Banks must lend most of the money that is deposited with them so that they can earn interest and pay interest on those deposits. RIGHT!

If banks allowed money just to sit in the vault, no productive use could be made of the money. Banks are useful as the intermediary between savers, who have the money, and spenders, who wish to borrow the money. Through their lending activity, banks promote efficiency. That means the money is not sitting idle in the bank's vault.

•ANSWERS•

Using Key Terms
Across
1. bank reserves
5. excess reserves
7. transactions account
9. required reserves
10. money multiplier

Down

2. aggregate demand
3. deposit creation
4. barter
6. money supply
8. reserve ratio
10. money

True or False

1. F Transactions accounts permit direct payment to a third party by check or debit card. In addition to traditional checking accounts, NOW accounts, ATS accounts, credit union share drafts, and demand deposits at mutual savings banks also serve this purpose.
2. F Credit cards are a payment service, not a final form of payment, i.e. credit card balances must be paid by cash or check.
3. T
4. F The single action of withdrawal simply changes the composition of the money supply from, for example, a transactions account balance to cash. However, the banking system now has less money to lend out and the potential exists for a reduction in the money supply.
5. T
6. F The higher the reserve ratio, the lower the lending power of the banks.
7. T
8. F The amount any one bank can lend is equal to its excess reserves.
9. T
10. T

Multiple Choice

1. d	5. d	9. d	13. a	17. a
2. a	6. c	10. d	14. d	18. d
3. c	7. c	11. d	15. b	19. b
4. a	8. c	12. a	16. c	20. a

Problems and Applications

Exercise 1

1. 0.25, 4
2. excess reserves
3. $150,000; $100,000
4. $100,000
5. $666,666.67

Exercise 2

1. **Table 13.3 Answer**

Assets		Liabilities	
Required reserves	$22,000	Transaction accounts	$110,000
Excess reserves	8,000		
Other assets	80,000		
Total	$110,000	Total	$110,000

2. **Table 13.4 Answer**

Assets		Liabilities	
Required reserves	$21,600	Transaction accounts	$108,000
Excess reserves	6,400		
Other assets	80,000		
Total	$108,000	Total	$108,000

3. **Table 13.5 Answer**

Assets		Liabilities	
Required reserves	$21,280	Transaction accounts	$106,400
Excess reserves	5,120		
Other assets	80,000		
Total	$106,400	Total	$106,400

4. Bank A lent $8,000
   Bank B lent $6,400
   Bank C lent $5,120
   Total loans made so far $19,520
5. 1/reserve ratio = 1/0.20 = 5
6. potential deposit creation = initial excess reserves x money multiplier = $8,000 x 5 = $40,000

Exercise 3

1. $M1$
2. medium of exchange
3. "Scan does less than 3% of its business in cash . . ."
4. "Barter is poisoning the development of capitalism . . . because it consumes huge amounts of time that would be better spent producing goods."

Exercise 4

1. a. 10
   b. 5
   c. 3.33
2. decrease
3. decrease
4. T

CHAPTER 14

The Federal Reserve System

Quick Review

In the preceding chapter we saw how money was created and received strong signals that money must somehow be controlled if the economy is to perform according to our expectations. In this chapter we examine these questions:

- How does government control the amount of money in the economy?
- Which government agency is responsible for exercising this control?
- How are banks and bond markets affected by the government's policies?

The answer to all of these questions rests with the Federal Reserve System (the Fed), the central bank of the United States. All banks are subject to the reserve requirements imposed by the Fed. The Fed is independent of congressional whims and has a structure that is unique among the world's central banks because it is made up of twelve regional Federal Reserve banks. The Chairman of the Board of Governors is the chief spokesman for the Fed.

The Federal Reserve System has three basic tools that it can use to control the money supply: open-market operations, the reserve requirement, and the discount rate. Open-market operations are implemented by the Fed Open Market Committee, and are the most important. To increase the size of the money supply, the Open Market Committee orders the purchase of government securities (bonds) in the open market. These purchases increase bank reserves and lending potential and may have the additional effect of raising bond prices (lowering yields).

The Fed could accomplish the same objective, although with less certainty, by lowering the discount rate. A lower discount rate encourages member banks to borrow reserves and acquire lending potential. The Fed can also modify reserve requirements, but these are not changed often or by large amounts. When the reserve requirement is raised, excess reserves are transformed into required reserves; when the reserve requirement is lowered, required reserves are transformed into excess reserves. In addition, there is an inverse relationship between the size of the reserve requirement and the size of the money multiplier. Any change in the reserve requirement will, *ceteris paribus*, affect the lending potential of the banking system.

There are occasions when the Fed will restrain the economy with a "tight money" policy—by selling bonds in the open market, raising reserve requirements and raising the discount rate. In practice, restraint is basically applied through open-market operations.

The idea of what constitutes a "bank" has changed dramatically in the last twenty years. Before 1980, the Fed's power over the money supply was weakening because so many financial institutions remained outside its control. As a result, Congress passed the Monetary Control Act of 1980 to allow the Fed to reassert control over the money supply and foster competition among financial institutions. Over the intervening period banks have declined in importance while "nonbanks" have grown more important. The nonbanks hold accounts and make loans too. Banks now must compete more vigorously against money-market mutual funds, brokerage houses, foreign and domestic corporations, and so on. Banks are certainly less important than they used to be. The Fed must focus more on nonbank financial institutions as well if it is to maintain control of the money supply in the future.

Learning Objectives

After reading Chapter 14 and doing the following exercises, you should:

1. Be familiar with the organization, structure, and purposes of the Federal Reserve System.
2. Know how the reserve requirement can be changed to achieve a money-supply objective.
3. Know what the money multiplier is and how it is used.
4. Know the meaning of "federal funds" and the "federal funds rate."
5. Know how the discount rate can be changed to achieve a given policy objective.
6. Understand the distinction between the interest rate on a bond and the yield from a bond.
7. Be able to demonstrate the inverse relationship between interest rates and bond prices.
8. Understand how the Fed's activities in the bond market alter portfolio decisions of bond sellers and bond buyers.
9. Understand how the Open Market Committee can achieve a given policy objective by buying or selling securities.
10. Know the background and provisions of the Monetary Control Act of 1980 and recent changes in the structure of the financial system.

Using Key Terms

Across

5. The interest rate one bank charges another bank when lending reserves.
6. Equal to total reserves minus required reserves.
7. The interest rate the Fed charges a bank when lending reserves.
10. Represent a leakage from the flow of money because they cannot be used to make loans.
12. The choice of where to place idle funds.

Down

1. The reciprocal of the required reserve ratio.
2. The use of money and credit controls to influence the macroeconomy.
3. The purchase and sale of government securities by the Fed in order to change bank reserves.
4. The annual interest payment divided by the bond's purchase price.
7. Controlled by the Fed through the use of the reserve requirement, the discount rate, and open market operations.
9. Refers to the Fed lending reserves to private banks.
11. A certificate acknowledging a debt and terms for repayment.

Puzzle 14.1

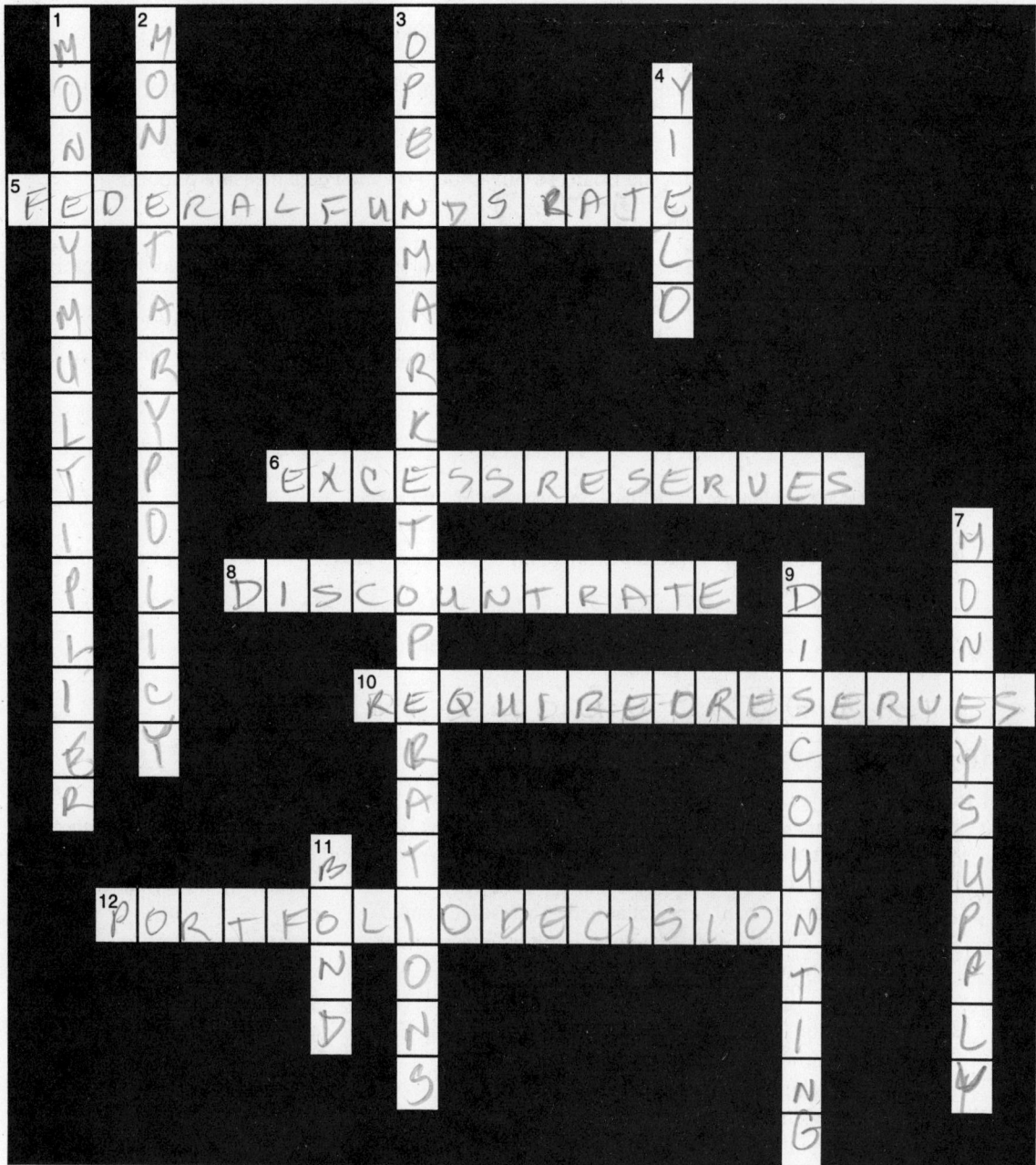

True or False: *Circle your choice and explain why any false statements are incorrect.*

T **F** 1. The Federal Reserve banks hold deposits of banks and other business firms.

T F 2. The Board of Governors is responsible for setting monetary policy.

T F 3. The Fed is not one bank but is actually twelve regional banks with central control located in Washington D.C.

T F 4. The fourteen-year terms for the Board of Governors give the Fed a measure of political independence.

T **F** 5. Monetary policy is the use of money and government spending to influence macroeconomic activity.

T **F** 6. If the Fed wishes to create the conditions under which the money supply can be increased, it can increase the reserve requirement.

T F 7. When the reserve requirement is increased, excess reserves are reduced.

T **F** 8. The FOMC implements monetary policy by adjusting reserve requirements and discount rates.

T F 9. Open-market operations are the principal mechanism for altering the reserves of the banking system.

T **F** 10. To increase the lending capacity of banks, the Fed sells securities.

Multiple Choice: *Select the correct answer.*

_b_ 1. Suppose that Brian receives a check for $100 from a bank in Atlanta. He deposits the check in his account at his Baltimore bank. Brian's Baltimore bank will collect the $100 from the:
   (a)   Atlanta bank.
   (b)   Baltimore bank's regional Federal Reserve Bank.
   (c)   The central Federal Reserve Bank in Washington.
   (d)   Board of Governors.

_d_ 2. Which of the following is a service performed by the Federal Reserve banks?
   (a)   Clearing checks between commercial banks.
   (b)   Holding reserves of commercial banks.
   (c)   Providing currency to commercial banks.
   (d)   All of the above.

_d_ 3. The formulation of general Federal Reserve policy is the responsibility of the:
   (a)   Federal Open Market Committee.
   (b)   Federal Advisory Council.
   (c)   Regional Federal Reserve banks.
   (d)   Board of Governors.

d 4. Members of the Federal Reserve Board of Governors:
   (a) Are appointed to fourteen-year terms by the president of the United States.
   (b) Are relatively immune to short-term political pressures.
   (c) May not be reappointed after serving a full term.
   (d) All of the above are true.

c 5. Which of the following is responsible for buying and selling government securities to influence reserves in the banking system?
   (a) The Board of Governors.
   (b) The twelve regional Federal Reserve Banks.
   (c) The Federal Open Market Committee.
   (d) The Executive Branch of the government.

a 6. Which of the following is *not* one of the tools of monetary policy used by the Fed?
   (a) Expulsion from Fed membership.
   (b) Changing the reserve requirement.
   (c) Changing the discount rate.
   (d) Performing open-market operations.

a 7. When the Fed wishes to increase the excess reserves of the member banks, it:
   (a) Buys securities.
   (b) Raises the discount rate.
   (c) Raises the reserve requirement.
   (d) Sells securities.

a 8. The reserve requirement is:
   (a) A powerful tool which can cause abrupt changes in the money supply.
   (b) The most often used tool on the part of the Fed.
   (c) A tool which has little impact on the money supply.
   (d) Effective in changing excess reserves but not the money multiplier.

d 9. A bank can acquire additional reserves by:
   (a) Selling securities.
   (b) Borrowing from the discount window.
   (c) Borrowing in the Fed funds market.
   (d) All of the above.

a 10. The federal funds market is a market in which:
   (a) Banks lend excess reserves to other banks.
   (b) Government securities are bought and sold.
   (c) Reserves are discounted outside the Fed's control.
   (d) The Fed lends to member banks.

b 11. Discounting refers to the Fed's practice of:
   (a) Selling securities at the federal funds rate.
   (b) Lending reserves to private banks.
   (c) Lending at the prime rate.
   (d) Purchasing securities at the lowest available federal funds rate.

c 12. The most frequently used tool on the part of the Fed is:
   (a) The reserve requirement.
   (b) The discount rate.
   (c) Open-market operations.
   (d) The Fed funds rate.

a 13. Suppose that the Fed desires to sell more bonds than people are willing to purchase. The most likely result of this situation would be a:
   (a) Decrease in the price of bonds.
   (b) Switch to another type of monetary policy lever by the Fed.
   (c) Switch to fiscal policy.
   (d) Purchase of the unsold bonds by the Fed.

b 14. When the Fed buys bonds from the public:
   (a) It decreases the flow of reserves to the banking system.
   (b) It increases the flow of reserves to the banking system.
   (c) It decreases the money supply.
   (d) It decreases the discount rate.

d 15. If the Fed buys bonds from the public, which of the following changes are likely to occur?
   (a) The public's holdings of bonds would decrease.
   (b) M1 would increase.
   (c) Excess reserves would increase.
   (d) All of the above would occur.

b 16. The Fed can decrease the Federal Funds rate by:
   (a) Selling bonds.
   (b) Buying bonds.
   (c) Simply announcing a lower rate since the Fed has direct control of this interest rate.
   (d) Changing the money multiplier.

a 17. A growing economy needs a:
   (a) Steadily increasing supply of money to finance market exchanges.
   (b) Continually increasing supply of money to finance the government's expenditures.
   (c) Constant supply of money to keep inflation under control.
   (d) Decreasing supply of money to keep interest rates low.

b 18. An increase in the discount rate:
   (a) Reduces the cost of reserves borrowed from the Fed.
   (b) Signals the Fed's desire to restrain money growth.
   (c) Signals the Fed's desire to support credit creation.
   (d) Signals the Fed's eagerness to lend additional reserves.

d 19. The Monetary Control Act of 1980:
   (a) Created greater competition in the banking industry.
   (b) Extended the Fed's control of the money supply.
   (c) Gave all depository institutions access to the Fed's discount window.
   (d) All of the above.

d 20. Which of the following has contributed to the reduction in Fed control of the money supply?
   (a) A network of international money clearinghouses.
   (b) The fact that approximately two-thirds of the U.S. dollars in circulation are held abroad.
   (c) International credit cards.
   (d) All of the above contribute.

Problems and Applications

The first three exercises demonstrate how monetary policy might work in a hypothetical situation.

Exercise 1

This exercise is similar to a problem in the text, which shows how to understand the accounts for the entire banking system. The focus of this exercise is the reserve requirement.

Suppose the Fed wishes to expand $M1$. Carefully read the assumptions below and then work through the exercise step-by-step to achieve the policy objective. Assume:

- The banks in the system initially have $240 million of transactions deposits.
- The banking system initially has no excess reserves.
- The initial reserve requirement is 0.25.
- The banks make loans in the full amount of any excess reserves that they acquire.
- All loans flow back into the banking system as transactions deposits.
- The combined balance sheet of the banks in the system is as shown in Table 14.1.

Table 14.1
Balance sheet of banking system when reserve requirement is 0.25 (millions of dollars)

Total reserves	$ 60	Transactions accounts	$240
Required, $60			
Excess, $0			
Securities	80		
Loans	100		
Total	$240	Total	$240

1. Suppose the Fed lowers the reserve requirement to 0.20. How many dollars of excess reserves does this create? _____

2. How large are required reserves now? _____

3. How large are total reserves? _____

4. What is the additional lending capacity of the banking system as a result of the change in the reserve requirement from 0.25 to 0.20? _____

5. Assume the banks lend all excess reserves. Reconstruct the balance sheet in Table 14.2 to show the new totals for the accounts affected in the banking system because of the new loans.

Table 14.2
Balance sheet of banking system when reserve requirement is 0.20 (millions of dollars)

Total reserves	$_____	Transactions accounts	$_____
Required, _____			
Excess, _____			
Securities	_____		
Loans	_____		
Total	$_____	Total	$_____

6. The money supply (*M*1) expanded by _____ .

7. Total reserves have increased by _____ .

8. Loans have increased by _____ .

Exercise 2

Like a problem in the text, this exercise shows how the money supply can be changed. The focus of this exercise is open-market policy.

Suppose the Fed wants to expand the money supply using open-market operations and it is faced with the balance sheet of the banking system as shown in Table 14.3. Suppose further that:

- The banking system initially has no excess reserves.
- The reserve requirement is 0.20.
- The banks make loans in the full amount of any excess reserves that they acquire.
- All loans flow back into the banking system as transactions deposits.

Table 14.3
Balance sheet of banking system
(millions of dollars)

Total reserves	$ 60	Transactions accounts	$300
Required, $60			
Excess, $0			
Securities	80		
Loans	160		
Total	$300	Total	$300

1. Suppose the Open Market Committee buys $10 million of securities from the commercial banking system. In Table 14.4 show the changes and new totals for the various accounts on the balance sheet of the commercial banks after this transaction but before any new loans are made or called in.

Table 14.4
Balance sheet of commercial banking system after FOMC buys $10 million of securities
(millions of dollars)

Total reserves	$_____	Transactions accounts	$_____
Required, _____			
Excess, _____			
Securities	_____		
Loans	_____		
Total	$_____	Total	$_____

2. Suppose the banking system now expands its loans and transactions accounts by the maximum amount it can on the basis of its _____ in excess reserves.

3. The total lending capacity for the banking system will increase by _____ .

192

4. Assume banks fully utilize their new lending capacity. In Table 14.5 complete the balance sheet for the banking system showing the new totals for all of the accounts after loans have been made. (*Remember*: The reserve ratio is 0.20.)

Table 14.5
Balance sheet of banking system after expansion of loans and deposits (millions of dollars)

Total reserves	$_____	Transactions accounts	$_____
Required, _____			
Excess, _____			
Securities	_____		
Loans	_____		
Total	$_____	Total	$_____

5. As a result of the open-market operations, the money supply has expanded by a total of _____ .

6. Required reserves have gone up by _____ .

7. Loans have increased by _____ .

Exercise 3

This exercise demonstrates what might happen when the Fed lowers the discount rate.

Suppose the Fed wants to expand the money supply by changing the discount rate. It is faced with the balance sheet of the banking system as shown in Table 14.6. Carefully read the assumptions below and then work through the exercise step-by-step to achieve the policy objective. Assume that:

- The banking system initially has no excess reserves.
- The initial reserve requirement is 0.20.
- The banks in the system respond to each percentage point drop in the discount rate by borrowing $2 million from the Fed.
- The banks make loans in the full amount of any excess reserves that they acquire.
- All loans flow back into the banking system as transactions deposits.

Table 14.6
Balance sheet of banking system (millions of dollars)

Total reserves	$ 70	Transactions accounts	$350
Required, $70			
Excess, $0			
Securities	70		
Loans	210		
Total	$350	Total	$350

1. Suppose that the Fed now lowers the discount rate by 1 percentage point and that the banking system responds as indicated in the third assumption above. As a result of this policy initiative, the banks in the system will now borrow _____ from the Fed, all of which is (excess/ required) reserves. On the basis of this lending potential, the banks together can expand their loans by _____ .

2. In Table 14.7, assume the banks have made the additional loans. Complete the balance sheet to show the final effect of the change in the discount rate.

Table 14.7
Final balance sheet of banking system
(millions of dollars)

Total reserves	$_____	Transactions accounts	$_____
Required, _____			
Excess, _____			
Securities	_____		
Loans	_____	Discounts payable to Fed	_____
Total	$_____	Total	$_____

3. The effect of lowering the discount rate is an increase in the money supply of _____ .

Exercise 4

In order to understand how open-market operations work, it is important to understand how the bond market works. The following exercise will demonstrate how the Fed can make bonds more or less attractive for people to buy.

1. Assume you purchase a bond for $1000. The face value of the bond is $1000 and the bond pays 10 percent interest annually. What is the dollar amount of the annual interest payment? _____

2. What is the yield on the bond? (*Hint*: Refer to the formula on page 280 in the text.) _____

3. Now assume that instead of paying $1000 for the bond, you buy the same bond for $850. (The annual interest payment stays the same because it is based on the face value of the bond.) Calculate the yield on the bond now. _____

4. When the price of a bond decreases, the yield (increases, decreases) and the bond becomes (more, less) attractive to people. There is a (direct, inverse) relationship between the bond price and the bond yield.

Exercise 5

The media often provide information about changes in policy by the Federal Reserve System. This exercise will use one of the articles in the text to show the kind of information to look for.

Reread the article in the text entitled "Fed Cuts Deposit-Reserve Requirements." Then answer questions 1-5.

1. What central monetary authority is mentioned in the article?_____

2. What phrase in the article indicates the monetary instrument that is being used by the central monetary authority?_____

3. Which instrument is being used?
   (a) Reserve requirement.
   (b) Open-market operations.
   (c) Discount rate.
   (d) Other (Specify: _____)

194

4. What passage indicates in which direction the monetary instrument(s) is being changed by the central monetary authority to influence the money supply?_____

_____

5. The policy initiative (lowers, raises) the quantity of money relative to what it would have been without the change.

Common Errors

The first statement in each "common error" below is incorrect. Each incorrect statement is followed by a corrected version and an explanation.

1. Bank reserves are required for the safety of depositors' money. WRONG!

   Bank reserves are for control of the money supply. RIGHT!

   Many people have the idea that bank reserves provide for the safety of depositors' money. They don't. The statistics in this chapter indicate that the amount of demand deposits is several times larger than that of reserves. Reserves are for control of the money supply. The FDIC provides for safety of deposits by insuring them. Reserves are not principally for depositors' safety.

2. Deposits of cash are necessary to start the process of lending and deposit creation. WRONG!

   To start the lending process, the banks must acquire reserves from outside the banking system. RIGHT!

   Many find it difficult to understand that for deposit creation to occur, the banking system needs only to acquire reserves from outside the system or be able to stretch existing reserves further. It may acquire reserves by selling a security to the Fed or by borrowing from the Fed. An individual bank, however, may acquire reserves from another bank. So to the extent that it has increased its reserves, another bank's reserves have shrunk. Thus, the system has no more reserves after the transaction than it had before, and so the system's lending capacity is unchanged.

3. When the Fed sells government bonds in open-market operations, it is increasing the money supply. WRONG!

   When the Fed sells government bonds, the buyers pay with reserves, which means there are fewer reserves and less money. RIGHT!

   The key here is to realize that payment of reserves to the Fed means that there are fewer reserves available to the entire banking system. By selling bonds the Fed is tightening monetary policy.

Using Key Terms
Across
5.   federal funds rate
6.   excess reserves
8.   discount rate
10. required reserves
12. portfolio decision

Down
1.   money multiplier
2.   monetary policy
3.   open market operations
4.   yield
7.   money supply
9.   discounting
11. bond

True or False

1. F   Federal Reserve banks hold *reserves* for banks and other types of financial institutions.
2. T
3. T
4. T
5. F   Monetary policy is the use of changes in the money supply and credit conditions to influence the macroeconomy.
6. F   The Fed has to *reduce* the reserve requirement to increase the money supply.
7. T
8. F   The FOMC implements monetary policy by buying and selling bonds.
9. T
10. F   The Fed *buys* securities to increase the lending capacity.

Multiple Choice

1. b	5. c	9. d	13. a	17. a
2. d	6. a	10. a	14. b	18. b
3. d	7. a	11. b	15. d	19. d
4. d	8. a	12. c	16. b	20. d

Problems and Applications

Exercise 1

1. $12 million
2. $48 million
3. $60 million
4. $60 million

5. **Table 14.2 Answer**

Total reserves	$ 60	Transactions accounts	$300
Required, $60			
Excess, $0			
Securities	80		
Loans	160		
Total	$300	Total	$300

6. $60 million
7. Zero
8. $60 million

Exercise 2

1. **Table 14.4 Answer**

Total reserves	$ 70	Transactions accounts	$300
Required, $60			
Excess, $10			
Securities	70		
Loans	160		
Total	$300	Total	$300

2. $10 million
3. $50 million

4. **Table 14.5 Answer**

Total reserves	$ 70	Transactions accounts	$350
Required, $70			
Excess, $0			
Securities	70		
Loans	210		
Total	$350	Total	$350

5. $50 million
6. $10 million
7. $50 million

Exercise 3

1. $2 million; excess; $10 million

2. **Table 14.7 Answer**

Total reserves	$ 72	Transactions accounts	$360
Required, $72			
Excess, $0			
Securities	70		
Loans	220		2
Total	$362	Total	$362

3. $10 million

Exercise 4

1. $100
2. 10 percent
3. 11.76 percent
4. Increase, more, inverse

Exercise 5

1. The Federal Reserve Board
2. The title, "Deposit-Reserve Requirements"
3. a
4. "The Fed cut to 10% from 12% the percentage of checking-account deposits that banks are required to hold as reserves."
5. Raises

CHAPTER 15
Monetary Policy

Quick Review

In this chapter, the focus is on monetary policy and the Fed's role in attempting to move the economy toward its macroeconomic goals. Specifically, we look for answers to the following questions:

- What's the relationship between the money supply and aggregate demand?
- How can the Fed use its control of the money supply to alter macro outcomes?
- How effective is monetary policy, compared to fiscal policy?

By controlling the banks' ability to make loans ("create money"), the Federal Reserve System controls the money supply. The amount of money in the economy, however, reflects money demand as well as money supply.

The demand for money has three components:
1. The transactions demand, which reflects normal needs for coin, currency, and checking accounts in order to buy and sell goods and services.
2. The precautionary demand, which is what people feel they need for potential emergencies and other unforeseen needs that may arise.
3. The speculative demand, in which money is held temporarily as a secure liquid asset in anticipation of profiting from changes in interest rates.

Both the level of GDP and interest rates influence transactions and precautionary demand. Speculative demand, however, is most influenced by interest rates. The equilibrium rate of interest is the rate that equates the quantity of money demanded with the quantity of money supplied.

If the Fed wishes to stimulate aggregate spending, it will drive down interest rates by expanding the money supply. This lower interest rate stimulates components of aggregate demand (e.g., investment), which are influenced by interest rates. The success of monetary policy depends on the elasticity of the demand for money and the sensitivity of the spending decisions to changes in interest rates.

One way to visualize the transmission mechanism from the money market to aggregate demand is as follows: An increase in the money supply will, *ceteris paribus*, drive the interest rate down and stimulate greater investment spending, thus shifting the aggregate demand curve to the right. There are constraints to be considered though and things might not work so smoothly. Will the banks be willing to lend? Will the increase in the money supply force the interest rate down, or will it fall into the Keynesian liquidity trap? Will low expectations leave the business sector without incentives to increase investment? Or if monetary restraint is being applied and the money supply is reduced, will optimistic firms and households borrow more in spite of higher interest rates? Finally, since the money market is a global one, if domestic interest rates get too high, will borrowers look abroad?

There is substantial controversy over the transmission mechanism implied by the use of monetary policy. Monetarists believe that the link is direct. They use the equation of exchange ($MV = PQ$) to demonstrate this. Assuming V is constant, any increase in M must be translated into greater spending regardless of what happens to interest rates. The Monetarists further assert that Q is constant as well, creating a vertical aggregate supply curve at the natural rate of unemployment. Thus, an increase in M translates into an increase in P. Monetarists, as a result, advocate steady, predictable changes in the money supply.

Monetarists and Keynesians alike argue that monetary policy can affect nominal, if not real, interest rates. When interest rates rise, some market participants (e.g., corporations) fare better than others. This influences the content of GDP and can influence the distribution of income as well. The Monetarist-Keynesian debate hinges on which policy lever (M or V) is likely to be effective. Monetarists and Keynesians are led to radically different views as to the efficacy of monetary *and* fiscal policy. The Fed has adopted an eclectic approach to policy making and uses several measures of the money supply and interest rates to gauge the state of the economy. $M2$ proved unreliable as a policy guide.

Learning Objectives

After reading Chapter 15 and doing the following exercises, you should:

1. Understand the opportunity cost of holding idle funds.
2. Know the determinants of the transactions, precautionary, and speculative demands for money.
3. Be able to graph money-market equilibrium.
4. Understand how changes in the money supply lead to changes in the interest rate.
5. Understand how changes in the money supply are transmitted to aggregate demand.
6. Be able to contrast expansionary and restrictive monetary-policy initiatives.
7. Be able to describe the constraints on *both* expansionary and restrictive monetary policy.
8. Understand the equation of exchange and the assumptions on which it is based.
9. Understand the relationship between the natural rate of unemployment and the aggregate supply curve.
10. Know the mechanism by which changes in M affect GDP in the monetarist model.
11. Understand and be able to calculate the real rate of interest.
12. Be able to contrast Keynesian and monetarist views of how monetary policy works.
13. Be able to articulate the effects of monetary policy on the mix of output and the distribution of income.
14. Be able to contrast Keynesian and monetarist views of monetary and fiscal policy.

Using Key Terms

Fill in the puzzle on the opposite page with the appropriate term from the list of Key Terms at the end of the chapter in the text.

Across

2. The Federal Reserve System can use its powers to alter the _____.
4. Money held for future financial opportunities.
8. Equal to the nominal rate of interest minus the inflation rate.
9. The downward-sloping curve in Figure 15.1 in the text.
11. The choice of how and where to hold idle funds.
12. A decrease in private-sector borrowing and spending because of an increase in government spending.
14. The number of times per year a dollar is used to purchase final goods and services.
15. Determined by the intersection of the money demand curve and the money supply curve in Figure 15.2.
16. The curve that shifts to the right in Figure 15.3 as the result of an increase in the money supply.

Down

1. Money held for everyday purchases.
3. Money held for emergencies.
5. The mathematical formula used by monetarists to explain how monetary policy works.
6. The long-run rate of unemployment determined by structural forces.
7. The use of money and credit controls to influence the macroeconomy.
10. The horizontal portion of the money demand curve in Figure 15.4 in the text.
13. The price paid for the use of money.

Puzzle 15.1

True or False: *Circle your choice and explain why any false statements are incorrect.*

T **F** 1. People who hold idle money balances incur no costs.

T F 2. The downward slope of the money-demand curve indicates that the quantity of money people are willing and able to hold increases as interest rates fall.

T F 3. When the Fed buys securities and causes interest rates to fall, investment spending increases thereby increasing AD.

T **F** 4. Monetary policy affects the macro economy by shifting aggregate supply.

T F 5. If the interest rate is in the liquidity-trap range, monetary policy is ineffective.

T F 6. The liquidity trap occurs because the opportunity cost of holding money is low at low interest rates.

T **F** 7. Monetarists believe that changes in the money supply increase aggregate demand by lowering interest rates.

T F 8. According to the equation of exchange, total spending will rise if the money supply grows and velocity is stable.

T F 9. The assumption of a natural rate of unemployment implies that M is stable in the equation of exchange.

T F 10. Monetarists believe an increase in government spending will lead to the "crowding out" of an equal amount of private spending.

Multiple Choice: *Select the correct answer.*

_d_ 1. Those who hold idle balances for speculative purposes are willing to incur the opportunity costs of doing so because they expect:
   (a) Interest rates are going to rise.
   (b) Bond yields are going to fall.
   (c) Bond prices are going to rise.
   (d) All of the above.

_a_ 2. By adding together the speculative, transactions, and precautionary demands for money, one can obtain:
   (a) The market demand curve for money.
   (b) The Keynesian liquidity trap.
   (c) The monetarist demand-for-money curve.
   (d) The market supply curve for money.

_____ 3. The intersection of the market demand for money and the market supply of money establishes the:
   (a) Equilibrium of supply and demand of investment goods.
   (b) Real rate of interest.
   (c) Equilibrium rate of interest.
   (d) Equilibrium average price level for the economy.

✗ b ___ 4. If the supply curve of money is vertical, what should happen to the equilibrium interest rate and equilibrium quantity of money as a result of a recession, *ceteris paribus*?
    (a)   Equilibrium interest rate should go up.
    (b)   Equilibrium interest rate should go down, but equilibrium quantity would remain unchanged.
    (c)   Both equilibrium interest rate and equilibrium quantity should go up.
    (d)   Equilibrium interest rate should go down, and equilibrium quantity should go up.

✗ d ___ 5. There is an inverse relationship between the quantity of money demanded and:
    (a)   The price of money.
    (b)   The interest rate.
    (c)   The opportunity cost of owning money.
    (d)   All of the above.

✗ d ___ 6. In the Keynesian model, the effectiveness of monetary policy depends on which of the following?
    (a)   The Fed's ability to influence the money supply.
    (b)   The sensitivity of interest rates to changes in the money supply.
    (c)   The sensitivity of investment spending to changes in interest rates.
    (d)   All of the above.

✗ a ___ 7. Which of the following is a series of events used by Keynesians to describe the steps by which expansionary monetary policy works in the short run?
    (a)   Increase in M, decrease in interest rate, increase in I.
    (b)   Decrease in interest rate, increase in M, increase in I.
    (c)   Increase in M, decrease in I, decrease in interest rate.
    (d)   Increase in M, increase in interest rate, increase in I.

___ 8. Monetary policy will be most effective if:
    (a)   The demand curve for money is horizontal and the investment demand curve is downward-sloping.
    (b)   The demand curve for money is downward-sloping but the investment demand curve is vertical.
    (c)   The demand curve for money and the investment demand curve are downward-sloping, but neither is vertical nor horizontal.
    (d)   The demand curve for money and the investment demand curve are vertical or both curves are horizontal.

___ 9. What should happen to the equilibrium interest rate and the corresponding rate of investment if the Fed lowers the minimum reserve ratio?
    (a)   Equilibrium interest rate and the rate of investment should both go up.
    (b)   Equilibrium interest rate should go up, and the rate of investment should go down.
    (c)   Equilibrium interest rate should go down, and the rate of investment should go up.
    (d)   Equilibrium interest rate and the rate of investment should both go down.

___ 10. Which of the following Fed actions is most likely to increase the aggregate demand curve?
    (a)   Buying bonds in the open market.
    (b)   Raising the discount rate.
    (c)   Raising the reserve requirement.
    (d)   Raising the federal funds rate.

___ 11. Monetary stimulus will fail if:
    (a)   The investment demand curve is perfectly inelastic.
    (b)   Expectations of a boom cause the investment demand curve to shift to the right, offsetting interest-rate effects that would stimulate the economy.
    (c)   The investment demand curve is elastic.
    (d)   All of the above.

12. When the money market is in equilibrium in the liquidity trap:
    (a) The demand for money is perfectly insensitive to interest rates.
    (b) An increase in the money supply does not affect interest rates.
    (c) There is no speculative demand for money.
    (d) Investment spending falls to zero.

13. The effectiveness of restrictive monetary policy will be constrained because of:
    (a) High real rates of interest.
    (b) Low expectations.
    (c) Low real rates of interest.
    (d) The desire to hold excess reserves on the part of banks.

14. Which of the following positions can be attributed to the Monetarists?
    (a) "Only money matters."
    (b) "Velocity is constant."
    (c) "Government expenditures crowd out private expenditures."
    (d) All of the above are monetarist positions.

15. Which of the following is a monetarist assumption which plays a key role in explaining the monetarist view that fiscal policy is ineffective?
    (a) The liquidity trap.
    (b) Crowding out.
    (c) Unstable velocity of money.
    (d) A vertical aggregate demand curve.

16. Given monetarist assumptions about the shape of the aggregate supply curve, which of the following would most likely result if the Fed pursues expansionary monetary policy?
    (a) The equilibrium price level and output would both increase.
    (b) The equilibrium price level and output would both decrease.
    (c) The equilibrium price level would increase but output would stay the same.
    (d) The equilibrium output would increase but the price level would stay the same.

17. Monetarists argue that the income velocity of money:
    (a) Is constant.
    (b) Is reduced when fiscal policy puts idle money balances to work.
    (c) Increases when there is a recession because people accumulate money balances.
    (d) Increases as much as total spending falls so that MV remains constant.

18. The existence of a natural rate of unemployment implies that in the long run:
    (a) V in the equation of exchange is actually very unstable.
    (b) Monetary policy affects only the rate of inflation.
    (c) Q in the equation of exchange varies in proportion to M.
    (d) The rate of unemployment can be permanently reduced by more expansionary monetary and fiscal policies.

19. An increase in the money supply will:
    (a) Always cause inflation.
    (b) Cause inflation if aggregate supply is upward sloping or vertical.
    (c) Cause inflation only if aggregate supply is horizontal.
    (d) Never causes inflation.

_____ 20. Which of the following provides the correct policy targets of the three groups mentioned?
   (a) Keynesians target the money supply, monetarists target interest rates, and the Fed targets a mix of the two.
   (b) Keynesians target interest rates, monetarists target steady money growth, and the Fed targets a mix of the two.
   (c) The Fed targets the money supply, monetarists target interest rates, and Keynesians target a mix of the two.
   (d) The Fed targets interest rates, monetarists target steady money growth, and Keynesians target a mix of the two.

Problems and Applications
Exercise 1

This exercise focuses on the relationship between the money supply, interest rates, and aggregate demand.

Use Figure 15.1 to answer questions 1-7.

Figure 15.1

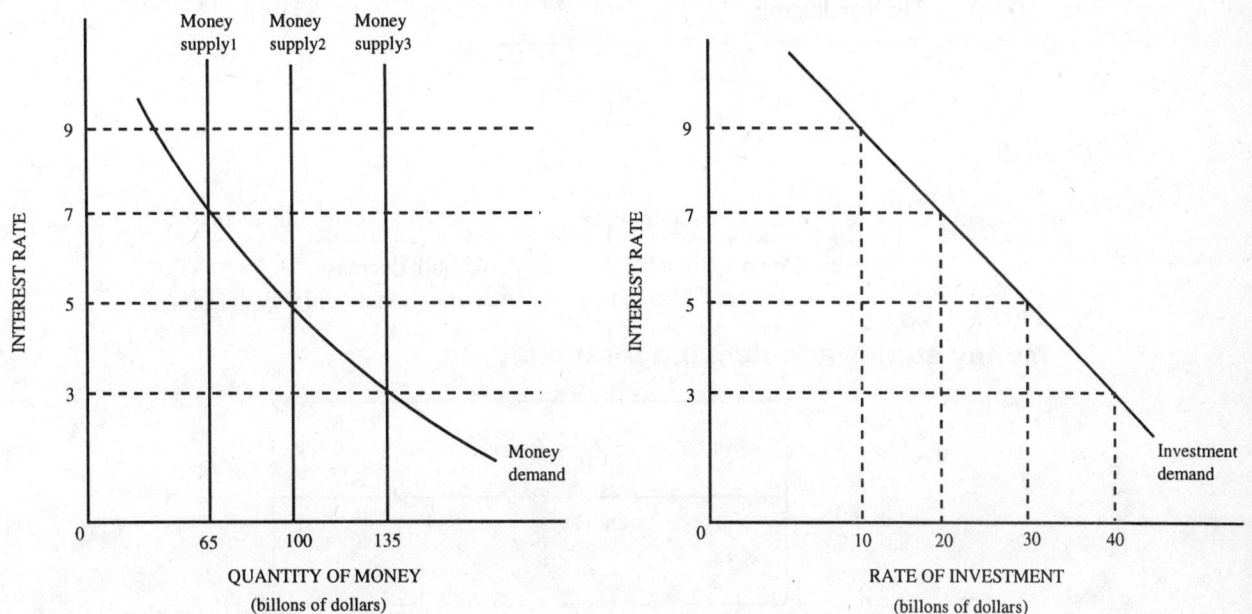

1. Assume the Federal Reserve sets the quantity of money at Money supply 2. The equilibrium interest rate is _____ percent and the equilibrium quantity of money is _____.

2. At the equilibrium interest rate in question 1 the rate of investment is equal to _____.

3. Now, suppose the Federal Reserve increases the money supply by $35 billion. The new equilibrium interest rate is _____ percent.

4. As a result of the (increase, decrease) in the interest rate, the rate of investment will (increase, decrease) to _____.

5. This (increase, decrease) in the rate of investment will cause aggregate _____ to (increase, decrease) or shift to the _____.

6. Now assume the Federal Reserve decides to change the money supply to Money supply 1. As a result of this change the equilibrium interest rate will (rise, fall) which will cause the rate of investment to (rise, fall).

7. Based on question 6, the change in the rate of investment will cause the level of aggregate demand to (rise, fall).

Exercise 2

This exercise examines what might happen if the Federal Reserve decided to increase the discount rate.

1. An increase in the discount rate will cause M1 to (increase, decrease, stay the same).

2. This change in the money supply will cause aggregate (demand, supply) to shift to the (left, right).

3. What other actions could the Fed take to achieve the same impact on aggregate demand? _____
_____

Exercise 3

The following exercise examines the relationship between monetary policy and changes in aggregate demand.

Table 15.3
Money supply and demand for money

Nominal interest rate (% per year)	Money demand ($ billions)	Supply of money ($ billions)
2	320	240
4	280	240
6	240	240
8	200	240

On the basis of Table 15.3, answer the indicated questions. Assume for every 1 percentage point decline in the interest rate, aggregate spending shifts upward by $20 billion.

1. In Table 15.3, the equilibrium interest rate is _____ percent per year.

2. If the interest rate in Table 15.3 is 8 percent, then there is a (surplus, shortage) of money, and the interest rate will (rise, fall, remain constant).

3. Assume the anticipated inflation rate is 4 percent. At the equilibrium nominal interest rate in Table 15.3, the real interest rate will be _____ percent per year.

4. If the real rate of interest is negative then, *ceteris paribus*:
   (a) The nominal interest rate is negative.
   (b) Monetary policy is tight.
   (c) The inflation rate is negative.
   (d) It pays to borrow.

5. Suppose the Fed buys $8 billion worth of securities on the open market and that the reserve requirement is 0.2. If the money supply expands to its maximum potential, the new equilibrium rate of interest in Table 15.3 would be, *ceteris paribus*, _____ percent per year.

6. The change in the equilibrium interest rate in Table 15.3 as a result of the Fed's purchase of $8 billion worth of securities would be _____ percentage points.

7. If every 1 percentage point decline in the interest rate causes investment to increase by $20 billion the change in the interest rate in question 6 would cause investment to (increase, decrease) by _____ .

Exercise 4

This exercise will help you check your understanding of how monetary and fiscal policy affect the economy.

1. Consider each of the statements in Table 15.2. Decide whether you think each was made by a Monetarist or a Keynesian, and place a check in the appropriate column. If you have difficulty, reread Tables 15.2 and 15.3 in the text.

Table 15.2
Comparing Keynesian and Monetarist views on monetary policy

	Monetarist	Keynesian
1. An increase in government spending will raise total spending.	_____	_____
2. A reduction in taxes will leave real output unaffected.	_____	_____
3. Real interest rates are determined by real growth.	_____	_____
4. Prices may be affected by increases in **G** or reductions in **T**.	_____	_____
5. Changes in the money supply definitely affect both the price level and aggregate spending.	_____	_____
6. Changes in **M** definitely affect changes in the normal interest rate.	_____	_____
7. Changes in **M** may cause changes in **V** and **Q**.	_____	_____
8. Changes in **M** definitely cannot lower the unemployment rate.	_____	_____
9. The liquidity trap may prevent the nominal interest rate from falling.	_____	_____
10. Monetary and fiscal policy must be used together to stabilize aggregate demand.	_____	_____

Exercise 5

The media often feature articles about changes in government policies that affect the money supply or about events that change the demand for money. This exercise will use one of the articles in the text to show the kind of information to look for.

Reread the article entitled "Interest Rates Cut in Europe." Then answer the following questions.

1. What passage specifically indicates why the European countries decided to lower interest rates?
    _____

2. How will businesses and consumers respond to the change?_____
    _____

3. How should the economy respond to the change? _____

4. If monetary policy is too stimulative, it can cause _____.

Common Errors

The first statement in each "common error" below is incorrect. Each incorrect statement is followed by a corrected version and an explanation.

1. When the interest rate goes down, the demand for money increases. WRONG!

    When the interest rate goes down, the quantity of money demanded increases. RIGHT!

    Don't fail to distinguish between a change in demand and a change in quantity demanded. Remember that each demand schedule (speculative, transactions, precautionary) is drawn on the assumption of *ceteris paribus*. Unless there is a change in one of the things held constant (e.g., expectations), there will be no change in demand when the interest rate falls, only a change in quantity demanded.

2. High nominal rates of interest mean high real rates of interest. WRONG!

    High nominal interest rates and high real interest rates do not necessarily coincide. RIGHT!

    High nominal interest rates and high real interest rates will coincide only if the average level of prices is not changing rapidly enough to offset the differential. For example, if the nominal rate is 10 percent and prices are rising at 10 percent, the real rate of interest is zero.

3. Monetary policy is easy to determine and to administer. WRONG!

    Monetary policy is difficult to determine and to administer. RIGHT!

    One could easily get the idea that monetary policy is easy to administer and that the Fed always knows the rate at which the money supply should grow. This is not so. Many variables intervene to make monetary policy difficult to prescribe and implement. Such variables include timing and the duration of a given policy, unanticipated events on the fiscal side, and problems abroad. The Fed's policy makers analyze the data available and do the best they can to achieve a given objective, which often involves compromises. The process is much more difficult than turning a printing press on and off.

•ANSWERS•

Using Key Terms
Across
2. money supply
4. speculative demand for money
8. real rate of interest
9. demand for money
11. portfolio decision
12. crowding out
14. income velocity of money
15. equilibrium rate of interest
16. aggregate demand

Down
1. transactions demand for money
3. precautionary demand for money
5. equation of exchange
6. natural rate of unemployment
7. monetary policy
10. liquidity trap
13. interest rate

True or False

1. F Holding money balances incurs an opportunity cost, e.g. giving up interest that could be earned on those balances.
2. T
3. T
4. F Monetary policy affects the macro economy by shifting aggregate demand.
5. T
6. T
7. F Monetarists believe that, according to the equation of exchange (MV = PQ), a change in the money supply must alter total spending, regardless of how interest rates change, given the assumption of a constant V.
8. T
9. F A natural rate of unemployment implies that Q is constant in the equation of exchange.
10. T

Multiple Choice

1. a	5. d	9. c	13. c	17. a
2. a	6. d	10. a	14. d	18. b
3. c	7. a	11. a	15. b	19. b
4. b	8. c	12. b	16. c	20. b

Problems and Applications

Exercise 1

1. 5, $100 billion
2. $30 billion
3. 3
4. decrease, increase, $40 billion
5. increase, demand, increase, right
6. rise, fall
7. fall

Exercise 2

1. decrease
2. demand, left
3. An open-market purchase of government securities or an increase in the reserve requirement.

Exercise 3

1. 6
2. surplus, fall
3. 2
4. d
5. 4
6. -2
7. increase, $40 billion

Exercise 4

Table 15.1 Answer

	Monetarist	Keynesian
1.		x
2.	x	
3.	x	
4.		x
5.	x	
6.	x	
7.		x
8.	x	
9.		x
10.		x

Exercise 5

1. ". . . coordinated response to sagging economic growth."
2. ". . . stimulate the economy by reducing the cost of borrowing, encouraging consumers to buy and businesses to invest."
3. The change should accelerate short-run economic growth.
4. inflation

210

C H A P T E R   16

Supply-Side Policy: Short-Run Options

Quick Review

This chapter identifies some supply-side policy options which can be used to affect macro outcomes by examining two questions:

- How does the aggregate supply curve affect macro outcomes?
- How can the aggregate supply curve be shifted?

Again we rely on the equation of exchange;

$$MV = PQ$$

where M = the quantity of money
V = velocity of circulation
P = average price of goods
Q = goods sold in a period

The demand-side levers are on the left-hand side of the equation. The responses of the economy to demand side policies depend on the slope of the aggregate supply curve. Monetarists view the aggregate supply as vertical at the natural rate of unemployment; a strict Keynesian view is that it is flat until full employment is reached. The consensus view accepts a rather smooth, upward-sloping curve which turns vertical at full employment.

It is obvious that an output–price level tradeoff exists with the consensus view in cases where either stimulus or restraint is being applied. This is made visual by the so-called Phillips curve, which is a plot of the unemployment rate against the rate of change in price level. Evidence shows that during the 1970s, the Phillips curve shifted to the right, indicating a worsening of the tradeoff. The economy thus suffered from stagflation— simultaneous and unacceptable levels of inflation and unemployment. Fortunately, this was reversed in the mid 1980s when both measures fell.

On the other hand, it is obvious that a shift in the aggregate supply curve provides improvement in employment (and output), while leading to a reduction in the price level. The question then is how to trigger the desired shift from the supply side. Here are some options:

- Supply-side tax cuts.
- Deregulation.
- Elimination of structural bottlenecks.
- Wage–price controls.

Each type of policy change has been used at one time or another to combat stagflation.

Supply-side tax cuts are incentive-based and work on the assumption that people and firms will produce more if they get to keep a larger fraction of what they earn. Keynesian demand-side tax cuts emphasize the spending that takes place when more of every dollar earned becomes disposable income. In both cases all economists agree that the marginal tax rate plays a pivotal role. Just how much supply will respond to a tax cut is measured by:

$$\text{tax elasticity of supply} = \frac{\text{percentage change in quantity supplied}}{\text{percentage change in tax rate}}$$

If the tax elasticity of supply were greater than one it would be possible for a tax cut to increase the tax base so dramatically that tax revenues might even increase! In practice, the tax elasticity of supply has turned out to be about 0.15, a number so small that in 1993, President Clinton used it to convince Congress that a tax increase would not hurt aggregate supply much!

Supply-siders favor tax cuts to provide incentives to encourage saving *and* investment, thus providing for long-term growth in capital stock. Human capital incentives are important too, as they emphasize the quality of the labor force and attack structural employment barriers, thus helping shift the aggregate supply curve to the right. Worker training, spending on education and affirmative-action programs, and the like, all have positive impact on the stock of human capital. Deregulation of both product and factor markets has provided a powerful stimulus to aggregate supply since the process began in the 1980s, because it eliminates barriers to the efficient employment of resources, thus reducing costs at every level of output. Agreements like the North American Free Trade Agreement (NAFTA) which eliminates trade barriers between Canada, the United States and Mexico, have the potential to shift aggregate supply to the right by reducing the cost of imported inputs and finished goods.

Finally, emphasis on infrastructure, which was somewhat taken for granted in the United States, enhances aggregate supply by reducing costs in transportation, communication, and so on. Though still impressive by international standards, public investment fell during the 1970s and early 1980s. The Surface Transportation Act of 1991 raised federal spending to over $50 billion a year for investment in the nation's infrastructure.

Learning Objectives

After reading Chapter 16 and doing the following exercises, you should:

1. Be able to explain supply side policy using the equation of exchange.
2. Understand why the success of demand-side policies depends on the aggregate-supply response.
3. Understand the nature of the inflation–unemployment tradeoff and the Phillips curve.
4. Understand the impact of an upward-sloping aggregate supply curve when using demand-side policies.
5. Be able to tell why the Phillips curve might shift, using the AS-AD framework.
6. Understand the basic supply-side options for improving the inflation–unemployment tradeoff.
7. Understand why marginal tax rates affect work incentives, investment, and saving.
8. Be able to describe human capital and its relationship to structural unemployment.
9. Understand why deregulation of factor and product markets influences aggregate supply.
10. Know why the maintenance of infrastructure is important to aggregate supply.

Using Key Terms

Fill in the puzzle on the opposite page with the appropriate term from the list of Key Terms at the end of the chapter in the text.

Across

4. The amount of output produced by a worker in a given time period.
5. The percentage change in quantity supplied divided by the percentage change in tax rates.
8. The simultaneous occurrence of unemployment and inflation.
10. The vertical curve in Figure 16.1 (b) in the text.
11. Payments such as Social Security, welfare, and unemployment benefits.
12. The transportation, communications, judicial, and other systems that facilitate market exchanges.
13. Business expenditure on new plant and equipment and inventory changes.

Down

1. The skills and knowledge of the workforce.
2. Unemployment because of a mismatch between the skills of the workforce and the requirements of jobs.
3. A lump-sum refund of taxes paid.
6. Disposable income minus consumption.
7. The tax rate imposed on the last dollar of income received.
9. The curve drawn in Figure 16.2 in the text.

Puzzle 16.1

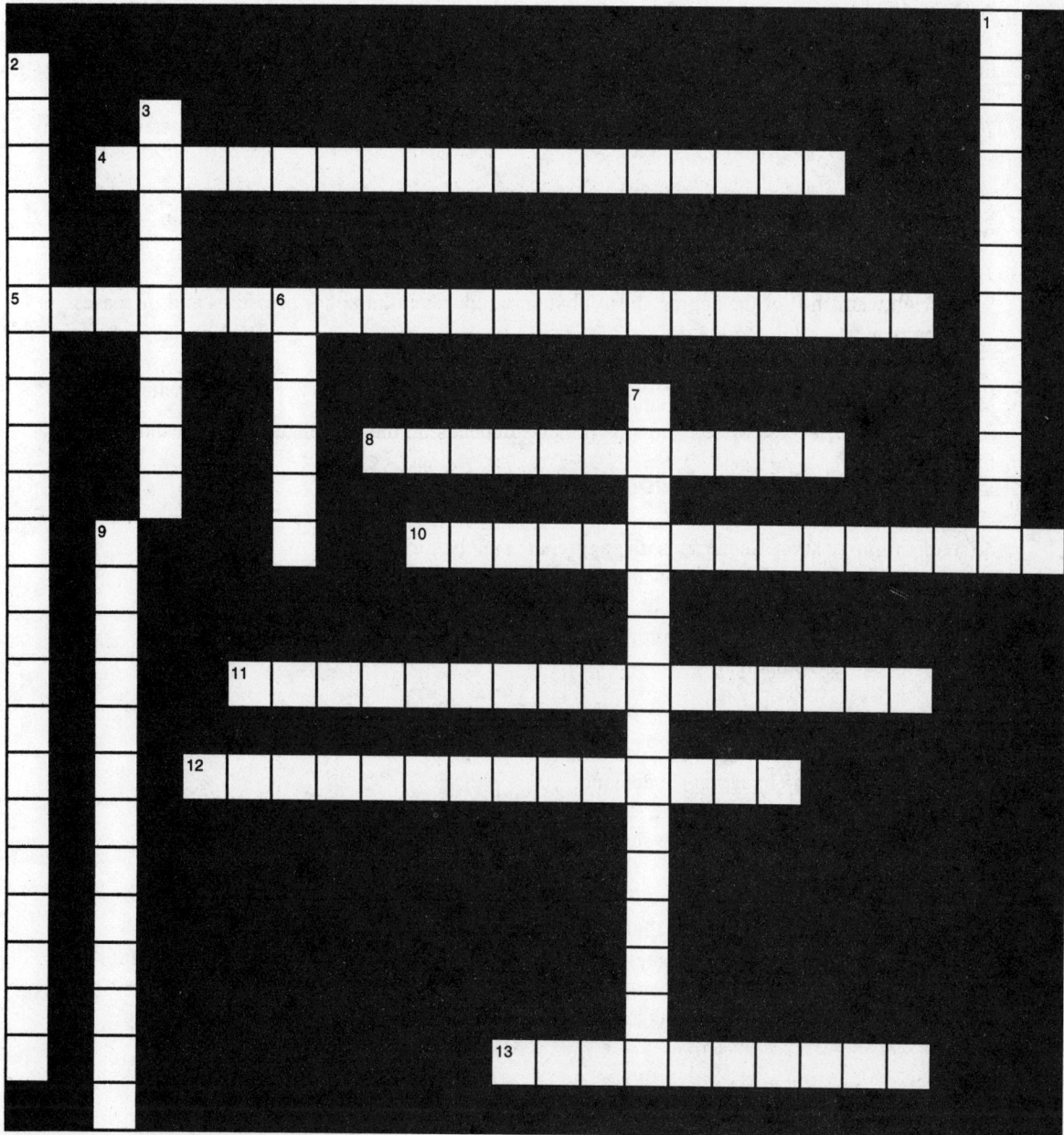

True or False: *Circle your choice and explain why any false statements are incorrect.*

T F   1.   Below full employment, strict Keynesians believe that increased aggregate demand raises output only, not prices (*P*).

T F   2.   Leftward shifts of the aggregate supply curve increase both price levels and output.

T F   3.   Investment in human capital reduces saving and shifts the aggregate supply curve leftward.

T F   4.   The Phillips curve shows a direct relationship between unemployment and the rate of inflation.

T F   5.   A basic contention of supply-side economists is that we should decrease regulation of the production process.

T F   6.   In the consensus view, the aggregate supply curve has a gentle, accelerating upward slope.

T F   7.   A progressive tax system provides more incentives to work than a system with constant marginal tax rates.

T F   8.   A reduction in tax rates will yield larger tax revenues only if the absolute value of the tax elasticity of supply is greater than 1.0.

T F   9.   A rightward shift of the aggregate supply curve reduces inflationary pressures and increases employment.

T F 10. Discrimination against any group can shift the aggregate supply curve to the left when the best person for a given job is not hired.

Multiple Choice: *Select the correct answer.*

_____ 1.   According to strict Keynesians, the aggregate supply curve is:
(a)   First horizontal, then upward-sloping, and finally vertical.
(b)   Vertical.
(c)   Horizontal until full employment is reached, and then it becomes vertical.
(d)   Upward-sloping.

_____ 2.   Stagflation is caused by:
(a)   An increase in aggregate demand.
(b)   A decrease in aggregate demand.
(c)   An increase in aggregate supply.
(d)   A decrease in aggregate supply.

_____ 3.   Lower unemployment and a lower inflation rate can best be achieved with:
(a)   A rightward shift of the Phillips curve.
(b)   A rightward shift of the aggregate supply curve.
(c)   A rightward shift of the aggregate demand curve.
(d)   A leftward shift of the aggregate supply curve.

_____ 4. Arthur Laffer predicted that tax revenue:
  (a) Would increase when taxes were cut because the absolute value of the tax elasticity of supply was greater than 1.
  (b) Would be maximized when the absolute value of the tax elasticity of supply was equal to zero.
  (c) Would be maximized when the absolute value of the tax elasticity of supply was equal to minus 1.
  (d) Would be maximized when the absolute value of the tax elasticity of supply was equal to the price elasticity of supply.

_____ 5. What is the slope of the aggregate supply curve according to Monetarists?
  (a) Horizontal until full employment is reached, and then vertical.
  (b) Upward-sloping.
  (c) Horizontal at all production levels.
  (d) Vertical.

_____ 6. Supply-side policies are designed to achieve:
  (a) A leftward shift in the Phillips curve.
  (b) A rightward shift of the aggregate supply curve.
  (c) Both a lower inflation rate and a lower unemployment rate.
  (d) All of the above.

_____ 7. In contrast to Monetarists and Keynesians, the Supply-siders focus on policies designed to:
  (a) Shift the Phillips curve leftward.
  (b) Raise inflation and lower unemployment.
  (c) Increase the left side of the equation of exchange.
  (d) Move leftward along the Phillips curve.

_____ 8. Which of the following shifts, _ceteris paribus_, will cause lower rates of both unemployment and inflation?
  (a) An increase in aggregate demand.
  (b) A decrease in aggregate demand.
  (c) An increase in aggregate supply.
  (d) A decrease in aggregate supply.

_____ 9. The impact on the economy of a given shift in aggregate demand depends on the:
  (a) Shape of the aggregate supply curve.
  (b) Response of consumers to a change in spending.
  (c) Position of the aggregate supply curve.
  (d) All of the above.

_____ 10. Declining investment in infrastructure:
  (a) Will lead to greater delays and higher opportunity costs.
  (b) Has characterized the United States since 1960.
  (c) Shifts both aggregate demand and aggregate supply.
  (d) All of the above.

_____ 11. According to supply-side theory, which of the following would cause a rightward shift in the aggregate supply curve?
  (a) Lifting trade restrictions.
  (b) Increasing transfer payments to the unemployed.
  (c) Eliminating government-funded training programs for the structurally unemployed.
  (d) Eliminating job-search assistance.

_____ 12. Which of the following will definitely lead to a larger value on the misery index?
   (a) A movement along the Phillips curve.
   (b) An outward shift of the aggregate demand curve.
   (c) Stagflation.
   (d) A rightward shift of the money supply curve.

_____ 13. Which of the following policies is a supply-side lever?
   (a) Tax incentives for saving.
   (b) Deregulation.
   (c) Human capital investment.
   (d) All of the above.

_____ 14. The tradeoff between unemployment and inflation is the result of an aggregate supply curve which is:
   (a) Horizontal.
   (b) Vertical.
   (c) Upward sloping.
   (d) Downward sloping.

_____ 15. Which of the following groups would use a decrease in government regulation to increase the incentive to work and produce?
   (a) Supply-siders.
   (b) Monetarists.
   (c) Keynesians.
   (d) All of the above.

_____ 16. If the absolute value of the tax elasticity of supply is 0.5, a tax _cut_ of 5 percent would:
   (a) Increase output by 2.5 percent and decrease tax revenues.
   (b) Increase output by 10 percent and decrease tax revenues.
   (c) Increase output by 2.5 percent and increase tax revenues.
   (d) Decrease output by 2.5 percent and decrease tax revenues.

_____ 17. Which policy was based on a supply-side justification?
   (a) The New Deal of Franklin Roosevelt.
   (b) World War II.
   (c) The Reagan tax cuts of 1981-84.
   (d) The Clinton plan to reduce the deficit.

_____ 18. The marginal tax rate indicates:
   (a) The change in taxes resulting from a change in fiscal policy.
   (b) The tax rate imposed on total income.
   (c) The tax rate imposed on taxable income.
   (d) What percent of the last dollar of income earned is paid in taxes.

_____ 19. If a new tax policy raises the tax rate 2% but causes the quantity supplied to fall by 10%, the absolute value of the tax elasticity of supply is:
   (a) 0.5.
   (b) 2.
   (c) 5.
   (d) 10.

_____ 20. According to supply-side theory, which of the following programs cause unemployment?
  (a) Agricultural acreage restrictions by the government.
  (b) The minimum wage.
  (c) More regulation by the government.
  (d) All of the above.

Problems and Applications

Exercise 1

This exercise will focus on how aggregate supply and demand changes affect the equilibrium output and price index.

The aggregate demand curve and aggregate supply curve for all of the goods in an economy are presented in Figure 16.2. The economy is assumed to be on aggregate demand curve B in the current fiscal year.

Figure 16.1
Aggregate supply and demand curves

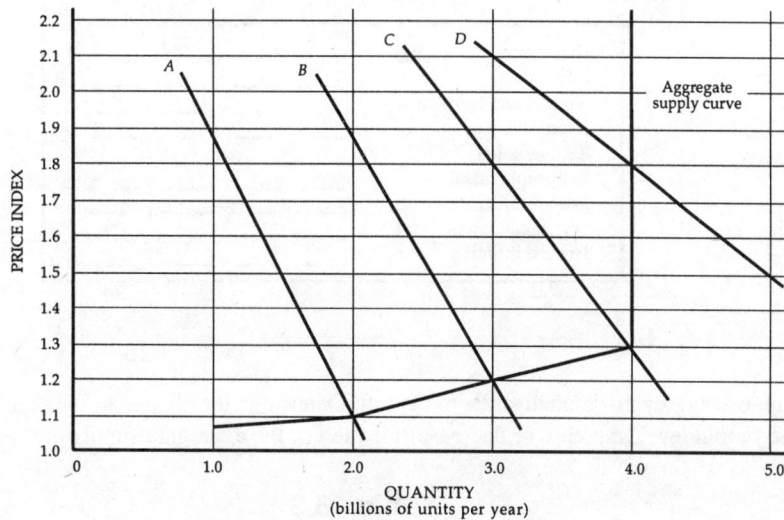

1. Four aggregate demand curves are shown in Figure 16.1, corresponding to four alternative government policies for the coming fiscal year.

   For the following four government policies, choose the aggregate demand curve in Figure 16.1 that best portrays the expected impact of each policy. Place the letter of your choice in the blank provided.

   _____ Money supply is expanded, taxes are cut, government increases its expenditures.
   _____ Government does nothing.
   _____ Government decides to balance the budget by reducing government spending and by raising taxes.
   _____ Government increases expenditures and cuts taxes.

2. Indicate the equilibrium price index and output for each policy in Table 16.1.

Table 16.1
Equilibrium prices for four government policies

Aggregate demand curve	A	B	C	D
Equilibrium price index	———	———	———	———
Equilibrium output	———	———	———	———

3. Place a check under the appropriate column in Table 16.2 to indicate the aggregate demand curve that is most likely to result in each of the macroeconomic outcomes listed. There can be more than one answer per outcome.

Table 16.2
Macroeconomic outcomes

(Place check mark)	Aggregate demand curve			
	A	B	C	D
Depression	——	——	——	——
Deflation	——	——	——	——
Highest unemployment	——	——	——	——
Recession	——	——	——	——
Zero inflation	——	——	——	——
Full employment	——	——	——	——
Price stability	——	——	——	——
Maximum output	——	——	——	——
Highest inflation	——	——	——	——

4. Suppose aggregate demand shifts to the left. Determine the change to the equilibrium price level and output level (increase or decrease) for each of the aggregate supply curves in Table 16.3.

Table 16.3

Aggregate supply curve	Change in price level	Change in output level
upward sloping	———————	———————
horizontal	———————	———————
vertical	———————	———————

Exercise 2

1. Suppose the price index is currently 1.2 as shown by demand curve B in Figure 16.1. Compute the inflation rate under each of the four policies, assuming the supply curve remains the same. The formula is:

$$\frac{\text{equilibrium price index} - 1.2}{1.2} \times 100\%$$

Enter your answers for each policy in the appropriate blank of column 1 in Table 16.4.

Table 16.4 Inflation rates, equilibrium output, and unemployment rates under four government policies

Aggregate demand curve	(1) Equilibrium price change	(2) Equilibrium output (billions of units per year)	(3) Unemployment rate
A	_____ %	_____	_____ %
B	_____	_____	_____
C	_____	_____	_____
D	_____	_____	_____

2. In column 2 of Table 16.4, indicate the equilibrium output associated with each of the policies. Use Figure 16.1 to find this information.

3. Which of the following best represents the U.S. unemployment rate?
   (a) The number of people divided by the U.S. labor force.
   (b) The number of people employed divided by the U.S. population.
   (c) The number of people counted as unemployed divided by the U.S. labor force.
   (d) The number of people unemployed divided by the U.S. population.

4. Table 16.5 shows the hypothetical population, the labor force, the number of people who are employed, and the number of people who are unemployed at each production rate for the economy. Compute the unemployment rate at each production rate in the table.

Table 16.5 Computation of the unemployment rate

Production rate (billions of units per year)	2	3	4
U.S. population (millions)	200	200	200
Labor force (millions)	100	100	100
Number of people unemployed (millions)	15	8	5
Number of people employed (millions)	85	92	95
Unemployment rate (percent)	_____	_____	_____

5. Using the information in Table 16.5, complete column 3 in Table 16.4, which shows the unemployment rate corresponding to each government policy.

6. The government's dilemma is:
   (a) That it cannot reach an unemployment level of 5 percent without experiencing inflation of at least 8 percent.
   (b) That it cannot reach stable prices (0 percent increase) without experiencing an unemployment rate of 8 percent or more.
   (c) That when it makes gains in holding inflation below 8 percent, unemployment increases.
   (d) Expressed by all of the above statements.

7. Which of the four aggregate demand curves from Figure 16.1 places the economy closest to full-employment output and moderate inflation?
   (a) Aggregate demand curve A.
   (b) Aggregate demand curve B.
   (c) Aggregate demand curve C.
   (d) Aggregate demand curve D.

Exercise 3

Suppose corporate taxes are reduced to encourage productivity and as a result firms (sellers) lower prices by $50 per unit of output. As a result, the average price level decreases by $50 at every level of real GDP.

Figure 16.2

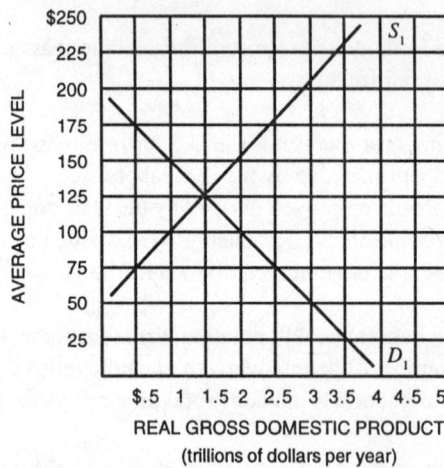

AVERAGE PRICE LEVEL (vertical axis): $250, 225, 200, 175, 150, 125, 100, 75, 50, 25

REAL GROSS DOMESTIC PRODUCT
(trillions of dollars per year)
$.5 1 1.5 2 2.5 3 3.5 4 4.5 5

1. Draw the new aggregate demand curve (label it D$_2$) or aggregate supply curve (label it S$_2$) in Figure 16.2.

2. What is the new equilibrium price level? _____

3. What is the new equilibrium output level? _____

4. Which type of economic policy is this tax change most consistent with? _____

5. This shift is consistent with:
   (a) Stagflation (inflation and a higher unemployment rate).
   (b) Inflation and a lower unemployment rate.
   (c) Deflation and a higher unemployment rate.
   (d) A lower price level and lower unemployment rate.

Exercise 4

Suppose taxpayers are required to pay a base tax of $400 plus 20 percent on any income over $1,000.

1. Compute the amount of taxes to be paid at the income levels in Table 16.6 by filling in columns 2, 3, and 4.

Table 16.4
Tax calculations

(1) Income ($ per year)	(2) Base tax ($ per year)	+	(3) Tax on income over $1,000 ($ per year)	=	(4) Total tax ($/year)	(5) Total tax after change In base tax	(6) In marginal tax rate
$ 5,000	____		____		____	____	____
$10,000	____		____		____	____	____
$15,000	____		____		____	____	____

2. Suppose further that the taxing authority wishes to raise taxes by $500 for people with incomes of $10,000. If the marginal tax rates remain unchanged, what will the new base tax have to be? _____

3. In column 5 of Table 16.6, compute the resulting taxes at each income level with the new base tax.

4. If the base tax of $400 is to remain unchanged, what will the *marginal tax rate* have to be if $500 is to be added to the tax paid by people with incomes of $10,000? _____

5. Use the new marginal tax rate to complete column 6.

6. If taxes are to be increased (columns 5 and 6), a change in the base is:
   (a) More progressive and helpful to work incentives than raising taxes by changing the marginal tax rate.
   (b) More progressive and harmful to work incentives than raising taxes by changing the marginal tax rate.
   (c) More regressive and helpful to work incentives than raising taxes by changing the marginal tax rate.
   (d) More regressive and harmful to work incentives than raising taxes by changing the marginal tax rate.

Common Errors

The first statement in each "common error" below is incorrect. Each incorrect statement is followed by a corrected version and an explanation.

1. Labor productivity increases when more is produced per dollar of wages. WRONG!

   Labor productivity increases when more units of product are produced per unit of labor. RIGHT!

   Productivity changes are not directly related to wage levels. Wage levels reflect a large number of influences embodied in the demand and supply curves for labor. Productivity, however, is a physical measure of the relation between units of product and the amount of labor needed to produce them.

2. The Phillips curve is simply a demand curve. WRONG!

Although the Phillips curve is related to supply and demand curves, it is not the same as either a demand or a supply curve. RIGHT!

Table 16.7 shows some of the major differences separating Phillips curves, market demand curves, and aggregate demand curves. The axes of the three curves are very different.

Table 16.7
Characteristics of three types of demand curve

Type of curve	Sources of differences		
	x-axis	y-axis	Market
Phillips curve	Unemployment	Inflation	Aggregate labor market
Market demand curve	Quantity per time period	Price	Single market
Aggregate demand curve	Quantity per time period	Price index	Aggregate product market

3. We can't have full employment with price stability. WRONG!

Full employment with price stability is possible, although it may be difficult to achieve. RIGHT!

Look at the definition of full employment again. It is the lowest rate of unemployment with price stability. Although we may be able to increase production above full employment, it will cause inflation.

4. Minimum-wage legislation provides more income to workers. WRONG!

Minimum-wage legislation eliminates low-paying jobs, which may decrease total income received by workers. RIGHT!

A higher wage may mean that businesses cannot afford to hire as many people. The lost wages of those people who are unemployed because of the minimum wages must be weighed against the higher wages received by those who are able to hold onto their jobs.

•ANSWERS•

Using Key Terms
Across
4. labor productivity
5. tax elasticity of supply
8. stagflation
10. aggregate supply
11. transfer payments
12. infrastructure
13. investment

Down

1. human capital
2. structural unemployment
3. tax rebate
6. saving
7. marginal tax rate
9. Phillips curve

True or False

1. T
2. F Decreases in AS increase price levels but decrease output.
3. F Investment in human capital can shift AS rightward.
4. F The Phillips curve indicates an inverse relationship between unemployment and inflation.
5. T
6. T
7. F There is less incentive to work when the additional income earned is taxed at a higher rate.
8. T
9. T
10. T

Multiple Choice

1. c	5. d	9. d	13. d	17. c
2. d	6. d	10. d	14. c	18. d
3. b	7. a	11. a	15. a	19. c
4. a	8. c	12. c	16. a	20. d

Problems and Applications

Exercise 1

1. D or C, B, A, C

2. **Table 16.1 Answer**

Aggregate demand curve	A	B	C	D
Equilibrium price index	1.1	1.2	1.3	1.8
Equilibrium output	2.0	3.0	4.0	4.0

3. **Table 16.2 Answer**

(Place check mark)	Aggregate demand curve			
	A	B	C	D
Depression	X	—	—	—
Deflation	X	—	—	—
Highest unemployment	X	—	—	—
Recession	—	X	—	—
Zero inflation	—	X	—	—
Full employment	—	—	X	—
Price stability	—	X	(8% is not stable)	—
Maximum output	—	—	X	X
Highest inflation	—	—	—	X

4. **Table 16.3 Answer (millions of dollars)**

Aggregate supply curve	Change in price level	Change in output level
upward sloping	decrease	decrease
horizontal	no change	decrease
vertical	decrease	no change

Exercise 2

1. See Table 16.4 answer, column 1.

Table 16.4 Answer

Aggregate demand curve	(1) Equilibrium price change	(2) Equilibrium output (billions of units per year)	(3) Unemployment rate
A	− 8.3%	2.0	15%
B	0.0	3.0	8
C	8.3	4.0	5
D	50.0	4.0	5

2. See Table 16.4 answer, column 2.
3. c

4. **Table 16.5 Answer**

Production rate (billions of units per year)	2	3	4
Unemployment rate (percent)	15	8	5

5. See Table 16.4 answer, column 3.

6. d
7. c

Exercise 3

1. See Figure 16.2 answer, S_2.

Figure 16.2 Answer

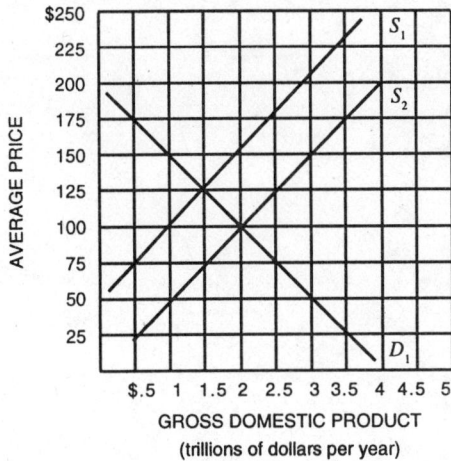

GROSS DOMESTIC PRODUCT
(trillions of dollars per year)

2. $100
3. $2 trillion
4. Supply-side policy
5. d

Exercise 4

1. See Table 16.6 Answer, columns 2-4.

Table 16.6 Answer

(1) Income ($ per year)	(2) Base tax ($ per year)	+	(3) Tax on income over $1,000 ($ per year)	=	(4) Total tax ($/year)	(5) Total tax after change In base tax	(6) In marginal tax rate
$ 5,000	$400	$	800 (= $ 4,000 × 0.2)		$1,200	$1,700	$1,424
$10,000	400		1,800 (= 9,000 × 0.2)		2,200	2,700	2,704
$15,000	400		2,800 (= 14,000 × 0.2)		3,200	3,700	3,984

2. $900 (= $400 + $500)
3. See Table 16.6 Answer column 5.
4. 25.6 percent. This is found by solving the following equation, which indicates people with $10,000 in income have a tax of $2,700 (= $2,200 + $500):

$$\$2,700 = \$400 + (\$10,000 - \$1,000)X$$
$$\$2,300 = \$9,000X$$
$$X = 25.6 \text{ percent}$$

5. See Table 16.6 Answer column 6.
6. c

CHAPTER 17

Growth and Productivity: Long-Run Possibilities

Quick Review

Economic growth has been the major source of the ever-rising standard of living of the human race. However, the nature of growth and possible limits to it have long been debated. In this chapter we focus on the following concerns:

- How important is economic growth?
- How does an economy grow?
- Is continued economic growth possible? Is it desirable?

Although short-term growth may be accomplished by moving to the production-possibilities frontier, long-term growth requires an expansion of an economy's productive capacity. For a nation's people to become better off, real GDP must increase at a rate that exceeds the rate of population growth. This is an important point. Since growth is an exponential process, changes which appear to be small can actually make a very big difference. For example, if real GDP grows at 2.5% annually, real GDP doubles every 28 years; at 3.5%, every 20 years!

Growth is a complex process and is not completely understood, but the best sources of increased productivity (increased output per worker) appear to be:

- Higher skills - an increase in labor skills.
- More capital - an increase in the ratio of capital to labor.
- Technological advance - the development and use of better capital equipment and products.
- Improved management - better use of available resources in the production process.

Given this list, it is obvious that the saving–investment process is a critical ingredient and government can do much to influence both. By pulling the right policy levers, growth may be accelerated. Government at all levels can influence the quantity and quality of schooling made available and immigration policy may target people with particular skills. Both bear on the quality of labor available in the production process. Increases in the capital-labor ratio may be nurtured by tax policies which favor both saving and investment. Much can be gained by creating a framework in which government policy makers are viewed as pursuing stable monetary and fiscal policies thus reducing risk and uncertainty for private sector decision makers.

Not everyone feels growth is necessarily good or sustainable. This feeling is best exemplified by the writing of the "doomsday prophets." In this regard, every generation of students rediscovers the work of the eighteenth-century clergyman Thomas R. Malthus. Malthus believed that the means of subsistence could not keep ahead of population growth. Population, he noted, grew geometrically while the means to subsistence grew arithmetically. Hence, the human race was doomed to starvation unless steps were taken to stave off disaster. Other "doomsday prophets" have surfaced from time to time and raised the question of limited growth by forecasting exhaustion of some particularly strategic resource.

However, technological advance and adaptive capacity are automatically encouraged by economic forces. As resources become relatively scarce, their prices rise. These higher prices discourage resource use and provide incentives for exploration of new sources of supply and the substitution of alternative resources in the production process. From the perspective of resource requirements, growth may be limitless. The pollution problem is perhaps more serious because the market mechanism does not adequately allocate the costs of pollution and thus does not provide the incentives necessary for its correction. Public policy to allocate costs or to set standards is needed to correct for this weakness.

Growth is possible for the foreseeable future. But is it desirable? Most seem to think it is, as long as it means a higher standard of living. On the other hand, an argument can be made that rather than seeking continued growth, we simply need to change the mix of output we are producing to bring about an increase in economic well-being.

Learning Objectives

After reading Chapter 17 and doing the following exercises, you should:

1. Know the difference between the way output changes in the short run and in the long run.
2. Know and be able to calculate some indexes of growth.
3. Understand some of the sources of productivity growth.
4. Understand how government policy can promote the growth process.
5. Be familiar with the history of the doomsday prophets.
6. Understand the nature of environmental constraints that can limit growth.
7. Recognize what society can do to mitigate the external costs imposed by economic growth.
8. Understand how the market mechanism automatically generates solutions to resource exhaustion and constraints on growth.

Using Key Terms

Fill in the puzzle on the opposite page with the appropriate term from the list of Key Terms at the end of the chapter in the text.

Across

4. According to the text, Malthus believed food supplies would increase in this manner.
8. The annual increase for the U.S. averaged 1.1 percent in the 1990s according to Figure 17.5 in the text.
11. All persons over the age of sixteen who are working for pay or are looking for work.
12. An increase in quantity by a constant proportion each year.
13. Gross investment minus depreciation.

Down

1. The percentage change in real output from one period to another.
2. This curve is used in Figure 17.1 in the text to demonstrate long-run growth.
3. The time period used for comparative analysis.
5. A decrease in private-sector borrowing and investment because of increased government borrowing.
6. The knowledge and skills possessed by the labor force.
7. Used to measure average GDP and equal to $31,481 for the U.S. in 1998 according to the text.
9. Shown in Figure 17.1(b) in the text as a rightward shift in the production-possibilities curve.
10. The actual quantity of goods and services produced, valued in constant prices.

Puzzle 17.1

True or False: *Circle your choice and explain why any false statements are incorrect.*

T   F   1.   World economic growth has virtually eliminated poverty in most of the world.

T   F   2.   Once an economy is on its production-possibilities curve, further increases in output require an expansion of productive capacity.

T   F   3.   An increase in nominal GDP always means there has been an outward shift in the production-possibilities curve.

T   F   4.   Growth in real GDP per capita is achieved when population grows more rapidly than output.

T   F   5.   A primary determinant of labor productivity is the rate of capital investment.

T   F   6.   Malthus believed that population grew arithmetically and that the means of subsistence grew geometrically.

T   F   7.   Economic growth is an exponential process because gains made in one year accumulate in future years.

T   F   8.   Increases in the size of the labor force and capital stock have been less important than productivity advances in causing U.S. real GDP to grow.

T   F   9.   Over time, research and development are credited with the greatest contributions to economic growth in the U.S.

T   F   10.   Overall, immigration has had a negative impact on the U.S. economy over time.

Multiple Choice: *Select the correct answer.*

_____   1.   A major difference between short-run and long-run economic growth is that short-run growth:
  (a)   Moves the economy to the production-possibilities curve, while long-run growth shifts the curve outward.
  (b)   Increases capacity utilization, while long-run economic growth increases capacity.
  (c)   Moves the economy up the aggregate supply curve, while long-run economic growth shifts the aggregate supply curve outward.
  (d)   All of the above.

_____   2.   Which of the following would likely contribute to an improvement in the productivity of labor?
  (a)   Greater expenditures on training and education.
  (b)   Policies to stimulate the saving and investment process.
  (c)   Greater expenditures on research and development.
  (d)   All of the above.

_____   3.   In order to produce a combination of goods and services outside the production-possibilities curve, an economy:
  (a)   Would have to use more of its existing resources.
  (b)   Would have to raise the prices of goods and services so that firms would produce more.
  (c)   Would have to find more resources or develop new technology.
  (d)   Will never be able to produce a combination of goods and services outside its current production-possibilities curve.

_____ 4. A sustained net growth in real output of 3.5 percent per year will cause real output to double in about:
(a) 10 years.
(b) 20 years.
(c) 30 years.
(d) 35 years.

_____ 5. The best measure of productivity could be calculated with data on:
(a) Real GDP and hours worked by the labor force.
(b) Real GDP and the population of the United States.
(c) Nominal GDP and the number of people in the U.S. labor force.
(d) Nominal GDP and the population of the United States.

_____ 6. A major goal of short-run macroeconomic policy is to:
(a) Shift the production-possibilities curve outward.
(b) Move toward the production-possibilities curve.
(c) Shift the aggregate supply curve leftward.
(d) Shift the aggregate supply curve rightward.

_____ 7. Which of the following is the best measure of the standard of living?
(a) The ratio of current GDP to GDP in the base period.
(b) Investment as a percentage of GDP.
(c) GDP per capita.
(d) GDP per worker.

_____ 8. Which of the following statements can be attributed to Malthus?
(a) Population grows geometrically and the means of subsistence grows arithmetically.
(b) Starvation serves as a natural check to population growth.
(c) Continued economic growth is impossible because food production cannot keep pace with population growth.
(d) All of the above are Malthusian statements.

_____ 9. Which of the following measures the growth rate of an economy?
(a) The ratio of current real GDP to real GDP in the base period.
(b) Investment as a percentage of GDP.
(c) Real GDP divided by nominal GDP.
(d) GDP per worker.

_____ 10. Which of the following measures productivity?
(a) The ratio of current GDP to GDP in the base period.
(b) Percentage increase in GDP.
(c) GDP per capita.
(d) GDP per worker.

_____ 11. When the production possibilities curve shifts outward, we can also be sure that:
(a) Aggregate supply has increased.
(b) Output has increased.
(c) GDP per capita has increased.
(d) All of the above occur when the production possibilities curve shifts outward.

_____ 12. Which of the following series of annual GDP growth rates would result in the highest level of GDP in ten years?
(a) A constant 4 percent annual rate of growth.
(b) Annual rates of 8 percent, 0 percent, 8 percent, 0 percent, etc. for ten years.
(c) Annual rates of 6 percent, -6 percent, 6 percent, -6 percent, etc. for ten years.
(d) All of these patterns of growth would result in the same level of GDP after ten years.

_____ 13. Which of the following policy levers definitely enhances productivity?
    (a)   Higher taxes.
    (b)   More government regulation.
    (c)   Development of human capital.
    (d)   A higher labor to capital ratio.

_____ 14. Whenever nominal GDP increases:
    (a)   Living standards improve.
    (b)   Output increases.
    (c)   The production possibilities curve shifts outward.
    (d)   The value of production has increased.

_____ 15. Sources of productivity growth include:
    (a)   Higher skills.
    (b)   More capital.
    (c)   Improved management.
    (d)   All of the above.

_____ 16. Which of the following could impede productivity improvements?
    (a)   Crowding out.
    (b)   Technological advances.
    (c)   Higher ratios of capital to labor.
    (d)   All of the above.

_____ 17. The easiest kind of economic growth comes from:
    (a)   Expansion of the production-possibilities curve.
    (b)   Shifting the aggregate demand curve to the right.
    (c)   Increased use of our productive capabilities.
    (d)   An increase in population.

_____ 18. Current U.S. problems with congested highways, air quality and global warming are primarily the result of:
    (a)   Too many goods and services.
    (b)   The mix of output produced.
    (c)   Too much government regulation.
    (d)   Excessively high levels of GDP per capita.

_____ 19. Growth in GDP per capita is attained only when:
    (a)   There is growth in population.
    (b)   There is growth in output.
    (c)   The growth of output exceeds population growth.
    (d)   Population is held constant.

_____ 20. From the long run perspective of economic growth, household saving:
    (a)   Threatens growth because of the paradox of thrift.
    (b)   Is the basic source of investment financing in the U.S.
    (c)   Is a leakage which constrains economic growth.
    (d)   Shifts the institutional production-possibilities curve inward.

Problems and Applications

Exercise 1

This exercise focuses on the difference in short-run growth versus long-run growth.

Refer to Figure 17.1 to answer questions 1-4.

Figure 17.1

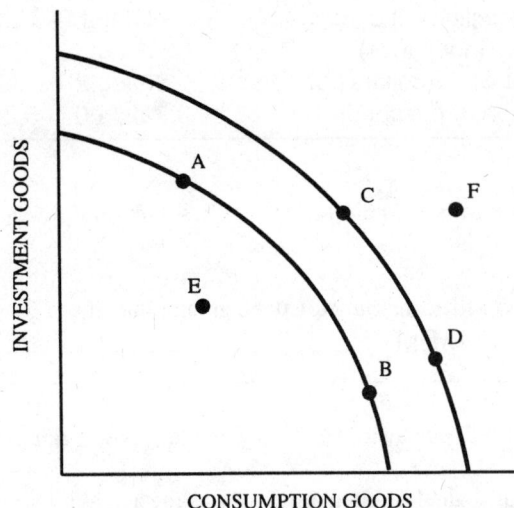

1. Assume the economy is producing at point E. A movement to point B represents an increase in (short-run, long-run) growth.

2. The movement from point E to point B results in increased output because of (increased use of existing capacity, increased capacity).

3. Assume the economy is now producing at point B. A movement to point D represents an increase in (short-run, long-run) growth.

4. The movement from point B to point D results in increased output because of (increased use of existing capacity, increased capacity). This type of growth implies a (leftward, rightward) shift in the _____ curve.

Exercise 2

The following exercise shows how gross domestic product can be used to indicate the standard of living and the rate of economic growth in an economy.

1. Using the data provided complete Table 17.1.

Table 17.1

	1970	1990	Percentage change
(1) U.S. real GDP (billions of dollars)	$3388.2	$6138.7	_____
(2) U.S. population (thousands)	205,052	249,924	_____
(3) U.S. per capita GDP (dollars per person)	$3388.2	$6138.7	_____
(4) World population (thousands)	3.722,000	5,329,000	_____

2. Using the information in Table 17.1, the U.S. standard of living (increased, decreased) from 1970 to 1990.

3. Why must the world economic growth be greater than the U.S. economic growth to maintain the same standard of living? _____

_____

4. From 1970 to 1990, what was the average annual growth rate for real GDP in the U.S? _____

5. If the growth rate calculated in question 4 was the actual growth rate each year (not the average), how long should it take for real GDP to double according to Table 17.1 in the text? _____

Exercise 3

The focus of this exercise is on the value of investment in spurring economic growth. This exercise will help you with a problem at the end of the chapter.

Suppose that every additional five percentage points in the investment rate (I/GDP) boosts economic growth by two percentage points. Assume also that all investment must be financed with household saving. Suppose the economy is currently characterized by the following data:

GDP:	$5 trillion
Consumption:	4 trillion
Saving:	1 trillion
Investment:	1 trillion

1. What is the current investment rate (I/GDP)? _____

2. If the goal is to raise the growth rate of income by one percentage point, by how much must investment increase? _____

3. By how much must consumption decline to permit the necessary growth in the investment rate to reach the 1% target? _____

4. How much does income increase in the first year due to the 1% growth rate? _____

5. Assuming that income each year in the future is 1% higher as a result of the one-year change in the investment rate, how many years will it take for the economy to recoup the amount of consumption goods given up to finance the increase in investment? _____

Common Errors

The first statement in each "common error" below is incorrect. Each incorrect statement is followed by a corrected version and an explanation.

1. Zero economic growth treats everyone equally. WRONG!

   Zero economic growth treats groups unequally. RIGHT!

   Zero economic growth in its simplest dimensions means that GDP would not grow from year to year. Income per capita therefore could not grow unless population declined. Yet we know that U.S. population is growing, although slowly, as a result of new births and increased longevity, and more recently as a result of immigration. If GDP were not to grow, the only way for those at the bottom of the income distribution to have more would be for someone at the top to take less.

2. There is no way to hold off the doomsday prophecy. WRONG!

   Much has been done in the last decade to avoid the cataclysmic predictions of the doomsday prophets. RIGHT!

   It's been over two decades since the deluge of new doomsday literature hit the newsstands. Before that, pollution, the environment, and ecology were issues popularized in the turbulent 1960s. Since then, much has been done by federal, state, and local governments to overcome some of the problems that seemed most acute. The air is cleaner in many areas. So is the water. Even the OPEC actions of the 1970s and early 1980s were of help in this regard. Higher oil prices spurred research into new sources of power and new ways to conserve energy. All of this activity helped us meet the doomsday challenge once again.

3. Zero economic growth will alleviate the pollution problem. WRONG!

   Zero economic growth will maintain the rate of pollution. RIGHT!

   Some people mistakenly think that stifling economic growth is a way to cut down on pollution. It isn't. The best that a zero economic growth policy could do is cut down on the *growth* in pollution. With the same output level and output mix, the rate of pollution would be the same from year to year. To cut pollution would require cutting GDP—that is, a *negative* economic growth policy! The economy has the capability of cleaning up pollution as well as generating pollution as it grows.

Using Key Terms
Across
4. arithmetic growth
8. productivity
11. labor force
12. geometric growth
13. net investment

235

Down

1. growth rate
2. production possibilities
3. base period
5. crowding out
6. human capital
7. GDP per capita
8. economic growth
10. real GDP

True or False

1. F   Over half of the world's population lives in poverty.
2. T
3. F   An increase in *nominal* GDP does not necessarily mean that production has increased.
4. F   Growth in real GDP per capita is achieved when output grows more rapidly than population.
5. T
6. F   Malthus believed that population grew geometrically but the means of subsistence grew only arithmetically.
7. T
8. T
9. T
10. F   Immigration has significantly increased the labor force and contributed to the outward shift of the U.S. production possibilities curve over time.

Multiple Choice

1. d	5. a	9. a	13. c	17. c
2. d	6. b	10. d	14. d	18. b
3. c	7. c	11. a	15. d	19. c
4. b	8. d	12. a	16. a	20. b

Problems and Applications

Exercise 1

1. short-run
2. increased use of existing capacity
3. long-run
4. increased capacity, rightward, long-run AS

Exercise 2

Table 17.1 Answer

	1970	1990	Percentage change
(1) U.S. real GDP (billions of dollars)	$3388.2	$6138.7	69.7%
(2) U.S. population (thousands)	205,052	249,924	21.9%
(3) U.S. per capita GDP (dollars per person)	$3388.2	$6138.7	39.2%
(4) World population (thousands)	3,722,000	5,329,000	43.2%

2. increased
3. Since the world population growth rate is faster than that of the U.S., it takes higher economic growth to maintain the same standard of living.
4. 4.06%
5. 18 years

Exercise 3

1. I /GDP is $1 trillion/$5 trillion = 0.20 or 20 percent
2. To raise the income level by 1 percent the I /GDP ratio must rise by 2.5 percent.
   0.025 x $5 trillion = $0.125 trillion or $125 billion.
3. Saving must rise by the same amount ($0.125 trillion) as investment increases, so consumption must fall by that amount as well.
4. One percent of $5 trillion is $50 billion.
5. $0.125 trillion is $125 billion. $125 billion divided by 50 billion is 2.5. It will take two and a half years to recoup the lost consumption.

CHAPTER 18
Global Macro

Quick Review

Up to this point, we have not paid much attention to economic events in the rest of the world. However, the economies of all nations are becoming increasingly interdependent. We need to consider these questions:

- How does the U.S. economy interact with the rest of the world?
- How does the rest of the world affect U.S. macro outcomes?
- How does global interdependence limit macro policy options?

One facet of our interaction with other countries is the export and import of goods and services. Exports (X) are an injection and imports (IM) are a leakage. The additional leakage from imports reduces the size of the income multiplier by lowering the amount of *additional* spending on domestic output that results from any increase in our income. In a model of the closed economy, the multiplier is $1/MPS$. However, the multiplier in a model of an open economy must reflect the consumers' desire to spend a little out of every extra dollar for imports, which is called their marginal propensity to import (MPM). The multiplier for the open economy becomes $1/(MPS + MPM)$. The graphic equivalent of this is a reduced slope of the aggregate expenditure curve in an open economy as compared with a closed economy.

The marginal propensity to import may hinder our application of fiscal policy to achieve domestic goals. Because the multiplier is smaller in an open economy than in a closed economy, any tax or spending change will have to be larger to achieve a given income or employment goal. In an open economy we must also consider the export of our goods. When we import goods, foreigners receive dollars, which they may turn around and spend on goods that we produce. When they decide to buy more goods from us, the aggregate spending curve will shift upward, with a resulting multiplier effect on income. Our exports (determined abroad) are seldom equal to our imports (determined at home). We expect either a trade surplus, $(X - IM) > 0$, or a trade deficit, $(X - IM) < 0$. Although the trade deficit permits us to consume more goods than we produce, it may complicate fiscal policy. A fiscal expansion will worsen any trade deficit, *ceteris paribus*.

While we're worrying about our domestic goals and the impact foreign trade has on our potential to achieve them, foreigners are doing the same thing. Our exports are their imports; our imports, their exports. If we have a trade deficit, $(X - IM) < 0$, and consume more than we produce, our trading partners must have an overall trade surplus, $(X - IM) > 0$, and consume less than they produce. Our domestic goals may not be compatible with theirs, or theirs with ours. This may mean that our economy competes with their economies with respect to employment and inflation goals. Policy makers face additional constraints in the open economy.

While trade flows involve the movement of new goods across international boundaries, capital flows involve the purchase of various forms of wealth or of titles to capital across international boundaries. Individuals and corporations purchase securities, bonds, and property in foreign countries or repatriate earnings from abroad. Their actions result in massive dollar flows—capital inflows when foreigners lend to us (e.g., by purchasing a Treasury bond) and outflows when we purchase securities from them (e.g., building up a bank account in Switzerland). Capital flows are seldom in balance. When the outflow of dollars exceeds the inflow of dollars, the U.S. experiences a capital deficit; when the inflow exceeds the outflow, a capital surplus. Capital imbalances can alter macro outcomes too. Inflationary pressures can be fought, *ceteris paribus*, by slowing the growth of the money supply and driving up domestic interest rates. But this action would attract foreigners to our bonds, which they would purchase with accumulated dollars, frustrating the Fed's attempt to reduce the money supply. Domestic goals of various countries are often in conflict.

The critical link between economies in both trade and finance is the exchange rate. The expected imbalance between trade and capital flows implies that the exchange rates fluctuate like other prices determined by supply and demand. For example, if the United States runs persistent trade deficits and foreigners suddenly begin to withdraw their investments from the United States, the value of the dollar will go down in terms of other currencies.

The exchange rate also responds to changes in the specialization and productivity of firms worldwide. Specialization and trade increase world efficiency and output, and stimulate improvements in productivity as producers anywhere must compete with producers everywhere. However, if one country makes dramatically greater improvements in productivity than other countries, then it is likely to run persistent trade surpluses, causing its currency to become more valuable. Significant "swings" in exchange rates sometimes overwhelm productivity changes and reduce the competitiveness of many firms within a country.

Thus, three kinds of rates must be watched very carefully in an open economy: inflation rates, interest rates, and exchange rates. Changes in these rates reflect changes in trade and capital flows. The effectiveness of both fiscal and monetary policy is influenced by changes in these rates.

The gains from trade and cooperation among nations are enormous and have been pursued with great resolve by blocks of countries. The International Monetary Fund, the Group of Seven, and the European Union are all attempts at global coordination.

Learning Objectives

After reading Chapter 18 and doing the following exercises, you should:

1. Understand how international transactions affect U.S. economic performance and the ability to use macroeconomic policy.
2. Be able to explain why the open-economy multiplier is smaller than the closed-economy multiplier.
3. Understand why the marginal propensity to import *changes the slope* of the aggregate expenditure curve.
4. Be able to demonstrate how a change in exports *shifts* the aggregate expenditure curve.
5. Be able to show how trade and capital flows can counteract normal macro policy initiatives.
6. Be aware of the foreign repercussions of U.S. policy initiatives.
7. Know the principal vocabulary of the trade and capital accounts.
8. Be able to relate exchange rate changes to the question of competitiveness in international trade.
9. Understand the various attempts at global coordination.

Using Key Terms

Fill in the puzzle on the opposite page with the appropriate term from the list of Key Terms at the end of the chapter in the text.

Across
2. The ability of a country to produce a specific good at a lower opportunity cost than its trading partners.
3. Income diverted from the circular flow, such as imports.
9. Equal to 1-MPC.
12. Equal to exports minus imports.
13. The amount by which exports exceed imports.
14. Equal to 1/1-MPC.
15. The amount by which the capital outflow exceeds the capital inflow.

Down

1. The fraction of each additional dollar of income that is spent on imports.
4. Goods and services purchased from foreign sources.
5. A situation in which capital inflows are greater than capital outflows.
6. A decrease in private-sector borrowing and spending because of an increase in government borrowing.
7. A situation in which imports exceed exports.
8. Output per unit of input.
10. Goods and services sold to foreign sources.
11. The price of one country's currency in terms of another country's currency.

Puzzle 18.1

True or False: *Circle your choice and explain why any false statements are incorrect.*

T F 1. The main reason countries specialize and trade with each other is to acquire goods and services they cannot produce themselves.

T F 2. A larger marginal propensity to import (MPM) means a larger multiplier, *ceteris paribus*.

T F 3. Increases in exports increase the size of the multiplier, *ceteris paribus*.

T F 4. A reduction in net exports will lower the equilibrium level of income, *ceteris paribus*.

T F 5. When the United States has a trade deficit, the value of what the United States consumes is more than the value of what it produces.

T F 6. When the dollar gets weaker, U.S. products become less competitive in the world market.

T F 7. Stimulative fiscal policy will increase both aggregate demand and a trade deficit, *ceteris paribus*.

T F 8. Trade stimulates improvements in productivity because of increased competition.

T F 9. A trade deficit is accompanied by a capital inflow; a trade surplus, by a capital outflow.

T F 10. The "Group of Seven" is an informal attempt to coordinate the global macro policy of the seven largest industrial countries.

Multiple Choice: *Select the correct answer.*

_____ 1. The open-economy multiplier is smaller than the closed-economy multiplier:
  (a) Because imports are a leakage from the circular flow.
  (b) Because the marginal propensity to import is greater than zero.
  (c) Because the denominator is greater for the open-economy multiplier than for the closed-economy multiplier.
  (d) For all of the above reasons.

_____ 2. The marginal propensity to import relates:
  (a) Domestic consumption to the foreign level of income.
  (b) Changes in the domestic level of income to changes in the foreign level of income.
  (c) Changes in the domestic imports with changes in domestic income.
  (d) Changes in domestic consumption with changes in imports.

_____ 3. An increase in U.S. exports:
  (a) Must increase unemployment in the rest of the world.
  (b) Means the rest of the world must be importing more.
  (c) Means the rest of the world must have a trade deficit.
  (d) Means the rest of the world must have a trade surplus.

_____ 4. If the marginal propensity to import is 0.2 and the marginal propensity to save is 0.2, the open-economy multiplier is:
  (a) 0.4.
  (b) 2.5.
  (c) 4.0.
  (d) 2.0.

_____ 5. An increase in the marginal propensity to import will:
  (a) Reduce the size of the open-economy multiplier.
  (b) Increase the size of the closed-economy multiplier.
  (c) Shift the aggregate supply curve rightward.
  (d) Shift the aggregate demand curve rightward.

_____ 6. With respect to the circular flow of economic activity:
  (a) Exports are a leakage.
  (b) Imports are a leakage.
  (c) Imports and exports are both leakages.
  (d) Exports and imports are both injections

_____ 7. World output of goods and services increases with specialization because:
  (a) The world's resources are being used more efficiently.
  (b) Each country's production possibilities curve is shifted outward.
  (c) Each country's workers are able to produce more than they could before specialization.
  (d) All of the above are correct.

_____ 8. When a trade deficit rises:
  (a) Exports rise, imports fall, or both.
  (b) Net exports fall.
  (c) The aggregate demand curve increases.
  (d) The level of income will rise, _ceteris paribus_.

_____ 9. An increase in U.S. imports:
  (a) Means the rest of the world must be exporting more.
  (b) Must increase unemployment in the rest of the world.
  (c) Means the rest of the world must have a trade deficit.
  (d) Means the rest of the world must have a trade surplus.

_____ 10. There is a tradeoff between the objective of reducing a trade deficit and the objective of reaching full employment because:
  (a) Net exports rise as income increases.
  (b) As income increases, the trade deficit rises.
  (c) Imports fall as income increases.
  (d) Fiscal policy and monetary policy must be used to achieve the objective.

_____ 11. Comparative advantage refers to the ability of a country to:
  (a) Produce a specific good with fewer resources than other countries.
  (b) Sell a good at a higher price than other countries.
  (c) Produce a specific good at a lower opportunity cost than other countries.
  (d) Maximize its economic welfare by producing all the goods and services it needs domestically.

_____ 12. French wine producers would gain an advantage over U.S. wine producers in world markets if:
  (a) The French franc weakened relative to the U.S. dollar.
  (b) The American dollar weakened against other currencies.
  (c) The French inflation rate rose relative to the American inflation rate.
  (d) French interest rates rose relative to American interest rates.

13. A net capital inflow into the U. S. means that the U. S. is:
    (a) Consuming more than it produces, and net exports are positive.
    (b) Consuming more than it produces, and net exports are negative.
    (c) Consuming less than it produces, and net exports are positive.
    (d) Consuming less than it produces, and net exports are negative.

14. The International Monetary Fund (IMF):
    (a) Receives its funds from contributions from all the countries of the world.
    (b) Lends funds to nations whose currency is in trouble.
    (c) Often insists on changes in a nation's monetary, fiscal and/or trade policies as a condition for an IMF loan.
    (d) All of the above are correct.

15. A capital outflow occurs for the U.S. when, *ceteris paribus*:
    (a) Citizens of the United States buy foreign stock.
    (b) U.S. corporations abroad repatriate their profits.
    (c) Foreigners purchase real estate in the United States.
    (d) All of the above occur.

16. The existence of a trade deficit can be financed by:
    (a) A capital surplus.
    (b) A strengthening of the exchange rate for the currency.
    (c) Stimulation of the economy to full employment.
    (d) A decrease in capital inflows.

17. When the U.S. dollar is strong, *ceteris paribus*:
    (a) Imports become more expensive.
    (b) U.S. producers become more competitive in foreign markets.
    (c) U.S. exports should increase.
    (d) U.S. goods become more expensive for foreigners to buy.

18. A common currency, like the Euro, facilitates trade by:
    (a) Eliminating the uncertainties associated with fluctuating exchange rates.
    (b) Eliminating currency conversion costs.
    (c) Easing the flow of financial capital across national boundaries.
    (d) All of the above facilitate trade.

19. For a given amount of fiscal stimulus, an open economy will experience, *ceteris paribus*, a shift in aggregate demand that is:
    (a) Greater than in a closed economy resulting in a larger increase in GDP.
    (b) Less than in a closed economy resulting in a larger increase in GDP.
    (c) Greater than in a closed economy resulting in a smaller increase in GDP.
    (d) Less that in a closed economy resulting in a smaller increase in GDP.

20. Gains from international trade include which of the following?
    (a) Increased world output of goods and services.
    (b) Greater efficiency in the use of the world's resources.
    (c) Higher standards of living throughout the world.
    (d) All of the above.

Problems and Applications

Exercise 1

Using the consumption function and the marginal propensity to import, it is possible to compare the multiplier effect for an open economy versus the multiplier effect for a closed economy.

Assume that an economy is characterized by the consumption function

$$C = 100 + 0.8Y_D$$

where all figures are in billions of dollars.

1. What is the marginal propensity to consume for this closed economy? _____

2. Compute the marginal propensity to save for the closed economy. _____

3   Compute the multiplier for this closed economy. _____

4. If government expenditures were to increase $250 billion, how much would income increase in this closed economy? _____

5. Now suppose the economy has been opened up to imports and has a marginal propensity to import equal to 0.30.

    Assuming that the consumption function is the same as in the beginning of this exercise, compute the multiplier for this open economy. _____

6. If government expenditures increase $250 billion, how much does income increase in this open economy? _____

7. T   F   Imports reduce the effectiveness of fiscal policy. (Compare your answers in questions 4 and 6 above.)

Figure 18.1

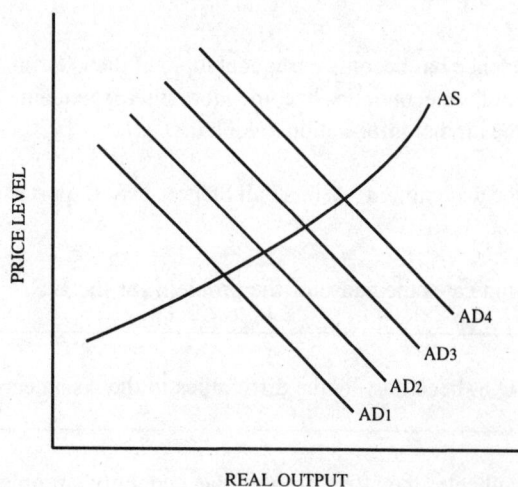

245

8. Refer to Figure 18.1. Assume the economy is originally on AD$_1$. For a closed economy, a fiscal policy stimulus shifts aggregate demand to AD$_3$. In an open economy, the same fiscal policy stimulus would shift aggregate demand to _____, *ceteris paribus*.

Exercise 2

This exercise shows the impact of fiscal policy on the trade balance.

Assume the following information for a hypothetical economy.

Table 18.1 Data in billions of dollars

	Year 1	Year 2
GDP	$800	$_____
Exports	50	50
Imports	60	_____
Net exports	_____	_____
Import/GDP ratio	_____	_____

1. Calculate the level of net exports in Year 1 in Table 18.1.

2. Assume the government increases spending form Year 1 to Year 2 which causes GDP to increase by $200 billion. Calculate GDP for Year 2 in Table 18.1.

3. As a result of the increase in government spending, the demand for imports increases. Assume imports increase by $10 for every $100 increase in GDP. Calculate the level of imports for Year 2 in Table 18.1.

4. Assume exports do not change. Calculate the level of net exports for Year 2 in Table 18.1.

5. Calculate the import/GDP ratio for Year 1 and for Year 2 in Table 18.1.

6. In an open economy, fiscal stimulus tends to (increase, decrease) a trade deficit by (increasing, decreasing) imports.

Exercise 3

Economic interdependence has become a frequent topic of the U.S. media. As countries forge greater links through trade and investment their economies become more interdependent. This exercise will use one of the articles in the text to show the kind of information to look for.

Reread the article in the text entitled "Asia's Fall Starves U.S. Export Market." Then answer the following questions.

1. What phrase indicates the cause of the problem for the U.S.? _____
   _____

2. How has the U.S. been hurt by the difficulties in the Asian economy? _____
   _____

3. What phrase indicates the effect of the Asian economy's problems on the level of U.S. exports?
   _____

4. What phrase suggests the current state of the U.S. economy? _____

_____

Common Errors

The first statement in each "common error" below is incorrect. Each incorrect statement is followed by a corrected version and an explanation.

1. A stronger dollar means American firms are stronger and more competitive. WRONG!

   A stronger dollar puts U.S. firms at a competitive disadvantage, *ceteris paribus*. RIGHT!

   The problem is how the word "competitive" is used. It is quite possible that because American firms were strong, productive, and competitive *in the past,* many countries bought U.S. goods and the dollar was strengthened. However, when the dollar strengthens *in the present* and nothing else changes (*ceteris paribus*), American firms are placed at a competitive disadvantage. It may be true that the stronger dollar will force them to be more competitive *in the future,* but they may also simply go out of business. Generally, a stronger dollar today means American firms are less able to compete with foreign companies today, because their output becomes more expensive relative to that of foreign producers.

2. The reason American firms can't compete is that foreign wages are so low. WRONG!

   American firms compete with other American firms, not just with foreign firms, for American dollars abroad. RIGHT!

   In a *given* market, an American firm competes with other American firms as well as with foreign firms. However, the firm is also competing indirectly with *all* American firms.

   When Americans buy foreign goods and send American dollars abroad, they provide the money with which foreigners can buy American goods. If American goods are being bought in large quantities by foreigners and Americans are buying few foreign goods, a trade imbalance will develop. The value of the dollar will rise as foreign exchange markets move to eliminate such an imbalance. This rise in the value of the dollar can make all American goods less competitive internationally—*even if the productivity of the companies producing those goods has risen.*

   It is not surprising that a manager who makes a firm more productive will become angry when foreign costs seem to be dropping faster than foreign productivity changes. However, the firm may really be experiencing the effects of a strengthening currency. A stronger currency reflects the productivity gains of *all* American firms. The manager's firm is effectively racing with other American firms in all other markets for the dollars held by foreigners.

3. Trade surpluses are good for the economy, and trade deficits are bad for the economy. WRONG!

   Trade surpluses and deficits are neither *inherently* bad nor *inherently* good. RIGHT!

   When we run a trade deficit, we get the benefits of foreign resources *net*. That's good. But persistent deficits can be bad for the economy if they lead to restrictive policies designed to cut down on imports and to a continual depreciation of the exchange rate. Our persistent trade deficits (foreigners' trade surpluses) mean foreigners will eventually accumulate more of our currency than they want to hold. Capital inflows will not be able to stem the glut of the currency. As a result, our currency will depreciate and foreign goods will become more expensive.

4. The U.S. trade deficit means U.S. producers are inefficient. WRONG!

The U.S. trade deficit means U.S. producers are having difficulty competing. RIGHT!

The trade deficit reflects more than our (in)efficiency. As an example, U.S. agricultural producers are extremely efficient, but they have had difficulty exporting because the dollar was so strong for so long. A weaker dollar helps our producers compete. Before we believe the rhetoric concerning competitiveness, we need to know what is happening to exchange rates.

•ANSWERS•

Using Key Terms
Across
2. comparative advantage
3. leakage
9. marginal propensity to save
12. net exports
13. trade surplus
14. multiplier
15. capital deficit

Down
1. marginal propensity to import
4. imports
5. capital surplus
6. crowding out
7. trade deficit
8. productivity
10. exports
11. exchange rate

True or False

1. F Getting goods and services they can't produce themselves is one reason to trade, but the main reason countries specialize and trade is to increase total output, incomes, and living standards.
2. F A larger marginal propensity to import results in a smaller multiplier because less spending stays in the nation's circular flow.
3. F Exports have no impact on the size of the multiplier because exports are not a leakage from the circular flow.
4. T
5. T
6. F U.S. products become more competitive (i.e. relatively lower priced) when the U.S. dollar becomes weaker.
7. T
8. T
9. T
10. T

Multiple Choice

1.	d	5.	a	9.	a	13.	b	17.	d
2.	c	6.	b	10.	b	14.	d	18.	d
3.	b	7.	a	11.	c	15.	a	19.	d
4.	b	8.	b	12.	a	16.	a	20.	d

Problems and Applications

Exercise 1

1. 0.8. See the consumption function.
2. 0.2 (= 1 - 0.8)
3. 5 (= 1/*MPS*)
4. $1,250 billion (= $250 billion x 5)
5. 2 [= 1/(MPS + MPM) = 1/(0.2 + 0.3)]
6. $500 billion (= $250 billion x 2)
7. T
8. AD_2

Exercise 2

1. **Table 18.1 Answer**

	Year 1	Year 2
GDP	$800	$1,000
Exports	50	50
Imports	60	80
Net exports	-10	-30
Import/GDP ratio	0.075	0.080

2. See Table 18.1 Answer
3. See Table 18.1 Answer
4. See Table 18.1 Answer
5. See Table 18.1 Answer
6. increase, increasing

Exercise 3

1. "Asia's financial turmoil has rolled across the USA . . ."
2. A decrease in exports and concern about job losses in virtually every state.
3. "U.S. exports to Asia . . . have dropped 11% in the last year. "
4. "The U.S. economy remains robust, marked by low unemployment, inflation, and interest rates."

CHAPTER 19
Theory and Reality

Quick Review

Designing economic policy for an economy as large and diverse as that of the United States is a very difficult job, and using the many available tools in a complementary fashion to implement the policy adds to the complexity. It is thus appropriate that we consider the following questions:

- What's the ideal "package" of macro policies?
- How well does our macro performance live up to the promises of that package?
- What kinds of obstacles prevent us from doing better?

We begin by noting that the president and congress are responsible for making economic policy and pursuing economic goals. One goal that is unanimously supported is that of eliminating the business cycle because achieving that goal alone would solve many problems all at once.

There are a number of policy tools or policy levers in the arsenal that can be used to fight upswings and downswings in the economy. Monetary-policy tools (open-market operations, changing reserve requirements, and the like) and fiscal-policy tools (changing taxes and spending) are the most powerful ones. Supply-side policy (deregulation, retraining, and so on) is used as well. Economic forecasters, who advise policy makers, follow a variety of indicators and use econometric models to predict problems. Many valuable economic resources are devoted to the study and development of economic policy, yet our policies seem often to fail. Why? There are many reasons. One is the lack of unanimity among the economists about how the economy works. Several "groups" of economists can be identified—Keynesians, Monetarists, Supply-siders, Rational Expectationists, and so on—who have somewhat different views about how to achieve economic stability.

Other serious problems plague us, too:

- *Goal conflicts*. Our economy has many macroeconomic goals, including some that impact other economies, so conflict seems inevitable. Some would argue that goal conflict has been institutionalized because the Fed is the guardian of the price level and the president and congress are more concerned with jobs, growth, and the like.
- *Measurement problems*. It's difficult to measure what we want to know, to make current measurements when measurement is possible, or to make accurate forecasts even with current information.
- *Design problems*. We don't know *exactly* how the economy responds to specific policies. Perverse reaction to government policies may actually worsen the problem the policy was intended to solve.
- *Implementation problems*. It takes time for Congress and the president to agree on an appropriate plan of action. Four types of lag seem to prevent policies from being implemented quickly:

recognition lag, lag in formulation of a response, lag in the response itself, and lag in the impact of the policy.

For all of these reasons the fine-tuning of economic performance rarely lives up to its theoretical potential. In addition, the continual changes of policy lead to a lack of credibility on the part of policy makers. Because of their rational expectations about the continually changing policies, people are likely to act in ways that defeat policy initiatives of the government.

Learning Objectives

After reading Chapter 19 and doing the following exercises, you should:

1. Know the three basic types of policies and each of the policy levers.
2. Know how the concept of "opportunity cost" defines the basic policy tradeoffs faced in the economy.
3. Be able to prescribe policies to eliminate an AD shortfall.
4. Be able to design policies to deal with excess AD.
5. Be able to suggest policies to control stagflation.
6. Know the general theories of several groups of economists.
7. Evaluate how effective policy makers have been in battling inflation and unemployment.
8. Be able to explain how measurement problems impede the development of effective policies.
9. Understand the concept of a leading indicator.
10. Understand the design problems encountered in administering policy and the problems which are inherent in economic forecasting.
11. Know the "rational-expectations" argument about the effectiveness of policy.
12. Recognize the lags involved in policy implementation.
13. Know the advantages and problems of both rules and discretion in making policy.

Using Key Terms

Fill in the puzzle on the opposite page with the appropriate term from the list of Key Terms at the end of the chapter in the text.

Across
1. Alternating periods of economic expansion and contraction.
3. Federal revenues at full employment minus federal expenditures at full employment.
7. Spending or revenue item that responds automatically and countercyclically to changes in national income.
8. Spending increases or tax cuts intended to increase aggregate demand.
9. The difference between full-employment GDP and equilibrium GDP.
10. The use of money and credit controls to change macroeconomic outcomes.
12. Spending decreases or tax hikes intended to decrease aggregate demand.
13. Focuses on providing incentives to work, invest, and produce.
14. The idea that people make decisions on the basis of all available information, including the anticipated effects of government intervention.
15. The number of times money turns over in a given time period.
16. A situation of inflation and substantial unemployment.

Down
2. The lowest rate of unemployment compatible with price stability.
4. Equal to 1/1-MPC.
5. The use of spending and revenue items to change macroeconomic outcomes.
6. A period during which real GDP grows, but at a rate below the long-term trend.
11. Continuous responses to changing economic conditions.

Puzzle 19.1

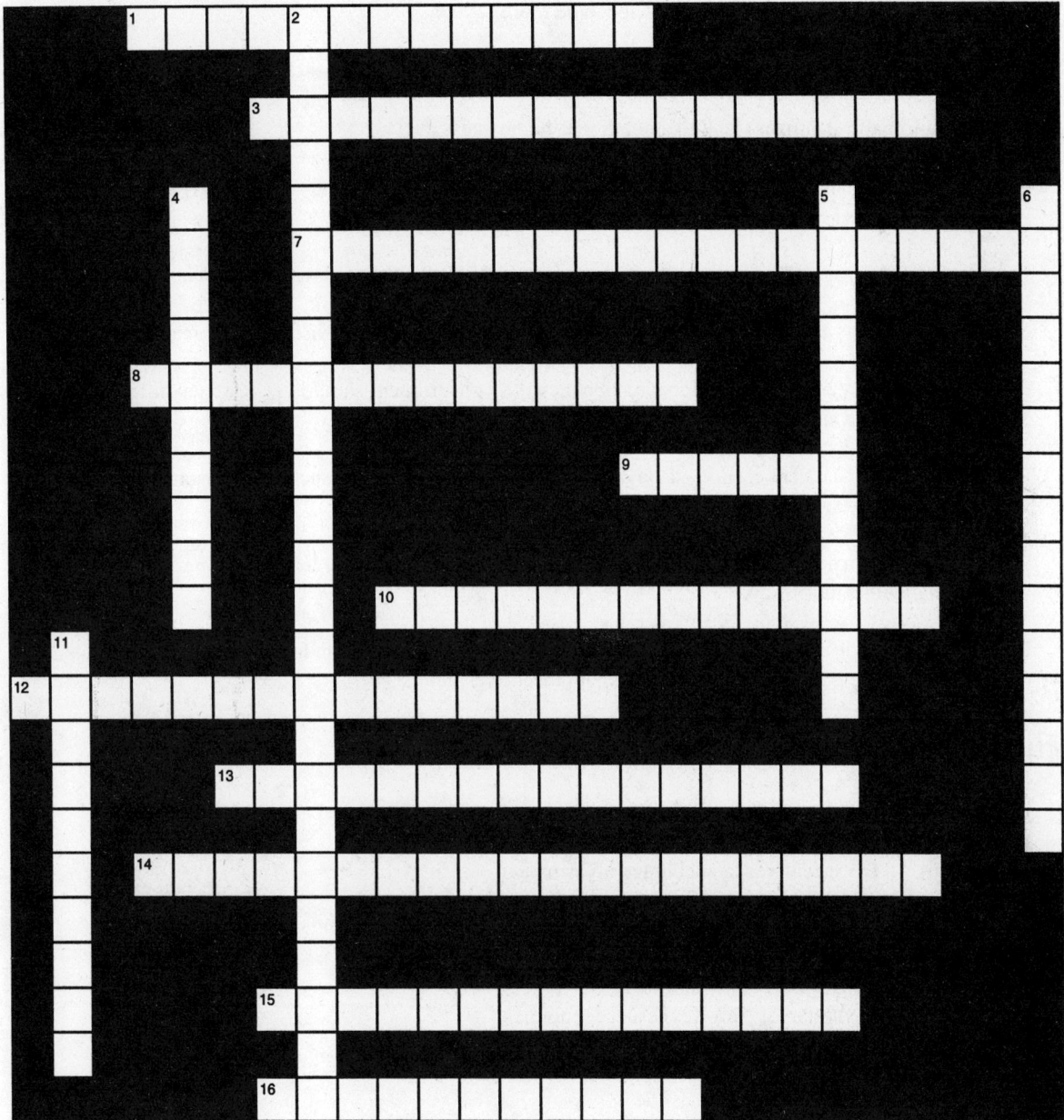

True or False: *Circle your choice and explain why any false statements are incorrect.*

T   F   1.   The failure of macroeconomic policy is reflected in the fact that since World War II, the ups and downs of the business cycle have become more severe.

T   F   2.   It is often the case that good economic policy and political objectives are in conflict.

T   F   3.   Automatic stabilizers tend to smooth out the business cycle.

T   F   4.   Macroeconomic forecasts from different computer models are usually surprisingly similar because the models are based on the same macroeconomic theories.

T   F   5.   Even if we agreed on policy priorities, we would still be confronted with tradeoffs.

T   F   6.   Monetarists and New Classical economists favor rules rather than discretionary macro policies.

T   F   7.   Modern Keynesians and Monetarists believe the government should use changes in the money supply as a method to eliminate a GDP gap.

T   F   8.   The New Classical economists favor steady, predictable policies, such as a constant growth rate in the money supply.

T   F   9.   Rational expectations about the effect of a government policy may lead to private-sector actions that defeat the policy.

T   F 10.   Supply-side economists focus on the expansion of capacity through lower marginal tax rates and policies to increase work and investment incentives.

Multiple Choice: *Select the correct answer.*

_____ 1.   A supply-side policy cure to stagflation would include:
        (a)   Reduced government spending.
        (b)   Tax incentives to encourage investment.
        (c)   Open-market operations when the Fed buys securities.
        (d)   A higher reserve requirement.

_____ 2.   Fine-tuning is most consistent with:
        (a)   Keynesian or Neo-Keynesian economics.
        (b)   Monetarist or New Classical economics.
        (c)   Supply-side economics or New Classical economics.
        (d)   Laissez faire.

_____ 3.   Which of the following is an accurate statement concerning the performance of macroeconomic policy in the United States?
        (a)   We have frequently failed to reach our goals of full employment, price stability and vigorous economic growth.
        (b)   The business cycle continues to exist.
        (c)   The ups and downs of the business cycle have been less severe since World War II.
        (d)   All of the above are accurate.

_____ 4. Monetary policy to eliminate an AD shortfall would include:
- (a) A lower reserve requirement.
- (b) The sale of securities in the open market by the Fed.
- (c) The Monetary Control and Deregulation Act.
- (d) A rise in the discount rate.

_____ 5. When Federal Reserve Board chairman Alan Greenspan announced a goal of "zero inflation," which of the following was most consistent with his new goal?
- (a) A lower discount rate.
- (b) A lower minimum reserve ratio.
- (c) Sales of securities in the open market.
- (d) Increased government spending.

_____ 6. Which of the following groups feels that output and employment gravitate to a long-term rate determined by structural forces in the labor and product markets?
- (a) Monetarists.
- (b) Keynesians.
- (c) New Classical economists.
- (d) Supply-side economists.

_____ 7. An increase in the discount rate during an inflationary period would be a policy consistent with the views of:
- (a) Monetarists.
- (b) Modern Keynesians.
- (c) Monetarists and Supply siders.
- (d) New Classicals and "Old" Keynesians

_____ 8. A supply-side policy to curb AD excess would include:
- (a) Reduced government spending.
- (b) Tax incentives to encourage saving.
- (c) The purchase of securities by the Fed.
- (d) A higher reserve requirement.

_____ 9. Which of the following is the Monetarist policy for fighting a recession?
- (a) Increase government spending.
- (b) Expand the money supply at a faster rate.
- (c) Provide tax incentives to increase investment.
- (d) Patience (i.e. laissez faire).

_____ 10. Which of the following supply-side efforts did the Clinton administration embrace?
- (a) Wage-price controls.
- (b) Infrastructure development.
- (c) The Budget Enforcement Act.
- (d) All of the above.

_____ 11. Expansionary fiscal and monetary policy are _not_ effective when the:
- (a) Aggregate supply curve is horizontal.
- (b) Aggregate supply curve is vertical.
- (c) Aggregate supply is upward sloping but not vertical.
- (d) Aggregate demand curve is vertical.

_____ 12. The opportunity costs of different policies must be weighted to solve which of the following obstacles?
    (a) Design problems.
    (b) Measurement problems.
    (c) Goal conflicts.
    (d) Implementation problems.

_____ 13. Which of the following is a reason that many economic policies fail, even if they are properly designed to achieve economic goals?
    (a) Measurement difficulties prevent policy makers from correctly identifying what is actually happening in the economy.
    (b) People often react in ways that may undercut new government policies.
    (c) There are significant lags in response to policy.
    (d) All of the above are reasons for the failure of economic policy.

_____ 14. Advocates of "fixed policy rules" believe:
    (a) That "fixed policy rules" can improve macro outcomes.
    (b) Appropriate macro policy would include constant increases in the money supply and balanced federal budgets.
    (c) That in view of the many practical problems associated with implementing fiscal and monetary policy, the economy would be better off if discretionary policy were abandoned.
    (d) All of the above.

_____ 15. Marxists differ from other economists by:
    (a) Focusing on budget restraint and monetary policy when the economy overheats.
    (b) Believing people's rational expectations will lead them to offset government policy.
    (c) Believing that failures of the economy are inherent in a capitalist economy and require capitalist economies to be changed.
    (d) Wanting to use tax cuts and government spending to increase demand and output.

_____ 16. Which of the following groups feels that output and employment gravitate to their natural levels?
    (a) Keynesians.
    (b) Monetarists.
    (c) New Classical economists.
    (d) Marxists.

_____ 17. The reason that economic forecasting of the economy is most important and useful is that:
    (a) Economists need employment.
    (b) Business managers need to be able to anticipate government policy changes.
    (c) Policymakers need to be able to anticipate what needs to be done and take action in time to be effective in achieving the desired result.
    (d) Consumers can find out when they are going to lose their jobs and income.

_____ 18. Congress is responsible for:
    (a) Monetary policy.
    (b) Fiscal policy and supply-side policy.
    (c) Monetary and fiscal policy.
    (d) Monetary, fiscal, and supply-side policy.

_____ 19. The order of policy lags can best be stated as follows:
    (a) Formulation, recognition, and implementation lags.
    (b) Implementation, formulation, and recognition lags.
    (c) Recognition, formulation, and implementation lags.
    (d) Formulation, implementation, and recognition lags.

_____ 20. Because of rational expectations about government policy changes, New Classical economists recommend that government policy consist of:
(a) Unalterable rules.
(b) Discretion.
(c) Faster measurement.
(d) Surprise policy shocks to the economy.

Problems and Applications

Exercise 1

This exercise will help you recognize the inherent trade-offs in the economy.

Table 19.1 presents data on interest rates, government expenditures, taxes, exports, imports, investment, consumption, a price index, and unemployment for four levels of equilibrium income (GDP). These items appear frequently in newspaper articles about the economy.

Table 19.1 Level of key economic indicators, by GDP level (billions of dollars per year)

Interest rate	30%	20%	10%	0%
Government expenditures	$ 100	$ 100	$ 100	100
Taxes	25	75	125	175
Budget balance	___	___	___	___
Exports	300	300	300	300
Imports	260	280	300	320
Investment	10	90	170	250
Consumption	750	790	830	870
Nominal GDP				
Price index	1.00	1.00	1.02	1.10
Real GDP (constant dollars)	___	___	___	___
Unemployment rate	15%	7%	4%	3.5%

1. Compute the federal budget balance, nominal GDP, and real GDP in Table 19.1, for each level of interest rate. (*Hint:* Remember the formula $C + I + G + [X - M] = $ GDP.)

2. Which policy is the government most likely using to reach each of the income levels in Table 19.1?
(a) Fiscal policy.
(b) Monetary policy.
(c) Wage and price controls.
(d) Labor policy.

3. Which of the following statements best explains why the amount paid in taxes might change as income changes, as shown in Table 19.1?
(a) Taxpayers experience stagflation as income increases.
(b) As taxpayers' incomes rise, their marginal tax rates rise.
(c) The income tax is regressive.
(d) Automatic stabilizers link taxes with income.

257

4. The reason that the price index changes as income changes, as shown in Table 19.1, is most likely that:
   (a) As people receive greater income, they can be more discriminating buyers and find the lowest prices.
   (b) As firms receive more orders, productivity rises allowing inflation to ease.
   (c) As people receive greater income, they spend it even when the economy is at full capacity, thus bidding up prices.
   (d) As businesses receive greater income, they have an incentive to expand capacity and must pass the cost of the increased capacity on to consumers in the form of higher prices.

5. The reason that unemployment changes as income changes, as shown in Table 19.1, is most likely that:
   (a) As income rises, people do not need jobs and leave the labor force.
   (b) As income rises, automatic stabilizers provide increased benefits to the unemployed, keeping them out of the labor force.
   (c) As income rises, inflation causes real income and employment to fall.
   (d) As income rises, aggregate demand rises, stimulating the derived demand for labor.

Exercise 2

This exercise shows the difficulties faced by policy makers because of the inevitable tradeoffs in the economy.

Table 19.2 presents data on government expenditure, taxes, the price index, unemployment, and pollution for four levels of equilibrium income (GDP). These items appear frequently in newspaper articles about the economy.

Table 19.2 Level of key economic indicators, by GDP level (billions of dollars per year)

Indicator	Nominal GDP			
	$120	$160	$200	$240
Government expenditure	$ 0	$ 20	$ 35	$ 50
Taxes	$ 18	$ 24	$ 30	$ 36
Budget balance	$_____	$_____	$_____	$_____
Price index	1.00	1.00	1.02	1.20
Real GDP (constant dollars)	$_____	$_____	$_____	$_____
Unemployment rate	15%	7%	4%	3.5%
Pollution index	1.00	1.10	1.80	1.90

1. Compute the federal budget balance and real GDP in Table 19.2 for each level of nominal GDP.

2. What government expenditure level would best accomplish all of the following goals according to Table 19.2? $_____
   • Lowest taxes.
   • Lowest pollution.
   • Lowest inflation rate.

3. Which of the following might induce a policy maker to choose a higher government expenditure level than the one that answers question 2?
   (a) High unemployment.
   (b) Government's inability to provide public goods and services.
   (c) Low real income.
   (d) All of the above.

4. What government expenditure level would best accomplish all of the following goals? $_____
   • Lowest unemployment rate.
   • Highest amount of public goods and services.
   • Highest real income.

5. For the policy that best satisfies the goals in question 4, there would most likely be:
   (a) A recession.
   (b) Rapid economic growth accompanied by inflation.
   (c) Stagflation.
   (d) None of the above.

6. Which government expenditure level would best accomplish all of the following goals? $_____
   • Balancing the federal budget.
   • Maintaining pollution at reasonably low levels.
   • Maintaining price stability.

7. At which government expenditure level does full employment occur? (Use 4 percent unemployment as full employment.) $_____

8. If you were a policy maker faced with the alternatives in Table 19.2, would you be able to say that one of the alternative government expenditure levels was clearly best? _____

Exercise 3

This exercise tests your ability to choose the appropriate policy initiative to overcome various undesirable economic conditions.

Choose a policy from the list below that would be appropriate to correct the economic conditions at the top of Table 19.3. Place the letter of each item in Table 19.3 only once.

a. Deregulation.
b. Discount rate lowered.
c. Discount rate raised.
d. Government spending decreases.
e. Government spending increases.
f. Open-market operations (Fed buys government securities).
g. Open-market operations (Fed sells government securities).

h. Reserve requirement higher.
i. Reserve requirement lower.
j. Skill training and other labor market aids.
k. Tax cuts.
l. Tax incentives to alter the structure of supply and demand.
m. Tax incentives to encourage saving.
n. Tax increases.

Table 19.3 Economic policies

	Recession	Inflation	Stagflation
Fiscal policy	1._____	6._____	
	2._____	7._____	
Monetary policy	3._____	8._____	
	4._____	9._____	
	5._____	10._____	
Supply-side policy		11._____	12._____
			13._____
			14._____

Exercise 4

The media often provide information about the government's slow response to the economy's needs. This exercise will use one of the articles in the text to show the kind of information to look for.

Reread the article in the text titled "Deficit-Cutting Wilts in Heat from Voters: Entitlements Remain Mostly Off-Limits." Then answer the following questions.

1. Which *one* of the following obstacles to success is best illustrated by the article?
   (a) Goal conflicts.
   (b) Measurement problems.
   (c) Design problems.
   (d) Implementation problems.

2. What passage specifically mentions the obstacle you have chosen? _____
   _____

3. What passage indicates the decision-maker who is responsible for determining the policy?
   _____

4. What passage indicates the situation which requires a policy response? _____
   _____

Common Errors

The first statement in each "common error" below is incorrect. Each incorrect statement is followed by a corrected version and an explanation.

1. Fiscal and monetary policy should be consistently applied to stimulate the economy. WRONG!

   Fiscal and monetary policies must be tailored to the specific economic problems faced by the government. RIGHT!

The government sometimes needs to apply apparently contradictory monetary and fiscal policies in order to attain quite different goals. For example, an expansionary fiscal policy may be needed to stimulate the economy, but a contractionary monetary policy may be needed to raise interest rates so that foreign capital will be enticed into the United States. A policy maker must weigh the various goals and decide on the appropriate mix of tools to achieve them.

2. Fiscal, monetary, and stagflation policies are effective regardless of the income level of the economy. WRONG!

   The state of the economy in relation to full employment is important in determining the effectiveness of the various policies. RIGHT!

   If the economy is experiencing an excess aggregate demand, wage–price controls will prove ineffective in curbing inflation. At relatively low levels of GDP, however, wage–price controls can be effective in holding down inflation. Work-force policies are often more effective in matching people with jobs when many people are looking for work than when unemployment is low. It is easier for the government to increase expenditures to stimulate the economy when there is a recession than to cut them back when there is excess aggregate demand.

3. The government has the power to prevent unemployment and inflation, but it just doesn't want to use it. WRONG!

   While the government has the power to move the economy closer to any one goal, it faces a tradeoff between different goals that prevents it from achieving all of them. RIGHT!

   Remember that the Phillips curve shows that a tradeoff exists between unemployment and inflation. Government policies to lower unemployment may lead to a worsening of inflation. The government must choose between the different goals.

•ANSWERS•

Using Key Terms
Across
1. business cycle
3. structural deficit
7. automatic stabilizer
8. fiscal stimulus
9. GDP gap
10. monetary policy
12. fiscal restraint
13. supply-side policy
14. rational expectations
15. velocity of money
16. stagflation

Down
2. natural rate of unemployment
4. multiplier
5. fiscal policy
6. growth recession
11. fine tuning

True or False

1.	F	The ups and downs of the business cycle have become less severe since World War II, possibly indicating partial success.
2.	T	
3.	T	
4.	F	Macroeconomic forecasts often differ because the models are based on different macroeconomic theories (e.g. Keynesian, supply-side).
5.	T	
6.	T	
7.	F	Modern Keynesians would agree to the use of changes in the money supply but Monetarists would take a "hands off" approach believing that as sales and output decline, interest rates will decline (because of lower demand) and the lower rates will stimulate investment, without government intervention.
8.	F	New Classicals believe that the only policies that work are those that are unexpected because rational people will anticipate the impact of announced policies and take protective actions that will render the announced policies ineffective.
9.	T	
10.	T	

Multiple Choice

1.	b	5.	c	9.	d	13.	d	17.	c
2.	a	6.	a	10.	b	14.	d	18.	b
3.	d	7.	b	11.	b	15.	c	19.	c
4.	a	8.	b	12.	c	16.	b	20.	a

Problems and Applications

Exercise 1

1. **Table 19.1 Answer (billions of dollars per year)**

Interest rate	30%	20%	10%	0%
Budget balance	$ −75	$ −25	$ 25	$ 75
Nominal GDP	900	1,000	1,100	1,200
Real GDP (constant dollars)	900	1,000	1,078	1,091

At the 30 percent interest rate, the following calculations should have been made, in billions of dollars per year:

Budget balance = $25 − $100 = − $75

Nominal GDP = $750 + $10 + $100 + $40 = $900

2. b   3. b   4. c   5. d

262

Exercise 2

1. **Table 19.2 Answer (billions of dollars per year)**

Indicator	Nominal GDP			
	$120	$160	$200	$240
Budget balance	$ 18	$ 4	$ -5	$ -14
Real GDP (constant dollars)	120	160	196	200

2. $0
3. d
4. $50 billion
5. b
6. $20 billion
7. $35 billion
8. No

Exercise 3

1. **Table 19.3 Answer**

	Recession	Inflation	Stagflation
Fiscal	1. k Tax cuts 2. e Government spending increases	6. n Tax increases 7. d Government spending decreases	
Monetary policy	3. b Discount rate lowered 4. f Open-market operations (Fed buys government securities) 5. i Reserve requirement lower	8. c Discount rate raised 9. g Open-market operations (Fed sells government securities) 10. h Reserve requirement higher	
Supply-side policy		11. m Tax incentives to encourage saving	12. a Deregulation 13. l Tax incentives to alter the structure of supply and demand 14. j Skill training & other labor market aids

Exercise 4

1. a   However, there is implicit evidence of design problems concerning the best way to cut the deficit.
2. "Even before his proposal [to cut the deficit] took shape, more than 3,000 New Mexico constituents sent him identical postcards opposing any effort to cap entitlement programs." The passage shows the conflict between deficit cutting and the need for inflation-indexed entitlement programs to protect different groups.
3. "Senate, which voted 69 to 28 to reject the proposal"
4. "digging out of the massive federal deficit"

C H A P T E R 20

The Demand for Goods

Quick Review

Demand and supply were introduced in Chapter 3 to demonstrate how markets operate. In this chapter we look at demand in greater depth. Specifically, the chapter looks at the following questions:

- How do we decide how much of any good to buy?
- How does a change in a product's price affect the quantity we purchase or the amount of money we spend on it?
- Why do we buy certain products but not others?

Other concepts are developed too, but these three questions organize our early discussion.

Demand for goods and services is more than just the desire for goods and services and it has nothing to do with the sellers of those goods or services or even with the availability of the goods or services. In fact, demand can exist even if there are no purchases by buyers at all. When people starve as a result of a drought, they have the desire for food but not the ability to pay for it. Demand reflects both the willingness and the ability to buy goods and services. Consumers' tastes, their incomes, the prices (and availability) of other goods, and people's expectations (about tastes, incomes, and prices) determine what individuals are willing and able to buy. If any of these determinants of demand change, then the demand curve shifts. Shifts in the demand curve are likely to cause changes in price and purchases in the marketplace. To understand the market, we must look carefully at tastes, incomes, prices, and expectations.

Utility theory helps clarify much of what we know about consumer tastes and preferences. Consumers buy only those things that give them satisfaction, or utility. Since consumers have a limited income, they must ask what gives them maximum satisfaction for that income. Usually a variety of goods and services is available. Consumers compare the available goods and services—and their relative prices—then choose the amounts that will give them the greatest satisfaction, or utility, for the income available. As a person consumes more and more of any one product, other goods and services become relatively more desirable. This is the law of diminishing marginal utility at work: as we consume more of a product, we receive smaller and smaller *increments* of pleasure from it.

The law of diminishing marginal utility translates readily into the law of demand. The law of demand asserts that we will be willing to buy increasing quantities of a product as its price falls; that is, an inverse relationship exists between quantity demanded and price. This law is graphically illustrated by a downward-sloping demand curve. The demand curve itself relates the quantity of a good demanded to its price, under the assumption that all other things are held constant (*ceteris paribus*). The downward slope of the demand curve indicates that larger quantities of a good will be purchased at lower prices.

The demand curve provides information about the total revenue that a firm could receive. By computing the price elasticity of demand, the firm can even determine how its total revenue changes for a given change in price and how responsive quantity demanded is to a change in price. Income elasticity and cross-price elasticity provide information on how demand curves shift in response to changes in income and the prices of other goods, respectively. The role of advertising can be understood in terms of demand theory—it is to shift the demand curve for a product to the right.

Learning Objectives

After reading Chapter 20 and doing the following exercises, you should:

1. Be able to distinguish the demand for a good from the desire for it.
2. Be able to show how any change in the price of a good, in the price of a substitute, in the price of a complement, in incomes, in tastes, or in expectations will affect the demand curve.
3. Know how the law of diminishing marginal utility and the law of demand relate to each other.
4. Be able to draw a demand curve from a demand schedule and create a demand schedule by looking at a demand curve.
5. Be able to distinguish between a change in demand (a shift of the curve) and a change in quantity demanded (a movement along the demand curve).
6. Know the determinants of elasticity.
7. Be able to compute the price elasticity of demand between two points on the demand curve.
8. Be able to determine on the basis of the elasticity of demand what will happen to total revenue when price changes.
9. Understand income elasticity, cross-price elasticity and their role in demand theory.
10. Know how a consumer makes the optimal consumption decision.
11. Understand the role of advertising in the theory of demand.

Using Key Terms

Across

1. Items for which an increase in the price of good X causes a decrease in the demand for good Y.
6. In the cartoon in the text, the fourth hamburger does not provide as much satisfaction as the first hamburger because of the law of _____.
12. Explains why the curve in Figure 20.3 in the text is downward sloping.
13. The satisfaction obtained from the entire consumption of a good.
14. The quantity of a product sold times the price at which it is sold.
15. According to Figure 20.8 in the text, candy and popcorn are _____.
17. Equal to the percentage change in quantity demanded divided by the percentage change in income.
18. Equal to the percentage change in quantity demanded of good X divided by the percentage change in the price of good Y.
19. The best forgone alternative.

Down

2. Influenced by tastes, income, expectations, and other goods.
3. Measures the response of consumers to a change in price.
4. The combination of goods which maximizes the total utility attainable from available income.
5. Positive but diminishing for the first five boxes of popcorn in Figure 20.2 in the text.
7. The result of a successful advertising campaign in Figure 20.9 in the text.
8. An item for which quantity demanded falls when income rises.
9. Affected by advertising in Figure 20.9 in the text.
10. Consumers buy more of such an item when their incomes rise.
11. The assumption that everything else is constant.
16. Satisfaction obtained from goods and services.

Puzzle 20.1

Across

1. COMPLEMENTARY GOODS
6. DIMINISHING MARGINAL UTILITY
12. LAW OF DEMAND
13. TOTAL UTILITY
14. TOTAL REVENUE
15. SUBSTITUTE GOODS
17. INCOME ELASTICITY OF DEMAND
18. CROSS PRICE ELASTICITY
19. OPPORTUNITY COST

Down

2. DEMAND
3. PRICE ELASTICITY OF DEMAND
4. OPTIMAL CONSUMPTION
5. MARGINAL UTILITY
7. SHIFT IN DEMAND
8. INFERIOR GOOD
9. DEMAND CURVE
10. NORMAL GOOD
11. CETERIS PARIBUS
16. UTILITY

267

True or False: *Circle your choice and explain why any false statements are incorrect.*

(T) F 1. Sellers use advertising to change the consumer's utilities, thus causing a shift in the consumer's demand curve.

(T) F 2. The law of demand differs from the law of diminishing marginal utility in that it considers what a person is able to pay for a good or service, not just the person's desire for a good or service.

T **(F)** 3. When the price of a good is expected to fall next month, then the current demand curve should shift to the right.

T **(F)** 4. According to the law of diminishing marginal utility, the total utility we obtain from a product declines as we consume more of it.

(T) F 5. If there is no budget constraint, utility maximization is achieved when marginal utility is zero.

T **(F)** 6. If demand is elastic, a rise in price raises total revenue.

T **(F)** 7. Elasticity of demand is constant along straight-line demand curves.

T **(F)** 8. The price elasticity of demand is influenced by all the determinants of demand.

(T) F 9. A demand curve is perfectly elastic if consumers reduce their quantity demanded to zero if price rises by even the slightest amount.

T F 10. A negative cross-price elasticity indicates goods are substitutes because a positive percentage increase in one good results in a negative percentage increase in the other.

Multiple Choice: *Select the correct answer.*

A 1. As more of a good is consumed, then total utility typically:
   - (a)   Increases at a decreasing rate.
   - (b)   Decreases as long as marginal utility is negative.
   - (c)   Decreases as long as marginal utility is positive.
   - (d)   Is negative as long as marginal utility is decreasing.

C 2. Which of the following statements exemplifies the law of diminishing marginal utility?
   - (a)   Spinach gives me no satisfaction, so I won't spend my income for any of it.
   - (b)   The more soda I drink, the more I want to drink.
   - (c)   The more I go to school, the more I want to do something else.
   - (d)   Since we need water more than we need diamonds, water is more valuable.

B 3. Both the law of demand and the law of diminishing marginal utility:
   - (a)   State that quantity and price are inversely related.
   - (b)   Reflect declining increments of satisfaction from consuming additional units of product.
   - (c)   Reflect both the willingness and the ability of buyers to buy goods and services.
   - (d)   Can be illustrated by means of demand curves.

_D_ 4. Which of the following is a reason why a demand curve is typically downward sloping?
   (a) The law of diminishing marginal utility.
   (b) Consumers are not willing to pay as much for a good with low marginal utility than for a good with a high marginal utility.
   (c) Consumers have limited budgets.
   (d) All of the above are reasons.

_B_ 5. The price elasticity of demand:
   (a) Compares the absolute change in quantity demanded with the percentage change in price.
   (b) Provides information about how responsive consumers are to a change in price.
   (c) Is the same as the slope of the demand curve.
   (d) Refers to the response of producers to a change in price.

_C_ 6. Which of the following causes demand to be more elastic with respect to price?
   (a) Shorter periods of time to adjust to a change in price.
   (b) A steeper demand curve for a given price and quantity.
   (c) More substitutes.
   (d) If the good takes up a larger portion of the consumer's budget.

✗ _D_ 7. Which of the following is likely to have the most elastic price elasticity of demand?
   (a) Food.
   (b) Fruit.
   (c) Peaches.
   (d) Farmer Betty's peaches (which are exactly like all the other farmer's peaches).

✗ _A_ 8. Assume that the price elasticity of demand for U.S. Frisbee Co. frisbees is -0.6. If the company increases the price of each frisbee from $6 to $8, the number of frisbees sold will:
   (a) Decrease by 17.1 percent. $\frac{\Delta Q \downarrow}{\Delta P \uparrow} = -.6$
   (b) Decrease by 47.6 percent.
   (c) Increase by 28.6 percent. $.33\%$
   (d) Increase by 17.1 percent.

_B_ 9. A demand curve is described as perfectly elastic if:
   (a) The same quantity is purchased regardless of price.
   (b) The same price is charged regardless of quantity sold.
   (c) Only price can change.
   (d) It is vertical.

~~A~~ _B_ 10. Total revenue declines when demand is:
   (a) Elastic and price rises, causing a demand shift.
   (b) Elastic and price rises, causing a movement along the demand curve.
   (c) Inelastic and price rises, causing a demand shift.
   (d) Inelastic and price rises, causing a movement along the demand curve.

_B_ 11. One of the airline industry's arguments against deregulation of air fares was that the resulting fall in prices would lower airline total revenue. Instead, total revenue rose. Assuming the increase in total revenue was due solely to the lower fares, it can be concluded that:
   (a) Airline representatives thought demand for plane trips was elastic.
   (b) Quantity demanded of airline service increased by a greater percentage than the percentage fall in price.
   (c) Demand for airline service increased with the fall in prices.
   (d) Airlines were more profitable after deregulation.

269

_C_ 12. If a state legislature wishes to raise revenue by increasing certain sales taxes, it would increase sales taxes on goods that:
   (a) Are illegal.
   (b) Are bought by those with high incomes.
   (c) Have inelastic demand.
   (d) Have elastic demand.

_D_ 13. Assume that a good has a downward sloping, linear demand curve. As the price of this good increases, total revenues:
   (a) Increase indefinitely.
   (b) Decrease indefinitely because the quantity sold will decrease.
   (c) Remain constant.
   (d) Increase then decrease.

_a_ 14. Assume that the price elasticity of demand for Great Fit Shoe Co. shoes is -1.5. If the company decreases the price of each pair of shoes, total revenues will:
   (a) Increase because more shoes will be sold.
   (b) Decrease because the company will be receiving less revenue per pair of shoes.
   (c) Increase because the percentage increase in the number sold is greater than the percentage decrease in the price.
   (d) Impossible to predict because we do not know the percentage change in price.

_D_ 15. When the price of postage stamps increases, the demand for long-distance telephone service increases, *ceteris paribus*. Postage stamps and long-distance service are therefore:
   (a) Elastic.
   (b) Inelastic.
   (c) Complements.
   (d) Substitutes.

_A_ 16. Which of the following elasticities would be most useful in determining the impact of a recession on the demand for airline travel?
   (a) The income elasticity of air travel.
   (b) The price elasticity of demand for air travel.
   (c) The cross-price elasticity of demand for air travel with respect to income.
   (d) The cross-price elasticity of income with respect to air travel.

_____ 17. Suppose the cross-price elasticity of demand for automobiles with respect to the gasoline price is -0.20. If gasoline prices rise 20 percent, then automobile sales should, *ceteris paribus*:
   (a) Fall 4 percent.
   (b) Fall 100 percent.
   (c) Rise 4 percent.
   (d) Rise 100 percent.

_____ 18. Optimal consumption when two or more goods are being consumed is achieved when:
   (a) Opportunity costs relative to utility are zero for all goods.
   (b) Marginal utility equals zero.
   (c) Marginal revenue equals zero.
   (d) The ratio of marginal utility to price is the same for all goods.

_____ C 19. To maximize utility when purchasing two or more goods, the consumer should choose that good which:
- (a) Is priced the lowest.
- (b) Has the highest price elasticity.
- (c) Delivers the most marginal utility per dollar.
- (d) Provides the most satisfaction.

_____ B 20. The objective of advertising is to:
- (a) Increase demand and increase the price elasticity of demand.
- (b) Increase demand and decrease the price elasticity of demand.
- (c) Increase demand only.
- (d) Decrease demand and make the price elasticity of demand unitary.

[CHAPTER 20 APPENDIX QUESTIONS]

_____ 21. An indifference curve shows:
- (a) The maximum utility that can be achieved for a given consumer budget.
- (b) The maximum utility that can be achieved for different amounts of a good.
- (c) The combinations of goods giving equal utility to a consumer.
- (d) The optimal consumption combinations between two goods.

_____ 22. A budget line represents:
- (a) Consumption possibilities.
- (b) The combinations of goods giving equal utility to a consumer.
- (c) The combinations of goods a consumer can afford.
- (d) The amount of income that is required to purchase a given amount of a good.

_____ 23. Where the budget line and an indifference curve are tangent, there is:
- (a) An optimal consumption point.
- (b) A point indicating the quantity and price that would appear on a demand curve.
- (c) A point where the ratio of marginal utility to price is equal for two goods.
- (d) All of the above.

Problems and Applications

Exercise 1

This exercise will help you draw demand curves using demand schedules. It should also give you practice in constructing market demand curves.

1. Market demand is:
   - (a) The total quantity of a good or service that people are willing and able to buy at alternative prices in a given period of time, *ceteris paribus*.
   - (b) The sum of individual demands.
   - (c) Represented as the horizontal sum of individual demand curves.
   - (d) All of the above.

2. Table 20.1 presents a hypothetical demand schedule for cars manufactured in the United States.

Table 20.1 Demand for U.S. cars

Price	Number of new U.S. cars (millions per year)
$10,000	9.0
9,000	10.0

Graph this demand curve in Figure 20.1.

Figure 20.1

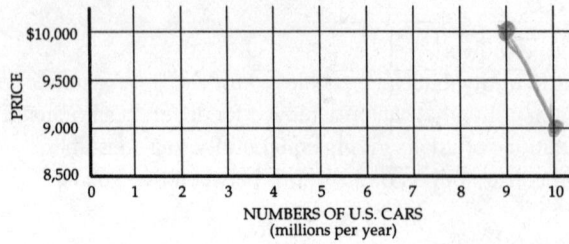

NUMBERS OF U.S. CARS
(millions per year)

3. Table 20.2 presents a similar demand schedule for imported cars.

Table 20.2
Demand for foreign cars

Price	Number of new foreign cars (millions per year)
$10,000	1.0
9,000	2.0

Graph this demand curve in Figure 20.2.

Figure 20.2

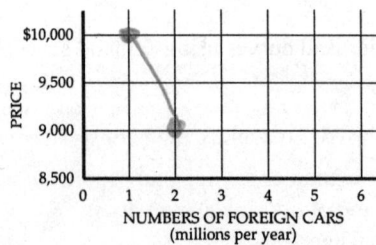

NUMBERS OF FOREIGN CARS
(millions per year)

4. In Table 20.3 calculate the demand schedule for cars (both foreign and domestically produced) at the two prices shown.

Table 20.3
Market demand for new cars

Price	Number of new cars (millions per year)
$10,000	*10.0*
9,000	*12.0*

5. In Figure 20.3 draw the domestic market demand curve for both foreign and domestic cars.

Figure 20.3

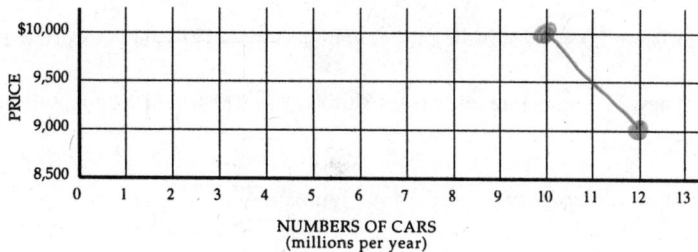

NUMBERS OF CARS
(millions per year)

Exercise 2

This exercise should give you practice in computing and interpreting the price elasticity of demand. This exercise is similar to a problem in the text.

1. T (F) The midpoint formula for the price elasticity of demand is

$$\frac{(p_2-p_1)/[1/2(p_1+p_2)]}{(q_2-q_1)/[1/2(q_1+q_2)]}$$

2. If you answered "true" to problem 1, you goofed. The percentage change in quantity, $(q_2 - q_1) \div [1/2(q_1 + q_2)]$, should be on the top, not the bottom. The correct formula is

$$\frac{(q_2-q_1)/[1/2(q_1+q_2)]}{(p_2-p_1)/[1/2(p_1+p_2)]}$$

Apply this formula to the information in Table 20.4, which represents a hypothetical demand schedule for cars. Remember to use the absolute value of this expression, which makes the coefficient always positive. (When calculating elasticities, answers will vary depending on the number of decimal places used. To achieve the book answer you will need to round each calculation to 2 decimal places.)

$$P \quad \frac{8,000-9000}{\frac{9000+8000}{2}} = \frac{1000}{17000} = .058$$

$$\frac{.153}{.058}$$

$$.88$$

$$Q \quad \frac{14-12}{\frac{12+14}{2}} = \frac{2}{13} = .153$$

273

Table 20.4
Market demand schedule for cars

Price	Number of new U.S. cars (millions per year)	Elasticity of demand
$10,000	10.0	—
9,000	12.0	1.64
8,000	14.0	1.25
7,000	16.0	1.0

3. According to Table 20.4, the price elasticity of demand for U.S. cars is (elastic, inelastic) between $9000 and $8000.

4. According to Table 20.4, what is the total revenue for new U.S. cars at a price of $8000? $112,000

5. If the price of new U.S. cars increases from $8000 to $9000, total revenue will (increase, decrease, stay the same).

6. Graph the first two columns of Table 20.4 in Figure 20.4.

Figure 20.4
Market demand curve

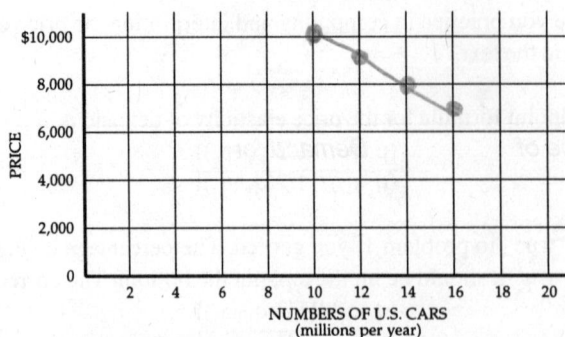

7. T F   The curve is a linear demand curve.

8. What is the slope of the demand curve? _____

9. Moving down a linear demand curve results in:
   (a) More inelastic demand and a changing slope.
   (b) More inelastic demand but a constant slope.
   (c) More elastic demand and a changing slope.
   (d) More elastic demand and a constant slope.

10. T F   While elasticity reflects a ratio of percentage changes in two variables, the slope reflects only changes in the variables, not percentage changes.

274

Exercise 3

This exercise focuses on calculating income elasticity and cross-price elasticity. It is similar to a problem in the text.

1. Use Table 20.5 to calculate the income elasticity of demand for peanut butter. Refer to the formula in the text. (Remember to round to 2 decimal places.)

Table 20.5

	Income (per year)	Demand for peanut butter (jars per year)		Income elasticity of demand
a	$10,000	12		
b	$20,000	7	a to b	-.79
c	$40,000	3	b to c	-1.20
d	$80,000	1	c to d	-1.50

2. Based on Table 20.5, peanut butter is a (normal, inferior) good because as income rises, the quantity demanded of peanut butter (rises, falls), and the income elasticity of demand is (negative, positive).

3. Use Table 20.6 to calculate the cross-price elasticity of demand for jelly when the price of peanut butter changes. Refer to the formula in the text. (Remember to round to 2 decimal places.)

Table 20.6

	Price of peanut butter (per jar)	Demand for jelly (jars per year)		Cross-price elasticity of demand
a	$2.00	12		
b	$3.00	10	a to b	_____
c	$4.00	7	b to c	_____
d	$5.00	2	c to d	_____

4. Based upon Table 20.6, peanut butter and jelly are (substitute, complementary) goods because as the price of peanut butter rises, the demand for jelly (falls, rises) and the cross-price elasticity of demand is (negative, positive).

Exercise 4

This exercise shows the relationship between total and marginal utility. It also gives practice in identifying the law of diminishing marginal utility.

Suppose there are two types of entertainment you enjoy - an evening at home with friends and an "event" entertainment, such as a sports event or a rock concert. The number of times that you experience each type of entertainment during a month determines the total utility of each type of entertainment for that month. Suppose Table 20.7 represents the total utility you achieve from consuming various quantities of the two types of entertainment.

Table 20.7
Total and marginal utility of two types of entertainment per month

Days of entertainment per month	Evening at home Total utility	Evening at home Marginal utility	Event Total utility	Event Marginal utility
0	0	0	0	
1	170	170	600	600
2	360	190	1,250	650
3	540	180	1,680	430
4	690	150	2,040	360
5	820	130	2,350	310
6	930	110	2,550	200
7	1,030	100	2,720	170
8	1,110	80	2,820	100
9	1,170	60	2,820	0
10	1,170	0	2,760	-60
11	1,120	-50	2,660	-100
12	1,020	-100	2,460	-200

1. Complete Table 20.7 by computing the marginal utility of each type of entertainment.

2. The law of diminishing marginal utility means:
    (a)   The total utility of a good declines as more of it is consumed in a given time period.
    (b)   The marginal utility of a good declines as more of it is consumed in a given time period.
    (c)   The price of a good declines as more of it is consumed in a given period of time.
    (d)   All of the above.

3. The law of diminishing marginal utility is in evidence in Table 20.7:
    (a)   For both types of entertainment.
    (b)   For home entertainment only.
    (c)   For event entertainment only.
    (d)   For neither type of entertainment.

    (Hint: You should be able to tell by looking at the marginal utility columns in Table 20.7. Does the marginal utility become smaller as you go down the column?)

4. In Figure 20.5 graph the total utility curve for evenings at home.

Figure 20.5

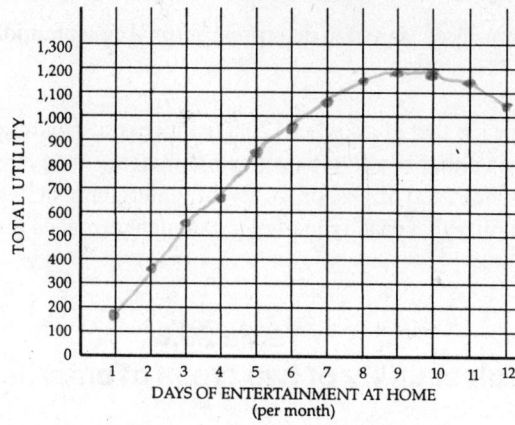

Figure 20.6

5. In Figure 20.6 graph the marginal utility curve for evenings at home.

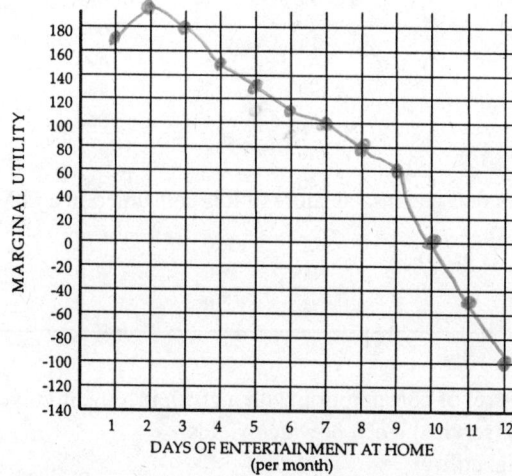

6. On the basis of the two graphs above, marginal utility becomes zero only when:
    (a) Total utility is zero.
    (b) Total utility reaches a maximum.
    (c) Total utility is rising.
    (d) Total utility is falling.

7. When total utility is rising, then:
    (a) Marginal utility is rising.
    (b) Marginal utility is negative.
    (c) Marginal utility is positive.
    (d) Marginal utility is zero.

277

Exercise 5

The principle of utility maximization is used to determine optimal consumption. This exercise builds on the previous exercise.

Suppose you hold a part-time job that gives you $120 a month extra spending money. On any day of the month you can spend that money on either of two types of entertainment—an evening at home with friends, for which you usually spend $10 for snacks and drinks, or an "event" entertainment, which costs $30. Table 20.8 shows the hypothetical marginal utility that each type of entertainment provides for you during the month.

Table 20.8
Total and marginal utility of two types of entertainment per month

Days of entertainment per month	Evening at home (price = $10)		Event entertainment (price = $30)	
	Marginal utility	MU/price	Marginal utility	MU/price
0	0	0	0	—
1	180	18	600	_____
2	180	18	600	_____
3	170	17	480	_____
4	140	14	360	_____
5	140	14	360	_____
6	140	14	360	_____
7	100	10	360	_____
8	100	10	0	_____
9	100	10	0	_____
10	0	0	0	_____

1. Finding the optimal level of consumption with a given income involves choosing successive *increments* of a good (service), *each of which* yields:
   (a) The largest total utility.
   (b) The largest marginal utility per unit of product or activity purchased.
   (c) The largest marginal utility for each dollar spent.
   (d) All of the above.

2. Divide marginal utility by the price of the event entertainment to complete Table 20.8.

Before you spend any money on any activity:

3. Which activity has the highest MU/p ratio? _____

4. Judging by the MU/p ratio, how many days of event entertainment should you buy before spending anything on at-home entertainment? _____

5. If you had $120 to spend on entertainment, how much money would you have left after buying two days of event entertainment? _____

6. Should you spend the entire balance from question 5 on at-home entertainment? _____

7. After you have bought three at-home nights and two events, how much income is left from the original $120? _____

8. Based on MU/*p*, which activity should you purchase with the income remaining in question 7? _____

9. T F When your income is $120, optimal consumption occurs with three evenings of each type of entertainment.

Appendix Exercise 6

This exercise provides practice in interpreting an indifference map and total utility.

For questions 1-7 refer to Figure A.2 in the appendix for Chapter 20.

1. At point E, the consumption combination includes ___3___ cokes and ___5___ video games.

2. At point D, the consumption combination includes ___2___ cokes and ___8___ video games.

3. Based on the indifference map, the consumer receives:
   (a) Greater satisfaction at point E than at point D.
   (b) Greater satisfaction at point D than at point E.
   (c) Equal satisfaction at point D and at point E.
   (d) Satisfaction cannot be determined from an indifference map.

4. At point B, the consumption combination includes ___2___ cokes and ___5___ video games.

5. At point C, the consumption combination includes ___3___ cokes and ___4___ video games.

6. Compare combinations B and C to point E. In each case, point E provides (greater, lesser) satisfaction than point B or point C.

7. For the given indifference map, the level of total utility is greatest at any point along curve ___I_2___.

Common Errors

The first statement in each "common error" below is incorrect. Each incorrect statement is followed by a corrected version and an explanation.

1. The law of demand and the law of diminishing marginal utility are the same. WRONG!

   The law of demand and the law of diminishing marginal utility are not the same. RIGHT!

   Do not confuse utility and demand. Utility refers only to expected satisfaction. Demand refers to both preferences and ability to pay. This distinction should help you to keep the law of diminishing marginal utility separate from the law of demand.

2. Figures 20.8a and 20.8b represent simple graphs drawn from a demand schedule.

Figure 20.8a

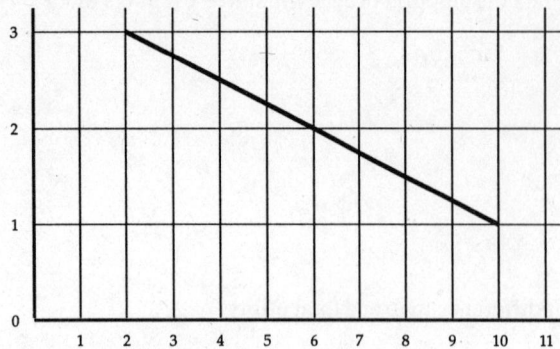

Price (dollars per unit)	Output quantity per unit of time
10	1
2	3

WRONG!

Figure 20.8b

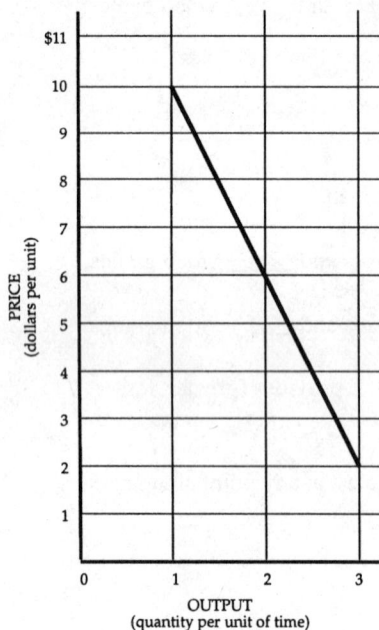

OUTPUT
(quantity per unit of time)

Price (dollars per unit)	Output quantity per unit of time
10	1
2	3

RIGHT!

The first graph has been drawn without any units indicated. It is something of an accidental tradition in economics to show price on the *y*-axis and quantity on the *x*-axis. This convention is sometimes confusing to mathematicians, who want to treat quantity as a function of price, according to the definition in the text. In Figure 20.8a the axes have been reversed and incorrect points have been chosen.

Be careful! When you are drawing a new graph, make a special effort to understand the units that are placed on the axes. Also, make sure you know the kinds of units in which each axis is measured. If you are drawing a graph from a table (or schedule), you can usually determine what should be on the axes by looking at the heading above the column from which you are reading the numbers.

Make sure price is shown on the *y*-axis (vertical) and quantity on the *x*-axis (horizontal). If you mix up the two, you may confuse a graph showing perfectly elastic demand with one showing perfectly inelastic demand.

280

3. The formula for the price elasticity of demand is

$$\frac{\text{Change in price}}{\text{Change in quantity}} \qquad \text{WRONG!}$$

The formula for the price elasticity of demand is

$$\frac{\text{Percentage change in quantity}}{\text{Percentage change in price}} \qquad \text{RIGHT!}$$

The concept of elasticity allows us to compare relative changes in quantity and price without having to worry about the units in which they are measured. In order to do this, we compute percentage changes of both price and quantity. A change in price *causes* people to change the quantity they demand in a given time period. By putting the quantity changes in the numerator, we can see that if the quantity response is very large in relation to a price change, the elasticity will also be very large. If the quantity response is small in relation to a price change, then demand is price inelastic (elasticity is small).

Be careful! Do not confuse slope and elasticity. The formula for the slope of the demand curve is the *wrong* formula shown above. The formula for the price elasticity of demand is the *right* formula. Remember to take the absolute value of the elasticity too.

4. A flat demand curve has an elasticity of zero. WRONG!

A flat demand curve has an infinite elasticity. RIGHT!

When price remains constant even when quantity changes, the elasticity formula requires us to divide by a zero price change. In fact, as demand curves approach flatness, the elasticity becomes larger and larger. By agreement we say it is infinite.

5. The person for whom a good or service has the greatest utility has the greatest desire for more of it. WRONG!

The good that has the greatest *marginal* utility for a person, with respect to price, is the good of which he or she desires more. RIGHT!

Utilities of one good for many people cannot be compared. Utilities of various goods for one person can be compared. Marginal utility with respect to price, not total utility, is the best indicator of how to make a choice.

6. An expected price change has the same effect as a change in the current price. WRONG!

An unexpected price change shifts the demand curve, whereas a current price change is a movement along the demand curve. RIGHT!

If prices are expected to rise in the near future, people will demand more of the commodity today in order to beat the rise in price. Demand increases and the quantity demanded will rise. However, if the price rises today, by the law of demand people reduce the quantity demanded! Furthermore, demand itself does not change. A current price change and an expected price change have very different effects.

7. When a buyer purchases a good, the demand for the good decreases. WRONG!

When a buyer purchases a good, demand is not affected. RIGHT!

Demand refers only to the *willingness* and *ability* of a buyer to buy. The potential for purchase, not the actual purchase, is the focus of demand. Demand is defined over a given period of time. If a buyer buys a good during that period of time, he or she is still counted as demanding the good—even after it is purchased.

8. Both income and cross-price elasticities must be interpreted using absolute values. WRONG!

The absolute value is used only for the price elasticity of demand. RIGHT!

The law of demand guarantees that the price elasticity of demand would always have a negative sign. However, the income and cross-price elasticities may be either positive or negative, and the sign provides important information about the demand for a good. The sign of the income elasticity indicates if a good is a normal good or an inferior good. The sign on the cross-price elasticity indicates whether a good is a substitute or a complement.

•ANSWERS•

Using Key Terms

Across

1. complementary goods
6. diminishing marginal utility
12. law of demand
13. total utility
14. total revenue
15. substitute goods
17. income elasticity of demand
18. cross-price elasticity
19. opportunity cost

Down

2. demand
3. price elasticity of demand
4. optimal consumption
5. marginal utility
7. shift in demand
8. inferior good
9. demand curve
10. normal good
11. ceteris paribus
16. utility

True or False

1. T
2. T
3. F Consumers will plan to wait until next month's lower prices to purchase this good. The current demand curve will shift to the left.
4. F The marginal utility will decline. The total utility will increase as long as the marginal utility is positive.
5. T
6. F A rise in the price will result in lower total revenues. A *decrease* in the price will raise total revenues if demand is elastic.
7. F Price elasticity of demand will be more elastic (i.e. consumers more responsive) at higher prices. Elasticity cannot be compared to slope.
8. T
9. T
10. F A *positive* cross-price elasticity indicates substitutes. An *increase* in the price of one good, for example, would result in an *increase* in the demand for the substitute.

Multiple Choice

1. a	5. b	9. b	13. d	17. a	21. c
2. c	6. c	10. b	14. c	18. d	22. c
3. b	7. d	11. b	15. d	19. c	23. d
4. d	8. a	12. c	16. a	20. b	

Problems and Applications

Exercise 1

1. d

2. **Figure 20.1 Answer**

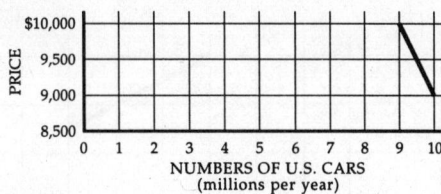

3. **Figure 20.2 Answer**

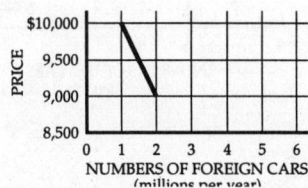

4. **Table 20.3 Answer**

Price	Number of new cars (millions per year)
$10,000	10.0
9,000	12.0

5. **Figure 20.3 Answer**

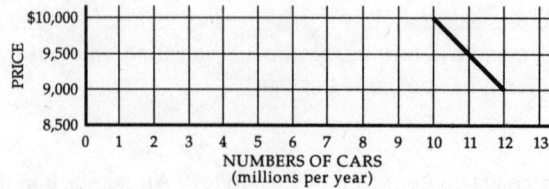

6. **Figure 20.4 answer**

Exercise 2

1. F
2. **Table 20.4 Answer**

Price	Number of new U.S. cars (millions per year)	Elasticity of demand
$10,000	10.0	----
9,000	12.0	1.64
8,000	14.0	1.25
7,000	16.0	1.00

3. elastic
4. $112,000
5. decrease
6. **Figure 20.4 answer**

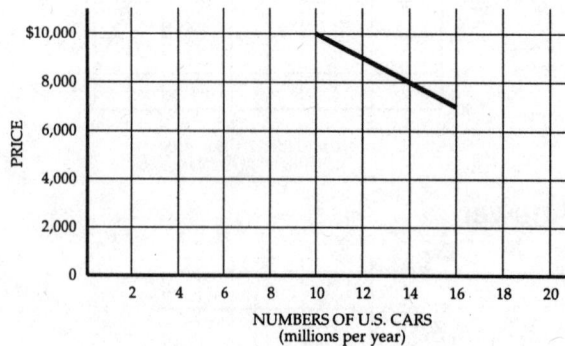

7. T

8. The slope can be estimated by using the coordinates of any two points on the demand curve. The slope is computed by dividing the change in the variable on the y-axis by the change in the variable on the x-axis. For example, using the first two points in Table 20.4, we would have

$$\frac{\text{Change in } y\text{-axis}}{\text{Change in } x\text{-axis}} = \frac{p_1 - p_2}{q_1 - q_2} = \frac{10,000 - 7,000}{10,000,000 - 16,000,000} = \frac{3,000}{-6,000,000} = -.0005 \text{ per car}$$

Regardless of what pair of points is chosen, the slope should be the same (except for differences that result from rounding).

9. b   As noted in the previous problem, the slope is the same regardless of which pair of points is tried.

10. T

Exercise 3

1. **Table 20.5 Answer**

	Income (per year)	Demand for peanut butter (jars per year)		Income elasticity of demand
a	$10,000	12		
b	$20,000	7	a to b	-0.79
c	$40,000	3	b to c	-1.19
d	$80,000	1	c to d	-1.49

2. inferior, falls, negative.

3. **Table 20.6 Answer**

	Price of peanut butter (per jar)	Demand for jelly (jars per year)		Cross-price elasticity of demand
a	$2.00	12		
b	$3.00	10	a to b	-0.45
c	$4.00	7	b to c	-1.21
d	$5.00	2	c to d	-5.05

4. complementary, falls, negative.

Exercise 4

Table 20.7 Answer

Days of entertainment per month	Evening at home Marginal utility	Event Marginal utility
0	—	—
1	170	600
2	190	650
3	180	430
4	150	360
5	130	310
6	110	200
7	100	170
8	80	100
9	60	0
10	0	−60
11	−50	−100
12	−100	−200

2. b
3. a

4. **Figure 20.5 Answer**

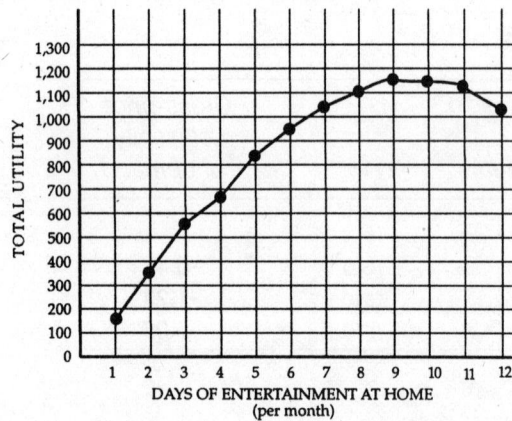

5. **Figure 20.6 Answer**

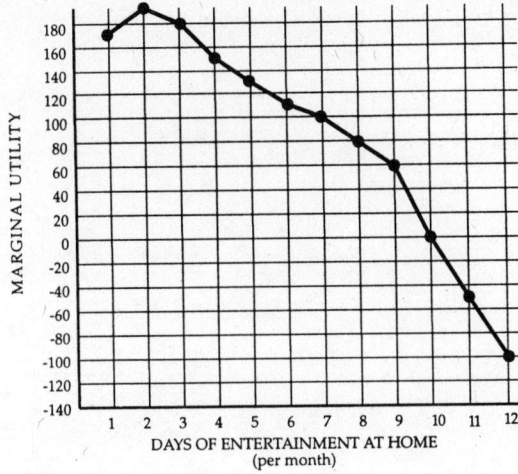

DAYS OF ENTERTAINMENT AT HOME
(per month)

6. b
7. c

Exercise 5

1. c
2. **Table 20.8 Answer**

	Event entertainment (price = $30)	
Days of entertainment per month	Marginal utility	$\dfrac{MU}{price}$
0	0	0
1	600	20
2	600	20
3	480	16
4	360	12
5	360	12
6	360	12
7	360	12
8	0	0
9	0	0
10	0	0

3. event entertainment
4. 2
5. $60 [= $120 - ($30 x 2)]
6. no
7. $30 [= $120 - $60 - (3 x $10)]
8. event entertainment
9. T

Exercise 6

1. 3 cokes, 5 video games
2. 2 cokes, 8 video games
3. C
4. 2 cokes, 5 video games
5. 3 cokes, 4 video games
6. greater
7. I_2

CHAPTER 21
The Costs of Production

Quick Review

In this chapter we attempt to identify the costs of producing goods and services. We begin by looking at some basic questions:

- How much output can a firm produce?
- How do the costs of production vary with the rate of output?
- Do larger firms have a cost advantage over smaller firms?

Managers of firms must know how costs change when output is changed. Without such knowledge they cannot determine what they should be willing and able to supply in the marketplace. Costs can be computed at different levels of production if management keeps track of all factors that are used in producing output. The production function establishes the maximum quantity that can be produced from a given combination of factors. The production function is therefore the cornerstone for computing a firm's costs at various output levels.

If we know the production function, it is possible to determine factor productivity, efficiency, and various categories of costs. Productivity is simply the amount of output per unit of input that can be produced by a firm. Efficiency is attained if the firm is able to achieve the maximum output from a given set of resources. The law of diminishing returns says that the marginal product of any factor decreases as more of it is employed in the production process when all other factors are held constant. These concepts have important implications for the behavior of cost.

In the short run (when firms are unable to vary some factors of production), the law of diminishing returns causes the marginal costs and average variable costs of production to rise with increased output. In effect, the variable factors of production are limited by the fixed factors, which, by definition, cannot be expanded. Even though average fixed costs fall as output increases, these limitations eventually cause average total costs to rise.

In the long run (when there are no fixed factors), changes in average total cost may occur when the rate of output is increased. If an increase in plant size (scale) causes average total cost to rise, there are diseconomies of scale. If average total cost falls with increased plant size, there are economies of scale. However, it is quite possible that average costs will not change over a wide range of output, in which case there are constant returns to scale.

The short-run cost curves are related to the long-run cost curves. The long-run average total cost curve runs along the lowest points of all possible short-run average total cost curves at each level of output.

Certain rules relate the different cost curves, in both the long-run and the short-run. Whenever the marginal curve is below the average curve, the average curve will fall as output increases. However, if the marginal curve is above the average curve, the average curve will be rising. The marginal cost curve always intersects the average variable cost and average total cost curve at their lowest points.

Global competitiveness of American firms has been called into question. Cheap foreign labor is frequently used as an excuse for the recent trade deficits of the United States. But labor is only one factor in the production process, and low wages generally mean low productivity. Thus, unit labor costs, the wage rate divided by marginal physical product, are the key to measuring labor efficiency. Looked at this way, American labor is highly competitive relative to "cheap" foreign labor.

Learning Objectives

After reading Chapter 21 and doing the following exercises, you should:

1. Know the relationship between the production function and the firm's ability to produce goods and services.
2. Understand the nature and determinants of marginal productivity.
3. Be able to draw a graph relating the marginal physical product and total product curves.
4. Be able to define and explain the law of diminishing returns.
5. Understand the relationship between the production function and the short-run cost curves.
6. Understand the difference between variable costs and fixed costs.
7. Know how to define and calculate the total, average, and marginal costs of production and be able to show their relationship to marginal productivity.
8. Understand the relationship between average and marginal cost curves.
9. Understand the distinction between economic costs and accounting costs.
10. Know the distinction between long-run costs and short-run costs.
11. Be able to explain economies of scale, diseconomies of scale, and constant returns to scale.
12. Understand the impact of technological improvements on the production function.

Using Key Terms

Fill in the puzzle on the opposite page with the appropriate term from the list of Key Terms at the end of the chapter in the text.

Across
1. The resources used to produce a good or service.
5. The horizontal curve at $120 in Figure 21.4 in the text.
7. Equals $245 when producing 15 pairs of jeans per day according to Table 21.2 in the text.
9. Equal to the wage rate divided by marginal physical product.
10. The marginal physical product of a variable input declines as more of it is employed with a given quantity of other (fixed) inputs.
12. Maximum output of a good attainable from the resources used.
13. Average total costs minus average fixed costs.
15. Includes both explicit and implicit costs.
16. Equal to 15 for the first worker hired in Figure 21.1 in the text.
19. Used in Table 21.1 in the text to tell how the output of jeans would change if some sewing machines were leased.
20. Output per unit of input.
21. A period in which some inputs are fixed.

Down
2. Drawn with a U-shape in Figure 21.5 in the text.
3. The most desired forgone alternative.
4. Helps to explain why one large firm dominates the funeral business according to the article in the text titled "Funeral Giant Moves In on Small Rivals."
6. A situation in which an increase in plant size does not reduce minimum average costs.
8. Equal to $6 per pair of jeans at an output rate of 20 pairs per day in Figure 21.5 in the text.

11. Determine how fast total costs rise.
14. This curve is typically rising because of the law of diminishing returns.
17. The difference between total revenue and total costs.
18. A period in which all inputs are variable.

Puzzle 21.1

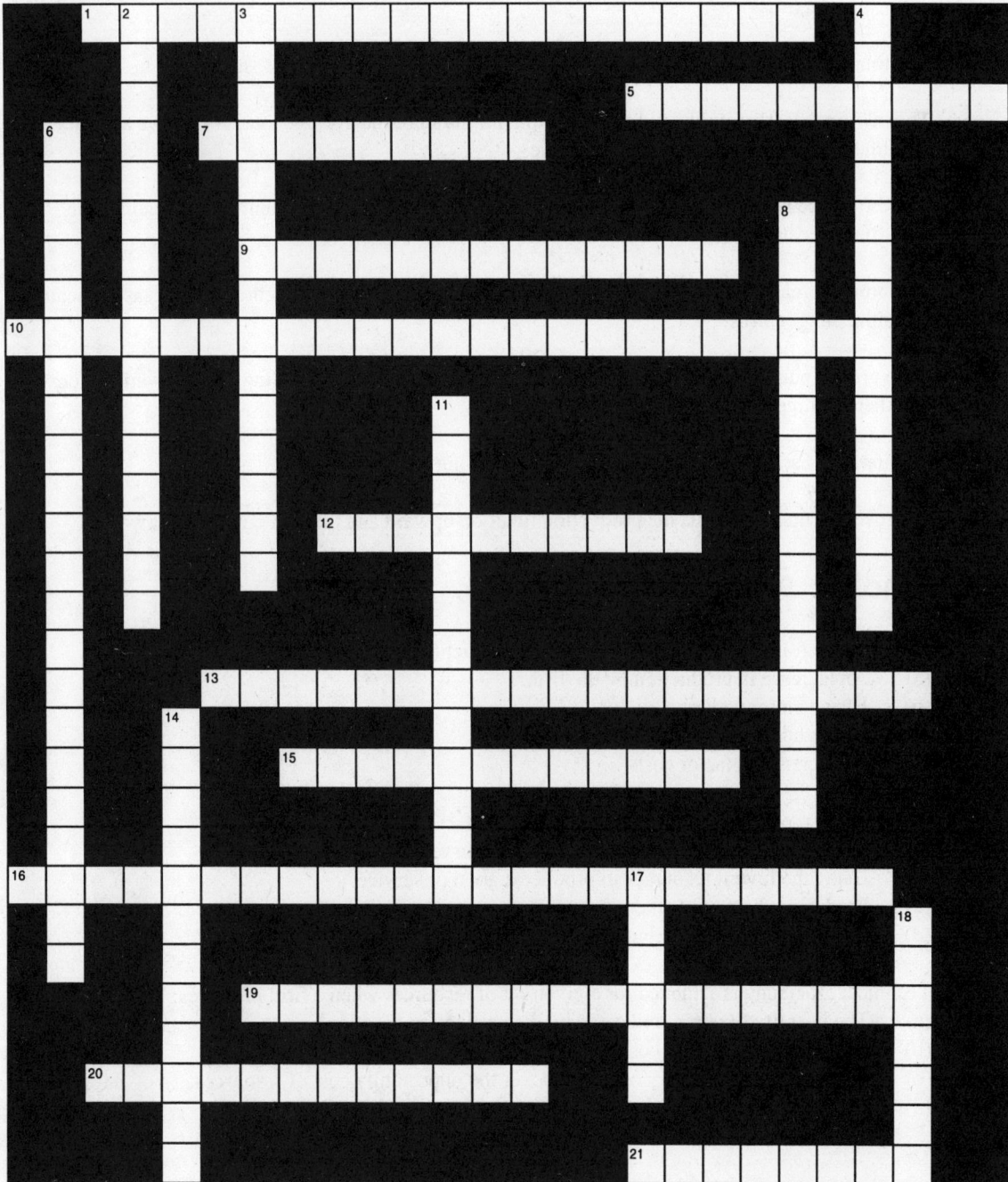

True or False: *Circle your choice and explain why any false statements are incorrect.*

T F 1. The production function can be increased by working the labor input harder.

T F 2. The productivity of labor is affected by changes in the mix of other factors being used in the production process.

(T) F 3. Whenever MPP is increasing with output, the marginal cost of producing a good must be falling, *ceteris paribus*.

T F 4. The total cost at a zero level of output is always the amount of variable costs.

(T) F 5. The marginal cost curve always intersects the minimum of the average total cost curve and the minimum of the average variable cost curve.

T (F) 6. The difference between the accountant's and the economist's measurement of costs equals the opportunity costs of resources that do not have a value.

(T) F 7. As output increases, marginal costs eventually increase and the MPP eventually decreases because of diminishing returns.

T F 8. With greater output, falling average fixed costs eventually outweigh falling average variable costs, and then average total cost starts to rise.

T F 9. Economies of scale result from the law of diminishing returns.

T F 10. Improved technology shifts the production function upward and the cost curves downward.

Multiple Choice: *Select the correct answer.*

_____ 1. Which of the following would cause a firm's production function to shift upward?
(a) An increase in production by the firm.
(b) Hiring more workers.
(c) Increased training for the firm's workers.
(d) An increase in factor costs.

_____ 2. When a firm produces at the least-cost output level, it is:
(a) Producing the output at the minimum MC curve.
(b) Using the fewest resources to produce a good or service.
(c) Producing the output where the AVC curve is at a minimum.
(d) Producing the best combination of goods and services.

_____ 3. Technical efficiency is achieved for a given set of resources when a firm produces:
(a) The quantity of output indicated by the production function.
(b) Below the opportunity cost for the resources.
(c) The minimum necessary output to cover the opportunity cost of resources.
(d) All of the above.

_D_   4. The law of diminishing returns indicates that the greater use of a variable input, holding other factors fixed, results in:
     (a) A declining rate of increase in total output for each additional unit of input.
     (b) A rising MC curve.
     (c) A declining MPP curve.
     (d) All of the above.

_D_   5. Rising marginal costs are the result of:
     (a) The *law of diminishing returns.*
     (b) Decreasing MPP.
     (c) Adding more variable factors of production to a fixed quantity of other factors of production.
     (d) All of the above are correct.

_____ 6. Given the cost of the variable input, marginal cost will increase with greater output if:
     (a) Marginal physical product is declining.
     (b) Marginal physical product is increasing.
     (c) Total variable cost is decreasing.
     (d) Total fixed cost is increasing.

_C_   7. For which of the following costs would the cost curve appear as a flat line and the associated average cost curve decline continuously?
     (a) Total costs.
     (b) Variable costs.
     (c) Fixed costs.
     (d) Marginal costs.

_____ 8. If an additional unit of labor costs $10, and has an MPP of 20 units of output, the marginal cost is:
     (a) $0.20.
     (b) $0.50.
     (c) $10.00.
     (d) $200.00.

_A_   9. Which of the following can you compute if you know only the total cost at an output level of zero?
     (a) Fixed cost.
     (b) Variable cost.
     (c) Marginal cost.
     (d) Average total cost.

_D_ 10. When output increases and the marginal cost curve is:
     (a) Below the ATC, the ATC is downward sloping.
     (b) Equal to the ATC, the ATC is at its lowest point.
     (c) Above the ATC, the ATC is upward sloping.
     (d) All of the above.

_____ 11. Changes in short-run total costs result from changes in only:
     (a) Variable costs.
     (b) Fixed costs.
     (c) Profit.
     (d) The price elasticity of demand.

_B_ 12. Which of the following is equivalent to ATC?
     (a) FC + VC.
     (b) AFC + AVC.
     (c) Change in output divided by change in total cost.
     (d) Total cost times the quantity produced.

_D_ 13. The ATC at a given output level multiplied by the number of units produced at that output level equals:
  (a) Marginal cost.
  (b) Total fixed cost.
  (c) Total variable cost.
  (d) Total cost.

_D_ 14. Which one of the following curves is falling when marginal cost is below it?
  (a) Average variable cost curve.
  (b) Average total cost curve.
  (c) Average fixed cost curve.
  (d) All of the above.

_A_ 15. Which of the following costs will always increase as output increases?
  (a) Total costs.
  (b) Average total costs.
  (c) Marginal costs.
  (d) Fixed costs.

_____ 16. Economies of scale are reductions:
  (a) In average total cost that result from declining average fixed costs.
  (b) In average fixed cost that result from reducing the firm's scale of operations.
  (c) In average total cost that result from increasing the firm's scale of operations.
  (d) In average fixed cost resulting from improved technology and production efficiency.

_____ 17. Which of the following contributes to the typical U shape of the ATC curve?
  (a) The initial dominance of diminishing returns.
  (b) The eventual dominance of the rising AVC curve.
  (c) The steady impact of a rising AFC curve.
  (d) All of the above.

_____ 18. The length of the long run in economics is:
  (a) A variable time depending on the nature of the business.
  (b) Six to nine months.
  (c) One year.
  (d) More than two years.

_____ 19. In defining economic costs, economists recognize:
  (a) Only explicit costs while accountants recognize only implicit costs.
  (b) Only explicit costs while accountants recognize explicit and implicit costs.
  (c) Explicit and implicit costs while accountants recognize only implicit costs.
  (d) Explicit and implicit costs while accountants recognize only explicit costs.

_____ 20. The long-run average cost curve is constructed from:
  (a) The minimum points of the short-run marginal cost curves.
  (b) The minimum points of the short-run average cost curves.
  (c) The lowest average cost for producing each level of output.
  (d) The minimum points of the long-run marginal cost curves.

Problems and Applications

Exercise 1

This exercise shows how to compute and graph the marginal physical product of a factor of production. It also demonstrates the law of diminishing returns.

In Table 21.1 of the text, an example of jeans production was used to show how many sewing machines and workers were needed per day to produce various quantities of jeans per day. This table is very similar.

Table 21.1
The production of jeans
(pairs per day)

Capital input (sewing machines per day)	Labor input (workers per day)							
	0	1	2	3	4	5	6	7
0	0	0	0	0	0	0	0	0
1	0	15	34	44	48	50	51	46
2	0	20	46	64	72	78	81	80
3	0	21	50	73	82	92	99	102

1. Suppose a firm had only two sewing machines and could vary only the amount of labor input. On the basis of Table 21.1, fill in the column 2 of Table 21.2 to show how much can be produced at different levels of labor input when there are only two sewing machines.

Table 21.2
The production of jeans with two sewing machines

(1) Labor input (workers per day)	(2) Production of jeans (pairs per day)	(3) Marginal physical product (pairs per worker)
0	_____	‒‒‒
1	_____	_____
2	_____	_____
3	_____	_____
4	_____	_____
5	_____	_____
6	_____	_____
7	_____	_____

2. Graph the total output curve in Figure 21.1.

Figure 21.1

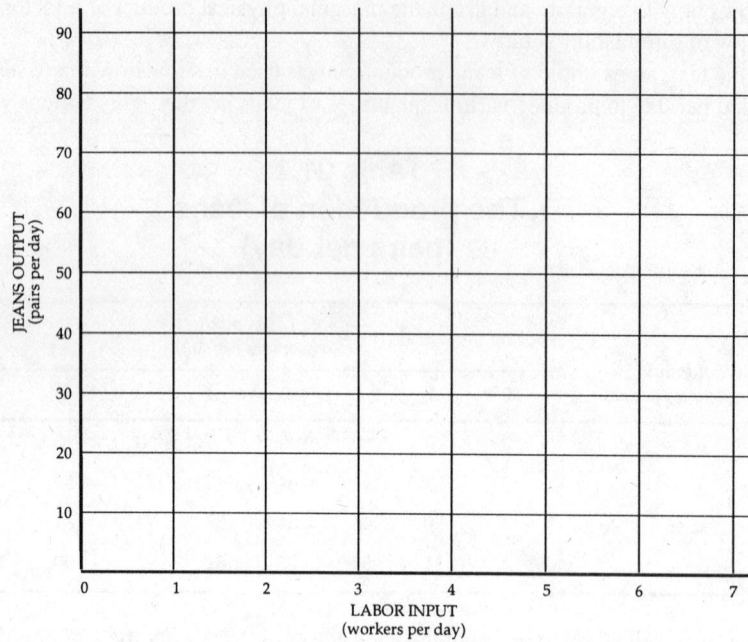

3. Compute the marginal physical product of each extra worker per day. (*Hint:* See Figure 21.2 in the text.) Place the answers in column 3 of Table 21.2.

4. Graph the marginal physical product curve in Figure 21.2.

Figure 21.2

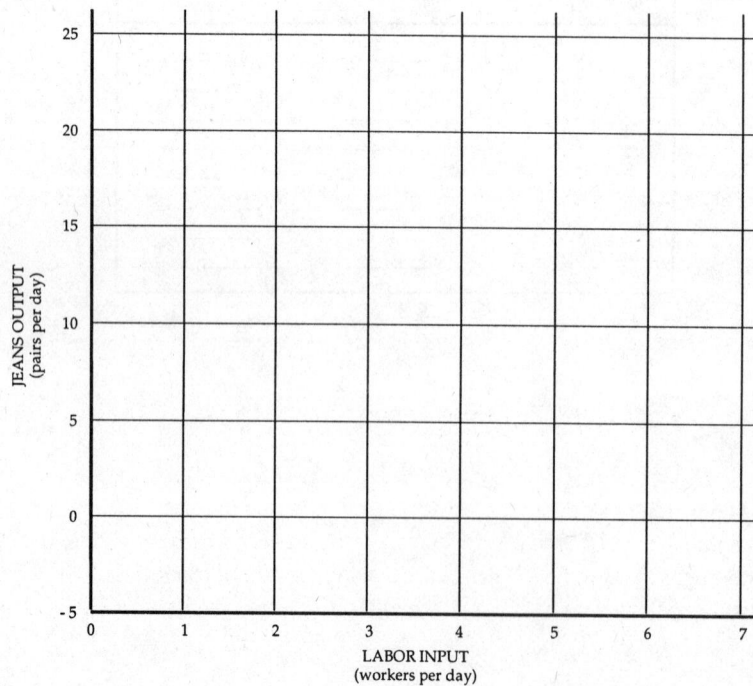

5. The law of diminishing returns states that the marginal physical product of a factor:
   (a) Will become negative as output increases.
   (b) Will decline as output increases.
   (c) Will increase and then decline as output increases.
   (d) Will decline as the amount of a factor used increases.

6. At what amount of labor input does the law of diminishing returns first become apparent in Figure 21.2?
   (a) 0-1.
   (b) 1-2.
   (c) 2-3.
   (d) 3-4.

7. In Figure 21.1 at 3 units of labor, total output:
   (a) Is rising with increased labor usage.
   (b) Is falling with increased labor usage.
   (c) Remains constant with increased labor.

8. T F When marginal physical product declines, total output declines.

Exercise 2

This exercise shows the relationship between the various costs of production.

1. Complete Table 21.3 using the information given about output and the costs of production. (Hint: refer to Figure 21.5 in the text if you need help getting started.)

Table 21.3 Costs of Production

Rate of Output	Fixed Cost	Variable Cost	Total Cost	Average Total Cost	Marginal Cost
0	$ 10	$ 0	$ 10	--------	-------
1	10	6	16	$ 16	$ 6
2	10	10	20	10	4
3	10	16	26	8.67	6
4	10	26	36	9	10
5	10	40	50	10	14
6	10	58	68	11.33	18

2. When the average total cost is rising, marginal cost is (above, below, equal to) average total cost.

3. When the average total cost is falling, marginal cost is (above, below, equal to) average total cost.

Exercise 3

This exercise shows the relationship between fixed costs, variable costs, accounting cost, and economic cost.

1. Fixed costs are defined as:
   (a) Costs that do not change with inflation.
   (b) Costs that are set firmly (without escalator clauses) in a contract.
   (c) Costs of production that do not change when the rate of production is altered.
   (d) Average costs that do not change when the rate of production is altered.

2. Variable costs include:
   (a) Costs of production that change when the rate of production is altered.
   (b) All costs in the long run.
   (c) The difference between total and fixed costs.
   (d) All of the above.

Table 21.4 Expense statements for parachute business (dollars per week)

Weekly expense	Parachutes produced per week		
	0	100	200
Lease on building	$1,200	$1,200	$1,200
Sewing machines	500	500	500
Nylon	0	300	700
Utilities (electricity, etc.)	0	150	200
Labor	0	650	650
Testing and certification	800	800	800

Use the information in Table 21.4 to answer the following questions.

3. Which items are considered to be fixed costs?

4. Calculate variable costs at an output level of 100 parachutes per week.

5. Calculate total costs at an output level of 100 parachutes per week.

6. Now assume the owner of the parachute business buys the building he is currently leasing so he no longer has a lease expenditure. Calculate the accounting cost at an output level of 200 parachutes per week.

7. Assume the owner still owns the building. Calculate the economic cost at an output level of 200 parachutes per week. Explain why there is a difference in the accounting cost at an output level of 200 parachutes and the economic cost.

Exercise 4

This exercise focuses on average total costs. It will help you solve the problems at the end of Chapter 21 in the text.

Table 21.5 represents the cost data for producing cement in three different plants, where Plant 1 is the smallest and Plant 3 is the largest.

Table 21.5
Costs associated with three plants

Output (tons per day)	1	2	3	4	5	6	7	8	9	10
Average total cost:										
Plant 1	$10	9	8	7	8	9	10	11	12	13
Plant 2	12	10	8	6	5	4	5	6	8	10
Plant 3	13	12	11	9	7	5	3	2	3	4

1. Given the three plant sizes in Table 21.5, the cement industry experiences (economies of scale, diseconomies of scale, constant returns to scale) because as plant size increases the minimum average total cost (increases, decreases, stays the same).

2. Which plant should be used to produce 2 tons of cement per day? _____

3. Which plant should be used to produce 8 tons of cement per day? _____

4. For which levels of output is Plant 2 the best choice? _____

Exercise 5

Suppose the marginal physical product of worker A is 10 units per hour and her wage is $15 per hour. Suppose the marginal physical product of worker B is 5 units per hour and her wage is $10 per hour. Given this information, answer questions 1-4.

1. Calculate the unit labor cost for worker A. _____

2. Calculate the unit labor cost for worker B. _____

3. T   F   Worker B is less costly per unit because her wage rate is lower.

4. T   F   Unit labor costs can be used to measure productivity.

Exercise 6

The news media often provide information on events that affect productivity and costs. This exercise will use one of the articles in the text to show the kind of information to look for.

Reread the article in the text titled "Funeral Giant Moves In on Small Rivals," and then answer the following questions.

1. What is the strategy employed by SCI to achieve economies of scale? _____
   _____

2. What phrase(s) indicates how SCI grew to more than 230,000 units? _____
   _____

3. What phrase indicates one way that SCI achieves lower costs than its rivals? _____
   _____

4. What phrase demonstrates that economies of scale have allowed SCI to reap greater profits than its smaller rivals? _____

Common Errors

The first statement in each "common error" below is incorrect. Each incorrect statement is followed by a corrected version and an explanation.

1. A rising marginal cost means average cost is rising. WRONG!

   A rising average cost curve means the marginal cost curve is above the average cost curve. RIGHT!

It is important to remember the basic relationships between the average cost curves and the marginal cost curve:

(a)   When the average cost curve rises, the marginal cost curve is above the average cost curve.
(b)   When the average cost curve falls, the marginal cost curve is below the average cost curve.
(c)   When the average cost curve is flat, the marginal cost curve equals the average cost curve.

2.   Total output starts falling when diminishing returns occur. WRONG!

Diminishing returns set in when marginal physical product begins to decline. RIGHT!

The law of diminishing returns describes what happens to *marginal physical product,* not total output. Marginal physical product will typically begin to decline long before total output begins to decline. For total output to decline, the marginal physical product must be negative.

3.   A firm's productivity increases when labor is willing to accept lower wages. WRONG!

A firm's productivity increases when more output can be produced per unit of labor used. RIGHT!

Productivity is not defined on the basis of the prices of factors of production. Productivity depends simply on the amount of output that is produced by the factors of production.

4.   The term "economies of scale" refers to the shape of the short-run average cost curve. WRONG!

The term "economies of scale" refers to the shape of the long-run average cost curve. RIGHT!

The short-run average cost curve and the long-run average cost curve may have similar shapes. But the shape of the short-run curve results from the law of diminishing returns. In the long run, all factors, and therefore all costs, are variable. Thus the shape of the long-run average cost curve is the result of other forces, such as the specialization and division of labor, the use of different sources of power, and so on. Remember, even though the long-run average cost curve is a summary of many short-run average cost curves, and even though the shapes of the two curves may be similar, the reasons for the shapes of the curves are quite different. The term "economies of scale" applies only to the long-run average cost curve.

5.   The marginal cost curve rises because factor prices rise when more of a good is produced. WRONG!

The marginal cost curve rises because the marginal productivity of the variable factor declines. RIGHT!

The marginal cost curve moves in the direction opposite to that of marginal product curve. Changes in factor prices would shift the whole marginal cost curve but would not explain its shape and would not affect the marginal product curve.

6.   Marginal physical product begins to decline because inferior factors must be hired to increase output. WRONG!

Declining marginal physical product occurs even if all of the factors are of equal quality. RIGHT!

Many people incorrectly attribute diminishing returns to the use of inferior factors of production. Diminishing returns result from an increasing ratio of the variable input to the fixed input. There is always a point where the variable input begins to have too little of the fixed input to work with. Result? Diminishing marginal product! The quality of the factors has nothing to do with it. Generally, factors of production are considered homogeneous in economics.

7. Diminishing returns means there are diseconomies of scale. WRONG!

Diminishing returns refers to the short run shape of a marginal physical product curve and diseconomies of scale refers to the shape of the long run average cost curve. RIGHT!

As suggested in the previous Common Error, diminishing returns is a short run phenomenon; at least one input in the production process is fixed. Diminishing returns is reflected in diminishing marginal productivity and a rising short run marginal cost curve. However, when all factors are variable—as they are in the long run—then it is possible to talk about economies or diseconomies of scale. Diseconomies of scale results in a rising long run average cost curve. It is quite common to have short run diminishing returns and long run economies of scale, particularly in the public utilities.

•ANSWERS•

Using Key Terms
Across
1. factors of production
5. fixed costs
7. total cost
9. unit labor cost
10. law of diminishing returns
12. efficiency
13. average variable cost
15. economic cost
16. marginal physical product
19. production function
20. productivity
21. short run

Down
2. average total cost
3. opportunity cost
4. economies of scale
6. constant returns to scale
8. average fixed cost
11. variable costs
14. marginal cost
17. profit
18. long run

True or False

1. F The production function represents the maximum output that can be obtained from a given mix of inputs, i.e. technical efficiency.
2. T
3. T
4. F The total cost at a zero level of output is fixed costs.

5. T
6. F   The difference is the opportunity costs of resources that are not given an explicit payment.
7. T
8. F   Rising AVC (MC) will eventually overcome falling AFC and cause the ATC to increase.
9. F   Economies of scale is a long-run phenomenon. The law of diminishing returns does not apply in the long run because there are no fixed inputs in the long run.
10. T

Multiple Choice

1.	c	5.	d	9.	a	13.	d	17.	b
2.	b	6.	a	10.	d	14.	d	18.	a
3.	a	7.	c	11.	a	15.	a	19.	d
4.	d	8.	b	12.	b	16.	c	20.	c

Problems and Applications

Exercise 1

1. See Table 21.2 Answer, column 2.

Table 21.2 Answer

(1)	(2)	(3)
0	0	---
1	20	20
2	46	26
3	64	18
4	72	8
5	78	6
6	81	3
7	80	- 1

2. Figure 21.1 Answer

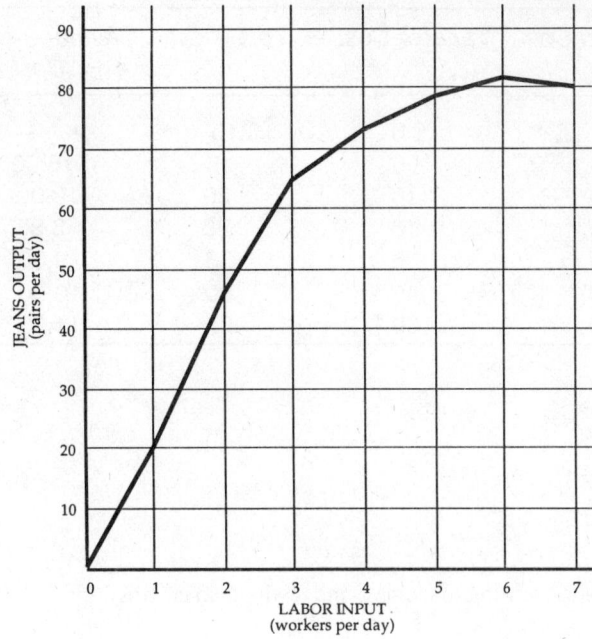

3. See Table 21.2 Answer, column 3.

4. **Figure 21.2 Answer**

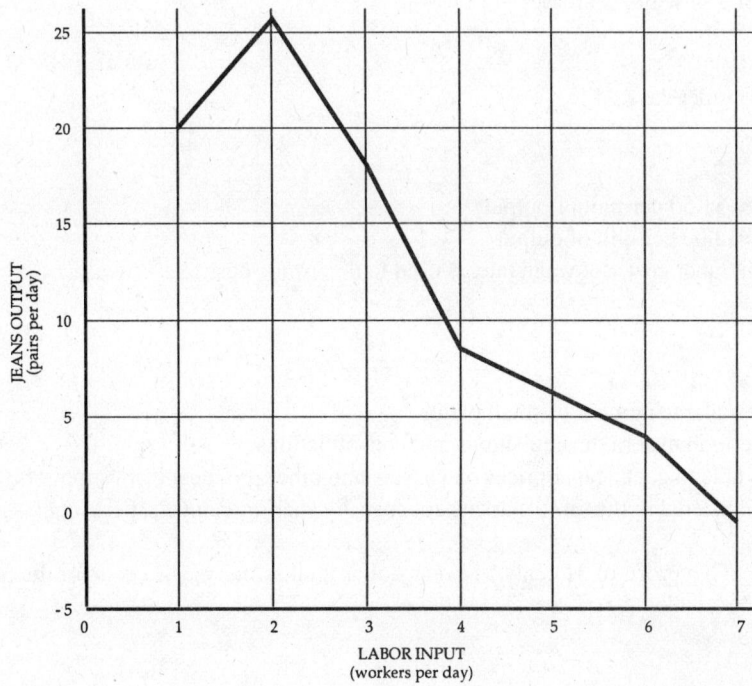

5. d   6. c   7. a   8. F

Exercise 2

1. Table 21.3 Answer

Rate of Output	Fixed Cost	Variable Cost	Total Cost	Average Total Cost	Marginal Cost
0	$ 10	$ 0	$ 10	---------	-------
1	10	6	16	$16.00	$ 6
2	10	10	20	10.00	4
3	10	16	26	8.67	6
4	10	26	36	9.00	10
5	10	40	50	10.00	14
6	10	58	68	11.33	18

2. above
3. below

Exercise 3

1. c
2. d
3. lease on the building, sewing machines, and testing and certification
4. $1,100
5. $3,600
6. $2,850
7. $4,050; The economic cost is greater because it includes the implicit cost of the building; the accounting cost does not.

Exercise 4

1. economies of scale, decreases
2. Plant 1
3. Plant 3
4. 4 to 6 tons per day

Exercise 5

1. $15/10 = $1.50 per unit of output
2. $10/5 = $2.00 per unit of output
3. F   Unit labor cost, not wage rate, is used to determine cost.
4. T

Exercise 6

1. SCI uses a large number of small plants.
2. "But we're in the era of acquisitions and consolidations..."
3. "SCI is able to get cheaper prices on caskets and other products from suppliers," and "if funeral homes clustered in the same markets cut costs by sharing vehicles, personnel, services, and supplies."
4. "...give SCI a profit of 31 cents on every dollar it takes in...vs. 12 cents for the industry as a whole."

CHAPTER 22
The Competitive Firm

Quick Review

The pursuit of profits is the motivating, driving force in the management of firms in the U.S. and other market economies. In this chapter we examine the profit motive and pay particular attention to how competitive firms answer the following questions:

- What are profits?
- What are the unique characteristics of competitive firms?
- How much output will a competitive firm produce?

To start with, firms are the suppliers of goods and services. Large and small firms alike want to earn profits. Profits are the difference between total revenue and total cost, and a profit-maximizing firm must consider how revenues and costs change when the rate of production changes. The profit-maximizing producer compares marginal cost with marginal revenue. As long as marginal revenue exceeds marginal cost, profits increase as the production rate increases. This additional profit gives the producer an incentive to speed up production. As the rate of production increases, however, marginal costs usually rise while prices remain constant or decline.

Why does increased production push up marginal costs? Marginal costs rise when crowding and waste occur as a result of the increased rate of production. Why does increased production lower prices and marginal revenue? The law of demand is at work.

At some rate of production, marginal cost will exceed marginal revenue. Further increases in production will then lower profits. Consequently, a firm achieves maximum profits at the production rate at which marginal cost equals marginal revenue $(MC = MR) = P$.

The manager can tell how total revenue will change in response to a change in price if he or she knows the price elasticity of demand. The response of total revenue to a change in price depends on the price elasticity of demand as indicated in the table below.

If elasticity of demand is:	Then for a	
	Rise in price:	Decline in price:
Greater than 1 (elastic demand)	Total revenue falls	Total revenue rises
Equal to 1 (unit elasticity)	Total revenue remains the same	Total revenue remains the same
Less than 1 (inelastic)	Total revenue rises	Total revenue falls

For competitive firms, demand is perfectly elastic. The demand curve is flat from the point of view of the firm, and the marginal revenue curve is equal to the demand curve. Because they possess no market power, competitive firms are price takers and simply respond to changes in the *market price*—increasing output when *MR* exceeds *MC* and decreasing output when *MC* exceeds *MR*.

A firm is faced with various types of costs. Fixed costs, which a firm cannot change in the short run, can be altered by the long-run investment decision. Production decisions, however, involve changes in variable costs, which can be manipulated in the short run by changing the rate of output. In the short run, a firm continues to operate as long as it can cover its variable costs. In the short run a firm *shuts down* if variable costs of production cannot be covered. In the long run a firm must cover all costs, both explicit and implicit, or exit from the market. This is the firm's investment decision.

For competitive firms, that part of the marginal cost curve that lies above the average variable cost curve is equivalent to its short-run supply curve. The supply curve shifts as a result of certain determinants which include the prices of resources, technology, taxes, expectations (about prices, technology, and so on), and the number of suppliers. A change in price causes a movement along the supply curve to a new quantity supplied but no change in the supply curve itself.

Economic and accounting ideas of profit and cost are different. Accountants recognize all costs that are paid an explicit wage. Economists recognize explicit costs, but they also identify other factors in the production of a good that are not paid an explicit wage. Because economists include implicit costs in assessing the costs of production, economic profits are smaller than accounting profits. If a firm earns zero economic profits, it is able to maintain its operations in the long run. In fact, there may be quite substantial accounting "profits" even when economic profits are zero!

Changes in tax laws can affect both the production decision (short run) and the investment decision (long run). The key to understanding how changes in taxes affect business decisions is to determine whether the tax is viewed by the firm as a variable cost (like the social security tax) or a fixed cost (like a lump sum tax or license fee).

Learning Objectives

After reading Chapter 22 and doing the following exercises, you should:

1. Know the difference between economic profits and accounting profits, and how profits are maximized.
2. Be able to compute profits and relate them to prices, costs, and the price elasticity of demand.
3. Understand why competitive firms are "price takers" and recognize the differences between the firm's demand and the market demand.
4. Know the relationships among total, average, and marginal costs (or revenue).
5. Recognize the difference between long-run and short-run decisions.
6. Know the profit maximization rule and the importance of marginal revenue and marginal cost.
7. Understand graphically how a firm determines profit, price, and production rate in the short run.
8. Understand how the firm makes the "shutdown" decision and the long-run investment decision.
9. Know how changes in the determinants affect the market supply curve.
10. Understand how various taxes affect the firm's output decision.

Using Key Terms

Fill in the puzzle on the opposite page with the appropriate term from the list of Key Terms at the end of the chapter in the text.

Across

2. The value of all resources used in production.
4. Equal to $10 per day at all rates of output in Figure 22.6 in the text.
6. The competitive _____ is summarized in Table 22.3 in the text.
7. Equal to $13 at every output level in Figure 22.7 in the text.
9. The opportunity cost of capital.
11. The short-run _____ is equal to the marginal cost curve in Figure 22.10 in the text.
12. Equal to $5 at the output rate of one bushel per hour in Figure 22.7 in the text.

13. The ability to alter the market price of a good or service.
14. The long-run decision to enter or exit an industry.
17. Ranges from perfect competition to monopoly in Figure 22.1 in the text.
18. Equal to $52 at an output rate of four bushels per day in Figure 22.7 in the text.
19. Costs of production that change when the rate of output changes.
20. A period of time long enough for all inputs to be varied.

Down

1. A market in which no buyer or seller has market power.
3. The sole supplier of a good or service.
5. A firm that must take whatever price the market offers for the goods it produces.
6. The choice of a short-run rate of output by Farmer Kitt.
8. Total revenue minus total economic cost.
10. Occurs at a price of $5 in Figure 22.9 in the text.
15. The period in which the quantity of some inputs cannot be changed.
16. Eventually becomes zero in a competitive industry because of market entry.

Puzzle 22.1

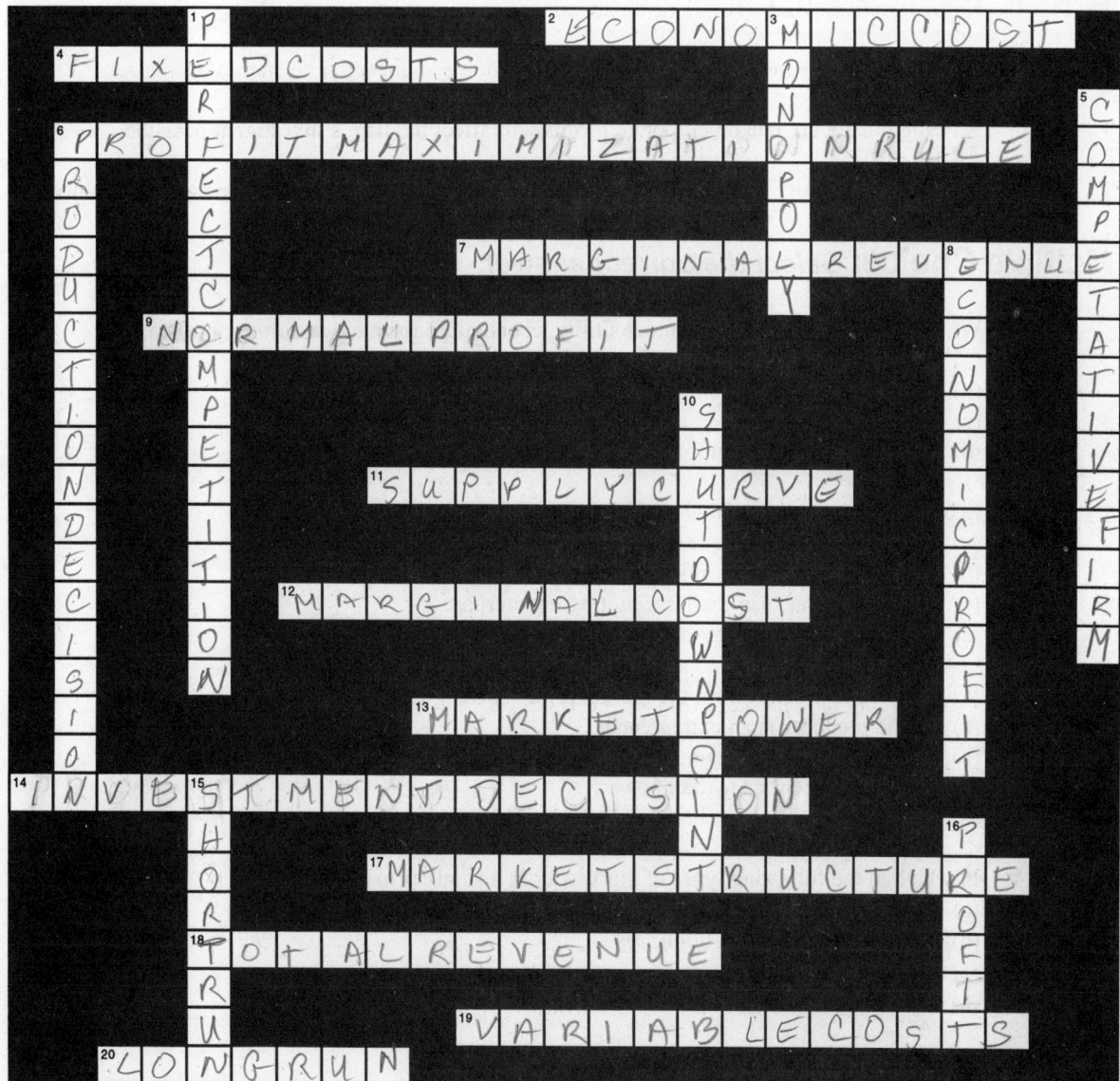

True or False: *Circle your choice and explain why any false statements are incorrect.*

(T) F 1. *466* A firm should produce until the next unit produced would raise marginal costs above marginal revenues. T

(T) F 2. *462* If the price of a good remains the same regardless of the rate of output that a firm produces, the demand curve faced by the firm is perfectly elastic. T

468 *471* T (F) 3. For a competitive firm, the supply curve is that part of the marginal cost curve that is above the short-run average total cost curve. F

467 T (F) 4. Since a firm's goal is to maximize profits, it should expand production as long as it is making profits. F

466 T (F) 5. If a firm maximizes revenue, it is maximizing profit. F

468 (T) F 6. A firm can minimize its losses by continuing to produce in the short run when price is less than ATC but greater than AVC. T

456 (T) F 7. Normal profit is when a firm's revenues just cover its economic costs. T

456 T (F) 8. When businesses earn zero economic profit, they have no incentive to stay in business. F

no (T) F 9. A change in the tax rate on corporate profits will affect the firm's investment decision.

458 (T) F 10. Perfectly competitive firms face horizontal demand curves because they have no market power. T

Multiple Choice: *Select the correct answer.*

__A__ 1. Whereas consumers try to maximize utility, economists assume that firms try to maximize: A
    (a) Profits.
    (b) Revenues.
    (c) Sales.
    (d) Production in a given period of time, *ceteris paribus.*

454 *455* __A__ 2. Economic costs and economic profits are typically: A
    (a) Greater and smaller, respectively, than their accounting counterparts.
    (b) Smaller and greater, respectively, than their accounting counterparts.
    (c) Both smaller than their accounting counterparts.
    (d) Both larger than their accounting counterparts.

457 __C__ 3. When a producer can control the market price for the good it sells:
    (a) The producer is an entrepreneur.
    (b) The producer is certain to make a profit. C
    (c) The producer has market power.
    (d) The producer is a perfectly competitive firm.

456 __D__ 4. In which of the following types of markets does a single firm have the most market power?
    (a) Perfect competition.
    (b) Monopolistic competition.
    (c) Oligopoly. D
    (d) Monopoly.

_D_ 5. Normal profit implies that:
  456
(a) Economic profit is zero.
(b) All factors employed are earning an amount equal to their opportunity costs.
(c) The factors employed are earning as much as they could in the best alternative employment.
(d) All of the above. _D_

_B_ 6. The market equilibrium price occurs where:
  459
(a) Price equals the minimum of average variable cost.
(b) Market supply crosses market demand. _B_
(c) A firm's marginal revenue equals marginal cost. — no because profit maximing rule
(d) A firm's marginal cost equals average cost.

_B_ 7. A competitive firm:
(a) Has a large advertising budget.
(b) Has output so small relative to the market supply that is has no effect on market price. _B_
(c) Can alter the market price of the good(s) it produces.
(d) Can raise price to increase profit.

_C_ 8. If a perfectly competitive firm can sell 100 computers at $500 each, in order to sell one more computer, the firm:
(a) Must lower its price. _C_
(b) Can raise its price.
(c) Can sell the 101st computer at $500.
(d) Cannot sell an additional computer at any price because the market is at equilibrium.

_C_ 9. A competitive firm's profits are maximized where:
(a) Market supply crosses the firm's marginal cost.
(b) Price equals the minimum of total cost.
(c) Price equals marginal cost. _C_
(d) Marginal cost equals total revenue.

_B_ 10. If price is greater than marginal cost, a perfectly competitive firm should increase output because:
(a) Marginal costs are increasing. _B_
(b) Additional units of output will add to the firm's profits (or reduce losses). profit maximize rule
(c) The price they receive for their product is increasing.
(d) Total revenues would increase.

_B_ 11. If a perfectly competitive firm wanted to maximize its total *revenues*, it would produce:
  460
(a) The output where MC equals price.
(b) As much output as it is capable of producing. _B_
(c) The output where the ATC curve is at a minimum.
(d) The output where the marginal cost curve is at a minimum.

_D_ 12. Total profit is:
  453
(a) _TR - TC_.
(b) $Q \times (P - ATC)$.
(c) $(P \times Q) - TC$. _D_
(d) All of the above.

_B_ 13. When price exceeds average variable cost but not average total cost, the firm should, in the short run:
(a) Shut down.
(b) Produce at the rate of output where price = MC. _B_
(c) Minimize per-unit losses by producing at the rate of output where ATC is minimized.
(d) Raise the price it charges.

A 14. A firm should shut down (stop producing) whenever:
  (a) Minimum average variable cost exceeds price.
  (b) Minimum average total cost exceeds price.
  (c) It is taking a loss.
  (d) Marginal cost exceeds marginal revenue.

A 15. A firm that makes an investment decision views all factors of production as:
  (a) Variable over the long run.
  (b) Variable over the short run.
  (c) Fixed over the long run.
  (d) Fixed over the short run.

D 16. The marginal cost curve:
  (a) Will be affected by changes in the cost of inputs.
  (b) Will eventually slope upward to the right as output increases.
  (c) Above the AVC is the short run supply curve for a competitive firm.
  (d) All of the above.

A 17. The market supply curve is calculated by:
  (a) Summing the quantities supplied of individual supply curves at each price.
  (b) Averaging the quantities supplied of individual supply curves at each price.
  (c) Summing the prices of individual supply curves at each price.
  (d) Averaging the prices of individual supply curves.

C 18. The supply curve is upward-sloping, i.e. it takes a *higher* price to induce greater production, because of:
  (a) Increasing total costs.
  (b) Increasing fixed costs.
  (c) Increasing marginal costs.
  (d) The decreasing skill level of additional workers.

A 19. Taxes affect average total cost and marginal cost curves as follows:
  (a) Profit taxes affect neither, property taxes affect only average total cost, and payroll taxes affect both average and marginal costs.
  (b) Payroll taxes affect neither, property taxes affect only average total cost, and profit taxes affect both average and marginal costs.
  (c) Payroll taxes affect neither, property taxes affect only marginal cost, and profit taxes affect both average and marginal costs.
  (d) Property taxes affect neither, payroll taxes affect only marginal cost, and profit taxes affect both average and marginal costs.

D 20. Which of the following would influence a firm's long-run decision making?
  (a) An increase in property tax assessments.
  (b) A charge on wages for unemployment and disability benefits.
  (c) An increase in profit taxes.
  (d) All of the above.

Problems and Applications
Exercise 1

This exercise uses total cost and total revenue to determine how much output a competitive firm should produce.

Refer to Figure 22.1 to answer questions 1-5.

Figure 22.1

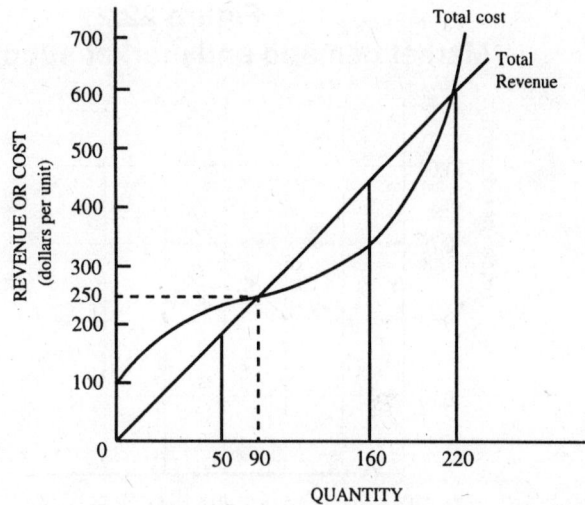

1. Profit is the difference between _Total Revenue_ and _Total Cost_.

2. This firm earns a profit at all output levels between _90_ and _220_ units.

3. What is the profit maximizing rate of output for this firm? _160_

4. This firm experiences losses at all rates of output below _90_ units.

5. Total costs increase more rapidly after 90 units of output because of the law of _diminishing returns_.

Exercise 2

This exercise shows how the equilibrium price is determined in a competitive market and how the profit maximizing rate of output is determined in a perfectly competitive market.

1. Using the information in Table 22.2 draw the market demand curve for chicken eggs in Figure 22.2. Label the curve D.

Table 22.2
Market demand for eggs

Quantity (millions of eggs per day)	Price (per dozen)
2	$ 1.00
4	$ 0.50

Figure 22.2
Market demand and market supply curves

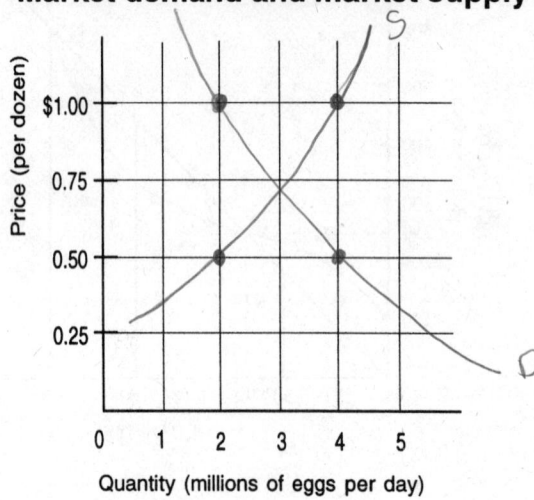

2. Using the information in Table 22.3 draw the market supply curve for chicken eggs in Figure 22.2. Label the curve S.

Table 22.3
Market supply of eggs

Quantity (millions of eggs per day)	Price (per dozen)
4	$ 1.00
2	$ 0.50

3. Use the information in Table 22.4 to determine the marginal cost at each output level for an individual egg farmer.

Table 22.4
Production costs for an individual egg farmer

Quantity (eggs per minute)	Total cost	Marginal cost
0	$ 4.00	---------
1	$ 4.20	.20
2	$ 4.65	.45
3	$ 5.40	.75
4	$ 6.50	1.10
5	$ 7.90	1.40

4. Use the information in Table 22.4 to draw the marginal cost curve for the individual egg farmer in Figure 22.3.

Figure 22.3
Costs of egg production

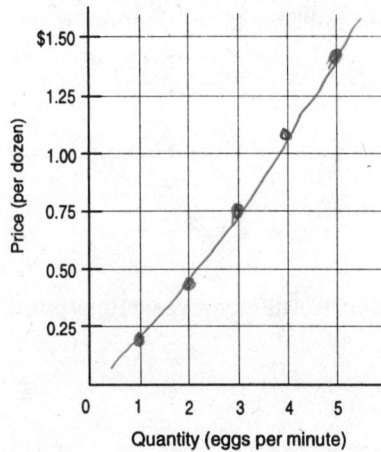

5. Use the market equilibrium price from Figure 22.2 to draw a line at the price that the individual farmer faces in Figure 22.3.

6. For a competitive firm, MR always equals _price_.

7. According to the profit-maximization rule, this egg farmer should produce _3_ eggs per minute.

8. At an output level of 5 eggs per minute, for the individual farmer, MC is (greater, less) than price and the farmer should (increase, decrease) output in order to maximize profit.

Exercise 3

This exercise provides practice in using graphs in a perfectly competitive market situation.

Figure 22.4
Production costs

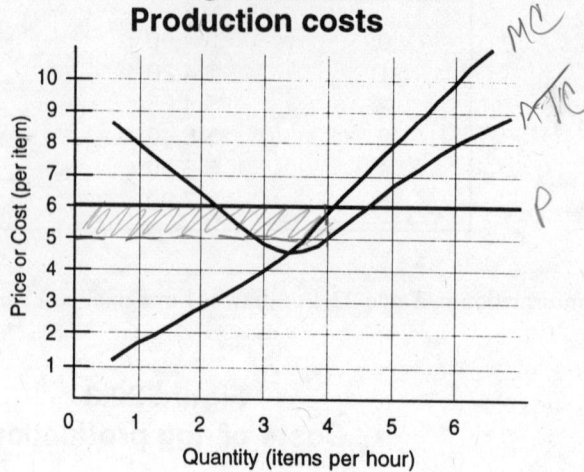

1. Label the three curves given in Figure 22.4 for a firm in a perfectly competitive market situation.

2. What is the profit maximizing rate of output for this firm? 6

3. Shade the area that represents total profit at the profit maximizing rate of output.

Exercise 4

This exercise gives you a chance to calculate total revenue, total profit, and marginal cost and to find the output that will yield maximum profit.

1. Fill in the blanks for the formulas below.
   (a) Price x quantity = _Total Revenue_
   (b) Change in total cost / change in output = _Marginal cost_
   (c) Total revenue - total cost = _profit_

2. After checking your answers for question 1, complete Table 22.5.

Table 22.5
Cost and revenue data

Qty.	Price	Total revenue	Total cost	Profit	Marginal cost
0	$7	$ 0	$ 5.00	-$ 5.00	--------
1	7	7.00	7.00	+ 0	$ 2.00
2	7	14.00	11.00	+ 3.00	4.00
3	7	21.00	18.00	+ 3.00	7.00
4	7	28.00	27.00	+ 1.00	9.00
5	7	35.00	39.00	- 4.00	12.00

314

3. In Figure 22.5, graph price and marginal cost.

Figure 22.5

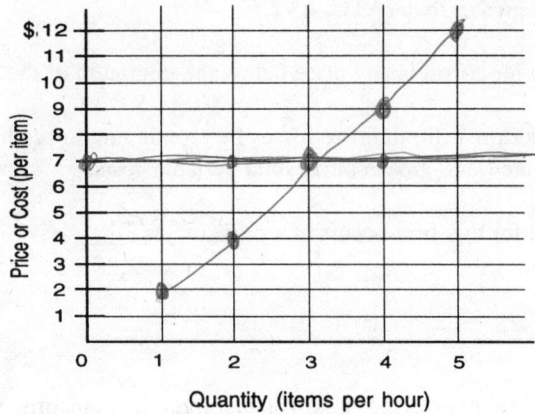

Quantity (items per hour)

4. What is the profit maximizing level of output for this firm? _____3 items per day_____

5. At an output level of 2 items this firm could (increase, decrease) profit by producing more.

Exercise 5

This exercise focuses on the shutdown decision.

Refer to Figure 22.6 to answer questions 1-6.

Figure 22.6

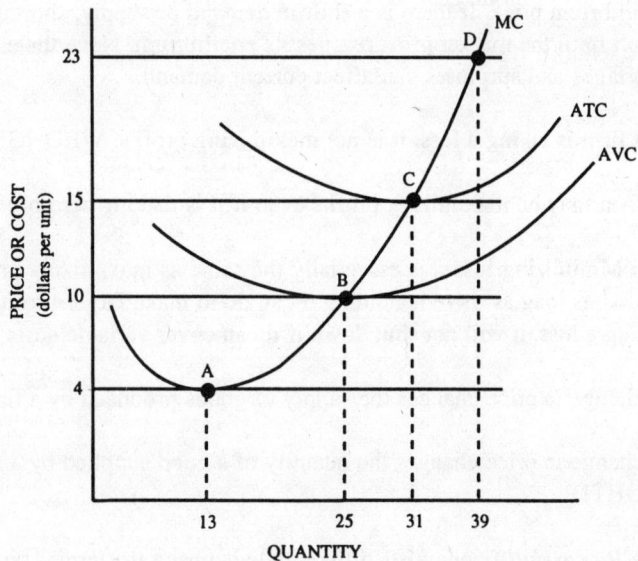

QUANTITY

315

1. What is the profit-maximizing production rate for the firm if the price is $23? __39__

2. What is the profit-maximizing production rate for the firm if the price is $15? __31__

3. At a price of $12 this firm is earning a (profit, loss) and should (continue to produce, shut-down) because the price is greater than (ATC, AVC).

4. The shutdown price for a firm is any price below the minimum of the __AVC__ curve.

5. At a price of $8 this firm will minimize losses by (continuing to produce, shutting down). In this case total revenues are (less, greater) than total variable costs.

6. The shutdown point for this firm occurs at a price of __10__.

Common Errors

The first statement in each "common error" below is incorrect. Each incorrect statement is followed by a corrected version and an explanation.

1. Higher prices yield greater profits. WRONG!

   The effect of price increases on total revenue depends on the elasticity of demand. RIGHT!

   The law of demand tells us that when prices rise, quantity falls; total revenues may actually decrease (remember the $4 ice cream cones). Costs also change; if they don't fall as quickly as total revenues, then *profits* fall.

2. Surpluses and shortages are determinants of demand and supply that shift demand and supply curves. WRONG!

   Surpluses and shortages often result from shifts of demand or supply curves, but they do not cause such shifts themselves. RIGHT!

   Surpluses or shortages may appear in a market if the market price does not adjust to the equilibrium price. If there is a shift in demand or supply, shortages or surpluses may temporarily result until the market price reaches its equilibrium. Nevertheless, expectations of future shortages and surpluses can affect current demand.

3. If a firm is taking a loss, it is not maximizing profits. WRONG!

   A firm may be maximizing profits even if it is making zero profits or taking a loss. RIGHT!

   Minimizing losses is essentially the same as maximizing profits. A firm is maximizing profits as long as there is nothing it can do to make larger profits. Remember, even if the firm is taking a loss, it will not shut down if it can cover variable costs.

4. A change in price changes the supply of goods produced by a firm. WRONG!

   A change in price changes the quantity of a good supplied by a firm in a given time period. RIGHT!

   Be careful! Economists differentiate between the terms "quantity supplied" and "supply." A change in the quantity supplied usually refers to a movement along a supply curve as a result of a change in price or production rate. A change in supply refers to a shift of the supply curve as a result of a change in technology, the price of a resource, or the number of sellers.

5. A firm should always increase the rate of production as long as it is making a profit. WRONG!

A profitable firm should increase production rates only as long as additional revenues from the increase in production exceed the additional associated costs. RIGHT!

If the increase in production rates generates more costs than revenue, the firm will be less profitable. In this case, continued expansion will ultimately result in zero profits.

•ANSWERS•

Using Key Terms

Across

2.   economic cost
4.   fixed costs
6.   profit maximization rule
7.   marginal revenue
9.   normal profit
11. supply curve
12. marginal cost
13. market power
14. investment decision
17. market structure
18. total revenue
19. variable costs
20. long run

Down

1.   perfect competition
3.   monopoly
5.   competitive firm
6.   production decision
8.   economic profit
10. shutdown point
15. short run
16. profit

True or False

1. T
2. T
3. F   The supply curve is that part of the marginal cost curve above the AVC curve.
4. F   The firm should expand production as long as it is making a profit on *additional* units. A firm could produce an output greater than the profit-maximizing output but still have an profit.
5. F   To maximize revenue, a firm would produce as much output as it possibly can. To maximize profit, the firm should produce the output where the difference between TR and TC is the greatest.

6. T
7. T
8. F   A firm that earns zero economic profits is covering all its economic costs, including a normal profit to the entrepreneur.   There is no better use for the firm's resources (i.e. it is earning exactly what it could earn in the next best option).
9. T
10. T

Multiple Choice

1.	a	5.	d	9.	c	13.	b	17.	a
2.	a	6.	b	10.	b	14.	a	18.	c
3.	c	7.	b	11.	b	15.	a	19.	a
4.	d	8.	c	12.	d	16.	d	20.	d

Problems and Applications

Exercise 1

1. total revenue, total cost
2. 90, 220
3. 160 units
4. 90
5. diminishing returns

Exercise 2

Figure 22.2 Answer

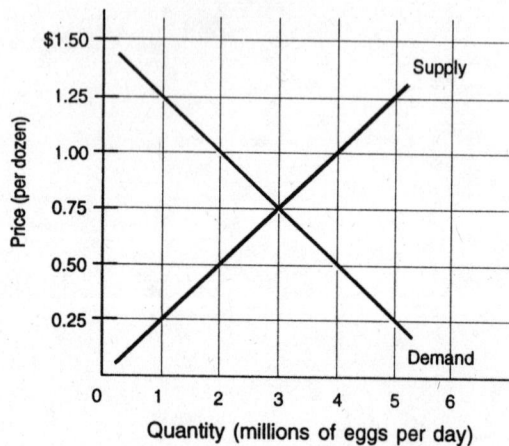

1. See Figure 22.2 answer.
2. See Figure 22.2 answer.

3. **Table 22.4 Answer**

Quantity	Marginal cost
0	$ ------
1	0.20
2	0.45
3	0.75
4	1.10
5	1.40

Figure 22.3 Answer

4. See Figure 22.3 answer.
5. See Figure 22.3 answer.

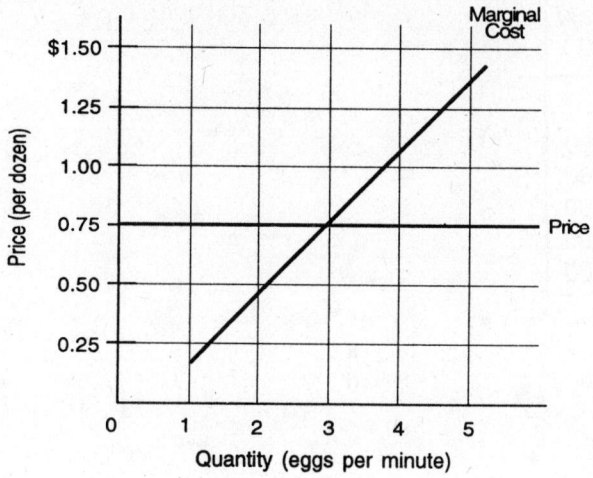

6. price
7. 3
8. greater, decrease

Exercise 3

1. **Figure 22.4 Answer**

2. 4 items per hour
3. See Figure 22.4 answer.

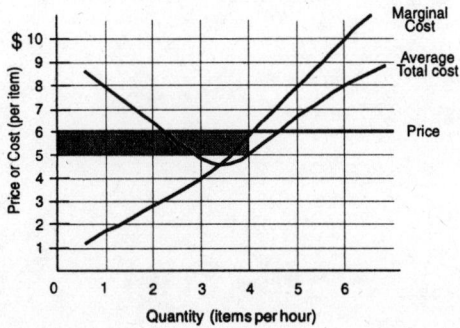

Exercise 4

1. a. total revenue
   b. marginal cost
   c. profit

2. **Table 22.5 Answer**

Quantity	Total revenue	Profit	Marginal cost
0	$ 0.00	$ -5.00	-------
1	7.00	+ 0.00	$ 2.00
2	14.00	+ 3.00	4.00
3	21.00	+ 3.00	7.00
4	28.00	+ 1.00	9.00
5	35.00	- 4.00	12.00

3. **Figure 22.5 Answer**

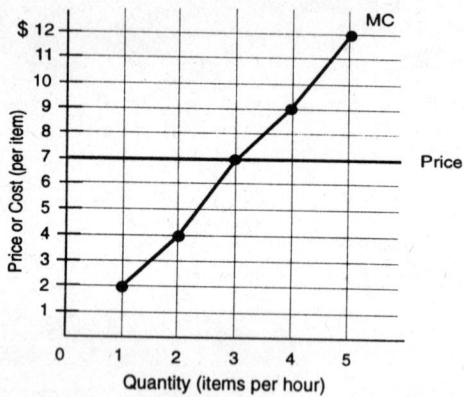

4. 3 items per day
5. increase

Exercise 5

1. 39 units
2. 31 units
3. loss, continue to produce, AVC
4. AVC
5. shutting down, less
6. $10

CHAPTER 23

Competitive Markets

Quick Review

The purely competitive market provides the standard by which all other market structures are judged. Other markets are labeled efficient or inefficient, depending on how their long-run equilibrium price and output compare with what would be achieved in a competitive market.

The essence of a competitive market is that the actors are powerless to influence product prices and resource flows. They are powerless because such a market is characterized by (1) a product that is homogeneous, (2) a large number of very small buyers and sellers, (3) prices that are free of artificial restrictions, and (4) an absence of barriers to entry into or exit from the market.

In this chapter we consider three principal questions:

- How are prices determined in competitive markets?
- How does competition affect the profits of a firm or industry?
- What does society gain from market competition?

Of course, firms sometimes incur losses. In that case, the market has sent a signal that some firms should leave the market. Supply is thereby reduced, price rises, *ceteris paribus,* and long-run equilibrium is established at a higher price. Resources that left the market will move to higher-valued uses elsewhere. Society's efficient allocation of scarce resources owes as much to losses as it does to profits.

Firms in a competitive market are called "price takers." The price that they "take" is the equilibrium price, at which market supply equals market demand. Because each firm is so small relative to the market, each entrepreneur recognizes that he or she alone cannot influence the price of the product by altering his or her share of the total supply. The price dictated by the market becomes, therefore, the marginal revenue. Following the rules described earlier, entrepreneurs produce at that rate of production at which $MR = MC$. This is the best they can do.

Let's suppose that at the current market price, profits are above the normal rates of return earned by similar resources in alternative uses. Owners of those resources will enter the market, start new firms, and produce output. But by doing so they will increase the supply of the product and, *ceteris paribus,* drive down the market price (each firm's marginal revenue). The entry of firms will continue until the above-normal returns are eliminated. Thus, each firm is forced by the competition (or threat of competition) from other firms to operate efficiently. In other words, the producer is forced to the minimum average total cost (*ATC*) of producing goods.

When the long-run equilibrium is reached in a competitive market, several important conditions result. First, consumers are willing to pay an amount (*P*) for the last unit produced that is just equal to the amount required (*MC*) to get firms to produce it. Furthermore, *MC* = minimum *LATC*, because if price were any higher, returns would be above average and new firms would enter the industry and drive the price down.

Consumers get what they want at the lowest possible price. The economy's resources are used most efficiently in perfectly competitive markets.

Examples of competitive markets are easy to find. Personal computers, agricultural products, VCRs, and so on are just a few. This chapter uses the story of the personal computer to illustrate how competitive markets work and how the consumer benefits as a result. We should expect to see the same thing happen in the market for HDTV very soon.

Learning Objectives

After reading Chapter 23 and doing the following exercises, you should:

1. Know how the absence of market power relates to the shape of demand and supply curves from the point of view of buyers and sellers.
2. Be able to tell why the demand curve facing a competitive firm is flat.
3. Be able to list the characteristics of the competitive market structure and describe the role of competition in the U.S. economy.
4. Know how barriers to entry influence the competitive process.
5. Know the difference between the firm's demand curve and the market demand curve.
6. Know why above-normal profits disappear in competitive industries.
7. Understand how a competitive market structure affects prices, cost, output, and profits in the short and long run.
8. Be able to identify the signals for the entry and exit of firms.
9. Be able to show the effects of shifts of market demand or supply on individual demand or supply.
10. Describe how marginal cost pricing leads to efficiency in the allocation of resources.

Using Key Terms

Fill in the puzzle on the opposite page with the appropriate term from the list of Key Terms at the end on the chapter in the text.

Across

3. The choice of a short-run rate of output by catfish farmers.
4. The offer of goods at a price equal to their marginal cost.
6. Competitive markets promote _____ because price is driven down to the level of minimum average costs.
7. According to Table 23.2 in the text, firms will enter an industry if _____ exists.
8. A market in which no buyer or seller has market power.
10. Equal to $300 at an output rate of 600 computers per month in Table 23.1 in the text.
11. This curve shifts to the right in Figure 23.2 in the text as more firms enter the industry.
12. The rate of output at which price equals minimum AVC.
13. The price signal the consumer receives in a competitive market is an accurate reflection of _____.
14. Equal to marginal revenue at an output rate of 600 computers per month in Table 23.1 in the text.
15. Total cost divided by the quantity produced.
16. Determined by the intersection of market demand and market supply.
17. Allows for indirect communication between producers and consumers by way of market sales and purchases.

Down

1. Occurs where price equals minimum ATC in Figure 23.6 in the text.
2. Occurs where price equals marginal cost in Figure 23.6 in the text.

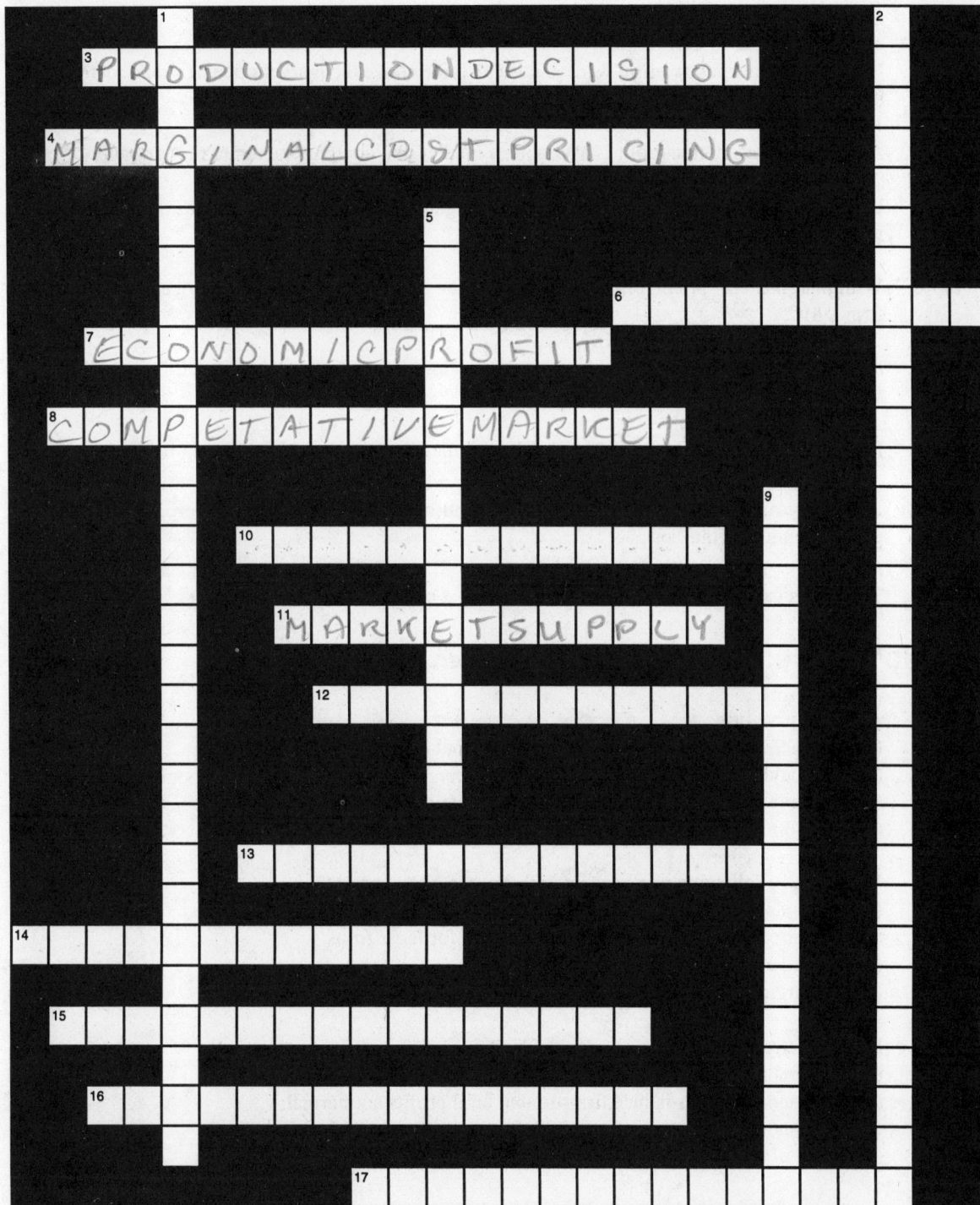

5. Obstacles that make it difficult or impossible for new firms to enter an industry.
9. The decision to build, buy, or lease plant and equipment.

Puzzle 23.1

3. PRODUCTIONDECISION
4. MARGINALCOSTPRICING
7. ECONOMICPROFIT
8. COMPETATIVEMARKET
11. MARKETSUPPLY

True or False: *Circle your choice and explain why any false statements are incorrect.*

T F 1. The market supply curve is a horizontal summation of the *MC* curves above minimum *AVC* of the individual firms.

T F 2. A competitive firm's production decision aims to maximize profits at the production rate where the ATC is at a minimum.

T F 3. If a perfectly competitive firm were to raise its price above the market price, it would increase its total revenues.

T F 4. As long as an economic profit is available, a market will continue to attract new entrants.

T F 5. In competitive markets, economic losses are a signal to firms that better options are available for its resources.

T F 6. With marginal cost pricing, firms will produce the output where the market price equals the firm's MC.

T F 7. Since perfectly competitive firms earn zero economic profits in the long run, all firms will leave the industry.

T F 8. Perfectly competitive firms are forced to be technically efficient by government regulations.

T F 9. In the long-run equilibrium for a perfectly competitive market, the price of the product will equal the minimum marginal cost.

T F 10. Technological changes shift the average total cost curve and the marginal cost curve downward.

Multiple Choice: *Select the correct answer.*

_____ 1. A competitive firm:
  (a) Is able to keep other potential producers out of the market.
  (b) Would like to keep other potential producers out of the market but cannot do so.
  (c) Is powerless to alter its own rate of production.
  (d) Will not care if more producers enter the market.

_____ 2. Which of the following is consistent with a competitive market?
  (a) A small number of firms.
  (b) Exit of small firms when profits are high for large firms.
  (c) Zero economic profit in the long run.
  (d) Marginal revenue lower than price for each firm.

_____ 3. In a perfectly competitive market in the long run:
  (a) Economic profits induce firms to enter until profits are normal.
  (b) Economic losses induce firms to exit until profits are normal.
  (c) Economic profit is zero at equilibrium.
  (d) All of the above.

C 4. The exit of firms from a market:
        (a) Shifts the market supply curve to the right.
        (b) Reduces profits of existing firms in a market.
        (c) Reduces the equilibrium output in the market.
        (d) All of the above.

D 5. Which of the following conditions is *not* characteristic of a perfectly competitive market?
        (a) There are many firms.
        (b) Products are homogeneous.
        (c) Barriers to enter the industry are low.
        (d) The market price is determined by an organization of sellers.

B 6. In a competitive market, if the market demand curve is tangent to the minimum point of the ATC curve, a firm may seek to earn economic profits by:
        (a) Producing at the rate of output where price equals demand.
        (b) Decreasing production costs through technological improvements.
        (c) Decreasing price.
        (d) Increasing price.

D 7. The entry of firms into a market:
        (a) Pushes the equilibrium price downward.
        (b) Reduces profits of existing firms in the market.
        (c) Shifts the market supply curve rightward.
        (d) All of the above.

C 8. The perfectly competitive market model is important because:
        (a) It characterizes most markets in the U.S. economy.
        (b) It shows how laissez faire can overcome market failures.
        (c) Many markets function much like the competitive model.
        (d) All of the above.

C 9. A competitive market promotes technical efficiency in the long run by pushing prices to the minimum of:
        (a) Short-run AVC.
        (b) Short-run MC.
        (c) Long-run ATC.
        (d) Long-run TC.

B 10. Which of the following conditions always characterizes a firm that is in short-run competitive equilibrium where profits are maximized?
        (a) Price equals minimum average total cost.
        (b) Price equals marginal cost.
        (c) There are no economic profits.
        (d) All of the above characterize such a firm.

D 11. The market supply curve will shift as a result of all of the following *except:*
        (a) Changes in technology.
        (b) Changes in the number of supplying firms.
        (c) Changes in expectations about making profits in an industry.
        (d) Changes in the current income of buyers.

_A_ 12. In a competitive market where firms are incurring losses, which of the following should be expected as the industry moves to long-run equilibrium, *ceteris paribus?*
  (a) A higher price and fewer firms.
  (b) A lower price and fewer firms.
  (c) A higher price and more firms.
  (d) A lower price and more firms.

_A_ 13. In long-run competitive equilibrium, price equals:
  (a) The minimum of the long-run average total cost curve.
  (b) The minimum of the long-run average variable cost curve.
  (c) Long-run marginal cost.
  (d) All of the above.

_B_ 14. In which of the following cases would a firm enter a market?
  (a) P = short-run ATC.
  (b) P > long-run ATC.
  (c) P < short-run ATC.
  (d) P < long-run ATC.

_D_ 15. The constant quest for profits in competitive markets results in:
  (a) Zero economic profits in the long run.
  (b) The production of goods and services that consumers demand.
  (c) Product and technological innovation.
  (d) All of the above are correct.

_A_ 16. When economic profits exist in the market for a particular product, this is a signal to producers that:
  (a) Consumers would like more scarce resources devoted to the production of this product.
  (b) That the market is oversupplied with this product.
  (c) The best mix of goods and services are being produced with society's scarce resources.
  (d) Price is at the minimum of the ATC curve.

_A_ 17. In a competitive market where firms are experiencing economic losses, which of the following would not be expected?
  (a) A decrease in MR for the remaining firms.
  (b) A decrease in market supply.
  (c) An increase in total revenue for the remaining firms.
  (d) An increase in output for the remaining firms.

_B_ 18. Economic losses are a signal to producers:
  (a) That they are using resources in the most efficient way.
  (b) That they are not using resources in the best way.
  (c) That consumer demand is being satisfied.
  (d) That consumers are content with the allocation of resources.

_D_ 19. When a computer firm is producing an output where the price is greater than the MC, then from society's standpoint:
  (a) The firm is producing too much because society is giving up more to produce additional computers than the computers are worth.
  (b) The firm is producing too much because society would be willing to give up more alternative goods in order to get additional computers.
  (c) The firm is producing too little because society is giving up more to produce additional computers than the computers are worth.
  (d) The firm is producing too little because society would be willing to give up more alternative goods in order to get additional computers.

326

20. Marginal cost pricing in competitive markets results in:
    (a)   Economic efficiency.
    (b)   Output being produced where price equals the opportunity cost of the last unit being produced.
    (c)   Necessary information for consumers to make rational choices between alternative goods and services.
    (d)   All of the above are correct.

Problems and Applications

Exercise 1

This exercise focuses on the market supply curve and how a competitive industry adjusts to long-run equilibrium.

Assume the HDTV industry is a competitive market and initially there are economic profits in the industry.

1. The lure of economic profits will cause (more, less) firms to enter the industry over time which will cause the market supply curve to _shift to the right_.

2. Market price is determined by the intersection of _market supply & market demand_.

3. If the market supply shifts to the right, *ceteris paribus*, market price will (increase, decrease).

4. As long as new producers enter the market, market output will (expand, contract) and economic profits will (increase, decrease).

5. Economic profits will approach _zero_ for this industry in the long run.

6. In long-run competitive equilibrium, price will be equal to minimum _ATC_.

Exercise 2

This exercise uses information from a table to determine revenues, costs, and profits.

Use Table 23.1 to answer questions 1-9.

Table 23.1

Output	Price	Total revenue	Total cost	Total profit	Marginal revenue	Marginal cost	Average total cost
0	----	----	$10	____	----	----	----
1	$13	____	15	____	____	____	____
2	13	____	22	____	____	____	____
3	13	____	31	____	____	____	____
4	13	____	44	____	____	____	____
5	13	____	61	____	____	____	____

1. It is obvious that Table 23.1 refers to a perfectly competitive firm because _____ is constant regardless of the level of output.

2. The fixed cost for this firm is equal to _____.

3. Calculate total revenue, total profit, marginal revenue, marginal cost, and average total cost for this firm.

4. What is the profit maximizing rate of output for this firm? _____

5. The short-run competitive equilibrium occurs where _____.

6. The long-run competitive equilibrium occurs where _____.

7. The minimum for average total cost for this firm is _____. This amount is (greater, less) than the current price so this firm is operating in the (short, long) run.

8. In this case, firms will _____ the industry because economic _____ exist.

9. What happens to price as new firms enter the market? _____

Exercise 3

When the hand-held calculator was invented in the 1970s, the market responded in competitive fashion. This exercise focuses on the adjustments made in a competitive market in both the short run and the long run.

Figure 23.1 presents the cost curves that are relevant to a firm's production decision, and Figure 23.2 shows the market demand and supply curves for the calculator market. Use Figures 23.1 and 23.2 and the knowledge of cost curves that you have gained from the text to answer questions 1-10.

**Figure 23.1
Firm**

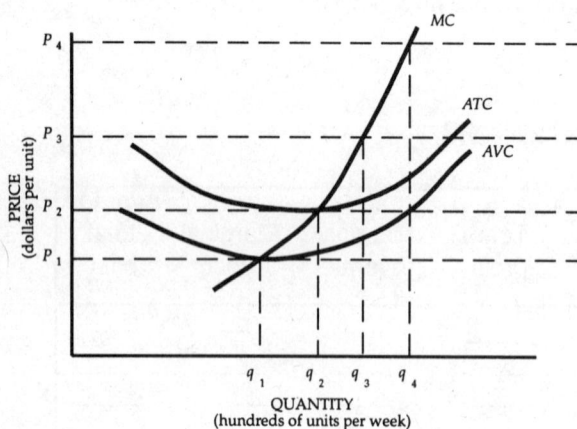

**Figure 23.2
Market (all firms)**

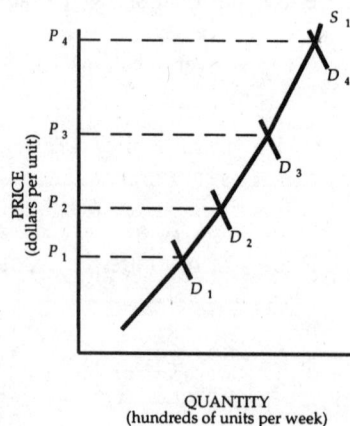

1. If the market demand and supply curves are S_1 and D_1, the market equilibrium price will be:
   - (a) P_1.
   - (b) P_2.
   - (c) P_3.
   - (d) P_4.

2. Suppose the demand for calculators shifts to D_4. This shift might be caused by:
   - (a) An increase in the number of consumers.
   - (b) An increase in consumers' incomes.
   - (c) A rise in the price of a substitute good.
   - (d) All of the above.

3. If the demand curve is at D_4, the quantity supplied by the *firm* will be:
   - (a) q_1.
   - (b) q_2.
   - (c) q_3.
   - (d) q_4.

4. Suppose a recession results in a shift in the demand curve for calculators to D_1. Then the *firm* will produce:
   - (a) q_1.
   - (b) q_2.
   - (c) q_3.
   - (d) q_4.

5. In the short run, the firm will continue to produce some output until demand changes enough to drive price below:
   - (a) P_1.
   - (b) P_2.
   - (c) P_3.
   - (d) P_4.

6. At prices below P_1, the firm will shut down (produce no output) because:
   - (a) Its loss will be less than if it produces at any level of output.
   - (b) Its loss will be limited to its fixed costs.
   - (c) Total revenue is less than total variable cost.
   - (d) All of the above are the case.

7. The fact that the quantity supplied by the firm changes whenever the market price changes indicates that:
   - (a) The firm is a price setter.
   - (b) The firm is a price taker.
   - (c) The firm has monopoly power.
   - (d) The firm has no control over the quantity it produces.

8. Since the firm will not produce any output if the market price falls below P_1:
   - (a) The firm's supply curve is that part of the *MC* curve above the minimum point on the *ATC* curve.
   - (b) The average variable cost curve is the firm's supply curve.
   - (c) The average total cost curve is the firm's supply curve.
   - (d) The firm's supply curve is that part of its marginal cost curve that lies above its average variable cost curve.

9. If the price is P_3, and the demand curve is D_3 in the long run:
    (a) Returns to the firm are below average, and firms will leave the industry.
    (b) Returns are above average, and new firms will have an incentive to enter the market.
    (c) Returns are about average, and there is no incentive for firms to move into or out of the industry.
    (d) We really can't say without more information.

10. Long-run competitive equilibrium occurs at a price of:
    (a) P_1.
    (b) P_2.
    (c) P_3.
    (d) P_4.

Exercise 4

Many newspapers provide information from competitive markets, such as the want ads, market prices, and advertising.

Reread the article in the text entitled "Fish Farms Fall Prey to Excess." Then quote the words that give an example of each of the following types of information which can help verify that a market is really competitive.

1. *Structural characteristics.* What phrases indicate that large numbers of farmers are involved?
    _____.

2. *Conduct.* What passage(s) indicate entry into or exit from the catfish market? _____
    _____

3. *Performance.* What passage(s) indicate information about prices, profits, or quantity of output that is consistent with the performance in a competitive market? _____
    _____
    _____

4. *Market boundaries.* On the basis of information in the article only, which of the following best characterizes the market boundaries of the catfish market? It appears to be strictly:
    (a) A local market.
    (b) A regional market.
    (c) A national market.
    (d) An international market.

5. What passage provides a clue about the extent of the market boundaries? _____
    _____

Common Errors

The first statement in each "common error" below is incorrect. Each incorrect statement is followed by a corrected version and an explanation.

1. The demand curve for a competitive market is flat. WRONG!

    The demand curve for a competitive firm is flat. RIGHT!

The error above results from failure to distinguish between the market and the firm. Review Exercise 3 if this distinction is not clear.

2.   Competitive firms do not make profits. WRONG!

Competitive firms can make economic profits in the short run. RIGHT!

In the long run, firms enter an industry and compete away economic profits. In the short run, a change in demand or supply may cause price to change and may bestow temporary economic profits on a firm. In the personal computer example in the text, technological changes shifted the supply curve and provided temporary profits.

Be careful! Always distinguish between short-run profit-maximizing production rates and price levels and long-run equilibrium production rates and price levels. While industries have a tendency to move toward long-run equilibrium, they may never reach it because of shocks that buffet a market.

3.   Since competitive firms make zero profits in the long run, they cannot pay their stockholders and so they should shut down. WRONG!

Since competitive firms make zero economic profits in the long run, they are able to pay all factors of production, including the entrepreneurs, to keep the firms in existence. RIGHT!

Be careful! Keep the accounting and economic definitions of such words as "profit" separate and distinct. Keep movements along the supply curve (firms increase production rates) separate from shifts of the supply curve (firms enter or exit). Avoid confusing short-run responses (increasing production rates in existing plants) with long-run responses (entry or exit).

•ANSWERS•

Using Key Terms
Across
3.   production decision
4.   marginal cost pricing
6.   efficiency
7.   economic profit
8.   competitive market
10.   profit per unit
11.   market supply
12.   shutdown point
13.   opportunity cost
14.   marginal cost
15.   average total cost
16.   equilibrium price
17.   market mechanism

Down
1.   long-run competitive equilibrium
2.   short-run competitive equilibrium
5.   barriers to entry
9.   investment decision

True or False

1. T
2. F The firm maximizes profits at the output rate where price (MR) = MC.
3. F Total revenues would decrease to zero because the firm could not sell any output at a price above the market price.
4. T
5. T
6. T
7. F Zero economic profits are an indication that there is no better use for a firm's resources. As a result, once economic profits reach zero, there is no further exit (or entry).
8. F Competition forces perfectly competitive firms to be technically efficient.
9. F The price of the product will equal the minimum ATC.
10. T

Multiple Choice

1.	b	5.	d	9.	c	13.	a	17.	a
2.	c	6.	b	10.	b	14.	b	18.	b
3.	d	7.	d	11.	d	15.	d	19.	d
4.	c	8.	c	12.	a	16.	a	20.	d

Problems and Applications

Exercise 1

1. more, shift to the right
2. market supply and market demand
3. decrease
4. expand, decrease
5. zero
6. ATC

Exercise 2

1. price
2. $10
3. **Table 23.1 Answer**

Output	Price	Total revenue	Total cost	Total profit	Marginal revenue	Marginal cost	Average total cost
0	----	----	$10	$-10	----	----	----
1	$13	$13	15	-2	$13	$5	$15.00
2	13	26	22	4	13	7	11.00
3	13	39	31	8	13	9	10.33
4	13	52	44	8	13	13	11.00
5	13	65	61	4	13	17	12.20

4. 4 units of output
5. p=MC
6. p=MC=minimum ATC
7. $10.33, less, short
8. enter, profits
9. decreases

Exercise 3

1.	a	3.	d	5.	a	7.	b	9.	b
2.	d	4.	a	6.	d	8.	d	10.	b

Exercise 4

1. "estimated that half of the state's 300 growers"
2. "luring cotton farmers such as Redditt, who converted almost 200 acres of his land into ponds" and "about as many as one-third could go bankrupt"
3. "Catfish are selling for about 60 cents a pound, but producing a pound of catfish costs about 65 cents"; "But when so many farmers produced so many fish, the dam burst and panic selling began"; "Prices have been in a free fall for months."
4. c
5. "The economies of large regions of Arkansas, Louisiana, Texas, Alabama and Mississippi have become intertwined."

CHAPTER 24

Monopoly

Quick Review

In this chapter we are concerned with monopoly—a market structure at the other end of the spectrum from a competitive market. In the former there is a single producer. The latter, as we learned in the previous chapter, has a large number of producers.

Let's focus on the following questions:

- What price will a monopolist charge?
- How much output will the monopolist produce?
- Are consumers better or worse off when only one firm controls an entire market?

The key to each of these questions rests with market power. Market power is the ability to influence significantly the market price of goods and services. The extreme case of market power is monopoly. The demand curve facing the monopolist and the market demand curve are identical. To sell larger quantities of output in a given time period, a monopoly must lower the price of its product. Such price reductions cause marginal revenue and price to diverge. A firm without market power has no such problem; it may sell as much output as it desires at the prevailing market price.

Like all profit-maximizing firms, a monopolist will produce that rate of output at which marginal revenue equals marginal cost. The monopolist will attain a higher level of profit than a competitive firm because of its ability to equate marginal revenue and marginal cost. By contrast, a competitive firm ends up equating marginal cost and price. In addition, monopolists are sometimes able to charge different prices to different buyers (a practice called "price discrimination") and extract high prices and profits even when market demand is relatively elastic.

The higher profits earned by a monopolist are sure to attract the envy of other entrepreneurs. A market-power position and its related profits are maintained only if barriers to entry keep others out of the market.

Monopolists charge a price which is higher than marginal cost. They also fail to fully utilize available resources. Finally, monopolists do not necessarily pick the least-cost production process. By contrast, competitive firms are compelled by the market to achieve these economic objectives in order to survive.

The principal arguments in favor of market power focus on the alleged ability of large firms to pursue long-term research and development, on the incentives implicit in the opportunity to attain market power, and on the greater efficiency that larger firms may attain. The first two arguments are weakened by the fact that competitive firms are under much greater pressure to innovate and can stay ahead in the profit game only if they do so. Nevertheless, larger firms may be able to achieve economies of scale—lower minimum average costs brought about by a larger scale of plant—and thus may be considered desirable on the grounds of efficiency. A firm with economies of scale over the entire range of market output is called a natural monopoly. Larger firms are not necessarily more efficient, however, since either constant returns to scale or even diseconomies of scale may arise as firm size increases. Few firms are natural monopolies.

Recently economists have investigated the restraining power of potential competition in markets where the barriers to entry are not too high. This idea is included in the concept of "contestable markets."

Because monopolies have so many adverse impacts on the economy, governments at all levels have been empowered to prevent or regulate the concentration of market power. The Sherman Act, the Clayton Act, and the Federal Trade Commission Act form the legal foundation for antitrust activities.

Learning Objectives

After reading Chapter 24 and doing the following exercises, you should:

1. Know the meaning of market power.
2. Know why a monopolist has market power and a downward-sloping demand curve and why price and marginal revenue diverge.
3. Be able to show the relationship between the market demand and individual demand curve for a monopolist.
4. Know the difference between marginal cost pricing for a competitive firm and profit maximization for a monopoly.
5. Be able to determine a monopolist's most profitable rate of production.
6. Be able to show why a monopoly typically results in higher profits, less output, and higher prices than would occur in a competitive market.
7. Be able to contrast the long-run results in a competitive market with that of a monopoly.
8. Be able to describe the advantages and disadvantages of monopoly versus competition.
9. Be able to distinguish price discrimination from other types of pricing.
10. Be able to distinguish economies of scale from constant returns to scale and diseconomies of scale.
11. Understand why a natural monopoly occurs.
12. Know how and why antitrust policy is used to control monopoly.
13. Understand the idea of "contestable" markets.

Using Key Terms

Fill in the puzzle on the opposite page with the appropriate term from the list of Key Terms at the end of the chapter in the text.

Across

2. This curve lies below the demand curve at every point except the first in Figure 24.2 in the text.
7. Used to determine that the most profitable rate of production is four bushels per hour in Figure 24.3 in the text.
9. The ability to alter the market price of a good or service.
10. An industry in which one firm can achieve economies of scale over the entire range of market supply.
11. Total cost divided by the quantity produced in a given time period.
12. Government intervention to alter market structure or prevent abuse of market power.
13. For a monopolist, this short-run choice is made by locating the intersection of marginal cost and marginal revenue.

Down

1. The sale of an identical good at different prices to different consumers by a single seller.
2. The market structure that Pepsi accuses Coke of trying to duplicate in the article titled "Pepsi Takes Coke to Court" in the text.
3. The percentage change in quantity demanded divided by the percentage change in price.
4. According to the article "Foxy Soviets Pelt the West" in the text, the Soviet Union erected _____ by not letting live sables leave the country.
5. Gives one producer an advantage over several smaller producers and acts as a barrier to entry.

6. An imperfectly competitive industry which is restrained by potential competition.
8. The pricing method characteristic of competitive markets but not a monopoly.

Puzzle 24.1

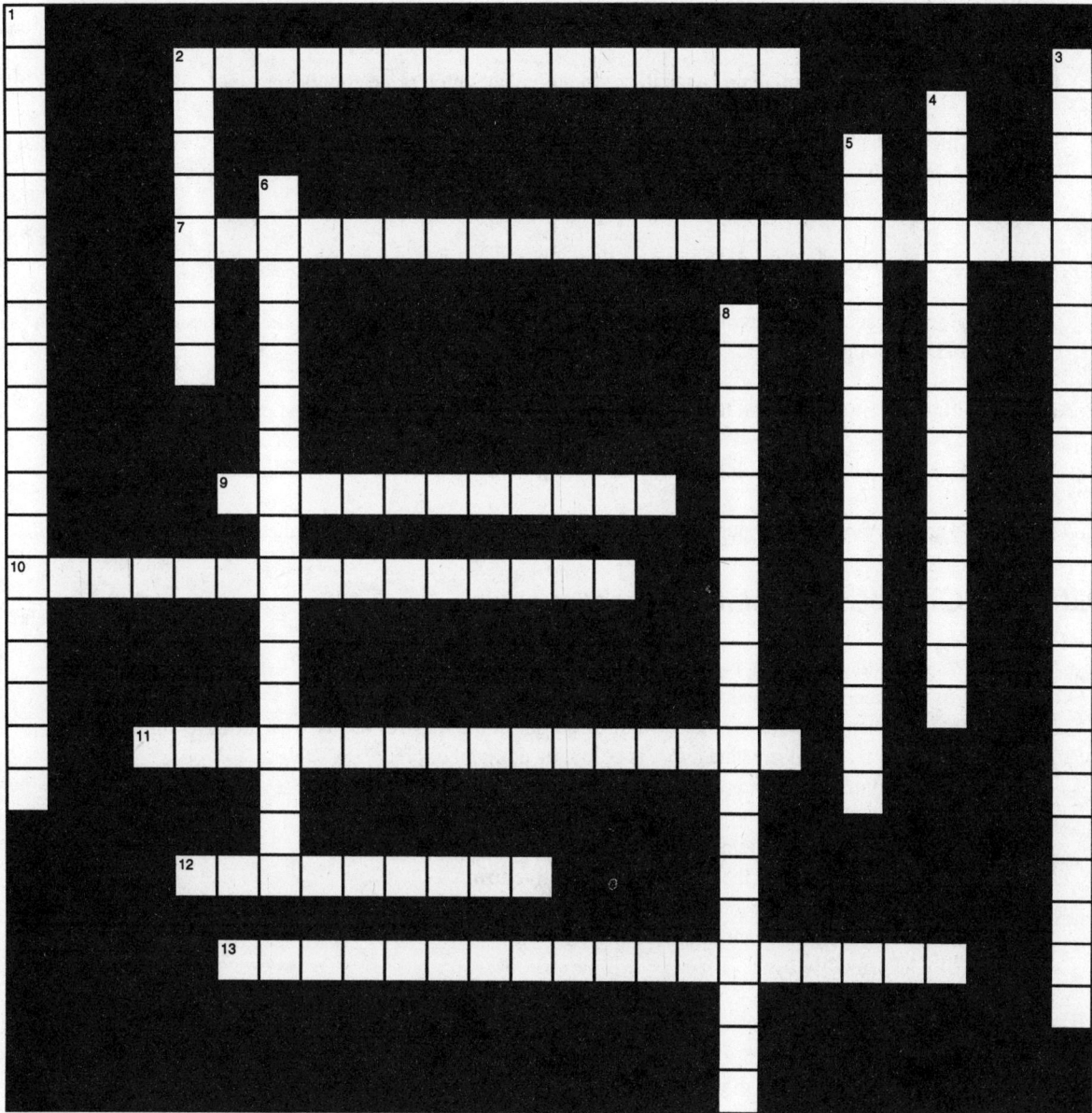

True or False: *Circle your choice and explain why any false statements are incorrect.*

T F 1. Since a competitive firm can sell unlimited quantities of output at the prevailing price, it can affect the market price of a good or service.

T F 2. The monopolist has a flat (i.e. horizontal) demand curve because of high barriers to entry.

T F 3. The demand curve for the monopolist is exactly the same as the market demand curve.

T F 4. Monopolists maximize profits at the output level at which price equals marginal cost.

T F 5. Since both monopolists and competitive firms maximize profits at the output level at which marginal revenue equals marginal cost, monopolists and competitive markets with the same marginal cost curves and market demand curves will produce the same output.

T F 6. In the long run, a monopolist can continue to earn economic profits.

T F 7. Monopolists have an advantage over competitive markets in receiving the full benefit of research and development efforts.

T F 8. Price discrimination can occur because of the differences in the demand curves among buyers.

T F 9. The theory of contestable markets focuses on market structure rather than market behavior.

T F 10. A natural monopoly experiences economies of scale over the entire range of market output.

Multiple Choice: *Select the correct answer.*

_____ 1. Which of the following is the result of a monopolist's market power?
(a) It faces a downward-sloping demand curve.
(b) When it produces an extra unit of output, it must lower its price on all of its units.
(c) Its marginal revenue curve is below its demand curve.
(d) All of the above are results.

_____ 2. For a monopolist, the demand curve facing the firm is:
(a) The same as for the perfectly competitive firm.
(b) The same as the market-demand curve.
(c) Always below marginal revenue.
(d) Perfectly elastic.

_____ 3. When a monopolist sells an additional unit of output, the marginal revenue will be lower than the price because:
(a) The price of all the units sold will have to be lowered in order to sell the additional unit.
(b) The monopolist faces a flat (horizontal) demand curve for its product.
(c) Costs increase as more output is produced.
(d) Economies of scale exist for monopolists.

_____ 4. Which of the following is most likely *not* a monopolist?
(a) The only doctor in a small community.
(b) A large soft-drink firm such as Coca-Cola.
(c) The electric power company in your area.
(d) The water company in your area.

_____ 5. Which of the following rules will always be satisfied when a firm has maximized profit?
(a) P = lowest level of long-run average costs.
(b) P = MC.
(c) MR = MC.
(d) P = ATC.

_____ 6. In a monopoly and perfect competition, a firm should expand production when:
(a) Price is below marginal cost.
(b) Price is above marginal cost.
(c) Marginal revenue is below marginal cost.
(d) Marginal revenue is above marginal cost.

_____ 7. The supply curve for a monopolist:
(a) Slopes upward.
(b) Is the same as the marginal cost curve.
(c) Is the same as the marginal revenue curve.
(d) Doesn't exist.

_____ 8. If a monopolist finds that demand for its product is inelastic, it can:
(a) Increase total revenue by lowering price.
(b) Increase total revenue by raising price.
(c) Reduce total costs by lowering prices.
(d) Reduce total costs by raising production rates.

_____ 9. Which of the following does not act as a barrier to entry into a monopoly market?
(a) Profits of the monopolist.
(b) Government regulation.
(c) Patents.
(d) Difficulty of obtaining resources.

_____ 10. A monopolist with many plants produces less than would be produced if all of the plants were competing with one another in a competitive market:
(a) Because the market demand curve is perfectly inelastic for the monopolistic firm but not for the competitive firms.
(b) Because the market demand curve slopes downward for the monopolistic market and for the competitive market.
(c) Because the marginal revenue curve is below the demand curve for the monopolistic firm but not for the competitive firms.
(d) Because profit is maximized where MR = MC for the monopolistic firm but not for the competitive firms.

_____ 11. The price charged by a profit-maximizing monopolist in the long run occurs:
(a) At the minimum of the long-run average cost curve.
(b) Where P = MR = MC.
(c) At a price on the demand curve above the intersection where MR = MC.
(d) At a price on the long-run average cost curve below the point where MR = MC.

_____ 12. When a monopoly continues to make above-normal profits in the long run, you can be sure that:
(a) It produces more efficiently than a competitive market can.
(b) Barriers to entry prevent other firms from competing away the above-normal profits.
(c) There is a conspiracy between the government and the monopolist to maintain high prices.
(d) It has an inelastic demand curve, which gives it greater revenues at every price.

13. If a monopoly used marginal cost pricing to determine its output and price, which of the following statements would be true?
    (a) The monopolist would not be maximizing its profits.
    (b) The monopolist would produce a higher level of output than it would if it was maximizing its profits.
    (c) The monopolist would produce the optimal level of output from the consumer's standpoint.
    (d) All of the above would be true.

14. The allocatively efficient output for a firm is the output where:
    (a) $MC = MR$.
    (b) The ATC is at a minimum.
    (c) The AVC is at a minimum.
    (d) $MC = Demand$.

15. Price discrimination allows a producer to:
    (a) Reap the highest possible average price for the quantity sold.
    (b) Increase the elasticity of consumer demand.
    (c) Minimize marginal costs.
    (d) Decrease total costs.

16. A family doctor charges patients for a particular service on the basis of what the patient can afford to pay. Which type of pricing is being used?
    (a) Monopoly pricing (price making).
    (b) Competitive pricing (price taking).
    (c) Price discrimination.
    (d) $P = MR$.

17. The argument that concentration of market power enhances research and development efforts may be weak because:
    (a) Monopolies cannot afford basic research.
    (b) A monopoly may have no clear incentive to pursue new research and development.
    (c) No one has attempted to gather any empirical evidence.
    (d) No existing monopoly has a research and development program.

18. According to the theory of contestable markets, monopoly may *not* be a problem if:
    (a) The structure of a market is competitive.
    (b) Firms can exit from the market.
    (c) Antitrust regulations are enforced.
    (d) Potential competition exists.

19. The primary purpose of anti-trust policy in the United States is to:
    (a) Issue patents.
    (b) Encourage competition.
    (c) Limit foreign competition.
    (d) Regulate monopolies.

20. Which of the following was the first to prohibit conspiracies in restraint of trade?
    (a) The Sherman Act.
    (b) The Clayton Act.
    (c) The Federal Trade Commission Act.
    (d) The Gramm-Rudman Act.

Problems and Applications

Exercise 1

This exercise provides practice in calculating total revenue and marginal revenue, and shows the relationship between marginal revenue and demand.

1. Use the information given in Table 24.1 to calculate total revenue and marginal revenue.

Table 24.1 Revenue data

	Quantity	Price	Total Revenue	Marginal Revenue
A	0	$12.00	$ _____	-------
B	1	11.00	_____	$ _____
C	2	10.00	_____	_____
D	3	9.00	_____	_____
E	4	8.00	_____	_____
F	5	7.00	_____	_____
G	6	6.00	_____	_____

2. Use the information from Table 24.1 to graph the demand curve and the marginal revenue curve in Figure 24.1. Label each curve and label the points (B through G) on the demand curve.

Figure 24.1 Demand and marginal revenue curves

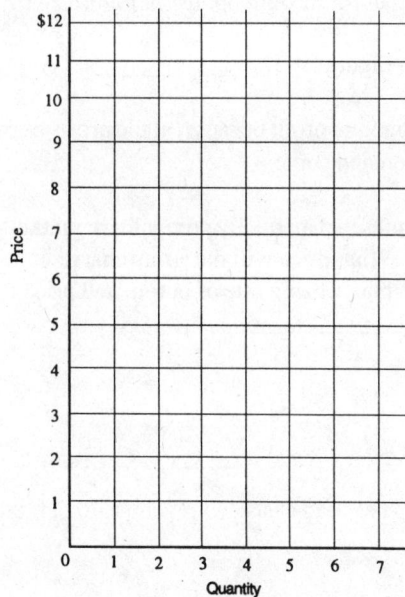

3. For a monopoly, price is determined from the _____ curve, directly above the point where _____ .

341

4. For a monopoly, marginal revenue is always (greater, less) than price, after the first unit, because the firm must (raise, lower) its price to sell additional output.

Exercise 2

This exercise reviews costs and revenues and provides further experience with profit maximization.

Figure 24.2 represents cost curves for a monopolist. Use Figure 24.2 to answer questions 1-4.

Figure 24.2 Cost curves and profit maximization

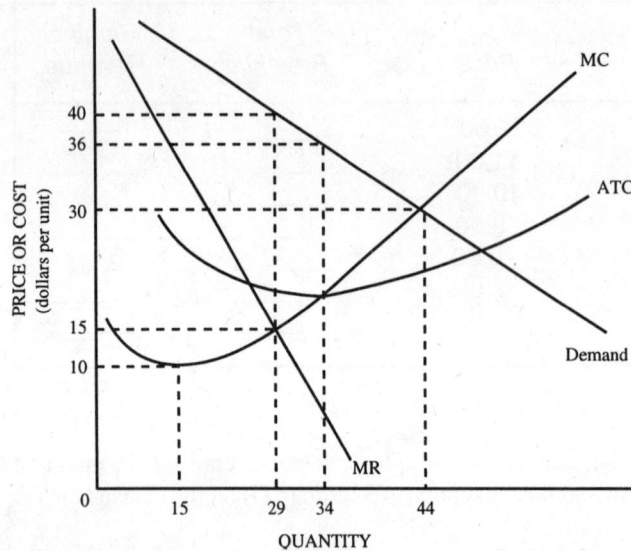

1. What is the profit-maximizing rate of output for the monopolist in Figure 24.2? ___29___

2. What price will the monopolist charge in Figure 24.2? ___$40___

3. This monopolist (is, is not) earning an economic profit because, at the profit-maximizing rate of output in Figure 24.2, ATC is (above, below) the demand curve.

4. Now assume the curves in Figure 24.2 represent a perfectly competitive market. What is the profit-maximizing rate of output? ___44___ What price will the firms charge at this output? ___30___ How do price and output compare to the profit-maximizing rate of output and price for a monopolist?
   _____

Exercise 3

This exercise emphasizes the relationship between costs and revenues for a monopolist and determination of profit maximization.

1. Use the data in Table 24.2 to calculate total revenue, marginal revenue, and marginal cost for a monopolist.

Table 24.2 Revenue and cost data

Quantity	Price	Total revenue	Marginal revenue	Total cost	Marginal cost
0	$14	$ 0	----	$13	----
1	13	13	$ 13	15	$ 2
2	12	24	11	18	3
3	11	33	9	23	5
4	10	40	7	30	7
5	9	45	5	39	9
6	8	48	3	51	12

2. For a monopolist, the profit-maximizing rate of output occurs where marginal revenue equals _____.

3. In this case, the profit-maximizing rate of output is _____ units.

4. At the profit-maximizing rate of output, the monopolist will charge _____ for the product.

5. At the profit-maximizing rate of output, this monopolist earns a profit of _____.

6. In order to sell one additional unit, the monopolist would have to (decrease, increase, make no change in) price.

7. Since this monopolist is earning a profit, the ATC curve must be (above, below, equal to) the demand curve at the profit-maximizing rate of output.

8. Now suppose the data in Table 24.2 represent a perfectly competitive market. The profit-maximizing rate of output occurs where marginal cost equals _____.

9. In this case, the profit-maximizing rate of output would be _____ units at a price of _____.

10. At the competitive profit-maximizing rate of output, profits equal _____.

11. Compared to a perfectly competitive markets, a monopoly charges a (higher, lower) price, produces a (higher, lower) output, and earns a (greater, smaller) profit.

Exercise 4

Reread the article titled "New Competition May Mean Bad News for CNN" and then answer the following questions.

1. What phrase indicates that CNN has monopoly power in the 24-hour news market? _____
_____

2. What barriers to entry have kept other networks from competing with CNN? _____
_____

3. Why are competitors trying to overcome the barriers to entry? _____
_____

343

Common Errors

The first statement in each "common error" below is incorrect. Each incorrect statement is followed by a corrected version and an explanation.

1. Monopolists have supply curves. WRONG!

   Monopolists have marginal cost curves, but not supply curves. RIGHT!

   The marginal cost indicates the quantity that a competitive firm will supply at a given price. (*Remember*: Price equals marginal cost for the profit maximizing competitive firm.) But we cannot tell what a monopolist will supply at a given price by looking at the marginal cost curve. We need to know marginal revenue and therefore the demand curve before we can tell what quantity the firm will supply. (*Remember*: Marginal cost equals marginal revenue when profits are maximized.)

   Be careful! Do not label the marginal cost curve of a monopolist (or any noncompetitive firm) as a "supply" curve in your diagrams.

2. When there are economies of scale, a firm can simply increase production rates in the short run and unit costs will decline. WRONG!

   When there are economies of scale, a firm can choose a plant size designed for increased production rates at lower unit costs. RIGHT!

   Economies of scale are not realized through production decisions in the short run. They are realized through investment decisions, by the choice of an optimal-sized plant for higher production rates. Scale refers to plant size or capacity, not to production rates within a plant of a given size. Think of economies of scale in terms of investment decisions concerning choices of optimal capacity for the long run, not production decisions concerning the lowest cost production in the short run.

•ANSWERS•

Using Key Terms
Across
2. marginal revenue
7. profit maximization rule
9. market power
10. natural monopoly
11. average total cost
12. antitrust
13. production decision

Down
1. price discrimination
2. monopoly
3. price elasticity of demand
4. barriers to entry
5. economies of scale
6. contestable market
8. marginal cost pricing

True or False

1. F A competitive firm has no control over the market price because it is such a tiny part of the relatively huge market. Because it is relatively insignificant, it can sell as much as it wants at the market price.
2. F The monopolist typically has a relatively inelastic demand curve because of barriers to entry, i.e. few substitutes.
3. T
4. F Monopolists maximize profits where $MR = MC$.
5. F Monopolists will tend to produce less than the output that would be produced in a competitive market because the MR curve is below the demand curve for the monopolist.
6. T
7. T
8. T
9. F The theory focuses on behavior rather than structure, i.e. not how many producers exist in a market but how many could potentially exist.
10. T

Multiple Choice

1. d	5. c	9. a	13. d	17. b
2. b	6. d	10. c	14. d	18. d
3. a	7. d	11. c	15. a	19. b
4. b	8. b	12. b	16. c	20. a

Exercise 1

1. **Table 24.1 Answer**

Quantity	Total revenue	Marginal revenue
0	$ 0.00	-----
1	11.00	$ 11.00
2	20.00	9.00
3	27.00	7.00
4	32.00	5.00
5	35.00	3.00
6	36.00	1.00

2. **Figure 24.1 Answer**

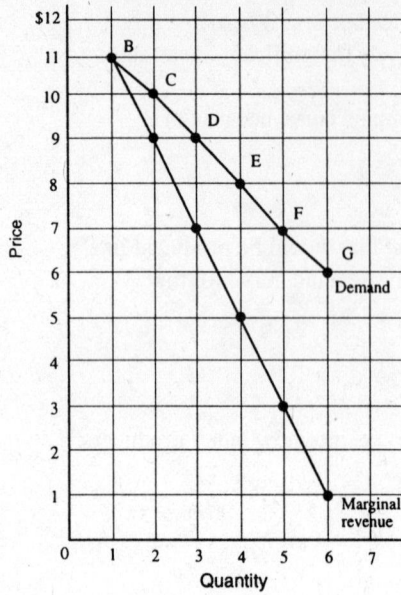

3. demand, MC = MR
4. less, lower

Exercise 2

1. 29 units
2. $40
3. is, below
4. 44 units, $30, price is less and output is greater for the perfectly competitive firm

Exercise 3

1. **Table 24.2 Answer**

Quantity	Price	Total revenue	Marginal revenue	Total cost	Marginal cost
0	$14	$ 0	----	$13	----
1	13	13	$ 13	15	$ 2
2	12	24	11	18	3
3	11	33	9	23	5
4	10	40	7	30	7
5	9	45	5	39	9
6	8	48	3	51	12

2. marginal cost
3. 4

4. $10
5. $10
6. decrease
7. below
8. price
9. 5, $9
10. $6
11. higher, lower, greater

Exercise 4

1. ". . . with the market to itself . . ."
2. ". . . huge distribution hurdles caused by lack of space on crowded cable systems . . ."
3. "Last year . . . CNN . . . generated about $227 million in operating profit for Turner Broadcasting System Inc."

CHAPTER 25
Oligopoly

Quick Review

This chapter takes up the following questions:

- What determines how much market power a firm has?
- How do firms in an oligopoly set prices and output?
- What problems does an oligopoly have in maintaining price and profit?

There are many gradations of market power, running from perfect competition on one end to monopoly on the other. The market power of the firms in each market structure ranges from very weak to very strong along the continuum. The determinants of market power, that is, the extent to which the firm can influence market outcomes, are determined by the number of producers, the size of each firm, barriers to entry, and the availability of substitute products.

Market power is commonly measured by calculating concentration ratios: the proportion of total market output produced by the four largest domestic producers. The concentration ratio is very high in industries such as autos, long-distance telephone services, and diapers, and nonexistent in competitive markets such as wheat or catfish farming. Concentration ratios can be misleading since they deal with national markets and ignore power in local markets and do not take account of the competition from foreign producers.

An oligopoly is a market structure consisting of a few interdependent firms referred to as oligopolists. It is frequently argued that oligopoly behavior can be understood by utilizing a kinked demand curve. The argument is that once an acceptable price, output, and market shares are established, firms are reluctant to change price because they fear that their rivals will follow any price decrease, but will not follow any price increase. In either case, little would be accomplished if a firm changes its price. This leads to a demand curve which is flatter above the equilibrium price and steeper below. The kink imparts a vertical section to the marginal revenue curve, which means that firms, while still using the profit-maximizing rule, will maintain both price and output in the face of moderate increases in marginal costs.

Because of the small number of firms involved in an oligopoly, it is obvious that they have, potentially, a shared monopoly and should they behave as such, could reap monopoly profits as a group. To do this, they must somehow band together to choose the monopoly price and output and find a way to ensure that each oligopolist is satisfied with the firm's share of the market. The possibilities for doing so seem limited only by the imagination of the persons involved. Schemes involving price fixing, price leadership, and direct allocation of market shares have all been tried and firms have been frequently prosecuted because of the illegal nature of such schemes.

Barriers to entry are the key to maintaining monopoly profits in the long run. Patents, control of a distribution system, government regulation, nonprice competition, even the cost of switching suppliers (because of retraining which may be required) can all serve as barriers to entry. Market power contributes to market failure when it results in significant misallocation of resources; thus society's concern is with the behavior of firms. Antitrust laws—the Sherman Act, the Clayton Act and the Federal Trade Commission Act—explicitly forbid many of the practices described in this chapter. Oligopolists may be very powerful and mount costly defenses in antitrust suits. Some contend that they are being prosecuted for being successful. Since resources of the antitrust agencies are limited, they must choose which cases should be prosecuted. To do so, they use a numerical measure called the Herfindahl-Hirshman Index (HHI). Since 1992, the Justice Department has examined existing market structure and entry barriers. Low barriers to entry may mean the market is contestable even though it is very concentrated!

Learning Objectives

After reading Chapter 25 and doing the following exercises, you should:

1. Be able to describe the continuum of market structures.
2. Understand the implications of market power for the optimal mix of the economy's output.
3. Know the determinants of market power.
4. Be able to calculate and interpret concentration ratios and the Herfindahl-Hirshman Index.
5. Be aware of some of the economy's most concentrated industries.
6. Know how market structure affects market behavior and market outcomes.
7. Understand and be able to describe the kinked demand curve model of oligopoly.
8. Know the difference between the long-run market outcomes resulting from perfectly competitive markets and oligopoly.
9. Understand the setting in which game theory is useful in studying business decision making.
10. Be able to describe the coordination problem inherent in the shared-monopoly idea of oligopoly.
11. Know some techniques which oligopolists have used to implement coordination and enforcement of market shares.
12. Be able to list and describe several barriers to entry.
13. Know three prominent antitrust laws and their major provisions.
14. Be able to determine whether an antitrust case should be prosecuted using the HHI.

Using Key Terms

Fill in the puzzle on the opposite page with the appropriate term from the list of Key Terms at the end of the chapter in the text.

Across

1.	The number and relative size of firms in an industry.
4.	Trans World Airlines, Delta Air Lines, and Northwest Airlines were accused of using this tactic in an *In the News* article in the text.
7.	Government intervention to prevent the abuse of market power.
8.	One way a firm can establish the market price for all firms in the industry.
9.	A measure of industry concentration that accounts for the number of firms and the size of each.
11.	One of the dominant firms in an oligopoly.
15.	Used by a firm to make its product appear different and superior to other products.
16.	The curve drawn with a gap in Figure 25.6 in the text.
17.	Obstacles that help to keep potential competitors out of an industry.
18.	A market structure with high barriers to entry, substantial market power, and a few firms.

Down

2.	A group of firms with an explicit agreement to fix prices and output shares.
3.	Firms produce at the rate of output where MR=MC.

5.   An imperfectly competitive industry subject to potential entry if prices or profits increase.
6.   The study of how decisions are made when strategic interaction exists.
10.   The proportion of total industry output produced by the largest firms.
12.   Occurs when market power leads to resource misallocation or greater inequity.
13.   The percentage of total market output produced by a firm.
14.   An explicit agreement among producers regarding the price at which a good is to be sold.

Puzzle 25.1

351

True or False: *Circle your choice and explain why any false statements are incorrect.*

T   F   1.   Firms are divided into specific market structures based on their ability to earn a profit.

T   F   2.   In imperfect competition, individual firms do not have direct influence on the market price of a particular product.

T   F   3.   Firms in an oligopoly market are highly independent because of their relatively small number.

T   F   4.   An increase in the market share of one oligopolist will not necessarily reduce the shares of the remaining oligopolists if the industry is growing.

T   F   5.   An attempt by one oligopolist to increase its market share by cutting prices will leave competitors unaffected.

T   F   6.   The shape of the demand curve facing an oligopolist depends on the responses of its rivals to a change in the price of its own output.

T   F   7.   The reason that changes in marginal cost may have no effect on the output of an oligopoly characterized by a kinked demand curve is that the accompanying marginal revenue curve contains a vertical segment or gap.

T   F   8.   The kinked demand curve demonstrates that if an oligopolist raises its price, it is likely to lose market share.

T   F   9.   One type of explicit price fixing is known as price leadership.

T   F   10. The antitrust agencies prohibit certain structural characteristics of a market, not behavioral characteristics.

Multiple Choice: *Select the correct answer.*

_____   1.   The only market structure in which there is significant interdependence among firms with regard to their pricing and output decisions is:
(a)   Monopolistic competition.
(b)   Monopoly.
(c)   Oligopoly.
(d)   Perfect competition.

_____   2.   Structural characteristics of a market include:
(a)   The number of firms in the market.
(b)   Long run profitability.
(c)   Entry and exit.
(d)   Pricing behavior.

_____   3.   Which of the following is evidence of the interdependence which characterizes the relationship among oligopolists?
(a)   Retaliation.
(b)   Price wars.
(c)   Gamesmanship.
(d)   All of the above.

_____ 4. Characteristics of an oligopolistic market include:
  (a)   Tacit collusion.
  (b)   High barriers to entry.
  (c)   High concentration ratios.
  (d)   All of the above.

_____ 5. A kinked demand curve indicates that rival oligopolists match:
  (a)   All price changes.
  (b)   No price changes.
  (c)   Price reductions but not price increases.
  (d)   Price increases but not price reductions.

_____ 6. The gap in the marginal revenue curve of an oligopolist is caused by:
  (a)   The existence of two alternative demand curves that apply to the oligopolist, depending on whether it raises prices or lowers prices.
  (b)   The failure of the marginal cost curve to intersect the demand curve at the profit-maximizing level.
  (c)   The ability of oligopolists to make above-normal profits if they cooperate with each other.
  (d)   All of the above.

_____ 7. Because of the gap in the marginal revenue curve, when the marginal cost curve rises, the kinked demand curve oligopolist may have an incentive to:
  (a)   Speed up production and lower prices—behavior that leads to greater profits.
  (b)   Maintain both production rates and prices—behavior that leads to lower profits but not necessarily to losses.
  (c)   Lower production rates and maintain prices—actions that raise profits by counteracting cost increases.
  (d)   Speed up production rates and maintain prices—actions that result in losses.

_____ 8. If an oligopolist is going to change its price or output, its concern is:
  (a)   The response of consumers.
  (b)   The possibility of losing market share.
  (c)   Gamesmanship practiced by its competitors.
  (d)   All of the above are concerns.

_____ 9. If a firm is producing at the kink in its demand curve and increases its price, according to the kinked-demand model:
  (a)   It will gain market share.
  (b)   It will lose market share to the firms that do not follow the price increase.
  (c)   Its market share will not be affected.
  (d)   It will not gain market share but it will definitely increase profits.

_____ 10. Which of the following is an explanation of why oligopolists have an incentive to collude?
  (a)   The demand for each firm's product would be kinked.
  (b)   Each firm would face a perfectly inelastic demand for its product.
  (c)   Each firm would face a relatively inelastic demand for its product rather than a relatively elastic demand when firms raise prices independently.
  (d)   The market demand curve would become perfectly inelastic.

_____ 11. Game theory is:
  (a)   The study of price fixing and collusion.
  (b)   The study of how decisions are made when interdependence between firms exists.
  (c)   An explanation of how oligopolists become monopolists.
  (d)   Only useful in perfectly competitive markets.

_____ 12. Oligopolists will maximize total market profits at the rate of output where:
- (a) MR = MC for the largest firms.
- (b) MR = MC for the average firm.
- (c) MR = MC for the marginal firm.
- (d) The market's MC equals the market's MR.

_____ 13. Open and explicit agreements concerning pricing and output shares transform an oligopoly into a:
- (a) Monopoly.
- (b) Cartel.
- (c) Differentiated oligopoly.
- (d) Perfectly competitive firm.

_____ 14. Price leadership:
- (a) Typically results in greater price stability in oligopolistic markets.
- (b) Is observed in oligopolistic markets.
- (c) Permits oligopolistic firms in a given market to coordinate market-wide price changes without formal collusion.
- (d) All of the above.

_____ 15. For an oligopoly, above-normal profit cannot be maintained in the long run unless:
- (a) A cartel is formed.
- (b) Barriers to entry exist.
- (c) A firm has a high concentration ratio.
- (d) The market is contestable.

_____ 16. An example of nonprice competition in the automobile market is:
- (a) Advertising.
- (b) Availability of service on weekends.
- (c) Providing financing for the purchase of an automobile.
- (d) All of the above.

_____ 17. Imperfectly competitive firms use nonprice competition to:
- (a) Shift the demand curve leftward.
- (b) Differentiate their product.
- (c) Shift the supply curve upward.
- (d) Threaten potential entry.

_____ 18. Market power leads to market failure when it results in:
- (a) Decreased market output.
- (b) Increased market prices.
- (c) Long lasting, above normal economic profits.
- (d) All of the above.

_____ 19. Which of the following are problems associated with pursuing anti-trust policy based on the behavior of firms rather than the structure of a market?
- (a) It is more expensive to investigate behavior rather than structure.
- (b) It is more difficult to prove anti-competitive behavior.
- (c) The general absence of public awareness and interest in the problem of collusion.
- (d) All of the above are problems.

_____ 20. The 1992 and 1996 anti-trust guidelines adopted by the Justice Department and the Federal Trade Commission:
    (a) Moved anti-trust focus away from a strict reliance on structural criteria.
    (b) Increased the focus on market contestability.
    (c) Allowed a consideration of potential greater efficiencies when mergers and acquisitions occur.
    (d) All of the above are correct.

Problems and Applications

Exercise 1

This exercise shows how to compute concentration ratios and market shares for an industry.

1. Market share is:
    (a) The percentage of total market output produced by the largest firms (usually the four largest).
    (b) The percentage of total market output produced by the largest firm.
    (c) The percentage of total market output produced by a given firm.
    (d) A type of stock issued by the firms in a market.

2. Concentration usually refers to:
    (a) The percentage of total market output produced by the four largest domestic firms.
    (b) The percentage of total market output produced by any four large domestic firms.
    (c) The percentage of total market output produced by a given domestic firm.
    (d) The percentage of total market output produced by the four largest domestic or foreign firms.

3. Table 25.1 gives the sales of the top four firms (A, B, C, D) in a market. Insert the total sales for the top four firms and total sales for the market. Then, using this information, compute the market share for each firm separately, and then the market share for the "Top four firms" and the market share for "All other firms."

Table 25.1
Sales and market shares of top four firms, by company

Firm	Sales (millions of dollars per year)	Market share
A	$ 60	_____%
B	40	_____
C	30	_____
D	20	_____
Top four firms	$____	_____%
All other firms	50	_____%
All firms	$____	100 %

4. T F   The sum of the market shares of the top four firms is the same as the four-firm concentration ratio.

Exercise 2

This exercise illustrates the differences between using the concentration ratio and the Herfindahl-Hirshman Index to measure market power. It also will help you complete a problem in the text.

Table 25.2 presents the market shares for two separate markets. Each market has only four firms.

Table 25.2
Market shares for calculating concentration ratios and the Herfindahl-Hirshman Index

First market		Second market	
Firm	Market share	Firm	Market share
A	25%	E	97%
B	25%	F	1%
C	25%	G	1%
D	25%	H	1%

1. The four-firm concentration ratio for the first market is _____ and for the second market is _____ .

2. The Herfindahl-Hirshman Index for the first market is _____ and for the second market is _____ .

3. Would you expect the market power exerted in the two markets to be the same? _____ Why or why not? _____ _____

4. According to the Justice Department guidelines:
    (a) Mergers would be permitted in both markets.
    (b) A merger would be permitted only in the first market.
    (c) A merger would be permitted only in the second market.
    (d) Mergers would not be permitted in either market.

Exercise 3

This exercise reviews costs and revenues and provides further experience with profit maximization.

Figure 25.1 represents cost curves for an oligopolist. Use Figure 25.1 to answer questions 1-4.

Figure 25.1

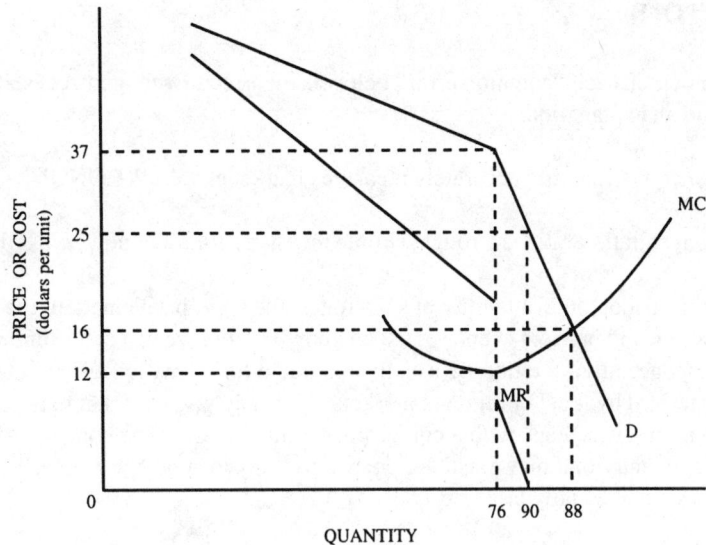

1. What is the profit-maximizing rate of output for the oligopolist in Figure 25.1? _____

2. What price will the oligopolist charge in Figure 25.1? _____

3. If the MC curve shifts up by a small amount, $4 or less, the profit maximizing oligopolist will (increase, decrease, not change) price because of the gap in the (MR, demand) curve.

4. The demand curve for the oligopolist is kinked because rival oligopolists will match price (increases, reductions) but not price (increases, reductions).

Exercise 4

The media often provide information about the strategies, both successful and unsuccessful, employed by oligopolists as they attempt to compete in the marketplace. By using one of the articles in the text, this exercise will show you what to look for.

Reread the article in the text entitled "Pop Culture: RC Goes For the Youth Market" and then answer the following questions.

1. What is the concentration ratio in the U.S. soft drink market? _____

2. What was the Royal Crown strategy in the 1980s? What phrase indicates the result? _____
   _____

3. What is the new Royal Crown strategy? What is their target? _____
   _____

357

4. What barriers to entry exist in the soft drink market? _____
_____

5. Calculate an HHI on the basis of the information in the pie chart in the article._____

6. Would game theory be useful in analyzing behavior in this market? Why? _____
_____

Common Errors

The first statement in each "common error" below is incorrect. Each incorrect statement is followed by a corrected version and an explanation.

1. The concentration ratio accurately measures market power. WRONG!

   The concentration ratio is a rough, simple measure of market power. RIGHT!

   Information on availability of substitutes, the appropriate market, the relative size of firms in the market, and barriers to entry must be known before we can determine whether market power exists. Concentration ratios are usually computed for the nation as a whole, but many industries are characterized by local or regional markets. Also, any given market may produce a variety of different products, each with a unique concentration ratio. The concentration ratio gives no idea of barriers to entry that may exist, nor does it give any idea whether a market contains one dominant firm or several equally large firms.

2. American industry consists mostly of monopolies. WRONG!

   There are only a few monopolies in the U.S. economy. RIGHT!

   The text has shown that many U.S. markets are imperfectly competitive, but concentration ratios of 100 percent are rare. Monopolies are most likely to occur in the utility industries, which are then heavily regulated by government.

3. All large firms have market power. WRONG!

   The largest firms in concentrated markets are *likely* to have market power. RIGHT!

   Control of a market is more important than actual firm size in determining market power. Relative size as measured by concentration is more important than absolute size as measured by sales. For example, while conglomerates may be very large, they may play only small roles in many different markets and have no ability to influence prices in any of them.

4. Oligopolists have unlimited power to raise prices and curtail production to make large profits. WRONG!

   Oligopolists' ability to raise prices is limited by demand and their competitive rivalry. RIGHT!

   The demand for oligopolists' products is limited by foreign competition, availability of substitutes, and potential entry by other firms. Such markets as the railroad-car market, the market for rifles, and the auto market contain only a few large firms, but they are limited by potential competition from other countries or at home.

Furthermore, there is no guarantee that oligopolists will cooperate with each other. Oligopolists may use their market power cooperatively through collusion, price leadership, or indirect means of supporting prices above competitive levels. Such cooperative activity *may* lead to profits in the long run as well as in the short run. Changes in demand and costs, however, can force oligopolists to take losses or even to fail. Most importantly, oligopolists may not cooperate with each other. They may conduct price wars and engage in nonprice competition in order to erode each other's market share. Such conduct often leads to instability and substantial losses.

5. Oligopolistic firms compete with each other. MISLEADING!

Oligopolies are often characterized by competitive rivalry. RIGHT!

When firms have market power, they become aware of their interdependence. The often warlike or conspiratorial conduct—rivalry—that occurs is quite different from the conduct of competitive firms. Since no competitive firm can affect market prices, no one firm sees any other as a threat, nor is there any possibility of colluding to fix prices. True competition is often marked on the one hand by independent behavior of the competing firms and on the other by cooperation to hold down costs. For example, while farmers rarely succeed in increasing the prices of farm products by cooperative efforts, they may share the use of farm equipment with neighboring farmers to lower costs. There is certainly no reason for one farmer to engage in a price war with another farmer, since both represent such a small part of the market.

•ANSWERS•

Using Key Terms
Across
1. market structure
4. predatory pricing
7. antitrust
8. price leadership
9. Herfindahl-Hirshman Index
11. oligopolist
15. product differentiation
16. marginal revenue
17. barriers to entry
18. oligopoly

Down
2. cartel
3. profit maximization rule
5. contestable market
6. game theory
10. concentration ratio
12. market failure
13. market share
14. price fixing

True or False

1. F The division is based on market power.
2. F Firms do have varying degrees of control over the market price in imperfect competition.
3. T
4. F Market share is a percentage measure. If one firm's percentage share of the market increases, other firms must experience a reduction in market share.
5. F Oligopolists are interdependent, i.e. a change in one firm's price or output will affect its competitors.
6. T
7. T
8. T
9. F Price leadership is an example of tacit collusion, not explicit price fixing.
10. F Anti-trust policy prohibits anti-competitive behavior.

Multiple Choice

1.	c	5.	c	9.	b	13.	b	17.	b
2.	a	6.	a	10.	c	14.	d	18.	d
3.	d	7.	b	11.	b	15.	b	19.	d
4.	d	8.	d	12.	d	16.	d	20.	d

Problems and Applications

Exercise 1

1. c
2. a
3. **Table 25.1 Answer**

Firm	Sales	Market share
A	$ 60	30%
B	40	20
C	30	15
D	20	10
Top four firms	$150	75%
All other firms	50	25%
All firms	$200	100%

4. T

Exercise 2

1. 100 percent; 100 percent
2. 2,500 (= $25^2 + 25^2 + 25^2 + 25^2$); 9,412 (= $97^2 + 1^2 + 1^2 + 1^2$)
3. No. The second market would exhibit much more market power since firm E is the dominant firm and would effectively determine the price. By contrast, market power would be more diffused among the four equally sized firms in the first market.
4. d Both markets have a Herfindahl-Hirshman Index above 1800.

Exercise 3

1. 76 units
2. $37
3. not change, MR
4. reductions, increases

Exercise 4

1. The four firm concentration ratio is 92.6%, the sum of the shares of the four largest producers.
2. The strategy was, apparently, not to spend on advertising. The result was ". . . we lost a whole generation of cola drinkers . . . ."
3. Their new strategy is to spend $15 million on advertising, the largest amount in their history, and to toss out a ". . . bunch of beverages targeted toward younger drinkers."
4. The article indicates that Pepsi and Coke ". . . have huge amounts of marketing muscle, financial resources, experience and bottling agreements, . . ." which will deter new entrants.
5. Based on the information in the pie chart, the HHI is 3117.5
   $(41.5^2 + 32.3^2 + 16.9^2 + 7.4^2 = 3117.5)$
6. Very likely, since Coke and Pepsi dominate the soft drink market. There are numerous opportunities for moves and countermoves by these oligopolists, and this is where game theory is very useful.

CHAPTER 26
Monopolistic Competition

Quick Review

Monopolistic competition is a type of market that we see frequently in malls, downtown shops, and among other small businesses. Studying monopolistic competition will allow us to understand the effects of advertising and customer loyalty. The following questions will help us understand monopolistic competition:

- What are the unique features of monopolistic competition?
- How are market outcomes affected by this market structure?
- What are the long-run consequences of different market structures?

Each market structure can be identified by its structural characteristics. A market characterized as "monopolistic competition" has many firms and each firm has some market power; that is, each firm also has a downward-sloping demand curve for its product or service. The firms are relatively independent because modest changes in price or output have no noticeable effect on the sales of any other firm. The barriers to entry are also characteristically low. Though some of the firms in monopolistically competitive industries are household names (IBM, Goodyear, Starbucks), their market power is constrained. Concentration ratios in these industries are relatively low and even then the firms must often contend with significant competition from foreign entrants.

The market power possessed by monopolistically competitive firms is the direct result of product differentiation. Advertising is very important in creating brand loyalty. This gives the firm demand curve a downward slope. Firms in monopolistic competition use the same profit-maximizing rule ($MC = MR$) as firms in other markets. In the short run firms may earn economic profits, but low barriers to entry permit the entry of new firms with the consequent erosion of those profits. In the long run only normal profits can be earned. Because the demand curves of the firms slope downward, the long-run equilibrium will be one in which $P = LATC$, but will occur at a point to the left of the minimum of the $LATC$ curve. Thus there is production inefficiency ($P > \min LATC$) and allocative inefficiency because the wrong mix of output is produced.

Firms in monopolistic competition spend tremendous amounts on advertising aimed at increasing demand and hopefully reducing the price elasticity of demand for their output. Other forms of nonprice competition are also used. In the process, the consumer's opportunity to choose between more service and lower prices frequently vanishes. The presumption follows that nonprice competition leads to a less desirable use of society's resources. We can expect, however, that this type of *behavior* will persist as long as imperfectly competitive market *structures* exist.

363

Learning Objectives

After reading Chapter 26 and doing the following exercises, you should:

1. Be able to describe structural characteristics of monopolistic competition.
2. Know how firms in monopolistic competition achieve their market power.
3. Know why the demand curve faced by the firms in monopolistically competitive markets is downward-sloping.
4. Be able to tell why monopolistically competitive firms use the $MC = MR$ rule in making the production decision.
5. Be able to describe the process by which the economic profits are eroded away by the entry of new firms.
6. Be able to explain why the long-run equilibrium in monopolistic competition suffers from production *and* allocative inefficiency.
7. Understand the difference between price competition and nonprice competition and how it may lead to an undesirable use of resources.

Using Key Terms

Fill in the puzzle on the opposite page with the appropriate term from the list of Key Terms at the end of the chapter in the text.

Across

3. Features that make one product appear different from competing products in the same market.
5. Obstacles that make it difficult or impossible for new firms to enter a market.
6. The ability to alter the market price of a good or service.
7. The choice of the short-run rate of output.
8. The offer of goods at prices equal to their marginal cost.

Down

1. A market in which firms produce a similar product but each maintains some independent control of price.
2. The proportion of total industry output produced by the largest firms.
4. The difference between total revenue and total economic costs.

True or False: *Circle your choice and explain why any false statements are incorrect.*

T F 1. A monopolistically competitive firm confronts a downward-sloping demand curve and, as a result, has some market power.

T F 2. In monopolistic competition, changes in the output or price of any single firm will have no significant influence on the sales of other firms.

T F 3. In monopolistic competition, each firm competes with other firms offering identical substitutes.

T F 4. When marginal costs rise, monopolistically competitive firms do not change output or price.

T F 5. For a monopolistically competitive firm, low barriers to entry tend to push economic profits toward zero in the long run.

T F 6. As new firms enter a monopolistically competitive industry, the demand curve for individual firms will shift to the right.

T F 7. The monopolistically competitive firm charges prices at the minimum of the long-run average total cost curve in the long run.

T F 8. Monopolistic competition tends to be less efficient than a perfectly competitive industry because the price is always above the minimum ATC.

T F 9. Monopolistic competition results in allocative efficiency.

T F 10. Advertising plays a role in reducing the importance of substitute goods in determining market power.

Multiple Choice: *Select the correct answer.*

_____ 1. One of the main differences between oligopoly and monopolistic competition is:
   (a) The amount of advertising that firms do.
   (b) The amount of nonprice competition that occurs.
   (c) The degree of interdependence among firms.
   (d) That the profit maximizing output level occurs where MR = MC.

_____ 2. One of the main similarities of perfect competition and monopolistic competition is:
   (a) That in the long run, price equals average total cost and marginal revenue equals marginal cost.
   (b) The amount of product differentiation.
   (c) The point on the long-run average total cost curve at which firms maximize profits.
   (d) All of the above.

_____ 3. A major difference between monopoly and monopolistic competition is:
   (a) One maximizes profits by setting MR equal to MC, and the other does not.
   (b) The number of firms.
   (c) One type of firm has market power, and the other does not.
   (d) One has a downward-sloping demand curve, and the other does not.

_____ 4. In monopolistic competition:
  (a) Firms have market power.
  (b) Entry is easy.
  (c) A firm's demand curve is downward-sloping.
  (d) All of the above.

_____ 5. "Product differentiation" refers to:
  (a) Different prices for the same product in a certain market.
  (b) The selling of identical products in different markets.
  (c) Features that make one product appear different from competing products in the same market.
  (d) The charging of different prices for the same product in different markets.

_____ 6. A monopolistically competitive firm maximizes profits or minimizes losses in the long run by producing where:
  (a) MR = MC.
  (b) The demand curve is tangent to the long-run average total cost curve.
  (c) P = ATC.
  (d) All of the above.

_____ 7. If more firms enter a monopolistically competitive market, we would expect:
  (a) The demand curves facing existing firms to shift to the left and become more price inelastic.
  (b) The demand curves facing existing firms to shift to the left and no change in price elasticity.
  (c) The demand curves facing existing firms to shift to the left and become more price elastic.
  (d) The demand curves facing existing firms to shift to the right and no change in price elasticity.

_____ 8. Exit from a market characterized by monopolistic competition:
  (a) Is rare because firms have market power.
  (b) Occurs frequently because barriers to entry are high.
  (c) Occurs when a firm's demand is below its long-run average cost curve at all levels of output.
  (d) Results from economies of scale.

_____ 9. Entry into a market characterized by monopolistic competition:
  (a) Is rare because firms have market power.
  (b) Is frequent because barriers to entry are low.
  (c) Occurs when a firm's demand is below its long-run average cost curve at all levels of output.
  (d) Results from economies of scale.

_____ 10. Firms in a monopolistically competitive market will:
  (a) Produce efficiently.
  (b) Make zero economic profits in the long run.
  (c) Use the profit-maximizing rule TC = TR.
  (d) All of the above.

_____ 11. Compared to marginal cost pricing, a monopolistically competitive firm will:
  (a) Produce a lower output and charge a higher price.
  (b) Produce a greater output and charge a higher price.
  (c) Produce a lower output and charge a lower price.
  (d) Produce a greater output and charge a lower price

_____ 12. Monopolistically competitive firms are productively inefficient because long-run equilibrium occurs at an output rate where:
   (a) MC is greater than MR.
   (b) Price is greater than MC.
   (c) ATC is greater than the minimum ATC.
   (d) Diseconomies of scale exist.

_____ 13. In monopolistic competition there is allocative inefficiency because:
   (a) Price is greater than the minimum ATC.
   (b) Production is not at the minimum ATC.
   (c) Of excess capacity.
   (d) Price is greater than MC.

_____ 14. A monopolistically competitive firm can raise its price somewhat without fear of great change in unit sales because of:
   (a) Brand loyalty.
   (b) Economies of scale.
   (c) Perfectly elastic demand.
   (d) Large market shares of firms in the market.

_____ 15. Advertising is:
   (a) An efficient form of competition.
   (b) Less important than price competition in oligopolistic and monopolistic competition.
   (c) A major component of competition in perfectly competitive markets.
   (d) A form of nonprice competition.

_____ 16. When a monopolistically competitive firm advertises, it is attempting to increase:
   (a) The demand and decrease the price elasticity of demand for its product.
   (b) The demand and increase the price elasticity of demand for its product.
   (c) Long-run profits.
   (d) Market demand.

Select the letter of the diagram representing long-run equilibrium in Figure 26.1 that best matches the type of market named in questions 17-20. Use each diagram *only once*.

Figure 26.1 Long-run cost curves

Firm A

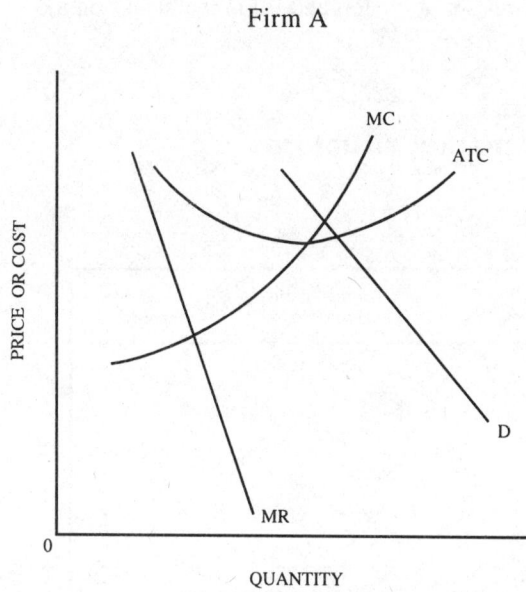

Firm B

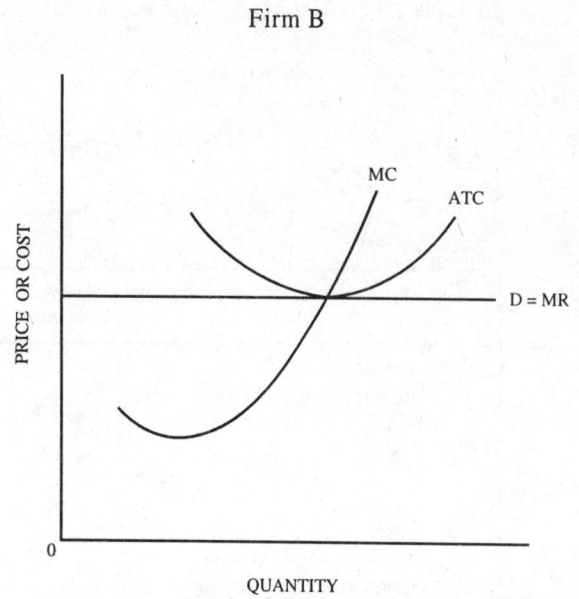

Firm C

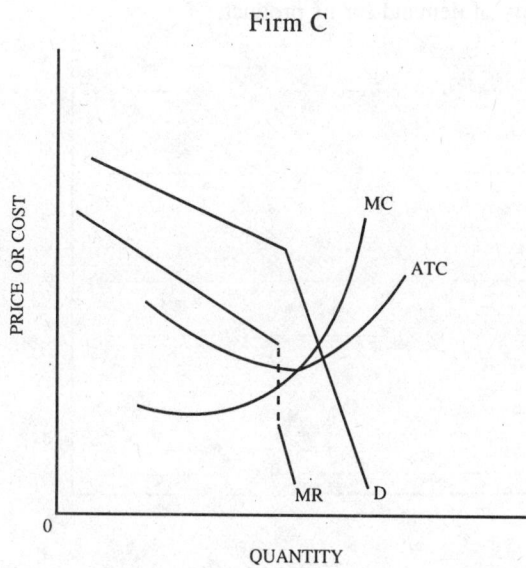

Firm D

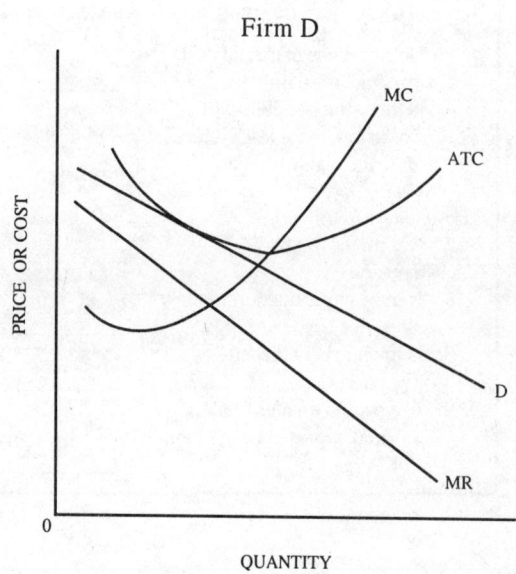

_____ 17. Perfect competition.

_____ 18. Oligopoly.

_____ 19. Monopolistic competition.

_____ 20. Monopoly.

Problems and Applications

Exercise 1

This exercise contrasts monopoly, oligopoly, monopolistic competition, and competition, and summarizes their differences.

In Table 26.1 select the appropriate answer given in parentheses at the left and fill in the blanks on the right.

Table 26.1
Characteristics of four market structures

	Monopoly	Oligopoly	Monopolistic competition	Competition
Characteristic				
1. How many firms are there? (many, few, one)	_____	_____	_____	_____
2. Product is_____ . (standardized, differentiated, unique)	_____	_____	_____	_____
3. Entry is _____ . (blocked, impeded, easy)	_____	_____	_____	_____
4. Is there market power? (yes, no)	_____	_____	_____	_____
Conduct				
5. Do firms use marginal cost pricing? (yes, no)	_____	_____	_____	_____
6. Is there the possibility of collusion, price leadership, or price wars? (yes, no)	_____	_____	_____	_____
Performance (long run)				
7. Are prices too high? (yes, no)	_____	_____	_____	_____
8. Is market production too low? (yes, no)	_____	_____	_____	_____
9. Is the market efficient? (yes, no)	_____	_____	_____	_____
10. Are profits greater than normal expected in the long run? (yes, no)	_____	_____	_____	_____

Exercise 2

This exercise examines the characteristics of monopolistic competition using a graph.

Use Figure 26.2 to answer questions 1-6.

Figure 26.2

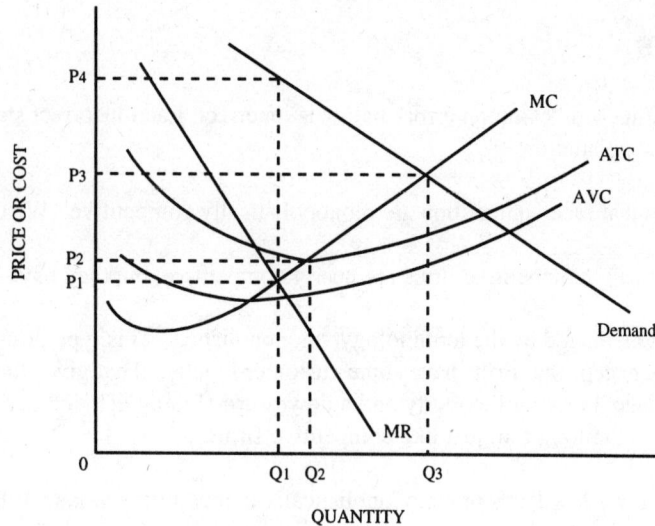

1. The profit-maximizing rate of output for a monopolistically competitive firm occurs where
   _____.

2. According to Figure 26.2, the profit-maximizing rate of output is _____ units and the price is
   _____.

3. Does Figure 26.2 represent a short run or a long run situation? _____

4. This firm is earning a (profit, loss) because at the profit-maximizing output level, the demand
   curve is above the _____ curve.

5. In the long run, the average total cost curve will be tangent to the _____ curve and
   economic profits will be _____.

6. A perfectly competitive firm would maximize profits at an output of _____ and a price of _____.

Exercise 3

This exercise will use one of the articles in the text to show what kind of information to look for to
determine whether a market is characterized by monopolistic competition.

Reread the article entitled "JNCO Jeans: Teen Cool." Then answer the following questions.

1. What phrase gives information about the number of firms competing in the jeans market?
   _____

2. How do the firms differentiate their products?_____
   _____

3. Through its advertising campaigns and by sponsoring extreme athletes, JNCO hoped to establish _____ for its product.

4. In the jeans market there is evidence of:
    (a) Nonprice competition.
    (b) Easy entry.
    (c) Product differentiation.
    (d) All of the above.

Common Errors

The first statement in each "common error" below is incorrect. Each incorrect statement is followed by a corrected version and an explanation.

1. Monopolies that face competition are monopolistically competitive. WRONG!

    Monopolistically competitive firms are nearly competitive, but they have brand loyalty. RIGHT!

    Do not be misled by the terminology "monopolistic." This type of industry is essentially competitive except that firms have some customer loyalty. That gives them a little ("monopolistic") pricing flexibility and a downward-sloping demand curve. But they still make zero profit in the long run, just like competitive firms.

2. There are only a few firms in a monopolistically competitive market. WRONG!

    There are many firms in a monopolistically competitive market. RIGHT!

    Again don't let the word "monopolistic" fool you. Firms can easily enter or exit from a monopolistically competitive market. Each firm is likely to have excess capacity—which suggests there may be too many firms in a monopolistically competitive market. The restaurant business is a good example of a monopolistically competitive market.

3. Because price equals average cost in the long run in a monopolistically competitive firm, such firms must be efficient. WRONG!

    Because price equals average cost in the long run in a monopolistically competitive firm, profits are zero in the long run, but the firm is inefficient. RIGHT!

    Long-run profits are normal (zero economic profits) because competition forces prices to equal long-run average cost. The firm does not reach the *lowest* long-run average cost level, however, and so it is inefficient. The firm's demand curve touches the long-run average cost curve, but not at its lowest point.

•ANSWERS•

Using Key Terms
Across
3. product differentiation
5. barriers to entry
6. market power
7. production decision
8. marginal cost pricing

Down

1. monopolistic competition
2. concentration ratio
4. economic profit

True or False

1. T
2. T
3. F In monopolistic competition, each firm offers slightly different products.
4. F The MR curve for monopolistically competitive firms does not have a vertical segment because there is no significant interdependence between firms. As a consequence, a shift in MC will result in an intersection between MC and MR at a new output level.
5. T
6. F As new firms enter, individual firms will experience a decrease in the number of customers resulting in a shift in demand to the left.
7. F A monopolistically competitive firm will charge a price above the minimum ATC because of product differentiation.
8. T
9. F A monopolistically competitive firm will produce less than the allocatively efficient output level because of a downward sloping demand curve facing each firm.
10. T

Multiple Choice

1. c	5. c	9. b	13. d	17. b
2. a	6. d	10. b	14. a	18. c
3. b	7. c	11. a	15. d	19. d
4. d	8. c	12. c	16. a	20. a

Problems and Applications

Exercise 1

Table 26.1 Answer

	Monopoly	Oligopoly	Monopolistic competition	Competition
1.	one	few	many	many
2.	unique	standardized or differentiatiated	differentiated	standardized
3.	blocked	impeded	impeded or easy	easy
4.	yes	yes	yes	no
5.	no	no	no	yes
6.	no	yes	no	no
7.	yes	yes	yes	no
8.	yes	yes	yes	no
9.	no	no	no	yes
10.	yes	yes	no	no

373

Exercise 2

1. MC=MR
2. Q_1, P_4
3. short run
4. profit. ATC
5. demand, zero
6. Q_3, P_3

Exercise 3

1. " . . . throngs of competitors from trying to steal a share of the market."
2. " . . . with distinctive stitching and hot ad campaigns."
3. brand loyalty
4. d

CHAPTER 27

(De)Regulation of Business

Quick Review

Perfectly competitive markets provide a model for economic efficiency. However, the strict requirements for the model to operate are seldom encountered in the real world. Free markets thus may fail to provide optimal answers to the WHAT, HOW, and FOR WHOM questions, and government may intervene in hopes of making things better. But, devising the appropriate social and economic regulations is difficult. Optimal intervention, an elusive concept at best, is required or intervention might make things worse! During the early 1970s many economists and government officials came to the conclusion that regulation of the economy had gone too far and that in fact considerable *deregulation* was required to redress this "government failure." However, the development of services like the Information Superhighway may require some form of government intervention in some parts while crying out for deregulation in others.

This chapter considers government's role in the marketplace by discussing the following questions:

* When is government regulation necessary?
* What form should that regulation take?
* When is it appropriate to deregulate an industry?

Historically, economists and politicians have recognized many reasons why an industry should be regulated. "Market failure" means that the market provides an inadequate output mix. Sources of market failure include natural monopoly, market power, externalities, public goods, and the inequitable distribution of income.

The existence of any one of these failures prevents the market from providing satisfactory answers to the economic problem. To improve market outcomes where market failure occurs, governments intervene in several ways. Most frequently the intervention takes the form of antitrust activity, economic and social regulation, public-sector production, taxation, or subsidies.

The clearest case for intervention is in "natural monopolies," where a market is best served by a single firm because it alone can capture continuous economies of scale. In regulating natural monopolies, regulators may pursue three basic, but potentially conflicting goals including price efficiency, production efficiency, and equity. Finding the right combination of policy levers—such as regulating price, output, or profit—is a very difficult job and the risks of regulating badly are unfortunately quite high.

In addition, it has become increasingly clear that regulation itself may impose significant opportunity costs on the economy. Resources are used in devising and administering regulations. The firms in a regulated market use resources to comply with (or get around!) regulations. In addition to these administrative and compliance costs, efficiency costs that result from bad decisions, incomplete information, and so on may worsen the mix of output; moreover, their effects may be compounded over time!

Because many industries are viewed as operating in suboptimal fashion, the process of deregulation has begun. Railroads, trucking, telephone service, and airlines are industries in which deregulation has basically been completed. However, there are still many industries that are regulated and even some where regulation has increased, as in the health industry. Moreover, some cable TV was deregulated in 1986 with arguably unsatisfactory results and modified reregulation was required in 1992.

In markets as dynamic as telecommunications, traditional industry boundaries become blurred. The market once dominated by telephone companies now includes cable tv, satellite services, electric utilities, etc. Much effort now goes into breaking down barriers to entry for new participants. The Telecommunications Act of 1995 required the Baby Bells to improve access to their own local telephone markets before they could have permission to enter new markets like those for video and data services. The scope for error in designing regulations is enormous and even good regulation may quickly be outdated by the pace of technological advance.

The question to be answered is always, "Do the benefits of the regulation exceed the cost of regulation?" These are questions which must be evaluated on an industry-by-industry basis. Deregulation in practice seems to have served the consumer well. Prices are lower and output greater in the deregulated markets.

Learning Objectives

After reading Chapter 27 and doing the following exercises, you should:

1. Know several sources of market failure and several techniques of intervention.
2. Be able to distinguish social regulation from economic regulation.
3. Be able to demonstrate natural monopoly graphically and verbally.
4. Understand economies of scale.
5. Understand the potential conflict among the goals of price efficiency, production efficiency, and equity.
6. Know the difficulties associated with regulating the price, output, or profits of natural monopolies.
7. Understand the difficulty of devising regulations and why second-best solutions are a realistic goal.
8. Be able to distinguish between administrative, compliance, and efficiency costs of regulation.
9. Know the history of regulation and deregulation in the U.S. economy, and be able to cite some results of deregulation.

Using Key Terms

Fill in the puzzle on the opposite page with the appropriate term from the list of Key Terms at the end of the chapter in the text.

Across
3.   The market structure in Figure 27.1 in the text.
5.   An imperfectly competitive industry subject to potential entry if prices or profits increase.
6.   The doctrine of nonintervention by government.
8.   Occurs when the market mechanism results in a suboptimal outcome.
9.   Obstacles that make it difficult or impossible for new firms to enter a market.
10. The decrease in minimum average costs because of an increase in the size of plant and equipment.
12. Equal to total revenue minus total economic profit.
13. The goods and services that must be given up in order to obtain something else.
14. A form of nonprice competition to make a product appear different from competing products.

Down
1.   Government intervention that fails to improve economic outcomes.
2.   The use of high prices and profits on one product to subsidize low prices on another product.
4.   The offer of goods at prices equal to their marginal cost.
7.   Government intervention to alter the behavior of firms.
11. Laws to prevent the abuse of market power.

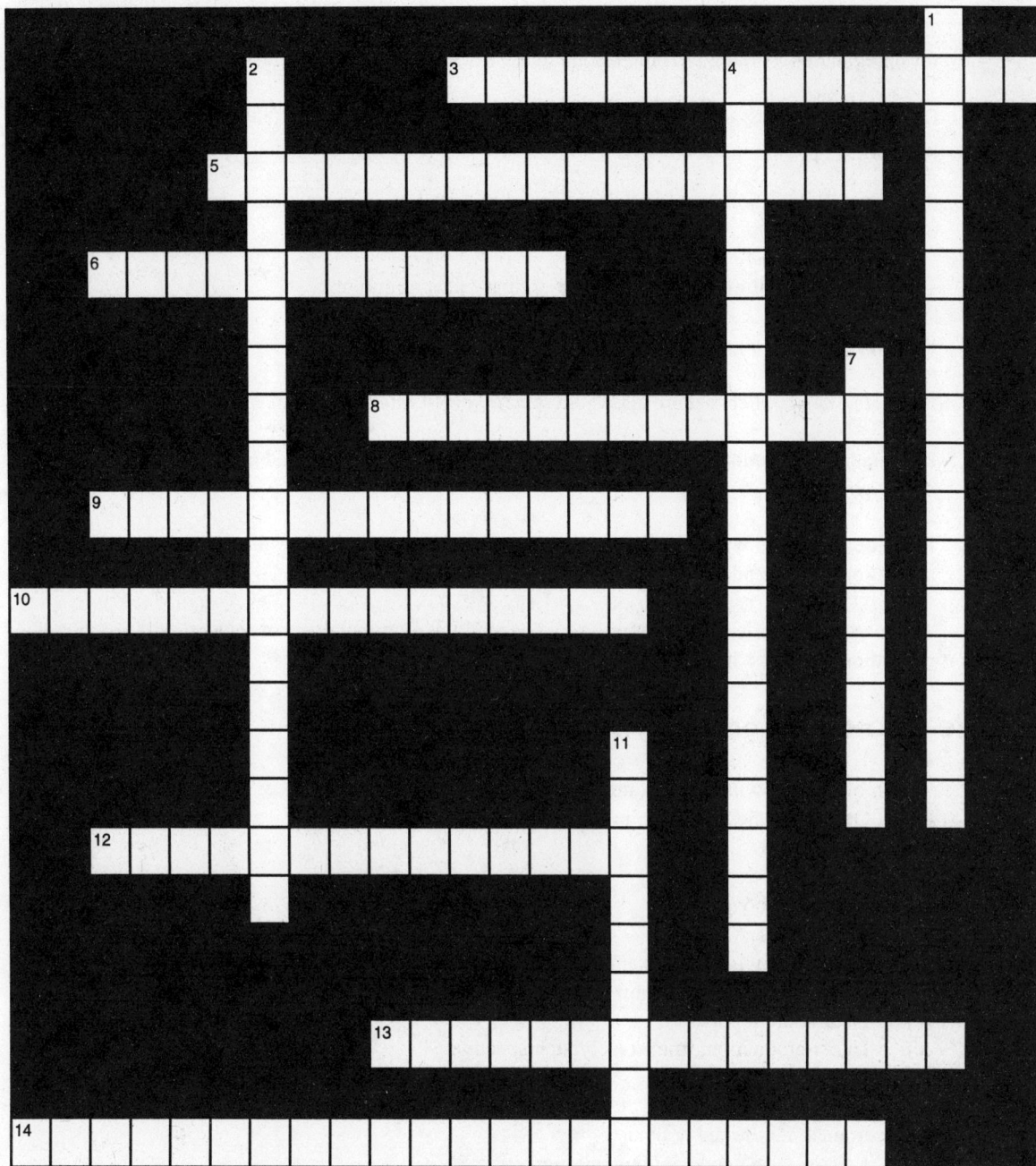

True or False: *Circle your choice and explain why any false statements are incorrect.*

T F 1. Economic regulation focuses on prices, production, and the conditions for industry entry or exit.

T F 2. The argument for regulation is that markets can generate imperfect outcomes, and the argument for deregulation is that government sometimes worsens market outcomes

T F 3. Deregulation implies that government failure is worse than the market failure that regulation is designed to correct.

T F 4. Since social regulation is concerned with workplace safety, discrimination, and other undesirable outcomes, it does not affect prices or output.

T F 5. Unregulated natural monopolies produce optimal rates of output.

T F 6. Price regulation of a natural monopoly does not require a subsidy.

T F 7. Regulated monopolies that are allowed a specific profit rate have an incentive to hold down costs.

T F 8. Eliminating the economic profit of a natural monopolist can be justified on the basis of society's equity goal.

T F 9. Recent experiences with deregulation in the cable TV and telephone industries imply that all regulation should end.

T F 10. The marginal benefits of regulation should exceed the marginal costs of regulation if additional regulations are to be imposed.

Multiple Choice: *Select the correct answer.*

_____ 1. Which of the following is an example of government failure?
   (a) Over regulation resulting in wasted resources.
   (b) Public goods.
   (c) Externalities.
   (d) All of the above.

_____ 2. Which of the following is an example of market failure?
   (a) Inequities in the output mix and the distribution of income.
   (b) Natural monopoly.
   (c) Under production, from society's perspective.
   (d) All of the above.

_____ 3. If government failure did not exist:
   (a) Laissez faire would apply to all markets.
   (b) Deregulation would be unnecessary.
   (c) The invisible hand would be the most efficient and equitable way to run the economy.
   (d) All markets would be regulated.

_____ 4. Government can intervene in the structure or behavior of a market. Which of the following correctly distinguishes between antitrust and regulation?
- (a) Antitrust focuses on both, while regulation focuses mostly on behavior.
- (b) Antitrust focuses on both, while regulation focuses mostly on structure.
- (c) Regulation focuses on both, while antitrust focuses mostly on behavior.
- (d) Regulation focuses on both, while antitrust focuses mostly on structure.

_____ 5. Economic regulation focuses on:
- (a) Prices in a market.
- (b) Production by the market.
- (c) Conditions under which firms enter and exit from an industry.
- (d) All of the above.

_____ 6. To produce at the greatest possible allocative efficiency, a natural monopoly:
- (a) Should be allowed to maximize profit without government interference.
- (b) Sets price equal to average cost.
- (c) Must be subsidized by the government to overcome losses if $P = MC$.
- (d) Produces where $MC = ATC$.

_____ 7. Which of the following problems results from output regulation of a natural monopoly?
- (a) Losses and bankruptcy for the natural monopoly.
- (b) Loss of quality.
- (c) Excess output.
- (d) All of the above.

_____ 8. If the government regulated a natural monopolist to achieve price efficiency without subsidies or price discrimination, the monopolist would:
- (a) Earn economic profits.
- (b) Earn only normal profits.
- (c) Have no incentive to stay in the market.
- (d) Earn less of a profit than before, but still earn a profit.

_____ 9. Which of the following problems results from profit regulation of a natural monopoly?
- (a) Production does not occur at a socially optimal rate.
- (b) The firm has no incentive to strive for efficiency.
- (c) There is an incentive to "pad costs".
- (d) All of the above are problems.

_____ 10. The economic cost of a manufacturer's complying with an "air bag" law would be:
- (a) The additional money required to buy an automobile with an air bag.
- (b) The resources that were used to produce the air bag.
- (c) The best alternative goods and services forgone when the air bag is produced.
- (d) All of the above.

_____ 11. The basic issue in regulatory policy is:
- (a) Whether or not the benefits of government regulation exceed the costs.
- (b) How to achieve second-best solutions in all markets.
- (c) How to eliminate all natural monopolies.
- (d) How to achieve profit regulation in all industries.

_____ 12. Second-best solutions:
- (a) Are options that should never be implemented.
- (b) Reflect the realistic choices that society must make between imperfect markets and imperfect government intervention.
- (c) Are not consistent with utility maximization in the "real world."
- (d) Will always have cost greater than benefits.

_____ 13. When market outcomes are improved after government regulation is enforced:
   (a) Technical efficiency is being achieved.
   (b) The net effect of government intervention on society in this case has been beneficial.
   (c) Government intervention still may not be justified if the economic costs of regulation are too high.
   (d) All of the above are correct.

_____ 14. When there is market failure:
   (a) Government intervention is always beneficial.
   (b) A laissez-faire approach is the best policy.
   (c) Government intervention is beneficial only in the case of natural monopolies.
   (d) Government intervention is beneficial only when the marginal benefit of intervention exceeds its marginal cost.

_____ 15. The first major regulatory target in the United States was:
   (a) Airlines.
   (b) Railroads.
   (c) Trucking firms.
   (d) Telephone companies.

_____ 16. Deregulation of the trucking industry led to:
   (a) A reduction in most truck rates.
   (b) A significant increase in the number of trucking firms.
   (c) The elimination of monopoly profits and increased quantity and variety of service.
   (d) All of the above.

_____ 17. As a consequence of the deregulation of the telephone industry:
   (a) Many telephone companies have abandoned the market.
   (b) Long-distance phone rates have increased sharply.
   (c) Local telephone rates have risen in the absence of cross-subsidization of local costs from long-distance profits.
   (d) Long-distance users now subsidize local users of phone service to a greater extent than before deregulation.

_____ 18. The inefficiency of regulation of interstate airlines was revealed by:
   (a) The absence of nonprice competition among interstate airlines.
   (b) The long history of losses and bankruptcies among major regulated airlines.
   (c) The regulatory practice of allowing unrestricted entry into interstate markets.
   (d) Fares that were as much as 60 percent higher on interstate routes than on comparable (unregulated) intrastate routes.

_____ 19. Deregulation of the airline industry has been followed by:
   (a) Lower fares on shorter, less-traveled routes.
   (b) Increased concentration in the airline industry.
   (c) Higher average cost of service by surviving airlines.
   (d) Reduced competition in most airline markets.

_____ 20. The electric utility industry became a target for deregulation when:
   (a) The cost of constructing nuclear power plants declined.
   (b) New technology allowed the transmission of power from region to region with insignificant power loss.
   (c) Local utility companies began behaving like monopolies.
   (d) All of the above.

Problems and Applications

Exercise 1

This exercise provides practice in identifying market imperfections, finding an appropriate form of government intervention, and recognizing the possible side effects of government intervention.

Table 27.1 lists market imperfections, means for the government to intervene, and some of the side effects of government policy.

Table 27.1
Market imperfections, government interventions, and side effects

Market imperfections	Means of government intervention	Side effects of government policy
I. Externalities	A. Taxes, subsidies, or transfers	1. Inefficiency (unnecessarily high costs)
II. Inequities	B. Regulation of prices, output, or entry	2. Shortages or surpluses
III. Natural monopoly	C. Antitrust activity	3. Lack of quality
IV. Nonexclusive goods	D. Provision of information	4. Inefficient government bureaucracy
V. Market power	E. Production of goods by the government	5. Dynamic inefficiencies
VI. Lack of information about tastes, costs, or prices		
VII. Lack of information about profitability or technology		

1. For each of the situations described in Table 27.2, choose the roman numeral(s) for each market imperfection that applies, the letter(s) that represent appropriate action by the government, and the number(s) that indicate possible side effects of government involvement.

Table 27.2
Market imperfections and government intervention

Situation	Market imperfection	Government intervention	Possible side effects of government policy
1. Because of severe balance-of-trade deficits, the United States needs to export more goods abroad. If not, foreign exchange markets will be increasingly disrupted. However, many small American companies do not know enough about foreign markets to become exporters of goods and services.	_____	_____	_____
2. It is not economical to have firms compete to provide sewage facilities for residential areas. Each house needs only one set of pipes and it is most efficient to attach all pipes from houses to one major sewer conduit.	_____	_____	_____
3. Many workers at a firm find they are becoming nauseated in the workplace. Futhermore, the cancer rate among the employees appears to be very high. They cannot get management to study the problem because the firm can simply fire them and hire new employees.	_____	_____	_____
4. Farmers are willing to use the latest techniques for growing crops. However, they have difficulty determining what the newest techniques are by themselves and the market does not undertake the continuous research process necessary to develop them.	_____	_____	_____
5. If the farmers do not change continually to the latest disease-resistant seed varieties, it is likely that there will be a disastrous spread of disease that will threaten the economy's food supply. However, new varieties of grain are expensive to develop, and the private market would not undertake the continuous research process necessary to develop them.	_____	_____	_____
6. At the beginning of World War II, the United States found that it was cut off from important suppliers of rubber, sugar, and hemp by the Japanese. The private market had not kept enough inventories of these goods on hand in case of war.	_____	_____	_____
7. The St. Joe Mineral Company dumped taconite tailings filled with asbestos into the Great Lakes. While St. Joe suffered no bad side effects from this activity, many people who used the lakes began to suffer such effects.	_____	_____	_____
8. Many older people are poor and as they age and become weaker are beset by various problems and cannot take care of themselves adequately. Private charities do not do enough to maintain a standard of care that society as a whole considers desirable.	_____	_____	_____
9. It is very costly to run electrical lines into a house; thus, it is not economical to put more than one set of electric lines into a home. Electrical services are most economically provided by only one firm.	_____	_____	_____
10. General Electric and Westinghouse decided to coordinate their activities and conspired to set the price of electronic equipment on which they were bidding.	_____	_____	_____

Exercise 2

This exercise emphasizes the characteristics of a natural monopoly using a graph.

Use Figure 27.1 to answer questions 1-6.

Figure 27.1

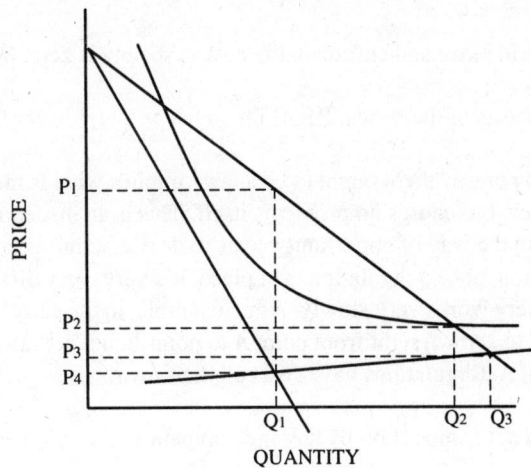

1. Label the ATC curve, the MC curve, the MR curve, and the demand curve in Figure 27.1.

2. What is the profit-maximizing price and output level for the unregulated natural monopolist in Figure 27.1?

3. At the unregulated output level, the natural monopolist (will, will not) earn an economic profit.

4. Regulation designed to achieve price efficiency would result in a price of _____ and an output level of _____.

5. At the output level in question 4, the natural monopoly will earn a (profit, loss) because ATC is (greater, less) than the price.

6. Profit regulation for the natural monopoly would result in a price of _____ and an output level of _____.

Exercise 3

This exercise focuses on market failure and government intervention.

Reread the In the News article "Calif. Consumers Can Choose Power Company" in the text.

1. What passage indicates increased government intervention in the electricity market?

    _____

2. Which of the following forms of market failure justified government intervention?
    (a) Externalities
    (b) Public good
    (c) Natural monopoly
    (d) Inequity

3. Which phrase indicates the benefit of deregulation?_____

4. How are power companies responding to the deregulation?_____

Common Errors

The first statement in each "common error" below is incorrect. Each incorrect statement is followed by a corrected version and an explanation.

1. Once regulations are in place and enforced, the cost to society is zero. WRONG!

   Regulations impose costs of their own. RIGHT!

   The often-heard phrase "there ought to be a law" implies what is meant here. It seems that the law solves the problem but causes no problems itself. This is an inadequate assessment. It costs society a great deal in the way of opportunity costs to devise, administer, and comply with regulations. In addition, once a regulation is in place, it's very, very difficult to remove because bureaucratic machinery works very slowly. As an example, in the early days of the energy crisis, trucks were allowed to carry freight from point A to point B, but not allowed to haul anything back from point B to point A. Regulations have costs all their own!

2. The government can aid competition by helping competitors in a market to survive. WRONG!

   The government interferes with free entry and exit when helping competitors survive, and this interferes with competition. RIGHT!

   When the government prevents exit from the market, it is interfering with the contestability of the market. By not allowing inefficient firms to exit from the market, the government makes it more difficult for the more efficient firms to enter the market. Barriers to exit lead to barriers to entry, which interfere with the competitive process.

•ANSWERS•

Using Key Terms
Across
3. natural monopoly
5. contestable market
6. laissez faire
8. market failure
9. barriers to entry
10. economies of scale
12. economic profit
13. opportunity cost
14. product differentiation

Down
1. government failure
2. cross subsidization
4. marginal cost pricing
7. regulation
11. antitrust

True or False

1. T
2. T
3. T
4. F   Complying with social regulations, e.g. workplace safety, can involve significant costs. As a result, prices and output can be significantly affected.
5. F   Unregulated natural monopolies tend to produce less than optimal levels of output.
6. F   Price regulation occurs where MC = demand which is below the firm's ATC, making a subsidy necessary.
7. F   When a firm is allowed a specific profit rate, it has no incentive to keep costs in check.
8. T
9. F   The regulation of natural monopolies can improve outcomes.
10. T

Multiple Choice

1.	a	5.	d	9.	d	13.	c	17.	c
2.	d	6.	c	10.	c	14.	d	18.	d
3.	b	7.	b	11.	a	15.	b	19.	b
4.	a	8.	c	12.	b	16.	d	20.	b

Problems and Applications

Exercise 1

1. **Table 27.2 Answer**

Situation	Market imperfections	Government interventions	Possible side effects of government policy
1.	VI, VII	D	1, 4
2.	III, V	B or E	1, 2, 3, 4, 5
3.	I, IV	B, D	1, 2, 3, 4, 5
4.	VI, VII	D	1, 4, 5
5.	I, III, IV, VI, VII	A, D, E	1, 3, 4, 5
6.	I, IV	A, E	2, 4, 5
7.	I	A or B	1, 2, 4, 5
8.	II, IV	A	1, 4, 5
9.	III, V	B	1, 2, 3, 4, 5
10.	V	C	1, 2, 4, 5

Exercise 2

1. **Figure 27.1 Answer**

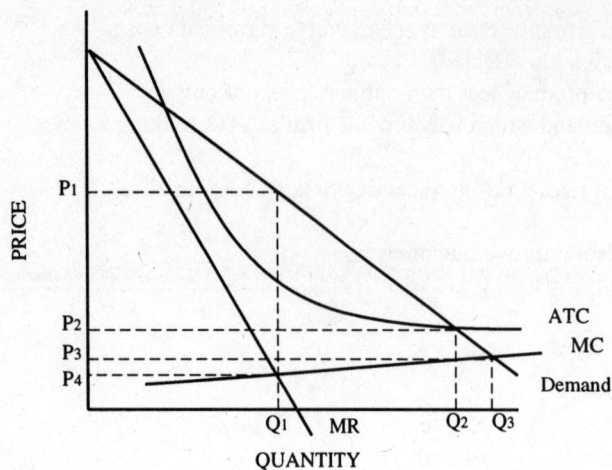

2. P_1, Q_1
3. will
4. P_3, Q_3
5. loss, greater
6. P_2, Q_2

Exercise 3

1. "So far, 16 states have laws to deregulate electricity." ". . . the Clinton administration proposed legislation for nationwide competition by 2003."
2. c
3. ". . . the average family could save $232 a year."
4. They are advertising in an effort to segment the market.

CHAPTER 28
Environmental Protection

Quick Review

Nearly everyone is concerned about the environment and agrees that we ought to protect it. It wasn't always that way. Until the 1960s the problems associated with polluting the environment were not widely understood and certainly did not attract the attention they do today. Of course, a clean environment is only one of the things we want, and as with nearly everything else we desire, there is the cost of obtaining it. In this chapter we consider four questions that are crucial to understanding environmental protection and the least costly ways of obtaining the optimal amount of it:

- How do (unregulated) markets encourage pollution?
- What are the costs of greater environmental protection?
- How much of our (scarce) resources should be allocated to environmental protection?
- How can government policy best ensure an "optimal" environment?

Today we are well aware of many kinds of pollution: problems associated with the earth's ozone layer and global warming, other forms of air pollution, water pollution, and noise pollution, just to name a few.

One wonders why producers pollute (although we all contribute to the problem in one way or another). The answer lies in market incentives. In making production decisions, producers will choose the profit-maximizing rate of output and attempt to produce it at the lowest possible cost—even if by doing so they push some real costs onto society as a whole. When they are successful in pushing these costs onto third parties, we say that an "externality" has been created. It represents a divergence between social cost (the full resource cost of an economic activity) and private costs (those borne directly by the producer or the consumer of a good).

The solutions to the pollution problem lie in two basic areas: (1) using market incentives and (2) bypassing the market and using direct controls. We shouldn't lose sight of the fact that a pollution-free economy would be very difficult and expensive to achieve. Resources would have to be reallocated to fight pollution and would have to be taken away from the production of other goods and services that we also desire. Prices and patterns of employment would change. That partly explains *why we do not desire to eliminate all pollution.* Indeed, the optimal rate of pollution would be one at which the marginal costs of cleaning up the environment is equal to the value of the marginal benefits from cleaning it up.

The Clean Air Act and its amendments of 1990 moved the economy away from the direct-regulation (command and control) approach which specified mandatory pollution reductions *and* the specific technologies for achieving them. This approach, while effective in achieving pollution reduction goals, did not do so at the lowest possible cost. Government agencies are now moving toward market-based systems which achieve given reductions at lower costs and also provide incentives for new, more cost-efficient technologies to be developed. The system relies on a market for "pollution credits" on the Chicago Board of Trade. Those with the highest marginal costs of pollution reduction are the buyers; those with the lowest marginal costs are the sellers. Both parties gain, as does society, because the total resource cost of reducing pollution is reduced.

Learning Objectives

After reading Chapter 28 and doing the following exercises, you should:

1. Know the principal types and sources of pollution.
2. Understand how to apply the notion of opportunity cost to the pollution problem.
3. Understand how market forces influence the production and efficiency decisions for the producer.
4. Be able to distinguish between private costs and social costs.
5. Understand the term "externality," and how externalities arise.
6. Be able to show how taxes, emission charges, marketable pollution rights, and effluent charges can be used to control pollution.
7. Be able to show how regulation can be used to control pollution.
8. Understand the international dimensions of the pollution problem.
9. Understand how the optimal rate of pollution is determined and know why it is *not* zero.
10. Know the theory behind the Clean Air Act and its amendments.
11. Understand the rationale for the market for pollution credits.

Using Key Terms

Fill in the puzzle on the opposite page with the appropriate term from the list of Key Terms at the end of the chapter in the text.

Across

1. A fee imposed on polluters based on the quantity of pollution.
5. Occurs when government intervention fails to improve economic outcomes.
9. The most desired goods and services that are given up in order to obtain something else.
10. Costs or benefits of a market activity borne by a third party.

Down

2. Occurs when the marginal social benefit of pollution control equals its marginal social cost.
3. The total costs of all resources used in an economic activity.
4. The choice of a short run rate of output using existing plant and equipment.
6. The choice of a production process that minimizes costs for any rate of output.
7. Occurs when the market mechanism results in a suboptimal outcome.
8. The resource costs borne by the specific producer.

Puzzle 28.1

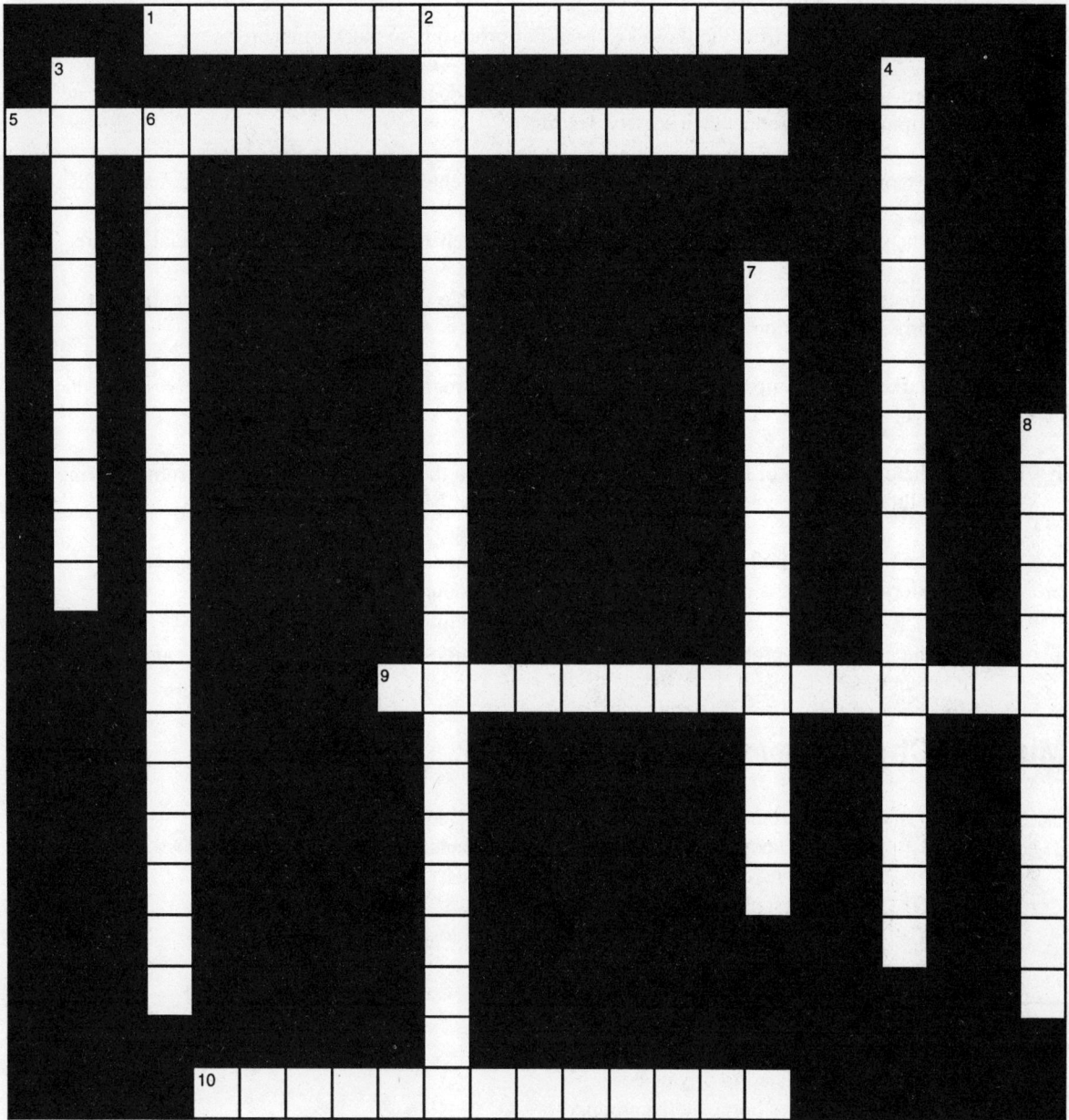

True or False: *Circle your choice and explain why any false statements are incorrect.*

T F 1. Pollution abatement imposes opportunity costs on society.

T F 2. Pollution results from the flawed response of producers to market incentives.

T F 3. Firms that are able to push part of their costs onto society by polluting will produce a greater output of their product than society desires.

T F 4. Externalities are a measure of the divergence between social costs and private costs.

T F 5. When externalities exist, firms will not allocate their resources to maximize social welfare.

T F 6. Direct government regulation is generally preferable to alteration of market incentives in correcting pollution problems.

T F 7. Marketable pollution permits rely on government regulation, not market incentives, to reduce the level of pollution.

T F 8. The optimal rate of pollution will be attained when the total benefits received from lowering the pollution level are equal to the total costs that must be incurred to achieve it.

T F 9. The problem of pollution applies to market economies where the market fails as a result of externalities, but is not a problem in command economies without markets.

T F 10. The greenhouse problem is evidence of market failure in both the United States and other countries.

Multiple Choice: *Select the correct answer.*

_____ 1. In making the production decision, polluting firms equate:
   (a) Marginal social cost with marginal social benefits.
   (b) Marginal revenue and private marginal costs.
   (c) Marginal social cost and marginal revenue.
   (d) Marginal private costs and marginal social costs.

_____ 2. Social costs:
   (a) Are less than private costs.
   (b) Include private costs.
   (c) Are unrelated to private costs.
   (d) Are always borne by the producer.

_____ 3. When social costs and private costs of consumption and production diverge, then inevitably:
   (a) Producers have an incentive to produce too little.
   (b) Consumers have an incentive to consume too little.
   (c) Both producers and consumers have an incentive to produce and consume too much.
   (d) External costs are zero.

_____ 4. When external costs result from the production of some good, the output level of that good tends to be:
   (a)   Larger than is desirable.
   (b)   Smaller than is desirable.
   (c)   Neither too small nor too large.
   (d)   Too small if the private costs exceed the external costs.

_____ 5. The market will overproduce goods that have external costs because:
   (a)   Producers experience lower costs than society.
   (b)   Producers experience higher costs than society.
   (c)   The government is not able to produce these goods.
   (d)   Producers cannot keep these goods
         from consumers who do not pay so they have to produce greater amounts.

_____ 6. A firm that dumps its waste products into our waterways will be:
   (a)   Paying the full cost of production.
   (b)   Paying more than the full cost of production.
   (c)   Able to sell its product at a lower price than if it cleaned up its wastes.
   (d)   Internalizing externalities.

_____ 7. Other things being equal, if a perfectly competitive firm is forced to switch to a more expensive, nonpolluting production process:
   (a)   The average cost curve will shift downward.
   (b)   The profit-maximizing level of output will be increased.
   (c)   The marginal cost curve will shift downward or to the right.
   (d)   Total profits will decrease.

_____ 8. When firms are allowed to pollute the environment without bearing the costs of polluting, then:
   (a)   Their marginal cost curve is too low.
   (b)   Their average variable cost curve is too low.
   (c)   Their average total cost curve is too low.
   (d)   All of the above.

_____ 9. Solution to the pollution-abatement problem involves:
   (a)   Eliminating the divergence between internalized private costs and social costs.
   (b)   Compelling firms to internalize all costs resulting from their production.
   (c)   Forcing polluters to pay all social costs.
   (d)   Doing all of the above.

_____ 10. If emission charges were affixed to all production and consumption activities:
   (a)   The relative price of highly polluting activities would increase.
   (b)   People would stop producing and consuming.
   (c)   Pollution would be eliminated.
   (d)   There would be no redistribution of income.

_____ 11. The purpose of an emission charge is to:
   (a)   Increase the difference between social and private costs.
   (b)   Internalize externalities.
   (c)   Reduce the socially optimal rate of output.
   (d)   Externalize the costs of pollution.

_____ 12. The primary purpose of tradable pollution permits is to:
  (a) Reduce, but not eliminate, the level of pollution.
  (b) Reduce the cost of pollution control.
  (c) Reduce both the level of pollution and the cost of pollution control.
  (d) Completely eliminate pollution.

_____ 13. The 1990 Clean Air Act relied on which of the following strategies to clean up the environment?
  (a) Marketable pollution permits.
  (b) "Command and control" approach to regulation.
  (c) Subsidizing new pollution-control technologies.
  (d) All of the above.

_____ 14. When there are external costs of production, then the social optimum occurs where marginal revenue equals:
  (a) Private marginal cost.
  (b) Social marginal cost.
  (c) The minimum of the average cost curve.
  (d) Social marginal benefit.

_____ 15. An optimal amount of pollution can be described as:
  (a) The minimal amount technically possible.
  (b) The amount that would result when polluting firms spend revenues on pollution-control equipment until they earn only normal profits.
  (c) The amount for which a $1 increase in pollution-control expenditures creates $1 in additional social welfare.
  (d) Zero.

_____ 16. The marginal benefit of reducing pollution:
  (a) Rises as the environment gets cleaner.
  (b) Falls as the environment gets cleaner.
  (c) Is constant.
  (d) Is not an issue in determining the optimal rate of pollution.

_____ 17. The pursuit of a pollution-free environment is:
  (a) The morally correct strategy and costs should not be a consideration.
  (b) Probably not in society's best interests, in view of the extremely high opportunity costs.
  (c) The economically correct strategy.
  (d) The economically correct strategy as long as benefits accrue to society.

_____ 18. In cost-benefit analysis, the government should intervene as long as:
  (a) Government corrects market failures without incurring resources costs.
  (b) The value of government failure exceeds the value of market failure.
  (c) Government's improvement of market outcomes exceeds costs of government intervention.
  (d) Government corrects market failures in spite of government failure.

_____ 19. The costs of pollution control will:
  (a) Always be borne entirely by the polluting producer.
  (b) Always be passed on completely to the consumer.
  (c) Be distributed between producer and consumer depending on factors like the price elasticity of demand.
  (d) Be borne entirely by the taxpayers in the United States.

20. When human lives are involved, a cost-benefit ratio:
   (a) Should have no bearing on decision making.
   (b) Must be considered because it provides a measure of the opportunity costs of government policies.
   (c) Is useless because human lives cannot be measured in dollars and cents.
   (d) Is an indication that a policy should be implemented if it is a very high value.

Problems and Applications

Exercise 1

This exercise shows how to compute the optimal rate of pollution and will help with a problem in the text.

Table 28.1 indicates various levels of pollution that might be experienced in a lake near your home. It also contains information concerning the value of damages imposed on society by the pollution and the cost to society of cleaning the lake to particular levels. For example, the lake could be made pollution-free with an expenditure of $280,000. The question is: "Is it worth it?" Complete questions 1-7 to find out.

Table 28.1
Annual value of damages associated with polluted water and costs of reducing pollution

(1) Quantity of pollution (units of waste material per 100 cubic feet of water)	(2) Monetary value of damages (thousands of dollars)	(3) Marginal benefits of pollution abatement (thousands of dollars)	(4) Costs of treating polluted water (thousands of dollars)	(5) Marginal cost of pollution abatement (thousands of dollars)
6	$140	$ ---	$ 0	$ ---
5	100	40	5	5
4	70	_____	15	_____
3	45	_____	30	_____
2	25	_____	50	_____
1	10	_____	100	_____
0	0	_____	280	_____

1. Assume that without any controls, polluters will annually impose $140,000 of damages on the lake's users by generating 6 units of waste for every 100 cubic feet of water. To clean out the sixth unit of pollutants (that is, lower the quantity of pollution from 6 units to 5) costs $5,000. The value of the benefits gained is $40,000. Complete the rest of column 3.

2. Complete column 5 in Table 28.1 in the same way. The first calculation has been done for you.

3. Should the annual level of pollution be reduced from 6 units to 5? _____

4. Which of the following reasons explains why annual pollution should (or should not) be reduced from 6 to 5 units of pollution?
   (a) The optimal rate of pollution has been reached.
   (b) The marginal social benefits exceed the marginal social cost from reducing the pollution.
   (c) The marginal social costs exceed the marginal social benefits from reducing the pollution.

5. Should pollution be reduced annually from 5 units to 4? _____

6. What is the optimal rate of pollution? _____

7. Which of the following reasons explains why the lake should not be made free of pollution?
   (a) The optimal rate of pollution has been reached when the lake is free of pollution.
   (b) The marginal social costs incurred in eliminating the pollution would exceed the total social benefits achieved.
   (c) The marginal social costs incurred in eliminating all of the pollution would be less than the marginal social benefits achieved.
   (d) None of the above are the case.

Exercise 2

This exercise shows how externalities affect third parties. This exercise will help you complete the problems in the text.

A chemical plant and a plastics factory are located adjacent to the same stream. The chemical plant is located upstream. The downstream plastics factory requires pure water for its production process. Its basic supply is the stream that runs past both firms.

Figure 28.1
Markets for plastics and chemicals

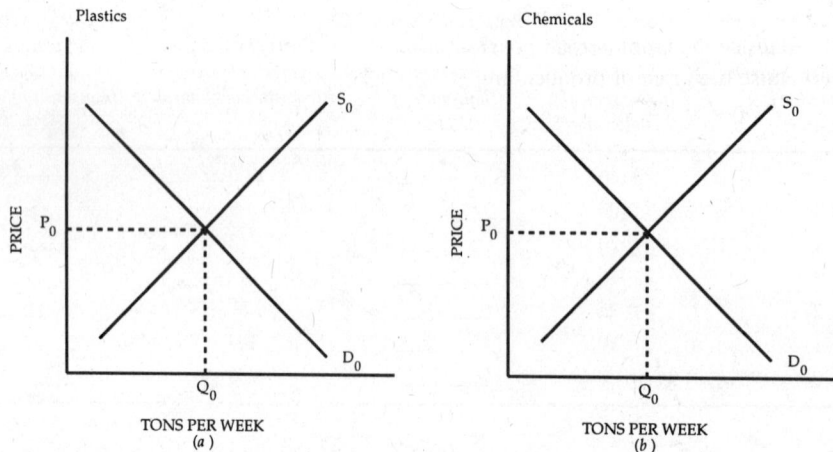

In Figure 28.1, diagrams a and b, S_0 and D_0 represent the supply and demand for plastics and chemicals, respectively. Assume that the economy is initially competitive and resources are allocated efficiently. Equilibrium price and quantity are P_0 and Q_0 in each case. But then the chemical producer decides to dump waste products into the stream rather than dispose of them with the costly process that had been used.

1. In Figure 28.1 diagram b, draw in a new supply curve for chemicals after the dumping in the stream begins. Label it S_1. (*Hint:* There are many ways to draw the curve.)

2. The pollution from the chemical plant forces the plastics manufacturer to use a costly water-purifying system. Draw a new supply curve for plastics in Figure 28.1 diagram a. Label it S_1. (There are many ways to draw this curve correctly.)

3. The effect of the decision to pollute on the quantity of chemicals sold is the same as if:
   (a) A new, improved technology were discovered.
   (b) Wages to its labor force were reduced.
   (c) The Social Security tax on employers had been abolished.
   (d) All of the above were the case.

4. As a result of the chemical plant's polluting activities:
   (a) The price of chemicals has risen.
   (b) The price of chemicals has fallen.
   (c) The price of plastics has not changed.
   (d) None of the above is the case.

5. As a result of the chemical plant's activities:
   (a) More chemicals are produced and sold than society desires.
   (b) More labor is used to produce chemicals than society desires.
   (c) More capital inputs are used to produce chemicals than society desires.
   (d) All of the above are the case.

6. The effect of the chemical firm's pollution is to:
   (a) Raise the price of plastics and reduce the quantity sold.
   (b) Lower the price of plastics and increase the quantity sold.
   (c) Raise the price of plastics and increase the quantity sold.
   (d) Do none of the above.

7. The impact of the pollution on the plastics industry in this example is, *ceteris paribus*, to:
   (a) Reduce the output of plastics below the level that society desires.
   (b) Reduce the employment possibilities in the plastics industry.
   (c) Raise the price of products made with plastics.
   (d) Do all of the above.

Exercise 3

This exercise shows the difference between private marginal costs and social marginal costs.

1. An iron-producing firm mines iron ore. Assume the iron ore industry is competitive. Table 28.2 depicts the private costs and social costs of the firm's iron production at each daily production rate. Complete Table 28.2.

Table 28.2 Costs of producing iron

Production rate (tons per day)	Total private cost (dollars per day)	Private marginal cost (dollars per ton)	Total social cost (dollars per day)	Social marginal cost (dollars per ton)
0	$ 0	$ ---	$ 0	$ ---
1	40	_____	80	_____
2	90	_____	170	_____
3	150	_____	270	_____
4	220	_____	380	_____
5	300	_____	500	_____
6	390	_____	630	_____
7	490	_____	770	_____
8	600	_____	920	_____
9	720	_____	1,080	_____
10	850	_____	1,250	_____
11	990	_____	1,430	_____
12	1,140	_____	1,620	_____

2. In Figure 28.2, the price of the iron in the competitive market is $140 per ton. Draw the private marginal cost curve and label it *PMC*. Draw the social marginal cost curve and label it *SMC*. Label the demand curve "Demand."

Figure 28.2

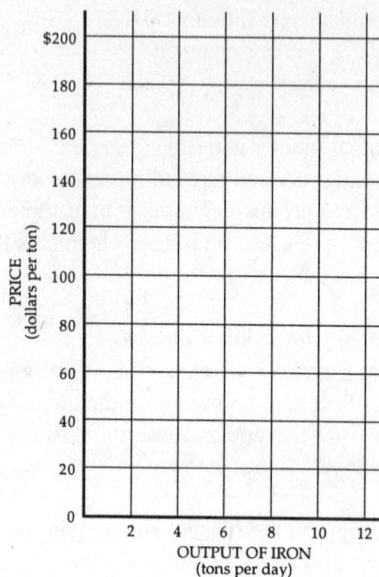

3. What is the profit-maximizing production rate for the firm if it considers only its private costs?
   (a) 5 tons per day.
   (b) 7 tons per day.
   (c) 9 tons per day.
   (d) 11 tons per day.

4. What is the profit-maximizing production rate if the firm is required to pay all social costs?
   (a) 5 tons per day.
   (b) 7 tons per day.
   (c) 9 tons per day.
   (d) 11 tons per day.

5. How much should the pollution (emission) fee be in order to induce the iron-producing firm to produce the socially optimal rate of output?
   (a) $4 per ton.
   (b) $40 per ton.
   (c) $100 per ton.
   (d) $50 per ton.

Exercise 4

The effects of pollution have become an increasingly important topic in the media. This exercise will use one of the articles in the text to show the kind of information to look for to identify the effects of pollution.

Reread the In the News article entitled "Dirty Air Can Shorten Your Life." Then answer the following questions.

1. What are the three general sources of pollution mentioned in the article?_____
   _____

2. What phrase tells you that EPA standards do not guarantee healthy air to breathe?_____
   _____

3. How is the author implicitly measuring the cost of pollution in affected areas?_____
   _____

4. What phrase indicates that the effects of breathing polluted air are like those associated with smoking cigarettes?_____

5. The effect of new and tougher standards on the polluting industries by the monitoring agency would cause the MC and ATC curves to shift (upward, downward)?

Common Errors

The first statement in each "common error" below is incorrect. Each incorrect statement is followed by a corrected version and an explanation.

1. We should eliminate all pollution. WRONG!

   There is an optimal rate at which pollution can take place given the limited resources of our economy. RIGHT!

   Eliminating pollution involves some significant costs. Would it be practical to make sure that every cigarette butt on campus was picked up—even those that might have been flipped into the bushes? No, because the additional costs necessary to achieve a 100 percent pollution-free environment would exceed the additional benefits of doing so. We stop short of that 100 percent pollution-free level—at the point where the marginal social benefits equal the marginal social costs. It would be inefficient to do otherwise.

2. If business firms have a social conscience, they won't pollute. WRONG!

   Even if business firms have a social conscience, there will still be pollution. RIGHT!

   Firms produce goods and services to make profits. In so doing, they serve the rest of society by providing the goods and services society wants and jobs for millions of workers in the process. To avoid polluting, the firms would have to raise their own costs beyond what society could support, and firms would close down or never exist.

•ANSWERS•

Using Key Terms
Across
1. emission charge
5. government failure
9. opportunity cost
10. externalities

Down
2. optimal rate of pollution
3. social costs
4. production decision
6. efficiency decision
7. market failure
8. private costs

True or False

1. T
2. F   Pollution is the result of the rational responses of producers to market incentives (i.e. private costs).
3. T
4. T
5. T
6. F   Market incentives are typically more efficient than direct government regulation.
7. F   Pollution permits rely on market incentives.
8. F   The optimal rate of pollution is attained when marginal benefits are equal to marginal costs.
9. F   Pollution also occurs as a result of government failure when government planners place a low priority on environmental quality.
10. F   It is an indication of both market and government failure.

Multiple Choice

1. b	5. a	9. d	13. a	17. b
2. b	6. c	10. a	14. b	18. c
3. c	7. d	11. b	15. c	19. c
4. a	8. d	12. b	16. b	20. b

Problems and Applications

Exercise 1

1. See Table 28.1 Answer, column 3.

Table 28.1 Answer

Quantity of pollution	(3) Marginal benefits	(5) Marginal cost
6	$ ---	$ ---
5	40	5
4	30	10
3	25	15
2	20	20
1	15	50
0	10	180

2. See Table 28.1 Answer, column 5.
3. Yes, because the marginal benefits are worth $40,000 annually, while the marginal costs are only $5,000 annually.
4. b
5. yes
6. when pollution has been reduced to 2 parts per 100 cubic feet of water annually.
7. c

Exercise 2

1. See Figure 28.1 Answer, diagram b, line S_1.

Figure 28.1 Answer

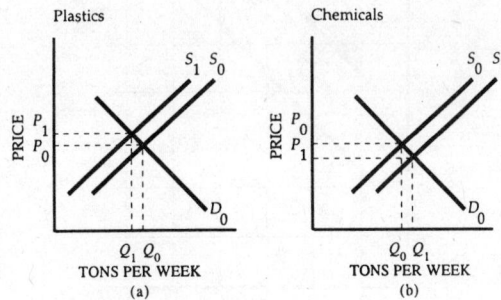

2. See Figure 28.1 Answer, diagram a, line S_1.

3. d   4. b   5. d   6. a   7. d

Exercise 3

1. **Table 28.2 Answer**

Production rate	Private marginal cost	Social marginal cost
0	$ ---	$ ---
1	40	80
2	50	90
3	60	100
4	70	110
5	80	120
6	90	130
7	100	140
8	110	150
9	120	160
10	130	170
11	140	180
12	150	190

2. **Figure 28.2 Answer**

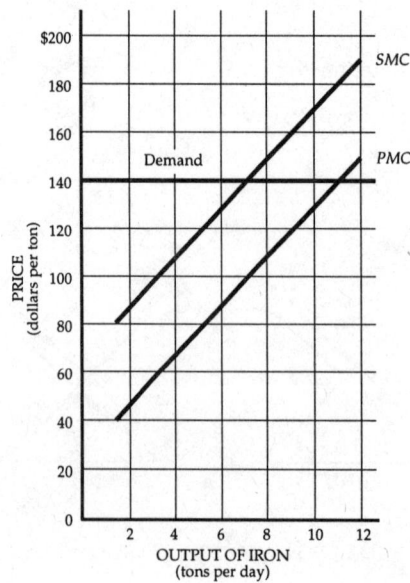

3. d   4. b   5. b

Exercise 4

1. Large particles, small particles, gases.

2. ". . . this form of pollution is killing citizens even in areas that meet Environmental Protection Agency air quality standards. . ."

3. By estimating the probability of premature death due to breathing polluted air.

4. ". . . run a risk of premature death about one sixth as great as if they'd been smoking for 25 years."

5. upward

CHAPTER 29

The Farm Problem

Quick Review

This chapter discusses the "farm problem." Even the title indicates the need for a solution. The federal government has been working on the problem since the 1930s and the programs they've put in place now cost taxpayers upwards of $15 billion annually. Many voters view this crazy quilt of policies as a good example of government failure! The questions that arise in examining the problem are:

- Why are farm prices and profits so unstable?
- Why has the farm sector shrunk so much?
- How do government farm programs affect farm output, prices, and income?

In answer to the first question, farming has always been an uncertain occupation at best, and there have been many farm depressions. The farm depression of the early 1980s was the worst on record. Real farm income was actually lower in 1983 than in 1933! The problems now seem more deep-seated and intractable than before, and the impact of changes taking place will be felt for a long, long time. Some go so far as to say that traditional farming is dead.

On the supply side there have always been the forces of nature to deal with. Sudden droughts, freezes, or blights have always raised havoc with supply. On the demand side, both price and income elasticities are perverse. A low income elasticity (low sensitivity of the demand for agricultural goods to changes in income) causes domestic demand to grow slowly. Political considerations have prevented the expansion of export markets, and the period in which the dollar was strong only made exporting more difficult.

As if this weren't enough, tremendous productivity advances, which would be welcome in most other markets, have resulted in much lower prices and farm incomes because the price elasticity of market demand is low (low sensitivity of the quantity demanded of agricultural goods to changes in price). In addition, the producers in this competitive market are beset by the same problems that hampered firms in many other sectors and brought even giant firms to their knees. Farming is now dominated by huge farms, which must contend with foreign competition, high interest rates, and unanticipated fluctuations in the prices of other inputs. The results have been falling land prices, a continuous decline of the farm population, farms lost, and the destruction of a way of life.

Well-intentioned government policy has produced perverse results. The price-support programs encourage production of products already in surplus, raise prices to consumers, and distort the allocation of resources. Direct income-support programs seem to provide more income to those who need it least and set-aside programs pay people for not producing. Deficiency payments encouraged farmers to subdivide their farms to circumvent a provision which limited the payment to $50,000 for a single farm. The dairy termination program reduced the size of the dairy herd, and the price of dairy products rose. Nothing seems to work well.

Farmers say they want parity, not charity, and continue to call for price supports to reestablish the *relative* purchasing power that farm commodities commanded some seventy years ago. The Reagan administration moved in the opposite direction with the Farm Security Act of 1985 arguing that farmers must be made more responsive to market forces. For example, supporting dairy prices at artificially high levels and then giving away the surplus strikes many as government run amok once again. Subsequent legislation continued the inexorable trend.

Farm-support legislation must be renewed every five years, and the 1990 legislation took additional steps to free farmers from government target prices and selling (rather than accumulating) surpluses. The 1995 legislation, entitled the "Freedom to Farm Act," established a gradual phase-out of support prices and set-asides for major commodities. As a result of the Asian crisis farm prices fell in 1997 and 1998 and farmers demanded more federal aid.

Learning Objectives

After reading Chapter 29 and doing the following exercises, you should:

1. Know the dimensions and nature of the farm problem.
2. Understand the role of income and price elasticities in the farm problem.
3. Be able to relate the farm problem to forces on both the supply side and demand side of the market.
4. Understand the impact of supply- and demand-induced changes in prices of inputs on farm decision-making and profits.
5. Be able to describe several types of farm policies and their effects on the farming economy.
6. Be able to describe the causes and dimensions of the two great farm depressions.
7. Understand the direction and rationale of the Freedom to Farm Act of 1995.

Using Key Terms

Fill in the puzzle on the opposite page with the appropriate term from the list of Key Terms at the end of the chapter in the text.

Across
1. Income transfer paid to farmers for the difference between target and market prices.
3. Total revenue minus total economic costs.
7. Percentage change in quantity demanded divided by the percentage change in price.
10. The ability to change the market price of a good or service.
11. The implicit price paid by the government for surplus crops taken as collateral.
12. Land withdrawn from farm production in an effort to increase crop prices.

Down
2. Percentage change in quantity demanded divided by percentage change in income.
4. The relative price of farm products from 1910-1914.
5. An incentive to engage in undesirable behavior.
6. Obstacles that make it difficult or impossible for new producers to enter a market.
8. Equal to q_2 minus q_D at a price of p_f in Figure 29.4 in the text.
9. Total revenue minus total cost.

Puzzle 29.1

405

True or False: *Circle your choice and explain why any false statements are incorrect.*

T F 1. Because there are 2 million farms in the U.S., individual farmers have some market power.

T F 2. Agricultural price-supports lead farmers to produce more goods than consumers want.

T F 3. When prices for farm commodities fall, total revenue will go down because the market demand for farm commodities is price inelastic.

T F 4. The demand for farmland is derived from the demand for agricultural commodities.

T F 5. Price supports have lowered the price of farm products, increased consumption, and reduced production.

T F 6. Deficiency payments are designed to establish the same ratio of farm to nonfarm income as would parity prices.

T F 7. Direct income payments to farmers are less efficient at raising farm incomes than are price-support programs.

T F 8. When a large crop is produced by American farmers, farmers receive higher incomes because the price elasticity for agricultural products is low.

T F 9. The intent of the 1996 Freedom to Farm Act was to increase the level of federal aid to farmers.

T F 10. When the government continually bails out farmers during economic crises, rather than relying on the farmers themselves to manage their risks, the government has created a "moral hazard."

Multiple Choice: *Select the correct answer.*

_____ 1. If an agricultural market is perfectly competitive, then:
  (a) A farmer is a price taker.
  (b) A farmer uses price discrimination.
  (c) The market demand curve is perfectly elastic.
  (d) Each firm's demand curve is perfectly inelastic.

_____ 2. The 1996 Freedom to Farm Act:
  (a) Eliminated target prices and deficiency payments.
  (b) Focused farm policy toward stabilizing farm incomes rather than prices.
  (c) Eliminated many restrictions on acreage set-asides.
  (d) The 1996 Act did all of the above.

_____ 3. Which of the following would result from a price-support program when the support price is set above the equilibrium price?
  (a) The price paid by consumers would be higher.
  (b) The consumption of the product would be reduced.
  (c) Output would increase, *ceteris paribus*.
  (d) All of the above would result.

_____ 4. When government subsidizes the purchase of irrigation water by farmers, the result is:
  (a) Higher marginal costs of production.
  (b) Lower fixed costs to farmers.
  (c) Increased output because marginal costs are lower.
  (d) Higher fixed costs to farmers.

_____ 5. Which of the following programs will raise farm incomes without generating market distortions?
  (a) Set-aside programs.
  (b) Direct income-support programs.
  (c) Import restrictions.
  (d) All of the above.

_____ 6. The primary intent of the 1996 Freedom to Farm Act was to:
  (a) Make farmers more dependent on market forces.
  (b) Increase prices paid to farmers.
  (c) Increase set-aside acreage.
  (d) All of the above.

_____ 7. Which of the following is consistent with farming as a competitive market?
  (a) A small number of firms.
  (b) Marginal revenue lower than price for each firm.
  (c) Exit of small firms when profits are high for large firms.
  (d) Zero economic profit in the long run.

_____ 8. When effective price floors are set for an agricultural market:
  (a) Quantity demanded will be less than the equilibrium quantity, and price will be greater than the equilibrium price.
  (b) Quantity demanded will be less than the equilibrium quantity, and price will be less than the equilibrium price.
  (c) Quantity demanded will be greater than the equilibrium quantity, and price will be greater than the equilibrium price.
  (d) Quantity demanded will be greater than the equilibrium quantity, and price will be less than the equilibrium price.

_____ 9. The surplus induced by farm price-support programs can be eliminated by all of the following *except*:
  (a) Export sales.
  (b) Reduced demand.
  (c) Government purchases and stockpiling.
  (d) Supply restrictions.

_____ 10. What impact did the "Asian crisis" have on U.S. agriculture beginning in 1998?
  (a) Decreased farm exports to Asia.
  (b) A decrease in grain prices.
  (c) A decrease in employment in the U.S. farm equipment industry.
  (d) All of the above.

_____ 11. Which of the following is *not* generally a characteristic of agriculture?
  (a) Ease of entry and exit.
  (b) Market power.
  (c) Homogeneous products.
  (d) Artificial restraints on prices.

12. Individual farmers view the demand curve they face for agricultural commodities as very price elastic, and:
    (a) They are correct even though the market demand curve tends to be quite inelastic.
    (b) They are correct, and the market demand curve is quite elastic as well.
    (c) They are incorrect because the market demand curve tends to be price inelastic.
    (d) They are incorrect because price and quantity demanded are inversely related in the product market.

13. Which of the following characterizes the price and income elasticities for farm products?
    (a) When prices fall, consumers respond by buying a great deal more; when income increases, consumers respond by buying less.
    (b) When prices and income fall, consumers respond by buying less.
    (c) When prices fall, farmers get less revenue; when income rises, consumers do not change purchases much.
    (d) All of the above are characteristic.

14. The government creates a "moral hazard" when it:
    (a) Encourages the type of behavior that leads to an undesirable allocation of resources.
    (b) Ignores the plight of a group suffering economic depravation, e.g. farmers during the third farm depression.
    (c) Passes laws it knows can't be enforced.
    (d) Doesn't provide the same level of moral leadership that it expects from U.S. citizens.

15. If the price of corn falls by 20 percent on world markets, causing American corn consumption to increase by 5 percent, *ceteris paribus*, the absolute value of the price elasticity of demand for corn in the United States would be:
    (a) 0.25.
    (b) 0.5.
    (c) 4.0.
    (d) 25.0.

16. The relationship between farm and nonfarm prices which existed during the period 1910 to 1914 has come to be known as:
    (a) The payment-in-kind program.
    (b) The farm parity price.
    (c) The target price.
    (d) Price supports.

17. A program of deficiency payments is best classified as a federal:
    (a) Price-support program.
    (b) Income-support program.
    (c) Farm cost subsidy.
    (d) Acreage set-aside.

18. If the market price of wheat is below the government's "loan rate":
    (a) The Commodity Credit Corporation lends the farmer an amount equal to the loan rate times the farmer's wheat output and takes the farmer's wheat crop as collateral.
    (b) The wheat farmer defaults on the loan but keeps the crop; the CCC keeps the money.
    (c) The wheat farmer, in effect, "buys" the crop from the CCC.
    (d) All of the above.

19. An advantage of set-aside programs over price-support programs is that they:
    (a) Reduce the price of agricultural goods.
    (b) Transfer more income to farmers.
    (c) Raise the price of agricultural production but do not lead to a surplus of output.
    (d) Affect the demand side as well as the supply side of the farm problem.

_____ 20. Which of the following agricultural programs reduces agricultural output, rather than increasing it?
   (a)   Direct income-support programs.
   (b)   Farm cost subsidies.
   (c)   Marketing orders.
   (d)   Export sales.

Problems and Applications

Exercise 1

This exercise shows the impact of farm subsidies on the market and consumers.

Figure 29.1 represents the agricultural market. Use this figure to answer questions 1-6.

Figure 29.1

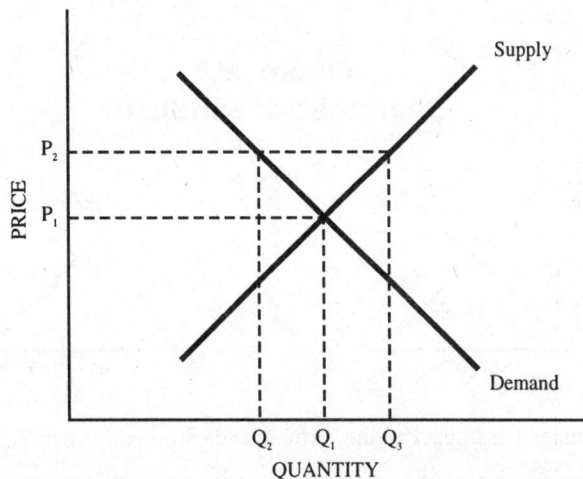

1.   Without government intervention, the price of farm goods is determined by the intersection of

_____.

2.   The equilibrium price is _____ and farmers supply farm goods equal to _____.

3.   Individual farmers are price (makers, takers) and will always produce the level of output where price equals _____.

4.   Government price supports would (increase, decrease) the price of farm goods and cause price to move to _____.

5.   At the new price farmers would supply farm goods equal to _____.

6.   The price support caused a (shortage, surplus) of output in the agricultural market equal to the distance _____.

Exercise 2

Articles about agriculture often provide information about shortages or surpluses. This exercise will use one of the articles in the textbook to show the kind of information to look for to determine whether shortages or surpluses exist.

Reread the In the News article entitled "EU Farm Subsidies." Then answer the following questions.

1. The article indicates there are:
   (a) Shortages.
   (b) Surpluses.

2. What passage in the article indicates the existence of the shortage or surplus? _____
   _____

3. Which diagram in Figure 29.3 best represents the shortage or surplus mentioned in the article?
   _____

Figure 29.3
Shortages or surpluses

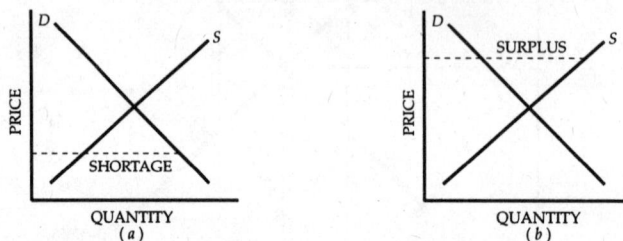

4. What phrase indicates the impact of the farm subsidies on consumers? _____
   _____

Common Errors

The first statement in each "common error" below is incorrect. Each incorrect statement is followed by a corrected version and an explanation.

1. Advances in farm productivity should be accompanied by improved profitability. WRONG!

   Competition translates improved productivity into lower prices, which can cause lower profitability. RIGHT!

   The spectacular increases in farm productivity that have occurred in the past decades have resulted in lower prices and lower incomes. Increases in supply coupled with price-inelastic and slow-growing demand have lowered rather than raised net farm income. Yet competition forces the adoption of the newest techniques of scientific farming.

2. When farmers have a bumper crop because of good weather, they will receive high incomes. WRONG!

   When farmers have a bumper crop, their income is likely to fall to low levels. RIGHT!

Because the demand for farm goods is price inelastic, a large percentage increase in output will cause an even larger percentage reduction in price.

•ANSWERS•

Using Key Terms
Across
1. deficiency payment
3. economic profit
7. price elasticity of demand
10. market power
11. loan rate
12. acreage set-aside

Down
2. income elasticity of demand
4. parity
5. moral hazard
6. barriers to entry
8. market surplus
9. profit

True or False

1. F The fact that there are so many farmers in the U.S. means that individual farmers have no market power.
2. T
3. T
4. T
5. F Price supports have raised the price of farm products, reduced consumption, and encouraged production.
6. F Deficiency payments are payments made to farmers to make up the difference between target and market prices. Target prices may or may not be designed to reach parity.
7. F Direct income payments are more efficient because they do not cause market distortions, e.g. surpluses.
8. T
9. F The primary intent of the 1996 Freedom to Farm Act was to wean farmers away from federal aid, i.e. make farmers more dependent on market forces.
10. T

Multiple Choice

1. a	5. b	9. b	13. c	17. b
2. d	6. a	10. d	14. a	18. a
3. d	7. d	11. b	15. a	19. c
4. c	8. a	12. a	16. b	20. c

411

Problems and Applications

Exercise 1

1. market supply and market demand
2. P_1, Q_1
3. takers, MC
4. increase, P_2
5. Q_3
6. surplus, Q_3-Q_2

Exercise 2

1. b
2. The article says, ". . . governments also agree to purchase any surplus production."
3. diagram b (surplus)
4. "All this protection costs the average EU consumer over $200 a year."

PART 10 Factor Markets: Basic Theory

CHAPTER 30

The Labor Market

Quick Review

Most of us do not think of ourselves in the abstract as "inputs," or factors of production, but in the language of the circular flow of economic activity, that's what we are. In the circular-flow model there are markets for products and markets for factors of production. People are demanders in the product market but suppliers in the factor market. This chapter discusses the supply side of that market first and then looks at the demand side. It considers these questions:

- How do people decide how much time to spend working?
- What determines the wage rate an employer is willing to pay?
- Why are some workers paid so much and others so little?

Let's begin with the first question. People choose between leisure and the satisfaction of material needs. Given the institutional structure of our economy, material needs are satisfied mainly by working for income. When we work, however, we sacrifice leisure. Hence, the opportunity cost of goods and services obtained by working is the number of hours of leisure that must be sacrificed to earn the required income. Conversely, the opportunity cost of leisure is the amount of goods and services that cannot be bought because of the time not spent working. Psychological and social needs may also motivate people to work. These needs affect the utility of both leisure and the income gained from work.

The marginal utility of labor reflects the satisfaction to be gained from added income as well as any direct pleasure a job may provide. A worker compares the marginal utility of labor with that of leisure and chooses either more labor or more leisure, depending on which offers greater marginal utility.

The supply curve of labor reflects the tradeoff between material needs and leisure. People feel two conflicting emotions when they receive an increase in their wage. The substitution effect makes a person want to work more. (An hour of work is worth more in terms of goods and services that can be obtained; the opportunity cost of leisure has risen.) The income effect diminishes the need to work. (The same quantity of goods and services can be obtained with less labor after the wage increase.)

Usually these two effects result in an upward-sloping supply curve for labor; a wage increase encourages a person to work more hours. But if a person dislikes work or feels enough of his or her needs are already met, a higher wage may result in fewer hours worked, so that his or her supply curve bends backward. In this case the income effect overpowers the substitution effect.

The demand for labor depends on the demand for the goods that labor produces. The demand for labor is thus a derived demand; the marginal revenue product curve is a derived demand curve. It shows the additional revenue generated by an additional unit of labor. An employer will not want to pay a worker more than the extra revenue that the worker creates. Hence, the marginal revenue product curve sets an upper limit to wages.

The more labor a business employs, the less revenue each additional unit of labor brings to the firm.

This reflects the law of diminishing returns: employing more workers in a given firm implies that each worker has less plant and equipment with which to work. As a result, each worker's marginal product declines as more workers are hired. The other factors of production also experience diminishing returns.

The interaction of market demand and market supply determines the equilibrium market wage. When either the market supply or market demand curve shifts as a result of changes in its nonprice determinants, surpluses or shortages may result. The labor market adjusts just as a product market does. Shortages lead to wage increases; surpluses, to wage decreases.

Firms choose among factors on the basis of the increase in product that each extra factor generates for the input price. A profit-maximizing producer will always choose the most cost-efficient input, that is, the one with the highest ratio of marginal product to factor price (not necessarily the factor with the lowest price).

The marginal revenue product (*MRP*) is not the only means by which wage rates are determined, however. Wage rates also reflect market power, custom, discrimination, and the opportunity wage. In cases where *MRP* is difficult to measure, such as the salary of a CEO, the opportunity wage is used.

Learning Objectives

After reading Chapter 30 and doing the following exercises, you should:

1. Understand the labor-supply curve and its nonprice determinants.
2. Be able to apply the law of diminishing marginal utility to the labor market.
3. Know how people determine the number of hours they want to work.
4. Be able to explain the shape of the labor-supply curve using the income and substitution effects of wages.
5. Know how to calculate the elasticity of the market supply of labor.
6. Understand why the demand for factors of production is derived from the demand for goods and services.
7. Be able to derive the marginal revenue product curve and know why it slopes downward.
8. Understand how market supply and market demand interact to determine market wage rates when their nonprice determinants change.
9. Understand cost efficiency and how the efficiency decision is made.
10. Know that the "opportunity wage" reflects a worker's productivity in his or her best alternative employment, *ceteris paribus*.

Using Key Terms

Fill in the puzzle on the opposite page with the appropriate term from the list of Key Terms at the end of the chapter in the text.

Across
1. The choice of a production process for any given rate of output.
7. Determined by the intersection of the market supply and market demand for labor.
13. The percentage change in quantity of labor supplied divided by the percentage change in wage rate.
14. The willingness and ability to work specific amounts of time at alternative wage rates.
15. A specific combination of resources used to produce a good or service.

Down
2. The quantity of resources purchased by a firm depends on the firm's expected sales and output.
3. An increased wage rate causes people to work more hours.
4. The MPP of labor declines as the quantity of labor employed increases.
5. The change in total output because of one additional unit of input.
6. An increased wage rate allows people to reduce the hours worked without losing income.
8. The change in total revenue because of one additional unit of input.

9. The total quantity of labor that workers are willing and able to supply at alternative wage rates.
10. The MPP of an input divided by its price.
11. The highest wage an individual would earn in his or her best alternative job.
12. The quantity of labor employers are willing and able to hire at alternative wage rates.

Puzzle 30.1

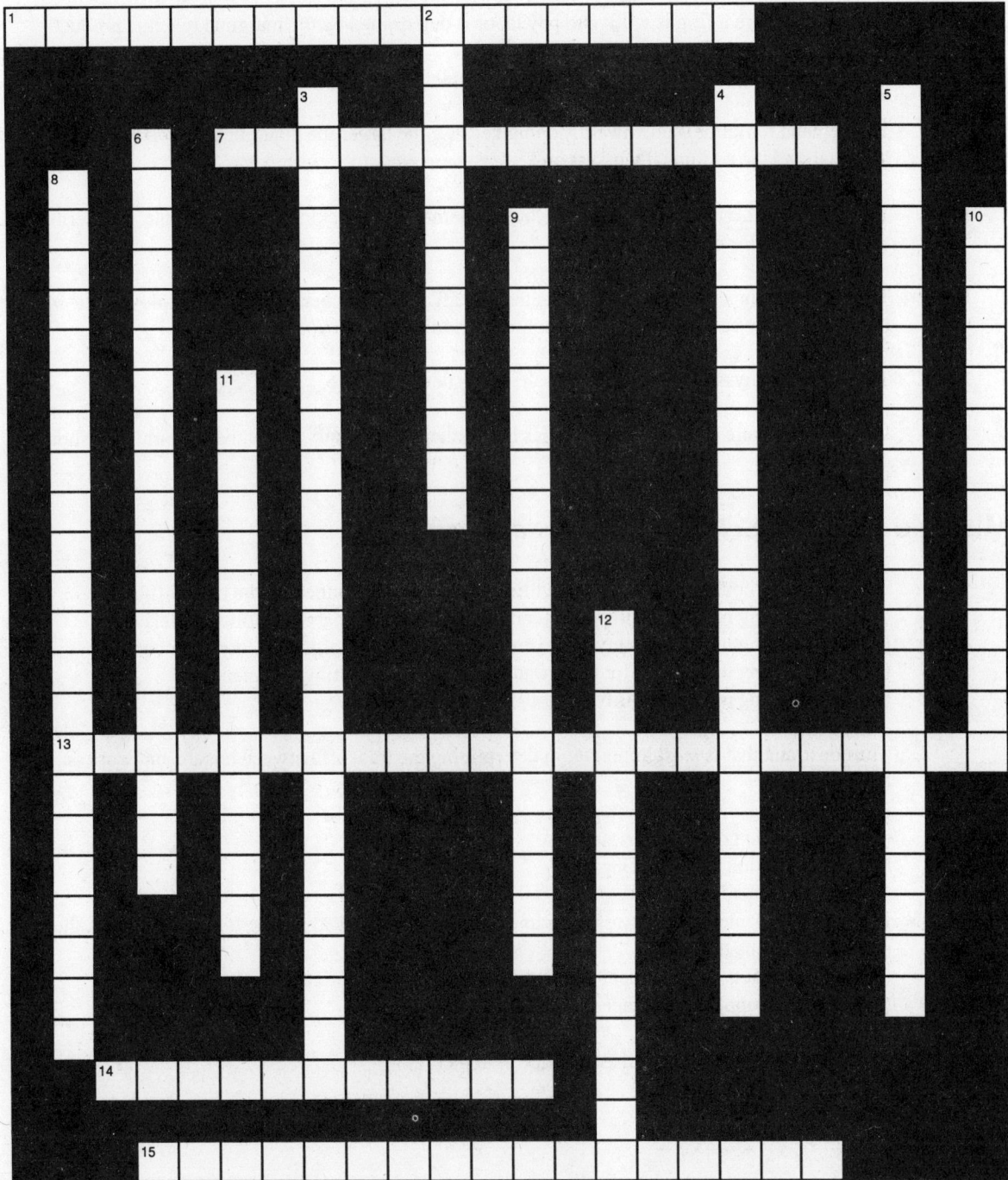

True or False: *Circle your choice and explain why any false statements are incorrect.*

T F 1. The supply curve for labor bends backward when the income effect of wages exceeds the substitution effect of wages.

T F 2. The intersection of the labor market supply and market demand curves establishes the minimum wage.

T F 3. For wages to be higher without sacrificing jobs, productivity must decrease.

T F 4. The highest wage a firm is willing to pay labor is determined by the marginal revenue product.

T F 5. The value of additional income decreases as total income increases.

T F 6. The demand for labor is downward sloping because the larger the quantities of workers hired the less qualified the additional workers are.

T F 7. The concept of derived demand means that the demand for bricklayers, for example, is determined by the demand for new brick houses.

T F 8. The law of diminishing returns suggests that the fewer the number of workers employed, the more total output they can produce in a given time period, *ceteris paribus.*

T F 9. The marginal physical product curve is the labor-demand curve.

T F 10. If salary caps were placed on CEO wages below their opportunity wage, there would be a shortage of CEOs.

Multiple Choice: *Select the correct answer.*

_____ 1. The number of hours that a worker is willing to work is determined by the trade-off between:
- (a) Increasing marginal utility for income and decreasing marginal utility for leisure.
- (b) Increasing marginal utility for leisure and decreasing marginal utility for income.
- (c) Increasing total utility for leisure and decreasing total utility for income.
- (d) Increasing marginal utility for both income and leisure.

_____ 2. The constraint that is *most* important in determining the tradeoff between leisure and work is:
- (a) Income.
- (b) Time.
- (c) Available goods and services.
- (d) Satisfaction from working.

_____ 3. If consumers wanted to increase wages and the number of jobs available for apple pickers, the best strategy would be to:
- (a) Insist that the government establish a minimum wage for apple pickers.
- (b) Boycott apples until wages increased.
- (c) Buy more apples.
- (d) Insist that the sellers raise the price of apples.

_____ 4. An upward-sloping labor-supply curve illustrates, *ceteris paribus*, that:
   (a) The supply of labor and the wage rate are inversely related.
   (b) The quantity supplied of labor and the hours of work per week are directly related.
   (c) The quantity supplied of labor and the hours of work per week are inversely related.
   (d) A greater quantity of labor would be supplied at higher wage rates.

_____ 5. The elasticity of labor supply does *not* depend on:
   (a) The demand for labor.
   (b) Income and wealth.
   (c) The prices of consumer goods.
   (d) Expectations for income or consumption.

_____ 6. A competitive firm should continue to hire workers until:
   (a) The MRP is equal to demand.
   (b) The MPP is equal to the number of workers hired.
   (c) The MRP is equal to the market wage rate.
   (d) The MRP is equal to zero.

_____ 7. Shifts of the labor-supply curve are caused by:
   (a) Changes in tastes for jobs.
   (b) Wage increases.
   (c) Changes in the number of job vacancies.
   (d) All of the above.

_____ 8. Which of the following policies is consistent with surpluses of labor in the labor market?
   (a) Price supports in the product market.
   (b) Minimum-wage legislation.
   (c) Wage controls (ceilings).
   (d) All of the above.

_____ 9. Which of the following helps explain why the wages received by two workers with different jobs are not the same?
   (a) Differences in marginal revenue products at their respective jobs.
   (b) The opportunity wages of the two workers differ.
   (c) The prices of the products they produce differ.
   (d) All of the above may contribute to the difference.

_____ 10. Which of the following is true about the equilibrium market wage?
   (a) All workers are satisfied with the wage.
   (b) All employers are satisfied with the wage.
   (c) There is no unemployment in this market at the equilibrium wage.
   (d) All of the above are correct.

_____ 11. At the market equilibrium wage:
   (a) MRP = wage rate.
   (b) The ratio of the MPP of each factor to the factor's price is the same for all factors.
   (c) The market demand curve for labor intersects the market supply curve of labor.
   (d) All of the above.

_____ 12. The cost efficiency of labor is equal to:
   (a) The marginal cost of output.
   (b) The MPP of labor times the wage rate.
   (c) The MPP of labor divided by the wage rate.
   (d) The MRP of labor divided by the unit price of labor.

_____ 13. In order to calculate marginal revenue product, we need to know:
  (a) The change in total output and the change in quantity of labor.
  (b) The marginal physical product and the unit price of the factor.
  (c) The marginal revenue and the amount of the product produced.
  (d) The marginal revenue and the cost of the factor.

_____ 14. The diminishing returns to a factor may be due to:
  (a) The declining utility of a good as we consume more of it.
  (b) Crowding or overuse of other factors as production is increased.
  (c) The decline in the demand curve for a product.
  (d) The decline in the marginal revenue curve for a product.

_____ 15. The efficiency decision involves choosing the input combination or process:
  (a) Which produces the greatest output.
  (b) Which results in the lowest output per dollar of input.
  (c) Which results in the greatest output for a given cost.
  (d) Which has the lowest ratio of *MPP* to input.

_____ 16. The marginal revenue product curve and marginal physical product curve have similar shapes:
  (a) Because marginal revenue product depends on marginal physical product.
  (b) Because the product demand curve slopes downward in accordance with the law of diminishing returns.
  (c) Because the law of demand and the law of diminishing returns are due to the same economic behavior.
  (d) For all of the above reasons.

_____ 17. Employment will definitely rise when:
  (a) Productivity and wages rise.
  (b) Productivity rises and wages fall.
  (c) Productivity falls and wages rise.
  (d) Productivity and wages fall.

_____ 18. A change in wages causes a:
  (a) Shift in the marginal revenue product curve for labor.
  (b) Shift in the marginal physical product curve for labor.
  (c) Shift in the derived demand curve for labor.
  (d) Movement along the labor-demand curve.

_____ 19. When the minimum wage is raised in a competitive market, ceteris paribus,:
  (a) All workers are better off.
  (b) All workers are worse off.
  (c) Some workers are better off and some are worse off.
  (d) Workers are not affected by a minimum wage increase, only by decreases.

_____ 20. "Opportunity wage" is defined as:
  (a) The highest wage an individual would earn in his or her best alternative employment.
  (b) The value of goods or services that an individual can purchase with the income earned by working 1 hour.
  (c) The income equivalent of a volunteer worker.
  (d) The income a worker loses when he or she quits a job.

Problems and Applications

Exercise 1

This exercise shows how to determine the supply of labor. It provides practice in graphing labor supply and examines backward-bending supply curves, the substitution effect, and the income effect.

Suppose you came to school without any means of support and your advisor suggests that you take a job at the school. Your only task is to correct true-false examinations (the professors give you all of the answers to the exams), add up the scores, and calculate each student's grade. You can work as many hours as you wish because opportunities are plentiful.

Drawing Labor-Supply Curves

If the work were offered to you on a volunteer basis, you would not work at all. But at $2 an hour you might work 1 hour per day—just to see how well your classmates are doing. Only at $4 an hour would it be worthwhile to work many hours—perhaps 4 hours per day. At $8 an hour you would work 6 hours per day and at $16 an hour you would make it a full-time job of 8 hours per day. But at $32 an hour you would decide to spend more time at leisure and work only 6 hours per day.

1. Fill in column 2 of Table 30.1, your labor-supply schedule, using the information in the paragraph above.

Table 30.1
Supply of labor

(1) Hourly wage (dollars per hour)	(2) Work effort (hours worked per day)	(3) Elasticity of supply
$ 0	_____	—
2	_____	_____
4	_____	_____
8	_____	_____
16	_____	_____
32	_____	_____

2. Graph the labor-supply curve in Figure 30.1. First label the axes for the graph and then draw the curve and label it. (The curve should pass through point *A*.)

Figure 30.1

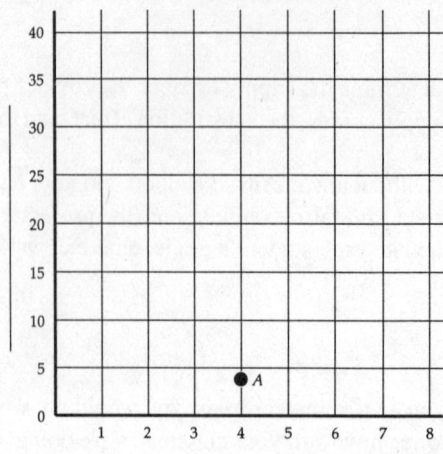

Backward-Bending Supply Curves

3. On the backward-bending segment of a supply curve, wage and quantity supplied are:
   (a) Directly (positively) related.
   (b) Inversely related.
   (c) Related by a horizontal line.
   (d) Related by a vertical line.

4. Which of the following circumstances might explain a backward-bending supply curve such as the one you have drawn in Figure 30.1?
   (a) You want to make a certain amount of income, and you want to spend the rest of your time sleeping and watching videos.
   (b) Because of the increased income you receive from an increase in your wage, you can increase your leisure without losing any income.
   (c) The marginal utility of each extra dollar falls as income rises.
   (d) All of the above might explain such a curve.

Substitution and Income Effects

5. An increase in wage rates:
   (a) Definitely increases hours worked through both the substitution and income effects.
   (b) Tends to increase hours worked through the substitution effect but may tend to decrease hours worked through the income effect.
   (c) Tends to increase hours worked through the substitution effect but definitely decreases hours worked through the income effect.
   (d) Tends to decrease hours worked through the substitution effect and may increase hours worked through the income effect.

6. On the backward-bending portion of the supply curve:
   (a) The income effect is greater than the substitution effect.
   (b) The substitution effect overpowers the income effect.
   (c) Both effects tend to decrease the quantity of labor supplied as a result of a wage increase.

7. In column 3 of Table 30.1, compute the elasticity of supply between each successive wage rate. Use the midpoint formula from the text.

Exercise 2

This exercise illustrates the relationship between marginal physical product and marginal revenue product for a company producing bottled water.

1. T F The marginal physical product (MPP) measures the change in total output that occurs when one additional worker is hired.

2. Which of the following formulas would provide a correct calculation of the marginal physical product?
   (a) Quantity / labor
   (b) Change in quantity /labor
   (c) Change in quantity / change in labor
   (d) Change in total revenue /change in labor

3. Calculate total revenue, marginal revenue product, and marginal physical product for Table 30.2.

Table 30.2. Marginal physical product and marginal revenue product

(1) Labor (workers per hour)	(2) Quantity produced (gallons per hour)	(3) Price (dollars per gallon)	(4) Total revenue (dollars per hour)	(5) Marginal revenue product (dollars per worker)	(6) Marginal physical product (gallons per worker)
0	0	$1	_____	_____	_____
1	15	1	_____	_____	_____
2	27	1	_____	_____	_____
3	36	1	_____	_____	_____
4	42	1	_____	_____	_____
5	45	1	_____	_____	_____
6	46	1	_____	_____	_____

_____ 4. The law of diminishing returns implies that:
   (a) The marginal revenue declines as additional labor is employed in a given production process.
   (b) The marginal revenue product declines as additional labor is employed in a given production process.
   (c) The marginal physical product of labor increases as additional labor is employed in a given production process.
   (d) None of the above.

5. T F There are diminishing returns to labor with increased production in Table 30.2.

Exercise 3

This exercise provides experience in computing and graphing derived demand as well as determining the number of workers to hire.

1. You are the producer of a sports drink called EnerG, which sells for $1 per gallon. You have to pay $6 an hour for labor. Complete Table 30.3.

Table 30.3 EnerG production, by labor hours

(1) Wage (dollars per hour)	(2) Labor (workers per hour)	(3) Quantity produced (gallons per hour)	(4) Price (dollars per gallon)	(5) Total revenue (dollars per gallon)	(6) Marginal revenue product (dollars per worker)
6	0	0	$1	$ _____	$ _____
6	1	15	1	_____	_____
6	2	27	1	_____	_____
6	3	36	1	_____	_____
6	4	42	1	_____	_____
6	5	45	1	_____	_____
6	6	46	1	_____	_____

2. T   F   The demand curve for EnerG workers is found by plotting the marginal revenue product curve.

3. In Figure 30.2 draw the demand curve for labor from Table 30.3. Label it demand or MRP.

Figure 30.2

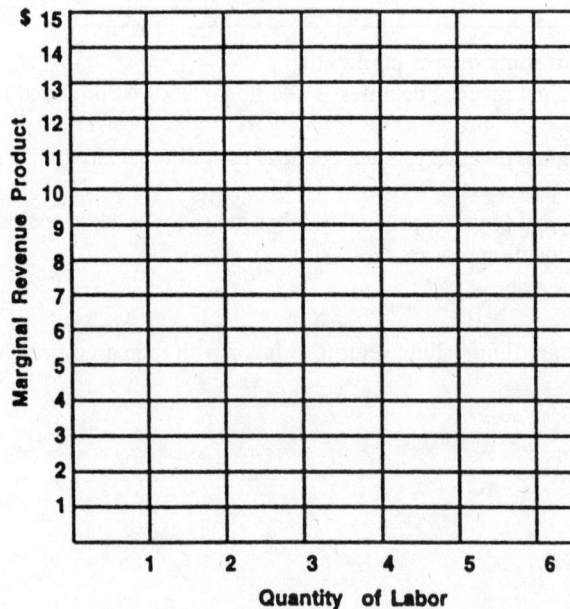

422

4. Draw a straight line at a wage of $6 in Figure 30.2 and label it wage rate.

5. How many workers are you willing to hire to produce EnerG?
   (a) 0.
   (b) 1.
   (c) 2.
   (d) 3.
   (e) 4.
   (f) 5.
   (g) 6.

6. How much EnerG will be produced per hour? _____

Exercise 4

This exercise examines the impact of a minimum wage on a labor market.

Figure 30.3

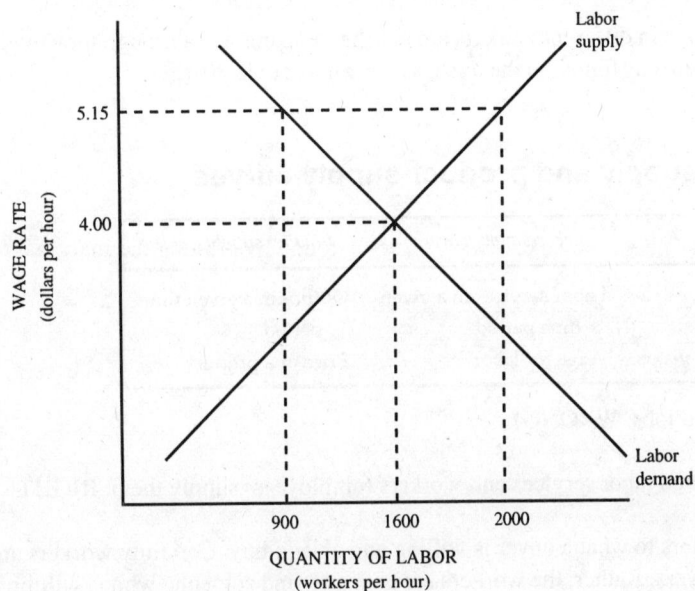

1. Figure 30.3 shows the labor market for unskilled workers. The equilibrium wage rate occurs at _____ per hour and at a quantity of _____ workers.

2. Now assume that the minimum wage is set at $5.15 per hour. The result of this government intervention is to create a (shortage, surplus) of labor.

3. At the new minimum wage _____ workers keep their jobs and _____ workers lose their jobs.

4. According to the article in the text titled "Clinton Wants Minimum Wage Up $1 by 2000", why does Clinton believe a minimum wage is important? _____

5. An increase in labor productivity in Figure 30.3 would cause the labor (supply, demand) curve to shift to the (left, right).

423

Common Errors

The first statement in each "common error" below is incorrect. Each incorrect statement is followed by a corrected version and an explanation.

1. People work because they have to. WRONG!

    Generally, people work in order to buy the goods and services they want. RIGHT!

    People have flexibility in choosing the conditions under which they will work. What they *choose* to do reflects their utility of leisure compared with their utility of the goods and services they can buy with their income from work. If their needs for goods were satisfied, they might not work at all.

2. The labor-supply curve is the same as the supply curve of the products that labor produces. WRONG!

    The labor-supply curve is a supply curve in a factor market, whereas a product supply curve applies to a product market. RIGHT!

    Supply curves in different markets are not the same curves, although they may look the same. The chief difference is found on the axes, as shown in Table 30.4.

Table 30.4
Axes of labor-supply and product-supply curves

Axis	Labor-supply curve	Product supply curve
x-axis	Labor services in a given time period	Output in a given time period
y-axis	Wage for labor	Price of a product

3. Workers demand jobs. WRONG!

    Employers demand labor services and workers (employees) supply them. RIGHT!

    Demand refers to what a buyer is willing and able to buy. Certainly workers are not seeking to pay their employers. Rather, the workers are trying to find someone who is willing and able to pay them for their labor.

4. Employers employ those factors that are least expensive. WRONG!

    Employers want to employ those factors that are most cost-effective. RIGHT!

    If a factor is cheap, there may be a reason for it. It may not last long, may not work correctly, or may require heavier use of other factors of production—for example, maintenance workers. The marginal productivity of the cheap factor may therefore be low. An apparently more expensive factor might perform its proper function well and even save on the costs of other factors. The marginal productivity of the more expensive input would more than make up for its higher cost. Businesses would choose the more expensive factor of production.

5. Marginal revenue product is the same as marginal revenue. WRONG!

The marginal revenue product curve applies to the factor market, while the marginal revenue curve applies to the product market. RIGHT!

The formula for marginal revenue product is

$$\frac{\text{Change in total revenue}}{\text{Change in quantity of input}}$$

while that for marginal revenue is

$$\frac{\text{Change in total revenue}}{\text{Change in quantity of output}}$$

Marginal revenue shows changes in total revenue as a result of increased output and therefore is appropriate in analyzing what happens in the product market.

Marginal revenue product shows how total revenue changes as a result of the increased use of a factor and therefore is appropriate in analyzing what happens in the factor market. Both curves are derived from the demand curve in the product market. However, in order to find marginal revenue product, it is necessary also to know the relationship between the quantity of input and quantity of output. That is why the marginal physical product becomes important.

6. The law of diminishing returns means that average total costs will rise as a firm expands. WRONG!

The law of diminishing returns applies only to changes in the use of one factor while all others remain constant. RIGHT!

If a firm could expand all factors of production proportionately, there might be no decline in productivity at all, and thus no increase in average total cost. If the firm could do so without affecting factor prices, there would then be no change in unit costs either. The law of diminishing returns applies to changes of only one factor or group of factors, *ceteris paribus* (all other factors being held constant).

7. No one is hurt when companies are taxed except the companies themselves. WRONG!

Part of the burden of taxes on a company may fall on the factors of production that a company employs. RIGHT!

Remember that the demand for factors is derived from the product market. If the sales tax, for example, affects the demand curve for a product, it will affect the demand curve for the factors used to produce the product.

•ANSWERS•

Using Key Terms
Across
1. efficiency decision
7. equilibrium wage
13. elasticity of labor supply
14. labor supply
15. production process

Down

2. derived demand
3. substitution effect of wages
4. law of diminishing returns
5. marginal physical product
6. income effect of wages
8. marginal revenue product
9. market supply of labor
10. cost efficiency
11. opportunity wage
12. demand for labor

True or False

1. T
2. F The intersection of supply and demand establishes the equilibrium wage. The minimum wage is typically set above the equilibrium wage by the government.
3. F For wages to be higher without sacrificing jobs the MPP must increase (or the price of the product must increase).
4. T
5. T
6. F The demand for labor is downward sloping because of diminishing returns caused by the fact that the amount of capital and space available to each worker decreases.
7. T
8. F When fewer workers are hired total output is typically lower. It is also usually true, however, that when fewer workers are hired the MPP of the last worker increases.
9. F The MPP multiplied by the price of the product equals the MRP which is the labor-demand curve.
10. T

Multiple Choice

1. b	5. a	9. d	13. b	17. b
2. b	6. c	10. c	14. b	18. d
3. c	7. a	11. d	15. c	19. c
4. d	8. b	12. c	16. a	20. a

Problems and Applications

Exercise 1

1. See Table 30.1 Answer, column 2.

Table 30.1 Answer

(1) Hourly wage (dollars per hour)	(2) Work effort (hours worked per day)	(3) Elasticity of supply
$ 0	0	----
2	1	1.0
4	4	1.8
8	6	0.6
16	8	0.429
32	6	-0.429

2. **Figure 30.1 Answer**

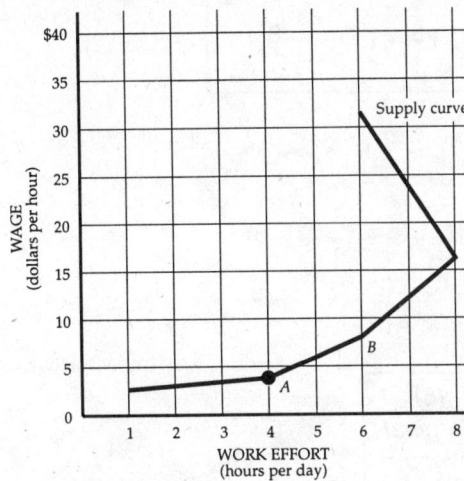

3. b   4. d   5. b   6. a

7. See Table 30.1 Answer, column 3. The formula for the elasticity of labor supply is

$$\frac{\text{Percentage change in quantity of labor supplied}}{\text{Percentage change in wage rate}}$$

The elasticity of labor supply can be estimated (just as the elasticity of demand was estimated) by using the following midpoint formula:

$$\frac{(L_2 - L_1) \div [1/2 \times (L_2 + L_1)]}{(W_2 - W_1) \div [1/2 \times (W_2 + W_1)]} = \frac{(6 - 8) \div [(1/2 \times (6 - 8)]}{(32 - 16) \div [(1/2 \times (32 - 16)]} = \frac{3}{7}$$

In the formula, L_1 is the amount of labor offered at the wage W_1 in period 1 and L_2 is the amount of labor offered at the wage W_2 in period 2. (*Note:* Elasticity is negative only on the backward-bending part of the supply curve.)

Exercise 2

1. T
2. c
3. **Table 30.2 Answer**

(1) Labor	(4) Total revenue	(5) Marginal revenue product	(6) Marginal physical product
0	----	----	----
1	$15	$15	15
2	27	12	12
3	36	9	9
4	42	6	6
5	45	3	3
6	46	1	1

4. b
5. T

Exercise 3

1. **Table 30.3 Answer**

(2) Labor	(5) Total revenue	(6) Marginal revenue product
0	$ 0	$ ----
1	15	15
2	27	12
3	36	9
4	42	6
5	45	3
6	46	1

2. T

3. **Figure 30.2 Answer**

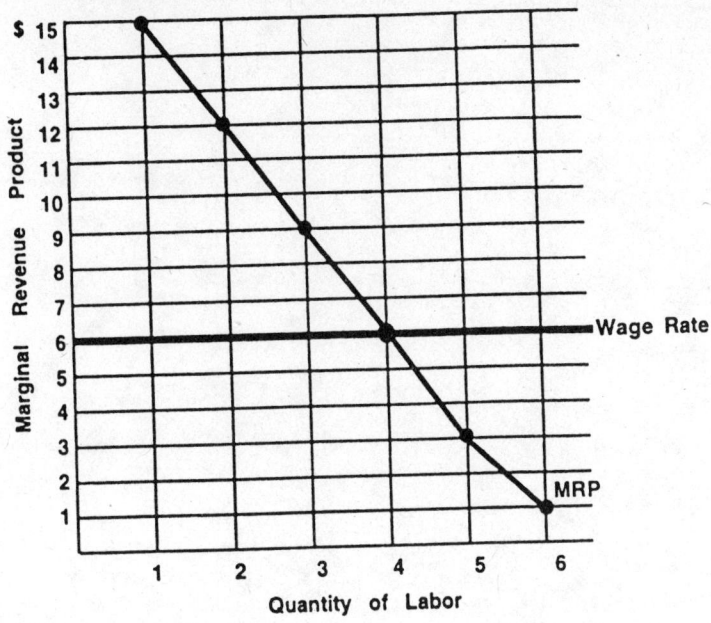

4. See Figure 30.2 Answer
5. 4
6. 42

Exercise 4

1. $4.00, 1600
2. surplus
3. 900, 700
4. ". . . to help families coming off welfare."
5. demand, right

CHAPTER 31

Labor Unions

Quick Review

The outcomes in the labor market, including the wage rate and level of employment, can be distorted by market power on either the supply or demand side. This chapter investigates power in labor markets by looking first at labor unions and then at powerful employers. We examine the following:

- How do large and powerful employers affect market wages?
- How do labor unions alter wages and employment?
- What outcomes are possible from collective bargaining between management and unions?

Power in labor markets means the ability to influence wage rates. Where the labor market is segmented by geographical, occupational, or industrial boundaries, a very few firms or unions may have market power. In extreme cases, a single labor union may contract all of one type of labor and thus be a monopoly, or a single firm may be the only buyer in a particular market, thereby becoming a monopsonist.

Unions typically negotiate over a large number of objectives. The most important is usually the wage rate. But a union's power is based on its membership. If wages rise, the number of workers hired may decline (law of demand). Unions therefore tend to reduce the number of people they permit to be employed and to bargain for higher wages than they would seek if the labor market were competitive.

In a competitive labor market the market equates the supply of labor with the demand for labor to determine the equilibrium wage. However, unions may behave like monopolists. They may restrict employment so that supply and the marginal wage rate are equated. The marginal wage rate is the change in total wages that results from employment of an extra unit of labor. The union tries to negotiate a wage as far above this marginal wage rate as possible. If a firm has market power, it will try to keep wages down to the marginal wage rate.

The dilemma faced by firms that have market power is the opposite of the one confronting labor unions: the more labor an employer seeks, the higher the wages will have to be. And when wages are raised for any worker, they must be raised for everyone. The marginal factor cost is therefore higher than the market wage rate. The marginal factor cost is the change in total wage costs that results from the hiring of an extra unit of labor. It is the marginal factor cost, not the market wage rate (i.e., on the labor-supply curve), that a firm equates with marginal revenue product (found on the labor-demand curve). Like unions, monopsonists fail to employ the amount of labor that would be employed in a competitive labor market. Unlike unions, employers will try to pay *less* than the competitive wage. They will force the wage somewhere between the marginal revenue product of labor and the market wage rate.

In bilateral monopolies, where power exists on both sides of the labor market, unions and employers engage in collective bargaining to negotiate a final settlement. The ultimate settlement for wages and employment depends on the skill of the negotiators.

The percentage of workers in the U.S. economy who belong to a union has been declining for forty years and union power has thus waned as well. Two noticeable trends have emerged as a result. Old industrial unions are being supplanted by unions of service workers, especially in the public sector, and private sector unions have been merging to enhance their power.

Whether unions have been effective in achieving their goals is a question that must be addressed empirically. There is general agreement that unions have raised relative wages significantly. Labor's *share* of national income has also increased, but this is thought to be due largely to changes in the structure of the economy, not union power. Union work rules are thought to restrain *productivity growth*. If this is true, it certainly provides an incentive for firms to raise product prices if wage settlements exceed productivity improvements. Finally, even though the unionization ratio is significantly lower than it used to be, organized labor is still a potent political force.

Learning Objectives

After reading Chapter 31 and doing the following exercises, you should:

1. Understand the characteristics that are used to define the boundaries of labor markets.
2. Be able to demonstrate the meaning of the equilibrium wage rate.
3. Be able to describe the various types of labor buyers and suppliers.
4. Be familiar with the history of labor unions and their role in the economy.
5. Be able to define, compute, and graph the marginal wage curve and the demand curve for labor.
6. Be able to determine the optimal level of employment from a union point of view.
7. Know how to measure union power using the unionization ratio.
8. Be able to define, compute, and graph the marginal factor cost of labor and the supply curve of labor.
9. Be able to describe the monopsonist's desired equilibrium.
10. Understand how wages are determined in a market characterized by bilateral monopoly.
11. Be able to discuss the impact of unions in the U.S. economy.

Using Key Terms

Fill in the puzzle on the opposite page with the appropriate term from the list of Key Terms at the end of the chapter in the text.

Across

2. The change in total wages paid because of a one unit increase in the quantity of labor employed.
5. A market with only one buyer and one seller.
10. The change in total costs because of a one unit increase in the quantity of a factor employed.
11. A workplace in which all workers must join the union within 30 days after being employed.
12. The willingness and ability to work specific amounts of time at alternative wage rates.

Down

1. The quantity of labor employers are willing and able to hire at alternative wages.
2. The change in total revenue because of an additional unit of input.
3. Direct negotiations between employers and unions to determine labor market outcomes.
4. Output per unit of input.
6. The wage rate at which the quantity of labor supplied equals the quantity of labor demanded.
7. The percentage of the labor force belonging to a union.
8. The ability to alter the market price of a good or service.
9. A market in which there is only one buyer.

Puzzle 31.1

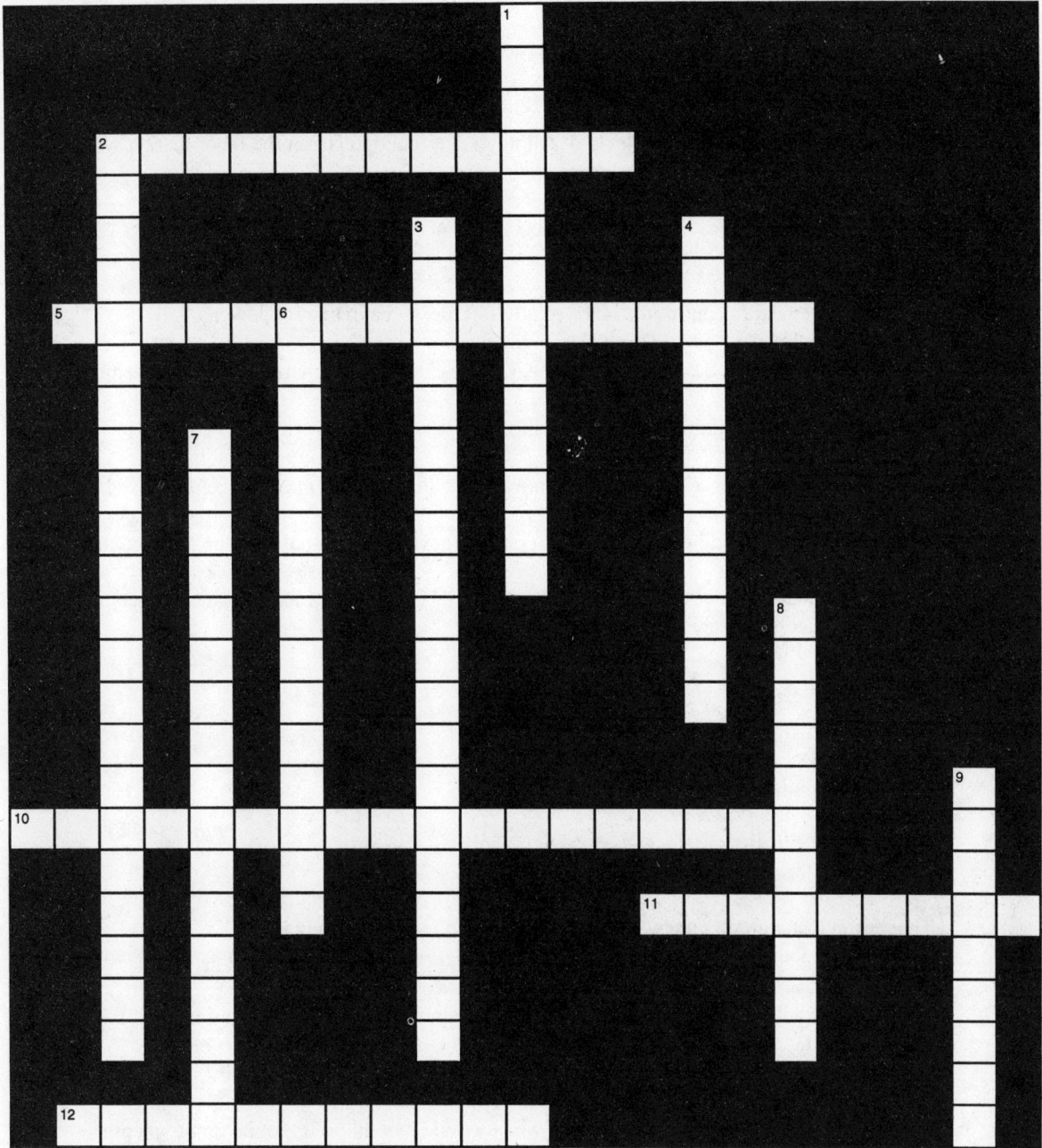

True or False: *Circle your choice and explain why any false statements are incorrect.*

T F 1. The equilibrium wage rate is the rate at which the quantity of labor demanded equals the quantity supplied.

T F 2. When determining the optimum level of employment, monopsonists will equate the marginal wage and the marginal revenue product.

T F 3. When determining the optimum level of employment, monopolists in the labor market will equate the marginal wage and the labor supply curve.

T F 4. The marginal wage curve lies below the labor-demand curve because all worker's wages are lowered when one more worker is hired.

T F 5. Unions do not need to control the labor supply in order to have market power.

T F 6. Wars have aided union development, whereas depressions tend to hurt the union movement.

T F 7. The U.S. unionization ratio is about one-half of the labor force.

T F 8. A monopsony employer seeks to establish a wage rate that is lower than competitive standards.

T F 9. The collective bargaining process results in prices above the marginal revenue product curve.

T F 10. Unions are thought to be responsible for the rise in labor's share of national income and the rise in relative wages for unionized workers.

Multiple Choice: *Select the correct answer.*

_____ 1. Typical goals of a labor union in the United States include:
   (a) Job security.
   (b) Wages.
   (c) Fringe benefits.
   (d) All of the above.

_____ 2. The reason that a union may worry about having too many members is that:
   (a) The union faces a downward-sloping marginal revenue product curve.
   (b) It may be unable to control all of its members.
   (c) It may not be able to reach optimal employment, at which the marginal labor cost curve intersects the demand curve.
   (d) None of the above.

_____ 3. Total wages paid to labor are maximized when workers are hired up to the point where:
   (a) The marginal wage is equal to the market wage.
   (b) The demand for labor is equal to the marginal factor cost.
   (c) The market wage equals the marginal factor cost.
   (d) The marginal wage equals zero.

_____ 4. Unions must distinguish between the marginal wage and the market wage, but nonunion workers generally do not:
(a) Because the demand curve for labor from the union point of view slopes downward.
(b) Because for a nonunion worker who has no market power, the demand curve appears flat.
(c) Because for a nonunion worker who has no market power, the demand curve is the same as the marginal wage curve.
(d) For all of the above reasons.

_____ 5. From a union's perspective, the optimal level of employment is determined by the intersection of:
(a) The labor-demand curve and the labor-supply curve.
(b) The marginal wage curve and the labor-supply curve.
(c) The labor-demand curve and the marginal wage curve.
(d) The labor-demand curve and the marginal factor cost curve.

_____ 6. The unionization ratio represents the:
(a) Percentage of the total labor force belonging to unions.
(b) Market power of unions relative to the market power of nonunion labor.
(c) Proportion of industries that are dominated by unions.
(d) Annual percentage growth in the total number of unions.

_____ 7. To be successful in changing wage rates and employment conditions, labor unions need to have control over only:
(a) Their own members.
(b) The supply of labor to the market.
(c) The _MRP_ of employers.
(d) The production decision of employers.

_____ 8. A craft union:
(a) Exerts market power by controlling the supply of labor to a particular industry.
(b) Exerts market power by controlling the supply of labor to a particular firm.
(c) Is an organization of workers with a particular skill.
(d) Is an organization of workers in a particular industry.

_____ 9. At a union-imposed level of employment:
(a) Employment is lower than at the competitive equilibrium.
(b) The marginal wage is negative.
(c) Employment and wages are both at the maximum possible levels.
(d) Employment would not be increased by reducing the wage rate.

_____ 10. A monopsonist must pay a higher wage rate to hire additional workers because:
(a) As a single seller in the market, it has market power.
(b) As a single buyer in the market, it faces an upward-sloping supply curve for labor.
(c) As a single seller in the market, it does not have to compete with other firms for customers.
(d) As a single buyer in the market, it faces a flat supply curve for labor.

_____ 11. The difference between a competitive labor market and a monopsonistic labor market is:
(a) That the monopsony will attempt to charge a higher wage than will be charged in a competitive market, _ceteris paribus._
(b) That the monopsony will hire less labor than will be hired in a competitive market, _ceteris paribus._
(c) That the shape of the marginal revenue product curve of a monopsony will differ from that of a competitive market.
(d) All of the above.

_____ 12. The marginal factor cost for labor is:
   (a) The net cost to a monopsonist of hiring an additional unit of labor.
   (b) The net gain to a monopolist seller of labor if an additional unit of labor is hired.
   (c) The demand for labor.
   (d) The supply of labor.

_____ 13. If the employers in a competitive labor market decided to collude, *ceteris paribus,* then most likely:
   (a) Wages would rise and employment would fall.
   (b) Wages would rise and employment would rise.
   (c) Wages would fall and employment would fall.
   (d) Wages would fall and employment would rise.

_____ 14. A profit-maximizing monopsonist will hire workers to the point where the marginal factor cost curve intersects the:
   (a) Marginal wage curve.
   (b) Equilibrium wage.
   (c) Marginal revenue product curve.
   (d) Labor-supply curve.

_____ 15. The buyer's profit-maximizing level of input use occurs at:
   (a) Marginal wage = marginal factor cost.
   (b) MRP = marginal wage.
   (c) Marginal wage = zero.
   (d) MRP = marginal factor cost.

_____ 16. A workplace that requires workers to become a member within thirty days of being hired by a firm is:
   (a) A craft union.
   (b) An industrial union.
   (c) A union shop.
   (d) The AFL-CIO.

_____ 17. Which of the following correctly assesses the impact of unions in the U.S. economy?
   (a) Unions have been successful in raising both the relative wages and the absolute wages of their members.
   (b) Union work rules have contributed to inflation because productivity increases have generally exceeded wage increases.
   (c) The political power of unions has grown because the unionization ratio has grown at the same rate as the labor force.
   (d) Unions have been successful at raising relative wages but not absolute wages.

_____ 18. The trend in the U.S. toward the merger of unions is driven by the labor movement's desire to:
   (a) Increase representation.
   (b) Increase financial support.
   (c) Enhance their political power.
   (d) All of the above.

_____ 19. In a bilateral monopoly, wages and employment are determined by:
   (a) Negotiation.
   (b) The intersection of market supply and demand.
   (c) The intersection of marginal cost and marginal revenue product.
   (d) The intersection of marginal wage and market demand.

_____ 20. Unions have had an adverse impact on the efficiency of U.S. firms by supporting which of the following types of legislation?
    (a)   Civil rights legislation.
    (b)   Tariffs and quotas.
    (c)   Health and education programs.
    (d)   All of the above.

Problems and Applications

Exercise 1

This exercise provides practice in calculating the marginal factor cost of labor (marginal wage) and the marginal revenue product of labor for a monopsony situation.

1. Suppose the data in Table 31.1 represent the wages, number of workers, and the price that you face when producing different amounts of Roaring Ripple, a new soft drink. Complete Table 31.1.

Table 31.1
Labor market with variable wage

(1) Labor (workers per hour)	(2) Wage (dollars per hour)	(3) Ripple (quarts per hour)	(4) Price (dollars per quart)	(5) TC (dollars per hour) (1) x (2)	(6) MFC (dollars per worker) ($\Delta TC/\Delta L$)	(7) TR (dollars per hour) (3) x (4)	(8) MRP (dollars per worker) ($\Delta TR/\Delta L$)
0	$1	0	$1	$ _____	$ ___	$ _____	$ ___
1	2	15	1	_____	_____	_____	_____
2	7	27	1	_____	_____	_____	_____
3	9	36	1	_____	_____	_____	_____

2. The amount of Roaring Ripple you will produce to maximize your profits is _____ ; the wage you will pay your workers is _____ ; the marginal cost of labor will be _____ ; the number of employees you will hire will be _____ .

3. T   F   For each new worker you hire, you must raise wages for all of the workers together, which means that the marginal cost of labor is different from the supply curve of labor.

4. T   F   The wage at which the marginal cost of labor curve intersects the marginal revenue product curve is the equilibrium wage rate.

Exercise 2

The differences in labor goals are the focus of this exercise.

Suppose that the supply and demand schedules in Table 31.2 apply to a particular labor market.

Table 31.2
Labor supply and demand

Wage rate (dollars per hour)	$14	13	12	11	10	9	8	7	6	5
Quantity of labor demanded (workers per hour)	0	1	2	3	4	5	6	7	8	9
Total wage bill (dollars per hour)	—	—	—	—	—	—	—	—	—	—
Marginal wage (dollars per worker)	—	—	—	—	—	—	—	—	—	—

Wage rate (dollars per hour)	$3	4	5	6	7
Quantity of labor supplied (workers per hour)	1	3	5	7	9
Total wage (dollars per hour)	—	—	—	—	—
Marginal factor cost (dollars per worker)	—	—	—	—	—

Figure 31.1

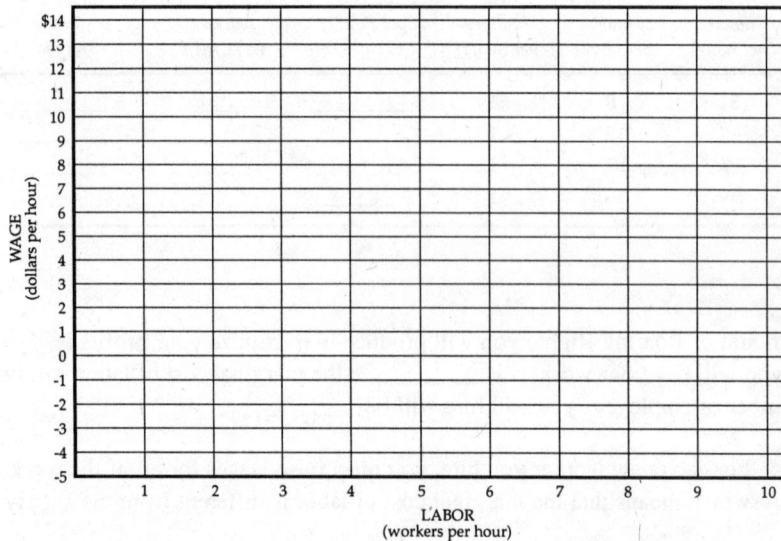

1. Compute the marginal wage and the marginal factor cost in the space provided in Table 31.2.

2. Graph labor demand, labor supply, marginal wage, and marginal factor cost curve in Figure 31.1.

3. The amount of labor hired in a competitive market would be _____ workers at a wage of _____ per hour.

4. The amount of labor that a union would want hired if it acted as a monopolist would be _____ workers at a wage of _____ per hour.

5. Suppose a union asks each member to contribute a certain percentage of income to the union. Therefore, when the wage bill is maximized the union maximizes the dues it receives. The amount of labor that would maximize union dues would be _____ workers at a wage of _____ per hour.

6. Suppose the union wishes to maximize the number of employees that it has so that it can become a political force at the ballot box. The maximum amount of labor that such a union would be able to recruit would be _____ workers at a wage of _____ per hour.

7. The amount of labor hired by a monopsonist would be _____ workers at a wage of _____ per hour.

Following are the names of the five types of labor market situations described in question 3-7:

    A.   Competition (question 3)
    B.   Union monopolist (question 4)
    C.   Union dues maximizer (question 5)
    D.   Union vote maximizer (question 6)
    E.   Monopsony (question 7)

8. Label the wage-labor combination in Figure 31.1 corresponding to the letter of each of these types of labor markets.

9. Rank this list of labor markets in order (highest to lowest) with respect to wage rates and then rank (lowest to highest) with respect to the total employment. When there is a tie, place both types of market on the same line.

	Wage		Amount of labor
(rank)	(highest to lowest)	(rank)	(lowest to highest)
1.	_____	1.	_____
2.	_____	2.	_____
3.	_____	3.	_____
4.	_____	4.	_____
5.	_____	5.	_____

10. T F Market power, regardless of whether it is possessed by the buyer or the supplier, results in output equal to or lower than in a competitive labor market.

11. T F Market power, regardless of whether it is possessed by the buyer or the supplier, results in wage rates higher than in a competitive labor market.

Exercise 3

Reread the *In the News* article entitled "Free Agents In Sports: A Threat to Monopsony." Then answer the following questions.

1. Before 1976, team owners had _____ power in the labor market.

2. As players were allowed to become "free agents," player salaries (increased, decreased, did not change).

3. For a monopsonist, the marginal factor cost is (greater, less) than the wage rate because additional workers can be hired only if the wage rate for all workers (increases, decreases).

4. A monopsonist hires (more, fewer) workers at a (higher, lower) wage rate than would occur in a competitive market.

Common Errors

The first statement in each "common error" below is incorrect. Each incorrect statement is followed by a corrected version and an explanation.

1. The marginal cost of labor curve is the same as the marginal cost curve, and therefore it is also the supply curve for a firm. WRONG!

    The marginal cost of labor curve is derived from the supply of labor and is applicable only to the labor market, not to the product market. RIGHT!

    The marginal cost of labor is given by the formula

    $$\frac{\text{Change in total wage cost}}{\text{Change in quantity of labor}}$$

    while the marginal cost curve is given by

    $$\frac{\text{Change in total wage cost}}{\text{Change in quantity of product}}$$

    While the marginal cost of labor applies only to labor costs in the labor market, the marginal cost curve applies to all costs in the product market.

2. In bilateral monopoly the optimal level of employment occurs where the marginal cost of labor curve intersects the marginal wage curve. WRONG!

    In bilateral monopoly, it is possible to determine the limits between which the labor employment and wage levels will fall but not the precise optimal levels. RIGHT!

    The buyer wishes to buy labor at the point where the marginal cost of labor curve intersects the labor-demand curve. Only through negotiation can a compromise be worked out. The final outcome reflects the relative market power of supplier and buyer.

3. Powerful unions can get whatever wage they want. WRONG!

    Powerful unions are limited by the demand for labor. RIGHT!

    If unions make and receive exorbitant wage demands, they may find the union membership dwindling as more employees are laid off. Frequently, unions moderate wage demands in order to prevent employers from going out of business, foreign competition from undercutting prices, and nonunionized workers from becoming attractive to employers. All of these considerations reflect the law of demand.

•ANSWERS•

Using Key Terms
Across
2. marginal wage
5. bilateral monopoly
10. marginal factor cost
11. union shop
12. labor supply

Down
1. demand for labor
2. marginal revenue product
3. collective bargaining
4. productivity
6. equilibrium wage
7. unionization ratio
8. market power
9. monopsony

True or False

1. T
2. F Monopsonists will equate marginal factor cost and marginal revenue product.
3. T
4. T
5. F To maintain higher than equilibrium wages labor supply must be reduced.
6. F Unions tend to gain power during downturns in the economy.
7. F Only about one-seventh of the U.S. labor force is unionized.
8. T
9. F The marginal revenue curve sets an upper limit for wages because it measures the value of each worker to the firm.
10. T

Multiple Choice

1. d	5. b	9. a	13. c	17. a
2. a	6. a	10. b	14. c	18. d
3. d	7. b	11. b	15. d	19. a
4. d	8. c	12. a	16. c	20. b

Problems and Applications

Exercise 1

1. **Table 31.1 Answer**

(1) Labor	(2) Wage	(5) TC	(6) MFC	(7) TR	(8) MRP
0	$1	$ 0	$ ---	$ 0	$ ---
1	2	2	2	15	15
2	7	14	12	27	12
3	9	27	13	36	9

2. 27 quarts per hour; $7 per hour; $12 per hour; 2 employees per hour
3. T
4. F

Exercise 2

1. **Table 31.2 Answer**

Wage rate (dollars per hour)	$14	13	12	11	10	9	8	7	6	5
Quantity of labor demanded (workers per hour)	0	1	2	3	4	5	6	7	8	9
Total wage bill (dollars per hour)	0	13	24	33	40	45	48	49	48	45
Marginal wage (dollars per worker)	—	13	11	9	7	5	3	1	-1	-3

Wage rate (dollars per hour)	$3	4	5	6	7
Quantity of labor supplied (workers per hour)	1	3	5	7	9
Total wage (dollars per hour)	$3	12	25	42	63
Marginal factor cost (dollars per worker)	3	4.5	6.5	8.5	10.5

2. **Figure 31.1 Answer**

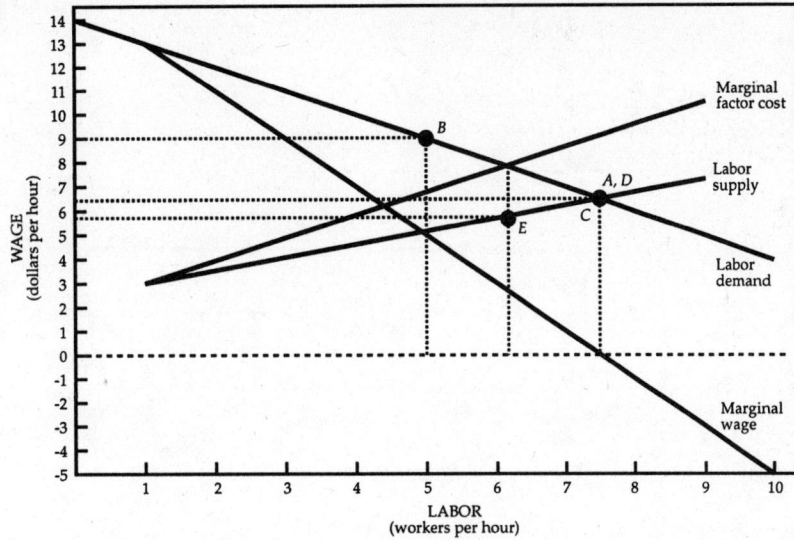

Note: When demand falls below the price at which workers are willing and able to work, there can be no greater employment. So the dues-maximizing and wage bill-maximizing unions will push employment to the competitive level. However, more inelastic demand can mean that wage bill-maximizing unions would produce less than the competitive level at a higher wage.

3. 7 (Labor supply and labor demand intersect at 7.5 workers.); $6.50
4. 5; $9.00
5. 7; $6.50. The wage bill is maximized where the marginal wage intersects the *x*-axis. But the equilibrium amount of labor, where labor supply equals labor demand, tells us the maximum number of workers which could be hired.
6. 7; $6.50
7. 6; $5.75. Remember that a monopsonist forces the wage down to the supply curve from which the wage is read.
8. See the letters marking the points in Figure 16.1 Answer.

9.

Wage (rank)	(highest to lowest)	Amount of labor (rank)	(lowest to highest)
1.	Union monopolist	1.	Union monopolist
2.	Competition	2.	Monopsony
	Union dues maximizer	3.	Competition
	Union vote maximizer		Union vote maximizer
3.	Monopsony		Union dues maximizer

10. T
11. F   Monopsony results in a lower price than the competitive price.

Exercise 3

1. monopsony
2. increased
3. greater, increases
4. fewer, lower

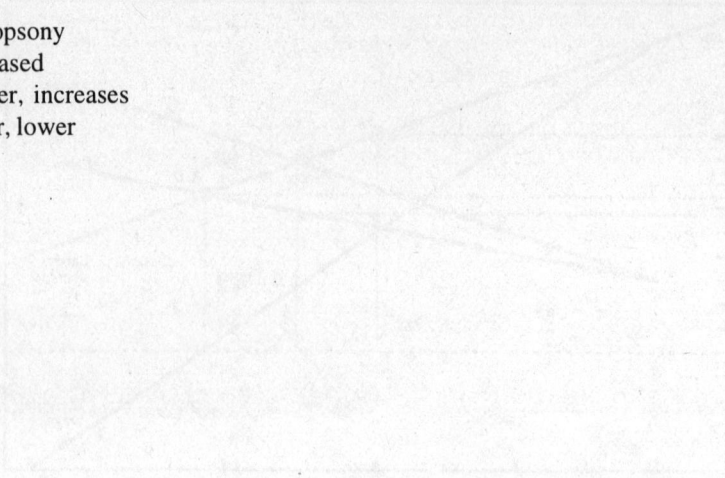

CHAPTER 32

Uncertainty, Risk, and Financial Markets

Quick Review

Financial markets play a critical role in the economy, but the way in which they do so remains a mystery to many people. The objective of this chapter is to provide a basic analysis of how financial markets work. To do this we will focus on the following questions:

- What is traded in financial markets?
- How do the financial markets affect the economic outcomes of WHO, WHAT, and FOR WHOM?
- Why do financial markets fluctuate so much?

In answering these questions we'll look at how financial markets bring together those who wish to save more than they spend (the savers) and those who wish to spend more than they save (the dissavers). Financial markets provide access to the savings pool of funds. This is vital to the process of "spreading the risk" of failure over a large number of individuals. Three distinct financial markets, the stock market, the bond market, and the futures market aid in financial intermediation through which risk spreading occurs. By bringing together savers and spenders, financial intermediaries also reduce the costs of information and search. In doing so, they make the financial markets more efficient.

Financial intermediaries are concerned with the present value of future profits. Future dollars must be discounted by the opportunity cost of money or the market interest rate. Higher interest rates and a longer time until future payment will cause a decrease in the present discounted value of a future payment. Risk also has an impact on the expected value of future payments.

The stock market allows firms to raise capital by selling equities, that is, claims to ownership in a corporation which are then listed on one of several stock exchanges. Naturally, a stock market has both a supply side and a demand side. Changes in the nonprice determinants of the supply of, and the demand for, stocks lead to shifts of the respective curves and, in the process, cause the price to change. Changing expectations regarding the future profitability of particular corporations and the future course of the economy are especially important nonprice determinants on both the supply side and the demand side.

The bond market is a market in which debt instruments called bonds are bought and sold. Each bond is essentially an IOU which states the principal amount, interest, and terms on which the debt must be repaid. While the initial purchasers lend directly to the borrower, the bonds can then be traded in an organized market where, again, their price is determined by the supply and demand for bonds at the time the trade is made. Changes in investors' expectations concerning future interest rates and the borrowers' potential ability to pay interest and repay principal will affect the supply and demand for bonds. Bond yields are inversely related to bond prices.

Venture capitalists provide initial funding for entrepreneurial ventures. If the project is a success, they get profits; if not, losses. Financial markets help the economy in its search for the optimal mix of output by helping to mobilize savings, manage risk, and signal desired resource allocations.

Learning Objectives

After reading Chapter 32 and doing the following exercises, you should:

1. Understand the primary function of financial markets.
2. Understand how financial markets increase efficiency.
3. Know what present discounted value means and how to calculate it.
4. Know that risk has an impact on the expected value of future payments.
5. Understand how companies raise funds through the stock market and the bond market.
6. Know some of the determinants of the demand for and supply of stocks and bonds, and know how changes in those determinants affect stock and bond prices.
7. Be able to explain why bond yields are inversely related to bond prices.
8. Understand the role of venture capitalists.

Using Key Terms

Fill in the puzzle on the opposite page with the appropriate term from the list of Key Terms at the end of the chapter in the text.

Across
1. Amount of corporate profit paid out for each share of stock.
8. The price of a stock share divided by earnings per share.
10. A limited liability form of business.
11. The rate of return on a bond is the current _____.
13. The face value of a bond.
14. The ability of an asset to be converted to cash.
15. The difference in rates of return on risky and safe investments.

Down
2. The first sale to the general public of stock in a corporation.
3. An increase in the market value of an asset.
4. Shares of ownership in a corporation.
5. An institution that brings savers and dissavers together.
6. The value today of future payments, adjusted for interest accrual.
7. The probable value of a future payment, including the risk of nonpayment.
9. An IOU issued by corporations and government agencies.
12. Failure to make scheduled payments of interest or principal on a bond.

Puzzle 32.1

447

True or False: *Circle your choice and explain why any false statements are incorrect.*

T F 1. Financial intermediaries change the mix of output by transferring purchasing power from dissavers to savers.

T F 2. If the opportunity cost of money was zero, the expected value of future dollars would be equal to their present value.

T F 3. A risk premium compensates people who invest in risky ventures that succeed.

T F 4. One reason present dollars are worth more than future dollars is that income-earning investment opportunities exist.

T F 5. The present discounted value of a future payment will decrease when interest rates decrease.

T F 6. Stock prices will increase, ceteris paribus, when the prevailing interest rate increases.

T F 7. When a corporation issues a bond, it is borrowing funds.

T F 8. Interest is a return on the use of money.

T F 9. The present value of a future payment is discounted by potential interest accumulation.

T F 10. Venture capitalists share in the risks and rewards by financing new ventures.

Multiple Choice: *Select the correct answer.*

_____ 1. The function of financial intermediaries is to transfer purchasing power from:
    (a) Dissavers to consumers.
    (b) Savers to dissavers.
    (c) Consumers to savers.
    (d) Dissavers to savers.

_____ 2. Financial intermediaries:
    (a) Reduce search and information costs for savers and investors.
    (b) Transfer purchasing power from spenders to savers.
    (c) Concentrate investment risk.
    (d) Do all of the above.

_____ 3. Present dollars are worth more than future dollars because:
    (a) Income-earning investment opportunities exist.
    (b) There is always a chance that you may not receive the future dollars.
    (c) Of the opportunity cost of money.
    (d) All of the above.

_____ 4. The term present discounted value means:
    (a) The future value of today's dollars.
    (b) The value today of future payments adjusted for inflation.
    (c) The value today of future payments adjusted for interest accrual.
    (d) The value today of future payments adjusted for risk.

5. Higher interest rates:
   (a) Reflect a higher opportunity cost of money.
   (b) Raise the future value of current dollars.
   (c) Lower the present value of future payments.
   (d) All of the above.

6. The present discounted value of a future payment will decrease when the:
   (a) Future payment is further into the future.
   (b) Interest rate decreases.
   (c) Risk of non-payment increases.
   (d) Opportunity cost of money decreases.

7. The possibility of non-payment is taken into account in the calculation of the:
   (a) Present discounted value.
   (b) Future discounted value.
   (c) Expected value.
   (d) Profits.

8. The term expected value means:
   (a) The future value of a current payment.
   (b) The present value of a future payment.
   (c) The probable value of a future payment.
   (d) The difference in the rates of return on risky and safe investments.

9. Suppose that Beth has a 20 percent chance of not collecting $1000 in 3 years. If the interest rate is 10 percent, what is the expected value of the future payment?
   (a) $150.
   (b) $601.
   (c) $751.
   (d) $1065.

10. A motivation for holding stocks is:
    (a) To receive interest payments on the firm's debt.
    (b) To receive potential capital gains.
    (c) To have a direct role in the operation of the corporation.
    (d) All of the above.

11. The purpose of an initial public offering is to:
    (a) Raise funds for investment and growth by selling shares of the company to the public.
    (b) Change the membership of the Board of Directors.
    (c) Borrow funds for investment and growth.
    (d) See if there is a demand for a company's new product.

12. Which of the following determines the price of a stock?
    (a) The amount of stock that people are willing and able to purchase.
    (b) The amount of stock that people offer for sale.
    (c) Expectations of future earnings.
    (d) All of the above.

_____ 13. The price of a stock will increase, *ceteris paribus*, when:
   (a)   When there is a shortage of the stock at the current price.
   (b)   The demand for the stock increases.
   (c)   The supply of the stock decreases.
   (d)   All of the above.

_____ 14. A bond is:
   (a)   A share in a corporation.
   (b)   A coupon used to collect a dividend.
   (c)   An insurance policy investors purchase to protect against the possibility of falling stock prices.
   (d)   A promise to repay a loan.

_____ 15. If a corporation issues bonds which they cannot sell, this is an indication that:
   (a)   Expectations of future sales are low.
   (b)   The coupon rate is too low.
   (c)   Dividends are too low.
   (d)   All of the above.

_____ 16. When investors expect greater future profits from a company, the:
   (a)   Demand for the company's bonds increases.
   (b)   Price of the company's bonds increases.
   (c)   Yield on the company's bonds decreases.
   (d)   All of the above occur.

_____ 17. When the interest rate rises:
   (a)   The demand for loanable funds falls and the supply of loanable funds falls.
   (b)   The demand for loanable funds rises and the supply of loanable funds rises.
   (c)   The demand for loanable funds falls and the supply of loanable funds rises.
   (d)   The quantity of loanable funds demanded falls and the quantity of loanable funds supplied rises.

_____ 18. The present value of $100,000 to be received every year for 3 years when the discount rate is 10 percent is:
   (a) $300,000.
   (b) $248,742.
   (c) $133,100.
   (d) $330,000.

_____ 19. As the interest rate increases, the opportunity cost of money:
   (a)   Increases for both lender and borrower.
   (b)   Increases for the borrower but not the lender.
   (c)   Decreases for both lender and borrower.
   (d)   Decreases for the borrower but not the lender.

_____ 20. As the interest rate increases, *ceteris paribus*, the tradeoff between present and future consumption:
   (a)   Is not affected.
   (b)   Encourages present consumption.
   (c)   Changes in favor of future consumption.
   (d)   Makes it less appealing to sacrifice present consumption.

Problems and Applications

Exercise 1

This exercise shows how to compute the present discounted value of an investment. It also shows how important the interest rate and length of time until payment are in the present value calculation.

1. Suppose you own 1,000 acres of forest land. Next year you could have the trees cut down for lumber and receive $1,320,000 (after taxes and all other expenses). The interest rate is 10 percent. Find the present discounted value of your 1,000 acres of forest land. _____

2. Suppose interest rates rose to 20 percent. What would the present discounted value of cutting down the forest for lumber be at the 20 percent interest rate if the cost and profit were the same as at 10 percent? _____

3. Suppose interest rates are at the original 10 percent. What would the present discounted value of cutting down the forest for lumber be if you had to wait two years to receive $1,320,000?

    _____

4. T F   When the interest rate rises, the present value of an investment rises.

5. T F   The longer one has to wait for a future payment, the less present value it has.

Exercise 2

This exercise uses the loanable funds market to determine the market interest rate and investment.

1. The supply and demand of loanable funds are shown in Figure 32.1. If the supply of loanable funds is S_1, then the equilibrium interest rate is _____ percent.

Figure 32.1
Investment demand, and the supply of loanable funds

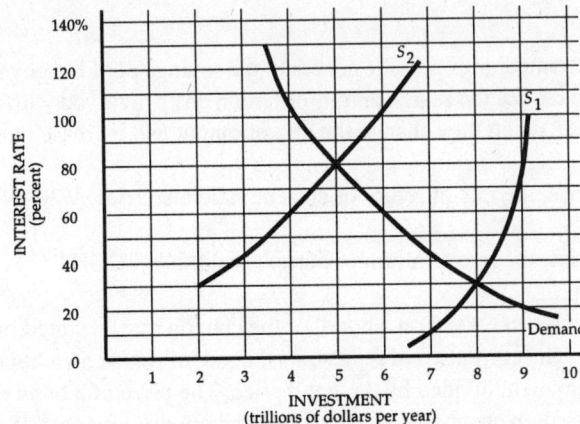

2. At the equilibrium interest rate, the level of investment would equal $_____ trillion.

3. If the supply of loanable funds shifts to S_2, this represents a(an) (increase, decrease) in loanable funds.

4. The equilibrium interest rate would (increase, decrease) to _____ percent and the level of investment would (increase, decrease) to $_____ trillion.

5. One reason for the shift in loanable funds in Figure 31.1 might be the (increase, decrease) in savings by consumers.

Exercise 3

The media often carry information about the amount of money won in lotteries. The reality is often different than what is reported.

Reread pages 653 through 654 in the text about Frank and Shirley Carpaci and their lottery winnings. Then answer the following questions.

1. What was the advertised amount of the payoff from the winning lottery? _____

2. When discounted at 6.2%, what was the present value of the payout? _____

3. What would happen to the present value of the payout if it were discounted at an interest rate greater than 6.2%? _____

4. How many payments was the winner of the lottery to receive? _____

5. If the payoff was made in ten annual installments instead, what would have happened to the present value? _____

Common Errors

The first statement in each "common error" below is incorrect. Each incorrect statement is followed by a corrected version and an explanation.

1. The primary function of financial intermediaries is to provide checking accounts for customers. WRONG!

   The primary function of financial intermediaries is to transfer income from savers to spenders. RIGHT!

   Financial intermediaries provide access to the savings pool for government and the business sector. They also reduce the search and information costs involved with lending and investment opportunities. As a result they change the mix of output and increase market efficiency.

2. As bond prices rise, the rate of return or current yield also rises. WRONG!

   As bond prices rise, the rate of return or current yield falls. RIGHT!

   The rate of interest earned on a bond, or the coupon rate, is stated on the bond certificate and does not change. The current yield represents the rate of return on a bond. It is calculated as the annual interest payment divided by the bond price. The price of a bond in the secondary bond market varies based on changes in expectations and opportunity cost. If the annual interest payment stays constant and the bond price increases, the rate of return or current yield falls.

•ANSWERS•

Using Key Terms
Across
1. dividend
8. price earnings ratio
10. corporation
11. yield
13. par value
14. liquidity
15. risk premium

Down
2. initial public offering
3. capital gain
4. corporate stock
5. financial intermediary
6. present discounted value
7. expected value
9. bond
12. default

True or False

1. F Financial intermediaries change the mix of output by transferring purchasing power from savers to dissavers.
2. F The expected value calculation takes into account the possibility of not getting the future payment. Whenever this is a possibility, future dollars will be worth less than current dollars.
3. T
4. T
5. F The present discounted value of a future payment will increase when interest rates decrease.
6. F Stock prices will decrease when the prevailing interest rate increases because the opportunity cost of holding stocks will increase making stocks a less desirable investment option (i.e. the demand for stocks will decrease).
7. T
8. T
9. T
10. T

Multiple Choice

1. b	5. d	9. b	13. d	17. d
2. a	6. a	10. b	14. d	18. b
3. d	7. c	11. a	15. b	19. a
4. c	8. c	12. d	16. d	20. c

Problems and Applications

Exercise 1

1. $\$1,320,000/(1.10)^1 = \$1,200,000$
2. $\$1,320,000/(1.20)^1 = \$1,100,000$
3. $\$1,320,000/(1.10)^2 = \$1,090,909$
4. F
5. T

Exercise 2

1. 30 percent
2. $8 trillion
3. decrease
4. increase, 80 percent, decrease, $5 trillion
5. decrease

Exercise 3

1. The advertised amount was $195 million.
2. $103.90 million.
3. If discounted at more than 6.2%, the present discounted value would be less than $103.90 million.
4. The text says that the payments were to be made over 24 years.
5. Ten annual installments would raise the present discounted value.

PART 11 Distributional Issues

CHAPTER 33

Taxes: Equity vs. Efficiency

Quick Review

Taxes are used to transfer command of resources from the private sector to the public sector and to redistribute income from the rich to the poor. The impact of taxes on the economy is not always easy to determine, and there appears to be a tradeoff between society's goals of equity and efficiency. Let's focus on the following questions:

- How are incomes distributed in the United States?
- How do taxes alter that distribution?
- How do taxes affect the rate and mix of output?

The distribution of income is a major concern of public policy; it concerns the FOR WHOM question. It should be remembered, however, that income is sometimes not required to get goods and services; welfare payments, for example, are sometimes made in kind. It is also necessary to distinguish between income and wealth, even though the two are obviously related, and both have implications for one's command over goods and services. Income is a flow and is measured over time; wealth is a stock and is measured at a point in time.

The size distribution of income concentrates on the way income is distributed among income-receiving units, such as households. For example, one may be interested in the fraction of total income received by those who constitute the lowest 20 percent of income recipients (households).

The Lorenz curve is a graph that compares the actual distribution of income with a distribution of income in which everyone receives the same income. The Lorenz curve is particularly useful in comparing income distribution before and after taxes. It is generally observed that in the United States, income is distributed somewhat more equally after taxes than before.

One must be extremely careful in talking about taxes and the tax system. Provisions in the tax law, called "loopholes," allow individuals to reduce the amount of income subject to tax. The loopholes also result in a violation of two important principles of taxation—horizontal equity and vertical equity. Because of this, economists use several tax rates—average tax rate, nominal tax rate, effective tax rate, and so on—to analyze the tax system. This is not an easy task. Taxes may also be shifted from one group to another. Even the employer's portion of the social security tax is thought to be borne by the employee. We should also not lose sight of the fact that other levels of government (state and local) tax income and property, too.

While the overall degree of inequality is difficult to determine, one cannot argue with the fact that income is distributed unequally in the United States. Whether the distribution is fair or not is an entirely different matter. Some feel more should be transferred from those with higher incomes to those with lower incomes. Others argue that such a redistribution of income would so damage the incentives of productive, high-income people that total production and income would decline.

Because of the many concerns about such issues as equity, efficiency, and the erosion of the tax base, Congress passed the Tax Reform Act of 1986. This act closed loopholes, reduced marginal tax rates, reduced the number of tax brackets, increased the tax burden of corporations relative to individuals, and provided tax relief for the poor. The new marginal tax rates didn't last long. Revisions in 1990 and 1993 added a fourth bracket, a new marginal tax rate and a surcharge.

Arguments over the equity of the federal income tax will not go away. Most recently Congressman Richard Armey has proposed a "flat tax" of 17% to replace the cumbersome, complex and sometimes contradictory IRS Code. His proposal would eliminate all deductions, credits and most exemptions and would not tax income from savings and investment (interest, dividends and capital gains). Armey's focus is on simplicity (all IRS forms would be eliminated in favor of a single postcard sized one) and on incentives to save and invest. Under this system, he argues, decisions to save and invest would be made on an economic basis rather than to simply avoid taxes.

Critics argue that many provisions Armey would throw out are there to encourage desired economic activity and that the flat tax would hit the middle class particularly hard and reduce the government's ability to alter the mix of output. Massive restructuring and redistribution of wealth and income are also a possibility.

Learning Objectives

After reading Chapter 33 and doing the following exercises, you should:

1. Be able to distinguish between wealth and income.
2. Understand the size distribution of income and be able to interpret a Lorenz curve.
3. Be aware of the impact of taxes and transfers on the distribution of income.
4. Understand the principles of horizontal and vertical equity.
5. Be able to distinguish the marginal and average tax rates, and nominal and effective tax rates.
6. Understand the impact of tax "loopholes."
7. Be able to distinguish arguments for equality from arguments for equity.
8. Be aware of major reforms embodied in the Tax Reform Act of 1986 and the changes in 1990 and 1993.
9. Be able to distinguish among progressive, regressive, and proportional taxes.
10. Recognize that the most serious potential cost of greater equality would be damaged incentives.
11. Be aware of the arguments for and against the proposed "flat tax."

Using Key Terms

Fill in the puzzle on the opposite page with the appropriate term from the list of Key Terms at the end of the chapter in the text.

Across
4. The percentage change in the quantity supplied divided by the percentage change in tax rates.
7. A tax system in which tax rates rise as incomes rise.
14. Taxes paid divided by total income.
15. Taxes paid divided by taxable income.
16. The proportion of total income received by a particular group.
17. The change in total revenue associated with one additional unit of input.
20. The idea that people with higher incomes should pay more taxes.
21. A tax system in which tax rates fall as incomes rise.

Down
1. The tax rate imposed on the last dollar of income.
2. The way total personal income is divided among households.
3. People with equal incomes should pay equal taxes.
5. Distribution of the real burden of a tax.
6. A graph that contrasts complete equality with the actual distribution of income.
7. Income received by households before taxes.
8. Goods and services received directly, without payment in a market transaction.

9. A mathematical summary of inequality based on the Lorenz curve.
10. A situation in which the market mechanism prevents optimal outcomes.
11. A situation in which government intervention fails to improve market outcomes.
12. A single-rate tax system.
13. Payments to individuals for which no current goods or services are exchanged.
18. The amount of income directly subject to nominal tax rates.
19. The market value of assets.

Puzzle 33.1

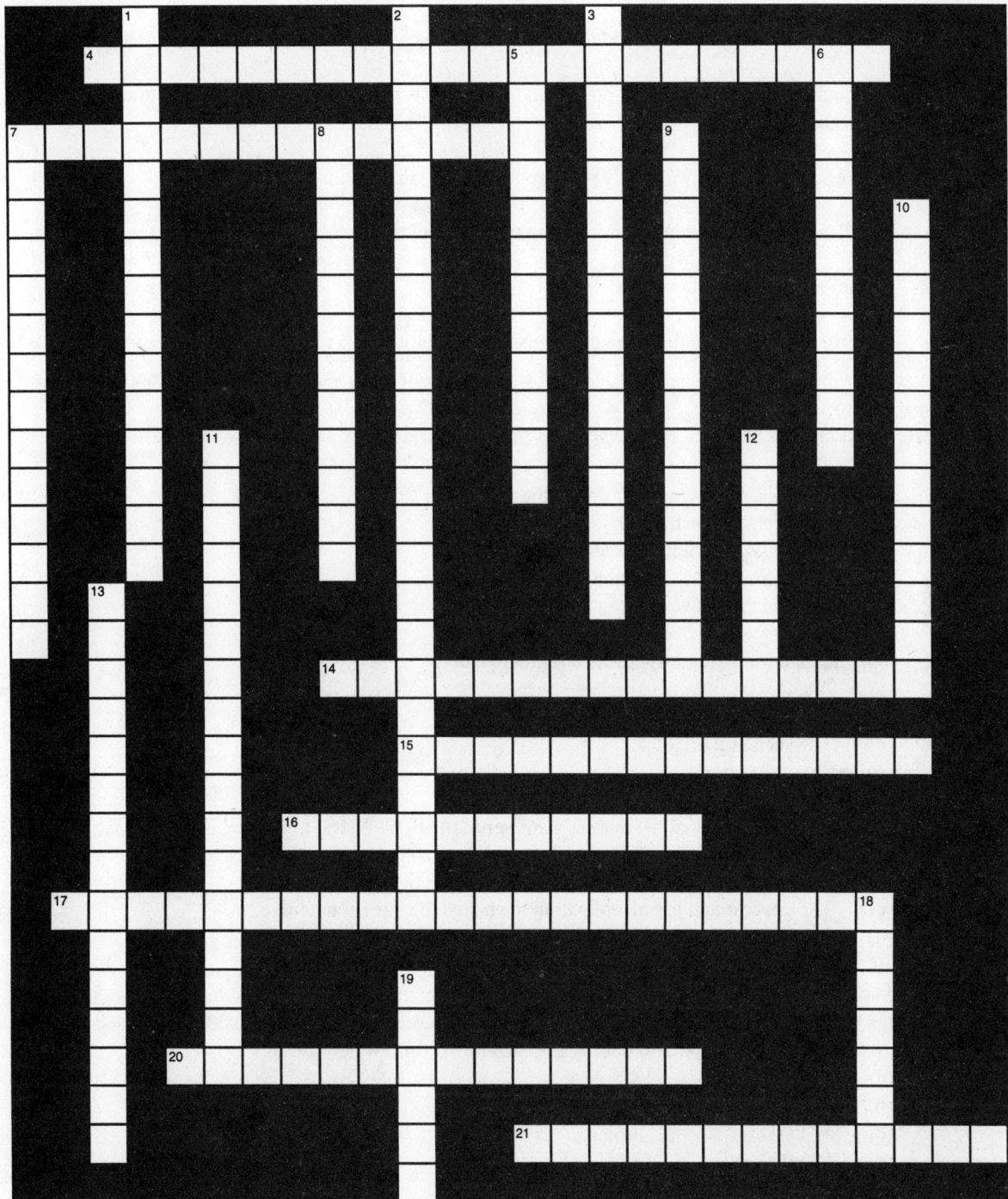

True or False: *Circle your choice and explain why any false statements are incorrect.*

T   F   1.   Marginal tax rates must increase as income increases for a tax to be progressive, *ceteris paribus*.

T   F   2.   When people believe that the market's answer to the FOR WHOM question is suboptimal, taxes can be used as a policy lever to address the problem.

T   F   3.   A flat tax rate would take the same dollar amount from each taxpayer.

T   F   4.   The efficiency issue in taxation refers to the negative impact of higher marginal tax rates on the incentive to produce and work.

T   F   5.   Fewer workers are employed and the net wage is reduced when a payroll tax is imposed.

T   F   6.   The combined effect of federal, state, and local taxes is to increase the degree of income inequality in the United States.

T   F   7.   Greater income equality has only positive impacts on an economy.

T   F   8.   The distribution of money income is synonymous with the distribution of goods and services.

T   F   9.   A sales tax is a proportional tax.

T   F   10.   Government failure results when government intervention fails to improve market outcomes.

Multiple Choice: *Select the correct answer.*

_____ 1.   The distribution of income is basically the answer to:
   (a)   The WHAT question for society.
   (b)   The HOW question for society.
   (c)   The FOR WHOM question for society.
   (d)   None of the above.

_____ 2.   Which of the following is typically a regressive tax?
   (a)   A sales tax.
   (b)   A property tax.
   (c)   The social security tax.
   (d)   All of the above.

_____ 3.   When people believe that the market's answer to the FOR WHOM question is suboptimal:
   (a)   Market failure exists.
   (b)   Taxes can be used as a policy to address the problem.
   (c)   The government has an obligation to change the market outcome.
   (d)   All of the above are correct.

_____ 4.   Suppose that in 1999 Ms. Gonzales had a taxable income of $80,000. Assume that the marginal tax rates are 10% of the first $20,000, 20% of the income in excess of $20,000 to $60,000, and 30% of any income over $60,000. Ms. Gonzales' tax bill was:
   (a) $8,000.
   (b) $16,000.
   (c) $24,000.
   (d) $36,000.

_____ 5. If income is distributed unequally:
  (a) The Lorenz curve would be a straight line.
  (b) The line of equality sags below the Lorenz curve.
  (c) The Lorenz curve sags below the line of equality.
  (d) The Gini coefficient would be greater than zero.

_____ 6. The U.S. tax system results in a slight reduction in inequality of after-tax income because:
  (a) Of the progressive nature of state and local taxes.
  (b) Of the progressive nature of the federal income tax.
  (c) The rich have fewer available loopholes than the poor.
  (d) The poor receive such generous welfare benefits.

_____ 7. Government attempts to create a more equitable income distribution by increasing marginal tax rates may:
  (a) Reduce output.
  (b) Increase unemployment.
  (c) Reduce government tax receipts.
  (d) All of the above.

_____ 8. The argument *in favor* of greater equality of income distribution in the United States hinges on:
  (a) The idea that greater equality does not affect incentives.
  (b) The idea that low-income earners would be more willing and able participants in the economy if income were distributed more equally.
  (c) The idea that those with high incomes wield greater political power and strengthen the democratic process.
  (d) All of the above.

_____ 9. In making comparisons of income among countries, care must be exercised because:
  (a) In poor countries much of what is produced does not pass through markets and thus does not get counted in the nation's income.
  (b) In countries such as Sweden and Great Britain, the government provides more goods and services directly than in the United States.
  (c) In-kind benefits should be included in real income in all countries.
  (d) All of the above are true.

_____ 10. The tax elasticity of labor supply measures the:
  (a) Response of workers to a change in the tax rate.
  (b) Response of workers to a change in prices.
  (c) Change in the amount of taxes workers must pay when tax rates change.
  (d) Response of employers to a change in the tax rate.

Use the following information to answer questions 11-12. The tax schedule is hypothetical to keep the calculations simple.

Suppose an individual has a total income of $100,000, has a taxable income of $50,000, and pays taxes of $5,000.

_____ 11. This individual's _____ tax rate is 5 percent.
  (a) Effective.
  (b) Nominal.
  (c) Marginal.
  (d) Incidence.

459

_____ 12. This individual's _____ tax rate is 10 percent.
   (a)   Marginal.
   (b)   Effective.
   (c)   Nominal.
   (d)   Incidence.

_____ 13. The principle of taxation that says people with equal incomes should pay equal taxes is called:
   (a)   Vertical equity.
   (b)   Horizontal equity.
   (c)   Progressive.
   (d)   Regressive.

_____ 14. Transfer payments are an appropriate mechanism for correcting:
   (a)   Market power.
   (b)   Government failure.
   (c)   Natural monopoly.
   (d)   Inequity.

_____ 15. Food stamps, public housing, and subsidized public education are examples of:
   (a)   Free goods.
   (b)   "In-kind" benefits or income.
   (c)   Tax expenditures.
   (d)   Money incomes.

_____ 16. If the tax elasticity of supply is negative 0.6 and tax rates increase by 20 percent, the quantity of labor supplied would:
   (a)   Increase by 12 percent.
   (b)   Decrease by 12 percent.
   (c)   Increase by 33.3 percent.
   (d)   Decrease by 33.3 percent.

_____ 17. The flat tax:
   (a)   Reduces the government's ability to alter the mix of output.
   (b)   Encourages economic activity through deductions and credits.
   (c)   Includes many tax brackets.
   (d)   All of the above.

_____ 18. By instituting a sales tax, a tax plan would:
   (a)   Be more progressive since it takes a larger fraction of income as income falls.
   (b)   Increase horizontal equity.
   (c)   Increase vertical equity.
   (d)   Shift the Lorenz curve for after-tax income away from the line of equality.

_____ 19. A tax is progressive if it takes a:
   (a)   Larger number of dollars as income rises.
   (b)   Larger number of dollars as income falls.
   (c)   Smaller fraction of income as income falls.
   (d)   Smaller fraction of income as income rises.

_____ 20. New loopholes in the personal income tax law tend to:
   (a)   Make the system more regressive.
   (b)   Increase horizontal equity.
   (c)   Increase the tax base.
   (d)   All of the above.

Problems and Applications

Exercise 1

This exercise will help you understand the Lorenz curve.

1. Complete column 3 in Table 33.1 using the data from column 2. Then draw a Lorenz curve based on column 3 in Figure 33.1.

Table 33.1
Size distribution of personal income, by household income group, 1988

(1) Quintile of income recipients (households)	(2) Percent of total household income received	(3) Percent of income received (cumulative)
Lowest fifth	3.8%	_____ %
Second fifth	9.6	_____
Third fifth	16.0	_____
Fourth fifth	24.2	_____
Highest fifth	46.3	_____

Figure 33.1
Lorenz curve

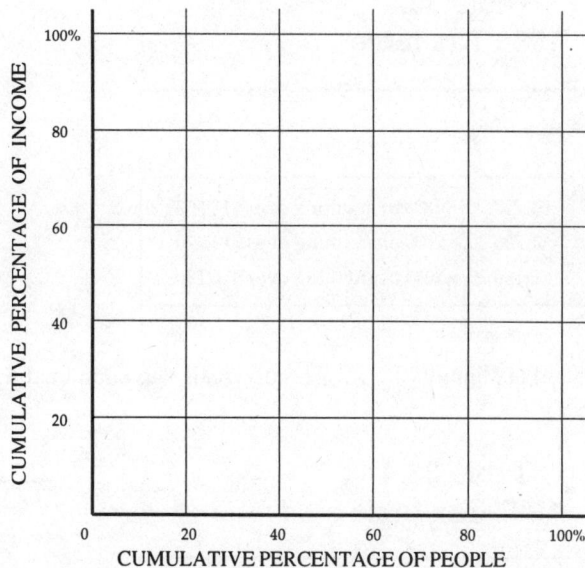

2. The information given in Table 33.1 is for 1988 income. Income in 1988 was distributed (equally, unequally).

3. Draw the line of absolute equality in Figure 33.1 and label it. Shade in the area between the Lorenz curve and the line of equality. The shaded area is a measure of the degree of _____ .

4. In Figure 33.1 draw a second Lorenz curve that indicates the distribution of wealth in the United States for the same year. Use the hypothetical data from Table 33.2. Calculate column 3 first.

Table 33.2
Hypothetical size distribution of wealth, by wealth-holding group

(1) Quintile of wealth owners	(2) Wealth owned	(3) Wealth owned (cumulative)
Lowest fifth	0.5%	_____ %
Second fifth	5.0	_____
Third fifth	12.0	_____
Fourth fifth	20.0	_____
Highest fifth	62.5	_____

5. Although the data in Table 33.2 are hypothetical, they do actually indicate the direction of inequality of wealth ownership relative to the distribution of income. Wealth is (more, less) equally distributed than income.

Exercise 2

This exercise will use the tax reform legislation for the 1987 tax year to show how to determine the impact of a tax change on vertical and horizontal equity. It will help you complete problem 1 for Chapter 33 in the text.

For the 1986 tax year the federal tax liability for single individuals was computed on the basis of the schedule shown in Table 33.3.

Table 33.3
1986 Tax table

If your taxable income Is above:	But below:	Then your tax is:
$11,650	$13,920	$1,297.70 + 18% of anything over $11,650
13,920	16,190	1,706.30 + 20% of anything over $13,920
16,190	19,640	2,160.30 + 23% of anything over $16,190

For the 1987 tax year the corresponding federal tax liability for single individuals was computed with the schedule found in Table 33.4.

Table 33.4
1987 Tax table

If your taxable income Is above:	But below:	Then your tax is:
$ 1,800	$16,800	$ 198.00 + 15% of anything over $ 1,800
16,800	27,000	2,448.00 + 28% of anything over $16,800

1. What would the marginal tax rates be for a single taxpayer with a taxable income of $17,000 in 1986? _____ In 1987? _____ On the basis of this information, does it appear that the tax reform of the Reagan administration increased work incentives for single taxpayers with a taxable income of $17,000? _____

2. For the three taxpayers listed in Table 33.5, compute the taxable income, taxes in the years 1986 and 1987, and difference in taxes for the two years.

Table 33.5
Taxable income and tax computations

Taxpayer	Gross income	Exemptions and deductions	Taxable income	1986 Tax	1987 Tax	Difference
1	$30,000	$18,000	$_____	$_____	$_____	$_____
2	30,000	13,000	_____	_____	_____	_____
3	50,000	38,000	_____	_____	_____	_____

3. On the basis of Table 33.5 did the tax reform package lower taxes for single taxpayers in the taxable income range of $12,000 to $17,000? _____

4. In Table 33.6 rank each taxpayer on the basis of the effective tax rate. Then complete the table by filling in the nominal, effective, and marginal tax rates for each taxpayer.

Table 33.6
Rankings for 1987

Rank	Tax payer	Nominal tax rate	Effective tax rate	Marginal tax rate
1	_____ (highest)	_____%	_____%	_____%
2	_____ (middle)	_____	_____	_____
3	_____ (lowest)	_____	_____	_____

5. How should horizontal equity be determined?
   (a) The two taxpayers with the same nominal incomes should be compared for their marginal tax rates.
   (b) The two taxpayers with the same nominal incomes should be compared for their effective tax rates.
   (c) The effective tax rate of the taxpayer with the highest nominal income should be compared with the effective tax rates of taxpayers with lower nominal incomes.
   (d) The marginal tax rate of the taxpayer with the highest nominal income should be compared with the marginal tax rates of taxpayers with lower nominal incomes.

6. How should vertical equity be determined?
   (a) The two taxpayers with the same nominal incomes should be compared for their marginal tax rates.
   (b) The two taxpayers with the same nominal incomes should be compared for their effective tax rates.
   (c) The effective tax rates of the taxpayer with the highest nominal income should be compared with the effective tax rates of taxpayers with lower nominal incomes.
   (d) The marginal tax rate of the taxpayer with the highest nominal income should be compared with the marginal tax rates of taxpayers with lower nominal incomes.

7. T F For single taxpayers with taxable incomes between $12,000 and $17,000, the tax-reform package reduced vertical equity from 1986 to 1987. (*Hint:* See last column in Table 33.5)

Exercise 3

Around April 15 of every year many articles appear which discuss changes in the tax laws from the previous year. This exercise will use one of the cartoons in the text to show the kind of information to look for to identify and classify changes in the tax system.

Look at the cartoon on page 682 in the text. Then answer the following questions.

1. What word indicates a change in policy has occurred or has been proposed?_____

2. What three words indicate a change in horizontal or vertical equity resulting from the change?
   _____

3. The change in equity indicated in the article concerns:
   (a) Vertical equity.
   (b) Horizontal equity.

Common Errors

The first statement in each "common error" below is incorrect. Each incorrect statement is followed by a corrected version and an explanation.

1. Income and wealth are the same thing. WRONG!

   Income and wealth mean distinctly different things. RIGHT!

   The distinction between income and wealth is critical to sound economic analysis. Income is a flow and has a time dimension. For example, one states one's income in dollars *per year*. Wealth is a stock and is measured at a point in time; for example, you may say you have $5,000 in your savings account *today*. Some people with apparently great wealth may have very little income, as in the case of someone who owns land known to contain oil. On the other hand, someone who has much income may have little wealth; some famous entertainers earn large incomes, save little (accumulate no wealth), and wind up in bankruptcy. Of course, wealth and income may go hand in hand: the incomes of some oil magnates flow *from* their wealth. But clearly the two terms imply different things about one's economic well-being and command over goods and services.

2. Equity and equality of income distribution mean the same thing. WRONG!

   Equity and equality of income distribution mean different things. RIGHT!

   Many arguments over the division of the income pie, whether at the national level, the corporate level, or the university level, are laced with the terms "equity" and "equality" used interchangeably. They are *not* interchangeable. Equality of income distribution means that each person has an equal share. Equity of income distribution implies something about fairness. In a free society some will surely be more productive than others at doing what society wants done. The brain surgeon's services have greater value than the hairdresser's. The surgeon's income will exceed that of the hairdresser—that is, they'll be unequal. But is that inequitable? This is a matter of judgment. It's safe to say, however, that if one were not allowed to keep some of the rewards for being more productive than average, our economy would suffer. An equitable distribution of income in our society will require some inequality. How much? There is no sure answer to that

464

question, only a series of compromises.

•ANSWERS•

Using Key Terms
Across
4. tax elasticity of supply
7. progressive tax
14. effective tax rate
15. nominal tax rate
16. income share
17. marginal revenue product
20. vertical equity
21. regressive tax

Down
1. marginal tax rate
2. size distribution of income
3. horizontal equity
5. tax incidence
6. Lorenz curve
7. personal income
8. in-kind income
9. Gini coefficient
10. market failure
11. government failure
12. flat tax
13. income transfers
18. tax base
19. wealth

True or False

1. T
2. T
3. F A flat tax takes the same percentage of income from each taxpayer.
4. T
5. T
6. F The combined effect is to slightly decrease the level of income inequality in the U.S.
7. F Greater income equality can have negative impacts on work incentives and efficiency.
8. F Wealth is also a determinant of who receives goods and services.
9. F A sales tax is a regressive tax because lower income groups tend to spend a higher proportion of their income than upper income groups.
10. T

Multiple Choice

1.	c	5.	c	9.	d	13.	b	17.	a
2.	d	6.	b	10.	a	14.	d	18.	d
3.	d	7.	d	11.	a	15.	b	19.	c
4.	b	8.	b	12.	c	16.	b	20.	a

Problems and Applications

Exercise 1

1. **Table 33.1 Answer**

(1) Quintile of income recipients (households)	(3) Percent of income received (cumulative)
Lowest fifth	3.8%
Second fifth	13.4
Third fifth	29.4
Fourth fifth	53.6
Highest fifth	99.9

See Figure 33.1 Answer.

Figure 33.1 Answer

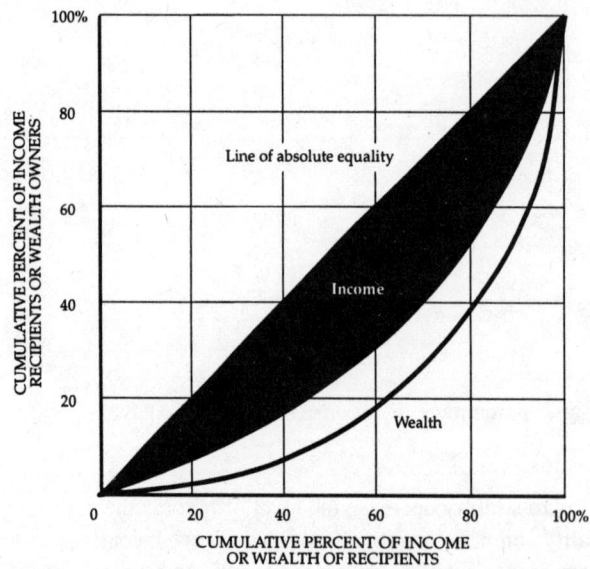

2. unequally
3. See line of absolute equality and shaded area in Figure 33.1 Answer; inequality.

4. **Table 33.2 Answer**

(1) Quintile of wealth owners	(3) Wealth owned (cumulative)
Lowest fifth	0.5%
Second fifth	5.5
Third fifth	17.5
Fourth fifth	37.5
Highest fifth	100.0

See Figure 33.1 Answer.

5. less

Exercise 2

1. 23 percent for 1986 (the percentage used in the formula is the marginal tax rate); 28 percent for 1987; no

2. **Table 33.5 Answer**

Taxpayer	Taxable income	1986 Tax	1987 Tax	Difference
1	$12,000	$1,360.70	$1,728	$367.30
2	17,000	2,346.60	2,504	157.40
3	12,000	1,360.70	1,728	367.30

3. no

4. **Table 33.6 Answer**

Rank	Tax payer	Nominal tax rate	Effective tax rate	Marginal tax rate
1	2	14.7% (=2,504/17,000)	8.4% (=2,504/30,000)	28%
2	1	14.4% (=1,728/12,000)	5.8% (=1,728/30,000)	15
3	3	14.4% (=1,728/12,000)	3.5% (=1,728/50,000)	15

5. b
6. c
7. T   The difference in total taxes paid was greater at a $12,000 taxable income than it was at a $17,000 taxable income, as shown in the last column of Table 33.5 Answer.

Exercise 3

1. "it," when referring to some generic policy that has changed
2. "favors the rich"
3. a

CHAPTER 34

Transfer Payments: Welfare and Social Security

Quick Review

The distribution of income is an age-old problem. Even in the most affluent societies some individuals and families have incomes and living standards that society feels are too low. This is certainly true in the United States where programs to provide relief have multiplied since the 1960s. Existing programs have been broadened to include more recipients and new programs have been funded. The programs are very costly to provide and administer and have become a political hot potato requiring every presidential candidate to declare the need for reform. We conduct our study of this topic by examining the following questions:

- What are the goals of major income transfer programs?
- How are transfer benefits computed?
- How do transfer payments alter market behavior?

Approximately half of every U.S. tax dollar is spent on income transfers, and almost every U.S. household receives some of these transfer dollars. Most of the transfer payments received by poor families are in the form of "in-kind" transfers such as food stamps, medical aid, and housing assistance. Other transfer payments, such as Social Security, are cash transfers. All income transfers result in a redistribution of income, but not all income transfers go to the poor. Welfare programs are means-tested and require some type of income eligibility test, while social insurance programs offer event-conditioned benefits. They insure people against events such as old age or unemployment. The majority of income transfer payments in the U.S. are the result of social insurance programs, not welfare.

In 1996, Congress created a new welfare program called Temporary Aid to Needy Families (TANF). This program allows states to play a much greater role in deciding who receives welfare, under what conditions, and for how long. But, the unintended impact of welfare is to encourage undesirable behavior. Welfare benefits perpetuate dependence, since they do not increase human capital or job opportunities, and welfare benefits may *worsen* the poverty problem by discouraging recipients from working.

The latter is known as the work-welfare dilemma as it is argued that income transfers reduce the incentive to seek earned income which allows individuals to fend for themselves. The designers of welfare programs recognize that many of the programs put in place result in a person being as well off without working as he or she is working! In fact, if work-related expenses are taken into account, a person might be worse off if he or she participates in the labor market. Modifications of existing programs have taken this into account by adjusting the marginal tax rate on earned income. The basic problem is that low marginal tax rates encourage more work effort, but make more people eligible for welfare. High marginal tax rates discourage work effort, but make fewer people eligible for welfare.

The Social Security program faces the same work disincentives as the welfare program. The program provides income for older people who do not work, but it imposes high marginal tax rates on those who do work. Because of the way the program is designed, people retire earlier than they would otherwise. The result is a reduction in total output. By eliminating the work test, the economic cost of the Social Security program could be reduced. The marginal tax rate on the wages of older workers would change from 50 percent to zero. The American Association of Retired Persons favors this change. This would eliminate the work disincentive and total output would increase. However, the total cost of the Social Security program would increase because all older people would receive their full retirement benefit. Payroll taxes would have to increase to cover the additional costs.

Learning Objectives

After reading Chapter 34 and doing the following exercises, you should:

1. Know the impact of transfer payments in the U.S.
2. Be able to distinguish between cash transfers and "in-kind" transfers.
3. Understand the role of human capital and derived demand in the poverty dilemma.
4. Know what the basic government welfare programs are, which level of government administers them, and who is eligible for the various programs.
5. Be able to describe the work disincentive that results from the welfare program and Social Security.
6. Understand how welfare eligibility changes as income increases.
7. Be able to describe how a welfare recipient's real income changes as money income increases.
8. Know some of the recent initiatives to reform the welfare system and Social Security.

Using Key Terms

Fill in the puzzle on the opposite page with the appropriate term from the list of Key Terms at the end of the chapter in the text.

Across
1. The willingness and ability to work specific amounts of time at alternative wage rates.
4. An incentive to engage in undesirable behavior.
5. The percentage of income transfers that goes to the intended recipients and purposes.
6. The shortfall between actual income and the poverty threshold.
7. Means-tested income transfer programs.
11. Programs that provide event-conditioned income transfers.
12. The percentage of base wages paid out in benefits is the _____ _____ rate.
13. Direct transfers of goods and services rather than cash.

Down
2. The income level at which welfare eligibility ceases.
3. Payment to individuals for which no good or service is exchanged.
4. The tax rate imposed on the last dollar of income.
8. The percentage change in quantity of labor supplied divided by the percentage change in tax rates is the _____ _____ of labor supply.
9. Income transfers of direct cash payments.
10. The _____ participation rate is the percentage of the working-age population working or seeking employment.

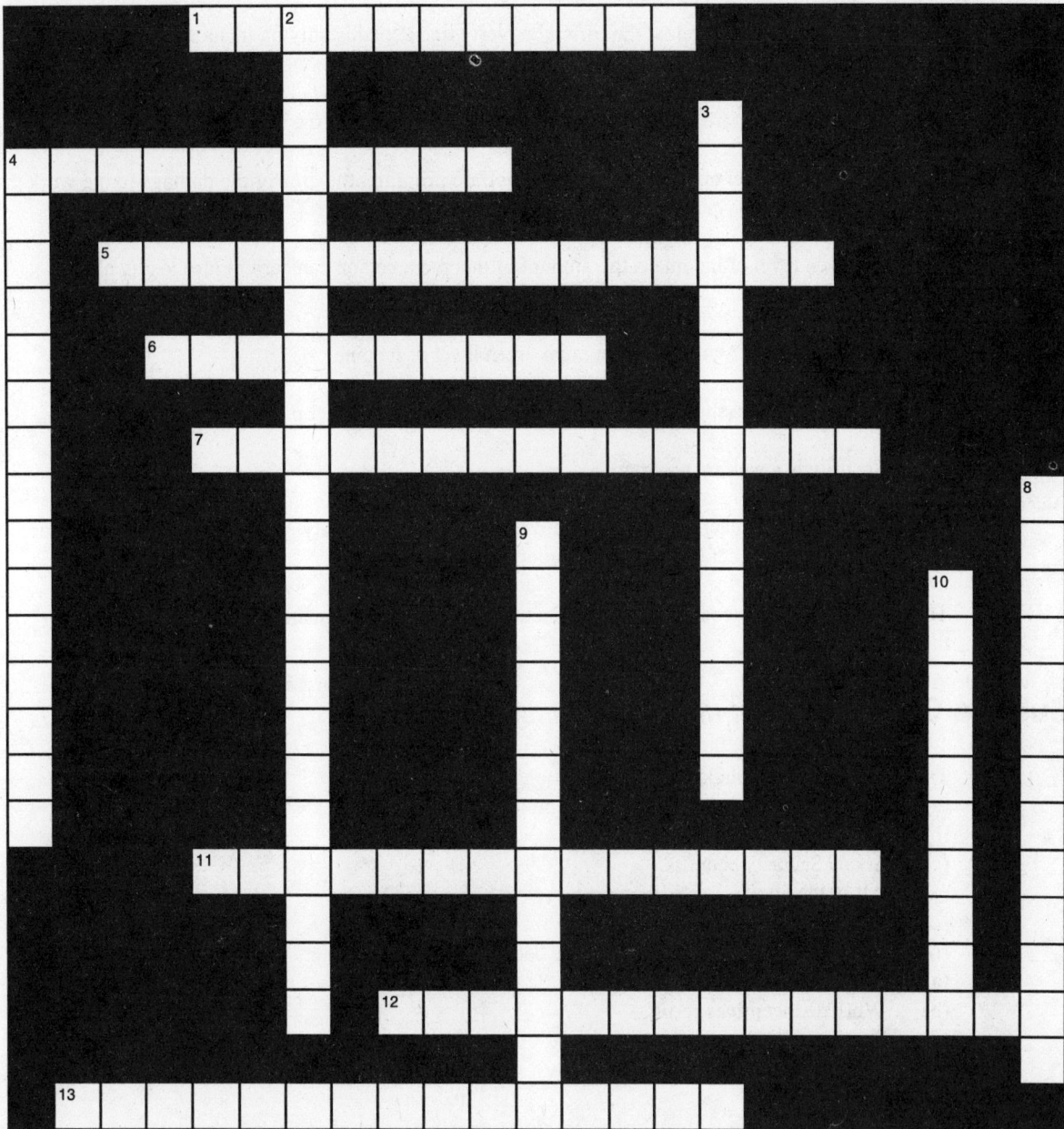

True or False: *Circle your choice and explain why any false statements are incorrect.*

T   F   1.   The Social Security payments received by retired persons are an in-kind transfer payment.

T   F   2.   Whether a given family is below the official poverty line depends only on its money income and the number of family members.

T   F   3.   The availability of welfare benefits shifts the labor supply curve to the right.

T   F   4.   The higher the marginal tax rate of any given welfare program, the greater the damage to the work incentives of recipients, *ceteris paribus*.

T   F   5.   The break-even level of income is the amount of income a person can earn before losing all welfare benefits.

T   F   6.   Increasing "disregards" will lower the break-even level of income.

T   F   7.   Almost every U.S. household receives some form of income transfer payments.

T   F   8.   Social Security is a welfare program.

T   F   9.   If welfare benefits for each household in poverty equaled the poverty gap, people who are not poor would have a strong incentive to become poor.

T   F   10.   The primary economic cost of the Social Security program is the financial costs of administering the program.

Multiple Choice: *Select the correct answer.*

_____   1.   Transfer payments include:
   (a)   Unemployment benefits for the unemployed.
   (b)   In-kind transfers.
   (c)   Social Security benefits.
   (d)   All of the above.

_____   2.   Increased income transfers are undesirable because:
   (a)   They create dependency.
   (b)   Work disincentives result.
   (c)   Total output decreased.
   (d)   All of the above.

_____   3.   Which of the following is a goal of an in-kind transfer program but not a cash transfer program?
   (a)   To change the market's answer to the WHO question.
   (b)   Equity.
   (c)   To insure that recipients get the type of aid intended.
   (d)   All of the above are correct.

_____   4.   Medicaid and food stamps are received by:
   (a)   Anyone that applies.
   (b)   Only the elderly.
   (c)   Only the poor.
   (d)   Mostly upper income households in the U.S. due to inequities in the system.

5. Social insurance programs:
   (a) Are event conditional.
   (b) Insure people against specific problems, e.g. unemployment.
   (c) Are not welfare programs.
   (d) All of the above are correct.

6. Income-transfer programs can:
   (a) Change the answer to the WHAT to produce question.
   (b) Change the answer to the FOR WHOM to produce question.
   (c) Result in reduced output.
   (d) All of the above are correct.

7. If welfare benefits for each household in poverty equaled the poverty gap:
   (a) The effective marginal tax rate for welfare recipients would be 100 percent.
   (b) People who are not poor would have a strong incentive to become poor.
   (c) Poverty would be eliminated.
   (d) All of the above would occur.

8. Suppose a poverty program provides a basic benefit of $3,000, and a marginal tax rate of 0.25. The break-even level of income is:
   (a) $8,000.
   (b) $12,000.
   (c) $18,000.
   (d) $4,000.

9. The official poverty index is based on:
   (a) Family size.
   (b) Cash income.
   (c) Age of the household head.
   (d) All of the above.

10. A good reason for excluding in-kind transfers from income calculations is:
    (a) That the more poor there are, the more jobs there will be for bureaucrats.
    (b) That people would be forced above the poverty line by consuming things like medical services.
    (c) That it is impossible to place a value on most of the services provided.
    (d) All of the above.

Use the following welfare benefit formula to answer the following questions.
Welfare Benefit = Maximum benefit - 3/4 [Wages - (work expenses + child care costs)]

11. Based on the information given above, the marginal tax rate is:
    (a) Zero percent.
    (b) 25 percent.
    (c) 75 percent.
    (d) 100 percent.

12. Suppose that Mr. Henry works 1200 hours per year at a wage of $8 per hour, has child care expenses of $1600 per year and work expenses of $1400. If Mr. Henry's state has a maximum welfare benefit of $8000 per year, based on the welfare formula given above, Mr. Henry's welfare benefit will be:
    (a) Zero. His income has exceeded the limit.
    (b) $3050.
    (c) $4950.
    (d) $6600.

13. Social security benefits paid by the federal government:
   (a) Are income transfers financed by taxes on workers and employers.
   (b) Are classified as in-kind benefits.
   (c) Have no effect on the decision regarding for whom output is to be produced.
   (d) All of the above.

14. Which of the following programs does *not* provide in-kind benefits?
   (a) The food stamp program.
   (b) The housing assistance program.
   (c) Temporary Aid to Needy Families (TANF).
   (d) Medicaid.

15. When authorities choose to "disregard" income earned by welfare recipients, they are:
   (a) Intentionally helping the welfare recipient cheat.
   (b) Attempting to improve work incentives.
   (c) Looking out for their own jobs because the more income they disregard, the more poor there will be.
   (d) Being arbitrary in their administration of the program.

16. Higher marginal tax rates in welfare programs will:
   (a) Decrease the incentive to work.
   (b) Decrease total welfare costs.
   (c) Reduce the number of people on welfare.
   (d) Do all of the above.

17. The Social Security program tends to:
   (a) Increase work incentives for both older and younger workers.
   (b) Increase work incentives for older workers but not younger workers.
   (c) Decrease work incentives for both older and younger workers.
   (d) Decrease work incentives for older workers but not younger workers.

18. If the Social Security program is privatized:
   (a) Work disincentives for younger workers will be reduced.
   (b) Income inequalities would increase.
   (c) Another kind of public transfer program may have to be implemented for those elderly who made bad investments.
   (d) All of the above could occur.

19. The primary economic cost of the Social Security program is the:
   (a) Financial costs of administering the program.
   (b) Reduction in total output the program causes because of work disincentives.
   (c) Redistribution of income from younger to older workers.
   (d) Benefits paid.

20. The primary benefit of the Social Security program is the:
   (a) Increased work incentives for older workers.
   (b) More equitable distribution of income that results.
   (c) Jobs created by the additional spending.
   (d) All of the above are benefits.

Problems and Applications

Exercise 1

This exercise examines welfare benefits and the marginal tax rate on benefits.

Assume the welfare benefit is calculated as:

$$Benefit = maximum\ benefit - wages$$

1. Every additional dollar of wages (increases, reduces) welfare benefits by the same amount.

2. T   F   In this case there is a disincentive to work because the marginal tax rate is 100 percent.

3. Now assume the welfare benefit formula changes to:

    $$Benefit = maximum\ benefit - 0.5(wages)$$

    What is the marginal tax rate? _____

4. A decrease in the marginal tax rate will encourage (more, less) work effort and make (more, fewer) people eligible for welfare.

5. Use the formula in question 3. Assume the maximum benefit is $10,000. If a welfare recipient earns $4000 in a part-time job, his or her total income will be _____.

6. The breakeven level of income is the amount of income a person can earn before losing (some, all) welfare benefits.

7. The breakeven level of income in question 5 is _____.

Exercise 2

This exercise focuses on the Social Security program.

1. The Social Security program is a _____ transfer program because it sends checks to recipients.

2. T   F   The primary economic cost of the Social Security program is benefits it pays to retired workers.

3. Assume a person is entitled to a maximum award of $12,000 in Social Security benefits. But this person continues to work upon reaching retirement age and earns $10,000 per year. Given the following benefit formula:

    $$Benefit\ amount = maximum\ award - 0.60(wage - \$6000)$$

    What is the Social Security benefit for this individual? _____

4. What is the total income for this individual? _____

Common Errors

The first statement in each "common error" below is incorrect. Each incorrect statement is followed by a corrected version and an explanation.

1. The federal government runs the welfare system. WRONG!

   The welfare system consists of programs administered by federal, state, and local governments. RIGHT!

   It's true that the federal government is heavily involved in the welfare system, but state and local governments are involved as well. As a matter of fact, the benefits that a poor person may receive vary from state to state. The differentials in benefits have been the reason for the migration of some poor people from low-benefit states to high-benefit states. The federal government is trying to reduce its role in this area, however.

2. Welfare recipients are typically minority families headed by able-bodied males. WRONG!

   There is no average welfare recipient. RIGHT!

   The stereotype of the welfare recipient seems firmly entrenched in the minds of American taxpayers. The poor are a very heterogeneous group, however, with many more whites than minority-group members. Most work when they can find employment. Some work all year long and are still poor.

•ANSWERS•

Using Key Terms

Across
1. labor supply
4. moral hazard
5. target efficiency
6. poverty gap
7. welfare programs
11. social insurance
12. wage replacement
13. in-kind transfers

Down
2. break even level of income
3. transfer payment
4. marginal tax rate
8. tax elasticity
9. cash transfers
10. labor force

True or False

1. F They are a cash transfer payment.
2. T
3. F The availability of welfare benefits reduces the incentive to work thus shifting the labor supply curve to the left.
4. T
5. T
6. F Increasing disregards will raise the break-even level of income.
7. T
8. F Social Security is event-based and is therefore not a welfare program.
9. T
10. F The primary economic cost of the Social Security program is the reduction in total output the program causes because of work disincentives.

Multiple Choice

1.	d	5.	d	9.	d	13.	a	17.	c
2.	d	6.	d	10.	b	14.	c	18.	d
3.	c	7.	d	11.	c	15.	b	19.	b
4.	c	8.	b	12.	b	16.	d	20.	b

Problems and Applications

Exercise 1

1. reduces
2. T
3. 50 percent
4. more, more
5. $10,000 - 0.5($4000) = $10,000 - $2000 = $8000 $8000 + $4000 = $12,000
6. all
7. $10,000/0.5 = $20,000

Exercise 2

1. cash
2. F The primary economic cost is the decrease in total output because workers retire early.
3. $12,000 - 0.6($10,000 - $6000) = $12,000 - 0.6($4000) = $12,000 - $2400 = $9600
4. $10,000 + $9600 = $19,600

PART 12 International Economics

CHAPTER 35

International Trade

Quick Review

Even the most casual observer of economic activity understands that trade between the United States and other nations is very important. Hardly a day goes by without hearing or reading some reference to exports, imports, the "trade deficit," the value of the dollar in foreign-exchange markets, and the like. In this chapter we ask some basic questions about trade, such as:

- What benefit, if any, do we get from international trade?
- How much harm do imports cause, and to whom?
- Should we protect ourselves from "unfair" trade by limiting imports?

In recent decades the United States has become much more dependent on foreign trade than ever before. We export a wide variety of goods, especially agricultural products and capital goods, to many countries, and import from advanced industrial nations such as Japan, Germany, and Canada and such poor countries as Mexico and Uruguay. Oil is our most important import. Each nation trades with many others and although overall trade must balance (total exports must equal total imports), exports and imports between pairs of countries seldom do. Bilateral trade imbalances (surpluses and deficits) are the rule rather than the exception.

Countries are motivated to trade because by doing so they can produce together more total output than they could in the absence of trade. Specialization and trade allow both members of a trading partnership to consume beyond their respective production-possibilities curves. That is, consumption possibilities will exceed production possibilities. The economic reason for this result is rooted in the "law of comparative advantage." This dictum says that as long as the opportunity costs of producing goods in two countries differ, it will always be possible for those countries to specialize and trade to their mutual advantage. Neither the absolute size of the countries nor their absolute costs of production are important. What does count is the relative (comparative) opportunity cost of producing alternative goods.

It is obvious that specialization and trade benefit trading nations. While trade increases total world output, it is the terms under which trade takes place that determine how the gains are distributed between trading partners. In spite of trade's overall benefits, special interest groups often exert strong pressure *against* foreign trade. Those who would lose their markets and jobs to imported goods and foreign workers often strongly and successfully oppose free trade.

Industries that need raw materials that are being exported may exert pressure on government to place restrictions on the export of those raw materials. The government may place a tariff or quota on imported goods or provide aid to the affected domestic industry. The government may subsidize industries that are hurt by foreign trade. We have occasionally asked our trading partners to voluntarily limit their exports to us so as to ease the pressure on threatened firms and industries. Government has sometimes made assistance (cash, training, or relocation) available to those whose jobs were lost to foreign competition.

Most of the world's industrialized countries belong to the General Agreement on Tariffs and Trade (GATT). This organization, which was created in 1947, commits the world's trading partners to pursue free-trade policies. This includes the dismantling of both tariff and nontariff barriers to trade in goods and services. The organization had significant success in early "rounds," but it has had more difficulty in making important gains recently. Overall, tariffs have been reduced from an average of 40 percent in 1948 to less than four percent today, and trade has expanded greatly as a result. The Uruguay round of GATT expanded the application of free trade rules to agricultural goods and to services and created the World Trade Organization to adjudicate disputes

The Economic Union (EU) and the North American Free Trade Agreement (NAFTA) are examples of trading blocks designed to reduce trade barriers. Any successful trading arrangement will bring about a reallocation of resources, but the overall effect will be a net gain in jobs and output for all the participants. NAFTA brought gains to U.S. producers of agricultural products, metal products, autos and others, and estimated losses in construction, medicine, lumber, etc.

Learning Objectives

After reading Chapter 35 and doing the following exercises, you should:

1. Know some basic facts about U.S. trade patterns.
2. Understand the macroeconomic impact of international trade.
3. Understand why specialization and trade increase both production possibilities and consumption possibilities.
4. Be able to explain comparative advantage using opportunity costs.
5. Know how to determine the limits to the terms of trade.
6. Be able to calculate the gains from specialization and trade at given terms of trade.
7. Be able to show how trade allows a country to consume beyond its production-possibilities curve.
8. Recognize the sources of pressure that result in restricted trade.
9. Know some of the arguments used by those wishing to restrict trade.
10. Be able to discuss tariff and nontariff barriers to trade.
11. Be able to discuss the reasons for the rise of regional trading arrangements.

Using Key Terms

Fill in the puzzle on the opposite page with the appropriate term from the list of Key Terms at the end of the chapter in the text.

Across

2. Alternative combinations of goods and services that can be produced with available resources and technology.
3. Alternative combinations of goods and services that a country can consume.
5. The ability to produce a good at a lower opportunity cost than another country.
9. A negative trade balance.
11. The sale of goods in export markets at prices below domestic prices.
13. A limit on the quantity of a good that may be imported.
14. The most desired goods and services that are foregone in order to obtain something else.
15. A tax imposed on imported goods.
16. The amount of good A given up for good B in trade.

Down

1. An agreement to reduce the volume of trade in a specific good.
4. Determined by the intersection of market demand and market supply.
6. The ability of a country to produce a good with fewer resources than other countries.

7. A prohibition on exports or imports.
8. The amount by which exports exceed imports.
10. Goods and services sold to foreign buyers.
12. Goods and services purchased from foreign sources.

Puzzle 35.1

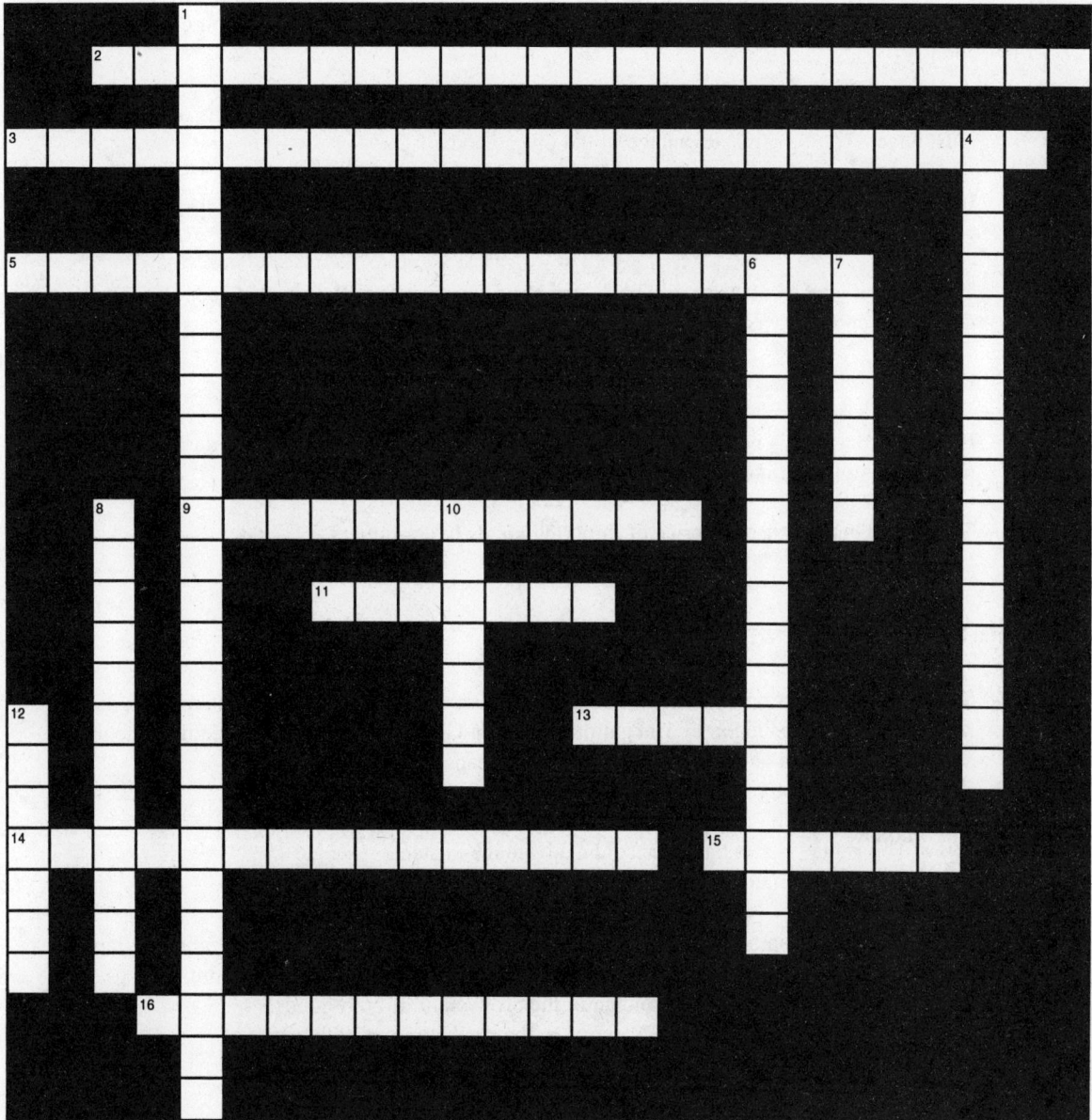

True or False: *Circle your choice and explain why any false statements are incorrect.*

T F 1. The United States buys large quantities of goods and services from other countries but foreign countries buy very few of our goods and services.

T F 2. A reduction of trade barriers should result in reduced prices and increased consumption, *ceteris paribus*.

T F 3. The United States has a higher reliance on foreign trade, as measured by the ratio of exports to GDP, than most other nations.

T F 4. Comparative advantage refers to the ability to produce output with fewer resources than any other country.

T F 5. If one country has a comparative advantage in producing one of two goods, the other country must have a comparative advantage in the other good.

T F 6. It is impossible for a country to consume a mix of goods and services beyond its production-possibilities curve.

T F 7. The terms at which countries will trade one good for another will occur between their respective domestic opportunity costs.

T F 8. Everybody wins when countries specialize and trade.

T F 9. From the consumer's point of view, quotas have the potential to inflict more damage than do tariffs because additional imports are not available at any price.

T F 10. Tariffs and quotas raise the price of imported goods to consumers.

Multiple Choice: *Select the correct answer.*

_____ 1. Suppose the production of 1 ton of steel in the United States requires the same amount of resources as the production of 100 gallons of oil. In Canada, 2 tons of steel requires the same amount of resources as 200 gallons of oil. This means that:
    (a) Neither country has a comparative advantage.
    (b) Canada has the comparative advantage in steel.
    (c) The United States has an absolute advantage in steel.
    (d) The United States has the comparative advantage in steel.

_____ 2. In Germany, suppose 6 cameras or 4 bicycles can be produced with 1 unit of labor. In Japan, suppose 9 cameras or 5 bicycles can be produced with 1 unit of labor. Therefore:
    (a) Japan has an absolute advantage in the production of both goods.
    (b) Japan has a comparative advantage in the production of both goods.
    (c) Germany has a comparative advantage in the production of cameras.
    (d) Japan has a comparative advantage in the production of bicycles.

_____ 3. If a country is completely self-reliant in producing goods for its own consumption needs, then:
    (a) It is consuming more than it could with trade.
    (b) Its consumption possibilities will equal its production possibilities.
    (c) It is promoting specialization.
    (d) It will achieve a higher standard of living by exporting.

_____ 4. The expansion of world output as a result of trade is mainly due to the effects of:
    (a)   Higher trade barriers.
    (b)   Improved terms of trade.
    (c)   Specialization according to comparative advantage.
    (d)   Specialization according to absolute advantage.

_____ 5. When one country can produce a given amount of a good using fewer inputs than any other country:
    (a)   It has an absolute advantage in producing the good.
    (b)   It has a comparative advantage in producing the good.
    (c)   Specialization will definitely increase worldwide consumption possibilities.
    (d)   All of the above.

_____ 6. "Terms of trade" refers to:
    (a)   The opportunity costs incurred in trade.
    (b)   The rate at which goods are exchanged.
    (c)   The degree to which one country has an absolute advantage.
    (d)   Which country pays the transportation costs when trade occurs.

_____ 7. To say that a country has a comparative advantage in the production of wine is to say that:
    (a)   It can produce wine with fewer resources than any other country can. _absolute_
    (b)   Its opportunity cost of producing wine is greater than any other country's.
    (c)   Its opportunity cost of producing wine is lower than any other country's.
    (d)   The relative price of wine is higher in that country than in any other.

_____ 8. America's tariffs on foreign goods result in:
    (a)   Lower domestic prices than those that would prevail in their absence.
    (b)   A stimulus to efficient American firms that are not protected.
    (c)   Higher employment and output in protected industries than would otherwise be the case.
    (d)   A more efficient allocation of resources than would occur in their absence.

_____ 9. A principal objective of GATT is to:
    (a)   Reduce barriers to trade.
    (b)   Settle domestic tax disputes internationally.
    (c)   Equalize income tax structures in various countries.
    (d)   Protect domestic producers from foreign competition.

_____ 10. World output of goods and services increases with specialization because:
    (a)   The world's resources are being used more efficiently.
    (b)   Each country's production possibilities curve is shifted outward.
    (c)   Each country's workers are able to produce more than they could before specialization.
    (d)   All of the above are correct.

_____ 11. A "beggar-thy-neighbor policy" is:
    (a)   An attempt by a poor country to get more foreign aid and assistance.
    (b)   The imposition of trade barriers for the purpose of expanding exports.
    (c)   The imposition of import barriers for the purpose of curbing inflation.
    (d)   The imposition of trade barriers to increase domestic employment.

Suppose the production possibilities of Japan and the U.S. are given in Table 35.1. Use Table 35.1 to answer questions 12 and 13.

Table 35.1
Output per worker day in the United States and Japan

Country	TV sets (per day)	Bicycles (per day)
Japan	2	10
United States	1	8

_____ 12. Which of the following statements is true?
   (a)   The United States has an absolute advantage in the production of bicycles.
   (b)   Japan has an absolute advantage in the production of bicycles only.
   (c)   Japan has an absolute advantage in the production of TV sets only.
   (d)   Japan has an absolute advantage in the production of both bicycles and TV sets.

_____ 13. Suppose the terms of trade are established in such a way that 1 TV set equals 5 bicycles. Which of the following statements would be true?
   (a)   These terms of trade provide gains for the United States, but Japan is worse off.
   (b)   These terms of trade provide gains for Japan, but the United States is worse off.
   (c)   These terms of trade provide gains for the United States, and Japan is no worse off.
   (d)   These terms of trade provide gains for Japan, and the United States is no worse off.

_____ 14. Suppose the country of Montgomery has specialized in the production of a good but has not yet entered into a trade. At this point in time, Montgomery:
   (a)   Has moved to a level of production outside its production possibilities curve.
   (b)   Has shifted its production possibilities curve outward.
   (c)   Has moved along its existing production possibilities curve.
   (d)   Has moved to a level of consumption outside its production possibilities curve.

_____ 15. "Dumping" is said to occur when:
   (a)   Foreign producers sell more of a particular good in the United States than domestic producers sell.
   (b)   Foreign producers sell their goods in the United States at prices lower than the U.S. average cost of production.
   (c)   Foreign producers sell their goods in the United States at prices lower than those prevailing in their own countries.
   (d)   The foreign countries have trade surpluses and the United States has a trade deficit.

_____ 16. What should happen to the equilibrium price and quantity in a market as a result of a tariff on imports?
   (a)   Equilibrium price and quantity should both go up.
   (b)   Equilibrium price should go up, and equilibrium quantity should go down.
   (c)   Equilibrium price should go down, and equilibrium quantity should go up.
   (d)   Equilibrium price and quantity should both go down.

_____ 17. With regard to international trade, the market mechanism:
   (a)   Provides a profit incentive to producers who specialize in the goods and services for which a comparative advantage exists.
   (b)   Provides a profit incentive to producers who trade in the goods and services for which a comparative advantage exists.
   (c)   Determines the terms of trade.
   (d)   Does all of the above.

_____ 18. International trade:
    (a)   Lowers prices to consumers.
    (b)   Alters the mix of domestic production.
    (c)   Redistributes income toward export industries.
    (d)   All of the above.

_____ 19. Suppose that Brazil has a comparative advantage in coffee and Mexico has a comparative advantage in tomatoes. Which of the following groups would be worse off if these two countries specialize and trade?
    (a)   Brazilian tomato producers.
    (b)   Brazilian coffee producers.
    (c)   Mexican tomato producers.
    (d)   Everyone is better off when specialization and trade take place.

_____ 20. If we add together all the gains from specialization and trade and then subtract all the losses, the net result would be:
    (a)   Zero; the gains and losses would cancel out.
    (b)   Positive; a net gain for the world and each country.
    (c)   Negative; a net loss for the world and each country.
    (d)   Impossible to tell; the net result could be zero, positive, or negative.

Problems and Applications

Exercise 1

This exercise shows how trade leads to gains by all trading partners through specialization and comparative advantage.

Suppose that Japan has 20 laborers in total and that the United States has 40 laborers. Suppose their production possibilities are given in Table 35.2. (*Be careful:* The table tells you that a worker in Japan can produce 2 TV sets per day *or* 10 bicycles per day, *not* two TV sets *and* 10 bicycles!)

Table 35.2
Output per worker day in the United States and Japan

Country	TV sets (per day)	Bicycles (per day)
Japan	2 or	10
United States	1 or	8

1.   Draw the production-possibilities curves for each country in Figure 35.1. Assume constant costs of production.

	L	TV	B
J	20	40 OR	200
US	40	40 OR	320

Figure 35.1

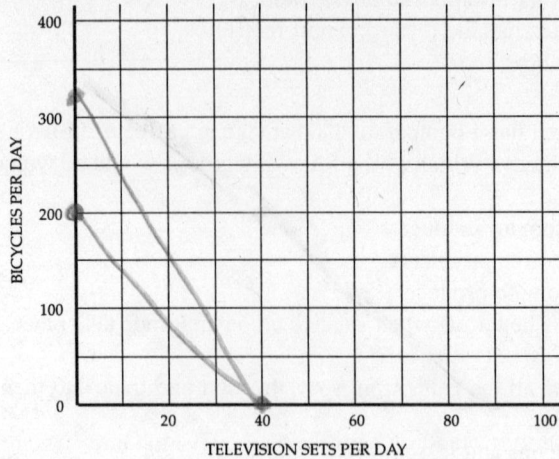

2. Suppose that before trade Japan uses 12 laborers to produce bicycles and 8 laborers to produce television sets; suppose also that in the United States 20 workers produce bicycles and 20 produce television sets. Complete Table 35.3.

Table 35.3
Output produced and consumed without trade

Country	TV sets (per day)	Bicycles (per day)
Japan	16	120
United States	20	160
Total	36	280

3. Before trade, the total output of television sets is ___36___ ; of bicycles, ___280___ .

4. What is the opportunity cost of 1 television set in Japan? ___5___ In the United States? ___8___

5. What is the opportunity cost of 1 bicycle in Japan? ___⅕___ In the United States? ___⅛___

6. If Japan and the United States specialize according to their respective comparative advantages, Japan will produce ___TV___ and the United States will produce ___bikes___ . They will do so because the opportunity cost of bicycles in terms of television sets is (lower, higher) in the United States than in Japan, and the opportunity cost of television sets in terms of bicycles is (lower, higher) in Japan than in the United States.

7. After specialization, the total output of television sets is ___40___ and the total output of bicycles is ___320___ . (*Hint:* Assume 20 Japanese produce only TV sets, and 40 Americans produce only bicycles.)

8. This output represents an increase of ___40___ bicycles and ___4___ television sets over the pre-specialization output. (*Hint:* Compare answers to problems 3 and 7.)

Exercise 2

This exercise will help you understand how the terms of trade are determined. Refer to Exercise 1 for the data.

If Japan and the United States are to benefit from the increased production, trade must take place. The Japanese will be willing to trade television sets for bicycles as long as they get back more bicycles than they could get in their own country.

1. The terms of trade will be between 1 television set equals ____5____ bicycles and 1 television set equals ____8____ bicycles.

2. If the terms of trade were 4 bicycles equals one television set:
   (a) Neither country would buy bicycles, but both would buy TV sets.
   (b) Neither country would buy TV sets, but both would buy bicycles.
   (c) Both countries would buy bicycles and TV sets.

3. Suppose that the two countries agree that the terms of trade will be 6 bicycles equals 1 television set. Let Japan export 20 television sets per day to the United States. Complete Table 35.4. Assume that Japan produces 40 television sets per day and the United States produces 320 bicycles.

Table 35.4
Consumption combination after trade

Country	TV sets (per day)	Bicycles (per day)
Japan	20	120
United States	20	200
Total	40	320

4. As a result of specialization and trade, the United States has the same quantity of television sets and ____40____ more bicycles per day. (Compare Tables 35.3 and 35.4.)

5. As a result of specialization and trade, Japan has the same number of bicycles and ____4____ more television sets per day.

Now suppose that at the exchange rate of 6 bicycles to 1 TV set, Japan would like to export 10 TV sets and import 60 bicycles per day. Suppose also that the United States desires to export 90 bicycles and import 15 television sets per day.

6. At these terms of trade there is a (shortage, surplus) of television sets.

7. At these terms of trade there is a (shortage, surplus) of bicycles.

8. Which of the following terms of trade would be more likely to result from this situation?
   (a) 5 bicycles equal 1 television set.
   (b) 6 bicycles equal 1 television set.
   (c) 7 bicycles equal 1 television set.

Exercise 3

When protection is provided to producers of a particular product, consumers of that product are harmed because they must pay higher prices than in the absence of protection. In addition, the effects of the protection in one market spill over into related factor and product markets, thus distorting both production and consumption patterns. This exercise will help you to discover how this occurs.

Reread the World View article entitled "Sugar Quota a Sour Deal," and then answer the following questions.

1. What was the estimated overall cost to U.S. consumers in 1995 due to the quota on sugar?

2. If the U.S. sugar quota was abolished, which of the following would be the most likely equilibrium world price for sugar, *ceteris paribus*?
    (a) 7 cents per pound.
    (b) 15 cents per pound.
    (c) 22 cents per pound.
    (d) 24 cents per pound.

3. If the sugar quotas were abolished, what would you predict to happen to the number of sugar producers in the United States?_____

4. Suppose the next best use of land used to produce sugar beets in the U.S. was to produce wheat. What would you predict to happen to the price of wheat in the U.S. market, *ceteris paribus*, if the sugar quota was abolished?_____

5. What would you predict to happen to the marginal revenue product of labor and the level of employment of labor in the Caribbean sugar industry, *ceteris paribus*?_____
    _____

Common Errors

The first statement in each "common error" below is incorrect. Each incorrect statement is followed by a corrected version and an explanation.

1. A country must have an *absolute advantage* in order to gain from trade with another country. WRONG!

    A country must have a *comparative advantage* in order to gain from trade with another country. RIGHT!

    Mutually advantageous trade requires only that the opportunity costs of producing goods differ between the two countries, *ceteris paribus*. Another way of stating this is that the production-possibilities curves of the two countries must have different slopes. The two circumstances noted above are indicated in Figure 35.2 below.

Figure 35.2

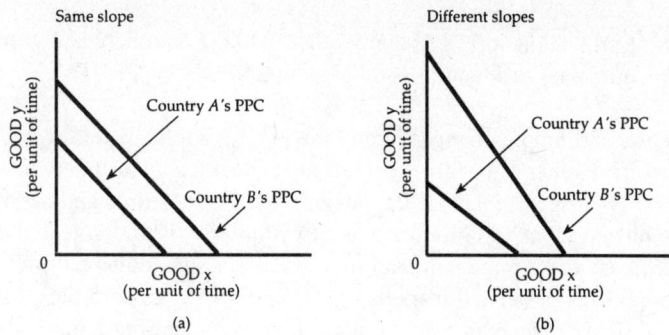

In diagram (a), in which country B has an absolute advantage over country A, the production-possibilities curves have the same slope; thus mutually advantageous trade *is not* possible. In diagram (b), each country has a comparative advantage because the production-possibilities curves of the two countries have different slopes; thus mutually advantageous trade *is* possible.

2. Foreign trade costs a country jobs. WRONG!

Although jobs may be lost, new ones will be created by the opportunities opened up with trade. RIGHT!

When countries specialize and trade according to the law of comparative advantage, some particular workers and firms may be hurt by imports, but the economy as a whole gains by trade. More output per resource input will be attainable. Because the economy is able to reach full employment with trade as well as without trade, there is no reason to assume there will be fewer jobs.

3. A country is well off only as long as it exports more than it imports. WRONG!

Countries may, at times, be well off when they experience a trade surplus; they may also be well off when they have a trade deficit. RIGHT!

Both trade deficits and trade surpluses can be problems if either situation persists for a long period of time. Trade surpluses mean that a country is giving more of its limited, precious resources in trade than it is acquiring from other countries. The currencies of deficit countries tend to depreciate, which means they will be unable to buy as many foreign goods with a unit of currency.

4. Countries tend to enter into trade to get things they cannot produce themselves. WRONG!

Countries very often trade for things they could produce themselves. RIGHT!

Be careful! Countries often trade for things they could produce themselves because the relative costs of domestic production would be prohibitive. Take baskets as an example. Producers in the U.S. could certainly produce baskets if they really wanted to. The technique is not difficult to learn and the materials are abundant. But baskets do not lend themselves to machine production, and hand labor is expensive here. The cost in terms of goods forgone would be tremendous. (So would the price of the baskets.) We're better off specializing in something like computers, where we have a comparative advantage, and trading for baskets, where we clearly do not have a comparative advantage.

5. The effects of protection affect only workers in the protected industry and the domestic consumers of the protected commodity. WRONG!

    The effects of protection spread to many other markets both here and abroad as producers and consumers adjust their production and consumption patterns. RIGHT!

    Protection and output changes in any market are bound to set off additional changes in related markets. Higher prices for a protected product lead consumers to seek out substitutes with lower prices. This should increase the demand for the substitute and set off a host of other changes in related input and product markets. Similarly, if the protected commodity is used as an input, an increase in its price will lead to a search for substitutes with lower prices and have consequent impacts on related markets. In the case of sugar, corn based high-fructose corn syrup has replaced sugar to such an extent that corn growers, fearing a reduction in the demand for their output, now lobby their congressional delegations to maintain the sugar quota! Similar impacts can be expected in the markets of foreign producers.

•ANSWERS•

Using Key Terms
Across
2. production possibilities
3. consumption possibilities
5. comparative advantage
9. trade deficit
11. dumping
13. quota
14. opportunity cost
15. tariff
16. terms of trade

Down
1. voluntary restraint agreement
4. equilibrium price
6. absolute advantage
7. embargo
8. trade surplus
10. exports
12. imports

True or False

1. F Approximately 11 percent of U.S. GDP is exported. In dollar terms, the U.S. is the world's largest exporter of goods and services.
2. T
3. F Despite the fact that the U.S. is the world's largest importer, the U.S. only exports and imports a relatively small percentage of its GDP.
4. F Comparative advantage refers to the ability to produce output at a smaller opportunity cost than another country, i.e. giving up fewer alternative goods and services.
5. T
6. F With specialization and free trade it is possible for a country to consume a mix of goods and services beyond its production-possibilities curve although it is never possible for a country to produce beyond its production-possibilities curve.

7. T
8. F Although countries as a whole benefit from specialization and free trade, there are always individuals and groups that may lose, e.g. import-competing firms.
9. T
10. T

Multiple Choice

1. a	5. a	9. a	13. c	17. d
2. a	6. b	10. a	14. c	18. d
3. b	7. c	11. d	15. c	19. a
4. c	8. c	12. d	16. b	20. b

Problems and Applications

Exercise 1

1. **Figure 35.1 Answer**

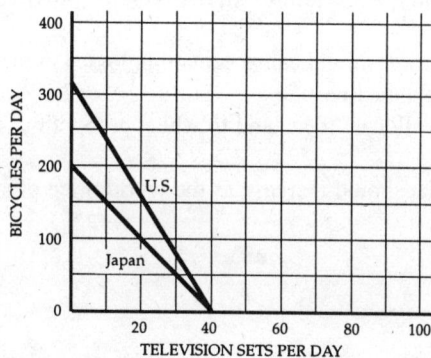

2. **Table 35.3 Answer**

Country	TV sets	Bicycles
Japan	16	120
United States	20	160
Total	36	280

3. 36; 280
4. 5 bicycles; 8 bicycles
5. 1/5 television set; 1/8 television set
6. television sets; bicycles; lower; lower
7. 40; 320
8. 40; 4

Exercise 2

1. 5; 8

491

2. a
3. **Table 35.4 Answer**

Country	TV sets	Bicycles
Japan	20	120
United States	20	200
Total	40	320

4. 40
5. 4
6. shortage, The Japanese wish to export fewer (10) TV sets than Americans want to import (15).
7. surplus, The Americans wish to export more (90) bicycles than the Japanese want to import (60).
8. c   The shortage of TV sets will cause their price to increase.

Exercise 3

1. The estimated cost to U.S. consumers due to the price difference between the U.S. market and the world market was $1.5 billion.
2. c   The market should reach equilibrium between the previous world price and the protected U.S. price.
3. The absence of protection should cause economic losses in the U.S. sugar industry and the number of firms should decline.
4. As sugar producers reallocate their land to wheat production, the market price of wheat should fall.
5. Their marginal product should increase as the world price of sugar rises; the level of employment should increase.

CHAPTER 36
International Finance

Quick Review

All of the trade between nations discussed in the previous chapter must somehow be financed. And since each country has its own money, we have to ask several critical questions:

- What determines the value of one country's money as compared to the value of another's?
- What causes the international value of currencies to change?
- Should government intervene to limit currency fluctuations?

To facilitate trade and to eliminate the need for barter, markets for foreign exchange have developed. Their function is to determine the exchange rate at which two currencies will trade. The foreign-exchange market is like any other market—it consists of a supply schedule and a demand schedule. Supply and demand mean the same thing here as they do in any other market. The commodity being traded in this case is the money of one country for the money of another. Demand and supply determine the equilibrium price (exchange rate) and quantity of foreign exchange that is traded.

When the international value of a currency increases, the currency is said to appreciate. When a currency's international value decreases, the currency is said to depreciate. The exchange rate responds to changes in underlying forces, as reflected in shifts of the supply and demand curves. Changes in relative income levels, changes in relative prices, changes in product availability, relative interest-rate changes, and speculative activities are examples of the determinants that cause supply and demand curves to shift and alter exchange rates.

To keep track of the foreign-exchange flows that accompany the flow of goods and services, each country summarizes its transactions in a statement called the "balance of payments." The balance of payments is based on double-entry bookkeeping and must therefore balance, even though individual accounts may not.

There are good reasons why countries resist exchange rate movements. On a micro level, those doing business involving foreign currency will know the current exchange rate, but must forecast its future value when making contracts. This is very difficult and causes a great deal of uncertainty. Furthermore, any change in a country's exchange rate automatically alters the price of all its exports and imports. The interests of exporters and importers are thus diametrically opposed when a currency appreciates or depreciates due to market forces. On a macro level, changes in exchange rates can complicate the conduct of domestic monetary and fiscal policy. As a result, governments sometimes feel forced to intervene in foreign exchange markets.

Under a fixed-rate system, governments enter on the supply side to prevent an unwanted appreciation and on the demand side to prevent a depreciation. The overall conduct of intervention requires a country to accumulate reserves (foreign currencies, gold, etc.) at some times and disburse them at others. Both trade policy (tariffs, quotas, etc.) and domestic monetary and fiscal policy are sometimes used to prevent undesirable trends in exchange rates. When monetary and fiscal policy are used to address balance of payments and currency problems the general rule is that deficit countries are required to forsake full employment and surplus countries must give up price stability.

The United States and its major trading partners abandoned the fixed-rate Bretton Woods system in 1973 and replaced it with a flexible exchange rate system. In an ideal setting, a flexible rate system would not require government intervention because the exchange rate would automatically adjust to the equilibrium rate. In practice this has not been the case, however, and a system of "managed rates" has evolved in which governments still intervene, but now with the idea of narrowing, rather than eliminating, fluctuations.

A change in the value of one country's currency can affect other countries if the countries are linked through trade, geography, or by agreement. Recently Asia, Mexico, Brazil, and Russia have all experienced currency crises. In each case, the countries asked for outside help in the form of a currency bailout. Typically a bailout is facilitated by the International Monetary Fund (IMF) and the world's strongest economies. There are arguments both for and against currency bailouts.

Learning Objectives

After reading Chapter 36 and doing the following exercises, you should:

1. Understand that an exchange rate is simply a price.
2. Know the forces that operate on the demand side of the foreign exchange market.
3. Know the forces that operate on the supply side of the foreign exchange market.
4. Understand how supply and demand interact to determine the equilibrium exchange rate.
5. Understand the essentials of balance-of-payments accounting.
6. Be able to demonstrate graphically the forces that cause a currency to appreciate or depreciate.
7. Understand why there is resistance to exchange-rate changes.
8. Be able to describe several exchange-rate systems and their consequences.
9. Understand the macroeconomic and microeconomic consequences of exchange-rate movements.
10. Be able to describe a balance-of-payments problem.
11. Be aware of the recent history of the international value of the dollar.

Using Key Terms

Fill in the puzzle on the opposite page with the appropriate term from the list of Key Terms at the end of the chapter in the text.

Across

2. Places where foreign currencies are bought and sold.
4. The amount by which the quantity demanded exceeds the quantity supplied.
6. A system in which governments intervene in foreign-exchange markets to limit exchange-rate fluctuations.
8. Stocks of gold held by a government to purchase foreign exchange.
9. A rise in the price of a currency relative to another.
10. The price of one currency in terms of another currency.
11. A fall in the price of one currency relative to another.
13. A mechanism for fixing the exchange rate.
14. The price at which the quantity demanded equals the quantity supplied.
15. An excess demand for domestic currency at current exchange rates.

Down

1. An excess demand for foreign currency at current exchange rates.
2. Holdings of foreign exchange by official government agencies.
3. Floating exchange rates.
5. A summary record of a country's international economic transactions.
7. An abrupt depreciation of a currency whose value was fixed or managed by the government.
12. A situation in which the value of imports exceeds the value of exports.

Puzzle 36.1

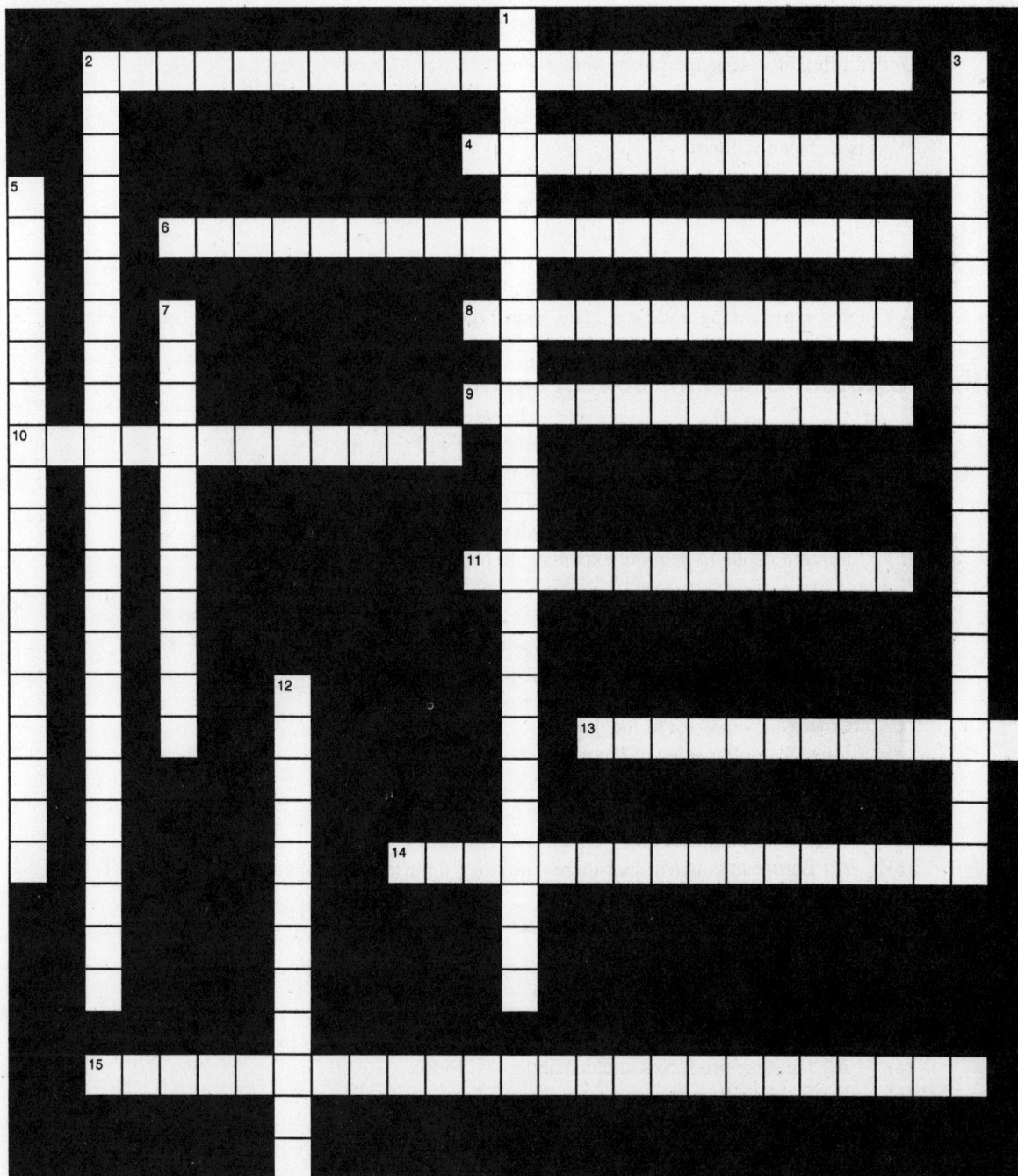

True or False: *Circle your choice and explain why any false statements are incorrect.*

T F 1. The U.S. demand for French francs represents a supply of dollars to the foreign-exchange market.

T F 2. Increased foreign travel by Americans tends to cause the dollar to appreciate, *ceteris paribus*.

T F 3. Trade protection can be used to prop up fixed exchange rates.

T F 4. When the dollar price of German marks increases, German machinery becomes more expensive to U.S. residents.

T F 5. If the dollar appreciates against the franc, this change will be harmful to California vineyard owners.

T F 6. Under a flexible-exchange-rate system, there is no need for foreign-exchange reserves.

T F 7. If the U.S. price level rises more rapidly than the Japanese price level, *ceteris paribus*, U.S. exports to Japan will rise.

T F 8. When exchange rates are fixed, the balance of payments is zero.

T F 9. If there is a deficit in the capital account, it must be offset by a surplus in the current account.

T F 10. A country experiencing trade surpluses faces higher foreign debt and interest costs.

Multiple Choice: *Select the correct answer.*

_____ 1. An increase in the dollar price of other currencies will tend to cause:
   (a) American goods to be cheaper for foreigners.
   (b) American goods to be more expensive for foreigners.
   (c) Foreign goods to be cheaper to residents of the United States.
   (d) Foreign goods to be more expensive to residents of foreign countries.

_____ 2. Suppose that a flexible exchange rate exists between the U.S. dollar and the Japanese yen. An increase in the supply of yen (a rightward shift in the supply curve of yen) will tend to:
   (a) Increase U.S. imports of Japanese goods.
   (b) Push the U.S. balance of trade in the direction of a surplus.
   (c) Lower the yen price of the dollar.
   (d) Raise the dollar price of the yen.

_____ 3. Changes in the value of the euro affect the economies of:
   (a) Only those countries using the euro as currency.
   (b) All European countries but there would no significant impact on countries outside Europe.
   (c) Potentially the entire world.
   (d) There would be no significant impact on any economies as long as exchange rates are flexible.

_____ 4. If the exchange rate between U.S. dollars and Japanese yen changes from $1 = 100 yen to $1 = 110 yen:
   (a) All Japanese producers and consumers will lose.
   (b) U.S. auto producers and autoworkers will gain.
   (c) U.S. consumers of Japanese TV sets will gain.
   (d) Japanese tourists to the U.S. will gain.

5. A country will experience a reduction in its balance-of-payments deficit, *ceteris paribus,* if:
   (a) Its level of GDP rises relative to foreign levels of GDP.
   (b) Its prices fall relative to foreign price levels, *ceteris paribus.*
   (c) The domestic price of the foreign currency falls.
   (d) It lowers its tariffs.

6. A result of the Asian Crisis of 1997-98 was:
   (a) A general increase in the value of the U.S. dollar in relation to Southeast Asian currencies.
   (b) A major decrease in the level of U.S. exports to Southeast Asia.
   (c) Political unrest in many Southeast Asian countries.
   (d) All of the above.

7. Greater volatility of floating exchange rates results in:
   (a) Greater costs because of uncertainty.
   (b) Balance-of-payments instability.
   (c) Smaller market shortages and surpluses of currencies.
   (d) Depletion of foreign reserves.

8. Which of the following changes will tend to cause a shift in the domestic demand curve for foreign currencies?
   (a) Changes in domestic incomes, *ceteris paribus.*
   (b) Changes in domestic prices of goods, *ceteris paribus.*
   (c) Changes in consumer taste for foreign goods, *ceteris paribus.*
   (d) All of the above.

9. An increase in the U.S. trade deficit could be caused by:
   (a) A depreciation of the dollar in terms of other currencies.
   (b) An appreciation of the dollar in terms of other currencies.
   (c) The imposition of a tariff on imported goods.
   (d) An increase in the capital-account deficit.

10. In a floating-exchange-rate system, the capital-account balance equals:
    (a) The negative of the current-account balance.
    (b) Foreign purchases of U.S. assets minus U.S. purchases of foreign assets.
    (c) The balance of payments minus the sum of the trade balance, the services balance, and unilateral transfers.
    (d) All of the above.

11. American citizens planning a vacation abroad would welcome:
    (a) Appreciation of the dollar.
    (b) Depreciation of the dollar.
    (c) Devaluation of the dollar.
    (d) Evaluation of the dollar.

12. A change in the exchange rate for a country's currency alters the prices of:
    (a) Exports only.
    (b) Imports only.
    (c) Both exports and imports.
    (d) Only domestic goods and services.

13. In a floating exchange-rate regime, the overall "balance" of the balance of payments must be:
    (a) Equal to zero.
    (b) Positive if exports of goods and services exceed imports of goods and services.
    (c) Positive if the capital account is in surplus.
    (d) Negative if the current account is in deficit.

_____ 14. When exchange rates are flexible, they are:
   (a)   Determined by proclamation of the monetary authorities of a country.
   (b)   Determined by the relative levels of gold reserves.
   (c)   Permitted to vary with changes in supply and demand in the foreign exchange market.
   (d)   Determined by the provisions of the Bretton Woods agreement.

_____ 15. If the U.S. dollar depreciates, the United States should experience in the long run:
   (a)   A lower inflation rate.
   (b)   A smaller deficit on the U.S. trade balance.
   (c)   A larger deficit on the U.S. current account.
   (d)   A larger deficit on the U.S. capital account.

_____ 16. The major drawback to a system of managed exchange rates is that:
   (a)   A country's efforts to manage exchange-rate movements may arouse suspicion and retaliation.
   (b)   A country's efforts to affect changes in exchange rates are almost totally ineffective.
   (c)   Government efforts to alter exchange rates usually result in violent disruptions of the domestic economy.
   (d)   It requires enormous gold reserves.

_____ 17. If French speculators believed the yen was going to appreciate against the dollar, they would:
   (a)   Purchase francs.
   (b)   Purchase dollars.
   (c)   Purchase yen.
   (d)   Sell yen.

_____ 18. Suppose that at the prevailing yen-dollar exchange rate, there is an excess demand for yen. To prevent the dollar from depreciating, the United States might:
   (a)   Raise taxes.
   (b)   Reduce government spending.
   (c)   Raise interest rates.
   (d)   Do all of the above.

_____ 19. A currency bailout:
   (a)   Occurs when an economy is lent money in order to increase or maintain the value of its currency.
   (b)   Can help avoid a "domino effect" of depreciating currencies in other economies.
   (c)   Can be ultimately self-defeating because it saves the country receiving the bailout from implementing politically unpopular domestic policies which could have prevented the problem in the first place.
   (d)   All of the above are correct.

_____ 20. The capital account includes:
   (a)   Trade in goods.
   (b)   Trade in services.
   (c)   Unilateral transfers.
   (d)   Foreign purchases of U.S. assets.

Problems and Applications

Exercise 1

This exercise provides practice in determining exchange rates.

1. Table 36.1 depicts the hypothetical demand for and supply of British pounds in terms of U.S. dollars. Use the information in Table 36.1 to plot the demand and supply of British pounds at the exchange rates indicated in Figure 36.1. Then answer questions 2-4.

Table 36.1
Monthly demand for and supply of British pounds in the United States

Dollars per British pound	Quantity demanded	Quantity supplied
4.50	100	700
4.00	200	600
3.50	300	500
3.00	400	400
2.50	500	300
2.00	600	200
1.50	700	100

Figure 36.1
Demand and supply curves for pounds

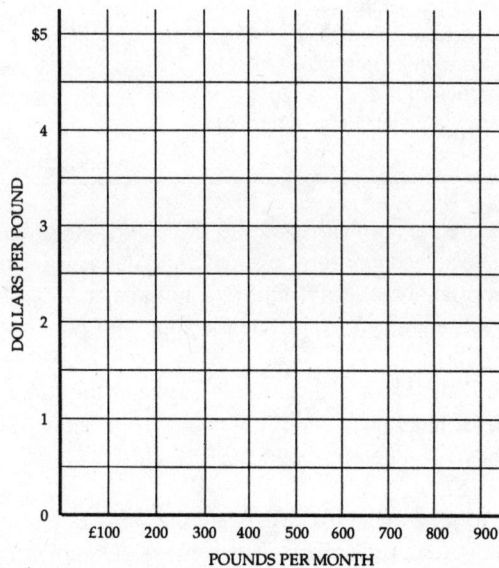

2. What is the equilibrium rate of exchange? _____

3. At a price of $2 per pound there would be excess:
   (a) Demand, and the exchange rate for pounds would rise.
   (b) Demand, and the exchange rate for pounds would fall.
   (c) Supply, and the exchange rate would rise.
   (d) Supply, and the exchange rate would fall.

499

4. Suppose that Americans suddenly increased their demand for British exports. The dollar price of pounds would (rise, fall).

5. T F Whenever one currency depreciates, another currency must appreciate.

6. As a result of the increased demand for British exports, the pound price of the dollar would (rise, fall).

Exercise 2

This exercise shows why one currency appreciates when another currency depreciates. It also shows why the demand for dollars represents the supply of other currencies, while the supply of dollars represents the demand for other currencies in the foreign-exchange markets. In learning these things, you will get practice in making calculations with exchange rates.

1. Table 36.2 includes the sources of demand and supply of dollars. In the first column, check off the items that are the source of the demand for dollars. In the second column, check off the items that are the source of the supply of dollars. (*Hint*: There are two kinds of speculators—those who think the dollar will rise and those who think it will fall. You must sort the two types of speculators to determine which type will supply dollars and which will demand dollars.)

Table 36.2
Sources of supply and demand for dollars and pounds

	(1) Demand for $	(2) Supply of $	(3) Demand for £	(4) Supply of £
Foreign demand for American exports	___	___	___	___
Foreign demand for American investments	___	___	___	___
Speculation that the dollar will appreciate	___	___	___	___
American demand for imports	___	___	___	___
American demand for investments in foreign countries	___	___	___	___
Speculation that the dollar will depreciate	___	___	___	___

2. If we assume there are just two currencies in the world, the dollar ($) and the pound (£), then the items in Table 36.2 also account for the supply and demand for the pound. Once again place checks in the appropriate blanks of Table 36.2 to indicate which items will constitute the demand for pounds and which items will constitute the supply of pounds.

3. T F In a two country world the sources of demand for dollars are the same as the sources of the supply of the pound, and the sources of the supply of dollars are the same as the sources of the demand for pounds.

4. T F The sources of demand for dollars are the same as the sources of supply for all other currencies in terms of dollars. The sources of supply of dollars are the same as the sources of demand for all other currencies in terms of dollars.

5. Let's return to our assumption that there are only two countries. Use your observations in the previous two questions and your knowledge of converting one currency into another to find the quantities of dollars supplied (column 3) and quantities of dollars demanded (column 6) in Table 36.3. Use the information in Table 36.3, which is the same as the data we used in Exercise 1 above, to compute the supply and demand for pounds.

Table 36.3
Supply and demand for dollars ($) and pounds (£)

(1) Price of a £ ($ / £)	(2) Quantity of £ demanded	(3) Quantity of $ supplied	(4) Price of a $ (£ / $)	(5) Quantity of £ supplied	(6) Quantity of $ demanded
4.50	100	_____	_____	700	_____
4.00	200	_____	_____	600	_____
3.50	300	_____	_____	500	_____
3.00	400	_____	_____	400	_____
2.50	500	_____	_____	300	_____
2.00	600	_____	_____	200	_____
1.50	700	_____	_____	100	_____

6. Complete column 4 of Table 36.3 by converting the price of pounds (£) in terms of dollars ($) in column 1 to the price of dollars in terms of pounds. (*Hint*: they are reciprocals of each other. Remember that to find the price of any good or currency, that good or currency appears in the denominator!)

7. From the data on the demand for the dollar (columns 4 and 6 of Table 36.3), draw the demand curve for the dollar in Figure 36.2. From the data on the supply of the dollar (columns 3 and 4 of Table 36.3), draw the supply curve for the dollar in Figure 36.2.

Figure 36.2
Demand and supply of dollars

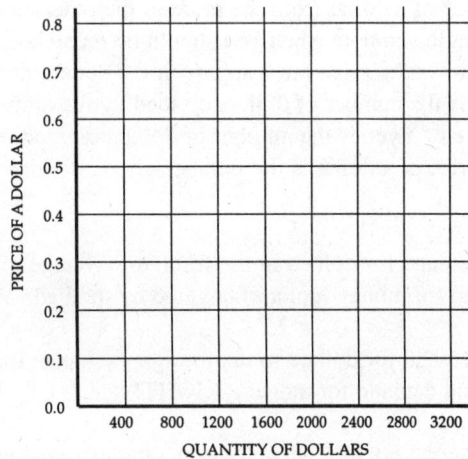

8. The equilibrium value of the dollar is _____ , and the equilibrium quantity of dollars is _____.

9. When you multiply the equilibrium quantity of dollars by the equilibrium exchange rate for the dollar in terms of pounds (£), you find the quantity of pounds is _____. When you find the reciprocal of the equilibrium exchange rate for the dollar, you find the exchange rate for pounds is _____.

10. T   F   When you multiply the equilibrium quantity of dollars by the equilibrium exchange rate for the dollar in terms of pounds (£), you have calculated the equilibrium quantity of pounds. (Compare your answer to question 9 in this exercise with your answer to question 2, Exercise 1 above.)

501

11. T F The equilibrium exchange rate for the dollar equals the equilibrium exchange rate for the pound.

Exercise 3

The media often feature articles about international financial issues.

Read the article entitled "Nobel Prize Was Nobler in October." Then answer the following questions.

1. According to the article, what was the dollar value of the Nobel Prize at the time it was announced?_____

2. How much was it worth two months later?_____

3. Why did the value change so much? _____

Common Errors

The first statement in each "common error" below is incorrect. Each incorrect statement is followed by a corrected version and an explanation.

1. The price of a dollar in terms of yen is the number of dollars per yen. WRONG!

    The price of a dollar in terms of yen is the number of yen per dollar. RIGHT!

    This mistake can cost a bundle if you are in a foreign country and don't know how to distinguish the price of a dollar from the price of the other currency. In Japan you don't want to give $100 for a single yen note when you should be receiving 100 yen for $1! Remember that the item for which you want a price must appear in the denominator of the price. For example, the price of tomatoes is the number of dollars divided by the number of tomatoes that are purchased. Similarly, the price of a yen is the number of dollars divided by the number of yen that are purchased. The price of a dollar is the number of yen divided by the number of dollars that are purchased.

2. The supply and demand for dollars in the foreign-exchange market is the same thing as the supply and demand for money (dollars) targeted by the Fed. WRONG!

    The supply and demand for dollars in the foreign-exchange market is a totally different concept from the supply and demand for money. RIGHT!

    Remember that the price of money was the interest rate when we were focusing on the supply and demand for money. In the foreign-exchange market the price is the exchange rate, not the interest rate. Furthermore, the supply and demand for money (dollars), which is the focus of the Fed, occurs geographically within the United States. The foreign-exchange market occurs between countries—literally on the phone lines between banks of different countries. We can visualize the foreign-exchange market as an area totally outside of borders in which money temporarily enters for the purpose of being exchanged. While domestic monetary policies may influence the amount of money going into the foreign-exchange market, the link is often indirect. In fact, when the Fed tightens monetary policy to reduce the supply of dollars, the foreign-exchange market may see an *increase* in the supply of dollars as foreigners seek the higher interest rates from a tighter U.S. monetary policy.

3. A country is well off if its currency appreciates steadily over a long period of time. WRONG!

   Both appreciating currencies and depreciating currencies create problems. RIGHT!

   Be careful! There are problems associated with steadily appreciating currencies *and* with steadily depreciating currencies. People sometimes view a depreciating currency as a source of national shame and dislike the higher cost (and inflation) associated with higher prices of foreign goods. However, depreciation may make a country's exports more competitive, may lead to more jobs, and may help correct a trade deficit. By contrast, a country with an appreciating currency develops employment problems and a loss of competitiveness against other countries, even if it has more buying power as a result of its stronger currency.

4. When countries have trade deficits, money really flows out. When they have surpluses, money really flows in. WRONG!

   Money is not physically sent in most transactions, but the claim to ownership is. RIGHT!

   Most foreign trade is transacted by check and is just a "flow" of bookkeeping entries. Even when gold is sold, it seldom *physically* flows anywhere. In the case of the United States, under a fixed-exchange-rate system, it stays in Fort Knox even though someone else owns it. Thus, it is the claim to ownership that flows, not the money. When countries run trade deficits, their trading partners add to their claims against them. For countries with a trade surplus, the reverse is true.

5. There are balance-of-payments surpluses and deficits under floating exchange rates. WRONG!

   The balance of payments is always zero under floating exchange rates. RIGHT!

   Under fixed exchange rates, the government must balance surpluses and deficits on the balance of payments with changes in reserves. With floating exchange rates, there is no reserve currency and any transfers abroad by the government are simply classified as unilateral transfers and are included in the current account. By definition, the current account and the capital account balance each other under a floating exchange-rate system.

•ANSWERS•

Using Key Terms
Across
2. foreign-exchange markets
4. market shortage
6. managed exchange rates
8. gold reserves
9. appreciation
10. exchange rates
11. depreciation
13. gold standard
14. equilibrium price
15. balance-of-payments surplus

Down
1. balance-of-payments deficit
2. foreign exchange reserves

3. flexible exchange rate
5. balance of payments
7. devaluation
12. trade deficit

True or False

1. T
2. F Increased foreign travel by Americans tends to increase the demand for foreign currency, thus increasing the supply of U.S. dollars and reducing the value of the dollar.
3. T
4. T
5. T
6. T
7. F U.S. goods will be relatively more expensive to Japan thus reducing exports.
8. F Fixed exchange rates tend to cause balance-of-payments deficits and surpluses because they cause shortages and surpluses of currencies.
9. T
10. F A country experiencing trade deficits will have higher foreign debt and interest rates because that country will have to borrow to finance the additional goods and services it is consuming over what it is producing.

Multiple Choice

1.	a	5.	b	9.	b	13.	a	17.	c
2.	a	6.	d	10.	d	14.	c	18.	d
3.	c	7.	a	11.	a	15.	b	19.	d
4.	c	8.	d	12.	c	16.	a	20.	d

Problems and Applications

Exercise 1

1. **Figure 36.1 Answer**

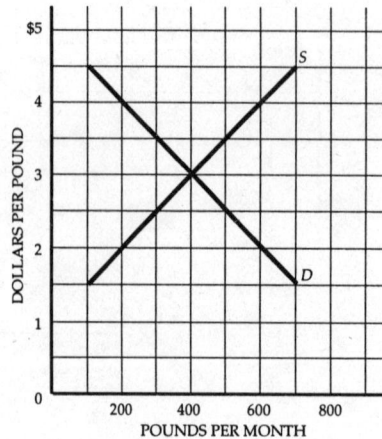

504

2. $3 per British pound   3. a   4. rise   5. T   6. fall

Exercise 2

Table 36.2 Answer

	(1) Demand for $	(2) Supply of $	(3) Demand for £	(4) Supply of £
Foreign demand for American exports	X	—	—	X
Foreign demand for American investments	X	—	—	X
Speculation that the dollar will appreciate	X	—	—	X
American demand for imports	—	X	X	—
American demand for investments in foreign countries	—	X	X	—
Speculation that the dollar will depreciate	—	X	X	—

3. T
4. T
5. and 6.   **Table 36.3 Answer**

Price of a £ ($/£) (1)		Quantity of £ demanded (2)		Quantity of $ supplied (3)	Price of a.$ (£/$) (4)	Quantity of £ supplied (5)	Quantity of $ demanded (6)
4.50	x	100	=	450	0.222 = 1/4.50	700	3,150
4.00	x	200	=	800	0.25 = 1/4	600	2,400
3.50	x	300	=	1,050	0.29 = 1/3.50	500	1,750
3.00	x	400	=	1,200	0.33 = 1/3	400	1,200
2.50	x	500	=	1,250	0.40 = 1/2.50	300	750
2.00	x	600	=	1,200	0.50 = 1/2	200	400
1.50	x	700	=	1,050	0.67 = 1/1.50	100	150

7.   **Figure 36.2 Answer**

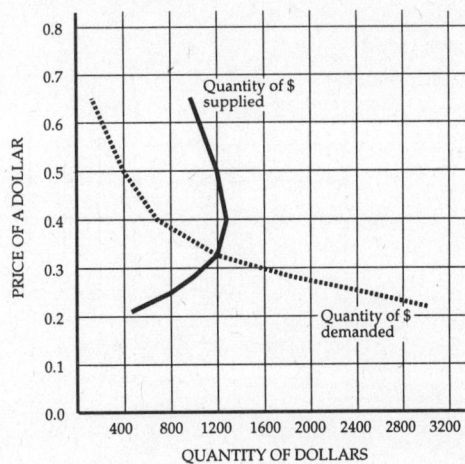

8. 1/3 £ per dollar; $1,200
9. 400 (= 1,200 x 1/3); $3 per pound [= 1/(1/3)]
10. T
11. F   The equilibrium exchange rate for the dollar equals the *reciprocal* of the equilibrium exchange rate for the pound.

Exercise 3

1. $1.2 million
2. $958,000
3. The Swedish krona depreciated which caused the value of the prize to decrease.

CHAPTER 37
The New Capitalist Revolutions: Russia, China, Cuba

Quick Review

The collapse of communism has accelerated since the late 1980s. In 1991 the Soviet Union became fifteen separate republics. Each of the republics had to establish their own methods for allocating their resources and developing answers to the WHAT, HOW, and FOR WHOM questions. It was inevitable that, with the collapse of the Soviet Union, Fidel Castro would have to decide how to run the Cuban economy without the massive Soviet subsidies which propped up his system for over three decades. China remains a centrally-planned economy, but it has recently allowed some capitalist innovation to occur. All around the world former communist countries are being forced to abandon central planning, however reluctantly, in favor of the market mechanism.

In this chapter we look back at the communist ideology and the central planning which was used to implement it. Then we investigate the inherent problems of attempting to plan a large, diverse, and complex economy. Finally, we look at "transitional problems" as the formerly planned economies move toward market-based systems of resource allocation. Specifically, we attempt to answer the following questions:

- What is the appeal of central planning?
- What are the basic problems of central planning?
- What impedes the transition to market economies?

Every economy has to answer the WHAT, HOW, and FOR WHOM questions. In the United States these questions are answered when consumers attempt to maximize satisfaction with limited incomes, business people attempt to maximize profits, and voters express their preferences about the way they are governed. In planned economies, the big decisions, such as the division of output between capital goods and consumer goods, are made by a central authority.

The central authority (i.e., the planners) attempts to allocate resources to achieve specific objectives. Very often these objectives include a particular income distribution and a strong military establishment. Planners use such techniques as input-output analysis to allocate their scarce resources; in contrast, in a market economy prices automatically signal where resources are to move. Prices are used in planned economies to perform a rationing function, but not the allocation function that they perform in a market economy.

Trade between nations is difficult in centrally planned economies because prices, which are set by planners rather than by markets, are not accepted internationally. Currencies are not convertible, barter results, and countries do not follow the dictates of comparative advantage. These are additional problems to be overcome during the transition from planning to markets.

The movement from central planning to market-based systems of resource allocation is not an easy task and every economy attempting this transition must experience changes in the form of price reform, currency reform, private ownership of property, and institutional reform. Price reform means abandoning prices set by planners in favor of prices established in free markets. The implicit surpluses and shortages which were suppressed under the old system must be allowed to bring about necessary changes in resource and product markets. Some prices shoot up and others collapse while the markets seek equilibrium. The inevitable inflation which follows must be followed by currency reform. Consumers and producers in both internal and external markets must be able to rely on the real value of the medium of exchange, or it will cease to play that role and inefficient barter will result. While currency and price reform are the foundation for a market-directed economy, the necessary cornerstone is the emergence of private property. Private property provides the incentives necessary for good economic decisions. This has been very difficult for the former communists to accept since virtually all property had been owned by the state. Privatization of former state assets (land and capital) has been accomplished in many countries, but it has never been easy.

Finally, institutional reform must take place. This means workers are no longer guaranteed employment with state owned firms where inefficiency and low productivity were rampant. Inevitably, unemployment skyrockets while currency, price and property reforms are in progress. It cannot be avoided. The cost in human terms, especially for the very old and very young, is great.

Learning Objectives

After reading Chapter 37 and doing the following exercises, you should:

1. Know the historical background of communism and the appeal of central planning.
2. Recognize that every economy is restricted by its production-possibilities curve and the choices that result.
3. Recognize the very serious difficulties encountered in "planning" for large economies.
4. Recognize that every economy, no matter how it's organized, must answer the WHAT, HOW, and FOR WHOM questions.
5. Understand the roles that prices play in market and planned economies.
6. Know what input-output analysis is and how it is used by planners.
7. Know the relative strengths and weaknesses of market and planned economies.
8. Understand that suppressed inflation is the symptom of even more serious underlying problems of planned economies.
9. Know that inconvertible currencies lead to inefficiency in the allocation of resources both domestically and internationally.
10. Know that price, currency, and institutional reforms must be accompanied by privatization in the transition to a market-directed economy and the difficulties which accompany the reforms.
11. Be aware of the Cuban approach to reform.

Using Key Terms

Fill in the puzzle on the opposite page with the appropriate term from the list of Key Terms at the end of the chapter in the text.

Across

3. Any currency widely accepted as payment in international markets.
5. An economy in which all nonlabor means of production are owned by the state.
10. Direct exchange of one good for another.
11. An economy that relies on the market mechanism to allocate goods and services.
12. An economy in which basic allocation decisions are made by market forces.
13. Alternative combinations of goods and services that can be produced with available resources and technology.
14. An increase in production possibilities.
15. The amount by which the quantity demanded exceeds the quantity supplied.

Down

1. Inflationary imbalances reflected in market shortages and the rationing of goods.
2. The ability to produce a specific good at a lower opportunity cost than another country.
4. A situation in which people are employed but contribute little or nothing to total output.
6. The use of prices and sales to signal desired output.
7. A stateless, classless economy with no private property in which everyone shares in production and consumption according to their abilities and needs.
8. Expenditures on new plant and equipment plus changes in inventories.
9. Consumer saving because of shortages of goods.
13. The difference between total cost and total revenue.

Puzzle 37.1

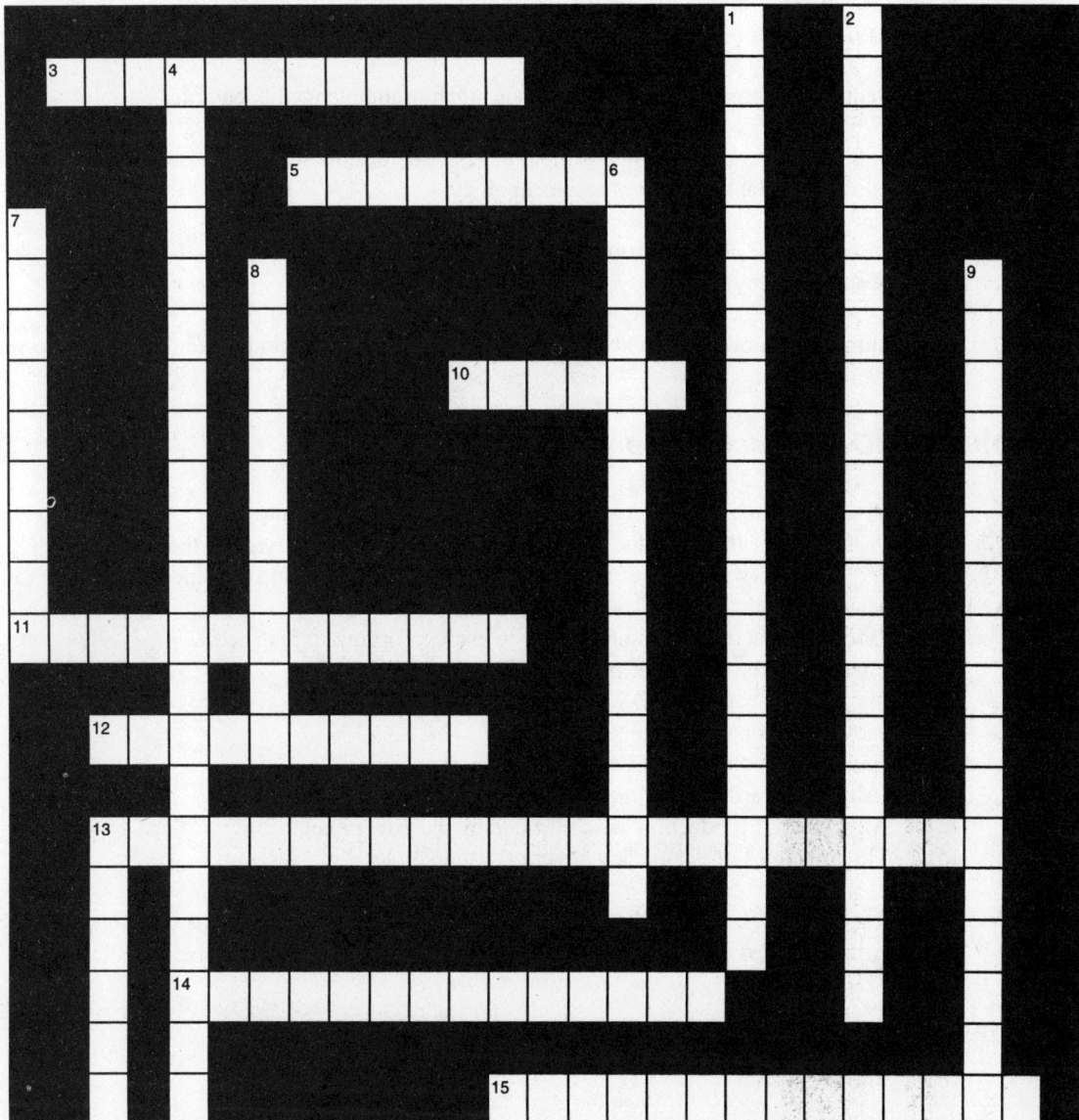

True or False: *Circle your choice and explain why any false statements are incorrect.*

T F 1. The historical order of Marx's stages is (from first to last) . . . capitalism, socialism, communism.

T F 2. When the official price for goods and services is below the equilibrium price in a market, prices no longer perform their rationing function efficiently.

T F 3. Marx envisioned communism as a state-controlled economy in which there would be no private property.

T F 4. In the planned economies of Eastern Europe unemployment was nonexistent.

T F 5. The basic function of prices in a centrally planned economy is to signal to producers that some products are relatively scarce and others are relatively plentiful.

T F 6. A system which requires complete income equality eliminates material incentives to motivate workers.

T F 7. Income equality is greater in the United States than in the planned economies.

T F 8. Central planning agencies use input-output tables to determine which goods and services can be produced with available resources and technology.

T F 9. When currencies are not convertible, they cease to perform their medium-of-exchange function in the domestic economy.

T F 10. When limited availability of goods leads to involuntary saving, workers are encouraged to work harder.

Multiple Choice: *Select the correct answer.*

_____ 1. The motivating principle of the communism Marx envisioned would be:
   (a) Protection for the capitalist class because they are the ones who do the saving.
   (b) Private ownership of factors of production because this would provide an incentive to accumulate.
   (c) "From each according to his ability, to each according to his need."
   (d) Freedom in the pursuit of private economic gain.

_____ 2. Capitalism is an economic system in which:
   (a) Basic allocation decisions are made by market forces.
   (b) Labor is rewarded according to need.
   (c) All factors of production are controlled by the government.
   (d) The principles of democracy govern the marketplace.

_____ 3. In a market economy, the coordination of producer and consumer decisions is accomplished by markets; in a planned economy, such decisions are typically coordinated by:
   (a) The workers.
   (b) The plant managers.
   (c) A central planning authority.
   (d) The proletariat.

_____ 4. In a socialist economy input-output tables can be used to:
    (a) Choose the best production processes.
    (b) Allocate the right amount of resources to each sector.
    (c) Choose the optimal amount of investment.
    (d) Choose the optimal amount of consumption.

_____ 5. Planned economies typically suffer from:
    (a) Underemployment but not unemployment.
    (b) Both unemployment and underemployment.
    (c) Neither unemployment nor underemployment.
    (d) Unemployment but not underemployment.

_____ 6. In both planned and market economies, increased capital formation requires:
    (a) Lower interest rates.
    (b) Increased saving.
    (c) Increased consumption.
    (d) Reduced business taxes.

_____ 7. In the move from a communist system to a market system which of the following changes have to be made?
    (a) State-owned property to privately-owned property.
    (b) Profits must be permitted.
    (c) Prices determined by supply and demand rather than central planners.
    (d) All of the above would have to change.

_____ 8. Resource allocation can be accomplished without major shortages and surpluses using:
    (a) Input-output analysis in a planned socialist economy.
    (b) Input-output analysis in the market mechanism.
    (c) Prices in an economy which relies on the market mechanism.
    (d) Prices in a planned socialist economy.

_____ 9. Suppressed inflation takes the form of:
    (a) Market surpluses.
    (b) Market shortages.
    (c) Prices above equilibrium levels.
    (d) Output above equilibrium levels.

_____ 10. The major communist criticism of market economies relates to the market's answer to the:
    (a) FOR WHOM question.
    (b) WHAT question.
    (c) HOW question.
    (d) EFFICIENCY question.

_____ 11. Which of the following statements justifies the rejection of the market mechanism by planned economies?
    (a) If prices were used to allocate resources, planning goals would be jeopardized.
    (b) If prices were used to allocate resources, capital-goods production would be reduced.
    (c) If prices were used to allocate resources, income-distribution goals would be impaired.
    (d) All of the above justify such a rejection.

_____ 12. In an effort to establish economic equity, central planners are likely to cause:
    (a) Uncontrolled inflation.
    (b) Economic inefficiencies.
    (c) Massive unemployment.
    (d) All of the above.

13. Involuntary saving occurred in the Soviet Union because:
    (a) Workers were provided pensions which were not available until the worker retired.
    (b) Workers purchased government securities in compulsory programs.
    (c) Consumer goods were not available because government used the resources for investment.
    (d) Workers were shoved into higher marginal tax brackets as their real incomes increased.

14. Using heavy price controls and severe quotas on the production of consumer goods, the Soviet Union:
    (a) Reduced suppressed inflation.
    (b) Created market shortages.
    (c) Lowered enforced saving.
    (d) All of the above.

15. Which of the following has been used as an incentive to increase worker productivity under the former Soviet Union?
    (a) Terror.
    (b) Income bonuses.
    (c) "Ownership" of small plots of land.
    (d) All of the above.

16. Planned socialist economies tend to hold prices of necessities:
    (a) Above market equilibrium prices, which results in surpluses.
    (b) Below market equilibrium prices, which results in shortages.
    (c) Below market equilibrium prices, which results in surpluses.
    (d) Above market equilibrium prices, which results in shortages.

17. A communist country's efforts to eliminate cyclical unemployment typically causes:
    (a) Disguised unemployment.
    (b) Inflation.
    (c) Structural unemployment.
    (d) Frictional unemployment.

18. When currencies are nonconvertible:
    (a) The official rate is determined in the black market.
    (b) The currency is not useful for trade in the domestic market.
    (c) Foreign suppliers often require hard currencies in payment for goods.
    (d) The official rate is determined by negotiations between governments.

19. Countries that use barter instead of currencies in international trade will:
    (a) Not be able to specialize in production to the extent they would if currencies were used.
    (b) Not be able to consume on their true consumption-possibilities curve.
    (c) Be forced to devote more resources to the arrangement of trade than if currencies were used.
    (d) All of the above.

20. The transition from communism to capitalism would most likely result in:
    (a) Massive unemployment.
    (b) Negative GDP growth rates.
    (c) Social and political tension.
    (d) All of the above.

Problems and Applications

Exercise 1

The production-possibilities curve for a planned economy is shown in Figure 37.1. Assume that the economy is operating at point A. Suppose the planners decide that the society must increase its production of defense goods from the amount indicated by D_1 to the amount indicated by D_2.

Figure 37.1
Production possibilities

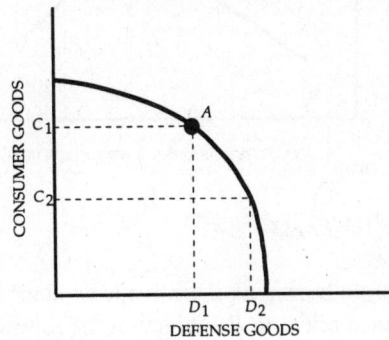

Production possibilities and opportunities

1. The opportunity cost of increasing the output of defense goods from D_1 to D_2 is:
    (a) Zero, since there are unemployed resources in the economy.
    (b) $0C_2$ of consumer goods.
    (c) $0C_1$ of consumer goods.
    (d) C_1C_2 of consumer goods.

2. To get the workers to switch from the production of consumer goods to the production of defense goods, the planners will be most successful if they:
    (a) Raise the wages of workers who produce defense goods.
    (b) Lower the wages of workers who produce consumer goods.
    (c) Raise the wages of workers who produce defense goods relative to those of workers who produce consumer goods.
    (d) Raise the wages of workers who produce consumer goods relative to those of workers who produce defense goods.

3. If more defense goods are to be produced, resources will have to be taken away from consumer goods, and consumers will have fewer consumer goods to purchase. Suppose the demand and supply of consumer goods are as indicated in Figure 37.2. The equilibrium price-quantity combination is:
    (a) P_2, C_1.
    (b) P_1, C_1.
    (c) P_2, C_2.
    (d) P_3, C_2.

Figure 37.2
Supply and demand for consumer goods

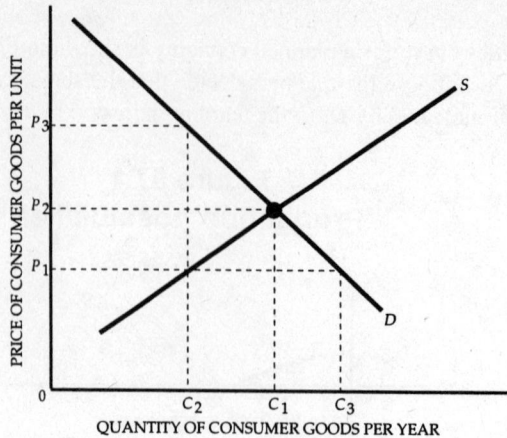

Taxes and price limitations (ceilings)

4. To prevent producers from having an incentive to produce too many consumer goods, the planners might hold down prices to P_1. Which of the following results would you expect?
   - (a)   Excess inventories.
   - (b)   Excess profits.
   - (c)   Long queues of people waiting to buy.
   - (d)   All of the above.

5. When the planners cut production from C_1 to C_2, the result is a:
   - (a)   Surplus at prices below P_1.
   - (b)   Shortage at prices below P_2.
   - (c)   New equilibrium at P_3, C_2.
   - (d)   None of the above.

6. To get consumers to restrain their consumption to output C_2, the planners could levy a tax equal to the distance:
   - (a) $0P_3$.
   - (b) $0P_1$.
   - (c) P_2, P_3.
   - (d) P_1, P_3.

Subsidies, price supports, and floors

7. Suppose the government wishes to control diseases by making more medical services available. Figure 37.3 shows the demand and supply curves for medical services. The equilibrium price-quantity is:
   - (a) P_1, M_1.
   - (b) P_2, M_2.
   - (c) P_3, M_3.
   - (d) P_1, M_3.

Figure 37.3
Supply and demand of medical services

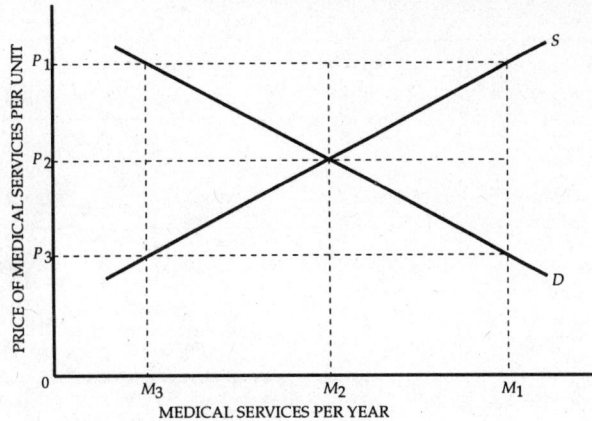

8. Suppose the government wants M_1 of medical services produced. If the government sets a price like P_1 so that the desired quantity of medical services would be supplied, you would expect:
   (a) Underemployment of medical personnel.
   (b) Shortages of medical services.
   (c) Improvements in health to the degree that the government targets.
   (d) All of the above.

9. In order to encourage fuller use of the services available at M_1, the government could introduce a subsidy per unit of medical service of:
   (a) P_1, P_3.
   (b) M_3, M_1.
   (c) P_2, P_3.
   (d) P_1, P_2.

10. If the government wanted M_1 of medical services to be offered, wanted to subsidize no one, and wanted to keep the price at P_3, it would have to build medical facilities to provide:
    (a) M_3, M_1 of medical services.
    (b) $0M_1$ of medical services.
    (c) $0M_2$ of medical services.
    (d) $0M_3$ of medical services.

11. At a price of P_3, private medical practices would provide:
    (a) M_3, M_1 of medical services.
    (b) $0M_1$ of medical services.
    (c) $0M_2$ of medical services.
    (d) $0M_3$ of medical services.

    (*Hint:* The supply curve reflects what would be provided in the private market.)

Exercise 2

This exercise should give you an idea of how to use input-output analysis. It should also give you an idea of how difficult it is to allocate resources without the use of prices.

Table 37.1
Soviet input-output relationships

(1)	(2)	(3)	(4)	(5)	(6)
			Input requirement per unit of:		
Sector number	*Inputs*	*Automobiles*	*Tractors and agricultural machinery*	*Bread, flour, and confections*	*Electric and thermal power*
1	Specialized M & E	0	0.00004	0.00054	0
2	Fish products	0	0	0.00040	0
3	Sugar	0.00000	0.00006	0.05334	0.00000

Source: U.S. Congress. *Soviet Economic Prospects for the Seventies: A Compendium of Papers Submitted to the Joint Economic*

1. You are a planner faced with the Soviet input-output relationships shown in Table 37.1 in the text and Table 37.1 above. You are responsible for ensuring that the bread, flour, and confections industry (column 5 in Table 37.1) has all of the required inputs needed to produce 100,000 rubles of bread, flour, and confections. You succeed in obtaining all of the necessary requirements except those produced by three industries. Table 37.2 shows the amounts (column 2) of the various requirements in these three industries that you are able to obtain. In column 3 of Table 37.2 write the input-output coefficients for each of these sectors (use Table 37.1 above).

2. You should be able to calculate the amounts of the three requirements in Table 37.2 that you would need to produce 100,000 rubles of bread, flour, and confectionery goods. Place these amounts in column 4 of Table 37.2. (*Hint:* The coefficients in column 3 tell the fraction of the total cost of bread, flour, and confectionery goods that goes into each input.)

Table 37.2
Shortfall for requirements in three industries to produce bread, flour, and confections

(1)	(2)	(3)	(4)	(5)	(6)
Industry	*Amount obtained (rubles)*	*Input-output coefficient*	*Amount (rubles) needed to produce 100,000 rubles of output* $100,000 \times (3)$	*Fraction of target that can be met* $(2) \div (4)$	*Maximum production possible given input available* $100,000 \times (5)$
Specialized M & E (sector 1)	45.0	_____	_____	_____	_____
Fish products (sector 2)	30.0	_____	_____	_____	_____
Sugar (sector 3)	533.4	_____	_____	_____	_____

3. You are now ready to find the percentage of bread, flour, and confectionery goods you can make with the available inputs that you have. In column 5 of Table 37.2 you can compute the ratio of what you have available of each input to the amount needed to reach your target of 100,000 rubles of bread, flour, and confection output. This same ratio tells the fraction of your 100,000-ruble production target that you will be able to produce. Compute this maximum production in column 6, Table 37.2.

4. Which input causes the production of bread, flour, and confectionery goods to be the lowest?
   (a)   Specialized M & E.
   (b)   Fish products.
   (c)   Sugar.

5. Assuming that production can be increased only if you have enough of each input and that production can be expanded only in proportion to the available inputs, the maximum output of bread, flour, and confectionery goods that can be produced with available inputs is:
   (a)   1,000 rubles.
   (b)   10,000 rubles.
   (c)   100,000 rubles.
   (d)   90,000 rubles.
   (e)   83,333 rubles.
   (f)   75,000 rubles.

6. Since you are able to meet only one-tenth of your target for bread, flour, and confectionery products, you will have (surpluses, shortages) of all of the inputs to these products except sugar.

7. For each of the commodities in Table 37.3, compute the amount of surplus you have of each of the listed inputs as a result of your inability to use them. The input-output coefficients are from Table 37.1 in the text. Since you had enough of each of these inputs to produce 100,000 rubles of bread, flour, and confectionery goods, you can assume that column 3 in Table 37.3 represents the amount of each input you were allocated. (*Hint:* Find the input coefficient and then compute the amount of factor needed as you did in Table 37.2.) Since you can use only 10 percent of the factors you were allocated, because of the sugar shortages, your surplus will be 90 percent (column 4) of what you were allocated (column 3).

Table 37.3
Excess inputs as a result of sugar shortage

(1) Input	(2) Input-output coefficient for bread, flour, and confections. (See Table 22.1 in the text.)	(3) Amount (rubles) needed to produce 100,000 rubles of output	(4) Amount unused 0.9 x (3)
Coal (sector 5)	_____	_____	_____
Electric and thermal power (sector 9)	_____	_____	_____

8. You are also the planner for automobile production. You have to produce 1 million rubles of output of automobiles. If you fail you will go to Siberia. You receive the allocation that you need from all sectors except for the two shown in Table 37.4. Complete Table 37.4 as you did Table 37.2 of this study guide, this time using the automobile column (column 1) in Table 37.1 in the text to find the input-output coefficients.

Table 37.4
Shortfall of requirements to produce one million rubles of automobiles

(1) Input	(2) Amount obtained (rubles)	(3) Input-output coefficient	(4) Amount (rubles) needed to produce 1 million rubles of output 1,000,000 x (3)	(5) Fraction of target that can be met (2) ÷ (4)	(6) Maximum production possible given available inputs 1,000,000 x (5)
Coal (sector 5)	1,945.8	_____	_____	_____	_____
Electric and thermal power (sector 9)	11,592.9	_____	_____	_____	_____

9. How would you be able to reach your automobile target?
   (a) Transfer bread, flour, and confectionery products to the automobile industry.
   (b) Transfer cars to the bread, flour, and confectionery industry.
   (c) Transfer sugar, fish products, and specialized M & E to the automobile industry.
   (d) Transfer coal and electric and thermal power from the automobile industry to the bread, flour, and confectionery industry.
   (e) Transfer coal and electric and thermal power from the bread, flour, and confectionery industry to the automobile industry.

10. How much more coal (in rubles) does the automobile industry need from the bread, flour, and confectionery industry in order to reach its target without any waste?
    (a) 1,171 rubles.
    (b) 214.2 rubles.
    (c) 117.1 rubles.
    (d) 2,160 rubles.

11. Are there still surpluses of inputs for some industry after the automobile target is reached?
    _____

Exercise 3

This exercise will use one of the articles in the text to show the kind of information to look for to identify the type of economic system used in another country.

Reread the article "China Debates Whether to Slow Reforms" in the text.

1. How would you classify the way the economy of this country has been organized in the past? (circle one)
   Communism   Socialism   Mixed economy   Free market

2. What passage is consistent with the way you have classified the past economy? _____
   _____

3. What passage indicates an example of the way the economy is changing to a new economic structure (for example, from communism to capitalism)? _____
   _____

4. What passage indicates the impact the Asian crisis has had on reforms? _____
   _____

Common Errors

The first statement in each "common error" below is incorrect. Each incorrect statement is followed by a corrected version and an explanation.

1. Prices serve no function in a planned economy. WRONG!

   Prices are used to allocate resources and goods in accordance with central plans. RIGHT!

   In planned economies prices are not allowed to perform the same functions as in a market economy. Prices do not generally provide the signal for resources to move (their allocation function), but they do perform the rationing function. Luxury goods have high prices, and necessities carry lower price tags.

2. The average city dweller in China subsists on an income of approximately $340 per year. WRONG!

   The average Chinese city dweller is at about the U.S. poverty line. RIGHT!

   This "common error" points up the difficulty of making comparisons of living standards across international boundaries. Simple dollar comparisons gloss over the radical differences in economic organization. Some of the things that carry high price tags in the United States, such as medical services, carry low price tags in China. Housing is another example. Many services that are provided without charge by the state in China must be paid for by the consumer in the United States. Such differences create significant distortions, so simple comparisons are very misleading. After adjustments, it appears that the average Chinese city dweller has an income roughly equivalent to that at the U.S. poverty line.

3. Capitalism is a system characterized by democracy. WRONG!

   Capitalism is an economic system in which individuals own the factors of production and use the market mechanism. RIGHT!

   Do not confuse the classification of political systems with the classification of economic systems. It is conceivable—even if not historically common—for tyrannies to practice capitalism and democracies to practice communism. An economic system focuses on the ownership of the means of production and the mechanism by which goods are exchanged. A political system focuses on the issue of collective decision making.

•ANSWERS•

Using Key Terms
Across
3. hard currency
5. socialism
10. barter
11. market economy
12. capitalism
13. production possibilities
14. economic growth
15. market shortage

Down

1. supressed inflation
2. comparative advantage
4. disguised unemployment
6. market mechanism
7. communism
8. investment
9. involuntary saving
13. profit

True or False

1. T
2. T
3. F Marx did envision a society in which there was no private property; however, he did not see the need for a central authority, i.e. a state, because in his view the only function of the state was to pursue the interests of the dominant class.
4. F Although, officially, unemployment did not exist, disguised unemployment (underemployment) was widespread.
5. F Prices in a centrally planned economy are typically government controlled and do not fluctuate in response to shortages and surpluses.
6. T
7. F One of the major objectives of planned economies is to create a more equal distribution of income.
8. T
9. F When currencies are not convertible, they do not perform their medium of exchange function in the international economy.
10. F Limited availability of goods is a disincentive to work harder because access to more goods and services is the primary reward for hard work.

Multiple Choice

1. c	5. a	9. b	13. c	17. a
2. a	6. b	10. a	14. b	18. c
3. c	7. d	11. d	15. d	19. d
4. b	8. c	12. b	16. b	20. d

Problems and Applications

Exercise 1

1. d	3. a	5. b	7. b	9. a	11. d
2. c	4. c	6. c	8. a	10. a	

Exercise 2

1-3. **Table 37.2 Answer**

(1) Industry	(2) Amount obtained	(3) Input-output coefficient	(4) Amount needed	(5) Fraction of target	(6) Maximum production
Specialized M & E	45.0	0.00054	54	5/6	83,333
Fish products	30.0	0.00040	40	3/4	75,000
Sugar	533.4	0.05334	5,334	1/10	10,000

4. c
5. b
6. surpluses
7. **Table 37.3 Answer**

(1) Input	(2) Input-output coefficient	(3) Amount needed	(4) Amount unused
Coal	0.00238	238	214.2
Electric and thermal power	0.00284	284	255.6

8. **Table 37.4 Answer**

(1) Input	(2) Amount obtained	(3) Input-output coefficient	(4) Amount needed	(5) Fraction of target	(6) Maximum production
Coal	1,945.8	0.00216	2,160	0.9008	900,800
Electric and thermal power	11,592.9	0.01171	11,710	0.9900	990,000

9. e   10. b   11. yes

Exercise 3

1. communism
2. Communist leaders
3. "Just over a year ago, the country was engaged in restructuring its obsolete state enterprises, inadequate housing system and insolvent banks."
4. "The crisis has . . . put on hold reforms . . . "